Explorations in Temperament

International Perspectives on
Theory and Measurement

PERSPECTIVES ON INDIVIDUAL DIFFERENCES

CECIL R. REYNOLDS, *Texas A&M University, College Station*
ROBERT T. BROWN, *University of North Carolina, Wilmington*

Current volumes in the series

THE CAUSES AND CURES OF CRIMINALITY
Hans J. Eysenck and Gisli H. Gudjonsson

EXPLORATIONS IN TEMPERAMENT
International Perspectives on Theory and Measurement
Edited by Jan Strelau and Alois Angleitner

HANDBOOK OF CREATIVITY
Assessment, Research, and Theory
Edited by John A. Glover, Royce R. Ronning, and Cecil R. Reynolds

HANDBOOK OF MULTIVARIATE EXPERIMENTAL PSYCHOLOGY
Second Edition
Edited by John R. Nesselroade and Raymond B. Cattell

HISTORICAL FOUNDATIONS OF EDUCATIONAL PSYCHOLOGY
Edited by John A. Glover and Royce R. Ronning

THE INDIVIDUAL SUBJECT AND SCIENTIFIC PSYCHOLOGY
Edited by Jaan Valsiner

LEARNING STRATEGIES AND LEARNING STYLES
Edited by Ronald R. Schmeck

METHODOLOGICAL AND STATISTICAL ADVANCES IN THE STUDY OF INDIVIDUAL DIFFERENCES
Edited by Cecil R. Reynolds and Victor L. Willson

THE NEUROPSYCHOLOGY OF INDIVIDUAL DIFFERENCES
A Developmental Perspective
Edited by Lawrence C. Hartlage and Cathy F. Telzrow

PERSONALITY DIMENSIONS AND AROUSAL
Edited by Jan Strelau and Hans J. Eysenck

THEORETICAL FOUNDATIONS OF BEHAVIOR THERAPY
Edited by Hans J. Eysenck and Irene Martin

A Continuation Order Plan is available for this series. A continuation order will bring delivery of each new volume immediately upon publication. Volumes are billed only upon actual shipment. For further information please contact the publisher.

Explorations in Temperament

International Perspectives on Theory and Measurement

Edited by
Jan Strelau
University of Warsaw
Warsaw, Poland

and

Alois Angleitner
University of Bielefeld
Bielefeld, Germany

Plenum Press • **London and New York**

Library of Congress Cataloging in Publication Data

Explorations in temperament: international perspectives on theory and measurement /
edited by Jan Strelau and Alois Angleitner.
    p.   cm. — (Perspectives on individual differences)
    Includes bibliographical references and index.
    ISBN 0-306-43782-1
    1. Temperament. 2. Temperament — Testing. I. Strelau, Jan. II. Angleitner,
A. (Alois) III. Series.
    [DNLM: 1. Temperament. BF 798 E96]
    BF798.E95   1991
    155. — dc20
DNLM/DLC   91-3681
for Library of Congress   CIP

ISBN 0-306-43782-1

© 1991 Plenum Press, New York
A Division of Plenum Publishing Corporation
233 Spring Street, New York, N.Y. 10013

Printed in the United States of America

Contributors

Manfred Amelang, Department of Psychology, University of Heidelberg, D-6900 Heidelberg, Federal Republic of Germany

Alois Angleitner, Department of Psychology, University of Bielefeld, D-4800 Bielefeld, Federal Republic of Germany

Arnold H. Buss, Department of Psychology, University of Texas at Austin, Austin, Texas 78712

Stella Chess, Medical Center, New York University, New York, New York 10016

Hans J. Eysenck, Department of Psychology, Institute of Psychiatry, University of London, London SE5 8AF, United Kingdom

Jochen Fahrenberg, Institute of Psychology, Albert-Ludwigs-University, D-7800 Freiburg i., Br., Federal Republic of Germany

H. H. Goldsmith, Department of Psychology, University of Oregon, Eugene, Oregon 97403-1227

Jeffrey A. Gray, Department of Psychology, Institute of Psychiatry, University of London, London SE5 8AF, United Kingdom

Charles F. Halverson, Jr., Department of Child and Family Development, University of Georgia, Athens, Georgia 30602

Willem K. B. Hofstee, Department of Psychology, University of Groningen, 9712 HV Groningen, The Netherlands

Paul M. Kohn, Department of Psychology, York University, North York, Ontario M3J 1P3, Canada

Jacqueline V. Lerner, Human Development and Family Studies, Pennsylvania State University, University Park, Pennsylvania 16802

Richard M. Lerner, Human Development and Family Studies, Pennsylvania State University, University Park, Pennsylvania 16802

Roy P. Martin, Department of Educational Psychology, University of Georgia, Athens, Georgia 30602

Albert Mehrabian, Department of Psychology, University of California, Los Angeles, California 90024

Judy Morrow, Department of Psychological Sciences, Purdue University, West Lafayette, Indiana 47907

Petra Netter, Department of Psychology, University of Giessen, D-6300 Giessen, Federal Republic of Germany

Katherine Nitz, Human Development and Family Studies, Pennsylvania State University, University Park, Pennsylvania 16802

Rainer Riemann, Department of Psychology, University of Bielefeld, D-4800 Bielefeld, Federal Republic of Germany

Mary Klevjord Rothbart, Department of Psychology, University of Oregon, Eugene, Oregon 97403-1227

Elizabeth H. Slabach, Department of Psychological Sciences, Purdue University, West Lafayette, Indiana 47907

Jan Strelau, Department of Individual Differences, Faculty of Psychology, University of Warsaw, 00-183 Warsaw, Poland

Rachna Talwar, Pennsylvania State University, University Park, Pennsylvania 16802

Alexander Thomas, Medical Center, New York University, New York, New York 10016

Ulrike Ullwer, Department of Psychology, University of Heidelberg, D-6900 Heidelberg, Federal Republic of Germany

Guus L. Van Heck, Department of Psychology, Tilburg University, 5000 LE Tilburg, The Netherlands

Theodore D. Wachs, Department of Psychological Sciences, Purdue University, West Lafayette, Indiana 47907

Marvin Zuckerman, Department of Psychology, University of Delaware, Newark, Delaware 19716

Preface

The growing interest in research on temperament during the last decade has been recorded by several authors (e.g., R. Plomin; J. E. Bates) from such sources of information as the *Social Sciences Citation Index* or *Psychological Abstracts*. The editors' inquiry shows that the number of cases in which the term *temperament* was used in the title of a paper or in the paper's abstract published in *Psychological Abstracts* reveals an essential increase in research on temperament.

During the years 1975 to 1979, the term *temperament* was used in the title and/or summary of 173 abstracts (i.e., 34.6 publications per year); during the next five years (1980–1984), it was used in 367 abstracts (73.4 publications per year), whereas in the last five years (1985 to 1989), the term has appeared in 463 abstracts, that is, in 92.6 publications per year. Even if the review of temperament literature is restricted to those abstracts, it can easily be concluded that *temperament* is used in different contexts and with different meanings, hardly allowing any comparisons or general statements. One of the consequences of this state of affairs is that our knowledge on temperament does not cumulate despite the increasing research activity in this field.

This situation in temperament research motivated the editors to organize a one-week workshop on *The Diagnosis of Temperament* (Bielefeld, Federal Republic of Germany, September 1987). This was the first time that researchers representing so many disciplines (psychology, psychiatry, pediatrics, behavior genetics, neurophysiology) and the broadest spectrum of theoretical and methodological backgrounds in temperament research met together. Although a total of 50 temperament experts from 12 countries representing Europe (West and East), North America (the United States and Canada), and Japan were able to find a common language, the meeting also showed the lack of communication and the diversity of theoretical and methodological approaches in many areas of temperament studies.

These circumstances gave the editors the idea of compiling a volume aimed at presenting as many different theoretical and methodological approaches to temperament as possible, and this conception seems to be the most specific characteristic of *Explorations in Temperament: International Perspectives on Theory and Measurement* compared to other books recently published in this field.

Because of space limitations, we have been obliged to reduce the original number of authors as well as the length of chapters. However, the fact that we were able to recruit authors who are among the most competent and distinguished researchers in temperament helps to compensate for these limitations.

Originally planned as a two-volume set, *Explorations in Temperament* consists of two parts: the first, Contemporary Conceptualizations, and the second, Diagnosis and Methodological Issues.

It has to be stressed that *Explorations in Temperament* should not be regarded as an alternative title to "Proceedings from the Workshop: The Diagnosis of Temperament." Nevertheless, this meeting gave the editors the opportunity to obtain an overview of the current state of research on temperament, and—what is most important—it highly influenced the idea and content of this volume as well as the recruitment of its contributors. These are just some of the reasons why we are greatly indebted to the Center for Interdisciplinary Research (ZIF) at the University of Bielefeld, the German Research Foundation (DFG), and the German Academic Exchange Program (DAAD), who financed the workshop.

We should also like to thank Urszula Chmurzynska for the preparation of references, Maria Stanko for extensive help in typing the manuscript, and Heide Meise for administering most of the correspondence concerned with editorial issues. Much of the editorial work was supported by a grant from the Polish Minister of Education (Grant RPBP III.25).

JAN STRELAU
ALOIS ANGLEITNER

Contents

PART II. DIAGNOSTIC AND METHODOLOGICAL ISSUES

15. Contemporary Instruments for Assessing Early Temperament by Questionnaire and in the Laboratory

H. H. Goldsmith and Mary Klevjord Rothbart

PART III. ADDENDUM

Jan Strelau

Introduction

Temperament Research: Some Divergences and Similarities

Jan Strelau and Alois Angleitner

The increasing interest in research on temperament that can be observed in the last decade goes together with the growing variety of theories as well as methodological issues regarding temperament. The book *Explorations in Temperament: International Perspectives on Theory and Measurement* exemplifies, to some extent, the spectrum of these diversities and richness of problems being discussed in the area of temperament. An attempt to summarize the current state of affairs in studies on temperament has been undertaken by Strelau in Chapter 19 of this volume. The aim of the Introduction is to bring into relief some of the actual problems in this field of study, taking as a starting point the contribution of the authors to this book. The following issues will be discussed:)

1. The concept of temperament
2. The structure of temperament
3. Developmental aspects of temperament
4. Biological bases of temperament
5. Diagnosis of temperament
6. Methodological issues in temperament research
7. Importance of temperament for practical application

Jan Strelau • Department of Individual Differences, Faculty of Psychology, University of Warsaw, 00-183 Warsaw, Poland   **Alois Angleitner** • Department of Psychology, University of Bielefeld, D-4800 Bielefeld, Federal Republic of Germany.

1

The Concept of Temperament

One of the most controversial problems regarding temperament studies is the notion of "temperament" itself. In a roundtable discussion, eight debaters, mostly experts in child temperament, have given eight different definitions of temperament (Goldsmith *et al.*, 1987). The diversity in the understanding of this notion has also been stressed by many other authors, especially when relating the concept of temperament to personality (e.g., Adcock, 1957; Strelau, 1987a).

The controversy in comprehending temperament is fully reflected in this volume. Some authors regard temperament as a synonym for personality (Eysenck, Gray), the latter concept being at the same time understood in a rather narrow way. The notion "personality" is often limited to dimensions, such as extraversion, neuroticism, and psychoticism (Eysenck), or to impulsivity and anxiety (Gray). The narrow understanding of personality is best exemplified by Eysenck, who writes that "concepts like values, interests, attitudes and others are related to personality but do not usually form part of its central core." Zuckerman, discussing in his chapter so-called basic personality traits, such as, for example, sensation-seeking, extraversion, and impulsivity, does not use the notion "temperament" at all. For him personality dimensions are mediated, however, by biological mechanisms, these being found even in very primitive animals. "A simple organism like a paramecium has two basic 'personality traits': approach and withdrawal" (Zuckerman).

The tradition to confine temperament to the emotional characteristics of behavior, as proposed by Allport (1937), and recently advocated by Goldsmith and Campos (1986), also has its proponents among authors in this volume (Gray, Mehrabian). In his chapter, Mehrabian states that " 'Temperament' is defined here as 'characteristic emotion state' or as 'emotion trait.' "

The most typical definition of temperament, which gained the highest popularity among child-centered researchers, especially in the United States, has been proposed by Chess and Thomas. This definition is that temperament should be understood "as the behavioral style or *how* of behavior" (see also Talwar, Nitz, Lerner, & Lerner; Martin & Halverson). The question "how" refers mainly to formal characteristics of behavior, such as reactivity, activity, or self-regulation. According to the definitions of temperament presented by Rothbart and Strelau (see also Van Heck, Angleitner & Riemann) these temperament characteristics are present since early childhood and have a strong biological background. The fact that temperament is present since infancy and has a clear-cut genetic determination has been consequently underlined in the definition of temperament given by Buss and Plomin (1984). In his chapter Buss writes that "temperaments are here regarded as a subclass of personality traits, defined by *appearance during the first year of life, persistence later in life, and the contribution of heredity.*" The fact that temperament should be regarded as a subclass of personality is strongly advocated by Hofstee, who represents a personological approach to personality psychology. Taking as his starting point the definition of "personality as the study of traits," Hofstee argues that "temperament is the core of personality . . . is a proper subset of it."

This brief insight to the understanding of temperament represented by the authors of this volume allows us to conclude that there is no agreement as to what temperament is. The question arises whether lack of consistency in defining temperament is typical for this phenomenon only; the answer is definitely no. There is no consensus among psychologists in the understanding of most of the concepts in psychology. A shift from theory to the operational level allows us, however, to compare some of the results obtained within different approaches to research on temperament. Data recorded under the "umbrella" of different conceptualizations regarding temperament are admitted, at least to some extent, to enrich our knowledge concerning individual differences in behavior characteristics.

The Structure of Temperament

Questions regarding the structure of personality have gained most popularity since the introduction of factor analysis to this field of study. The leaders in trait-oriented personality psychology have offered different solutions concerning the number and quality of traits (factors). In most considerations regarding the structure of personality the number of factors varies from three, as proposed by Eysenck, to sixteen, as suggested by Cattell. For several years past the so-called Big Five robust factors—Extraversion, Agreeableness, Conscientiousness, Neuroticism, and Openness (Intellect or Culture)—as introduced by Norman (1963) and Costa and McCrae (1985) have gained high popularity among trait-oriented personality psychologists. Angleitner (1990) emphasizes that the Big Five considered as broad dimensions for the classification of individual differences in behavior rating studies are now consensually acknowledged.

The question arises as to how the above-mentioned personality factors relate to the structure of temperament. Because of the differentiated view of the notions "temperament" and "personality," the answer cannot be unequivocal. If we take the position represented by Eysenck, for whom temperament and personality are synonyms (assuming that abilities are extracted from personality), it has to be stated that the structure of temperament may be described by three superfactors: extraversion, neuroticism, and psychoticism. A similar position is represented in this volume by Gray and Zuckerman. The former author proposes describing temperament, treated interchangeably with personality, by means of three dimensions which correspond with the three neurological constructs underlying emotion systems—Behavioral Inhibition System (BIS), Behavioral Approach System (BAS), and Fight/Flight System (F/FLS). Mehrabian, who, like Gray, limits the temperament domain to emotions, has also distinguished three basic traits: Pleasure–Displeasure, Arousal–Nonarousal and Dominance–Submissiveness. His bipolar characteristics, by means of which he describes the structure of temperament, have, however, little in common with Gray's theory. Zuckerman offers support for the three superdimensions, as proposed by Eysenck, and suggests adding to this model two further dimensions, namely Activity and Aggression/Hostility.

The opinion, found in many studies and by means of several methods (Digman, 1990), that the Big Five have much in common with temperament is not a novelty. A suggestion that the Big Five factors, with the exclusion of the latter—openness (Intellect or Culture)—be treated as temperament characteristics is expressed in Hofstee's chapter. They form the central variables in the personality domain and, as mentioned earlier, for Hofstee temperamental traits constitute a central subset of personality. A similar view has been presented recently by Angleitner (1990), who sees the first four factors of the Big Five as primarily temperamental dimensions. A temperament structure similar to this proposed by Eysenck, as well as the structure proposed by authors of the Big Five, has been postulated by Buss and Plomin (1984). The three basic temperament dimensions—Activity, Emotionality, and Sociability—have much in common with such factors as Extraversion, Neuroticism, and, to some extent, Agreeableness (Digman, 1990).

The Big Five, as well as the three superfactors, represent the broadest level in a hierarchical structure of traits. Temperament researchers, especially those who study temperament in children and/or who make a distinction between the notions "temperament" and "personality," delineate the structure of temperament using more specific dimensions. For example, Chess and Thomas, as well as Lerner and Windle (see Talwar et al.), describe temperament by means of nine traits. Among them, only four— Activity, Approach/Withdrawal, Quality of Mood, and Distractability—are to some extent identical in both theories. The temperament traits, as proposed by Windle and Lerner (1986), tend to describe behavior characteristics in a still more specific way. This is expressed in the distinction of three kinds of Rhythmicity: Rhythmicity–Sleep, Rhythmicity–Eating, and Rhythmicity–Daily Habits. Martin, who has taken the Thomas and Chess (1977) model as a starting point, has reduced the number of traits from nine to six: Activity Level, Adaptability, Approach/Withdrawal, Emotional Intensity, Distraction, and Persistence (Martin & Halverson).

The structure of temperament, as proposed by Thomas and Chess (see Chess & Thomas), Windle and Lerner (see Talwar et al.), and Martin (see Martin & Halverson), is based on a descriptive approach to temperament. The hypothetical–deductive strategy is an example of a different way in which the structure of temperament may be built. This strategy, applied by several temperament researchers (e.g., Eysenck, 1970, Strelau, 1983; Strelau, Angleitner, Bantelmann, & Ruch, 1990), is represented in this volume by Rothbart. Taking as a point of departure two basic temperament characteristics— Reactivity and Self-Regulation, which evoke to some extent Strelau's (1974) temperament concepts of Reactivity and Activity, Rothbart describes temperamental individuality by introducing such traits as Negative Reactivity, Positive Reactivity, Duration of Orienting, Behavioral Inhibition, and Effortful Control. Rothbart explains individual differences in these traits by appealing to given biological mechanisms as well as to developmental regularities.

As can be seen from this review, we are far from possessing a commonly accepted structure of temperament. The number of traits as well as proposed structures of temperament mentioned here are nowhere near exhausted. In the Addendum, Strelau has listed over 80 traits (factors) used in studies aimed at describing temperament in adults. To bring us closer to the solution regarding the structure of temperament, more systematic factor-analytic as well as cross-cultural studies are required in which different concepts are studied together and in which the developmental and cultural specificity of human beings is taken into account.

The Developmental Aspects of Temperament

Research on temperament in children gained high popularity, especially in the United States, due to the pioneering studies conducted by Thomas and Chess. The authors' New York Longitudinal Study (NYLS) on temperament, which began in 1956 and continues into the present, has thrown some light on the developmental aspects of human temperament. The NYLS experience, summarized after 20 years of studies in Thomas and Chess' monograph *Temperament and Development* (1977), allowed the authors to arrive at the following conclusion:

> As regards temperament specifically, the behavioral criteria for any temperamental trait must necessarily change over time as the child's psychological functioning develops and evolves. What remains consistent over time is the *definitional identity* of the characteristic (p. 159).

In other words, according to the authors, it is not the tendency to react in a given way (the temperament trait) that changes over time, but the developmentally determined kind of behavior in which the temperamental traits (the tendencies) are expressed. The view that temperamental traits are characterized by low changeability during ontogenesis can be found in many chapters of this volume (e.g., Hofstee, Mehrabian, Van Heck). According to Mehrabian, "environmental influences on temperament are hypothesized to be gradual and to be possible only when these influences are consistent and highly repetitious (amounting to hundreds of thousands of trials) over the course of the first dozen years of development."

The developmental psychologist Rothbart (Chapter 4) underlines the fact that temperament traits develop in ontogenesis (see also Goldsmith & Rothbart, Chapter 15). Under maturation, due to changes in the physiological mechanisms underlying temperament, the quality as well as the number of temperamental traits undergo changes (see also Goldsmith & Rothbart, Chapter 15). For example, such a temperamental trait as Effortful Control, present in preschool children, yet cannot be found in infants. The developmental specificity in temperamental characteristics is due mainly to the fact that during development the processes of self-regulation, as well as the child's own activity, reach continuously higher levels, thus resulting in qualitative and quantitative changes in temperament.

According to many conceptualizations of temperament also presented in this volume, the importance of temperament is mainly expressed in the fact that psychological development is the result of interaction between temperament, other characteristics of the individual, and the environment—primarily the social one. This idea is clearly expressed in the chapters by Chess and Thomas, Talwar *et al.*, and Van Heck. According to Talwar *et al.*, the significant increase in studies on child temperament has its roots in "the theoretical role that individual differences in temperament have been given in accounts of variations in person–social context relations." Developmental contextualism is the approach that underlies the research on temperament conducted by Lerner and his associates (Talwar *et al.*).

Even if one shares the position that temperament traits are relatively stable, their importance in the determination of human development is evident if we consider them within an interactionist approach. Thus, for example, behavior modification can be achieved when given temperament characteristics interact with adequate situational changes (Mehrabian). Van Heck and Buss, in their chapters, go one step further in considering the temperament–environment interaction by stressing the importance of genotype–environment interaction. Individuals with given temperament traits select situations that correspond with their temperament and undertake activities in order to modify situations in such a way as to match their temperament. The kinds of temperament–environment interactions cannot be neutral for human development.

To conclude, it might be stated that the developmental approach to temperament leads to different solutions. The one delineated in this volume by Rothbart consists of producing evidence that changes in temperament are in essence mainly developmental. The second outcome, represented by many authors in this volume, postulates that temperament (whether prone to changes or not) plays a significant role in psychological development. Both solutions are rather complementary to rather than competitive with each other.

Biological Bases of Temperament

Most temperament researchers agree that temperament, whatever the traits and structure to which this concept refers, has a strong biological determination. The biological mechanisms underlying temperament serve as the explanatory concepts by means of which individual differences in temperament characteristics are interpreted.

The biological determination of temperament and/or basic personality dimensions is one of the most crucial assumptions in temperament theories. This assumption has its roots in the facts that temperament characteristics can be observed from the first weeks of life (see, e.g., Rothbart) and individual differences in temperament traits have a strong genetic determination (in this volume, Buss, Eysenck, Zuckerman). To avoid oversimplification, the temperament/personality "traits are not directly inherited, but are only a manifestation of particular combinations of inherited biological traits" (Zuckerman). This idea has been expressed in other words by Eysenck when discussing the biological determination of Extraversion, Neuroticism, and Psychoticism:

> Clearly, genetic factors cannot act directly on behavior; there must be an intervening link between genes and chromosomes on the one hand, and social behavior on the other. This intervening link may be looked for in physiological factors, neurological structure, biochemical and hormonal determinants, or other biological features of the organism.

Arousal-oriented temperament researchers, who concentrate mostly on temperament traits in adults (in this volume Gray, Eysenck, Fahrenberg, Kohn, and Zuckerman), pay much attention to these neurological and biochemical mechanisms which regulate the energetic aspects of the emotional and behavioral components of temperament. The study conducted by Gray (Chapter 7) on the BIS, BAS, and F/FLS mechanisms underlying the emotional temperament, as well as by Zuckerman (Chapter 8) in the domain of sensation-seeking, belong to the most sophisticated research regarding the physiological and biochemical mediators of temperamental traits.

One of the crucial problems when studying biological mechanisms underlying temperament consists in the fact that the same physiological variables are often considered to be correlates of different temperamental traits. For example, the amplitude of the averaged evoked potential (AEP) is used as a physiological correlate of Augmenting/Reducing, Sensation-Seeking, Strength of the Central Nervous System (CNS), Extraversion and Impulsivity (see Strelau, 1987b). This suggests that physiological mechanisms responsible for the regulation of the level of arousal (activation) codetermine rather the energetic (intensity) characteristics of temperament traits (common for several dimensions) but not the specificity of these traits. Netter, in her chapter on biochemical variables employed in studying temperament, offers evidence which shows that one type of behavior is mediated by a variety of transmitters and biochemical variables and the reverse. The same transmitter and biochemical variable codetermines different temperament traits. One of the recommendations emerging from this kind of data proposes that it is necessary to study configurations of different physiological and biochemical correlates in order to get a consistent picture regarding the biological mechanisms underlying a given temperament trait. This procedure is explicitly or implicitly recommended by many authors of this volume (e.g., Eysenck, Netter, Fahrenberg, and Zuckerman).

Researchers who assume that temperament has a biological background prefer causal theories of temperament. They use knowledge about the functioning of neurophysiological and biochemical mechanisms in order to explain individual differences in temperament characteristics. It has to be added, however, that theories based on a purely descriptive level are not an exception in temperament studies, especially in children (see Kohnstamm, Bates, & Rothbart, 1989). The theory of temperament developed by Thomas and Chess is a good example here. The categories of temperament they identify have some empirical foundation; however, they "do not rest on any *a priori* conceptual neurobiologic, neurochemical, or psychophysiological basis." Hofstee, in his chapter, goes further, stating that the task of personality (including temperament) researchers is first of all to describe, not to explain, personality/temperament.

The kind of strategy one prefers—explanation or description—when studying temperament or basic personality traits has different consequences for theory and practice. For biologically oriented temperament researchers it is important not to fall into reductionism (see Hofstee), which consists in reducing the psychological phenomenon of temperament to physiological reactions and/or biochemical processes. For descriptivally oriented researchers it is crucial to show the predictive power of temperamental traits.

The Diagnosis of Temperament

The number of psychometric instruments aimed at measuring temperamental traits illustrates in a given way the expansion of research on temperament observed in the last years. Slabach, Morrow, and Wachs (Chapter 13) have catalogued almost 30 different diagnostic instruments in the area of infant and child temperament. Strelau (Addendum) gives a list of 25 "paper-and-pencil" methods used for the purpose of diagnosing temperamental traits in adults.

The large number of diagnostic instruments is mainly due to the many different theories and conceptualizations regarding temperament. Sometimes even modifications within the same approach result in constructing separate inventories. For example, in three chapters of this volume (Chess & Thomas, Talwar *et al.*, and Martin & Halverson), the same stylistic definition of temperament, as proposed by Thomas and Chess (1977), has served as the starting point for developing three different structures of temperament. As a consequence it has led to the development of different temperament inventories.

Specificities exist in psychometric tests, depending on whether they are aimed at diagnosing temperament in infants and children or in adults. Two factors on which these specificities are based are of special significance: (1) in children, permanent changes in temperament characteristics occur due to their fast development while, in adults, the temperament traits are more or less stable; and (2) because children (at least until school age) are not able to report their own behavior, ratings by others (parents, teachers) have to be used for diagnosing temperament. In adults, self-rating is the dominant psychometric method in studies on temperament.

The excessive developmental changes in children's behavior require the construction of inventories specific for a given developmental period (e.g., infant, toddler, preschooler). Goldsmith and Rothbart show in their chapter the frame for constructing such psychometric instruments. These assessment methods take into account the quantitative and qualitative developmental specificity typical for the different age periods. At the same time they allow a comparison of temperamental traits of the same person at different ages—a requirement needed in longitudinal studies.

The many psychometric tests used in studying temperament elicit a conclusion that effort should be expended to reduce them to a small, reasonable number. Slabach et al. (see Chapter 13), reviewing temperament questionnaires popular in the 1980s for diagnosing temperament in children (from birth until the age of 18), present evidence showing that different questionnaires are useful for different purposes. The reliability as well as the validity measures of questionnaires compiled by the authors (see also Hubert, Wachs, Peters-Martin, & Gandour, 1982) give a good orientation regarding the usefulness of these tests.

As mentioned before, the rating by others rather than self-rating is typical for diagnosing temperament in children. One of the major problems here is the low reliability of these measures when interrater agreement is taken into account (see Slabach et al. in this volume). A systematic study conducted by Martin and Halverson (Chapter 14) is consistent with this conclusion.

Many temperament inventories for adults refer to arousal-oriented theories. Some of these, to which reference has been made in this volume, as, for example, the Eysenck Personality Questionnaire, Zuckerman's Sensation-Seeking Scale, or the Strelau Temperament Inventory—Revised, may be mentioned here. One of the most popular ways of examining construct validity of the arousal-oriented temperament inventories is to use psychophysiological or psychophysical measures, supposed to be indicators of arousal (activation). As shown in many studies (Fahrenberg, Chapter 18; see also Fahrenberg, 1987; Strelau, 1990), when psychophysiological/physical measures, treated as markers of a given trait, are correlated with psychometric scores of this trait, the correlations are often very low or even zero. Amelang and Ullwer (Chapter 17) demonstrate the lack of consistency between laboratory measures and psychometric scores for extraversion and neuroticism. The lack of consistency has also been observed when biological correlates were compared with psychometric measures in children (Slabach et al., this volume). From the review of literature regarding cross-situational consistency in personality traits (see, e.g., Jackson & Paunonen, 1985; Olweus, 1980) it might be concluded that there is much higher consistency when psychometric measures are compared with behavioral characteristics instead of psychophysiological correlates. This finding has support in preliminary data reported by Goldsmith and Rothbart (Chapter 15). The authors show that assessment of temperament in children based on psychometric measures correlates with temperament characteristics expressed in natural behavior measured in laboratory conditions.

It is the editors' belief that the construction of a satisfactory temperament inventory, whatever the specificity of this instrument is, has to be based on a well-grounded theory. It must also fulfill the basic methodological and psychometric requirements. Goldsmith and Rothbart's (Chapter 15) study of the construction of tests for the assessment of temperament in children exemplifies this kind of approach. Not only constructors but also users of temperament inventories, when making a decision as to which of the many temperament inventories to select and apply, should take into account the criteria mentioned above.

Methodological Issues in Temperament Research

The aim of this section is to concentrate on selected issues concerned with the assessment of temperamental traits. If one distinguishes between the notions "temperament" and "personality," as do many authors of this volume, the question arises whether essential differences exist between temperament and personality inventories. This question was asked by Angleitner and Riemann (Chapter 12) who, referring to preliminary data, have given an affirmative answer. Whereas temperament scales are constructed by items that ask for overt and covert behavior (reactions), personality items refer mainly to attributes, wishes, interests, and biographical facts and attitudes.

One of the most essential differences between personality and temperament inventories, especially when arousal-oriented temperament questionnaires are considered, consists in the formal characteristics of items. It has recently been suggested by Angleitner (1990; see also Strelau, Addendum) that whereas personality items refer mainly to the "frequency" criterion (how often a given behavior occurs), temperament items mostly have to do with the "intensity" measure [how strong (intense) a given reaction (behavior) is expressed].

For the assessment of temperament as well as personality by means of inventories the psychometric principles to be followed when generating items and scales are very important. A kind of guideline for constructing temperament scales is presented by Angleitner and Riemann in this volume. In this respect the rules are similar to those drawn for constructing personality inventories (see Angleitner, John, & Loehr, 1986).

As mentioned earlier, self-rating is the source of information to which temperament inventories for adults refer. The question arises whether self-rating is the best way in which temperamental characteristics can be assessed. According to Hofstee (Chapter 11), "personality and temperament are best viewed as judgmental variables." He suggests that the best strategy to assess temperament is to use methods that refer to judges (observers), i.e., peer-rating instead of self-rating (the actor's point of view).

Among the many temperament traits there exist some the diagnosis of which is based mainly on psychophysiological or/and psychophysical measures. The reducing/augmenting dimension as proposed by Petrie (1967) and Buchsbaum (Buchsbaum & Silverman, 1968), as well as the Pavlovian properties of the CNS (Nebylitsyn, 1972; Strelau, 1983) exemplify this statement. The many studies reported in the literature (e.g., Fahrenberg, 1987; Strelau, 1983, 1990) show that psychophysiological and psychophysical measures lack generalizability. They are highly modality-specific and differ in response patterns. This means, among other things, that the application of single psychophysiological or biochemical measures for diagnosing temperament traits is obsolete. This also holds true when psychophysiological scores are used as markers of psychometrically measured traits (Fahrenberg, this volume). An essential step in the assessment of temperament based on psychophysiological measures "would be to acknowledge advances in differential psychophysiology concerning, for example, the multivariate approach, differentiation of response patterns, and multimodal assessment strategies." It is rather obvious that this very essential methodological requirement can be fulfilled only in best psychophysiological laboratories and can hardly be adapted for practical purposes.

Importance of Temperament for Practical Application

Concentration on the role temperament plays in everyday life is not the main purpose of the book. There are, however, some theoretical problems presented in this volume which are of special importance for application in practice. The concept of "goodness of fit," as discussed by Chess and Thomas and by Talwar *et al.* is probably the best example of this kind of issue.

Goodness of fit, as understood by Chess and Thomas implies an adequate interaction between the individual's temperament traits as well as other personality characteristics (including competencies) and the environment (demands, expectations, opportunities). If the individual with given temperamental traits (the core of our interest) is not able to cope with the environmental demands, then poorness of fit occurs. Chess and Thomas's concepts of goodness and poorness of fit have much in common with the concept of stress. This is especially evident when stress is understood as a state caused by the imbalance between the environmental demands and the individual's capacity/capability (codetermined by, among other factors, temperamental traits) to cope with these demands (Strelau, 1988). The role of temperament in human behavior is especially evident in extreme situations (Nebylitsyn, 1972; Strelau, 1983), it means when the individual is confronted with high discrepancy between the environmental demands and his/her capability of coping with them. Kohn's study (Chapter 16) is largely devoted to the relationship between temperamental traits and sensitivity as well as tolerance to pain, is an example of studying the relationship between stress and temperament in a laboratory situation. Chess and Thomas, in their chapter, make us aware of the usefulness of the concept of goodness of fit in everyday practice (educational problems, psychological health, etc.).

Taking as a starting point the assumption that temperament is significant for adaptive functioning through its links with the social context, Talwar *et al.* have developed a concept of goodness of fit which "emphasizes the need to consider both the characteristics of individuality of the person and the demands of the social environment, as indexed, for instance, by expectations or attitudes of key significant others with whom the person interacts." A match (fit) between the individual's temperament traits and the demands of the social context assures positive interaction, whereas a poor fit between individual temperament and a particular social context leads to negative adjustment. Another way of looking at the importance of temperament in real life has been proposed by Buss (see Chapter 3). The author underlines the role of temperamental traits themselves rather than the kind of demand-capacity interaction in choosing given environments (e.g., city living vs countryside) and/or activities (e.g., job in television news vs job as an accountant) in order to maintain positive adjustment. Also, problem behaviors, such as shyness or hyperactivity, are explained by Buss not by means of individual-environment interaction but by referring to extreme positions on given temperament traits or by a combination of traits.

Many studies are reported in the literature (see Carey & McDevitt, 1989; Chess & Thomas, 1986; Kohnstamm et al. 1989; Strelau, 1983) supporting the idea expressed in several chapters of this book (Buss, Chess & Thomas, Kohn, Talwar et al.), that temperament contributes essentially to the efficiency and adequacy of human behavior in everyday life, especially when confronted with extreme situations.

Many other issues, questions, and remarks may arise after getting acquainted with this volume. As mentioned earlier, it has been our intention to center on these which seem to be most characteristic of the current state of research on temperament. On the basis of the 19 chapters, written by experts in temperament, some recommendations may be suggested for further studies in this area. We postulate, among other premises, more systematic concentration on a cross-cultural approach, where much attention is paid to the universality of the structure of temperament, to the determinants of temperamental traits from a developmental perspective, and to behavior treated as the basic source of information regarding the individual's temperament and its significance in real life.

References

Adcock, C. J. The differentiation of temperament from personality. *The Journal of General Psychology*, 1957, *57*, 103–112.

Allport, G. W. *Personality: A psychological interpretation*. New York: Holt, 1937.

Angleitner, A. *Personality psychology: Trends and developments*. Presidential Address presented at the 5th European Conference of Personality Psychology, Arricia-Genzano, Italy, June 1990.

Angleitner, A., John, O. P., & Loehr, F. J. It's what you ask and how you ask it: An itemmetric analysis of personality questionnaires. In A. Angleitner & J. S. Wiggins (Eds.), *Personality assessment via questionnaires: Current issues in theory and measurement*. Berlin: Springer, 1986.

Buchsbaum, M. S., & Silverman, J. Stimulus intensity control and cortical evoked response. *Psychosomatic Medicine*, 1968, *30*, 12–22.

Buss, A. H., & Plomin, R. *Temperament: Early developing personality traits*. Hillsdale, NJ: Erlbaum, 1984.

Carey, W. B., & McDevitt, S. C. (Eds.), *Clinical and educational applications of temperament reserach*. Amsterdam/Lisse: Swets & Zeitlinger, 1989.

Chess, S., & Thomas, A. *Temperament in clinical practice*. New York: Guilford, 1986.

Costa, P. T., Jr., & McCrae, R. R. *The NEO Personality Inventory*. Odessa, FL: Psychological Assessment Resources, 1985.

Digman, J. M. Personality structure: Emergence of the five-factor model. *Annual Review of Psychology*, 1990, *41*, 417–440.

Eysenck, H. J. *The structure of human personality*. (3rd ed). London: Methuen, 1970.

Fahrenberg, J. Concepts of activation and arousal in the theory of emotionality (neuroticism): A multi-variate conceptualization. In J. Strelau & H. J. Eysenck (Eds.), *Personality dimensions and arousal*. New York: Plenum, 1987.

Goldsmith, H. H., Buss, A. H., Plomin, R., Rothbart, M. K., Thomas, A., Chess, S., Hinde, R. A., & McCall, R. R. Roundtable: What is temperament? Four approaches. *Child Development*, 1987, *58*, 505–529.

Goldsmith, H. H., & Campos, J. J. Fundamental issues in the study of early temperament: The Denver Twin Temperament Study. In M. E. Lamb, A. L. Brown, & B. Rogoff (Eds.), *Advances in developmental psychology*. Vol. 4. Hillsdale, NJ: Erlbaum, 1986.

Hubert, N. C., Wachs, T. D., Peters-Martin, P., & Gandour, M. J. The study of early temperament: Measurement and conceptual issues. *Child Development*, 1982, *53*, 571–600.

Jackson, D. N., & Paunonen, S. V. Construct validity and the predictability of behavior. *Journal of Personality and Social Psychology*, 1985, *49*, 554–570.

Kohnstamm, G. A., Bates, J. E., & Rothbart, M. K. (Eds.), *Temperament in childhood*. Chichester: Wiley, 1989.

Nebylitsyn, V. D. *Fundamental properties of the human nervous system*. New York: Plenum, 1972.

Norman, W. T. Toward an adequate taxonomy of personality attributes: Replicated factor structure in peer nomination personality ratings. *Journal of Abnormal and Social Psychology*, 1963, *66*, 574–583.

Olweus, D. The consistency issue in personality psychology revisited—with special reference to aggression. *British Journal of Social and Clinical Psychology*, 1980, *19*, 377–390.

Petrie, A. *Individuality in pain and suffering*. Chicago: University of Chicago Press, 1967.

Strelau, J. Temperament as an expression of energy level and temporal features of behavior. *Polish Psychological Bulletin*, 1974, *5*, 119–127.

Strelau, J. *Temperament—personality—activity*. London: Academic Press, 1983.

Strelau, J. The concept of temperament in personality research. *European Journal of Personality*, 1987a, *1*, 107–117.

Strelau, J. Personality dimensions based on arousal theories. In J. Strelau & H. J. Eysenck (Eds.), *Personality dimensions and arousal*. New York: Plenum, 1987b.

Strelau, J. Temperament dimensions as co-determinants of resistance to stress In M. P. Janisse (Ed.), *Individual differences, stress, and health psychology*. New York: Springer, 1988.

Strelau, J. *Are psychophysiological scores good candidates for diagnosing temperament/personality traits and for a demonstration of the construct validity of psychometrically measured traits?* Manuscript submitted for publication, 1990.

Strelau, J., Angleitner, A., Bantelmann, J., & Ruch, W. The Strelau Temperament Inventory—Revised (STI-R): Theoretical considerations and scale development. *European Journal of Personality*, 1990, *4*, 209–235.

Thomas, A., & Chess, S. *Temperament and development*. New York: Brunner/Mazel, 1977.

Windle, M., & Lerner, R. M. Reassessing the dimensions of temperamental individuality across the life-span: The Revised Dimensions of Temperament Survey (DOTS-R). *Journal of Adolescent Research*, 1986, *1*, 213–230.

I

Contemporary Conceptualizations

Part I presents a diversity of temperament theories. Some of these are mainly child centered (Chapter 1, Chess and Thomas; Chapter 2, Talwar, Nitz, Lerner, and Lerner; Chapter 3, Buss; Chapter 4, Rothbart). They illustrate the paths and directions of change in temperament research in the United States since the pioneering work of Thomas and Chess in the 1950s.

Another line of theorizing in temperament presented in this volume concentrates mainly on the concept of arousal, which has its roots in the Pavlovian tradition (Chapter 5, Mehrabian; Chapter 6, Eysenck; Chapter 7, Gray; Chapter 8, Zuckerman). A typical characteristic of the representatives of these theories, with the exception of Mehrabian, is that they treat the concepts "temperament" and "personality" as synonyms. According to them, personality/temperament dimensions (traits) have a clear-cut biological background.

Some of the chapters mentioned above (Chapters 7 and 8), as well as Chapter 9 (Netter), discuss the neurophysiological and/or biochemical mechanisms or at least correlates of temperament dimensions. No single book devoted to temperament presents such a broad perspective regarding the biology of temperament.

The last two chapters of Part I elaborate on some general issues in temperament research. Van Heck (Chapter 10) presents evidence showing that temperament plays an essential role in the person–environment interaction, while Hofstee (Chapter 11) discusses one of the most controversial problems in the relationship between temperament and personality.

1

Temperament and the Concept of Goodness of Fit

Stella Chess and Alexander Thomas

Research centers in various countries have formulated different theoretical viewpoints and methodological approaches to the diagnosis of temperament, to the definition of categories of temperament, and the rating schemes used to identify the categories. But no matter what the conceptual scheme and methodological techniques may be, a crucial question arises. How do we formulate the mechanism or mechanisms through which temperament exerts its influence on the psychological development of the individual from early childhood into adult life? In other words, given any diagnostic system of temperament, how do we examine its functional importance and its relationship to the values, demands, and expectations of the culture in which the person lives? A conceptual framework that serves as a basis for analyzing the dynamics of the influence of specific temperamental characteristics on any individual's life course gives us the ability to use our diagnosis of temperament in a number of important ways. We can counsel parents and teachers as to the best approach to children, which will vary according to the child's temperament. We can identify high-risk patterns of parent-child interaction, and intervene to prevent or treat more effectively the behavior disorders of children. Older children and adults can use their knowledge of their own temperaments to channel their behavior to achieve more effectively their personal and career goals.

The Goodness-of-Fit Concept

In our own studies of the functional significance of temperament we have found the formulation of *goodness of fit* to be a most useful conceptual framework. This formula-

Stella Chess and **Alexander Thomas** • Medical Center, New York University, New York, NY 10016.

15

tion stems from the conviction that normal or pathologic psychologic development does not depend on temperament alone. Rather, it is the nature of the interaction between temperament and the individual's other characteristics with specific features of the environment which provides the basic dynamic influence for the process of development.

Stated briefly, there is goodness of fit when the person's temperament and other characteristics, such as motivations and levels of intellectual and other abilities, are adequate to master the successive demands, expectations, and opportunities of the environment. If, on the other hand, the individual cannot cope successfully with the environmental demands, then there is poorness of fit. With a goodness of fit, psychologic development and functioning progresses favorably. With a poorness of fit, the individual experiences excessive stress and failures of adaptation, and his or her development takes an unfavorable course.

Goodness of fit does not imply an absence of stress and conflict. Quite the contrary. These are inevitable concomitants of the developmental process, in which new expectations and demands for change and progressively higher levels of functioning occur continuously as the child grows older. Demands, stresses, and conflicts, when in keeping with the person's developmental potentials and capacities for mastery, may be constructive in their consequences and should not be considered as an inevitable cause of behavioral disturbance. The issue involved in disturbed behavioral functioning is rather one of *excessive* stress resulting from poorness of fit between environmental expectations and demands and the capacities of the individual at a particular level of development.

The concept of goodness of fit has also been applied by the biologist René Dubos as a measure of physical health:

> Health can be regarded as an expression of fitness to the environment, as a state of adaptedness. . . . The words health and disease are meaningful only when defined in terms of a given person functioning in a given physical and social environment (1965, pp. 350–351).

Several specific examples from our longitudinal studies will illustrate our application of the goodness-of-fit concept to the analysis of the functional significance of temperament. These examples will be based on our own formulation of the definition and diagnosis of temperament. However, as will be indicated later on in this chapter, the concept of goodness of fit can be applied to other conceptualizations of temperament.

Diagnostic Formulation of Temperamental Categories

We have defined temperament, in line with the formulations of several psychologists in the American literature (Cattell, 1950; Guilford, 1959), as the behavioral style or *how* of behavior, as contrasted with the abilities, or *what* of behavior, and the motivations, or *why* of behavior. Two children may dress themselves with equal skillfulness or ride a bicycle with the same expertness and have the same motivations for engaging in these activities. Two adolescents may display similar learning ability and intellectual interests and their academic goals may coincide. Two adults may show the same technical expertise in their work and have the same reason for devoting themselves to their jobs. In other words, in all these instances, abilities and motivations may be similar. Yet these two children, adolescents, or adults may differ significantly with regard to the quickness with which they move, the ease with which they approach a new situation, the intensity and character of their mood expression, and the effort required by others to distract them when they are absorbed in an activity. These differences are differences in behavioral style, or temperament. Similarly, individuals may be alike in temperament, but different in abilities and/or motivations.

The rating and evaluation of the significance of temperament has been a major focus of interest throughout our studies. Our own diagnostic scheme for temperament has been based on an empiric inductive analysis of descriptive detailed behavioral data. These data were obtained in the childhood period primarily from parental interviews and secondarily from teachers. In the adolescent and adult age periods—thus far, extending to age 30, we have used direct interviews and questionnaires with the subjects themselves. Thus, the categories of temperament we have identified and the criteria used for their ratings have an empiric basis, and do not rest on any *a priori* conceptual neurobiologic, neurochemical or psychophysiologic basis. We are convinced that temperament does have biologic bases, though in individual cases it may be modified or even changed by environmental influences (Thomas & Chess, 1977). There is significant evidence for some genetic influence in the causation of our temperamental categories (Torgersen & Kringlen, 1978), though it is quite possible that variations in hormonal or other factors in the prenatal period may also affect the nature of the newborn child's temperament. This question of prenatal influence remains to be tested. As of now, studies of this issue have been fragmentary and inconclusive (Chess & Thomas, 1984).

The categories of temperament which we have identified and rated quantitatively and qualitatively include: (1) Activity level; (2) regularity of biologic functions, such as sleep-wake cycles, hunger and bowel elimination; (3) a positive versus negative response to a new situation, person, or environmental demand, which we have labeled approach/withdrawal; (4) ease or difficulty of adaptability to the requirement for change in an established behavior pattern; (5) sensory threshold; (6) quality of mood, rated as the preponderance of positive versus negative mood expression; (7) intensity of mood expression, irrespective of whether it is positive or negative; (8) ease or difficulty of distractibility of an ongoing activity by an extraneous stimulus; and (9) a double category of length of attention span, and degree of persistence with a difficult task.

We have also identified both clinically and by factor analysis three temperamental constellations which appear to have special functional significance. *Easy temperament* comprises a combination of regularity, positive approach responses to new stimuli, quick adaptability to change, and mildly or moderately intense mood that is preponderantly positive. Children in this group quickly develop regular sleep and feeding schedules, take to most new foods easily, smile at strangers, adapt easily to a new school, accept most frustrations with little fussing, and adapt to the rules of new games quickly. Such a child is easy to manage by parents, teachers, and pediatricians; hence the term easy temperament. Adults with this temperamental pattern adapt quickly to new jobs, make friends easily, and are usually mild-mannered in their emotional expressions.

At the opposite extreme to easy temperament is *difficult temperament*, which comprises irregularity in biological functions, negative responses to new situations or people, slow adaptability to change, and intense mood that is frequently negative. Such children characteristically show irregular sleep, feeding, and bowel elimination schedules, slow acceptance of new foods, prolonged adjustment periods to new routines, people, or places, and relatively frequent periods of loud crying. Laughter is also characteristically loud. Frustration typically produces a violent tantrum. Parents, teachers, and pediatricians most often find such children difficult to manage, hence the term difficult temperament. Adults with this temperamental pattern find themselves uneasy in new situations, new jobs, or with strangers, do not make friends easily, and are prone to violent expressions of anger or frustration. On the other hand, they may show great zest and enjoyment once they have adapted to some new interest or activity.

The third special pattern is what we have called *slow-to-warm-up temperament*, which comprises negative responses of mild intensity to the new, with slow adaptability after repeated contact. As children, the negative mild responses to the new can be seen in the first encounter with the bath, new foods, new people or places, or a new school setting. With repeated exposures to such new experiences, such a child gradually comes to show quiet and positive interest and involvement, hence the term slow-to-warm-up temperament. Adults with this temperamental pattern may be shy and cautious, but not necessarily timid or anxious. They typically prefer the familiar to the new, make new friends slowly, and are mild-mannered in their expression of their feelings.

Not all individuals fit neatly into one of these three temperamental patterns, because of the varying and different combinations of temperamental traits that are possible and do occur. Also, persons who fit one of these three patterns show a wide range in the degree of manifestation. Some demonstrate easy or difficult temperament to a marked degree in almost all situations. Others are relatively easy or difficult, but not necessarily in all types of life experiences. Some individuals predictably warm up slowly in any new situation, others warm up slowly with certain types of new stimuli or demands, but warm up quickly with others.

The nine temperamental categories and the three special patterns have by now been identified in a large number of studies in the United States, as well as in various European and Asian countries (Thomas & Chess, 1977; Ciba Foundation Symposium 89, 1982).

Examples of Goodness and Poorness of Fit

It should be emphasized that we consider all temperamental ratings, even when in the extreme ranges of very low or very high, to be within the normal limits of behavior. Thus, very high activity level, a temperamental trait, is normal, as contrasted to hyperactivity, which is a pathologic behavioral characteristic. This distinction is not an arbitrary one. Hyperactivity includes not only extremly high activity, but other abnormal symptoms, such as impulsive behavior, very brief attention span, and difficulty in organizing task activity. As another example, high persistence, as a normal temperamental trait, is to be distinguished from repetitive, rigid, and perseverative behavior which is found in organic brain syndromes.

A temperamental trait becomes a factor in pathologic behavior, not by itself alone, but when it is combined with a poorness of fit, that is, with environmental demands and expectations that are excessive and stressful for the individual with his or her specific temperament. Our examples will cite mainly cases from the childhood period, because the temperament-environment interaction is clearer in these early age periods. In adult life the same principle of goodness of fit does operate, but the behaviors one observes are more complicated, because of the increasing influence of developmental changes, abilities, motivations, special life experiences, and psychodynamic defense mechanisms as the individual matures.

One common example of the goodness-of-fit issue is the difference between the child who responds positively to new situations and adapts quickly to change, and the child with opposite temperament who has negative reactions to new situations and adapts slowly to change. The differences between these two children are evident, often dramatically so, when they first go to school, whether it be nursery school, kindergarden, or the first grade. The first child, who takes to the new positively and adapts quickly, will typically find the school experience a pleasant and even exciting one from the first day, will participate actively in the school program quickly, and soon makes friends with a group of his classmates. This is a goodness of fit from the beginning, unless the child has other problems—such as a borderline intellectual level or a physical handicap.

The second child, whose first reactions to the new are negative, and who adapts slowly, will typically show a very different initial adjustment to school. He will hold back, stand at the periphery of the group, cling to the mother, become engaged in the class activities slowly and make friends slowly. Whether this results in a goodness or poorness of fit will depend on the behavior of the parent and teacher. If they insist that the child participate actively from the beginning, and the parent does not remain nearby for the first days or weeks to reassure the child, the youngster can only feel pressured, inadequate and anxious. If, in addition, the child has a high intensity level, the distress may also include loud temper tantrums. This is a poorness of fit which all too often leads to a psychologic school problem. If, on the one hand, the parent and teacher recognize the meaning of the child's behavior, they will be patient, give the youngster time to adapt and encourage her tentative efforts to participate. If feasible, the parent can also remain nearby for several days or weeks to reassure the child. With such an approach which only makes demands on the child which he can master, a goodness of fit is achieved, and the youngster finally makes a good adjustment to school, as good as the first child with quick adaptability.

As older children or adults such individuals with negative reactions to the new and slow adaptability may be very shy and even timid, have difficulty in social situations and turn down new jobs or promotions if they are unfamiliar, especially if they have had many unpleasant and distressing experiences of being forced too quickly into new situations when growing up. If, however, their temperamental traits have been recognized and respected by parents and teachers, and they have been allowed to adapt comfortably at their own pace, the story in adult life will be different. The person may get to know that his first negative reactions to the new are only temporary, and will be able to participate actively in such situations, whether socially or at work, because he knows from his life experiences that the initial discomfort will disappear and he will then master and enjoy them.

Let us also take the example of the child with very high or very low activity level. The high activity child will become restless, impulsive, and difficult to manage if he does not have sufficient outlets for exercising his muscles. At home he may become a nuisance, and at school a disciplinary problem if required to sit still for long periods of time. All too often, when this happens, the child will be subjéct to criticism and punishment, which will only intensify his disturbed behavior, and his self-image as a "bad boy." This then can become a serious poorness of fit. If, on the other hand, parents and teachers recognize the child's need for adequate motor activity, the story will be different. The parents can seek out playground programs which emphasize active play and will not expect the child to sit quietly through a long dinner or automobile ride. The teacher can give the child a class responsibility which involves a good deal of motor activity, and send him on a brief errand when she notices that he is becoming particulary restless in his seat.

The issue of goodness versus poorness of fit in a high-activity child has been clearly demonstrated in the contrasting findings in our longitudinal studies of a middle-class sample, the New York Longitudinal Study Sample (NYLS) and a Puerto Rican working-class sample (PRWC) living in the congested and underprivileged East Harlem section of New York City. Half of the PRWC children with behavior disorders under 9 years of age were high-activity children who presented symptoms of excessive and uncontrollable motor activity, whereas only one NYLS youngster displayed these symptoms, and this was a brain-damaged child. The PRWC families usually had a relatively large number of children and lived in small apartments with little space for constructive motor activity that highly active children required. Furthermore, these very children were even more likely to be cooped up at home for fear that if they ran around in the streets they could be in particular danger of accidents. This was a realistic fear, given the conditions of the East Harlem area in which these families lived. In addition, safe playgrounds and recreational areas were not available to these families. By contrast, the NYLS families lived in spacious apartments or private homes with backyards, with safe streets and playgrounds also available. The high-activity children in these families therefore had ample opportunities to exercise their need for motor activity.

The differences in the incidence of behavior disorders in the temperamentally high-active children in these two contrasting populations was clearly due to the nature of the environmental restrictions and opportunities, which made for a goodness of fit for the NYLS children and a poorness of fit for the PRWC youngsters. This judgment was confirmed when one PRWC child who had been described by this teachers as "uncontrollably active," and by his parents as a "whirling dervish," became manageable when the family moved to a private house with a small yard.

The extremly low-active child is also vulnerable to a poorness of fit with her environmental expectations. This child moves slowly and usually requires more time to accomplish tasks than children with medium or high activity level. If her parents, teachers, or peers grow impatient at her slowness and pressure, scold or tease her, such a child may become pathologically passive and withdrawn. We have also seen teachers in the lower school grades evaluate a bright low-activity level child as subnormal intellectually and recommend incorrectly that the youngster repeat the school grade. A goodness of fit for such a child requires patience on the part of parents and giving her extra time to get dressed and otherwise prepared for school, meals, or family outings. The child's temperament should also be explained to the teacher, so that she also gives the child extra time when necessary, and also steps in to prevent the youngster's classmates from teasing her.

The above examples in no way exhaust the many ways in which the response of parents, teachers, mental health professionals, pediatricians, or peers will foster either a goodness or poorness of fit for a child with a particular extreme level of one temperamental trait or another. In general, this special concern for a child's temperamental characteristics is required when it is either at a very high or very low level. In the average range of temperament, which will usually be consonant with environmental demands and expectations, no special management techniques are required. Occasionally, a parent will expect, even demand, that his or her child function at an extreme level of temperament, such as with adaptability or persistence, when the child is only at an average level. This kind of excessive demand can also create a poorness of fit, with all its unfavorable consequences.

Variability in the Goodness of Fit

A number of factors can modify the functional significance of any particular temperamental trait. The age of the individual is one such variable. Thus, for example, regularity or irregularity of biologic functioning in early childhood is an important issue for most middle-class parents in our culture. The child who sleeps through the night at an early age, has a regular nap time, gets hungry at the same times each day and has a bowel movement on a regular daily schedule, makes the mother's management much easier. She can plan her day's activities with confidence that she will be free for other tasks at the same time each day when the baby naps. She can schedule meals ahead of time, and toilet training is relatively easier because of the child's regular timing of bowel movements. The irregular young child, by contrast, makes the mother's tasks more difficult. The infant's irregular nighttime sleep pattern, with unpredictable night awakenings, can leave the parent frequently groggy because of insufficient sleep at night. The irregular nap times can hinder the mother's planning of other tasks for specific times of the day, and the child's irregular hunger will make the scheduling of meals difficult. The irregular timing of bowel movements will usually prolong the period of toilet training.

However, for the older child and the adult, biologic irregularity usually becomes a minor insignificant problem. If his sleep schedule is irregular, this no longer needs to interrupt the parents' sleep. If his hunger is irregular, he can adjust to the family's mealtime schedule, perhaps with snacks in between. And once toilet training has been achieved, irregularity of bowel movements is no longer a problem.

By contrast, high distractibility and low persistence do not present problems in management in early years, but may do so in later childhood and adult life. The young child who is highly distractible may actually make for easier parental management. Such a child who resists dressing or bathing can be distracted with a toy and the task then accomplished. Or, if the baby begins to engage in potentially dangerous activities, such as poking at lamps or reaching for hot or sharp objects, she can easily be diverted by showing her a toy or some other attractive object. The infant with low distractibility, on the other hand, cannot be so easily diverted, and dressing, or removal from a dangerous object may require considerable energy. The infant with low persistence also presents no problems, since persistence at task performance is not an issue in this age period.

However, in older childhood and adult life, high distractibility and low persistence can easily make the individual vulnerable to a poorness of fit. In our culture the traditional work ethic emphasizes persistent and concentrated attention to a task until it is completed. This is an expectation that the individual with low distractibility and high persistence can achieve easily. The child with high distractibility or low persistence, or both, by contrast, will have difficulty meeting this demand. She may be able to accomplish tasks and assignments effectively, but will usually require several breaks and diversions in her efforts because of her temperamental characteristics. Unfortunately, all too often, parents, teachers, or employers may pay too much attention to such a person's inability to stick to a task to completion without any diversion, and lose sight of the fact that she does finish the assignment successfully and reliably.

This issue tends to come up first when the child starts school, and the parents notice that she does her homework intermittently rather than sitting down with it and not getting up until she has finished her work. Some parents interpret this behavior as "laziness" or "lack of willpower" and also worry that their child will not succeed in the professional or business world with this characteristic. They may then scold, criticize, and pressure the child to sit without interruption until her tasks are completed, which can only put the youngster under severe stress and make her feel inadequate and inferior. A severe poorness of fit is the inevitable result. If, on the other hand, the parents—and the teachers—recognize that the youngster is making a conscientious effort according to her own temperament, and does complete her tasks successfully, they will relax and encourage her. This achieves a goodness of fit.

One highly distractible boy in our NYLS sample had a different kind of problem with his mother. He would get distracted by something interesting he saw on his way home from school, forget that his mother was waiting to take him to a doctor or dentist appointment, and arrive home late. Or he would cheerfully start to do a chore at home, get distracted, and forget to finish it. The mother had her own psychologic problems involving a pathologic need to control her environment and her family. She interpreted the boy's behavior as willful disobedience and an attempt to control her, and engaged in a constant battle to force him to confirm immediately and fully with her demands. We pointed out to her repeatedly that his temperament was responsible for this behavior, and not any willful disobedience. We reminded her that she had told us herself that he showed this same distraction and forgetfulness with his friends and other people and not just her. But she refused to accept the logic of this explanation and continued her battles with her son, creating a potentially serious poorness of fit. The father was a benign but rather passive individual, who stayed aloof from these battles between mother and son.

Fortunately, when this boy became an adolescent, he spontaneously began to distance himself from his mother. He made friends easily, spent most of his time outside his home, and did not confide his activities and plans to his mother. This frustrated her, and she kept trying to intrude on his life, but he refused to let her do so. He also began to become aware himself of his tendencies to become easily distracted and learned to monitor himself and what he was doing. Now, as a young man of 30, he is successfully launched on a career of his own choosing. He comments that he is still likely to become distracted and to welcome an interruption on a job, but he is highly motivated not to allow these tendencies to interfere with his work accomplishments. It is of interest that as he has established himself as an independent adult, no longer subject to her pressures, his relationship with his mother has improved markedly.

Low sensory threshold is another temperamental trait which may create stress in childhood but not in later life. Carey (1974) has reported an association between frequent night awakening in infancy and low sensory threshold. This relationship is presumably due to such a child's sensitivity to extraneous noises and lights during the night. An infant's frequent night awakening means broken and inadequate nights' sleep for the parents, who may be irritable and annoyed at the child as a result, with a poorness of fit. This problem can be solved if the parents realize its basis, and take precautions to shield their sleeping infant as much as possible from outside noises. As the child grows older, this night awakening no longer involves the parents going in several times a night to soothe the youngster, and the problem is resolved spontaneously. Such a child may grow up to be a "light sleeper," but this is no longer a source of stress with the parents.

Occasionally, a child with a low sensory threshold will have a sensitivity to rough or tight clothing which may make the morning dressing routine an unpleasant experience. The parents may not understand why the youngster is objecting so strongly to wearing certain clothes, consider that she is being arbitrary and finicky, and a battle between parent and child may be the result. If the parent understands the nature of the youngster's reactions, and provide her with soft and loose clothing, this conflict can be avoided. As the child grows older, however, and begins to choose her own clothes, this problem disappears.

Sociocultural Factors

Socioeconomic and cultural factors may influence the development of a goodness or poorness of fit. An example is the difference in the consequencies of high-activity level in our middle-class NYLS sample versus the Puerto Rican working-class sample, given earlier. It is the demands, expectations, and opportunities of the individual environment which create ease or difficulty in functioning, depending on the person's temperament and other characteristics. And these environmental issues will vary from culture to culture, and one socioeconomic class to another. A dramatic example of this principle has been shown in the African studies conducted by DeVries (1984). In our middle-class culture, difficult temperament produces the greatest vulnerability of all the temperamental characteristics to behavior disorder development (Maziade, Caperaa, Laplante, Boudreault, Thivierge, Cote, & Boutin, 1985; Thomas & Chess, 1977). In our culture, children with this temperamental pattern are difficult to manage because of their irregularity and frequent intense negative responses to the new, and their slow adaptability to change.

Many parents assume this must somehow be their fault, and become guilty and anxious. Others may make a value judgment on the child, and condemn him for his behavior. One of our NYLS fathers, himself a mental health professional, kept insisting, in spite of all our explanations, that his daughter's difficult temperament meant that she was "just a rotten kid." Such negative parental attitudes usually gave rise to excessive pressure on the child to adapt quickly and modulate his intense expressiveness— impossible expectations for such a child. Poorness of fit was inevitable, and the majority of these children developed behavior disorders. On the other hand, if the parents understand the child's temperament, make allowances for his violent outbursts when upset, and patiently give him time to adapt at his own pace, then a goodness of fit could be achieved and the child could develop without becoming psychologically disturbed.

What DeVries (1984) did in the course of his African studies was to collect temperament ratings on a group of 47 infants of the Masai tribe in Kenya. This is a primitive tribe living in the sub-Sahara region. He used a translation of the Carey Infant Temperament Questionnaire, at a time when a severe drought was just beginning. With these ratings he identified the 10 infants with the most easy temperament, and the 10 with the most difficult temperament. He returned to this tribal area 5 months later, by which time the drought had killed of 97% of the cattle herd, on which the tribe depended for most of their food. He was able to locate the families of 7 of the easy babies and 6 of the difficult ones. The families of the other infants had moved in an effort to escape the drought. Of the 7 easy babies, 5 had died, whereas all of the difficult infants had survived! Clearly, the temperamentally difficult infants had received more attention and nutrition. Either because these qualities were more highly valued in that culture or because of their loud and prolonged crying when hungry, this behavior brought them more food. The difficult infants, in this tribe, and under conditions of partial famine, were favored over the easy children, a situation exactly the reverse in middle-class families in a comfortable environment in our culture.

Other Theoretical Approaches and Goodness of Fit

In recent years, a number of research workers in the field of developmental child psychology and psychiatry have also begun to use the concept of goodness and poorness of fit (see Chess & Thomas, 1984, p. 277). Some use the term goodness of fit, others speak of the synonymous term "match and mismatch." As an example, Murphy, in her Topeka Longitudinal Study, comments on the "interesting examples of misfit and fit between mothers and babies" (1981, p. 168). Strelau, from his theoretical framework, writes:

> Low-reactive individuals prefer activity of high stimulative value. Since human activity is mainly determined by social environment, it may happen that the stimulative value of the individual's activity does not develop in accordance with his/her reactivity level. In this case it may result in different disorders and disturbances in behavior. (1985, p. 31)

His colleague, Eliasz, in a discussion of high-reactive subjects, refers to several authors who have indicated that "any deviation of the stimulation from the optimum could impair the efficiency of the subject" (1985, p. 58). Eliasz concurs that for such individuals:

> the medium range of activation is conductive to the well-being of the subject. The high level of activation is connected with difficulties in concentration, psychic tension, and

several physical symptoms resulting from the autonomic system arousal. . . The low level of activation is associated with boredom, apathy and drowsiness. (1985, p. 58)

These formulations by Strelau and Eliasz, though they come from a different theoretical framework, are quite consonant with our concept of goodness and poorness of fit.

Goodness of Fit and Similarities of Temperament

We are frequently asked whether goodness of fit depends on a similarity of temperament between parent and child, or between teacher and child. The answer is emphatically *no*. As we have analyzed the interactions between parents and their children we have found all kinds of combinations. In some cases, similarity of temperament promoted a goodness of fit; in others it led to a poorness of fit. One parent who was himself slow-to-warm-up, with slow adaptation after an initial negative reaction to the new, empathized with his son, whose temperament was similar. On the other hand, one mother with intense emotional expressiveness, reacted to her daughter's temper tantrums, i.e., intense negative responses to frustration, with loud shouting and even screaming at the child. This only served to reinforce and intensify the child's tantrums.

The same variation of fit was true of parents and children of opposite temperament. One father who was a quietly expressive person with an easy temperament took delight in his young son's intensively expressive reactions, even when they were manifested by loud crying episodes at almost any new situation. He approvingly called his boy "lusty," even though his wife, at the same time, was feeling guilty and responsible for the boy's difficult behavior. Without this positive response from the father, given the mother's distress, there could have been a poorness of fit and this boy might very well have developed a behavior disorder. As it was, though he rated quantitatively as the subject with the most difficult temperament in our NYLS sample, the youngster did not develop any significant behavior disorder.

By contrast, another father, who himself was a persistent person with low distractibility, could not accept his son's low persistence and high distractibility. Though the boy was of high intelligence and motivated to learn, the father constantly criticized his inability to study and work without stopping until his task was completed. The father labeled his son as having "no character" and "lacking in self-discipline," and could not be swayed from this judgment by our discussions with him. The youngster inevitably finally accepted his father's judgment, and as an adolescent said, "Let's face it, my father is right, I am inferior." With this serious poorness of fit, this boy went on to become a non-functioning young adult in school and work. His father's judgment had become a self-fulfilling tragedy. We and several psychotherapists who attempted to treat the boy were unable to prevent this outcome.

Goodness of Fit, Self-Awareness, and Self-Esteem

Different theorists have proposed different mechanisms for the beginnings of self-differentiation and self-concept in infancy (Thomas & Chess, 1980, Chapter XIII).

Whatever may be the disputes over the infancy period, there can be no question as to the rapid development of the self-concept through the preschool and middle childhood years. Many elements help to shape the child's self-concept in a positive or negative direction—special abilities or handicaps, the nature of the family, a favorable or unfavorable socioeconomic environment, a stimulating or degraded school setting. Among these many factors, a goodness or poorness of fit between the child's temperament and her environment is often of major importance. This has been indicated in a number of the examples given above. If there is a goodness of fit between child and environment, the foundation for a healthy self-concept and stable self-esteem is laid down. If there is a poorness of fit, a negative, denigrated self-evaluation begins to crystallize. If, in later childhood or even in adult life, a poorness of fit can be altered, such as by the emergence of new positive capacities or a favorable change in the environment, then a negative self-image may be transformed into a positive one. What happens in childhood is important, but it does not fix the individual's psychological future irrevocably.

An important aspect of the self-concept development is whether or not the individual gains a recognition of his temperamental characteristics. This self-awareness can have positive consequences if the person then shapes his behavior so as to emphasize the potential strengths of his temperament, and to minimize their potential harmful effects. For example, one of our NYLS subjects is now launched on the beginning of a successful professional career. As a child she had a difficult temperament, with intense negative reactions when upset. She became a mild behavior problem because of loud, prolonged temper tantrums when criticized, teased, or in reaction to any unexpected change in her routines or schedules, combined with inconsistent handling and pressuring by her parents. The parents consulted us and we advised patient, relaxed, and consistent handling of the tantrum behavior. The parents followed our recommendations and the tantrums gradually disappeared. The girl had superior intelligence, enjoyed learning, and her subsequent development through adolescence and early adult life went smoothly. She is now 30 years old, and in our interview with her earlier this year she reported that she avoids direct confrontations with other people when there is a disagreement or other problem. She does not avoid the problem, but figures out some other way of dealing with it. She does this because she knows that if she gets angry in a confrontation she may lose control of herself because of the intensity of her emotional reaction.

For this young woman, as with many others, a knowledge of the potential problems her temperament might create was an important asset because she did not criticize herself for having a particular temperamental characteristic. However, a self-awareness of one's temperament can be harmful rather than helpful if a derogatory self-critical judgment is made as a result. An example of this outcome is the case of the NYLS subject cited above, with high distractibility and low persistence. He was aware of these temperamental traits, but accepted his father's inflexible judgment that this was unacceptable and made him into an inferior person. This unjustified self-condemnation led to serious difficulties in his psychological development.

Generalization of the Goodness-of-Fit Model

We have discussed the goodness-of-fit model as it applies to temperament because of the special usefulness of the concept in analyzing the functional significance of temperament. However, the same model can be applied to other aspects of an individual's psychological functioning. Thus, in the area of intellectual capacity, a child with borderline normal intelligence will suffer excessive stress if the parents or teachers demand that her academic achievement equal that of her classmates with average or superior intelligence. The child with average intelligence may suffer if her brothers and sisters have superior intelligence and her parents expect her to perform academically at the same level as her more gifted sibs. And the child with high superior intelligence can become bored and frustrated if her need for special academic stimulation is not recognized and provided by parents and teachers. Hunt (1980, pp. 34–35) has emphasized this issue, which he calls "the problem of the match" between the child's cognitive capacity and the demands made on him. If the demand is excessive for his cognitive level, the child will show "withdrawal and distress, and often tears." If the demand is not excessive, the task is performed with "interest and excitement." The same principle can be applied to other issues, such as athletic skills and special interests and talents; goodness or poorness of fit will depend on whether appropriate or excessive demands, or insufficient opportunities for stimulation are provided by the environment.

Prevention and Treatment of Behavior Disorders

We, and a number of other psychiatrists, pediatricians, and clinical psychologists have found the goodness-of-fit model to be extremely useful in the prevention and treatment of behavior disorders (Chess & Thomas, 1986). This is especially true in children, where overall behavior patterns are less complex than in adults and the identification of temperament is simpler and its influence more evident. In childhood, poorness of fit also usually involves primarily the interaction between child and parent, and counseling and guidance of the parents can be an effective approach for both prevention and treatment of childhood behavior disorders. Most parents are committed to the best welfare of their children, and are ready to modify their child-care practices and attitudes if this will benefit their youngsters. There are exceptions, in which the father or mother, or both, have rigid standards and expectations which the child cannot meet, and which the parent will not or cannot change. In such cases, parent guidance will be a failure, and direct treatment of the child may be necessary. A number of the specific examples given throughout this chapter illustrate both the successes and failures of parent guidance.

Parents can also be helpful in teaching their growing children to understand their own temperaments and how to deal with situations which are potentially very stressful because of one or another specific temperamental trait.

The identification of a temperamental factor in an adult's behavior problem may be more difficult than in children, but is feasible and sometimes essential. The goodness-of-fit model can also be useful in counseling couples with marital difficulties. A mutual understanding and respect for each other's temperament may be important in some such cases in dealing with the causes of the marital discord.

Conclusion

In conclusion, we wish to reemphasize the issue we raised at the beginning of this chapter. Temperament research is an important aspect of the study of human psychology.

This research can be approached from a variety of conceptual schemes and methodologic techniques and can explore a number of different biologic and behavioral relationships to temperament. These studies have been fruitful and promise to be even more productive in the coming years and decades. But we ourselves are concerned that temperament research should keep in mind its responsibility to broaden our knowledge of the behavior of real human beings in real life. Otherwise, there is the danger that our research, no matter how elegant and sophisticated its design and execution may be, will become abstract and sterile. It is for this reason that we have presented our goodness-of-fit model, as a useful approach to the analysis of the functional significance of temperament for an individual's psychological development. Other conceptual models may be developed by others which will prove to be as helpful or even more so. And the goodness-of-fit model itself will certainly benefit by further refinement of its conceptualization and application. Such developments will make temperament research more and more meaningful as an important field of scientific work.

References

Carey, W. B. Night wakening and temperament in infancy. *Journal of Pediatrics*, 1974, *81*, 823–828.

Cattell, R. B. *Personality: A systematic theoretical and factual study*. New York: McGraw-Hill, 1950.

Chess, S., & Thomas, A. *Origins and evolution of behavior disorders*. New York: Brunner/Mazel, 1984.

Chess, S., & Thomas, A. *Temperament in clinical practice*. New York: Guilford, 1986.

Ciba Foundation Symposium 89. *Temperamental differences in infants and young children*. London: Pitman, 1982.

Dubos, R. *Man adapting*. New Haven: Yale University Press, 1965.

Eliasz, A. Transactional model of temperament. In J. Strelau (Ed.), *Temperamental bases of behavior: Warsaw studies on individual differences*. Lisse: Swets & Zeitlinger, 1985.

Guilford, J. P. *Personality*. New York: McGraw-Hill, 1959.

Hunt, J. M. Implications of plasticity and hierarchical achievements for the assessment of development and risk of mental retardation. In D. B. Sarwin, R. C. Hawkins, L. O. Walker, & J. H. Penticuff (Eds.), *Exceptional infant*. Vol. 4. New York: Brunner/Mazel, 1980.

Maziade, M., Caperaa, P., Laplante, B., Boudreault, H., Thivierge, J., Cote, R., & Boutin, P. Value of difficult temperament among 7 year-olds in the general population for predicting psychiatric diagnosis at age 12. *American Journal of Psychiatry*, 1985, *142*, 943–946.

Murphy, L. B. Explorations in child personality. In A. I. Rabin, J. Aronoff, A. M. Barclay, & R. A. Zucker (Eds.), *Further explorations in personality*. New York: Wiley, 1981.

Strelau, J. *Temperament—personality—activity*. London: Academic Press, 1983.

Thomas, A., & Chess, S. *Temperament and development*. New York: Brunner/Mazel, 1977.

Thomas, A., & Chess, S. *Dynamics of psychological development*. New York: Brunner/Mazel, 1980.

Torgersen, A. M., & Kringlen, E. Genetic aspects of temperamental differences in infants. *Journal of the American Academy of Child Psychiatry*, 1978, *17*, 433–444.

de Vries, M. Temperament and infant mortality among the Masai of East Africa. *American Journal of Psychiatry*, 1984, *141*, 1189–1194.

2

The Functional Significance
of Organismic Individuality
The Sample Case of Temperament

Rachna Talwar, Katherine Nitz, Jacqueline V. Lerner,
and Richard M. Lerner

Developmental psychology, as a discipline, has tended to focus more on normative, developmental functions (Wohlwill, 1973) than on interindividual variation in developmental trajectories. This emphasis is changing, due to an increasing concern with biological bases of human individuality (Lerner, 1984; Plomin, 1986) and with multidirectional, life-span changes in psychological capacities and behavioral functions (Baltes, 1987). Research in our laboratory is associated with this latter concern, that is, with the nature, bases, and functional significance of interindividual variation in human development across life (e.g., Lerner & Lerner, 1983, 1987, 1989). It is because of this concern with the person's individuality that we have been drawn to the study of temperament.

In contemporary psychology, most approaches to study of temperament view this aspect of personality as pertaining to the stylistic component of an individual's mental or behavioral repertoire (Buss & Plomin, 1984; Windle, 1988). That is, temperament refers to *how* the person does whatever is done. Thus, neither the content of, nor the motivation underlying, behavior is of primary concern in the study of temperament. Instead, individual differences in the style in which a person manifests otherwise identical behaviors are of prime interest. For example, since all children eat and sleep, focus on these contents of the behavioral repertoire would not readily differentiate among them. However, children may differ in the rhythmicity of their eating or sleeping behaviors and/or in the vigor, activity level, or mood associated with these behaviors; such characteristics of individuality are temperamental attributes, by our definition.

Rachna Talwar, Katherine Nitz, Jacqueline V. Lerner, and Richard M. Lerner • Pennsylvania State University, University Park, Pennsylvania 16802.

Over the course of the past decade a significant increase has occurred in the study of temperament, especially during infancy and childhood (Lerner & Lerner, 1986). We believe that one reason for this growth in scientific attention is precisely because of the above-noted growing interest in interindividual variation in human development, and, more specifically, because of the theoretical role that individual differences in temperament have been given in accounts of variations in person-social context relations (Lerner & Lerner, 1986). Interindividual differences in temperament are seen as important moderators of children's and adolescents' success at coping with the stressors or demands encountered in the key settings of life (e.g., the family, the school, the peer group). In sum, then, the focus on temperament in our work is predicated on the belief that interindividual differences in temperament are important components of the bases for variation in person-context relations, bases which may be understood through the application of a perspective about the dynamic, reciprocal character of such relations: Developmental contextualism.

Features of a Developmental Contextual Perspective

We have indicated that we focus on temperamental individuality because it provides a means for us to test ideas associated with a developmental contextual view of human development (Lerner, 1986, 1989; Lerner & Kauffman, 1985). This perspective involves the idea that development occurs through reciprocal relations, or "dynamic interactions" (Lerner, 1978), between organisms and their contexts. A notion of integrated or "fused" levels of organization is used to account for these dynamic interactions (Novikoff, 1945a, 1945b; Schneirla, 1957; Tobach, 1981). Variables from levels of analysis ranging from the inner-biological, through the psychological, to the sociocultural, all change interdependently across time (history); as such, variables from one level are both products and producers of variables from the other integrated levels (Lerner, 1982; Lerner & Busch-Rossnagel, 1981). Accordingly, models where one represents the *relations* among levels, and not any level in isolation, are needed to study these dynamic interactions and their functional significance.

One such model is found in the goodness-of-fit concept we have been testing in the research in our laboratory (e.g., Lerner & Lerner, 1983, 1987, 1989). The goodness-of-fit concept derives from the view that the person-context interactions depicted within developmental contextualism involve "circular functions" (Schneirla, 1957), that is, person-context relations predicated on others' reactions to a person's characteristics of individuality: As a consequence of their characteristics of physical and behavioral individuality people evoke differential reactions in their significant others; these reactions constitute feedback to people and influence their further interactions (and thus their ensuing development). The goodness-of-fit concept allows the valence of the feedback involved in these circular functions to be understood (Lerner & Lerner, 1983, 1987; Thomas & Chess, 1977).

The goodness-of-fit concept emphasizes the need to consider both the characteristics of individuality of the person and the demands of the social environment, as indexed for instance by expectations or attitudes of key significant others with whom the person interacts (e.g., parents, peers, or teachers). If a person's characteristics of individuality match, or fit, the demands of a particular social context, then positive interactions and adjustment are expected. In contrast, negative adjustment is expected to occur when there is a poor fit between the demands of a particular social context and the person's characteristics of individuality.

To illustrate, if a particular characteristic of temperament (e.g., regular sleeping habits) is expected within a given social context (e.g., the family) by a significant other (e.g., the mother), then a child who possesses or develops that behavior will have a good fit with his or her environment. In such cases these children are expected to show positive behavioral interactions in regard to this characteristic, and ensuing developments are predicted to be favorable. If a child does not possess or develop behavior which matches or fits the demands of the context, then negative interactions and unfavorable outcomes are predicted.

In sum, then, within the framework of a developmental contextual perspective, we see temperament as a key instance of behavioral individuality. Through testing the goodness-of-fit concept, we seek to determine whether the functional significance of temperamental individuality for concurrent person-context relations and for subsequent development lies in the nature of the fit between: (1) The person's characteristics of temperamental individuality (i.e., his/her temperamental style); and (2) the demands (e.g., the expectations or attitudes) regarding temperamental style which are maintained by the significant others in the person's key contexts (e.g., the home, the peer group, the school). It is our view, then, that temperamental individuality, as an instance of organismic individuality, derives its significance for adaptive functioning through its link with the social context. This link is structured on the basis of circular functions between characteristics of temperamental distinctiveness and the reactions and feedback of significant others; the link is given its valence for developmental change by virtue of exchanges textured by the goodness of fit between temperament and the demands of the social context.

Our laboratory has been engaged over the course of about a decade with research testing this developmental contextual model of the functional significance of temperamental individuality for adaptive development. Much of this work has been reviewed elsewhere (e.g., J. Lerner, 1984; Lerner & Lerner, 1983, 1987, 1989; Lerner, Nitz, Talwar, & Lerner, 1989). Here, then, it may be of most use to present some of our more recent findings devoted to appraising the functional significance of individual temperament-context relations.

We discuss two of the main features of this research. First, we have developed questionnaire measures of temperament and of the attitudinal component of contextual demands, a component which we have operationalized through the assessment of "ethnotheories of temperamental difficulty." Second, we have utilized these measures in a longitudinal study of early adolescence, the Pennsylvania Early Adolescent Transitions Study (PEATS), an investigation wherein temperament-context fit has been related to psychosocial adjustment during the transition from elementary school to junior high school. We present first our scale development work and then turn to a discussion of the use of these scales in our substantive research aimed at studying the functional significance of temperamental individuality.

Measuring the Dimensions of Temperament and of Ethnotheories of Temperamental Difficulty

Our first current area of research involves developing and testing the empirical utility of measures of temperament and of contextual demands regarding temperament. It is useful to describe first our temperament measure.

The Dimensions of Temperament

The Revised Dimensions of Temperament Survey (DOTS-R; Windle & Lerner, 1986; Windle, Hooker, Lenerz, East, Lerner, & Lerner, 1986) is the instrument developed in our laboratory which we are using currently to assess the dimensions of people's temperamental individuality. The DOTS-R is a 54-item questionnaire which assesses young children's, early adolescents', and young adults' temperamental attributes. For the first two age groups the DOTS-R assesses nine orthogonal dimensions: Activity Level-General (i.e., the level of motor behavior displayed in daily functioning); Activity Level-Sleep (i.e., the level of motor behavior displayed while asleep); Approach-Withdrawal (i.e., the tendency to move toward or away from stimuli); Flexibility-Rigidity (i.e., the ease of adjustment to situations); Quality of Mood (i.e., the positive or negative valence of affect); Rhythmicity-Sleep (i.e., the cyclicality or regularity of sleep patterns); Rhythmicity-Eating (i.e., the regularity or predictability of eating); Rhythmicity-Daily Habits (i.e., the regularity or predictability of daily routines); and Task Orientation (i.e., the level of persistence on, attention to, and lack of distractibility from tasks). In young adulthood the Task Orientation attribute is differentiated as two dimensions, Distractibility and Persistence. In all versions of the DOTS-R the response format for each item is "1" = *usually false;* "2" = *more false than true;* "3" = *more true than false;* "4" = *usually true.* An example of a DOTS-R item (indexing Activity Level-General) is "I can't stay still for long."

Scoring the DOTS-R involves forming attribute scores by summing the scores on individual items. On the basis of the number of items per attribute the range of possible scores for each attribute is: 7–28 for Activity Level-General; 4–16 for Activity Level-Sleep; 7–28 for Approach-Withdrawal; 5–20 for Flexibility-Rigidity; 7–28 for Quality of Mood; 6–24 for Rhythmicity-Sleep; 5–20 for Rhythmicity-Eating; 5–20 for Rhythmicity-Daily Habits; and 8–32 for Task Orientation (or, within young adulthood, 5–20 and 3–12 for Distractibility and Persistence, respectively). Higher DOTS-R scores indicate higher levels of Activity Level-General and Activity Level-Sleep, a tendency to approach, higher flexibility, a positive mood, higher levels of rhythmicity in sleep, in eating, and in daily habits, and a higher task orientation level (for the young adult version higher DOTS-R scores indicate *lower* distractibility and higher persistence).

Internal consistency coefficients (Cronbach alphas) for the above nine childhood and early adolescent-age level DOTS-R attributes are: .84, .87, .84, .79, .91, .80, .80, .70, and .79, respectively, for a sample of 115 preschool children; and .75, .81, .77, .62, .80, .69, .75, .54, and 70, respectively, for a sample of 224 sixth graders (Windle & Lerner, 1986). In addition, for the above-noted ten DOTS-R attributes indexed in the

young adult version of the instrument, internal consistency coefficients are .8.
.70, .89, .78, .80, .62, .81, and .74, respectively, for a sample of 300 you
college students (Windle & Lerner, 1986). Construct validity for the DOTS-R
reported by Windle *et al.* (1986) in a study of temperament, perceived self-comp   ⌐uce,
and depression among early and late adolescents. Construct validity was also assessed
by Windle (1985) in an inter-inventory study among late adolescent college students. In
addition both convergent and discriminant relationships were found between the DOTS-
R attributes and the traits measured by the EASI-II (Buss & Plomin, 1975) and the
Eysenck Personality Inventory (Eysenck & Eysenck, 1969).

Contextual Demands Regarding Temperament

To assess contextual demands regarding temperament we have relied on the concepts of "developmental niche" and of "ethnotheory," as formulated by Super and
Harkness (1981, 1982, 1988). To explain the role these concepts play in our work, it is
useful to recall that Thomas and Chess (1977), in their New York Longitudinal Study
(NYLS), have found that particular attributes of a child's or an adolescent's temperament
were desired, wanted, or preferred by his or her parents or teachers. Positive mood and
rhythmicity of behavior are instances of such desired attributes. In turn, other attributes
were found to be unwanted, e.g., withdrawal and high intensity reactions (Thomas &
Chess, 1977). When a child possessed desired attributes, he or she was easy for the
parent or teacher to interact with; when a child possessed undesired attributes, others
found it difficult to interact with him or her (Thomas & Chess, 1977). In short, in the
NYLS possession of particular, i.e., wanted temperamental attributes afforded easy
interactions, while possession of other, unwanted, attributes afforded difficult interactions.

Given the existence of easy and difficult temperament attributes, one may ask what
influences whether a given attribute is regarded as easy or difficult by a parent, teacher,
or peer. What gives a given temperament attribute its particular meaning?

One answer is provided by Super and Harkness (1982, 1988). They point out that
the developing person's context is structured by three kinds of influences: The physical
and social setting; culturally regulated customs involved in socialization; and the "psychology" of the caregivers or the other significant people with whom the developing
person interacts. This psychology is termed an "ethnotheory" (Super & Harkness, 1980,
1981, 1988), that is, significant others' preferences, aversions, beliefs, or expectations
regarding the meaning or significance of particular behaviors. Together, the three types
of influence comprise the *developmental niche* of the person, that is, the set (or sets) of
structured demands on the developing person (Super & Harkness, 1981).

Super and Harkness indicate that not all groups have the same preferences or
aversions regarding temperament. Across cultures, and even *within* different subpopula-
tions within a culture (e.g., the peers versus the parents of adolescents), differences in
expectations, attitudes, and values regarding temperament may exist. These psychological differences are a product of the particular cultural or subcultural niche within which
the people holding these attitudes, values, and expectations exist. These psychological
differences in the meaning of temperament produce, then, differences in what is re-

garded as a wanted or an unwanted attribute. Thus, contextual or group differences might exist in how easy or difficult it would be to interact positively with an adolescent because differences may exist in different niches within the adolescent's general ecological milieu in the meaning of (the degree of preference for) a given temperament attribute. In other words, then, because specific cultural, subpopulation, or ecological groups may differ in how much they want particular temperamental attributes, they may differ therefore as well in their ethnotheories (i.e., their attitudes, values, and expectations) regarding the difficulty the possession of a particular temperamental attribute presents for interaction. For instance, an adolescent's peers may differ from his or her parents in their respective "ethnotheory of temperamental difficulty," i.e., their preferences for temperament and thus their beliefs about whether a particular temperamental attribute affords difficulty (or of course, conversely, ease) of interaction.

Based on this conception of the meaning of preferences about temperament for difficulty of social interaction, the DOTS-R items are used to assess the ethnotheories regarding temperamental difficulty which are maintained by the parents and by peers of early adolescents. The DOTS-R is used in order to produce scores for the same nine (or ten, in young adulthood) temperament attributes measured by the DOTS-R. For instance, with respect to parents of early adolescents, an item such as "My child gets sleepy at different times every night" is presented to parents who are told to consider the item in terms of how they *want their child to behave*. If the item describes the way the parent wants the child to behave, then the behavior would not make it difficult for the parent to interact with the child, even if the child *always* showed that behavior. However, if the item describes behavior the parent does not want quite as much, then more difficult interactions would exist if the child always showed this behavior. Similarly, if the parent wants the behavior still less, then even greater difficulty would exist in this case. Finally, if the parent does not want to see the behavior at all, and if the child always shows this behavior, the most difficulty for the interaction would exist. Thus, based on the degree to which the parent wants the behavior described in the item, he or she rates the item in regard to the level of difficulty for interaction which would be associated with the behavior. This preference-based rating reflects an ethnotheory component of the demands imposed on the adolescent in his or her developmental niche.

As with the original DOTS-R questionnaire, each DOTS-R ethnotheory questionnaire uses a four-choice format with high scores indicating greater difficulty of interaction. The response alternatives are "4" = most wanted and therefore *not difficult*, "3" = want somewhat and therefore only *a little difficult*, "2" = want only a little and therefore *somewhat difficult*, and "1" = do not want at all and therefore *very difficult*. If the item was considered not to be important or relevant to the parent then the corresponding response would be "not difficult."

The scoring procedures for the "DOTS-R: Ethnotheory" questionnaire are identical to that described for the scoring of the corresponding DOTS-R scale. For instance, for use with early adolescents, two "DOTS-R: Ethnotheory" forms are employed. The first is for use with the adolescent's parent. Only one parent per family is typically used and, in most cases in our research, the ethnotheory form is completed by the child's or adolescent's mother. In correspondence with this DOTS-R form, nine scores are derived, one score for each temperament attribute measured by this scale. These scores, then, represent a parent's ethnotheory about what he or she would find difficult about an adolescent's temperamental style based on the behaviors the parent desires or wants from the adolescent. A second ethnotheory form used with early adolescents is a Peer version and it is administered to the adolescents themselves, since their responses to this form represent the views of the peer group. Each adolescent's temperament is compared to the mean ethnotheory of his or her peers, as computed through use of the responses of the other students in his or her classroom.

Psychometric properties of the DOTS-R: Ethnotheory forms have been reported in Windle and Lerner (1986) and Windle *et al.* (1986). The internal consistency coefficients (Cronbach alphas) for the subscales of these two, above-noted versions of the ethnotheory form range from .65 to .92 with an average reliability of .81. All versions of the ethnotheory measure have comparable psychometric characteristics.

Fit Scores

In the work of the present authors, a fit score represents an index of relations between variables from two qualitatively distinct levels of analysis, that is, the individual and the developmental niche (or the context) of the individual. To obtain a fit score for the relation between, for instance, an early adolescent's temperament and the ethnotheory (for temperament) in the individual's developmental niche, discrepancy scores are obtained by substracting from each subject's DOTS-R score (for each of the nine temperament attributes) the corresponding parent (or peer) DOTS-R Ethnotheory score (i.e., DOTS-R score minus Ethnotheory score = fit score). Thus, each subject received nine fit scores for their parents and nine fit scores for their peer group. These scores indicate the amount of discrepancy between adolescent's self-rated temperament and parent's and peer's expectations of temperamental difficulty. Thus, higher discrepancy scores (positive or negative) reflect less of a fit between adolescent temperament and parental/peer demands, and lower discrepancy scores reflect a better fit between child temperament and parental/peer demands. A discrepancy score of zero indicates the best fit, i.e., the least mismatch between temperament and preferences.

This scoring procedure is represented in Table 2.1. To illustrate this scoring system, then, reference to this Table indicates that if an adolescent only showed a little of a given behavior (a score of 1) a fit score of -3 would exist if the parent (or peer group) wanted this behavior the most, while a fit score of zero would exist *if* the parent (or peer group) did not want this behavior at all; in turn, if the adolescent always showed a given behavior (a score of 4) a discrepancy score of zero would exist *if* the parent (or peer group) showed maximum preference for the behavior, while a discrepancy score of $+3$ would exist *if* the parent (or peer group) showed the minimum level of preference for the behavior. In addition to calculating these fit scores for each of the nine temperament attributes, absolute discrepancy scores can be derived by summing over the nine temperament attributes within each of the early adolescent's contexts (i.e., in our research to date the parent and peer group) to obtain an overall fit score. These scores indicate the total amount of absolute discrepancy between adolescent's temperament and demands, with higher scores indicating more of a mismatch between adolescent's self-rated temperament and preference and lower scores indicating more of a match between attributes and preferences.

Rachna Talwar *et al.*

Table 2.1.   Derivation of Fit (Discrepancy) Scores between Adolescent's Self-Rated Temperament (as Measured on the DOTS-R) and Parental (or Peer) Preferences Regarding Temperament (as Measured on the Corresponding "Ethnotheory of Temperamental Difficulty" Form)

	Ethnotheory Rating for Temperament			
DOTS-R Self-Rating— The behavior is shown:	Most want, and therefore not difficult = 4	Want somewhat, and therefore a little difficult = 3	Want only a little, and therefore somewhat difficult = 2	Do not want at all, and therefore very difficult = 1
A little = 1	−3	−2	−1	0
Somewhat = 2	−2	−1	0	+1
A Lot = 3	−1	0	+1	+2
Always = 4	0	+1	+2	+3

Given the above-noted reliability and validity data for the DOTS-R, and for the corresponding Ethnotheory scales, we have concluded that these measures are appropriate to employ in our tests of the use of the goodness-of-fit concept in understanding early adolescents' adjustments to the stressors they confront across the transition to junior high school. These tests relate to the second area of research focus within our laboratory which we shall discuss.

The Pennsylvania Early Adolescent Transitions Study (PEATS)

Our current tests of the goodness-of-fit concept have occurred within our conducting the Pennsylvania Early Adolescent Transitions Study (PEATS), a short-term longitudinal study of approximately 150 northwestern Pennsylvania early adolescents, from the beginning of sixth grade across the transition to junior high school and to the end of the seventh grade.

To illustrate our work here, we may note that East, Lerner, Lerner, and Soni (1991) determined the overall fit between adolescents' temperament and the demands of their peers regarding desired levels of temperament. Based on the circular functions notion involved in the goodness of fit concept, East *et al.* predicted that while no significant direct paths would exist between adjustment and either temperament, measured alone, or temperament-demands fit, fit would influence adolescent-peer social relations which, in turn, would influence adjustment. In short, significant mediated paths, but insignificant direct paths, were expected. These expectations were supported. For 9 of the 12 measures of adjustment employed (involving parents' ratings of behavior problems; teachers' ratings of scholastic competence, social acceptance, athletic competence, conduct adequacy, and physical appearance; and students' self-ratings of scholastic competence, social acceptance, athletic competence, conduct adequacy, physical appearance, and self-worth), both of the two mediated paths (between adolescent-peer group fit and peer relations, and then between peer relations and adjustment) were significant. In no case, however, was a significant direct path found.

Nitz, Lerner, Lerner, and Talwar (1988) found similar results regarding temperamental fit with parental demands and adolescent adjustment. At the beginning of sixth grade the number of significant relations between the adjustment measures and temperament-demands fit did not exceed the number of significant relations between temperament alone and adjustment. However, at both the middle and the end of sixth grade the percentage of significant relations involving adolescent temperament-parent ethnotheory fit scores and adjustment scores was significantly greater than the corresponding percentages involving adolescent temperament alone. Moreover, and underscoring the interconnections among the child-family relation and the other key contexts comprising the ecology of human development, such as the school context, Nitz *et al.* (1988) found almost interchangeable results when fit scores with the peer demands were considered.

In a related study, Talwar, Nitz, and Lerner (1990) found that poor fit with parental demands (especially in regard to the attributes of Mood and Approach-Withdrawal) at the end of sixth grade was associated in seventh grade with low teacher-related academic and social competence and negative peer relations. Corresponding relations were found in regard to fit with peer demands. Moreover, and again underscoring the importance of considering the context within which organismic characteristics are expressed, goodness-of-fit scores (between temperament and demands) were more often associated with adjustment than were temperament scores alone; this was true in regard to both peer and parent contexts at the end of sixth grade, and for the peer context after the transition to junior high school (at the beginning of seventh grade). Finally, Talwar *et al.* (1990) grouped the PEATS subjects into high vs low overall fit groups (by summing fit scores across all temperament dimensions). Adolescents in the low fit group in regard to peer demands received lower teacher ratings of scholastic competence, and more parent ratings for conduct and school problems, than did the adolescents in the high fit group in regard to peer demands. Comparable findings were found in regard to low vs high fit in regard to parent demands.

In a final study completed to date within our laboratory, Talwar, Schwab, and Lerner (1989) assessed whether the links among temperament and the PEATS subjects' academic competence, as indexed by Grade Point Average (GPA) and by standardized achievement test scores on the California Achievement Test, Form C (CAT/C), are (1) direct ones; or (2) are mediated by social appraisals (by the teacher) of the adolescent's scholastic competence and by the adolescent's appraisal of his/her own scholastic competence. From a developmental contextual perspective, these latter links would be expected to be significant. In turn, however, within a personological, acontextual view of temperament-psychosocial functioning relations (Plomin & Daniels, 1984; Sheldon, 1940, Sheldon & Stevens, 1942) only a direct link (or path) between temperament and academic competence should exist.

Talwar *et al.* (1989) used data from the end of the sixth grade and the end of the seventh grade to test these alternative models of the functional significance of temperament. In addition to the adolescents' self-ratings of temperament on the DOTS-R, their grade point averages for the sixth and for the seventh grades, and their total CAT/C scores for the sixth grade, teachers' ratings of the subjects' scholastic competence on the Teacher Behavior Rating Scale (Harter, 1983) and the subjects' ratings of their scholastic competence on the Harter (1983) Self-Perception Profile were involved in the data analyses conducted by Talwar *et al* (1989).

For the purpose of data reduction, the nine DOTS-R temperament variables were first factor-analyzed. Three second-order factors emerged. Factor one was labeled *Task Rhythmicity*, and was composed of task-orientation and rhythmicity in eating, sleeping, and daily habits. The second factor was labeled *Activity*, and was composed of sleep and of a general activity level. The third factor was labeled *Adaptation*, and was composed of flexibility, approach behaviors, and positive mood.

Analyses subsequent to this factor analysis resulted in corresponding findings for all three of the above-noted temperament factors. For instance, the temperament factor of Adaptation was correlated significantly with GPA and CAT/C scores at the end of grade 6 and with GPA at the end of grade 7. However, these correlations were *not* found to be the outcome of the direct influence of Adaptation on academic competence. Using the path analytic procedures illustrated in Figure 2.1, Talwar *et al.* (1989) compared (1) the direct link between temperament and academic competence with (2) the indirect paths which included the teacher's rating of scholastic competence and the adolescent's self-conception of his/her scholastic functioning. As shown in Figure 2.1, the data indicated that there were no significant paths between Adaptation and either GPA or

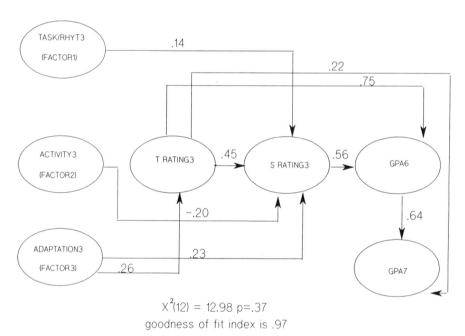

$$X^2(12) = 12.98 \ p=.37$$
goodness of fit index is .97

Figure 2.1. Results of a study by Talwar, Schwab, and Lerner (1989): Developmental contextual path model linking temperament factors, teachers' ratings (T Rating), and self-ratings (S Rating) to grade point average (GPA) at end of grade 6 and end of grade 7 (all paths are significant).

CAT/C scores. However, significant paths were found between this temperament factor, teacher ratings, self-ratings, and GPA and CAT/C scores at the end of grade 6. Corresponding findings involving GPA occurred at the end of grade 7. In respect to the Task Rhythmicity and the Activity factors, indirect paths were also found between these factors, adolescent self-ratings, and outcome measures of GPA and CAT/C scores. As with the Adaptation factor, no direct paths were found between these latter two temperament factors and either GPA or CAT/C scores at either grade level.

These findings, then, lend support to the developmental contextual view of the nature of the relation between adolescent temperament and psychological characteristics. In turn, the data suggest the importance of including in the assessment of early adolescent school functioning the study of temperament-context relations.

In sum, the above-described PEATS studies provide support for the developmental contextual idea that the understanding of the functional significance of temperament can be enhanced by evaluating the links between temperamental individuality and demands/expectations/appraisals of significant others (parents, peers, or teachers) in the key contexts of adolescence. Given such findings, our hope is that as our research continues it will provide a richer data base than has existed previously to evaluate the utility of the developmental contextual view of human development. This goal for our research may be usefully discussed in relation to some concluding observations about our approach to the study of the functional significance of temperament.

Conclusions and Future Directions

Together, the concepts of organismic individuality, of context, and of the relations between the two found in a developmental contextual perspective are quite complex. The simultaneous consideration of these concepts imposes formidable challenges on those who seek to derive feasible research from this perspective. As we have argued, this developmental contextual perspective leads to an integrated, multilevel concept of development, one in which the focus of inquiry is the organism-environment dynamic interaction. Furthermore, such an orientation places an emphasis on the potential for intraindividual change in structure and function—for plasticity—across the life span.

The data we have reviewed here, as well as those derived from other laboratories (e.g., see Baltes, 1987; Hetherington, Lerner, & Perlmutter, 1988, and Sorensen, Weinert & Sherrod, 1986, for reviews) underscore the current use—across the life span—of a developmental contextual orientation for the study of temperament. Nevertheless, for the future the major challenge for this perspective is, as we have noted, the further derivation and empirical testing of models reflecting the nature of dynamic, interlevel interactions across time. Such tests will profit by triangulation of the constructs within each of the level of analysis thought to interact dynamically within a given model.

For instance, in regard to the organism-context interactions assessed within the goodness-of-fit model, temperament could be simultaneously indexed both by more molecular biological measures (e.g., heart rate; see Kagan, Reznick & Snidman, 1986) and by more molecular behavioral measures. Similarly, demands (e.g., of parents) could be simultaneously appraised by assessing both attitudes/expectations about behavior and actual behavioral exchanges. In addition, temperament and demands could be assessed by both questionnaire and observational measures. Such triangulation would not only provide better convergent and discriminant validation information than currently exists. In addition, better insight would be gained about whether all modalities of functioning within a level of analysis are of similar import for adaptive functioning in particular person-context interactions. Moreover, the standard intercorporation of multiple measures into future research is important not only because of the new information it would provide about the developmental contextual model, but also because this information would provide insight into the most useful targets of interventions aimed at enhancing the social behavior of the developing person.

As we have indicated, one reasonably successful path we have taken for exploring the usefulness of a developmental contextual perspective involves the testing of the goodness-of-fit model of person-context relations. Nevertheless, our own work would profit from the sort of triangulation for which we call. In addition, of course, the goodness-of-fit model is not the only conception of person-context relations that may be derived from a developmental contextual orientation. There are perhaps an infinity of possible interlevel relations that may occur and a potentially similarly large array of ways to model them. In the future, those testing these perspectives should consider incorporation of multiple measures within each of the levels modeled. Indeed, since current tests of other models derived from a developmental contextual or life-span perspective also have found considerable empirical support (e.g., Baltes, 1987), we can expect that such extensions will be important additions to an already significant foundation. In sum, the relative plasticity of human development across the life span—a plasticity deriving from the dynamic interactions between organism and context which characterize human functioning—is already well documented (Baltes, 1987; Brim & Kagan, 1980; Featherman, 1983; Hetherington *et al.*, 1988; Lerner, 1984; Sorensen *et al.*, 1986). Thus a future research program including the sorts of directions we suggest should enrich greatly our understanding of the precise conditions promoting and constraining human plasticity and development. Given, then, the present literature, and the promise we see for tomorrow, we believe there is reason for great optimism about the future scientific use of the developmental contextual view of the biological and social bases of development.

ACKNOWLEDGMENTS. The writing of this chapter was supported in part by a grant to Richard M. Lerner and Jacqueline V. Lerner from the William T. Grant Foundation and by NIMH Grant MH39957.

References

Baltes, P. B. Theoretical propositions of life-span developmental psychology: On the dynamics between growth and decline. *Developmental Psychology*, 1987, *23*, 611–626.
Brim, O. G., Jr., & Kagan, J. Constancy and change: A view of the issues. In O. G. Brim, Jr. & J. Kagan (Eds.), *Constancy and change in human development*. Cambridge, MA: Harvard University Press, 1980.
Buss, A. H., & Plomin, R. *A temperament theory of personality development*. New York: Wiley, 1975.
Buss, A. H., & Plomin, R. *Temperament: Early developing personality traits*. Hillsdale, NJ: Erlbaum, 1984.

East, P. L., Lerner, R. M., Lerner J. V., & Soni, R. T. *Early adolescent-peer group fit, peer relations, and adjustment: A short-term longitudinal study.* Manuscript submitted for publication, 1991.

Eysenck, H. J., & Eysenck, S. B. G. *Personality structure and measurement.* San Diego: Robert R. Knopp, 1969.

Featherman, D. L. Life-span perspectives in social science research. In P. B. Baltes & O. G. Brim, Jr. (Eds.), *Life-span development and behavior.* Vol. 5. New York: Academic Press, 1983.

Harter, S. *Supplementary description of the Self-Perception Profile for Children: Revision of the Perceived Competence Scale for Children.* Unpublished manuscript, University of Denver, 1983.

Hetherington, E. M., Lerner, R. M., & Perlmutter, M. (Eds.), *Child development in life span perspective.* Hillsdale, NJ: Erlbaum, 1988.

Kagan, J., Reznick, S. J., & Snidman, N. Temperamental inhibition in early childhood. In R. Plomin & J. Dunn (Eds.), *The study of temperament: Changes, continuities and challenges.* Hillsdale, NJ: Erlbaum, 1986.

Lerner, J. V. The import of temperament for psychosocial functioning: Tests of a "goodness of fit" model. *Merrill-Palmer Quarterly,* 1984, *30,* 177–188.

Lerner, J. V., & Lerner, R. M. Temperament and adaptation across life: Theoretical and empirical issues. In P. B. Baltes & O. G. Brim, Jr. (Eds.), *Life-span development and behavior.* Vol. 5. New York: Academic Press, 1983.

Lerner, J. V., Nitz, K., Talwar, R., & Lerner, R. M. On the functional significance of temperamental individuality: A developmental contextual view of the concept of goodness of fit. In G. A. Kohnstamm, J. E. Bates, & M. K. Rothbart (Eds.), *Temperament in childhood.* West Sussex, England: Wiley, 1989.

Lerner, R. M. Nature, nurture and dynamic interactionism. *Human Development,* 1978, *21,* 1–20.

Lerner, R. M. Children and adolescents as producers of their own development. *Developmental Review,* 1982, *2,* 342–370.

Lerner, R. M. *On the nature of human plasticity.* New York: Cambridge University Press, 1984.

Lerner, R. M. *Concepts and theories of human development* (2nd ed.). New York: Random House, 1986.

Lerner, R. M. Contextualism and the life-span perspective on interaction. In M. Bornstein & J. S. Bruner (Eds.), *Interaction in human development.* Hillsdale, NJ: Erlbaum, 1989.

Lerner, R. M., & Busch-Rossnagel, N. Individuals as producers of their development: Conceptual and empirical bases. In R. M. Lerner & A. Busch-Rossnagel (Eds.), *Individuals as producers of their development: A life-span perspective.* New York: Academic Press, 1981.

Lerner, R. M., & Kauffman, M. B. The concept of development in contextualism. *Developmental Review,* 1985, *5,* 309–333.

Lerner, R. M., & Lerner, J. V. (Eds.), Temperament as a moderator of individual and social development in infancy and childhood. *New directions for Child Development.* San Francisco, CA: Jossey-Bass, 1986.

Lerner, R. M., & Lerner, J. V. Children in their contexts: A goodness of fit model. In J. B. Lancaster, J. Altman, A. S. Rossi, & L. R. Sherrod (Eds.), *Parenting across the life span: Biosocial dimensions.* Chicago: Aldine, 1987.

Lerner, R. M., & Lerner, J. V. Organismic and social contextual bases of development: The sample case of early adolescence. In W. Damon (Ed.), *Child development today and tomorrow.* San Francisco, CA: Jossey-Bass, 1989.

Nitz, K. A., Lerner, R. M., Lerner, J. V., & Talwar, R. Parental and peer demands, temperament, and early adolescent adjustment. *Journal of Early Adolescence,* 1988, *8,* 243–263.

Novikoff, A. B. The concept of integrative levels of biology. *Science,* 1945a, *101,* 405–406.

Novikoff, A. B. Continuity and discontinuity in evolution. *Science,* 1945b, *101,* 405–406.

Plomin, R. *Development, genetics, and psychology.* Hillsdale, NJ: Erlbaum, 1986.

Plomin, R., & Daniels, D. The interaction between temperament and environment: Methodological considerations. *Merrill-Palmer Quarterly,* 1984, *30,* 1449–162.

Schneirla, T. C. The concept of development in comparative psychology. In D. B. Harris (Ed.), *The concept of development.* Minneapolis: University of Minnesota Press, 1957.

Sheldon, W. H. *The varieties of human physique.* New York: Harper & Row, 1940.

Sheldon, W. H., & Stevens, S. S. *The varieties of temperament.* New York: Harper & Row, 1942.

Sorensen, A. B., Weinert, F. E., & Sherrod, L. R. (Eds.), *Human development and the life course: Multidisciplinary perspectives.* Hillsdale, NJ: Erlbaum, 1986.

Super, C. M., & Harkness, S. Figure, ground, and gestalt: The cultural context of the active individual. In R. M. Lerner & N. A. Busch-Rossnagel (Eds.), *Individuals as producers of their development: A life-span perspective.* New York: Academic Press, 1981.

Super, C. M., & Harkness, S. *Constitutional amendments.* Paper presented at the 1982 Occasional Temperament Conference, Salem, MA, October, 1982.

Super, C. M., & Harkness, S. *The development niche: Culture and the expressions of human growth.* Unpublished manuscript, Cambridge MA: Harvard University, 1988.

Talwar, R., Nitz, K., & Lerner, R. M. Relations among early adolescent temperament, parent and peer demands, and adjustment: A test of the goodness of fit model. *Journal of Adolescence,* 1990, *13,* 279–298.

Talwar, R., Schwab, J., & Lerner, R. M. Early adolescent temperament and academic competence: Tests of "direct effects" and developmental contextual models.*Journal of Early Adolescence,* 1989, *9,* 291–309.

Thomas, A., & Chess, S. *Temperament and development.* New York: Brunner/Mazel, 1977.

Tobach, E. Evolutionary aspects of the activity of the organism and its development. In R. M. Lerner & N. A. Busch-Rossnagel (Eds.), *Individuals as producers of their development: A life-span perspective.* New York: Academic Press, 1981.

Windle, M. *Inter-inventory relations among the DOTS-R, EASI-II and EPI.* Unpublished manuscript, Johnson O'Connor Research Foundation, Chicago, 1985.

Windle, M. Psychometric strategies of measures of temperament: A methodological critique. *International Journal of Behavioral Development,* 1988, *11,* 171–201.

Windle, M., Hooker, K., Lenerz, K., East, P. L., Lerner, J. V., & Lerner, R. M. Temperament, perceived competence, and depression in early- and late-adolescents. *Developmental Psychology,* 1986, *22,* 384–392.

Windle, M., & Lerner, R. M. Reassessing the dimensions of temperamental individuality across the lifespan: The Revised Dimensions of Temperament Survey (DOTS-R). *Journal of Adolescent Research,* 1986, *1,* 213–230.

Wohlwill, J. F. *The study of behavioral development.* New York: Academic Press, 1973.

3

The EAS Theory of Temperament

Arnold H. Buss

Temperaments are here regarded as a subclass of personality traits, defined by: *appearance during the first year of life, persistence later in life, and the contribution of heredity*. The three personality traits that meet these criteria are emotionality, activity, and sociability, from which are derived the acronym EAS (Buss & Plomin, 1984). There are other individual differences that may be observed in infants, and other personality traits that are inherited, but only the three EAS traits meet both criteria.

Their inheritance and appearance before socialization begins suggest that these three traits are especially stable. In this respect, they may be compared to body build. Consistent individual differences in physique are sufficiently stable by roughly two years of age to predict adult body build, but physique can change under the impact of diet and exercise.

Defining the nature of temperament is just the beginning of this formulation. Also specified for each temperament are its components, how it is measured, sex differences, the role of learning, and the impact of the person on the environment.

Activity

Activity is defined as the expenditure of physical energy. Specifically excluded is any psychological effort that might go into thinking, imagining, planning, or any other cognitive processes; also excluded is any arousal that accompanies emotional behavior. Activity consists solely of movements of the head, arms, legs, and body.

Components

During the first six months of life, individual differences in activity can be observed mainly in the total amount of movement by infants. Some infants seem to be continually

Arnold H. Buss • Department of Psychology, University of Texas at Austin, Austin, Texas 78712.

in motion, whereas those at the opposite extreme are relatively still. Once infants gain control of large and small body movements, activity differentiates into several components, for there is more than one way to expend energy. The various components are best observed in older children and adults, and they are best described by focusing on the extremes of the dimension of activity.

A major component is *tempo*: the pace of action. Energetic children tend to talk and walk faster, dash out of school, hop up steps, and in general, move faster than those around them. Energetic adults are brisk, bustling, and swift. At the other extreme, those low in activity tend to stroll along, speak slowly, straggle out of school, and in general, dawdle in relation to those around them.

The other major component of activity is *vigor*: responses of greater physical force or intensity. Vigorous children speak and scream louder than other children, yell more often, and bang harder on toys. Vigorous adults are likely to have a booming laugh, hit the floor hard when walking or climbing stairs, and push open doors with considerable force. At the other extreme are those who talk and laugh softly, rarely yell, tread lightly, and gently push open doors.

These examples of tempo and vigor suggest that activity is mainly a *stylistic* personality trait, the only one of the EAS temperaments to be stylistic. Style is defined as the way in which responses are delivered, not their content: the *how*, not the *what* of behavior. Thus the content of speech consists of vocabulary and grammar, but the style of talking consists mainly of the rate of speech and its loudness.

Active people tend to continue working or playing long after others have stopped—that is, they have more *endurance*, a minor component of activity. Of course, there may be other reasons for individual differences in endurance—health and physical fitness, for instance. But other things equal, active people tend to keep expending energy after others are resting.

Energetic people prefer to keep moving; from a need to expend energy is inferred the *motivational* component of activity. Active children want to play. Active adults want to keep busy and when forced into idleness, they become edgy and perhaps even irritable. Active children may be too restless to sit for long in a classroom, and their pent-up energy may seem to explode during play periods or at the end of the school day.

In brief, there are four components of activity. The major ones, tempo and vigor, are alternative means of expending energy. Thus some active people move rapidly but with little vigor; some active people move with considerable vigor but a slower pace. Of course, some active people display both tempo and vigor. The minor components are endurance and motivation.

Measures

Most measures blur the distinction between tempo and vigor, which is certainly acceptable if one wants to determine only total energy expenditure. A room can be marked off in squares, and observers can count how many squares are traversed in a given period of time, a procedure best used with children. Pedometers, which record distance traversed in walking, are available for all ages, but they measure only walking and so are poor measures of total energy expenditure.

The best and most popular objective device is the actometer, which is essentially a modified self-winding watch (Bell, 1968; Schulman & Reisman, 1959). It is reliable over time and correlates highly with parents' and teachers' rating of children (Eaton, 1983).

The rate of behaving can also be observed in everyday life, either by videotaping or by having observers watch and rate on the scene. The observers focus on the speed of walking, climbing, or descending stairs, gesturing, and the more general tendency to hurry. Some people dash to answer the door or the telephone, whereas others seem to approach in slow motion. Energetic people often bustle as they accomplish routine chores, whereas lethargic people are clearly in no hurry to finish. Videotaping or observing can also be used to assess the tempo of primates.

The best objective measures of vigor are loudness of voice and of clapping hands. For other responses, it is difficult to determine their physical force. We cannot easily measure the force of a foot striking the floor in walking nor how hard a door is shoved to open or close it. Therefore, vigor is usually measured by observing and rating the amplitude of gestures, head nods, door opening and closing, and pushing elevator buttons.

Beyond such direct measures of energy output, we can assess activity indirectly by the reaction to enforced idleness; this of course is the motivational component. What happens when people are forced to sit in one conference after another or work at a desk job for long hours? Energetic people become uncomfortable and start showing tension, irritability, or other signs of strain. The other indirect measure is the kind of activity selected when there are options. Does the person opt for fast-moving games and occupations (tempo) or is the choice play or work that requires high-amplitude responses (vigor); or is the choice leisurely, low-energy pursuits? Is there a preference for getting on the field to play or just being a spectator? Such decisions offer measures of activity that complement the direct measures of energetic behavior.

Finally, there are self-reports. One of the earliest consists of a factor in a larger questionnaire, the items being: exhibits a rapid pace, exhibits energy, has a drive for activity, and likes action. More recently, activity has been studied as a temperament, and similar self-reports have been developed as part of a temperament questionnaire (EASI; Buss & Plomin, 1975). The following modification of the original EASI activity scale separates tempo from vigor:

Tempo

1. I usually seem to be in a hurry.
2. My life is fast-paced.
3. I do not like to dawdle.
4. My friends tell me that my speech is rapid.
5. I walk faster than most people.

Vigor

1. My voice is on the loud side.
2. My gestures tend to be emphatic.
3. When I knock on a door, I usually knock hard.
4. I like using my strength.
5. My handshake is on the firm side.

Notice that most of the "vigor" items refer to specific behavior, whereas most of the "tempo" items refer to general tendencies. These items appear to reflect a difference between the two kinds of activity: It is easy to describe the general tendency to be quick in movements but difficult to describe the general tendency to be vigorous, so specific behaviors must be assessed.

Sex Differences

The play of boys is known to be more active than that of girls (Eaton & Enns, 1986). The difference could be innate, deriving from the way sex hormones differentiate the brains of male and female fetuses (Goy & McEwen, 1980). In this respect human children may be typical primates, for this sex difference also occurs in the higher apes, and it has been systematically observed in normal rhesus monkeys (Goy, 1978). Energetic, aggressive play in rhesus monkeys can be altered by manipulating prenatal male sex hormones (Goy & McEwen, 1980). Though similar research obviously cannot be tried with human subjects, there are "nature's experiments" that reveal a link in human children between rough-and-tumble play and prenatal levels of androgens:

> Girls with a history of prenatal androgenization were typically long-term tomboys, frequently involved in physically active play and sports behavior, and preferred boys to girls as playmates. (Ehrhardt, 1985, p. 45)

The other approach suggests that boys and girls are treated differently, their play being channeled into grooves deemed appropriate for each sex. How early does such socialization start? In one study, mothers of infants supervised the play of six-month-old infants who were not their own (Smith & Lloyd, 1987). The children were dressed as boys or girls regardless of their real sex, so that the mothers' reactions were based on perceived sex. Perceived boys were encouraged to be more physically active than were perceived girls. Dolls were offered only to girls; hammers, only to boys. Should we be surprised that boys subsequently are more active?

When all age groups are combined, how large is the sex difference in activity? Eaton and Enns (1986), after reviewing 90 studies, concluded that:

> Males were more active than females by roughly one-half of a standard deviation, a difference that accounts for a little less than 5% of the variation in the activity level distribution. (p. 24)

Learning

The five basic kinds of learning may be ordered from the simplest to the most complex: habituation, classical conditioning, instrumental conditioning, imitation, and cognitive learning. Of these, only instrumental conditioning appears to affect the activity. An individual's level of energy expenditure might be slightly elevated or diminished by contingencies of reinforcement, but the trait of activity appears to be little influenced by learning.

Person and Environment

The focus here is on the various ways that a person can affect the environment. The first is in *choosing environments*. A person with a fast tempo is likely to decide on city living rather than the countryside or a small town, where the pace is slower. Other things equal, such a person would try for a job in television news or the floor of a stock exchange, where events move at a frantic rate of speed, in preference to a job as an accountant or an architect, occupations marked by a slow tempo. Similarly, such a person would choose the fast-paced sports of tennis or soccer to the slower-paced sports of bowling or sailing.

The vigor required of participants is a less salient aspect of environments, but choices are available. Thus, other things being equal, such as education and social class, a vigorous person is more likely to apply for a job as a dockworker or construction worker than as a clerk or salesperson in a retail store. Such a person would choose an active avocation like rowing or weight lifting to an inactive game such as bridge or poker.

The motivation to keep busy may also influence the choice of environments. Highly active people are expected to prefer a job that keeps them on the go all day long. They want their time filled with work and are frustrated by periods of enforced idleness. Those who are low in activity are expected to avoid high-pressure jobs, and they welcome the opportunity to do nothing in particular.

Another way an individual can determine events is by *setting the tone* for others in social interaction. An active person may raise the level of sound and quicken the tempo of interaction. Consider two people engaged in animated conversation; by their rapid speech and vigorous gestures they set the tone for any third person who enters the conversation. And it takes only a few energetic people to make a party or other social gathering into a lively affair. Alternatively, a lethargic person can slow down a conversation; the long pauses, slow tempo, and general lassitude allow the interaction to slide into placidity and even boredom. Thus the activity level of the participants may be instrumental in setting the tone of a social interaction.

Individuals can also *modify the environment*. When active persons are confronted with a slow-moving situation, they may speed up the pace. If the music is a waltz, the active person can put on rock music; if others are strolling, an active person may attempt to get the group to walk faster. Those who lack energy may also modify the environment by slowing down the pace of events, but they tend to have less impact, deceleration being a weaker impetus than acceleration.

Energetic people, having more options, tend not to accept restrictions on activity. When an illness requires extended bed rest, they are eager to leave the bed early. If their legs become paralyzed and they are confined to a wheelchair, they are less content to have it motorized and instead prefer to move under their own (arm) power. Thus those high in activity are likely to make a strong effort to overcome physical limitations, whereas those low in activity tend to be more accepting of their fate.

Emotionality

Emotionality is defined as distress that is accompanied by intense autonomic arousal. The primordial distress seen in infants during the first few months of life is assumed to differentiate into fear and anger. From then on, these two emotions comprise the trait of emotionality.

Components of Fear

Fear consists of a complex of components that vary in how observable they are. Though the components can differentiate, leading to individual differences in their patterning, they are correlated, else they would not be grouped under the heading of fear. The sequence here will be from most to least observable components.

The most observable component consists of *motor acts*. We infer fear when an individual tries to escape from the threat by running, leaping, climbing, and even hiding. These actions are instrumental in putting distance between the person and the danger, after which the emotional components (to be described) gradually subside.

There is also a strong inhibition of ongoing behavior. Young children stop exploring and move immediately to the mother or other caretaker for reassurance. But not all youngsters react in the same way, and infants show marked variation in fear reactions (Buss & Plomin, 1975). Long after the immediate fear reaction has subsided, there is often an enduring residue: the tendency to avoid the threat or the area in which the danger occurred.

The emotion of fear is *expressed* largely in the face. Wrinkles appear mainly in the center of the forehead; the brows are elevated and drawn together, and the eyes are open wide to expose much of the white; the mouth is open, and the lips are tense (Ekman & Friesen, 1975). Extreme fear may be accompanied by a draining of facial blood to produce a striking pallor (even a dark skin appears lighter).

Fear may also be observed in motor tension. Typically, the hands are clenched, and the neck and shoulder muscles are rigid. The person may cringe, as if the crouching could in some way avoid the frightening stimulus. Often there is a spillover of tension which may be seen in pacing, sitting down and getting up repeatedly, aimless gesturing, or other random movements that signal restlessness. There may be nervous self-touching gestures: wringing the hands, wiping the brow, or touching the hair. Human children and primates of all ages whimper or even scream when they are afraid, and adult women may cry.

The third component of fear is *physiological*. Blood is diverted from the digestive tract to the large muscles of the body, sugar is released into the bloodstream, and more blood is pumped, as heart rate and blood pressure rise; sweat breaks out. After the emergency, homeostatic mechanisms eventually return the body to a resting state.

The last component is *cognitive*. Older children and adults report a variety of feelings that accompany fear. Some people experience a mounting tension, especially of the muscles of the stomach, arms, and legs. Nausea and cramps may occur or a vague experience described as butterflies in the stomach and a general feeling of weakness.

The second kind of cognition is a feeling of dread and the anticipation of disaster. Required here is the ability to conjure up future possibilities, which in the case of fear causes worry. This ability, absent in infants, matures during the course of cognitive development and is observed in young children.

Components of Anger

Anger may be divided into the same four components as fear—motor, expressive, physiological, and cognitive—but the contents of three of the categories are markedly different. The *motor* component comprises two kinds of behavior. The first is angry aggression, in which the aggressor is not only enraged but trying to hurt or harm the victim, as distinguished from instrumental aggression, in which anger is typically absent and there is no harmful intent (Buss, 1961). The second kind of motor behavior is temper tantrums, which are observed mainly in young children.

The *expressive* component is especially noticeable in the face: It is flushed, the eyes are narrowed, the lips are tense and scowling, and the jaw is firm or even jutting. The fists are often clenched, and bodily posture suggests a readiness to attack.

The *physiological* component is the same as that of fear. Cannon (1929) demonstrated in pioneering research that the bodily preparations for coping with threat involve mobilization of energy for the large skeletal muscles. It matters not whether the preparation is for escaping from the threat (fear) or attacking the threat (anger).

The *cognitive* component is hostility: dislike or hatred of others. It may be accompanied by fantasies of what one will do to the disliked person if the opportunity arises. In older children and adults, hostility also includes making negative attributions about the hated person, perhaps to justify the hatred.

Measures

Fear

Fear may be assessed by the *threshold* of the stimulus that elicits the reaction. Thus when stranger anxiety is studied, the stranger at first remains some distance from the child (weak stimulus) and then moves in close (strong stimulus). Children who become wary, clutch at the mother, or cry when the stranger is distant are obviously more fearful than children who can tolerate a distant stranger.

Another measure is the *duration* of the fear reaction. When a child remains upset long after the fear stimulus is gone and cannot be soothed, the fear reaction must be intense. When an adult narrowly misses being hit by a car and continues to tremble and verbalize feelings of panic long afterward, we infer that the fear is intense.

The motor component of fear is typically studied by examining *avoidance* behavior, such as the visual cliff paradigm that is used with young children. Some fears are sufficiently intense to be labeled phobias. The number of fears is also an index of fearfulness. A person may fear not only strangers but also dogs, spiders, snakes, and black cats.

The *physiological* indices of fear, described earlier, are typically measured by a polygraph. The expressive component is rarely used as a measure of fear. The most common way of assessing fear is the *self-report*. A recent questionnaire, deriving from factor analysis, contains these items (Buss & Plomin, 1984, p. 99): (1) I am easily frightened; (2) I have fewer fears than most people my age (reversed); (3) I often feel insecure; (4) When I get scared, I panic; and (5) I tend to be nervous in new situations.

Anger

Most of the measures are analogous to the measures of fear. One index of anger is the *threshold* of the eliciting stimulus: the threat or annoyance that leads to anger. Some children and adults are so explosive that even a slight irritant is enough to induce rage. At the other extreme are those who tolerate even strong stimuli.

Two measures involve time. The first is the *latency* between the onset of the anger stimulus and the anger reaction. The second is the *duration* of the rage reaction. The physiological measures of sympathetic activation during anger, which are the same as those in fear, have been described. The expressive component is rarely used as a measure of anger.

Perhaps the most frequent measure of the trait is the self-report. The most direct and explicit questionnaire on anger is the Irritability Scale of the Hostility Inventory (Buss & Durkee, 1975):

1. I lose my temper quickly but get over it quickly.
2. I am irritated a great deal more than people are aware of.
3. It makes my blood boil to have somebody make fun of me.
4. Sometimes people bother me just by being around.
5. I often feel like a powder keg ready to explode.
6. I sometimes carry a chip on my shoulder.
7. Lately, I have been kind of grouchy.

Sex Differences

Fear

Previous reviews of the literature on a sex difference in fear (Buss & Plomin, 1975; Maccoby & Jacklin, 1974) appear as valid today as then. Whether there is a sex difference depends on age. During the preschool years, there is no consistent sex difference. During the remainder of childhood, girls tend to be more anxious than boys, but the difference is slight. In adolescence and adulthood, females have more and more intense fears than males.

These facts appear to be consistent with how the two sexes are socialized. Girls are allowed to express their fears, but boys are expected to deny them. Girls are allowed to depend on others for protection, but boys are expected to stand up for themselves. If parents and other socialization agents transmit these expectations and follow up with contingencies of reinforcement, school-age children should start to behave in ways appropriate to their respective sex roles. And by adolescence the impact of socialization should be strong enough to produce a clear sex difference in fear.

Anger

Starting with the preschool years, males are consistently more aggressive than females, and this is true in most of the world's cultures (Rohner, 1976). But it is not clear whether males are angrier than females. To the extent that anger is linked to aggression, there is clearly a sex difference. But do young boys throw more temper tantrums than young girls? The Irritability scale of the Hostility Inventory (Buss & Durkee, 1975) yields no sex difference. In brief, there is no clear evidence of a sex difference in anger, though there is in aggression.

Learning

Fear

The simplest kind of learning, *habituation*, is important mainly for infants, who may tend to become so upset at a loud noise or a suddenly looming figure that the fear response habituates slowly. In those with an inherited tendency to be fearful, the reaction is more intense and habituates even slower than in youngsters low in the trait.

Classical conditioning is a major mechanism in the acquisition of fears, again especially in the young. When a child suffers necessary pain or discomfort at the hands of a dentist, the office becomes a cue for fear. Such conditioning involves mainly the physiological and subjective components of fear, but once these components are conditioned, avoidance behavior is sure to follow.

The motor component of avoidance may be an outcome of classical conditioning, but most avoidance is acquired through *instrumental conditioning*. Consider the rapid acquisition of a fear of dogs in children. Dogs often bark loudly and may even bite a child. After several repetitions, perhaps after only one such occurrence, the child may strongly fear dogs. Thereafter the child is unlikely to stay in the company of even friendly dogs long enough for the fear to wane. And those who are high in fearfulness will be especially susceptible to such conditioning.

Many fears are acquired by *imitation*, a prime example being fear of snakes. Watchers of television or movies can observe the frightened reaction of actors on the screen. Often it is a real-life family member who is observed by younger children. In some families, however, snakes are not feared but adopted as pets, and the children, after observing a parent handling snakes without fear, tend to handle snakes, of course, and a wide variety of fears can be acquired in this way.

Fear may also be acquired by means of *cognitive learning*. In addition to fear imagery stimulated by language, there is fear imagery itself, as portrayed in cartoons and in horror movies of monsters or the devil. Nightmares, especially those of children, are a source of new fears, for after dreaming of a menacing dog, a child may subsequently be afraid of dogs. These various kinds of cognitive learning comprise a powerful means of acquiring fears, and again, those high in the trait of fearfulness are expected to be especially susceptible to such learning.

Anger

Anger can be enhanced through *classical conditioning*. Places that are associated with outbursts of violence and fighting, such as saloons or, in some countries, soccer matches, can lower the threshold for anger. *Instrumental conditioning* of anger serves mainly to diminish it. Children may be punished for anger outbursts, and adolescents and adults who become enraged are likely to be called immature. *Imitation* and *cognitive learning* are especially important for the hostility component of anger. By watching their elders and characters on television and in the movies, and through reading and being taught by bigots, children can learn to hate those they do not know and may never meet. Presumably, children high in the trait of anger are especially susceptible to these various kinds of learning.

Person and Environment

Fear

We are sometimes able to *choose environments*. For those high in the trait of fearfulness, the choice is restricted to environments they regard as safe, which means that the trait severely limits choice of contexts. When the fear is severe, as in phobia, a given environment is completely avoided. Thus some people are so afraid of flying that they take trains or buses even when they must travel thousands of miles. For those who panic in closed spaces, an elevator is out of bounds, and they must climb stairs. In the most severe anxiety, agoraphobia, the person may be too scared to leave the house and is stuck at home, a prisoner of fear.

In a social context, each individual can *set the tone*, and fearful people can incubate anxiety. Consider family members at a hospital, awaiting the results of surgery on someone they love. A fearful family member is likely to be tense and restless in manner and apprehensive in verbalization, thereby intensifying the worries of members of the group. Of course, a person low in fearfulness can have an opposite effect. At the hospital, this person can lower tension by a calm demeanor and a verbal focus on the indications for a positive outcome.

In the face of threat or danger, individuals can also *modify the impact of the environment*. Driving a car in Los Angeles, Tel Aviv, or Rome poses a constant threat of a collision. An unsure, fearful driver may become so terrified that his or her ability to handle the car deteriorates, making a collision more likely. At the other end of the trait dimension, the absence of anxiety can minimize the impact of threat. The car driver is free to concentrate on driving, thereby lowering the probability of an accident.

Anger

The trait of anger can *set the tone* for an interaction. Some angry children or adults tend to be perennially grouchy and act as if they are ready to explode into rage. They are likely to trigger anger or at least annoyance in others, thereby escalating the potential for anger in all members of the group. Those at the low end of the trait dimension of anger have the opposite effect. Their expressive behavior is more benign, suggesting placidity and goodwill. They tend to minimize anger in a social setting and serve as peacemakers. In this way they also *modify the impact of the environment*.

Positive Emotionality

This theory of temperament has dealt with only the negative end of emotionality. Distress is characterized by bodily arousal, which is mediated by the sympathetic division of the autonomic nervous system (Cannon, 1929). Presumably, excessive sympathetic arousal is the inherited basis of individual differences in distress.

What about emotions such as elation and love, the positive end of emotionality? Positive emotions display little of the autonomic arousal that characterizes distress, fear, and anger (Buss & Plomin, 1984). The sympathetic division of the autonomic nervous system is hardly involved when positive emotions occur, offering one basis for excluding them as temperaments.

Another basis is the lack of evidence that they are inherited. Furthermore, if evidence did turn up that individual differences in elation and love were inherited, such inheritance might be attributed to the two other temperaments. Highly *active* people, being energetic and typically busy, tend to be upbeat in mood and, at the very least, not subject to dysphoria. *Sociability* correlates negatively with loneliness and positively with optimism (Perry & Buss, 1989), which suggest that sociable people are less subject to negative moods and tend to be happier.

Despite the adjectives *positive* and *negative*, these two kinds of emotions are not polar opposites. Instead, recent research has shown that the two kinds of emotions should be regarded as independent dimensions (Watson, 1988). In brief, the differences between positive and negative emotions provide sufficient bases for keeping them separate, and only negative emotionality—specifically, distress and its two developmental derivatives, fear and anger—meets the present definition of temperament.

Sociability

Sociability is defined as a preference for being with others rather than remaining alone. Those who are high in this trait are strongly motivated to seek out others and tend to become frustrated and upset during enforced privacy. Those who are low in the trait of sociability also like to be with others, but their motivation is weaker and they easily tolerate being alone. Like other primates, our species is strongly social, and no normal human seeks the life of a hermit. Thus even the most unsocial human is rewarded by the presence of others.

Components

The major component of sociability is *instrumental*: seeking out others and remaining in their company. What are the intrinsic social rewards that motivate this behavior? One reward is the *sharing of activities*. Children enjoy playing in the room or playground with other children. Sociable people prefer to eat, watch television, go to the movies, or just stroll down the street with others. There need be no interaction, just the company of others who are doing the some thing.

A second intrinsic reward is *attention from others*. Sociable people strongly want to be listened to or at least have their presence noted by others looking at or talking to them. No one wants to be ignored, but it is especially painful for social people.

Finally, there is *responsivity from others*. The height of social interaction is exemplified by conversation: What I say partly determines what you say, which in turn is a stimulus for what I say.

These three rewards, which can occur only when people are together, may be ordered in increasing social arousal, from sharing an activity, to attention from others, to responsivity from others. Highly sociable people may settle for the first or second reward, but what they strongly prefer is responsivity from others. Presumably, sociable people are motivated to seek the highest range of social arousal, which can be obtained only in back-and-forth interaction.

The minor component of sociability is *responsiveness* to social stimulation. Other things being equal, sociable people are enthusiastic when interacting with others. They are pleasantly aroused by conversation and nonverbal exchanges, as may be seen in tone of voice, facial expressions, and animation. Their behavior is a mirror image of the strong social reward they seek: responsivity.

Measures

One measure of sociability is the *number of acquaintances*, whether in work or play situations. Another measure is the number of *attempts* to come into contact with others. They can be physical, bringing the person closer to others, or they can be verbal, as in entering a conversation. Especially relevant to sociability are attempts to establish contact with those in the community who might become acquaintances. Presumably, people who are highly sociable are sufficiently motivated to seek interaction that they overcome any inhibitions about doing so, though the related issue of shyness must be taken into account.

The density of the population should be considered, as well as the nature of the residential or working community. Obviously, it is easier to maintain contact with others in an urban environment than in a sparsely populated rural area, just as it is easier when there is a sense of community than when people live in proximity (as in apartment houses) but are afraid to venture out in the neighborhood (parts of many cities). Thus another measure of the trait of sociability is the *overcoming of barriers to social contact*. When individuals have many friends despite being geographically or communally isolated, they must be regarded as highly sociable.

A measure that can be used in the laboratory is *choice*. A subject is allowed to decide whether to wait or to take part in the experiment alone or with others. This technique was used by Schachter (1959), who found that subjects preferred to wait with others when there was a threat of impending pain. In this study, the choice was determined mainly by the experimental manipulation, but in the absence of a manipulation, such choice would be an unequivocal measure of sociability.

At parties, some guests come early and leave late, whereas others come late and leave early. If such behavior is extrapolated to many social situations, it can be seen that *duration* of social contact is an excellent measure of sociability. The person who escapes quickly must be low in the motivation to remain, just as the person who stays must be high in social motivation.

The trait of sociability is most frequently assessed by means of a self-report. The questionnaire that specifically meets the present definition of sociability contains these items (Cheek & Buss, 1981): (1) I like to be with people; (2) I welcome the opportunity to mix socially with people; (3) I prefer working with others rather than alone; (4) I find people more stimulating than anything else; and (5) I'd be unhappy if I were prevented from making many social contacts.

Sex Differences

Females are reputed to be more sociable than males. Is this a fact, and if so, at what age does the sex difference become apparent? The research findings were reviewed some time ago (Buss & Plomin, 1975, Chapter 7), and nothing has since occurred that would substantially alter the conclusions drawn then. There is no consistent gender difference in mean level of sociability during the preschool period. Starting in late childhood, girls are slightly (but significantly) more sociable than boys, a difference that becomes more stable during adolescence and remains during adulthood. However, despite consistently greater sociability in females, the sex differences are slight and the male and female distributions overlap considerably.

Of greater significance is the way sociability becomes channeled in each sex. Women tend to be more sympathetic, understanding, and nurturant, and they disclose more and touch each other more than men do. Thus women's interactions are usually *interpersonal*, and there is an exchange of the affective rewards of praise, soothing, and affection.

Men, in contrast, tend to channel their sociability into groups or teams that have at least a vaguely defined goal:

> Men engage in collective instrumental action more often than women. Relations between men are governed by two apparently contradictory orientations: solidarity and peership, on the one hand, and competition for jobs, prestige, competence, and women, on the other. These tendencies are regulated by norms governing their appropriateness. The norms make it clear whether the goal of solidarity or of competence takes precedence in a particular situation. (Holter, 1970, p. 236)

Women tend to be less competitive and so can more easily express sociability interpersonally.

It has been suggested that the pattern for each sex derives from our evolutionary history. Tiger and Fox (1971) assume that these male and female roles may be seen in primates:

> In general, females occupy themselves with interpersonal matters involving face-to-face encounters and focusing on subjects that have to do with the bearing, nurturing, and training of the young . . . By contrast, males involve themselves with groups and activities that extend directly to the whole community. (p. 104)

This quotation would seem to apply just as much to primates as to humans, and that is precisely the point, for in this approach the gender differences in social behavior are rooted in our primate ancestry. In most primate species, adult females and their offspring tend to be in the center of the group, which makes it easier for the surrounding males to defend them. Virtually all nurturance of the young is offered by mothers, and young females are strongly drawn to mothers and their offspring. Males associate with each other and with females, but males regularly struggle for dominance, which opposes friendly interactions. And males tend to bond together to defend the group and, in some instances, to kill for meat. The sex difference in the qualitative nature of social interaction is assumed to be innate and perhaps linked to hormones.

The opposing position assumes that the sex difference in sociability originates in socialization practices. Boys are taught to compete and to bond together in groups or teams that have an instrumental goal. It follows from this approach that there should be differences from one culture to the next in how boys and girls are socialized. Consistent with this expectation, it has been reported that in the United States boys are urged to compete more strongly than are European boys (Block, 1973).

The socialization approach implies that a gender difference in the way sociability is channeled should appear only after a period of gender role of socialization, though no one has specified a precise timetable. The evolutionary approach assumes that the gender difference is innate and that socialization is of little consequence except to reinforce or disrupt an adaptive division of labor. It must be conceded that it makes adaptive sense for women to orient toward interpersonal relationships, for they bear the larger burden of child rearing; and it makes adaptive sense for men to orient toward individual and group achievement. But it is possible to discover adaptiveness in virtually any behavior, and we cannot assume that all innate tendencies are necessarily adaptive.

In the dispute between the two approaches, the question is whether biology is destiny. One approach assumes that it is the nature of men to interact with each another differently from the way women interact with each another, which means that the patterns are fixed and inflexible. The other approach suggests that each sex is taught a different gender role that involves social interaction, the implication being that these patterns are flexible because socialization practices can change. There is no evidence that decisively favors one perspective over the other, but the evolutionary approach clearly is more speculative.

Learning

Instrumental conditioning affects sociability, for it can link attempts to be with others to specific incentives. Whether the reward is sharing, attention, or responsivity from others, when an intrinsically social reward follows social behavior, such behavior is strengthened through instrumental conditioning.

The tendency to seek others can also be enhanced by two other social rewards. One is soothing, for when an individual is upset, being enfolded and calmed by others is a powerful reinforcer. Especially for those who tend to become distressed or fearful, receiving this kind of nurturance from others serves to intensify the need for being with others.

One of the more powerful social rewards is being liked or loved. Such acceptance and affection intensify the motive to be with others. Whatever the strength of the motive to affiliate with others, affection clearly should enhance it.

Flattery is not only strongly reinforcing but widely sought, starting with the praise offered by parents to their children. The most obvious aspect of any person that might be complimented is physical beauty, and it is well known that attractive people are regarded and treated with special favor (Berscheid & Walster, 1978). It follows that, other things being equal, attractive people should be more sociable. As they age and beauty fades, however, such people are no longer admired for their comeliness, and their sociability is likely to weaken, sometimes to the point of reclusiveness.

If the intrinsic social rewards strengthen the tendency to seek others, the absence of such rewards can weaken it. If individuals receive little or no attention from others and if there is only minimal sharing of activities, the motivation to be with others is thereby diminished.

Person and Environment

The trait of sociability influences how people *choose environments*. Sociable children seek out the playground rather than remaining alone in front of a television set or reading a book. Sociable adults are likely to become teachers, coaches, social workers, social scientists, interviewers, or filmmakers. They thrive where teamwork is essential—for example, in the space program or the military.

People may not always have a choice of vocations, but they can select avocations. Sociable people are more likely to opt for tennis, which involves considerable responsivity, or a team sport like soccer. They prefer interactive games such as checkers, chess, or poker, and especially a game like bridge, which involves both teamwork and competitive interaction. And sociable people tend to be *joiners*: active in clubs, organizations, political parties, and committees.

Those who are low in sociability may become forest rangers, mathematicians, writers, composers, artists, or astronomers. They do not mind being alone in these pursuits and enjoy the privacy of such a job as archivist in the depths of a large library or law firm. Those who have little need of people gravitate to outdoor activities that can be practiced or accomplished alone: long-distance running, archery, fishing, hunting, and riding horses. Their indoor avocations are likely to be be crossword or jigsaw puzzles, solitaire, knitting, reading, collecting stamps or coins, and listening to music, and they may enjoy reflection and introspection.

Individuals can also *set the tone* of social interaction. Sociable children tend to be lively, and when they assemble, the group is animated and talkative. Each sociable person tends to be responsive to others, thereby reinforcing their expressiveness. Unsociable people tend to be quieter, and their conversations are more subdued and interspersed with periods of silence. Being less responsive, they do not reinforce others' expressiveness, and their interactions lag and soon end.

The trait of sociability is also influential in *altering the environment*. Sociable people tend not to accept isolation and find some way of interacting. If they are stuck in the house because they must care for children or are ill, they telephone friends. Writing is usually a solitary activity, but sociable writers often collaborate; they can also talk with others about their work and seek frequent feedback. When all else fails, sociable people may fall back on substitutes for human interaction: playing with pet animals or computer games.

Problem Behaviors

This theory of temperament has implications for several kinds of behaviors that pose problems for parents or adjustment difficulties for individuals.

Shyness

Shyness is sometimes regarded as nothing more than low sociability, but the two traits are here regarded as related but distinct personality traits. Sociability, it bears repeating, is a preference for being with others. Shyness refers to how one behaves when with others: inhibited, anxious, self-conscious, and perhaps even disorganized. The two traits correlate $-.30$; fearfulness correlates $.50$ with shyness but only $-.09$ with sociability (Cheek & Buss, 1981). Thus there is evidence of a modest relationship between shyness and sociability, but it is worthwhile to distinguish between them.

Shyness is here regarded as deriving from the traits of sociability fearfulness. Shy individuals are afraid in novel social situations, which means that in infants shyness is the same as stranger anxiety. The child who is low in sociability is less rewarded by intrinsically social incentives and therefore does not tolerate aversive arousal when with others. A quick escape from social contexts means that the social fear does not habituate, nor can appropriate social skills fully develop. The outcome may be a person who is tentative and shy when with strangers or acquaintances.

Hyperactivity

Children who are both restless and inattentive in class and generally hard to control may be labeled *hyperactive*. Clearly, they are at the upper end of the activity dimension. They lack control, which means that the trait of impulsivity is also salient. But if there were not the powerful engine of the urge to move and expend energy, which defines the highly active child, there would be little need for control in such disciplined situations as the classroom. An active child who is not high in impulsivity can control his or her level of energy expenditure, at least for a while, only to delight in the freedom to move energetically afterward. Such children do not pose a problem so long as their motive to move around is channeled into socially acceptable avenues.

Difficult Children

Some children who cause problems for parents or teachers are called *difficult* (Bates, 1980; Thomas & Chess, 1977). Any of the three temperaments might underlie the behavior of such children. Shyness (low sociability and high fear) and hyperactivity have been mentioned, but activity and anger may be involved in two other kinds of difficult children.

Highly active children, by the tempo, vigor, and endurance of their movements, may bump into others, intrude on their space or privacy, and in general annoy others by their incessant activity. They may wear out parents or teachers, causing irritation, fatigue, or a sense of helplessness in the face of so much energy (even when the child is not impulsive).

Emotionality poses problems mainly when it differentiates into anger. Children who are quick to fly into a rage, stay angry, and throw temper tantrums cause problems in any family, nursery school, or playground. The only solution may be to isolate them and wait until the temper outburst dissipates. Attempting to avert their rage or minimizing it when it occurs is a challenge to any parent or teacher, who may be excused for labeling such children as difficult.

EAS Theory

The theory presented here is a modification of the original EASI theory of temperament (Buss & Plomin, 1975). The missing letter represents impulsivity, which now is not included as a temperament. The basic problem is that impulsivity is not a unitary trait. Our own factor analysis revealed four components, none of them strongly intercorrelated; and the evidence for the inheritance of impulsivity was mixed (Buss & Plomin, 1975). Perhaps one reason for the mixed evidence on inheritance is that impulsivity appears to consist of several subtraits. Furthermore, some components of impulsivity do not appear until after infancy, and some components correlate strongly with sensation-seeking (Zuckerman, 1979).

These various problems with the trait of impulsivity led to its being dropped as a temperament, an omission that carries with it some ambivalence. After all, there is some positive evidence for its inheritance. One of its components, distractibility, does occur in infancy and is included in other theories of temperament. In brief, though there is a reasonable argument for temporarily dropping impulsivity as a temperament, clarification of its nature may lead to a reconsideration of this issue.

References

Bates, J. E. The concept of difficult temperament. *Merrill-Palmer Quarterly*, 1980, *26*, 299–319.

Bell, R. Q. Adaptation of small wristwatches for mechanical recording of activity in infants and children. *Journal of Experimental Child Psychology*, 1968, *6*, 302–305.

Berscheid, E., & Walster, E. H. *Interpersonal attraction* (2nd ed.). Reading, MA: Addison-Wesley, 1978.

Block, J. H. Conceptions of sex role: Some cross-cultural and longitudinal perspectives. *American Psychologist*, 1973, *28*, 512–526.

Buss, A. H. *The psychology of aggression*. New York: Wiley, 1961.

Buss, A. H., & Durkee, A. An inventory for assessing different kinds of hostility. *Journal of Consulting Psychology*, 1957, *21*, 343–349.

Buss, A. H., & Plomin, R. *A temperament theory of personality development*. New York: Wiley, 1975.

Buss, A. H., & Plomin, R. *Temperament: Early developing personality traits.* Hillsdale, NJ: Erlbaum, 1984.

Cannon, W. B. *Bodily changes in pain, hunger, fear and rage.* New York: Appleton-Century-Crofts, 1929.

Cheek, J. M., & Buss, A. H. Shyness and sociability. *Journal of Personality and Social Psychology,* 1981, *41,* 330–339.

Eaton, W. O. Measuring activity level with actometers: Reliability, validity, and arm length. *Psychological Bulletin,* 1983, *100,* 19–28.

Eaton, W. O., & Enns, L. R. Sex differences in human motor activity level. *Psychological Bulletin,* 1986, *100,* 19–28.

Ehrhardt, A. A. Gender differences: A biosocial perspective. In T. B. Sonderegger (Ed.), *Nebraska symposium on motivation.* Lincoln, NE: University of Nebraska Press, 1985.

Ekman, P., & Friesen, W. V. *Unmasking the face.* Englewood Cliffs, NJ: Prentice-Hall, 1975.

Goy, R. W. Development of play and mounting behavior in female rhesus monkeys virilized prenatally with esters of testosterone or dihydrotestosterone. In D. J. Chivers & J. Herberts (Eds.), *Recent advances in primatology.* Vol. 1. New York: Academic Press.

Goy, R. W., & McEwen, B. S. *Sexual differentiation of the brain.* Cambridge, MA: MIT Press, 1980.

Harlow, H. F. Sexual behavior in rhesus monkeys. In F. A. Beach (Ed.), *Sex and behavior.* New York: Wiley, 1965.

Holter, H. *Sex role and social structure.* Oslo: Universitforlaget, 1970.

Maccoby, E. E., & Jacklin, C. N. *The psychology of sex differences.* Stanford, CA: Stanford University Press, 1974.

Perry, M., & Buss, A. H. *Correlates among social traits.* Unpublished research, University of Texas, 1989.

Rohner, R. P. Sex differences in aggression: Phylogenetic and enculturation perspectives. *Ethos,* 1976, *4,* 57–72.

Schachter, S. *The psychology of affiliation.* Stanford, CA: Stanford University Press, 1959.

Schulman, J. L., & Reisman, J. M. An objective measure of hyperactivity. *American Journal of Mental Deficiency,* 1959, *64,* 455–456.

Smith, C. & Lloyd, B. Maternal behavior and the sex of infants. *Child Development,* 1978, *49,* 1263–1265.

Thomas, A., & Chess, S. *Temperament and development.* New York: Brunner/Mazel, 1977.

Tiger, L., & Fox, R. *The imperial animal.* New York: Holt, Rinehart, & Winston, 1971.

Watson, D. Intraindividual and interindividual analyses of positive and negative affect: Their relation to health complaints, perceived stress, and daily activities. *Journal of Personality and Social Psychology,* 1988, *54,* 1020–1030.

Zuckerman, M. *Sensation seeking: Beyond the optimal level of arousal.* Hillsdale, NJ: Erlbaum, 1979.

4

Temperament
A Developmental Framework

Mary Klevjord Rothbart

In our theoretical work on temperament, Douglas Derryberry and I have defined temperament as individual differences in reactivity and self-regulation that are assumed to have a constitutional basis (Rothbart & Derryberry, 1981). By *reactivity*, we mean the arousability of multiple physiological and behavioral systems of the organism (e.g., somatic, endocrine, autonomic, and central nervous systems) as reflected in response parameters of threshold, latency, intensity, rise time and recovery time. By *self-regulation*, we refer to processes that act to modulate reactivity, including at the behavioral level selective attention and responsiveness to cues signaling reward and punishment, behavioral inhibition to novel or intense stimuli, and effortful control. When we say that temperament is *constitutionally based*, we are referring to the relatively enduring aspects of the makeup of the organism, as influenced over time by heredity, maturation and experience.

Having distinguished between reactivity and self-regulation, we must note that the two are not strictly differentiated. Thus, self-regulative systems have their own reactive aspects so that they may be assessed via parameters of threshold, latency, rise time and recovery time. In addition, reactivity within one system may affect reactivity and self-regulation in other systems (e.g., long-term endocrine changes influence both behavioral and autonomic reactivity and self-regulation). This model is not a simple one, but it allows for a degree of complexity of functioning we felt was necessary to capture temperamental individuality. Given this framework for viewing temperament, we were able to argue that as the child develops, self-regulative processes increasingly come to modulate reactive processes (Rothbart & Derryberry, 1981; Rothbart & Posner, 1985). We saw the young infant as very much influenced by the "other-regulation" provided by

Mary Klevjord Rothbart • Department of Psychology, University of Oregon, Eugene, Oregon 97403-1227.

the caregiver, with parental soothing and arousing of the infant through play seen as modulating the infant's reactive state. With peripheral mechanisms such as motor movement and orienting coming under voluntary control in later months, the child would come to provide this regulation itself (Posner & Rothbart, 1981).

We also argued that not all individual differences in temperament are present at birth, but that reactive and especially self-regulative processes emerge during early development. In this chapter, I review briefly some of the more recent developmental data that allow us to identify basic dimensions of temperamental individuality at the time when they can first be observed in the developing child. These data are reviewed in greater detail elsewhere (Rothbart, 1989a,b). The review is chiefly concerned with behavioral development, emphasizing temperamental individuality in emotional, attentional and motor activity during the period of infancy and early childhood. In the final section, temperamental dimensions we have identified in infancy and early childhood are related to some of the factors identified in the study of adult temperament and personality.

The Newborn Period

In our first review, we stressed the extent to which self-regulatory processes come to modulate initially reactive ones (Rothbart & Derryberry, 1981). The newborn infant is strongly dependent upon others for regulation of its state (e.g., soothing, feeding, changing) and this "other-regulation" is in turn influenced by the reactivity of the child, especially the child's distress reactions (see Figure 4.1). Thus, the child's distress elicits caregiver soothing, and the child who demonstrates distress more clearly may be, at least initially, more likely to accomplish its own contribution to parental soothing than the child who is less "easy to read" (Thoman, Becker, & Freese, 1978).

After reviewing the recent temperament literature (Rothbart, 1989b), I would wish to modify our original statement somewhat. The newborn infant demonstrates a number of regulative activities, including selective attention and movement toward and away from arousing stimuli. These regulative behaviors have been demonstrated in the work of Turkewitz and his colleagues on early approach and withdrawal processes (Lawson & Turkewitz, 1980; Lewkowicz & Turkewitz, 1981; McGuire & Turkewitz, 1979). The tendency of some infants to fall asleep under conditions of high intensity or prolonged stimulation may be seen as further evidence of early self-regulation (Brackbill, 1971, 1973). The infant engages in self-soothing from the earliest days via such activities as thumb or finger sucking. Although these self-regulative processes in the newborn to date have been reported with group data, little has been done to investigate neonatal individual differences in self-regulation and their longitudinal significance.

Much more research has been done investigating the dimension of emotionality that is most clearly present during the neonatal period, i.e., the child's susceptibility to distress or *negative reactivity*. Research from the Louisville Twin Study (Matheny, Riese, & Wilson, 1985; Riese, 1987) has found normative stability (i.e., individual predictability) of irritability from the newborn period, to distress and self-regulation of distress as assessed in standardized observations in the laboratory at 9 and 24 months.

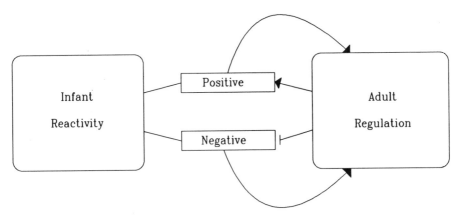

Figure 4.1. Infant reactivity and adult regulation.

Work by van den Boom (1989) has also demonstrated that infants who are irritable at two weeks as assessed by the Brazelton neonatal examination are especially likely to be later classified as having an "insecure attachment," that is, as showing avoidance during reunion with the caregiver after the infant has been left alone at twelve months. Stability of differences in distress-proneness has also been found from six months to later ages (Bates, 1987; Rothbart, 1986, 1987). In several reviews, infants' irritability or susceptibility to distress has also been identified as a dimension of temperament that is present from birth (Bates, 1987, 1989; Buss & Plomin, 1975; Rothbart, 1989b; Rothbart & Mauro, 1990a; van den Boom, 1989).

Because the direct expression of distress decreases across the early months of life (Rothbart, 1989b), and because children are socialized in the direction of not crying or showing distress in public, two problems are created for temperament research. First, there is a problem posed for the longitudinal assessment of distress proneness in that older subjects are not likely to show distress overtly. Thus, the student of infant temperament is likely to assess individual differences in negative affect by assessing how often and how intensely the infant cries; in older children and adults, we tend to ask subjects how they feel in situations that might be likely to elicit negative affect. There has been a tendency, possibly related to these different operationalizations of temperament dimensions, for theories of temperament in infants and adults to operate with little communication with one another. Our expectation is that these two quite different measures are getting at the same underlying dimensions of temperament, but only longitudinal studies will inform us about the degree of stability of susceptibility of temperament over major changes in its expression.

The basic point, however, is that negative reactivity is present early, shows some stability over time, and in the case of the Riese and van den Boom research, predicts forward to both distress and self-regulative strategies such as withdrawal and avoidance that might serve to decrease distress. This combination of reactivity and self-regulation is very similar to Strelau's homeostatic model of reactivity and activity described in Chapter 19 of this volume.

Infancy

By 2–3 months, a second major dimension of reactivity can be added to negative reactivity: the child's susceptibility to the positive emotions or *positive reactivity* as shown in smiling and laughter, and probably also in motor and vocal reactions (Kistiakovskaia, 1965; Rothbart, 1981, 1986). Kistiakovskaia (1965) has described this pattern as emerging in infants by 4 to 8 weeks of age, and as increasing in duration and decreasing in latency into the second and third month of life. She called it the "animation complex," including "smiling, quick and animated generalized movements with repeated straightening and bending of hands and feet, rapid breathing, vocal reactions, eyeblink, etc." (Kistiakovskaia, 1965, p. 39). We know that mothers have strong positive reactions to this complex of behaviors, and take it as evidence of the baby's love for them as well as a basis for their own love for the baby (Robson & Moss, 1970). The positive reaction from the caregiver to positive reactivity in the infant can lead to caregiver attempts to prolong the state through repetition of the eliciting stimulus (see Figure 1).

In infants we have observed longitudinally, we have found positive reactivity in the home to increase from 3 to 9 months and in the laboratory have found it to increase from 3 to 13.5 months (Rothbart, 1986). In the laboratory, we have found that the latency to an infant's positive reaction (smile or laugh) to the rapid opening of a parasol decreases, and the duration and intensity of the positive reaction increases across the periods 3, 6.5, 10 and 13.5 months of age. We have also found moderate longitudinal stability of positive reactivity in caregiver reports from 3 months to the end of the first year (Rothbart, 1981, 1986, 1987), and Worobey and Blajda (1989) have found stability in caregiver report from 2 months to 12 months, but not from 2 weeks to 12 months. This lack of longitudinal stability from the first month of life is consistent with the interpretation that at 2 weeks the underlying physiological systems have not matured to the point that long term stability can be demonstrated.

Emde and his associates have described a biobehavioral shift occurring by 2–3 months of age as indicating that the child has come to react to the external world in a new and more positively responsive way. By 2–3 months, evidence of individual differences in attention span or *duration of orienting* to external stimuli are clear, and Hageküll and Bohlin (1981) have found longitudinal stability of attentiveness from 4 months to 13 months using a caregiver-report measure. It is likely that visual orienting during the early months is controlled by what Posner and Peterson (1990) have called the posterior attention system, including activity of the parietal lobe, the superior colliculus and/or surrounding areas and the pulvinar nucleus.

We would expect later maturational events late in the first year of life to include development of an anterior attention system including the prefrontal cortex and anterior cingulate (Posner & Peterson, 1990). Development of the anterior system would be expected to allow the child to maintain an attentional focus in the presence of external distractors, giving the child a much greater degree of self-regulation through selection of activities with respect to events in the outer and inner world (Posner & Rothbart, in press). Development of this system may be related to the child's increasing tendency to monitor the presence of the adult caregiver, and to directly refer to the parent when in a state of distress (Rothbart & Ziaie, 1988).

Although this view stresses maturation of the systems underlying self-regulation, it is important to remember that experience will be involved in this development so that the timetable for maturation will not be solely a function of the genes regulating it (Valsinger, 1987). Nevertheless, we have argued that the introduction of new levels of self-control, e.g., the early onset of inhibited approach or behavioral inhibition, will have strong influences on the nature of the experience of the child over a period when another child has not yet developed this control (Rothbart & Derryberry, 1981). The child who is behaviorally inhibited may engage in a great deal of observational learning in novel situations, whereas the child without this behavioral control may learn about objects mainly through acting upon them.

Approach is a dimension of temperament that can be measured once the infant's motor capacities make movement toward objects possible. Aspects of approach can be seen in reflexive, defensive, and rooting movements during the newborn period, although only normative and not individual differences studies have been performed on the behaviors. By 5–6 months, approach tendencies of infants can be assessed through the study of the child's latency to make contact with objects by reaching and grasping. We have found some stability of the child's latency to approach relatively familiar and low-intensity toys from 6.5 to 10 and to 13.5 months of age in our longitudinal research (Rothbart, 1988a). Latency to approach is also positively related to the child's smiling and laughter. We have not yet looked at the relation between latency to approach a desired object and latency to withdraw from a disliked object, but following Gray's (1982) theoretical position, we might expect active avoidance and approach to be correlated across infants.

We have found that children's latency to approach intense and novel toys does not show stability across the 6.5–13.5 month period; this finding is consistent with the interpretation that the behavioral inhibition system to novelty and challenge is maturing rapidly during this time, so that some children's approach tendencies are modulated under novelty or intensity of stimulation. There is good evidence that physiological systems underlying motor approach involve the action of dopamine neurotransmitters (see review by Rothbart, 1989a). Physiological systems underlying behavioral inhibition have been seen to include the functioning of the hippocampus and the actions of the neurotransmitters serotonin and norepinephrine (see review by Rothbart, 1989a).

In considering the temperamental variable of *inhibition of approach* or behavioral inhibition, we see at least two dimensions of variability operating in situations where novel and/or intense stimuli are presented: the first is the child's approach tendency and the second is inhibition of approach, as proposed in Gray's (1982) model. Thus a child who shows strong positive reactivity and approach under safe and familiar circumstances may nonetheless, by the last quarter of the first year of life, show non-approach and distress toward a novel and intense stimulus. It is important to distinguish between these two aspects of temperament rather than considering them to be a single dimension extending from rapid approach through slower approach to inhibition or withdrawal, such as is described by Thomas and Chess' (1977) Approach-Withdrawal dimension. Positing two theoretical dimensions allows us to account for the *variability* of behavior demonstrated when a shy child shows positive activation and approach under familiar, safe circumstances but also shows behavioral inhibition and signs of distress under novel and/or intense stimulation (MacDonald, 1988; Rothbart, 1989c; Rothbart & Mauro, 1990b).

This is one way in which our model of reactivity and self-regulation differs from a solely homeostatic model of approach and inhibition. In the homeostatic view, more reactive individuals would be seen as more prone to distress and likely to engage in self-regulative activities functioning to reduce that distress. Thus, persons who do not show rapid approach to novel and intense stimuli would be thought to do so only because approaching would be distress-inducing, and not as a consequence of the additional possibility that the individual has less rapidly rising approach tendencies. In our view, approach is a separable self-regulative system that may be modulated by both behavioral inhibition and effortful control.

Initially we hypothesized that behavioral inhibition (inhibition of approach to novel and intense stimuli) and the child's ability to maintain a focus of attention when distractors are present (effortful control) would be manifestations of the same underlying process. However, for children 3–7 years, we have assessed children's shyness as an assay of behavioral inhibition (see Rothbart & Mauro, 1990b) and children's inhibitory effortful control through parental report, and have found these dimensions to be uncorrelated. We have also found fearfulness and inhibitory control to be uncorrelated in a self-report study with adult subjects (Derryberry & Rothbart, 1988). We expect, however, that the last half of the first year of life is an important period for both the development of inhibited approach (Rothbart, 1988a, 1989b and d) and for the development of components of the anterior attention system that will be involved in effortful inhibitory control (Diamond, 1981; Posner & Peterson, 1990; Posner & Rothbart, 1990, in press). It is likely that a combination of these two systems of control, one more active in the pursuit of goals (which we have called *effort*) and one more passive in the child's behavioral inhibition toward intense and novel stimuli, allows for the child's increasing regulation over his or her behavior during the preschool years (Rothbart & Mauro, 1990b).

As this brief review suggests, an increasing number of dimensions of individual differences in temperament can be observed across the first year of life. By the age of one year, these include *negative reactivity* (irritability or distress threshold), *positive reactivity* (the "animation complex" and approach), *behavioral inhibition* to novel and intense stimulation and to cues signaling punishment, and *duration of orienting* or attention span. We also see the beginnings of *effortful control*.

Recently, Jennifer Mauro and I have reviewed the major dimensions of infant temperament as assessed via parent-report questionnaires (Rothbart & Mauro, 1990a). Part of this exercise involved a conceptual analysis of dimensions assessed by each of the major infant temperament questionnaires. Because some questionnaires assessed dimensions that were conceptually overlapping, we were also especially interested in considering the results of studies that had employed item-level factor analyses to identify temperament dimensions. These studies were carried out by Sanson and her associates in Australia (Sanson, Prior, Garino, Oberklaid, & Sewell, 1987) and Hageküll and her associates in Sweden (Hageküll, 1985; Hageküll & Bohlin, 1981). To generate a basic list of dimensions, we looked for dimensions included in four or more of the major temperament questionnaires that had also emerged relatively intact from an item-level factor analysis. The six temperamental dimensions remaining after this analysis included: Irritability, Reaction to Novelty (distress and inhibition versus approach), Positive Affect, Activity Level, Rhythmicity and Attention Span. Dimensions originally posited by Thomas and Chess (Thomas & Chess, 1977; Thomas, Chess, Birch, Hertzig, & Korn, 1963) that did not survive this analysis included Adaptability (items from this scale joined the Reaction to Novelty factor), Threshold, Intensity (items from this scale joined the Activity Level factor), and Distractibility.

The dimensions on our list differed from those originally put forward by Thomas and Chess not only in that Adaptability, Threshold, Intensity, and Distractibility are lost in the analysis, but Mood was also differentiated into separate Distress and Positive Affect dimensions. Distress was further differentiated into Irritability and Distress to Novelty, but this distinction can be seen to have been anticipated by the separate Approach-Withdrawal and Mood dimensions in Thomas and Chess' original list of temperament dimensions.

The six temperamental dimensions listed above also correspond fairly closely to the dimensions emerging from our developmental analysis of temperament in infancy, as described above. Thus, irritability is seen in the newborn along with some reflexive aspects of attention and approach; positive affect, activity level, and duration of orienting or attention span are seen to emerge during the early weeks; distress and inhibition to novelty emerge later in the first year of life. Rhythmicity, or the child's regularity of sleep, eating, elimination, and amount of food usually consumed, is not included in the model of temperament described here, but it may prove to reflect aspects of self-regulation that are important to later development.

Because most temperament studies of children have not considered dimensions of temperament that might emerge beyond the age of six months, students of temperament in childhood might be tempted to think no further about possible dimensions of temperamental variability after having derived the temperamental variables listed above. It is important, however, to include within a developmental framework the dimension of effortful control that goes beyond fearful behavioral inhibition, and this requires us to consider individual differences observed in preschool aged children.

The Preschool Period

Over the preschool years (2–4 years), children demonstrate increasing ability to control their focus of attention and motor activity (see Eaton & Yu, 1989, and review by Rothbart, 1989a), and we expect this capacity to be influenced by both the development of the anterior attention system and by its susceptibility to verbal regulation (Luria, 1961; Posner & Rothbart 1990).

We call this temperamental dimension *effortful or inhibitory control* (Rothbart & Posner, 1985). To date, we have been able to assess this dimension in preschool age children, adolescents (Capaldi & Rothbart, 1990) and adults (Derryberry & Rothbart, 1988) through a scale of Inhibitory Control. Thus, our model includes two major levels of control, one similar to behavioral inhibition in that is assesses restraint versus expressiveness of emotions and behavior under exogenous stimulus control; the second more attentional (Derryberry & Rothbart, 1988). This latter dimension of effortful control represents a level of self-regulation that is not a part of most theories of temperament, e.g., those of Strelau, Gray, Eysenck, Thomas and Chess and other theorists of children's temperament such as Buss and Plomin (1975, 1984) and Goldsmith and Campos (1982).

The construct's major theoretical importance is that temperament is no longer seen as being chiefly a reflection of the individual's emotional makeup. Thus, in Strelau's (1983, 1989, in press) emotionally oriented theory, persons engage in regulative activities in order to either increase or decrease their reactive state. This kind of control would be in keeping with the level of approach versus behavioral inhibition and self-soothing versus stimulation-seeking activities also seen in our model (see Figure 2). The construct of effortful control, however, provides the possibility that a person can act in a way that is directly counter to the affective level of control. Depending on specific cultural programming and individual's semantic system, effortful control allows behaviors of the child or adult that can be more flexible and more intellectually governed than those of the very young child.

Each level of control in our model allows for increasing variability of behavior: behavioral inhibition provides for a child who may express a good deal of emotional and behavioral expression under safe and nonthreatening circumstances, and in fact be quite responsive to reward under those conditions, but who would be much less expressive under conditions of novelty, intensity or signals of punishment. Effortful control allows for the possibility that a person can tolerate momentary punishment for the sake of pursuing more distant goals.

Effortful Control and Ego-Control and Resiliency

Jeanne and Jack Block (1980) have identified two general dimensions of behavior in preschool and elementary school age children, labeled ego resiliency and ego control. In the Blocks' work, these dimensions have been assessed through parent and teacher Q-sorts. Ego control is defined as the characteristic expression versus containment of emotions and behavior (Block & Block, 1980); ego resiliency refers to the person's ability to modify his or her usual expression versus containment of emotions and behavior, depending upon the circumstances and task demands of the environment.

If we were to conclude our developmental analysis with only the temperamental dimensions clearly identified in infancy, then ego control would be seen as only another measure of behavioral inhibition; intentional effortful control would not be seen to contribute to it. We would also have great difficulty characterizing ego resiliency: if behavioral inhibition were the only variable controlling the child's expression versus containment of action and emotion, then novelty (or in our broader view, intensity of the stimulus and cues of reward or punishment) would be the major influence upon variability of behavior. We would not be able to account for situations in which a person inhibits contemporary behavior that would lead to great immediate satisfaction in order to serve some higher end or more distant goal, or approaches situations that are novel, intense or signal punishment, thereby acting in the face of imminent pain, in order to pursue a preeminent goal.

Similarities between Temperamental Dimensions Identified in Infancy and Early Childhood and Those Identified in Adult Subjects

There are strong similarities between the dimensions of temperament emerging from the developmental analysis described above and the major personality dimensions that have emerged from factor analyses of scales assessing personality in adulthood. In Tellegen's work (Tellegen, 1985; Watson & Tellegen, 1985) he has extracted two higher order personality factors labeled Positive Emotionality and Negative Emotionality. Tellegen identifies the Positive Emotionality dimension as assessing feelings of well-being, social potency, and pleasurable engagement, and the Negative Emotionality dimension as assessing feelings of stress, worry, resentment, and negative engagement. He has also identified a third higher order personality dimension labelled Constraint, which assesses characteristics of cautiousness, restraint, and timidity versus impulsivity and sensation-seeking. In the developmental model for temperament described above, these factors would correspond to negative reactivity, positive reactivity, and a combination of behavioral inhibition and inhibitory control.

Tellegen has noted that these three factors are similar to Eysenck's (1967, 1976; Eysenck & Eysenck, 1985) dimensions of Extraversion (positive emotionality), Neuroticism (negative emotionality) and Psychoticism (constraint), and has further noted similarities between Tellegen's Positive Emotionality and Gray's Approach, and Tellegen's Negative Emotionality and Gray's Anxiety dimensions. The "big five" personality dimensions that have frequently emerged from factor analytic studies include dimensions of Activity-Extraversion, Anxiety-Neuroticism, and Conscientiousness-Ego Control, which again are similar to the Positive Emotionality, Negative Emotionality and Constraint dimensions identified above (McCrae & Costa, 1985), and also to dimensions of positive and negative reactivity, behavioral inhibition and inhibitory control identified in childhood.

A Developmental Model for Temperament

Figure 2 depicts our current model for temperament (see also Rothbart, 1989c). It specifies the following eliciting conditions for reactivity: the intensity of stimulation, its signal qualities (cues of potential reward and/or punishment), the internal state of the organism, including illness or fatigue, as well as the individual's momentary expectations which may or may not be confirmed by stimulus events. If expectations are not confirmed (i.e., the person is surprised), reactivity involved in orienting will occur, leading to possibly multiple evaluations of the stimulus value of the event. In turn, signal qualities (cues of the potential rewardingness or punishment associated with the event) will influence the person's subsequent reactions and self-regulation.

Another aspect of signal quality importantly related to reactivity is the imminence of a positive or negative event, so that an upcoming negative event (e.g., an exam or trip to the dentist) can lead to increasing negative reactions. As the probability of occurrence of a positive event waxes and wanes, the individual's reaction can also shift from positive to negative. In general, individual processing of low or lowered probabilities of satisfying needs generates negative reactions; increased or high probabilities of satisfying needs generates positive reactions (Simonov, 1986).

In Figure 4.2, connecting lines without arrows indicate more specific instances of

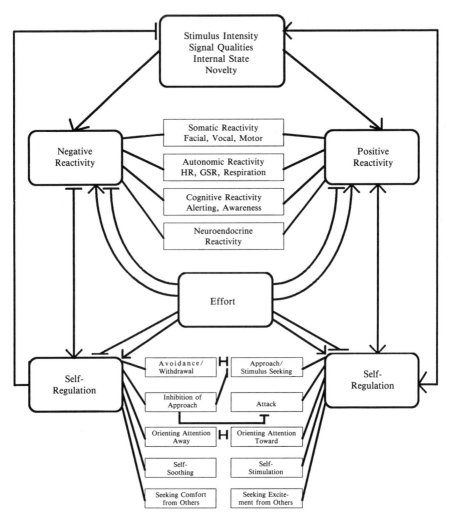

Figure 4.2. A framework for temperament. Arrows indicate facilitation; straight lines at the end of connecting lines, inhibition; direct connecting lines from larger to smaller boxes, more specific instances of a more general category. The figure does not describe all possible connections, but is designed to illustrate a general framework.

reaction indicated in the larger boxes. In this diagram, the more specific differences between positive and negative reactions as reflected in the somatic, autonomic, cognitive and neuroendocrine systems are not specified, but the possibility of individual variability in reactivity of each is allowed (Rothbart & Derryberry, 1981). It is beyond the scope of this chapter to deal with all the relationships and interactions outlined in the model depicted in Figure 4.2. However, we illustrate two aspects of the self-regulatory mechanisms postulated by the model: attentional control of negative affect and effortful control.

In our research with adult temperament (Derryberry & Rothbart, 1988), we have found a consistent negative relationship between self-reported fearfulness and frustration (negative affect) and the ability to shift attention from one focus to another. This attentional control over negative affect appears to begin early in life. In studies of infants we have found that those subjects who more frequently shift visual orientation show less fear in our laboratory scenarios (Rothbart, 1988b). These findings suggest that orienting of attention can be an important control device. Differences between people in their ability to direct attention away from arousing events can be seen when one individual cannot seem to get a negative event out of her or his mind, whereas another is able to switch focus easily.

An even more general control device is also postulated by this diagram. Effort involves pursuit of goals of the person in the face of conflicting response tendencies. Effort shows a special position in this diagram. Another name for effort is likely *will*, and it is interesting that some of the earliest studies of temperament in Great Britain by Webb (1915) identified "W" or "will" as an important dimension of temperamental variability. Simonov (1986) defines will as the process that directs behavior toward satisfying the individual's dominant need, regardless of the likelihood of negative events and in spite of other competing motives. The power and flexibility of this level of control is seen in its multiple influences on Figure 4.2.

Assessing effortful control or "will" is a difficult task because it is influenced by the full range of factors in socialization. Indeed, some traditional approaches to socialization have purposely attempted to "break the will" (Miller, 1984). Assessing effortful control by aggregating items from different areas of functioning may thus be difficult. However, problems of assessment and longitudinal stability of temperament apply to other temperament dimensions as well. By the time a person becomes an adult, a lifetime of criticism from others and internalized self-criticism may make it very difficult for a person to see the positive signal value of events. It is not unlikely that when clinicians ask their clients to contact the "small child within oneself," they are calling for the initial, more temperamentally governed reactions that preceded the child's adaptations to a social world where feelings are often not encouraged and actions are constantly at risk for being found unacceptable.

This outline for temperament has been created in order to be superseded, but it does allow for presentation of some basic psychological processes that appear to demonstrate important individual variability. It also allows us to think about the ways in which developmental events such as the onset of behavioral inhibition and effortful inhibitory control are likely to have widespread influences on the balance between reactivity and self-regulation in the individual.

References

Bates, J. E. Temperament in infancy. In J. D. Osofsky (Ed.), *Handbook in infant development* (pp. 1101–1149). New York: Wiley, 1987.

Bates, J. E. Concepts and measures of temperament. In G. Kohnstamm, J. Bates, & M. K. Rothbart (Eds.), *Temperament in childhood* (pp. 3–26). Chichester: Wiley, 1989.

Block, J. H., & Block, J. The role of ego-control and ego-resiliency in the organization of behavior. In W. A. Collins (Ed.), *Minnesota symposium on child psychology* (Vol. 13, pp. 39–101). New York: Erlbaum, 1980.

Brackbill, Y. Cumulative effects of continuous stimulation on arousal level in infants. *Child Development*, 1971, *42*, 17–26.

Brackbill, Y. Continuous stimulation reduces arousal level: Stability of the effect over time. *Child Development*, 1973, *44*, 43–46.

Buss, A. H., & Plomin, R. *A temperament theory of personality development.* New York: Wiley, 1975.

Buss, A. H., & Plomin, R. *Temperament: Early developing personality traits.* Hillsdale, NJ: Erlbaum, 1984.

Capaldi, D., & Rothbart, M. K. *Development of an adolescent temperament measure.* Paper presented at the meetings of the Society for Research on Adolescence. Atlanta, Georgia, 1990, March.

Derryberry, D., & Rothbart, M. K. Arousal, affect and attention as components of temperament. *Journal of Personality and Social Psychology*, 1988, *55*, 953–966.

Diamond, A. *Retrieval of an object from an open box.* Paper presented at the Society for Research in Child Development. Boston, MA, 1981.

Eaton, W. O., & Yu, A. P. Are sex differences in child motor activity level a function of sex differences in maturational status? *Child Development*, 1989, *60*, 1005–1011.

Eysenck, H. J. *The biological basis of personality.* Springfield, IL: Charles C. Thomas, 1967.

Eysenck, H. J. (Ed.), *The measurement of personality.* Baltimore, MD: University Park Press, 1976.

Eysenck, H. J., & Eysenck, M. W. *Personality and individual differences.* New York: Plenum, 1985.

Goldsmith, H. H., & Campos, R. Toward a theory of infant temperament. In R. Emde & R. Harmon (Eds.), *Attachment and affiliative systems* (pp. 161–193). New York: Plenum, 1982.

Gray, J. A. *The neuropsychology of anxiety.* Oxford: Oxford University Press, 1982.

Hageküll, B., & Bohlin, G. Individual stability in dimensions of infant behavior. *Infant Behavior and Development*, 1981, *4*, 97–108.

Hageküll, B. The Baby and Toddler Questionnaires: Empirical studies and conceptual considerations. *Scandinavian Journal of Psychology*, 1985, *26*, 110–122.

Kistiakovskaia, M. I. Stimuli evoking positive emotions in infants in the first months of life. *Soviet Psychology and Psychiatry*, 1965, *3*, 39–48.

Lawson, K. R., & Turkewitz, G. Intersensory function in newborns: Effect of sound in visual preferences. *Child Development*, 1980, *51*, 1295–1298.

Lewkowicz, D. J., & Turkewitz, G. Intersensory interaction in newborns: Modification of visual preferences following exposure to sound. *Child Development*, 1981, *52*, 827–832.

Luria, A. R. *The role of speech in the regulation of normal and abnormal behavior.* New York: Liveright, 1961.

MacDonald, K. *Social and personality development: An evolutionary synthesis.* New York: Plenum Press, 1988.

Matheny, A. P., Jr., Riese, M. L., & Wilson, R. S. Rudiments of infant temperament: Newborn to nine months. *Developmental Psychology*, 1985, *21*, 486–494.

McCrae, R. R., & Costa, P. T., Jr. Updating Norman's "Adequate Taxonomy": Intelligence and personality dimensions in natural language and in questionnaires. *Journal of Personality and Social Psychology*, 1985, *49*, 710–721.

McGuire, I., & Turkewitz, G. Approach-withdrawal theory and the study of infant development. In M. Bortner (Ed.), *Cognitive growth and development* (57–84). New York: Brunner/Mazel, 1979.

Miller, A. *For your own good: Hidden cruelty in child-rearing and the roots of violence.* New York: Farrar, Straus, Giroux, 1984.

Posner, M. I., & Peterson, S. E. The attention system of the human brain. In W. M. Cowan (Ed.), *Annual review of neuroscience,* in press.

Posner, M. I., & Rothbart, M. K. Intentional chapters on unintended thoughts. In J. S. Uleman & J. A. Bargh (Eds.), *Unintended thought: Limits of awareness, intention and control* (pp. 450–469). New York: Guilford, 1990.

Posner, M. I. & Rothbart, M. K. Attention mechanisms and conscious experience. In M. Rugg & A. D. Milner (Eds.), *Consciousness and Cognition,* in press.

Riese, M. L. Temperamental stability between the neonatal period and 24 months. *Developmental Psychology,* 1987, *23,* 216–222.

Robson, K. S., & Moss, H. A. Patterns and determinants of maternal attachment. *Journal of Pediatrics,* 1970, *77,* 976–985.

Rothbart, M. K. Measurement of temperament in infancy. *Child Development,* 1981, *52,* 569–578.

Rothbart, M. K. Longitudinal observation of infant temperament. *Developmental Psychology,* 1986, *22,* 356–365.

Rothbart, M. K. *Laboratory observations of the development of infant temperament.* Meetings of the Society for Research in Child Development, Baltimore, 1987, April.

Rothbart, M. K. Temperament and the development of inhibited approach. *Child Development,* 1988a, *59,* 1241–1250.

Rothbart, M. K. Attention and emotion in the development of temperament. In M. I. Posner (Ed.), *The role of attention in normal development and psychopathology: Proceedings of a symposium* (pp. 2–6). University of Oregon Center for the Study of Emotion, Technical Report No. 88-3, 1988b.

Rothbart, M. K. Biological Processes in temperament. In G. Kohnstamm, J. Bates, & M. K. Rothbart (Eds.), *Temperament in childhood* (pp. 77–110). Chichester: Wiley, 1989a.

Rothbart, M. K. Temperament and development. In G. Kohnstamm, J. Bates, & M. K. Rothbart (Eds.), *Temperament in childhood* (pp. 187–248). Chichester: Wiley, 1989b.

Rothbart, M. K. Temperament in childhood: A framework. In G. Kohnstamm, J. Bates, & M. K. Rothbart (Eds.), *Temperament in childhood* (pp. 59–76). Chichester: Wiley, 1989c.

Rothbart, M. K. Behavioral approach and inhibition. In S. Reznick (Ed.) *Perspectives on Behavioral Inhibition* (pp. 139–157). Chicago: University of Chicago Press, 1989d.

Rothbart, M. K., & Derryberry, D. Development of individual differences in temperament. In M. E. Lamb, & A. L. Brown (Eds.), *Advances in developmental psychology.* (Vol. 1, pp. 37–86). Hillsdale, NJ: Erlbaum, 1981.

Rothbart, M. K., & Mauro, J. A. Questionnaire measures of infant temperament. In J. Colombo & J. W. Fagen (Eds.), *Individual differences in infancy: Reliability, stability and prediction* (pp. 411–430). Hillsdale, NJ: Erlbaum, 1990a.

Rothbart, M. K., & Mauro, J. A. Temperament, behavioral inhibition and shyness in childhood. In H. Leitenberg (Ed.), *Handbook of social anxiety* (pp. 139–160). New York: Plenum, 1990b.

Rothbart, M. K., & Posner, M. I. Temperament and the development of self-regulation. In L. C. Hartlage, & C. F. Telzrow (Eds.), *The neuropsychology of individual differences: A developmental perspective* (pp. 93–123). New York: Plenum, 1985.

Rothbart, M. K., & Ziaie, H. *Infant behaviors that may modulate distress.* In J. L. Gewirtz, Chair, "Development and control of infant separation distress." Meeting of the International Conference on Infant Studies, Washington, DC, 1988.

Sanson, A., Prior, M., Garino, E., Oberklaid, F., & Sewell, J. The structure of infant temperament: Factor analysis of the Revised Infant Temperament Questionnaire. *Infant Behavior and Development,* 1987, *10,* 97–104.

Simonov, P. V. *The emotional brain.* New York: Plenum, 1986.

Strelau, J. *Temperament–personality–activity.* London: Academic Press, 1983.

Strelau, J. The regulative theory of temperament as a result of east-west influences. In G. Kohnstamm, J. Bates, & M. K. Rothbart (Eds.), *Temperament in childhood* (pp. 35–48). Chichester: Wiley, 1989.

Tellegen, A. Structures of mood and personality and their relevance to assessing anxiety, with an emphasis on self-report. In A. H. Tuma & J. D. Maser (Eds.), *Anxiety and the anxiety disorders* (pp. 681–706). Hillsdale, NJ: Erlbaum, 1985.

Thoman, E. B., Becker, P. T., & Freese, M. P. Individual patterns of mother-infant interaction. In G. P. Sackett (Ed.), *Observing behavior, Volume 1: Theory and applications in mental retardation* (pp. 95–114). Baltimore: University Park Press, 1978.

Thomas, A., & Chess, S. *Temperament and development.* New York: Brunner/Mazel, 1977.

Thomas, A., Chess, S., Birch, H. G., Hertzig, M., & Korn, S. *Behavioral individuality in early childhood.* New York: New York University Press, 1963.

Valsiner, J. *Culture and the development of children's action.* Chichester: Wiley, 1987.

van den Boom, D. Neonatal irritability and the development of attachment. In G. Kohnstamm, J. Bates, & M. K. Rothbart (Eds.), *Temperament in childhood* (pp. 299–320). Chichester: Wiley, 1989.

Watson, D., & Tellegen, A. Toward a consensual structure of mood. *Psychological Bulletin*, 1985, *98*, 219–235.

Webb, E. Character and intelligence. *British Journal of Psychology Monographs*, *1*, 3, 1915.

Worobey, J., & Blajda, V. M. Temperamental ratings at 2 weeks, 2 months, and 1 year: Differential stability of activity and emotionality. *Developmental Psychology*, 1989, *25*, 257–263.

5

Outline of a General Emotion-Based Theory of Temperament

Albert Mehrabian

Any theory of personality which is to be comprehensive must provide answers to the following questions. The first set of three *contemporaneous* questions addresses the interrelationships among behavioral, personality, and situational variables: (1) How is behavior a function of personality? (2) How is behavior a function of situation? (3) How is behavior a function of the interaction of personality and situation? The second set of *longitudinal* questions addresses issues of development and modification of personality over time: (4) How does personality develop over time? (5) What interventions are needed to modify personality?

The theory outlined below addresses all the preceding five basic questions. Also, it meets the essential requirement of incorporating all measures necessary to describe (1) behavioral, (2) personality, and (3) situational variables.

The core concept in the theory is "emotion state" which refers to transitory conditions of an individual's feelings or affect. Emotion states serve as mediating variables between situational and personality variables on the one hand and specific behavioral variables (e.g., actions, verbalizations) on the other.

Although the importance of emotions in human functioning is widely recognized, a strict behaviorist bias in the tradition of psychology resulted in only a limited study of emotions. Experimental psychologists dealt with the entire array of emotions by focusing narrowly on the concept of "drive" or "arousal." Typically, drive was manipulated in the laboratory by inducing shock or hunger and arousal was measured with GSR, blood pressure, or EEG desynchronization.

The broad and complex realm of emotions which could have been studied through exploration of verbalizations was shunned because verbal reports were not deemed

Albert Mehrabian • Department of Psychology, University of California, Los Angeles, California 90024.

legitimate data of study. Thus, with emotions essentially neglected by experimentalists, it was left to clinicians to deal with this important aspect of human function. Clinicians, of course, recognized the importance of emotions in their work and dealt with the topic using concepts such as "anxiety," "anger," or "depression." Unfortunately, however, clinical descriptions of emotion tended to be informal and loosely formulated, lacking precise definition and measurement.

Thus, it was not until the early 1960s that study of emotions employing both verbal and nonverbal behaviors commenced. The present formulation was one of those approaches and was stimulated by work in the field of nonverbal communication.

Emotion States: Core Mediating Variables of the Theory

Early studies of nonverbal communication identified facial expressions, gestures, postures, positions, gross bodily movements, qualities of voice accompanying verbalizations (e.g., loudness, intonation), speech rate and speech error rate as some of the many facets of behavior that had subtle communicative significance.

In an effort to organize and study all such behaviors, I found it useful to explore the other side of the communication equation—namely, *referents* or meanings of communication. The *symbols* of communication, the nonverbal behaviors noted above, were far too diverse and numerous. In contrast, the referents were emotions and attitudes. Extensive laboratory studies dealing with many facets of nonverbal communication resulted in the identification of three basic referent dimensions: liking, potency, and responsiveness (Mehrabian, 1972a, 1972b). Analogous sets of three dimensions had also been identified in the work of other researchers and particularly by Osgood (e.g., Osgood, Suci, & Tannenbaum, 1957)

Subsequent work in our laboratory directed at the comprehensive measurement of emotions led to the identification of pleasure-displeasure, arousal-nonarousal, and dominance-submissiveness as three nearly independent basic dimensions of emotion state (Mehrabian & Russell, 1974b). Pleasure-displeasure was the analogue of Osgood's evaluation and my liking dimension, and discriminated broadly between good and bad feelings. Arousal-nonarousal was the analogue of Osgood's activity and my responsiveness dimension, and was defined as a combination of physical activity and mental alertness levels. Dominance-submissiveness was the analogue of Osgood's and my potency dimension and was defined as the degree of control versus lack of control one experiences over one's physical and social environment.

Semantic differential type measures of pleasure-displeasure, arousal-nonarousal, and dominance-submissiveness were developed by factor-analyzing sets of bipolar emotion descriptors (e.g., satisfied-unsatisfied, excited-calm, controlling-controlled). The pleasure, arousal, and dominance factors accounted for 27, 23, and 14 (a total of 64) % of total variance, respectively. In addition, the pleasure factor correlated $-.07$ with the arousal, and .03 with the dominance, factor; the arousal and dominance factors correlated .18 (Mehrabian & Russell, 1974b).

A subsequent study employed the preceding three basic scales of emotion state and a total of 43 additional measures of emotions devised by other investigators. It was found that the pleasure-displeasure, arousal-nonarousal, and dominance-submissiveness scales were both necessary and sufficient to account for the reliable variance contained in the 43 scales (Russell & Mehrabian, 1977). Thus, the three dimensions of pleasure, arousal, and dominance (which had evolved from a broad and diverse experimental base in a variety of laboratories) could serve as a comprehensive framework to describe emotion states.

Indeed, additional data obtained by Russell and Mehrabian (1977, Table 4) provided specific definitions for 151 emotion states, with each state represented as a point in the three-dimensional emotion space. The following illustrate the definitions, with numeric scores ranging from -1 to $+1$, and numeric values for pleasure, arousal, and dominance given in that order. *Bold* (.44, .61, .66), *admired* (.81, .44, .51), *influential* (.68, .40, .75), *vigorous* (.58, .61, .49), *loved* (.87, .54, $-.18$), *impressed* (.41, .30, $-.32$), *disgusted* ($-.60$, .35, .11), *cruel* ($-.45$, .48, .42), *angry* ($-.51$, .59, .25), *frustrated* ($-.64$, .52, $-.35$), *distressed* ($-.61$, .28, $-.36$), *fearful* ($-.64$, .60, $-.43$), *upset* ($-.63$, .30, $-.24$), *shy* ($-.15$, .06, $-.34$), *bored* ($-.65$, $-.62$, $-.33$), *depressed* ($-.72$, $-.29$, $-.41$).

Mehrabian (1978) revised and expanded the three semantic differential scales measuring pleasure, arousal, and dominance to increase their reliabilities. The resulting pleasure-displeasure scale with 24 items had a KR-20 reliability coefficient of .91. The arousal-nonarousal scale with 8 semantic differential items had a reliability coefficient of .60. The dominance-submissiveness scale with 15 items had a KR-20 reliability coefficient of .84. The pleasure scale correlated $-.05$ with the arousal, and $-.03$ with the dominance, scale, The arousal and dominance scales correlated $-.06$.

In a subsequent study which employed the preceding three emotion scales to investigate the emotion connotations of product names, a very large sample of 1,147 observations was obtained. KR-20 internal consistency (reliability) coefficient for the pleasure scale was .97. The corresponding reliability coefficient for the arousal scale was .81 and the reliability for the dominance scale was .90 (Mehrabian & de Wetter, 1987).

Personality Described in Terms of Three Basic Temperament Variables

Description and Measurement of Temperament

"Temperament" is defined here as "characteristic emotion state" or as "emotion trait." In accordance with standard usage, "state" refers to a transitory condition of the organism, whereas "trait" refers to a stable, habitual, or characteristic condition of the organism. Thus, when an individual is said to possess an anxious temperament (or to rate high on trait anxiety), it means that the anxiety level of that individual, assessed across a representative sample of life situations, is above average in comparison to that of others.

It follows from the preceding definition that temperament or emotion traits can be described and measured by averaging emotion states across representative samples of situations. Further, since emotion states are described adequately with the three basic factors of pleasure, arousal, and dominance, it should be possible to obtain a comprehensive description of the averages of these states, or emotion traits, in terms of an analogous set of three factors.

Such a set of three basic temperament measures was developed by Mehrabian (1978). The semantic differential format was used and pairs of emotion terms constituted the poles of each item. Subjects were requested to place a check mark in one of nine spaces separating each pair (e.g., excited-enraged, affectionate-nasty) to show how they felt in general). Although the resulting trait pleasure and trait dominance measures were satisfactory, a reliable trait arousal measure was not obtained.

A more sensitive and reliable approach to the measurement of individual differences in arousal was achieved using the concept of stimulus screening (the cognitive counterpart of trait arousability).

According to the concept of stimulus screening, individuals differ in the degree to which they habitually and selectively process environmental information. One pole of this individual-difference dimension refers to persons who are best able to screen less relevant or irrelevant components of everyday stimuli and thereby to reduce the effective complexity and random character of the stimuli. These persons, the *screeners* or *unarousable* persons, show a less extreme arousal response to sudden increases in "information rate" (i.e., complexity, novelty, variability) of stimuli and exhibit more rapid declines of arousal to baseline levels.

The opposite pole refers to persons who habitually screen less of the irrelevant components of a situation in various sensory channels and who effectively experience situations as higher in information rate (i.e., more complex, more variable, more random). These *nonscreeners* or *arousable* persons have greater arousal responses to information rate spikes and less rapid declines of arousal to baseline levels.

Mehrabian (1976b, 1977; 1987, chap. 2) developed a questionnaire measure of trait arousability (or its converse and cognitive counterpart, stimulus screening). The questionnaire contains 40 items exemplified by "strong emotions don't have a lasting effect on me ($-$)," "extremes in temperature affect me a great deal ($+$)," "I am not one to be strongly moved by an unusual odor ($-$)," or "I am strongly moved when many things are happening at once ($+$)." The signs in parentheses indicate direction of scoring when the scale is scored for trait arousability. The 40-item trait arousability scale is balanced for direction of wording and has a KR-20 internal consistency (reliability) coefficient of .92.

To obtain a trait-dominance measure of greater reliability than the one devised by Mehrabian (1978), Mehrabian and Hines (1978) developed a questionnaire measure of trait dominance-submissiveness. The latter questionnaire is exemplified by "I go my own way instead of following others ($+$)," "I avoid talking about touchy subjects ($-$)," "I am often the center of attention in a group ($+$)," "I work best when someone has outlined a job for me ($-$)." It contains 20 positively, and 20 negatively, worded items to reduce response bias and has a KR-20 internal consistency coefficient of .95. This compares favorably with the corresponding reliability coefficient of .84 obtained by Mehrabian (1978) for his 15-item trait dominance scale which was in semantic differential format.

In sum, the three basic temperament measures employed in the present theory consist of a 24-item trait pleasure-displeasure scale which is in semantic differential format (Mehrabian, 1978), a 40-item trait arousability questionnaire (Mehrabian, 1976b, 1977; 1987, chap.2), and a 40-item trait dominance questionnaire (Mehrabian & Hines, 1978). The trait pleasure scale correlated .19 ($p < .01$) with the trait dominance scale, and correlated $-.07$ ($p > .05$) with the trait arousability scale. The trait arousability and trait dominance scales correlated .11 ($p > .05$) (Mehrabian, 1978; Mehrabian & Hines, 1978). Thus, as expected, and in line with the low intercorrelations obtained for the corresponding state measures of pleasure, arousal, and dominance, the present analogous trait measures also exhibited low intercorrelations, providing a parsimonious base for the general description of temperament.

The Three-Dimensional Temperament Space in Relation to Existing Personality Measures

Mehrabian and O'Reilly (1980) explored the heuristic value of the proposed three-dimensional temperament framework for describing personality. Thirty-four personality measures in common use were analyzed using regressions in which trait pleasure, trait arousability, and trait dominance served as independent variables.

One objective of the study was to categorize commonly used personality measures with reference to the three-dimensional temperament space. Personality *types* were described as points within this space. Personality *dimensions* and corresponding measures constituted lines (diagonals) drawn through the intersection-point of the three axes of the space.

To develop a shorthand taxonomy, each axis of the temperament space was dichotomized, resulting in octants, labeled as follows:

Exuberant	(+P+A+D)	vs	*Bored*	(−P−A−D)
Relaxed	(+P−A+D)	vs	*Anxious*	(−P+A−D)
Hostile	(−P+A+D)	vs	*Docile*	(+P−A−D)
Disdainful	(−P−A+D)	vs	*Dependent*	(+P+A−D)

Pleasant, arousable, and dominant, temperament are represented by the abbreviations +P, +A, and +D, respectively. −P, −A, and −D represent unpleasant, unarousable, and submissive, temperament, respectively. The four octants associated with above-average scores on trait pleasure (+P) define four distinct, adjusted or healthy, personality types; the remaining four octants associated with below-average scores on trait pleasure (−P) define four separate categories of abnormal or maladjusted personality.

Sample personality dimensions which extend along the Exuberant-Bored diagonal are:

Extraversion (Eysenck & Eysenck, 1968) =
 .21 P + .17 A + .50 D   R = .60
Sentience (Jackson, 1967) =
 .25 P + .36 A + .27 D   R = .53
Arousal-Seeking (Mehrabian & Russell, 1974a) =
 .14 P + .26 A + .55 D   R = .63
Affiliation (Jackson, 1967)=
 .44 P + .20 A + .26 D   R = .59
Nurturance (Jackson, 1967) =
 .41 P + .12 A + .17 D   R = .49

The preceding regression equations, taken from Mehrabian and O'Reilly (1980) are written for standardized variables. Thus, magnitudes of the coefficients can be used to compare the differential influence of trait pleasure, trait arousability, and trait dominance on each personality measure. Coefficients exceeding .11 in absolute value are significant at the .05 level. R stands for the multiple regression coefficient.

"Sentience" is defined as "notices smells, sounds, sights, tastes, and the way things feel" and "Nurturance" is defined as "gives sympathy and comfort; assists others whenever possible" (Jackson, 1967, Table 1). The preceding results show that trait measures that assess a somewhat intensified relationship of the individual with the environment (e.g., Sentience or Arousal-Seeking) and trait measures which assess intensified relationships of the individual with others (e.g., Extraversion or Affiliation) exemplify the Exuberant-Bored diagonal.

Measures of depression illustrate the opposite (Bored) end of the diagonal and the corresponding lack of involvement and withdrawal. In a study of major depression inventories in common use, Mehrabian and Bernath (1991) found that depression scales are significantly and highly weighted by trait displeasure and trait submissiveness and are essentially neutral with respect to trait arousability.

Several personality measures illustrate the Relaxed-Anxious diagonal. Those highlighting the Anxious end are illustrated by the Eysenck and Eysenck (1968) Neuroticism scale.

$$\text{Neuroticism} = -.26 \text{ P} + .49 \text{ A} - .25 \text{ D} \qquad\qquad R = .63$$

Measures highlighting the Relaxed end of the diagonal are represented by the Crowne and Marlowe (1960) Social Desirability scale.

$$\text{Social Desirability} = .34 \text{ P} - .26 \text{ A} + .17 \text{ D} \qquad\qquad R = .48$$

The Hostile-Docile diagonal is represented best by Jackson's (1967) Aggression measure. There were no representative measures in the study emphasizing the Docile end of the diagonal. Individual differences in docility may be of interest in studies of social conformity and in investigations of compatibility of mates. Docility is expected to be associated with conformity and with high compatibility.

$$\text{Aggression} = -.36 \text{ P} + .20 \text{ A} + .28 \text{ D} \qquad\qquad R = .43$$

Finally, the Disdainful-Dependent diagonal is represented by Jackson's Autonomy scale. At the Dependent end, it is exemplified by Jackson's Succorance (or dependency) measure, defined as "frequently seeks the sympathy, protection, love, advice, and reassurance of other people" (Jackson, 1967, Table 1).

$$\text{Autonomy} = -.10 \text{ P} - .13 \text{ A} + .35 \text{ D} \qquad\qquad R = .38$$
$$\text{Succorance} = .20 \text{ P} + .23 \text{ A} - .34 \text{ D} \qquad\qquad R = .45$$

Mehrabian and O'Reilly (1980) provided detailed interpretations for the equations given above and for those of their equations not reported here. The three-dimensional temperament space is a very effective device for analyzing the validity of various personality scales. Regression results such as the above readily expose the composition of a personality measure. If a personality measure is purported to assess positive interpersonal orientation, our findings suggest that it must be positively and moderately weighted by trait pleasure and trait arousability. Other findings, not reported here, showed that measures of emotional emphatic tendency are positively and strongly weighted by trait arousability and, secondarily, by trait pleasure. Thus, one's emotional responsiveness to others' feelings is a reflection of one's more general characteristic of greater arousability.

Disdainful and Hostile temperament types are distinguished by low trait arousability in the former and high trait arousability in the latter. In more extreme manifestations, Disdainful and Hostile temperaments exemplify two important varieties of criminal and/or psychopathic personality. The Disdainful temperament is more likely to be found among white-collar criminals engaged in non-violent, well-planned criminal activities. In contrast, the Hostile temperament is liable to be associated with violent and impulsive criminal activities and psychopathic personality types.

The Bored temperament type is associated with depression. However, measures assessing clinical depression have been found to confound boredom, as defined here $(-P -A -D)$ with anxiety $(-P +A -D)$. As a result, our overall findings for measures of depression indicated a neutral weighting with respect to trait arousability (Mehrabian & Bernath, 1991). But, measures of depression which highlighted the reactive (i.e., anxious, hostile, or panicked) component of depression tended to have a positive contribution from trait arousability.

The Relaxed-Anxious diagonal is helpful in defining one important variant of healthy personality. A Relaxed temperament $(+P -A +D)$, insofar as it represents an emotion constellation exactly opposite to anxiety, distress, and/or the emotional impact of stress $(-P +A -D)$, provides a temperament-based immunity to stress. Thus, in the same stressful situation, Relaxed persons are expected to experience less discomfort and/or anxiety than other temperament types.

Situations Described in Terms of Their Emotion-Eliciting Qualities

Attempts to describe situations comprehensively in terms of traditional perceptual distinctions result in a multitude of variables dealing with colors, textures, shapes, sizes, designs (visual), description of sound spectrum to characterize noise and/or music (auditory), and the more elusive characteristics of stimulation in the olfactory, kinesthetic, and tactual realms. Such descriptions involving literally hundreds of variables are unwieldy for scientific study. An alternative approach is to rely on a more fundamental level of experience—the emotional or connotative reactions which form the lowest common denominators of cognition (Osgood, 1960).

Since emotion states are described adequately in terms of the three relatively independent dimensions of pleasure, arousal, and dominance, it also is possible to obtain general and parsimonious descriptions of situations in terms of their pleasant, arousing, and dominance-inducing qualities. Such characteristics of situations can be assessed readily by averaging emotion-state responses of representative samples of individuals on the pleasure, arousal, and dominance measures.

Studies such as those reviewed by Mehrabian and Russell (1974a, Chap. 4) help describe relationships between specific perceptual characteristics of situations and their emotion-eliciting qualities. For instance, light intensity is a positive correlate of arousal state, blue and green hues elicit low arousal, whereas red, orange, and yellow hues elicit high arousal. Being in one's own or in a familiar territory elicits dominance, whereas being in another's territory or in an unfamiliar situation elicits submissiveness. Extensive data of this type have been reviewed and documented in our investigations of environmental psychology. The net effect is a ready translation of perceptual components of situations into their emotional impact, or vice versa.

Of the three aspects of situational stimulation, arousing quality is most readily and generally described in terms of the concept of "information rate." Using concepts of information theory, Mehrabian and Russell (1974c) proposed a general description of situational complexity, novelty, and/or variability (i.e., information rate) and devised a verbal-report measure for it. Their studies also showed that information rate of situations is a positive correlate of arousal state—thus, more complex, novel, and/or variable situations elicit greater arousal states from individuals exposed to the situations.

In short, a workable system of situational description can be achieved through reliance on the emotional impact of situations. This emotional impact is described succinctly in terms of pleasantness, arousing quality (or information rate), and dominance-inducing quality. In addition, summaries of findings relating emotional responses to specific characteristics of environments (e.g., size, density, crowding, disorganization) provide ready translations between emotional-impact descriptions and more common perceptual and/or verbal definitions of situations.

The following illustrate findings reported and discussed by Mehrabian (1976a, 1980; Mehrabian & Russell, 1974a): large-small (−A), people present vs absent (+P +A), comfortable (+P −A +D), colorful (+A), textured (+A), distant vs close (−A), large vs small scale (+A), crowded (+A), formal (−D), congested (+A −D), yellow (−P +A), green or blue (+P −A), natural vs man-made (+P −D), unsafe (−P +A −D), accessible (+P −A +D), disorganized (−P +A −D), unfamiliar (−D), elegant (+P +A), impressive (+P −D), functional (+P +D).

Hypotheses Outlining Answers to the Contemporaneous Questions

The first major group of questions addressed to any personality theory is: How is behavior a function of situation, personality, and interactions among situation and personality? In our approach, these questions are answered in most general form by first analyzing the combined effects of situation and personality on emotion states (the mediating variables in our framework).

Based on preliminary evidence obtained in our laboratory, situations have a distinctly stronger impact (70% of the influence) than temperament (30% of the influence). Thus, even though temperament characteristics dictate a certain level of consistency in emotional response as an individual moves among situations, the adaptive nature of humans necessitates a greater degree of responsiveness to situational characteristics. If, in contrast, temperament were to be the dominant force in determining emotional response, a person's behavior across a variety of situations would have the appearance of far greater uniformity, resembling that of an automaton.

The combined, largely additive, effects of situation and temperament on emotional response help explain the great variability in an individual's behaviors across situations, while identifying a certain stability of reaction for the same individual across situations. For instance, someone with a hostile temperament is expected to show greater than average degrees of anger, annoyance, disagreeableness, or unfriendliness across diverse situations. However, the same individual will show exuberant-like characteristics in a pleasant situation. This follows simply from a 70% weighting of the situation versus a 30% weighting of temperament. $[.7 \times P + .3 \times (-P + A + D) = .4P + .3A + .3D]$. In a similar way, a dependent person $(+P + A - D)$ who is generally sociable and affiliative is expected to evidence anxiety-related behaviors in unpleasant situations. Again, an anxious person is likely to evidence depressive characteristics in sustained low-information situations (e.g., when socially isolated). Finally, an anxious individual is likely to evidence hostile behaviors within his/her own territory (which induces feelings of dominance) while exhibiting discomfort and distress in unfamiliar situations.

The remaining and important link in our contemporaneous analysis is the relationship between emotion states and specific behavioral variables. A large number of studies conducted in our laboratory have yielded detailed relationships between emotion states as independent variables and specific behavioral responses. These include findings relating to the impact of emotion state on: approach toward vs avoidance of situations, people (socializing), and tasks (work) (Hines & Mehrabian, 1979); parent-infant interaction (Falender & Mehrabian, 1978); hunger and food consumption (Mehrabian, 1987, Chap. 8); alcohol consumption (Mehrabian, 1979); sexual desire and sexual dysfunction (Mehrabian & Stanton-Mohr, 1985); illnesses and accidents (Mehrabian & Ross, 1979).

The latter studies and others, reviewed by Mehrabian (1980), provide a wealth of information regarding effects of emotions on a great variety of behaviors. They illustrate the relative ease with which very general questions regarding the emotional determinants of any behavior can be answered experimentally when emotion states are described succinctly in terms of only three nearly independent factors.

Hypotheses Outlining Answers to the Longitudinal Questions

The two longitudinal questions addressed to any personality theory bear on personality development and personality modification. Within the present approach, the best personality characteristics are those which are most resilient to change and which, therefore, continue to manifest a consistency across situations and time. The rationale for this stance and evidence bearing on the stability and generality of temperament traits were reviewed by Mehrabian (1987, Chap. 3). One only need note animal breeding experiments to illustrate the close relationship between genetic and, therefore, highly stable emotional characteristics (or temperament).

In our approach, environmental influences on temperament are hypothesized to be gradual and to be possible only when these influences are consistent and highly repetitious (amounting to hundreds of thousands of trials) over the course of the first dozen years of development. Thus, parents who are typically loving, accepting, and tolerant manifest numerous behaviors daily which communicate this attitude. Over the course of years, a child exposed to such parental attitudes develops generalized positive expectations regarding social relationships and the outcomes of social interaction. Such expectations result in positive social behaviors by the child which, in turn, elicit positive reactions from others. Thus, the generalized positive expectations are reinforced and maintained (Mehrabian & Ksionzky, 1970). Similarly, generalized negative expectations, learned from repeated trials with parents, lead to negative interpersonal behaviors, negative reciprocated reactions from others, and maintenance of the negative expectations. These two patterns of positive and negative expectations are important correlates of pleasant and unpleasant temperament characteristics, respectively.

Trait arousability, in turn, may be determined in part by the typical information rate of the developmental environment. Children who grow up in neat, organized, sparsely decorated environments and with ordered and highly patterned activities will have diminished opportunities to learn to screen. They are thus more likely to be arousable than children who grow up in chaotic, noisy, ever-changing, crowded, and unpredictable homes.

Finally, dominant parents are expected to teach their children to be submissive and, conversely, submissive parents are expected to teach their children to be dominant. Here, however, genetic and learned influences are in conflict. The offspring of dominant parents who have learned to act submissive will tend to gradually manifest genetically determined dominant characteristics as they group up and leave the parental environment. Also, compared with the genetically submissive, they will show a greater differential in dominance with peers and subordinates compared with parents and/or authority figures. In short, such persons will manifest apparently contradictory dominant-submissive behaviors; however, the contradictions diminish with age and can be understood by noting the status of their targets in social interactions.

In all, our contention is that genetic factors determine at least 50% of temperament traits, with the balance being learned in the first dozen or so years of life. Just as environmental influences can have general and lasting effects on temperament following thousands of learning trials, by the same token, the modification of temperament would require similar, repetitious, and extensive training. Indeed, the more general a trait is that is to be modified, the greater the difficulty in modifying it.

Thus, for most practical purposes, attempts to modify temperament are doomed to failure. Instead, one only need note the following general relationship to discover approaches to behavior (and not temperament) modification. Behavior = f (temperament, situation, temperament × situation). If temperament is (for all practical purposes) reduced to a constant in the preceding equation, one realizes that behavior change can be achieved most readily through situational change. Here, we can borrow extensively from the literature on behavior modification, and of course, from findings bearing on the present theory which relate (1) situations to emotion states and (2) emotion states to behavior. For instance, boredom activates appetite (Mehrabian, 1987, Chaps. 8 & 9). Thus, overeating can be controlled temporarily by physical activity, exercise, social interaction, or exciting music.

Also, know-how regarding temperament-situation additive effects and interactions can be invaluable for determining the relative efficacy of different situational conditions for different temperament types. A pleasant and low-information setting may be far more helpful to an arousable person who has difficulty studying than to one who is unarousable. An unarousable mate is bound to be more beneficial to one who is anxious or hostile than to one who is relaxed or docile.

In sum, the present approach has numerous implications regarding behavior modification. Most importantly, application of the approach requires specific environmental findings relating situations to emotions, and emotions to behaviors. Once these links are known, therapy is reduced to an educational process in which clients are taught the linkages between situation, emotion, and behavior. They are trained to analyze situational factors in detail and, of course, to have an understanding of their own temperaments and the diverse ways in which temperament characteristics and situations interact to determine emotion states.

References

Crowne, D. P., & Marlowe, D. A new scale of social desirability independent of psychopathology. *Journal of Consulting Psychology*, 1960, *24*, 349–354.

Eysenck, H. J., & Eysenck, S. B. G. *Manual of the Eysenck Personality Inventory*. San Diego, CA: Educational and Industrial Testing Service, 1968.

Falender, C. A., & Mehrabian, A. Environmental effects on parent-infant interaction. *Genetic Psychology Monographs*, 1978, *97*, 3–41.

Hines, M., & Mehrabian, A. Approach-avoidance behaviors as a function of pleasantness and arousing quality of settings and individual differences in stimulus screening. *Social Behavior and Personality*, 1979, *7*, 223–233.

Jackson, D. N. *Personality Research Form Manual*. Goshen, NY: Research Psychologists Press, 1967.

Mehrabian, A. *Nonverbal communication*. Chicago, IL: Aldine-Atherton, 1972a.

Mehrabian, A. Nonverbal communication. In J. K. Cole (Ed.), *Nebraska symposium on motivation*. Vol. 19. Lincoln, NE: University of Nebraska, 1972b.

Mehrabian, A. *Public places and private spaces: The psychology of work, play, and living environments*. New York: Basic Books, 1976a.

Mehrabian, A. *Manual for the questionnaire measure of stimulus screening and arousability*. Psychology Department, University of California, Los Angeles, 1976b.

Mehrabian, A. A questionnaire measure of individual differences in stimulus screening and associated differences in arousability. *Environmental Psychology and Nonverbal Behavior*, 1977, *1*, 89–103.

Mehrabian, A. Measures of individual differences in temperament. *Educational and Psychological Measurement*, 1978, *38*, 1105–1117.

Mehrabian, A. Effect of emotional state on alcohol consumption. *Psychological Reports*, 1979, *44*, 271–282.

Mehrabian, A. *Basic dimensions for a general psychological theory*. Cambridge, MA: Oelgeschlager, Gunn & Hain, 1980.

Mehrabian, A. *Eating characteristics and temperament*. New York: Springer, 1987.

Mehrabian, A., & Bernath, M. S. Factorial composition of commonly used self-report depression inventories: Relationships with basic dimensions of temperament. *Journal of Research in Personality*, 1991.

Mehrabian, A., & de Wetter, R. Experimental test of an emotion-based approach to fitting brand names to products. *Journal of Applied Psychology*, 1987, *72*, 125–130.

Mehrabian, A., & Hines, M. A questionnaire measure of individual differences in dominance-submissiveness. *Educational and Psychological Measurement*, 1978, *38*, 479–484.

Mehrabian, A., & Ksionzky, S. Models for affiliative and conformity behavior. *Psychological Bulletin*, 1970, *74*, 110–126.

Mehrabian, A., & O'Reilly, E. Analysis of personality measures in terms of basic dimensions of temperament. *Journal of Personality and Social Psychology*, 1980, *38*, 492–503.

Mehrabian, A., & Ross, M. Illnesses, accidents, and alcohol use as functions of the arousing quality and pleasantness of life changes. *Psychological Reports*, 1979, *45*, 31–43.

Mehrabian, A., & Russell, J. A. *An approach to environmental psychology*. Cambridge, MA: MIT Press, 1974a.

Mehrabian, A., & Russell, J. A. The basic emotional impact of environments. *Perceptual and Motor Skills*, 1974b, *38*, 283–301.

Mehrabian, A., & Russell, J. A. A verbal measure of information rate for studies in environmental psychology. *Environment and Behavior*, 1974c, *6*, 233–252.

Mehrabian, A., & Stanton-Mohr, L. M. Effects of emotional state on sexual desire and sexual dysfunction. *Motivation and Emotion*, 1985, *9*, 315–330.

Osgood, C. E. The cross-cultural generality of visual-verbal synesthetic tendencies. *Behavioral Science*, 1960, *5*, 146–169.

Osgood, C. E., Suci, G. J., & Tannenbaum, P. H. *The measurement of meaning*. Urbana, IL: University of Illinois Press, 1957.

Russell, J. A., & Mehrabian, A. Evidence for a three-factor theory of emotions. *Journal of Research in Personality*, 1977, *11*,273–294.

6

Dimensions of Personality
The Biosocial Approach to Personality

Hans J. Eysenck

A Paradigm of Personality Description

It would seem difficult to doubt the truth of the proposition that man is a biosocial animal (Eysenck, 1980b). There is no longer any doubt about the strong determination of individual differences in personality by genetic factors (Eaves, Eysenck, & Martin, 1989), and much progress has been made in the study of physiological, neurological, and biochemical-hormonal factors in mediating this influence (Eysenck, 1981; Zuckerman, Ballenger, & Post, 1984; Stelmack, 1981). It has been suggested that the biological aspects of personality should be identified with the concept of *temperament* (Strelau, 1983) and this may prove an acceptable use, although the dictionary defines the term as equivalent to personality ("the characteristic way an individual behaves, especially towards other people"). What is not in doubt is the importance of considering individual differences as an important part of scientific psychology (Eysenck, 1984) and, indeed, it has been fundamental for any proper understanding of human behavior (Eysenck, 1983). Personality is more than superficial behavioral characteristics, easily acquired and easily abandoned; it is an indispensable part of any meaningful scientific investigation in educational, industrial, clinical, social or experimental psychology (Eysenck & Eysenck, 1985).

Concepts like values, interests, and attitudes are related to personality but do not usually form part of its central core. Undoubtedly they too are influenced by biological factors as shown, for instance, by the high heritabilities for social attitudes and interests (Eaves *et al.*, 1989); but too little work has been published on such determinants to deserve extended treatment here.

Hans J. Eysenck • Department of Psychology, Institute of Psychiatry, University of London, London SE5 8AF, United Kingdom.

The multiplicity of approaches to the descriptive analysis of personality should not mislead psychologists into thinking there is no agreement; Eysenck (1983) has argued that there is a paradigm in personality research, and Royce and Powell (1983), in a re-analysis of all large-scale psychometric analyses of personality to date have found that there are three major dimensions in this field. They appear again and again, and are very similar to the three major dimensions suggested by Eysenck, namely Psychoticism (P), Extraversion (E), and Neuroticism (N). There are several reasons for asserting that these three dimensions are firmly linked with biological determinants. These reasons are as follows:

1. As already noted, regardless of instrument of measurement or method of analysis, these three dimensions emerge from practically all large-scale investigations into personality, a result unlikely if environmental factors alone determined a person's position on these dimensions (Eysenck & Eysenck, 1985; Royce & Powell, 1983).

2. These same three dimensions are found cross-culturally in all parts of the world where studies have been carried out to investigate this universality (Barrett & Eysenck, 1984). Using the Eysenck Personality Questionnaire (EPQ; Eysenck & Eysenck, 1975), these authors analyzed results from 25 countries as diverse as Nigeria and Uganda in Africa, mainland China and Japan, European and Scandinavian countries, South American countries, Socialist countries like the USSR, Hungary, and Poland, as well as the former British colonies (USA, Canada, and Australia), testing 500 males and 500 females in each country with a translation of the EPQ, and carrying out factor analyses separately for males and females. It was found that, overall, practically identical factors emerged, showing indices of factor comparison which averaged .98. This identity of personality dimensions in fundamentally different cultures suggests a biological foundation.

3. Individuals tend to retain their position on these three dimensions with remarkable consistency (Conley, 1984a, b, 1985). This suggests that the events of everyday life have little influence on a person's temperament, and that biological causes are predominant in determining disposition.

4. Work on the genetics of personality (Eaves *et al.*, 1989) has powerfully reinforced this argument, as already pointed out; genetic factors determine at least half the phenotypic variance of the major dimensions of personality, and there is little if any evidence for between family environmental variance. This finding alone would seem to contradict all the major theories of personality advanced in psychological textbooks!

Clearly, genetic factors cannot act directly on behavior; there must be an intervening link between genes and chromosomes on the one hand, and social behavior on the other. This intervening link may be looked for in physiological factors, neurological structure, biochemical and hormonal determinants or other biological features of the organism. The proper theory of personality requires some knowledge of the relationships between social behavior, on the one hand, which gives rise to the descriptions of the major dimensions of personality, based on patterns of behavior, and specific biological features of the organism on the other. It is unlikely that simple heuristic findings will establish a convincing link; what is needed clearly is a set of theories relating the various dimensions of personality. Eysenck (1990) has given a detailed review of the theories and studies available to date in this very large and complex field; here we can only discuss some of the issues in question, with particular reference to the theory of "arousal" in relation to extraversion-introversion.

Biological Theories of Personality

Eysenck (1967) originally suggested a link between cortical arousal and extraversion-introversion. This was based essentially on the findings of Moruzzi and Magoun (1949) of the ascending reticular activating system (ARAS), the system activation of which elicited a general activation pattern in the cortical EEG. Collaterals from the ascending sensory pathways produce activity in the ARAS, which subsequently relays the excitation to numerous sites in the cerebral cortex. It was this excitation which produced the EEG synchronization observed by Moruzzi and Magoun. Much research has since shown that the reticular formation is implicated in the initiation and maintenance of motivation, emotion, and conditioning by way of excitatory and inhibitory control of autonomic and postural adjustments, and by way of cortical coordination of activity serving attention, arousal, and orienting behavior.

The link suggested by Eysenck (1967) between personality and the ARAS amounted to the suggestion that the extraversion-introversion dimension is identified largely with differences in level of activity in the cortico-reticular loop, introverts being characterized by higher levels of activity than extraverts, and thus being chronically more cortically aroused. In addition, Eysenck suggested that neuroticism was closely related to the activity of the visceral brain, which consists of the hippocampus-amygdala, singulum, septum, and hypothalamus. These two systems are independent, hence we have an orthogonal relation between extraversion-introversion and neuroticism-stability. However, this independence is only partial. One of the ways in which cortical arousal can be produced is through activity in the visceral brain which reaches the reticular formation through collaterals. Activity in the visceral brain produces autonomic arousal, and Eysenck has used the term *activation* to distinguish this form of arousal from that produced by reticular activity. Thus in a condition of high activation, we would expect high arousal; a person who is strongly affected by anger, or fear, or some other emotion will certainly also be in a state of high cortical arousal. Fortunately, such states of strong emotional involvement are relatively rare, but they do indicate that the independence of the two systems is only relative (Routtenberg, 1966).

A detailed discussion of the concept of arousal by many authors is given in a book edited by Strelau and Eysenck (1987). Clearly, the concept of general physiological arousal that was a core construct in Duffy's (1957) early theory and Hebb's (1955) optimal arousal approach does not seem viable any longer. The reticulo-cortical system of Moruzzi and Magoun (1949) now appears to be only one of several arousal systems (Zuckerman & Como, 1983), probably including the limbic arousal system, suggested by recent work (Aston-Jones & Bloom, 1981), as well as a monoamine oxidase system, the diffuse thalamocortical system and the pituitary-adrenocortical system (Zuckerman, 1983). This apparent diversity may not prevent the systems from operating in a relatively unitary fashion. Clearly, the way from the "conceptual nervous system" of Hebb to the "central nervous system" of the neurosciences is a hard one!

Problems in Theories Testing

At first sight it may seem relatively easy to test theories of this kind by taking groups of extraverts and introverts, or high and low N scorers, and submitting them to physiological tests of one kind or another. However, note the following:

1. There is no single measure of arousal or excitation in the neurophysiological field. As Lacey and Lacey (1958) have emphasized repeatedly, the underlying systems show *response specificity*, in that different systems are primarily activated by suitable stimulation in different people. Thus one person may react to emotional stimuli primarily through an increase in heart rate, another through increase in the conductivity of the skin, a third through more rapid breathing, etc. No single measure is adequate to portray the complexity of reactions; the recommended solution is to take measures of as many systems as possible, and score changes in the system maximally involved. But few experimenters have followed this advice, so that failure to support the theory may be due to faulty or too restricted choice of measuring instrument.

2. There is also *stimulus specificity*, in the sense that different people may be sensitive to different stimuli. Saltz (1970) has shown that failure, or the threat of failure, produces more anxiety among N+ subjects, whereas shocks generate greater anxiety among N− than N+ subjects. Genetic factors predispose individuals to condition anxiety responses to quite specific stimuli (Eysenck & Martin, 1987). Thus the usual stimuli chosen by experimenters, e.g., shocks, may result in quite different relationships between stimulus and response than some other stimuli.

3. Relations between stimulus and response are usually nonlinear. Both the Yerkes-Dodson Law (1908) and Pavlov's (1927) Law of Transmarginal Inhibition show that as stimuli get stronger, responses at first increase in strength, then they decline, producing a curvilinear regression. This leads to complex theoretical formulation which makes precise prediction difficult. We can predict that the high arousal of introverts will lead to a reversal of the stimulus-response correlation at a lower point of stimulus intensity than would be true of extraverts, but the precise point is difficult to establish. Nevertheless, the Law has shown impressive predictive powers in relation to a variety of behavioral responses (Eysenck, 1976; Eysenck & Eysenck, 1985).

4. Threshold and ceiling effects may make choice of measure difficult. Looking at the electrodermal response (EDR) as a measure of N, we could use as our response measure: (a) Size of response; (b) latency of response; or (c) duration of response, i.e., time to return to base-line. Only (c) seems to give useful correlations, but that could not have been predicted from what little we know of the EDR.

5. Resting levels are ill-defined, and are influenced powerfully by uncontrolled preexperimental variables. Subjects coming into our laboratories may have suffered an emotional shock quite recently, may have smoked or drunk alcohol heavily, have been frightened by rumors about the experiments to be performed, or may have been annoyed by being kept waiting; these and many other factors may determine decisively their reactions in the test. Eysenck (1981) has discussed in detail how anticipation in subjects produced quite contradictory results in two series of experiments. Spence had postulated, and found, that eyeblink conditioning was correlated with N, not with E. Eysenck had postulated, and found, that eyeblink conditioning was correlated with E, but not N.

Kimble visited both laboratories and discovered that while Eysenck reassured his subjects, told them explicitly that they would not receive electric shock, hid all the threatening apparatus, and avoided mechanical links with the eyelid, Spence went to the opposite extreme and thoroughly frightened his subjects. As a consequence, N played an important part in Spence's experiments, differences in activation drowning out differences in arousal, while activation played no part in Eysenck's experiment, allowing arousal to determine the observed correlations. Note that these preexperimental conditions were not discussed in the presentation of the experiments in question!

6. Neurological and hormonal systems interact in complex ways, and so do the dimensions of personality; it is never safe to assume that E+ and E− subjects are not influenced in their reactions by differences in P, or N, or intelligence, or whatever. At best these extraneous influences balance out, but they obviously constitute a goodly background of noise against which the signal may not be all that strong. The effects of such interactions deserve more detailed study than they have received hitherto. These difficulties are particularly critical in relation to neuroticism, because of the added complication that it is very difficult to manipulate experimentally states of depression, anxiety, guilt feelings, etc. Laboratory experiments are very restricted in what can and cannot be done ethically, and the very minor and weak manipulations of mood possible in the laboratory pay little relation to the very strong feelings elicited in a normal life. Cortical arousal, on the other hand, is much more manipulable, and hence work with the arousal theory of extraversion has been much more successful.

EEG Studies and Personality

Of the many different ways in which cortical arousal has been studied in relation to extraversion-introversion, the most prominent and indeed also the most obvious has of course been that of using electroencephalography. High levels of arousal are linked with low-amplitude, high-frequency activity in the alpha range of the EEG, and if it were found that extraverts showed low-amplitude and high-frequency alpha activity, this would certainly speak very strongly against the theory. It can of course be objected that the EEG, being recorded from the outside of the skull, represents a kind of composite amalgam of electrical energy generated from different parts of the cortex, and may thus produce a misleading impression of the actual activity in any specific area of the brain. In spite of this complication, evidence has consistently tended to support the hypothesis.

Gale (1983) has reviewed 33 studies containing a total of 38 experimental comparisons. Results are far from uniform, but nevertheless on this criterion extraverts were less aroused than introverts in 22 comparisons, while introverts were less aroused than extraverts in only five comparisons, no significant effects being reported in the remaining studies. The ratio of 22 to 5 in favor of the hypothesis is certainly a very positive finding, but one would like to be able to account for the 5 studies failing to show the predicted relationship.

Gale suggested that the effects of extraversion of the EEG were influenced by the level of arousal induced by the experimental conditions; in particular, he suggested that introverts are most likely to be more aroused than extraverts in moderately arousing conditions, with the differences between introverts and extraverts either disappearing or being reversed with conditions producing either very low or very high levels of arousal. These suggestions follow from the general theory, with high levels of arousal and introversion producing the paradoxical lowering of arousal postulated by Pavlov's Law of Transmarginal Inhibition. Conditions of very low arousal would paradoxically produce strong feelings of boredom in extraverts, which have been shown to lead to attempts at disinhibition.

Gale classified all the relevant EEG studies according to whether the test conditions were minimally, moderately, or highly arousing; he found that introverts appeared to be more aroused than extraverts in all eight of the studies using moderately arousing conditions that reported significant effects of extraversion; but the expected result was found in only 9 out of 12 significant studies using low-arousal conditions, and 5 out of 7 using high-arousal conditions. This result certainly suggests that in testing the hypothesis we should avoid extreme low arousal and high arousal situations, although even under such conditions likely to produce failure of the hypothesis, we still have 14 experiments supporting it, and only 5 giving the opposite result.

Later studies (O'Gorman & Mallise, 1984; O'Gorman & Lloyd, 1987; and Venturini, Pascalis, Imperiali, & Martini, 1981) found results which on the whole were in confirmity with the hypothesis. They also added new measures, such as the alpha attenuation response, which demonstrated that extraverts sometimes reacted to the auditory stimuli, while introverts did not. This greater responsivity to stimulation of introverts is of course in line with the theory.

Cortical evoked potentials furnish us with another possible way of testing the theory. Stelmack, Achorn, and Michaud (1977) found that introverts obtained greater amplitude of the average evoked response (AER) than extraverts with low-frequency stimulation, both with 55dB and with 80dB, while observing no differences between groups with high-frequency stimulation. This finding is explicable in terms of the known tendency of greater interindividual variability of the AER at low-frequency than at high-frequency levels (Davis & Zerlin, 1966; Rothman, 1970), as an increase in variance would obviously increase the possibility of obtaining significant covariance. The study is instructive in demonstrating the need to control details of the experimental manipulation, and pay attention to known features of the variables in question.

Another approach using evoked potentials is the augmenting/reducing effect, which relies on the assessment of cortical responses to stimuli of varying intensities. Increasing intensity of stimulation may produce corresponding increases or decreases in the amplitude of particular EP components recorded from different subjects. Augmenters are called such because increased stimulation produces increased amplitude, while for reducers increased stimulation produces decreased amplitude. The theory would predict an increase in amplitude with increases in stimulus intensity, up to a point where transmarginal inhibition would set in to lead to a reduction in amplitude. The point where reduction would be expected to set in would be expected to occur at *lower* levels of stimulus intensity for introverts than for extraverts. Thus introverts should be reducers, extraverts augmenters. This, indeed, has been the pattern in earlier studies (Friedman & Mears, 1979; Soskis & Shagass, 1974), and in studies using sensation-seeking measures, especially disinhibition, which is most closely related to extraversion (von Knorring, 1980; Zuckerman, Murtaugh, & Siegel, 1974). The only study out of line is one published by Haier, Robinson, Braden and Williams (1984). This only dealt with 11 augmenters and 10 reducers, which is a very small number, but nevertheless the results were significant and counter to the theory. Clearly, what is needed are more analytical studies to give us more information.

Two such studies have appeared recently. The first is by Lukas (1987) who used a Maxwellian-View Optical System to control retinal illuminance precisely, and carried out two studies comparing augmenting-reducing at O_z and C_z and their correlations with two personality measures, namely, Zuckerman's Sensation-Seeking Scale and Vando's Reducer Augmenter Scale (Vando, 1974). The occipital potential showed no correlation with the personality measures, but the vertex potentials, which are known to be affected by nonsensory factors, such as cortical arousal and attention, were significantly correlated with personality. Lukas argued that the vertex augmenter is a sensation-seeker, but this relationship was true only for the A/R slopes to the more intense light flashes. Lukas concluded that how the brain responds to intense sensory stimulation as measured by A/R determines how people respond behaviorally to intense sensations. Interestingly enough, Lukas extended his work to cats (Saxton, Siegel, & Lukas, 1987) and found that here too augmenters at a high-intensity range were more active and exploratory. This suggests that the relationship between sensory modulation and behavior is not confined to humans.

The most complete study of the augmenting/arousing effects in relation to personality has been done by Stenberg, Rosen, and Risberg (1988). They used 6 intensities of visual and 6 intensities of auditory stimuli, arguing that a superimposed mechanism of transmarginal or protective inhibition can account for the relationship with personality only if it generalizes across different modality and response definitions. They found that for the visual stimuli, the slope of the P90-N120 amplitude at the vertex correlated significantly with both the Extraversion and the Disinhibition scales in the way that augmenting/reducing theory predicts. However, over the primary visual area, no component showed the same personality relationship as the vertex wave, and one early component showed the opposite. This result, they argue, suggests that personality differences in VEPs may reflect different ways of allocating processing resources between primary and association areas, rather than a general tendency to inhibit strong stimuli. In the auditory modality, personality differences were not apparent in the amplitude slopes, possibly due to the confluence from primary and association areas in AEPs in the vertex lead. They finally state that "there was a general tendency for latencies to correlate positively with extraversion and disinhibition, in congruence with Eysenck's theory on the biological basis of extraversion" (Stenberg, et.al., 1988). These results powerfully indicate the need for very detailed and specific studies to look at the precise relationships involved, using different stimulus modalities, and different recording areas; only by thus enlarging our understanding will we be able to arrive at a more all-embracing theoretical formulation than is available at present. Perhaps an explanation will be found along these lines for the curious and unusual results of the Haier, et al., (1984) study.

Other studies using the EEG have employed the contingent negative variation (CNV), a technique in which EEG changes are observed between a warning signal and an effector signal. A summary of previous work, with original studies, is given by Werre (1983). The clearest differential effect on the CNV occurred when isolated, motivated, young adult students performed a constant 4-period reaction time task, which was novel to them, in the morning. Under those conditions there was a positive correlation between mean CNV amplitude and extraversion. Conditions not producing personality differences were those that existed when the students were repeating the standard tasks, and when they were performing a second task in addition to the standard one. This study is notable for varying conditions under which subjects perform, so that the author could clarify the relationship between conditions and personality in affecting the CNV. Yet other studies have used photic driving (Golding & Richards, 1985; Robinson, 1982). The Robinson study in particular is an example of how to relate experiment to theory, but is too complex to be reported here in detail.

Electrodermal Studies of Personality

Studies of electrodermal responses are almost as numerous as those using the EEG. In particular, relations have been studied to the orienting response (Lynn, 1966; Sokolov, 1963). Eysenck's theory would predict that introverts would show a stronger OR, and slower habituation. A large number of studies has been referenced by Eysenck (1990), most supporting the hypothesis, but many giving insignificant or contrary results. It can be noted that greater intensity of stimulation tends to produce differences where less intense stimulation does not. Thus, as far as auditory stimulation is concerned, which has been most widely used, studies using sounds in the region of 60–75 dB typically fail to differentiate introverts and extraverts, whereas stimuli in the 75–90 dB range tend to do so. As mentioned, interindividual variability of the auditory-evoked response has been found to be greater under low-frequency conditions, which also favor the differentiation of extraverts and introverts; similarly, low-frequency stimulation seems to be more effective in differentiating extraverts and introverts in the OR paradigm.

On the whole, it appears that conditions which favor differentiation between extraverts and introverts with the electrodermal measures of the OR can be described as moderately arousing, very much as in the case of the EEG. As Stelmack (1981) points out:

> From among the stimulus conditions in the studies reviewed here, low frequency tones in the 75–90dB intensity range and visual stimuli provide the base from which such an enquiry would commence. (p. 51)

The recommendation for visual stimuli rests on the fact that these have been found more likely to produce a differentiation.

In considering these studies, we should also remember the notion of autonomic response specificity mentioned earlier. An important study demonstrating the importance of this principle is provided by Stelmack, Bourgeois, Chain, and Pickard, (1979). This study was devoted to the habituation to neutral and affective words where multiple and autonomic measures were recorded. Multiple regression analysis was carried out which showed that a conjoint influence of cardiac, electrodermal and vasomotor OR components accounted for 54% of the variation in extraversion, which corresponds with a multiple correlation of .73; no single component accounted for more than 24%. As Stelmack (1981) points out:

The mechanism of the kind implied by the notion of autonomic response stereotypy can account for such an increase in prediction and suggests that the consideration of the individual autonomic response preference of subjects merits deliberate mention and that the application of multiple autonomic measurements may be worthwhile. (p. 32)

Another point of difference between studies relates to the different measures that have been taken. The technical points involved have been discussed in detail by Stelmack (1981). Differences in *phasic* response have been more frequently recorded than differences in *tonic* levels.

We must now turn to more recent developments. One of the most important papers to be noted here is one by Wilson (1989) which is innovative in several different ways. The most important point to note is that the 61 men and 50 women who measured their own skin conductance did so hourly throughout one working day, as well as recording drug intake and activities. Thus the study attempts to deal directly with a point originally raised by Blake (1967), who found that body temperature, which he and others considered an index of arousal, was higher for introverts in the morning, but higher for extraverts in the evening. Several recent studies have shown a similar crossover in the relative performance of introverts and extraverts according to whether the task is done in the morning or the evening (Colquhoun, 1960, 1971; Horne & Ostberg, 1975; von Knorring, Mörnstad, Forsgren, & Holmgren, 1986; Revelle, Anderson, & Humphreys, 1987). Generally it has been found that introverts show superior performance in the morning and extraverts in the evening, and this, too, has been interpreted in terms of differential arousal levels, the suggestion being that introverts are high in arousal in the morning, whereas in the afternoon or evening the arousal of extraverts overtakes that of introverts. Gray (1981) has made this the major point of his critique of the Eysenck theory, pointing out that it cannot be meaningful for people to be introverts in the morning, extraverts in the evening!

Figure 6.1 shows the major results. We should look at the age-corrected figures for introverts; there was a difference in age between introverts and extraverts, and it is well known that as people get older, the number of sweat glands decreases. It is clear from the figure that introverts throughout the day show higher skin conductance (are more aroused) than extraverts, with the difference being smaller in the evening and disappearing at midnight.

Why do the two groups came closer together in the evening? Examination of the particular aspects of introversion-extraversion that are critical suggested to the author that sociability was more instrumental than impulsiveness. This, he argued, is probably due to the fact that the activities which attract extraverts are more available in the evening, while the interests of introverts (e.g., task-oriented work in solitary activity) are more readily accommodated in the daylight hours. Supporting this idea is the fact that extraverts are more active, both generally and socially, in the evening, while introverts are more active in the morning.

The finding that extraverts also smoke and drink more than introverts in the evening may or may not be connected to the self-manipulation of arousal. It may simply reflect the fact that smoking and drinking are social activities, smoking giving opportunity for offering small gifts (cigarettes) to other people, helping them (striking the match) and generally establishing common ground by sharing the experience. Drinking alcohol is a

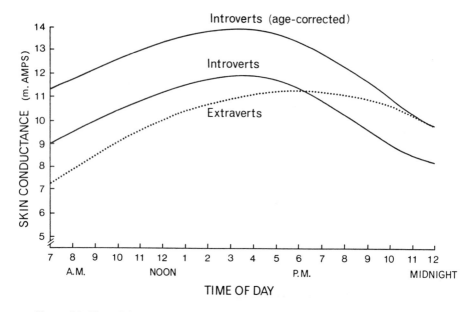

Figure 6.1. Time of day and skin conductance level in introverts and extraverts (Wilson, 1989).

notorious way of reducing social anxiety and facilitating companionship. Wilson concludes that:

> Overall, our results suggest that the evening activity of extraverts is responsible for the
> higher arousal in the evening. Apparently, vigorous activity leads to higher levels of
> arousal as indexed by skin conductance.

These results show the great importance of recording not only physiological measures of arousal, but also the activity preceding or accompanying the measurement.
Neglect to do so is one of the major criticisms of many of the studies summarized in this
chapter.

Miscellaneous Measures of Personality

In addition to EEG and electrodermal studies, there are a number of miscellaneous
measures which ought at least to be mentioned. The first of these concerns stimulated
salivation in its relation to extraversion. Eysenck's theory predicts that introverts would
react more strongly than extraverts to stimulation, such as drops of lemon juice on the
tongue, producing a greater flow of saliva. Deary, Ramsay, Wilson, and Riad (1988)
have summarized details on nine studies; they abstract their results as follows:

> The negative relation between extraversion and acid-stimulated salivation holds: for both
> male and female Ss with different saliva collection procedures; whether fresh or synthetic
> lemon juice or citric acid is used as a stimulus, (although fresh lemon juice appears the

most reliable); whether the stimulus is dropped or swabbed onto the tongue and whether the saliva is collected for ten seconds or ten minutes. There is, however, some evidence that the correlation is more robust when testing is performed in the morning when arousal differences are at their greatest. Swallowing the stimulus also appears to reduce the correlation. (p. 906)

S. P. G. and H. J. Eysenck (1967), tested the hypothesis that swallowing the stimulus, and thus increasing its intensity, would evoke transmarginal inhibition preferentially in introverts, and found that it in fact reversed the correlation. Overall results are certainly favorable to the hypothesis. In their own study, Deary, *et al.*, (1988) used 24 subjects, and reported replication of the findings outlined above.

Pupillometry is the next topic to be discussed in this section. In recent years there has been an increased interest in the use of the pupillary response as a psychophysiological measure relating to personality. Pupillary dilation is due primarily to sympathetic activity, whereas constriction reflects parasympathetic activity. We can thus use pupillometry to measure individual differences in responsiveness to stimulation, and tonic pupil size in the absence of specific stimulation can provide an index of general or autonomic arousal. In the first of this line of studies, Holmes (1967) measured speed of pupillary constriction to the onset of a light. The fast dilators tended to be extraverted, whereas the fast constrictors were introverted. Holmes argued that the rapid pupillary constriction of introverts indicated that they had greater amounts of acetylocholine at cholinergic synapses than extraverts.

Frith (1977) confirmed some of Holmes' findings, reporting that high scorers of the impulsivity component of extraversion showed less pupillary constriction than low impulsives in responses to a light flash, perhaps because they were less reactive to stimulation. He also found that impulsivity was negatively correlated with pupil size during an initial interval of no stimulation. This suggests that the more impulsive subjects (high P?) were less aroused than the less impulsive subjects.

The most important study in this field was reported by Stelmack and Mandelzys (1975); they also found that introverts had larger pupils than extraverts in the absence of specific stimulation, suggesting that the introverted subjects were more aroused throughout the experiment. As regards phasic pupillary responses to auditorily presented neutral, affective, and taboo words, they found that introverts showed significantly more pupillary dilation to these stimuli than extraverts, especially in response to taboo words. In other words, introverts responded more strongly than extraverts to the auditory stimuli. Altogether this line of research seems promising, and should be pursued in the future.

Studies of physique and constitution, as reviewed by Eysenck (1990), are also relevant to the concept of extraversion, although, because of a failure to link theoretically the work on body build, blood groups, etc. with the concept of arousal, these data will not be discussed in detail here. Suffice it to say that extraverts tend to be relatively broad, introverts elongated in body build (Eysenck, 1970; Rees, 1973), and that introversion is found to be significantly more frequent among persons having the AB blood group (Angst & Maurer-Groeli, 1974; Maurer-Groeli, 1974a, b). Eysenck (1977) has reported on national differences in personality as related to ABO blood group polymorphism.

Biochemical Determinants of Personality

As a final group of studies relating biological mechanisms to personality we must turn to biochemical influences, a group of determinants which have been studied more and more frequently in recent years, and work which has been surveyed in some detail by Zuckerman, Ballenger, and Post (1984). Of the more obvious hormones here we may mention the gonadal hormones, particularly testosterone. It is of course *prenatal* androgenization which has been shown to be particularly effective in producing masculine-type behaviors (Eysenck & Wilson, 1979), and there are obvious problems with correlational studies of testosterone and behavior, as well as with other biochemicals that show day-to-day fluctuations in level. Nevertheless, Daitzman, Zuckerman, Sammelwitz, and Ganjam (1978) found significant correlations between plasma androgen levels and the Disinhibition subscale of the Sensation-Seeking Scale, i.e., the scale most closely related to extraversion. In their later and more comprehensive study, Daitzman and Zuckerman (1980) again found high scorers on the Disinhibition scale to have higher levels of testosterone, and of estradiol and estrogen, than those with lower scores. They also used other indices of hormonal influence, and carried out a factor analysis too complex to be discussed here.

Another important biochemical agent is the enzyme MAO, which is present in all tissues including brain, with highest brain concentrations being found in the hypothalamus. MAO plays a role in the degradation of the monoamines norepinephrine, dopamine, and serotonin. The review by Zuckerman *et al.* (1984) indicates that MAO levels relate *negatively* to extraversion and sensation-seeking; these findings are consistent with behavioral observations of high- and low-MAO monkeys, and humans (Coursey, Buchsbaum, & Murphy, 1979). High-MAO monkeys in colony tended to be solitary, inactive, and passive; low-MAO monkeys tended to be active, to make many social contacts, and engage frequently in play. In rodents, too, MAO inhibitors produce hyperactivity and increase activity in a novel environment. Later studies by Schalling, Edman, Asberg, and Oreland, (1988), Calhoon (1988), Klinteberg, Schalling, Edman, Oreland, and Asberg (1987), and von Knorring, Oreland, and Wimblad (1984) bear out these major findings. Correlations have also been found between measures of impulsivity and CSF levels of the serotonin metabolite, 5-HIAA (Schalling, Asberg, Edman, & Levander, 1984), which is interesting in view of the associations assumed to exist between low-platelet MAO activity and central serotonergic hyperactivity. These results form a fairly congruent whole centering on the concept of impulsivity, and hence implicating P as well as E. Others have used the monoamine system (e.g., Ballenger, Post, Jimmerson, Lake, Murphy, Zuckerman, & Cronin, 1983), showing that CSF calcium correlated positively with extraversion and negatively with neurotic introversion and general neuroticism. Another interesting finding is that cortisol assayed from CSF correlated negatively with the Disinhibition scale from the Sensation-Seeking Scale.

Finally, we must mention the sedation threshold (Krishnamoorti & Shagass, 1963; Shagass & Jones, 1958; Shagass & Kerenyi, 1958). In these studies we start out with a group of introverts, ambiverts and extraverts who are administered some form of depressant or sedative, usually one of the barbiturates; also defined is a "sedation threshold," i.e., a point at which qualitative differences in behavior occur as a function of drug administration. Extraverts being characterized by lower arousal (or higher inhibition) than introverts, according to the theory, should require less of the drug to reach this threshold. The early studies certainly supported the hypothesis quite strongly, but later studies (e.g., Claridge, Donald, & Birchall, 1981) found that differences in neuroticism disturbed this clear-cut picture. The highest drug tolerance was shown by introverts with smallest neuroticism, and the lowest drug tolerance occurred among neurotic extraverts. Thus the hypothesis that introverts have higher sedation thresholds than extraverts was supported among those of medium neuroticism, whereas the opposite tendency was present among those of low neuroticism. While on the whole the data supports the hypothesis, it clearly requires amplification.

This rapid overview will suffice to show that there are meaningful and significant relationships between biological features of the organism and observable behavior patterns in social life. No doubt the arousal theory is simplistic, not sufficiently detailed, and certainly oversimplified; nevertheless it has given rise to large numbers of positive findings. Making a rough-and-ready calculation of all the available studies in this field, we may say that the ratio of successes to failures is roughly 4 or 5 to 1. This would seem to argue that while the theory is clearly along the right lines, it requires a good deal of modification, amplification, and explication, particularly with respect to the details of experimental manipulation. Predictions from the personality theory to behavioral indices and laboratory studies of memory, conditioning, vigilance, reminiscence, perception, and many other areas, have on the whole been somewhat more successful than predictions in the physiological, neurological, and hormonal fields (Eysenck, 1976, 1981), for reasons already given. Nevertheless, at the moment there is no alternative theory which could account for the facts anything like as well as that of cortical arousal.

It should perhaps be noted, if only as a final comment, that the arrow of causality does not necessarily always go from the biological to the behavioral side. Taking testosterone as an example, aggressive and sexual behavior can significantly change the level of testosterone, as well as being itself influenced by that level (Eysenck, 1990). This is not true of all the variables discussed (e.g., blood type polymorphisms are not affected by behavior), but it would be simple-minded to assume that the relationship is completely one-sided. The biosocial approach to human behavior, and to personality in particular, must take all possibilities into account. Nevertheless, it is clear that in the majority of cases genetic factors determine physiological, neurological and hormonal patterns, and these in turn affect behavior. This simple lesson is absolutely fundamental to an understanding of personality differences in particular, and behavior in general.

References

Angst, J, & Maurer-Groeli, J. Blutgruppen und Persönlichkeit. *Archiv für Psychiatrie und Nervenkrankheiten*, 1974, *218*, 291–300.

Aston-Jones, G., & Bloom, F. E. Norepinephrine-containing locus coeruleus neurons in behaving rats exhibit pronounced responses to non-noxious environmental stimuli. *Journal of Neuroscience*, 1981, *8*, 887–900.

Ballenger, J. C., Post, R. M., Jimmerson, D. C., Lake, C. R., Murphy, D., Zuckerman, M., & Cronin, C. Biochemical correlates of personality traits in normals: An exploratory study. *Personality and Individual Differences*, 1983, *4*, 615–625.

Barrett, P., & Eysenck, S. B. G. The assessment of personality factors across 25 countries. *Personality and Individual Differences*, 1984, *5*, 615–632.

Blake, M. F. Relationship between circadian rhythm of body temperature and introversion-extraversion. *Nature*, 1967, *215*, 896–897.

Calhoon, L. L. Exploration into the biochemistry of sensation-seeking. *Personality and Individual Differences*, 1988, *9*, 941–949.

Claridge, G. S., Donald, J., & Birchall, P. M. Drug tolerance and personality: Some implications for Eysenck's theory. *Personality and Individual Differences*, 1981, *2*, 153–166.

Colquhoun, W. P. Temperament, inspection efficiency and time of day. *Ergonomics*, 1960, *3*, 377–378.

Colquhoun, W. P. *Biological rhythms and human performance*. London: Academic Press, 1971.

Conley, J. J. The hierarchy of consistency: A review and model of longitudinal findings on adult individual differences in intelligence, personality and self-opinion. *Personality and Individual Differences*, 1984a, *5*, 11–26.

Conley, J. J. Longitudinal consistency of adult personality: Self- reported psychological characteristics across 45 years. *Journal of Personality and Social Psychology*, 1984b, *47*, 1325–1333.

Conley, J. J. Longitudinal stability of personality traits: A multitrait-multimethod-multioccasion analysis. *Journal of Personality and Social Psychology*, 1985, *49*, 1266–1282.

Coursey, R. D., Buchsbaum, M. S., & Murphy, D. C. Platelet MAO activity and evoked potentials in the identification of subjects biologically at risk for psychiatric disorders. *British Journal of Psychiatry*, 1979, *194*, 372–381.

Daitzman, R., & Zuckerman, M. Disinhibitory sensation-seeking personality and gonadal hormones. *Personality and Individual Differences*, 1980, *1*, 103–110.

Daitzman, R., Zuckerman, M., Sammelwitz, P., & Ganjam, V. Sensation-seeking and gonadal hormones. *Journal of Biosocial Science*, 1978, *10*, 401–408.

Davis, H., & Zerlin, S. Acoustic relations of the human vertex potential. *Journal of the Acoustic Society of America*, 1966, *39*, 109–116.

Deary, I. J., Ramsay, H., Wilson, J. A., & Riad, M. Stimulated salivation: Correlations with personality and time of day effects. *Personality and Individual Differences*, 1988, *9*, 903–909.

Duffy, E. The psychosocial significance of the concept of "arousal" or "activation". *Psychological Review*, 1957, *64*, 265–275.

Eaves, L., Eysenck, H. J., & Martin, N. *Gene, culture, and personality: An empirical approach*. New York: Academic Press, 1989.

Eysenck, H. J. *The biological basis of personality*. Springfield, IL: Thomas, 1967.

Eysenck, H. J. *The structure of human personality* (3rd Ed). London: Methuen, 1970.

Eysenck, H. J. (Ed.), *The measurement of personality*. Lancaster: Medical and Technical Publishers, 1976.

Eysenck, H. J. National differences in personality as related to ABO blood groups polymorphism. *Psychological Reports*, 1977, *41*, 1257–1258.

Eysenck, H. J. The biosocial model of man and the unification of psychology. In A. J. Chapman & D. M. Jones (Eds.), *Models of man*. Leicester: The British Psychological Society, 1980a.

Eysenck, H. J. Man as a biosocial animal: Comments on the sociobiology debate. *Political Psychology*, 1980b, *2*, 43–51.

Eysenck, H. J. (Ed.). *A model for personality*. New York: Springer, 1981.

Eysenck, H. J. Is there a paradigm in personality research? *Journal of Research in Personality*, 1983a, *17*, 369–397.

Eysenck, H. J. Personality as a fundamental concept in scientific psychology. *Australian Journal of Psychology*, 1983b, *35*, 289–304.

Eysenck, H. J. The place of individual differences in a scientific psychology. *Annals of Theoretical Psychology*, 1984, *1*, 233–286.

Eysenck, H. J. Biological dimensions of personality. In L. A. Pervin (Ed.), *Handbook of personality theory and research*. New York: Guilford Press, 1990.

Eysenck, H. J., & Eysenck, M. W. *Personality and individual differences: A natural science approach.* New York: Plenum, 1985.

Eysenck, H. J., & Eysenck, S. B. C. *Manual of the Eysenck Personality Questionnaire.* London: Hodder & Stoughton, 1975, San Diego: EDITS, 1975.

Eysenck, H. J., & Martin, I. *The theoretical foundations of behavior therapy.* New York: Plenum, 1987.

Eysenck, H. J., & Wilson, G. *The psychology of sex.* London: Dent, 1979.

Eysenck, S. B. G., & Eysenck, H. J. Physiological reactivity to sensory stimulation as a measure of personality. *Psychological Reports*, 1967, *20*, 45–46.

Friedman, J., & Meares, R. Cortical evoked potentials and extraversion. *Psychosomatic Medicine*, 1979, *41*, 279–286.

Frith, C. D. *Habituation of the pupil size and light responses to sound.* Paper presented at the meeting of the American Psychological Association. San Francisco, 1977.

Gale, A. Electroencephalographic studies of extraversion-introversion: A case study in the psychophysiology of individual differences. *Personality and Individual Differences*, 1983, *4*, 371–380.

Golding, J. F., & Richards, M. EEG spectral analysis, visual evoked potential and photic-driving correlates of personality and memory. *Personality and Individual Differences*, 1985, *6*, 67–76.

Gray, J. A. A critique of Eysenck's theory of personality. In H. J. Eysenck (Ed.), *A model for personality.* New York: Springer, 1981.

Haier, R. J., Robinson, D. L., Braden, W., & Williams, D. Evoked potential augmenting-reducing and personality differences. *Personality and Individual Differences*, 1984, *5*, 293–301.

Hebb, D. O. Drives and the C.N.S. (conceptual nervous system). *Psychological Review*, 1955, *62*, 243–259.

Holmes, D. S. Pupillary response, conditioning and personality. *Journal of Personality and Social Psychology*, 1967, *5*, 98–103.

Horne, J., & Ostberg, O. Time of day effects on extraversion and salivation. *Biological Psychology*, 1975, *3*, 301–307.

Klinteberg, B., Schalling, D. Edman, G., Oreland, L., & Asberg, H. E. Personality correlates of platelet monoamine oxidase (MAO) activity in female and male subjects. *Neuropsychobiology*, 1987, *18*, 89–96.

Knorring, von, L. Visual averaged evoked responses and platelet monoamine oxidase in patients suffering from alcoholism. In H. Begleiter (Ed.), *Biological effects of alcoholism.* New York: Plenum, 1980.

Knorring, von, L., Mörnstad, H., Forsgren, L., & Holmgren, S. Saliva secretion rate and saliva composition in relation to extraversion. *Personality and Individual Differences*, 1986, *7*, 33–38.

Knorring, von, L., Oreland, I. F., & Wimblad, B. Personality traits related to monoamine oxidase activity in platelets. *Psychiatric Research*, 1984, *12*, 11–26.

Krishnamoorti, S. P., & Shagaas, C. Some psychological test correlates of sedation threshold. In J. Wortis (Ed.), *Recent advances in biological psychiatry.* New York: Plenum, 1963.

Lacey, J. I., & Lacey, B. C. Verification and extension of the principle of autonomic response-stereotype. *American Journal of Psychology*, 1958, *71*, 50–73.

Lukas, J. N. Visual evoked potential augmenting-reducing and personality: The vertex augmenter is a sensation-seeker. *Personality and Individual Differences*, 1987, *8*, 385–395.

Lynn, R. *Attention, arousal and the orienting reaction.* New York: Pergamon, 1966.

Maurer-Groeli, J. Blutgruppen, Persönlichkeit und Schulabschluss: Eine Untersuchung mittels FPI. *Schweizarische Zeitschrift für Psychologie*, 1974a, *33*, 407–410.

Maurer-Groeli, J. Blutgruppen und Krankheiten. *Archiv für Psychiatrie und Nervenkrankheiten*, 1974b, *218*, 301–318.

Moruzzi, G., & Magoun, H. W. Brain stem reticular formation and activation of the EEG. *Electroencephalogical Clinical Neurophysiology*, 1949, *1*, 455–473.

O'Gorman, J. G., & Lloyd, J. E. M. Extraversion, impulsiveness, and EEG alpha activity. *Personality and Individual Differences*, 1987, *8*, 169–174.

O'Gorman, J. G., & Mallise, L. R. Extraversion and the EEG: II. A test of Gale's hypothesis. *Biological Psychology*, 1984, *19*, 113–127.

Pavlov, I. P. *Conditioned reflexes*. London: Oxford University Press, 1927.

Rees, L. Constitutional factors and abnormal behaviour. In H. J. Eysenck (Ed.), *Handbook of abnormal psychology*. London: Pitman, 1973.

Revelle, W., Anderson, K. J., & Humphreys, M. S. Empiracal tests and theoretical extentions of arousal-based thoeries of personality. In J. Strelau, & H. J. Eysenck (Eds.), *Personality dimension and arousal*. New York: Plenum, 1987.

Robinson, D. L. Properties of the diffuse thalamocortical system of human personality: A direct test of Pavlovian/Eysenckian theory. *Personality and Individual Differences*, 1982, *3*, 1–16.

Rothman, H. V. L. Effects of high frequencies and intersubject variability on the auditory-evoked cortical response. *Journal of the Acoustic Society of America*, 1970, *47*, 569–573.

Routtenberg, A. Neural mechanisms of sleep: Changing view of reticular formation function. *Psychological Review*, 1966, *73*, 481–499.

Royce, J. R., & Powell, A. *Theory of personality and individual differences: Factors, systems and processes*. Englewood Cliffs, NJ: Prentice-Hall, 1983.

Saltz, E. Manifest anxiety: Have we misread the data? *Psychological Review*, 1970, *77*, 568–573.

Saxton, P. M., Siegel, J., & Lukas, J. H. Visual evoked potential augmenting/reducing slopes in cats. 2. Correlations with behavior. *Personality and Individual Differences*, 1987, *8*, 511–519.

Schalling, D., Asberg, M., Edman, G., & Levanuer, S. Impulsivity, non-conformity, and sensation-seeking as related to biological markers for vulnerability. *Clinical Neuropharmacology*, 1984, *7*, 746–747.

Schalling, D., Edman, G., Asberg, M., & Oreland, L. Platelet MAO activity associated with impulsivity and aggressivity. *Personality and Individual Differences*, 1988, *9*, 597–606.

Shagass, L., & Jones, A. L. A neurophysiological test for psychiatric diagnosis. Results in 750 patients. *American Journal of Psychiatry*, 1958, *114*, 1002–1009.

Shagass, L., & Kerenyi, A. B. Neurophysiologic studies of personality. *Journal of Nervous and Mental Diseases*, 1958, *126*, 141–147.

Sokolov, E. N. *Perception and the conditioned reflex*. London: Pergamon, 1963.

Soskis, D. A., & Shagass, L. *Evoked potential tests of augmenting-reducing. Neurosis as pathology of brain's limbic system*. Symposium on Experimental and Clinical Neurosis. Habana, Cuba, February, 1980.

Stelmack, R. M. The psychophysiology of extraversion and neuroticism. In H. J. Eysenck (Ed.), *A model for personality*. New York: Springer, 1981.

Stelmack, R. M., Achorn, E., & Michaud, A. Extraversion and individual differences in auditory evoked response. *Psychophysiology*, 1977, *14*, 368–374.

Stelmack, R. M., Bourgeois, R. P., Chain, J., & Pickard, L. W. Extraversion and the orienting reaction habituation rate to visual stimuli. *Journal of Research in Personality*, 1979, *13*, 49–58.

Stelmack, R. M., & Madelzys, N. Extraversion and pupillary response to affective and taboo words. *Psychophysiology*, 1975, *12*, 536–546.

Stenberg, G., Rosen, I, & Risberg, J. Personality and augmenting/reducing in visual and auditory evoked potentials. *Personality and Individual Differences*, 1988, *9*, 571–579.

Strelau, J. *Temperament—personality—activity*. London: Academic Press, 1983.

Strelau, J., & Eysenck, H. J. (Eds.). *Personality dimensions and arousal*. New York: Plenum, 1987.

Vando, A. The development of the R-A Scale: A paper-and-pencil measure of pain tolerance. *Personality and Social Psychology Bulletin*, 1974, *1*, 28–29.

Venturini, R., Pascalis, V. de, Imperiali, M. G., & Martini, P. S. EEG alpha reactivity and extraversion-introversion. *Personality and Individual Differences*, 1981, *2*, 215–220.

Werre, P. P. Contingent negative variation and inter-individual differences. In R. Sinz, & M. K. Rosenweig (Eds.), *Psychophysiology, memory, motivation and event-related potentials in mental operations*. Amsterdam: Elsevier, 1983.

Wilson, G. D. Personality, time of day and arousal. *Journal of Research in Personality*, in press.

Yerkes, R. M., & Dodson, J. D. The relation of strength of stimulus to rapidity of habit formation. *Journal of Comparative and Neurological Psychology*, 1908, *18*, 459–482.

Zuckerman, M. (Ed.). *Biological bases of sensation seeking, impulsivity and anxiety*. Hillsdale, NJ: Erlbaum, 1983.

Zuckerman, M., Ballenger, J. C., & Post, R. M. The neurobiology of some dimensions of personality. *International Review of Neurobiology*, 1984, *25*, 391–436.

Zuckerman, M., & Como, P. Sensation-seeking and arousal systems. *Personality and Individual Differences*, 1983, *4*, 381–386.

Zuckerman, M., Murtaugh, T., & Siegel, J. Sensation-seeking and cortical augmenting/reducing. *Psychophysiology*, 1974, *11*, 535–542.

7

The Neuropsychology of Temperament

Jeffrey A. Gray

Some General Background

First, a word about "neuropsychology." This term has commonly been used in a quite restricted sense to delineate that part of psychology which is concerned with the study, in human beings, of the effects of known (even if often poorly known) structural damage to the brain. I use "neuropsychology," in contrast, in a much wider sense, as in my book, *The Neuropsychology of Anxiety* (Gray, 1982a), to mean the study, quite generally, of the role played by the brain in behavioral and psychological function, whether in human or animal subjects, and whether there is structural damage to the brain or not. Since I also take it as axiomatic (and few would, I think, disagree with the axiom) that all behavioral and psychological function depends upon the activities of the brain, it follows that "neuropsychology" has a breadth which shadows that of "psychology" itself: if there is a psychology of hunger, intelligence, love, or learning French, then there is *ipso facto* a neuropsychology of the same.

In this usage, "neuropsychology" is a term of the same kind as "physical chemistry" or "molecular genetics": it refers to a subject which arises at the frontier between two historically classical scientific disciplines as the barriers which (arbitrarily) divided them break down. In our case, the classical disciplines are psychology and "neuroscience" (the latter being itself a newly coined term, but covering the classical disciplines of neuroanatomy, neurophysiology, neurochemistry, etc.). The parallel with other such frontier hybrids is instructive. Roughly speaking, the subject higher up the scientific pyramid (chemistry, genetics, psychology) sets the functional agenda, while the one lower down (physics, molecular biology, neuroscience) seeks the mechanisms to account for function. Neither classical discipline has priority (though, for some reason, the "lower" one usually has greater scientific prestige); the two work in harness. And the

Jeffrey A. Gray • Department of Psychology, Institute of Psychiatry, University of London, London SE5 8AF, United Kingdom.

end product is a set of concepts which are simultaneously functional at the higher level and mechanistic at the lower.

"Neuropsychology" in this sense is already a thriving new discipline; though, as the discussion above illustrates well, not yet quite sure of its name. Our concern in this chapter is with just one part of it: the neuropsychology of temperament. How, then, to separate this from the rest of neuropsychology? A possible answer to this question is as follows.

A key feature of the research strategies adopted in neuropsychology is that much reliance is necessarily placed upon experiments with animals. One advantage which flows from the use of such strategies is the need for simple operational and/or behavioral definitions of theoretical concepts, allowing them to be applied in the animal laboratory; though, to be sure, this advantage is to some extent reduced by the subsequent need to demonstrate that there is sufficient continuity between animal and human neuropsychology for the same concepts also to apply at the human level. Two assumptions that have guided my own thinking (and that of many others, e.g., Millenson, 1967; Mowrer, 1960; Newman, 1987; Shapiro, Quay, Hogan, & Schwartz, 1988; and a number of authors in this volume) in thus rendering the term "temperament" amenable to such simple definition are (1) that temperament reflects individual differences in predispositions towards particular kinds of emotion, and (2) that emotions are states of the CNS elicited by reinforcing events. (The abbreviation "CNS" in assumption 2 is conveniently ambiguous between the "central" and "conceptual" nervous system; see Hebb, 1955, and Gray, 1972. This is intentional, since it correctly captures the symbiosis between the study of brain and behavior that constitutes neuropsychology.)

Rather than justify these assumptions *a priori*, I shall outline a general theoretical model of temperament that rests upon a wide range of experimental studies either derived from them or at least conforming to them. The judgment as to the potential usefulness of this model at the human level must rest with others who work at this level; and with explicit experimental tests of the model using human subjects (e.g., Boddy, Carver, & Rowley, 1986; Fowles, 1980; Newman, 1987; Shapiro *et al.*, 1988).

The Analysis of Emotion

Given the above assumptions, if we wish to approach the study of temperament, we first need an understanding of emotion. Such understanding is not easy to come by: a glance at a typical textbook of psychology will show that "emotion" is used to refer to a ragbag of apparently disconnected facts and is never itself clearly defined at all. Yet, within one branch of psychology, namely, animal learning theory, there has long been a reasonably clear consensus that emotions consist of states elicited by stimuli or events which have the capacity to serve as reinforcers for instrumental behavior. This, for example, is the framework within which Miller (1951) and Mowrer (1947), analyzed the concept of "fear" and its role in avoidance learning; Mowrer (1960) analyzed the concept of "relief," again in relation to avoidance learning; Amsel (1962) analyzed the concept of "frustration" and its role in the extinction of rewarded behavior; and I analyzed the concept of "anxiety" as an amalgam of fear and frustration (Gray, 1967, 1982a). Without further apology, therefore, I shall suppose that this is indeed the correct framework within which to analyze emotion and present here the results of one such analysis. The starting point for this analysis is the notion of an instrumental reinforcer. This has its standard Skinnerian definition: a reinforcer is any stimulus (or more complex event) which, if made contingent upon a response, alters the future probability of emission of that response. Figure 7.1 presents a more or less exhaustive outline of the possible variants upon this definition, created by the intersection of (1) whether the putative reinforcer is presented, terminated, or omitted (when otherwise it would have occurred) contingent upon a response (the rows in the figure); and (2) whether the observed change in the probability of emission of the response is an increase or decrease (the columns)—if no change is observed, the stimulus is not a reinforcer at all. As a matter of empirical fact, it turns out that stimuli (if they are reinforcers at all) come in two kinds: those which, when presented contingent upon a response (top row), increase response probability *and also*, when terminated or omitted (bottom rows), decrease response probability; and those which, when presented, decrease response probability *and also*, when terminated or omitted, increase response probability. This gives rise to the distinction (cross-hatching in Figure 7.1) between (in various terminologies) positive (the former class of stimuli) and negative reinforcers (the latter), rewards and punishments, or appetitive and aversive stimuli. Since the termination and omission procedures (bottom two rows of Figure 7.1) usually give the same results, the figure may be collapsed into a 2 × 2 table: rewards, when presented, increase response probability

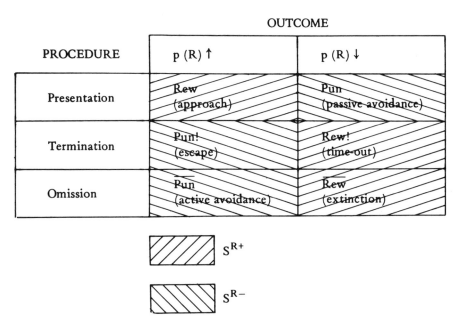

Figure 7.1. Possible reinforcing events as defined operationally. Events may be presented, terminated, or omitted (rows) contingent upon a response, and response probability (p^R) may in consequence increase or decrease (columns). S^{R+}, S^{R-}: positive and negative reinforcers, shown by cross-hatching.

and, when terminated/omitted, decrease it; punishments, when presented, decrease response probability and, when terminated/omitted, increase it.

To this 2 × 2 table one further complication has to be added: reinforcers may be primary (unconditioned) or secondary (conditioned). The former are stimuli or events which, without special learning, have innately reinforcing properties for the species concerned, e.g., food, water, a sex partner, pain. The latter are stimuli which are initially neutral (do not alter response probability), e.g., a tone or light of moderate intensity, but take on reinforcing properties as a consequence of entering into an association (most probably by Pavlovian conditioning; Gray, 1975) with an unconditioned reinforcer.

We are now armed with most of the tools of conceptual analysis that we need. They are to be used to address the following questions: how many separate emotions are there, and how is each to be defined? Or, in terms of the argument being developed here, if, in general, emotions consist of states of the CNS elicited by reinforcing events, can we parcel out the total set of reinforcing events (as defined by Figure 1, together with the unconditioned/conditioned distinction) into subsets, each corresponding to a different emotion which members of only that subset elicit?

At first sight, to someone steeped in human psychology, this question may seem simplistic to the point of absurdity. After all, if one looks into any good dictionary, one will find hundreds of words describing (apparently) different emotions. Consider: regret, nostalgia, indignation, schadenfreude, etc. Yet, on the analysis advanced here, there is only a maximum of eight (the multiple of our 2 × 2 × 2 orthogonal distinctions) separate emotions possible. This problem, however, is more apparent than real. The analysis developed here is not aimed at human linguistic behavior. How we *name* emotions is as separate from the way the CNS produces emotions as is how we name colors from the mechanisms that underlie color vision; and, in both cases, the *words* we use reflect as much the particular circumstances which give rise to the experience (e.g., "nostalgia," "shocking pink") as the experience itself. Just as, in the case of color vision, a mechanism based initially on just three color pigments is able to give rise to the great variety of experienced colors and thus to provide the basis for the even greater variety of color words, so (it is contended here) just a few emotion systems in the CNS are able to give rise to the variety of experienced emotional states and then to provide the basis for the vocabulary that is used to describe those states (Gray, 1985).

How, then, are we to arrive at subsets of reinforcing events, each corresponding to a separate emotion and therefore to a separate system in the brain responsible for that emotion? The distinctions we have made above are largely of a purely operational kind. It is a matter of experimental convenience that we decide, e.g., to measure changes in response probability separately as increases and decreases (the columns of Figure 1) or to classify stimuli as positive or negative reinforcers (the cross-hatching). But we do not know in advance whether the brain makes the same distinctions that we do: it may or may not use different mechanisms to acquire new behavior and to suppress the old; or to respond to positive and negative reinforcers; or to do both these things. Moreover, quite different theoretical positions have been taken on just this sort of issue. Thus, some theorists suppose that the brain has a "reward system" for dealing with positive reinforcers no matter how they affect behavior, together with a "punishment system" which similarly deals with negative reinforcers (e.g., Olds & Olds, 1965); while others suppose that there is one system for the acquisition of new behavior and another for behavioral inhibition (e.g., Gray, 1975). These theories are quite different; though, because they overlap if only the top row of Figure 1 is considered, they have often been confused with one another.

To take a position on these complex issues in the short space of a chapter inevitably appears arbitrary. In fact, however, the specific model I shall now present is based on an extensive data base, culled from a wide variety of experimental approaches in the study of animal learning and behavior, psychopharmacology, neuropsychology, and neuro-science (e.g., Gray, 1982a, 1987). A number of alternative models can be ruled out by data from one or other of these disciplines; the model that remains is, by contrast, at least consistent with (though far from proved by) the bulk of the data from all of them (this multiplicity of sources of critical data is, indeed, one of the great advantages of the whole neuropsychological enterprise).

The model posits in the mammalian CNS three fundamental emotion systems, each of which (1) responds to a separate subset of reinforcing events with specific types of behavior, and (2) is mediated by a separate set of interacting brain structures that processes specific types of information. The three systems are termed the behavioral inhibition system, the fight/flight system, and the behavioral approach system. The first of these has been extensively described before (see especially Gray, 1982a); the second has so far received little theoretical attention, especially at the cognitive level; while the third has recently become the object of such attention (Gray, Feldon, Rawlins, Hemsley, & Smith, 1991; Swerdlow and Koob, 1987). I shall therefore consider the fight/flight system only briefly, but the behavioral approach system in a little more detail than the other two systems. A further postulate, addressed at the end of the chapter, is that it is individual differences in the functioning of these three emotion systems, and their interaction, which underlie human temperament as measured by such dimensional analy-ses of personality as those of Eysenck (e.g., 1981) or Zuckerman, Kuhlman and Camac (1988). There will be no attempt to present the data on which the model rests; portions of these data are reviewed by Gray (1975,1977, 1982a, 1987), Gray and McNaughton (1983) and Gray *et al.* (1991).

The Model: I—The Behavioral Inhibition System

This is the best worked out part of the model, and the only one for which a corresponding human emotion (anxiety) can plausibly be identified. The input-output relations which define the behavioral inhibition system (BIS) at the behavioral level are presented in Figure 7.2. The critical eliciting stimuli are conditioned stimuli associated with punishment, conditioned stimuli associated with the omission or termination of reward ("frustrative nonreward"; Amsel, 1962), or novel stimuli. The appearance of novelty on this list may cause some surprise, since it is not at first obvious that this counts as a reinforcer at all, given the definition set out in Figure 1. In fact, however, novel stimuli possess rather complex reinforcing properties, which change as a function of the degree of novelty and also interact with stimulus intensity as well as a number of other factors (Berlyne, 1960). At high values of novelty and intensity, the stimulus

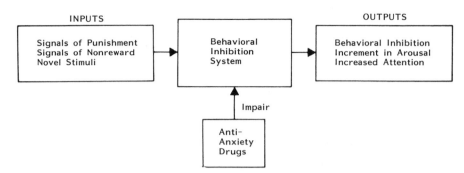

Figure 7.2. The Behavioral Inhibition System (BIS) as defined by its inputs and outputs.

principally elicits the type of behavior shown to the right of Figure 7.2; as (with stimulus prolongation or repetition) these values diminish, the elicited behavior shifts to approach (see the section on the Behavioral Approach System, below); with still further stimulus prolongation or repetition, complete habituation sets in and the stimulus ceases to elicit any response. The transition from behavioral inhibition to approach is not sudden; thus, over much of the range of values, novel stimuli elicit an approach-avoidance conflict (Gray, 1982a, 1987, Chapter 9; Zuckerman, 1982).

The behavior elicited by these stimuli (right-hand side of Figure 7.2) consists in behavioral inhibition (interruption of any ongoing behavior); an increment in the level of arousal, such that the next behavior to occur (which may consist in a continuation of the action that was interrupted) is carried out with extra vigor and/or speed; and an increment in attention, such that more information is taken in, especially concerning novel features of the environment. Any one of the inputs to the BIS elicits all the outputs; furthermore, a range of interventions is capable of blocking all the outputs to any of the inputs, while leaving intact other input-output relationships (including some that involve inputs to or outputs from the BIS but not both). These are among the reasons for regarding the BIS as indeed a unified system, rather than a congeries of separate input-output relationships. Among the interventions which specifically abolish the input-output relationships that define the BIS is the administration of drugs, such as the benzodiazepines, barbiturates, and alcohol, which reduce anxiety in human beings; indeed, the study of such drugs was a major impetus to the formation of the concept of the BIS (Gray, 1982a,b). On this basis, one may tentatively identify the subjective state that accompanies activity in the BIS as anxiety. This identification gains plausibility from the fact that it leads to a face-valid description of human anxiety: i.e., a state in which one responds to threat (stimuli associated with punishment or nonreward) or uncertainty (novelty) with the reaction, "stop, look and listen, and get ready for action" (right-hand side of Figure 7.2) (Gray, 1982a,b,c).

Neurologically, the set of structures which appear to discharge the functions of the BIS are as illustrated in Figure 7.3. The (tentative) identification of the BIS with activity in this set of structures depends upon a variety of sources of information (Gray, 1982a). Now, from the point of view of a psychologist attempting to understand temperament, it

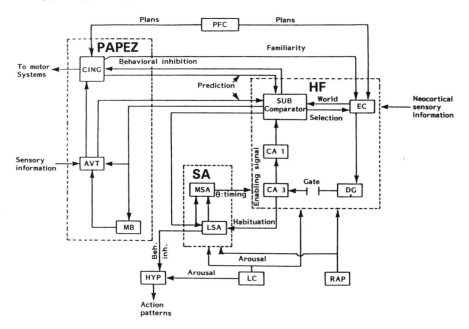

Figure 7.3. The Septohippocampal System: Major structures composing the neural basis of the Behavioral Inhibition System. The three major building blocks are shown in heavy print: HF, the hippocampal formation, made up of the entorhinal cortex, EC, the denate gyrus, DG, CA 3, CA 1, and the subicular area, SUB; SA, the septal area, containing the medial and lateral septal areas, MSA and LSA; and the Papez circuit, which receives projections from and returns them to the subicular area via the mammillary bodies, MB, anteroventral thalamus, AVT, and cingulate cortex, CING. Other structures shown are the hypothalamus, HYP, the locus coeruleus, LC, the raphe nuclei, RAP, and the prefrontal cortex, PFC. Arrows show direction of projection; the projection from SUB to MSA lacks anatomical confirmation. Words in lower case show postulated functions; beh. inhib., behavioral inhibition.

is on its own of no great importance to be told that one set of brain structures rather than another mediates the functions of the BIS. Indeed, there have been a number of valuable attempts to test, at the human level, predictions derived from the general concept of the BIS, together with related ideas, without reference to its supposed neurological underpinning (e.g., Boddy *et al.*, 1986). There is, however, a value to the psychologist in such "neurologizing." First, in the actual construction of a concept such as that of the BIS, the utilization of data from the neurosciences as well as from psychology is likely to lead to a more robust basis for further, purely psychological, theorizing. Second, understanding of the neural basis of a system such as the BIS can lead to specific psychological questions or hypotheses that would otherwise be unlikely to arise; we shall see some examples of this later in the chapter. Third, the neurological level leads inevitably back to mainstream issues in psychology. For the main function of the brain is to process information; and the task of describing how that information is processed, in other than neurological terms, belongs to cognitive psychology. Thus, faced with the kind of neurological flow diagram shown in Figure 7.3, one should ask not only how the structures illustrated therein produce the behavioral outputs of the BIS (Figure 7.2), but also what cognitive (i.e., information-processing) operations they perform in order to do so.

The information-processing functions attributed to the interlinked set of structures depicted in Figure 7.3 are themselves illustrated in Figure 7.4; detailed justification for the ideas that enter both figures can be found in Gray (1982a). At the cognitive level, the key concept is that of the comparator, i.e., a system which, moment by moment, predicts the next likely event and compares this prediction to the actual event. This system (1) takes in information describing the current state of the perceptual world; (2) adds to this further information concerning the subject's current motor program; (3) makes use of information stored in memory and describing past regularities that relate stimulus events to other stimulus events; (4) similarly makes use of stored information describing past regularities that relate responses to subsequent stimulus events; (5) from these sources of information predicts the next expected state of the perceptual world; (6) compares the predicted to the actual next state of the perceptual world; (7) decides either that there is a match or that there is a mismatch between the predicted and the actual states of the world; (8) if there is a match, proceeds to run through steps (1) to (7) again; but (9) if there is a mismatch, brings the current motor program to a halt, i.e., operates the outputs of the BIS (Figure 7.2), so as to take in further information and resolve the difficulty that has interrupted this program.

In the application of this model to anxiety, the focus of the analysis was on step (9) and the further consequences of this step (Gray, 1982a). More recently, Gray *et al.* (1991) have been concerned with the details of the monitoring process itself, and the way in which this interacts with the running of motor programs; we turn to this aspect of the problem below, in the section on the Behavioral Approach System.

Figure 7.4 depicts, as it were, the software of the comparator proposed by Gray (1982a); the corresponding hardware is illustrated in Figure 7.3. At this neural level, the core structure is the septohippocampal system (SHS, composed of the septal area, entorhinal cortex, dentate gyrus, hippocampus, and subicular area). Here we note only the following points. First, the heart of the comparator function is attributed to the

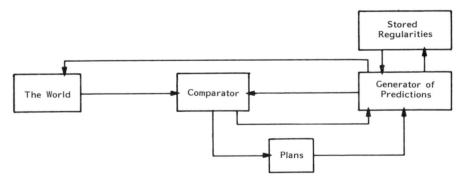

Figure 7.4. Information processing required for the comparator function of the septohippocampal system.

subicular area. This is postulated (1) to receive elaborated descriptions of the perceptual world from the entorhinal cortex, itself the recipient of input from all cortical sensory association areas; (2) to receive predictions from, and initiate generation of the next prediction in, the Papez circuit (i.e., the circuit from the subiculum to the mammillary bodies, the anteroventral thalamus, the cingulate cortex and back to the subiculum); and (3) to interface with motor programming systems (not themselves included in Figure 7.3) so as either to bring them to a halt or to permit them to continue. Second, the prefrontal cortex is allotted the role of providing the comparator system with information concerning the current motor program (via its projections to the entorhinal and cingulate cortices, the latter forming part of the Papez circuit). Third, the monoaminergic pathways which ascend from the mesencephalon to innervate the SHS (consisting of noradrenergic fibers originating in the locus coeruleus, and serotonergic fibers originating in the median raphe) are charged with alerting the whole system under conditions of threat and diverting its activities to deal with the threat; in the absence of threat, the information-processing activities of the system can be put to other, nonemotional purposes (Gray, 1984). Lastly, the system depicted in Figure 7.3 needs to be quantized in time, to allow appropriate comparison between specific states of the world and corresponding predictions, followed by initiation of the next prediction and next intake of information describing the world. This function is attributed to the hippocampal theta rhythm, giving rise to an "instant" within the model of about one-tenth of a second.

Much of the above analysis is inevitably speculative. Even so, the existence of a reasonably detailed sketch map of an emotion system covering several levels of analysis—behavioral (Figure 7.2), neural (Figure 7.3) and cognitive (Figure 7.4)— together with a plausible identification of a subjective state associated with the activity of this system (i.e., anxiety), has, I believe, heuristic value in indicating what a developed theory of a particular emotion might look like. In particular, we can now flesh out a little the notion of an "emotion system." Behaviorally, this consists, as we have seen, of a set of outputs jointly elicited by any one of several types of input. The plausibility of attributing such input-output relationships to an underlying system is increased by evidence that, say, certain drugs (e.g., Gray, 1977) or lesions to the brain (e.g., Gray & McNaughton, 1983) selectively alter these but not other input-output relationships; especially if one can show by independent arguments from neuroscientific data that the drugs and lesions concerned affect function in only a particular subset of neural structures (e.g., Gray, 1982a). The concept of a system gathers further strength from a consideration of the particular cognitive (information-processing) functions that it is likely to discharge; especially if such ideas can then be tested at the human level, as has recently been done for anxiety and the BIS (Mathews, 1988). Further important evidence at the human level comes from the recent application of imaging techniques to the living brain: using positron emission tomography, Reiman, Raichle, Butler, Hersovitch, and Robins (1984) showed that patients diagnosed as having panic disorder differed from normal controls in only one brain region, namely, the region containing the entorhinal cortex (the major input to the SHS) and the subicular area (the major output station from the SHS). Thus the program of research that commenced with the study in animals of drugs that reduce anxiety in human patients has come almost full circle back to the clinic.

The Model: II—The Fight/Flight System

The input-output relationships which define the fight/flight system (F/FLS) are set out in Figure 7.5; a tentative and highly schematic neurology (see Adams, 1979, and Graeff, 1987, for more detail), in Figure 7.6. Whereas the BIS responds to conditioned aversive stimuli, the F/FLS responds to unconditioned aversive stimuli; and, whereas the BIS responds with "Stop, look, and listen, and get ready for action," the F/FLS responds with unconditioned defensive aggression or escape behavior (Adams, 1979). Moreover, to these different patterns of behavior there correspond different pharmacologies. Thus, as noted above, the antianxiety drugs reduce the responses of the BIS to its adequate inputs, but these drugs do not reduce responses to unconditioned aversive (painful) stimuli; conversely, analgesics such as morphine reduce responses to painful stimuli but do not affect reactions to conditioned aversive stimuli (for review, see Gray, 1982a). Similarly, as will be evident from a comparison between Figures 7.3 and 7.6, the BIS and F/FLS have different neurologies, with indeed very little overlap (which is not to say with little interaction; see below). There are three important levels in the neuraxis at which stimulation and lesion experiments have pinpointed structures which appear to have the functions of the F/FLS: the amygdala, which inhibits the medial hypothalamus, which in turn inhibits the final output pathway in the central gray. As yet, there has been little if any work on the information-processing activities of the F/FLS; nor any direct link with a corresponding human emotion (though anger and/or terror are obvious possibilities).

The Model: III—The Behavioral Approach System

The input-output relations that define the behavioral approach system, or behavioral activation system (Fowles, 1980)—in either case, BAS—are set out in Figure 7.7. In essence, this depicts a simple positive feedback system, activated by stimuli associated with reward or with the termination/omission of punishment ("relieving non-punishment"; Mowrer, 1960), and operating so as to increase spatiotemporal proximity to such stimuli. By adding the postulate that conditioned appetitive stimuli of this kind activate the BAS to a degree proportional to their spatiotemporal proximity to the unconditioned appetitive stimulus ("goal") with which they are associated, we have in Figure 7.7 a system that is in general capable of guiding the organism to the goals it needs to attain (food, water, etc.) for survival (Deutsch, 1964; Gray, 1975, chapter 5).

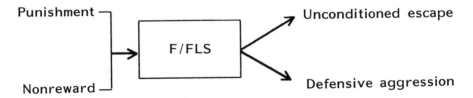

Figure 7.5. The Fight/Flight System (F/FLS) as defined by its inputs and outputs.

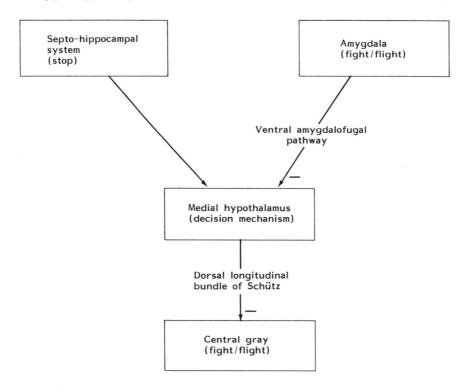

Figure 7.6. Major structures composing the neural basis of the Fight/Flight System.

At the neurological level the last decade has seen rapid progress (Groves, 1983; Penney & Young, 1981; Swerdlow & Koob, 1987; and see Gray *et al.*, 1991, upon which this section is closely based) in the construction of plausible neuropsychological models of the BAS (though, in the relevant literature, this phrase has not itself been used, terms such as "motor programming system" being preferred). The key components are the basal ganglia (the dorsal and ventral striatum, and dorsal and ventral pallidum); the dopaminergic fibers that ascend from the mesencephalon (substantia nigra and nucleus A 10 in the ventral tegmental area) to innervate the basal ganglia; thalamic nuclei closely linked to the basal ganglia; and similarly neocortical areas (motor, sensorimotor,

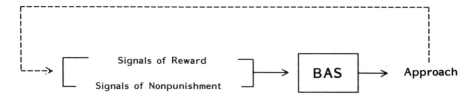

Figure 7.7. The Behavioral Approach System (BAS) as defined by its inputs and outputs.

and prefrontal cortex) closely linked to the basal ganglia. These components are best
seen as forming two closely interrelated subsystems, as illustrated in Figures 7.8 and 7.9
(based on Groves, 1983; Penney & Young, 1981; and chiefly Swerdlow & Koob, 1987).
Figure 7.8 shows the interrelations between non-limbic cortex (i.e., motor, sensorimotor, and association cortices), the caudate–putamen (or dorsal striatum), the dorsal
globus pallidus, nn. ventralis anterior (VA) and ventralis lateralis (VL) of the thalamus,
and the ascending dopaminergic pathway from the substantia nigra; for the sake of
brevity we shall refer to this set of structures as the "caudate" motor system. Similarly,
Figure 7.9 shows the interrelations between the limbic cortex (i.e., prefrontal and
cingulate cortices), n. accumbens (ventral striatum), the ventral globus pallidus, the

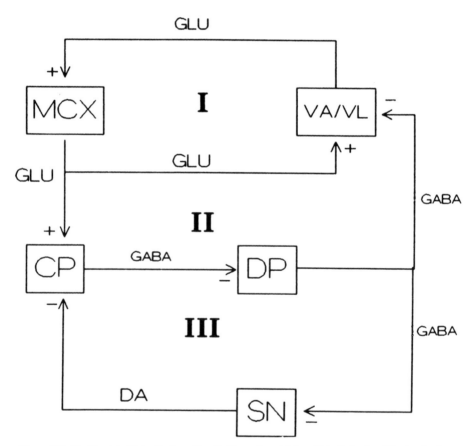

Figure 7.8. The Caudate Motor System. Non-limbic cortico-striato-pallido-thalamic-midbrain circuitry
making up the "caudate" component of the Behavioral Approach System. MCX: motor and sensorimotor
cortex. VA/VL: ventral anterior and ventrolateral thalamic nuclei. CP: caudate-putamen (dorsal striatum). DP: dorsal pallidum. SN: substantia nigra. GLU, GABA and DA: the neurotransmitters, glutamate,
gamma-aminobutyric acid and dopamine. +, −: excitation and inhibition. I, II, III: feedback loops, the
first two positive, the third negative. Based on Swerdlow and Koob (1987).

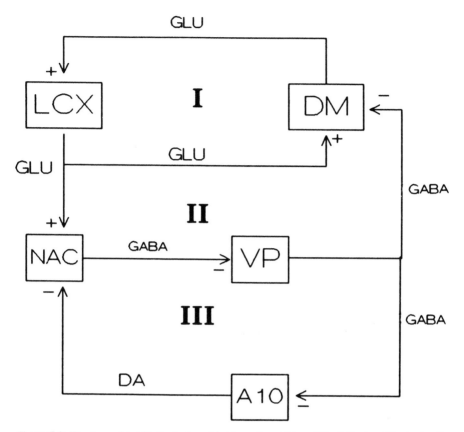

Figure 7.9. The Accumbens Motor System. Limbic cortico-striato-pallido-thalamic-midbrain circuitry making up the "accumbens" component of the Behavioral Approach System. LCX: limbic cortex, including prefrontal and cingulate areas. DM: dorsomedial thalamic nucleus. NAC: nucleus accumbens (ventral striatum). VP: ventral pallidum. A 10: dopaminergic nucleus A 10 in the ventral tegmental area. Neurotransmitters and feedback loops, as in Figure 7.8. Based on Swerdlow and Koob (1987).

dorsomedial (DM) thalamic nucleus, and the ascending dopaminergic projection from A 10; for brevity we shall call this set of structures the "accumbens" motor system. Importantly, n. accumbens also receives projections from two major limbic structures: the subiculum (output station for the SHS) and the amygdala.

As proposed by Swerdlow and Koob (1987), one can regard both the caudate and accumbens systems as being composed of three interacting feedback loops: a cortico-thalamo-cortical positive feedback loop (I in Figs. 7.8 and 7.9); a cortico-striato-pallido-thalamo-cortical positive feedback loop (II); and a striato-pallido-tegmento-striatal negative feedback loop (III), "tegmento" in this phrase referring to the two dopaminergic nuclei, substantia nigra or A 10. Loop I consists of a double excitatory input from cortex to thalamus and thalamus to cortex, and may therefore serve to maintain the continuous stream of impulses necessary to achieve one "step" in an ongoing motor program. Loop

II is more complex: the cortical excitatory (glutamatergic) input onto the Spiny I inhibitory (GABAergic) efferents from the striatum should have the effect of inhibiting the further inhibitory GABAergic pathway from the pallidum to the thalamus, thus further strengthening (by disinhibition) the excitatory interactions subserved by Loop I. To bring this reverberatory excitatory activity to an end, as proposed by Swerdlow and Koob (1987), Loop III is called into play: Excitation of the Spiny I GABAergic output from the striatum inhibits the pallidal GABAergic inhibition of the ascending dopaminergic input to the striatum, which is therefore increased. Since this dopaminergic input is itself also inhibitory, striatal activity is accordingly reduced; or rather (as proposed by, e.g., Evenden & Robbins, 1983, and Oades, 1985, and developed further below) it is permitted to switch from one pattern to another. A further important anatomico-physiological feature of the caudate and accumbens motor systems lies in the organization of the Spiny I output cells (Groves, 1983). These comprise about 96% of the entire population of striatal neurons. Each Spiny I cell appears to receive convergent inputs from many cortical and thalamic afferents, giving rise to the inference that these cells are "activated by the temporal coincidence of convergent excitatory input from several different sources" (Groves, 1983, p. 116). Single unit recording in behaving primates has thrown some light on the nature of these sources. As summarized by Rolls and Williams (1987, p.37):

> Neurons in the caudate nucleus, which receives inputs from the association cortex, have activity related to environmental stimuli that signal preparation for or initiation of behavioral responses. . . Neurons in the putamen, which receive inputs from the sensorimotor cortex, have activity related to movements. Neurons in the ventral striatum (including the nucleus accumbens), which receive inputs from limbic structures such as the amygdala and hippocampus, respond to emotion-provoking or novel stimuli.

The firing of some particular subset of Spiny I striatal neurons, then, will be triggered by some particular combination of environmental stimulation and patterns of movement. The excitatory loops (I and II) described above will ensure that this same subset will continue to fire for a period of time. Continuity of this pattern of activity is further assured by the interrelations between the Spiny I cells themselves. These are organized in the form of a lateral inhibitory network; thus, whichever subset of Spiny I cells is active at any one time, it will tend to inhibit firing in other such cells outside the set.

It remains to consider what might be represented by the particular set of cells that are active at a given moment. Basing their arguments both on the anatomical organization of the basal ganglia as described above, and on the general theory of random associative networks (Rolls, 1986a), Rolls and Williams (1987) have proposed an interesting answer to this question. Their proposal relates to the selection of an active subset of cells, not only in the striatum itself, but at all levels of the cortico-thalamo-pallidal midbrain circuitry depicted in Figures 7.8 and 7.9. I shall not here go into the details of this proposal. In brief, however, Rolls and Williams (1987) consider cells which, because of the particular chance patterns of connections they possess, receive inputs from both: (1) neurons that respond to environmental cues associated with reinforcement (i.e., reward or the avoidance of punishment), and (2) other neurons that fire when the animal makes a movement that affects the occurrence of this reinforcement; and they show how such cells might initially respond only to the conjunction of cue plus movement, but could come eventually to be activated by the cue alone, and so to participate in the production of the appropriate movement, given the cue. Thus the particular set of neurons firing at a particular time in the basal ganglia can be seen (1) as representing a step in a goal-directed motor program, and (2) as having been selected for this function by instrumental reinforcement mediated by the connectivity of the neurons that make up the set.

The discussion so far has distinguished anatomically between the caudate (Fig. 7.8) and accumbens (Fig. 7.9) motor systems, but not yet functionally. In now making this distinction I shall concentrate on the functions of the accumbens system; the function of the caudate system has already been given an adequate description (for our present purpose) in the preceding paragraph, i.e., that of encoding the specific content (in terms of relationships between stimuli, responses, and reinforcement) of successive steps in a goal-directed motor program. What, then, are the additional functions discharged by the accumbens system? A possible answer to this question (Gray et al., 1991) is twofold: (1) switching between steps in the motor program, and (2) in interaction with the SHS, monitoring the smooth running of the motor program in terms of progress towards the intended goal.

We have supposed above that the firing of a particular subset of output neurons in the dorsal striatum and its associated neurons in other related structures (pallidal, thalamic, etc.) represents a particular step in a motor program; and that the firing of the set is maintained for a period of time by the positive feedback loops designated I and II in Figure 7.8. For a motor program, conceived in this way, to proceed as an integrated whole, there has to be an orderly transition from one step in the program to the next. The "orderliness" of such a transition can best be defined in terms of spatiotemporal progression towards the reinforcer, or "goal," to which the program is directed and by mediation of which it was originally established; that is to say, the "next" step must be the one which will most effectively bring the subject into greater spatiotemporal proximity to the relevant goal. How is this next step to be determined?

Within the context of animal learning theory, the most common answers that have been given to this question depend upon the concepts of the goal gradient and incentive motivation. In essence the theories that employ these concepts make the following assumptions: (1) Stimuli which do not initially possess positively reinforcing properties come to acquire them as the result of Pavlovian conditioning in which they serve as conditioned stimuli (CS) for an unconditioned positive reinforcer; the latter may be either a definite reward, such as food or water (providing the basis for approach behavior), or the omission of an expected punishment (providing the basis for active avoidance). (2) The degree to which such CSs possess positively reinforcing properties is a direct function of their proximity (in terms of time, space, or position in a series of chained stimulus-response links) to the initial unconditioned stimulus (UCS). (3) If the subject is simultaneously in the presence of more than one such CS, he/she directs his/her behavior towards the one with the highest reinforcing power. These assumptions can in principle generate behavior that maximizes positive reinforcement (by approach to reward) and minimizes negative reinforcement (by active avoidance of punishment) (Gray, 1975).

If we use these notions to guide us to a means by which the basal ganglia can assure orderly transitions from one step to the next in their motor programs, we should seek then for a source of information concerning relationships between environmental stimuli that are not innately reinforcing, on the one hand, and primary reinforcers, on the other. Rolls' group, using single-unit recording techniques in behaving monkeys, has provided considerable evidence for just such a source of information, in the form of the input from the amygdala to n. accumbens; both these structures contain neurons that respond selectively to stimuli associated with reinforcement (Rolls & Williams, 1987). It is plausible to suppose, therefore, that this input is responsible both for determining the initial establishment of the sequence of steps that makes up a goal-directed motor program, and for guiding the orderly running of this sequence once its establishment is complete. This postulate is consistent with a range of other evidence (Rolls, 1986b; Gray, 1987) implicating the amygdala in the formation of Pavlovian stimulus-reinforcer association.

However, this is not all that is needed to ensure orderly transitions from one step to another in a motor program. As well as the selection and initiation of the next step in the program (a function we have just attributed to the input from the amygdala to n. accumbens), it is necessary also to consider the termination of the step that is in progress. This would be expected to depend upon feedback indicating success in attaining the subgoal to which that step is directed (a subgoal presumably consisting of one of the secondary reinforcing stimuli initially established by way of the amygdalo-accumbens input). Given the assumption, developed in detail elsewhere (Gray, 1982a; and see above), that the SHS performs just such a monitoring function (i.e., checking whether the actual and expected outcomes of motor programs match), it is natural to attribute the role of providing this feedback to the projection to n. accumbens from the subiculum. Furthermore, given the necessary correspondence between (1) the role of reinforcement in establishing an orderly sequence of motor steps and (2) the role of monitoring in determining that expected subgoals have been attained, we would expect a considerable degree of overlap in the projections from the subiculum and the amygdala, respectively, to n. accumbens. It is indeed known that both these projections are densest in the same, caudomedial, region of the nucleus accumbens (Phillipson & Griffiths, 1985), but information is as yet unavailable concerning the interrelations between them at the ultrastructural level.

These, then, are the major building blocks, both conceptual and anatomical, which go to make up the BAS. The chief assumptions they embody may be summarized as follows (and see Figure 7.10):

1. The caudate system (Fig. 7.8), by way of its connections with sensory and motor cortices, encodes the specific content of each step in a motor program (e.g., for a rat, turn left at a junction in a maze; or, for a human being, the next word to be spoken in a sentence).

2. The accumbens system (Fig. 7.9) operates in tandem with the caudate system so as to permit switching from one step to the next in a motor program.

3. Both the establishment of the sequence of steps that makes up a given motor program, and the subsequent orderly running of the program, are guided by the projection to n. accumbens from the amygdala; this projection conveys information concerning cue-reinforcement associations.

4. The septohippocampal system (Fig. 7.3) is responsible for checking whether the

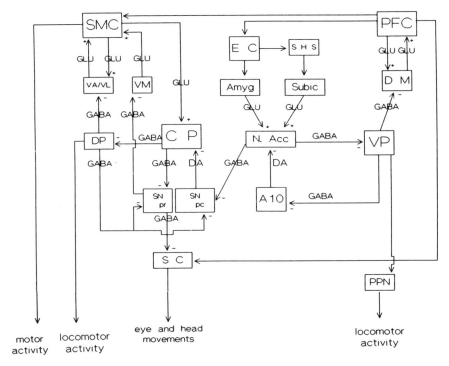

eye and head
motor   locomotor   movements   locomotor
activity   activity   activity

Figure 7.10. Major structures composing the neural basis of the Behavioral Approach System and its interrelations with the Behavioral Inhibition System. Structures: SMC = sensorimotor cortex; PFC = prefrontal cortex; EC = entorhinal cortex; SHS = septohippocampal system; Subic = subicular area; Amyg = amygdala; VA/VL = N. ventralis anterior and ventralis lateralis thalami; VM = N. ventralis medialis thalami; DM = N. dorsalis medialis thalami; DP = dorsal palladium; VP = ventral palladium; CP = caudate-putamen; N. Acc = N. accumbens; SNpr = substantia nigra, pars reticulata; SNpc = substantia nigra, pars compacta; A 10 = N. A 10 in ventral tegmental area; SC = superior colliculus; PPN = penduculopontine nucleus. Transmitters: GLU = glutamate; DA = dopamine; GABA = γ–aminobutyric acid.

actual outcome of a particular motor step matches the expected outcome; this information is transmitted to n. accumbens by the projection from the subiculum.

   5. The activities of the caudate, accumbens, and septohippocampal systems are coordinated and kept in step with one another by the prefrontal cortex, acting by way of its interconnections, respectively, with (a) the cortical components of the caudate system (Figure 7.8), (b) n. accumbens, dorsomedial thalamus and amygdala (Figure 7.9), and (c) the entorhinal and cingulate cortices (Figure 7.3).

   6. The maintenance of the pattern of activity in a subset of striatal, thalamic, and cortical neurons that makes up a motor step is due to the reverberatory excitatory activity in Loops I and II, together with lateral inhibition in the striatum. These patterns of activity are periodically interrupted by the firing of the dopaminergic inputs to the striatum at the termination of Loop III.

7. The duration of a step in a motor program corresponds to the joint operation, in both the caudate and accumbens systems, of Loops I-III (Figures 7.8 and 7.9).

8. Timing is coordinated between the septohippocampal monitoring system and the basal ganglia motor programming system. Given assumptions 6 and 7 above, and given the assumption that time is quantized in the SHS by the theta rhythm (Gray, 1982a), corresponding to an "instant" of about a tenth of a second, this must also be the duration of a motor step.

For further details of this model of the BAS, the reader is referred to Gray et al. (1991). There has been little work relating the BAS to human emotion; given the functions attributed to this system, we might expect it to underlie such states as pleasurable anticipation ("hope"; Mowrer, 1960), elation, or happiness. More dangerously, it is likely that activity in the BAS underlies the "high" experienced by users of a variety of recreational drugs. There is good evidence that conventional positive reinforcers, such as food or a sexually receptive member of the opposite sex, elicit the release of dopamine from the terminals of A 10 neurons in n. accumbens, and that this neurochemical effect is closely related to the approach behavior that such stimuli also elicit (and which, indeed, defines them as being positive reinforcers). It is significant, therefore, that compounds as chemically diverse as heroin, amphetamines, and cocaine (Stewart, de Wit, & Eikelboom, 1984), alcohol (Di Chiara & Imperato, 1985) and nicotine (Imperato, Mulas, & Di Chiara, 1986; Mitchell, Brazell, Joseph, Alavijeh, & Gray, 1989) have in common that they too cause the release of dopamine in n. accumbens, and sometimes very selectively in this region (e.g., Mitchell et al., 1989). It has in addition been reported that animals will work to self-administer the dopamine-releasing drug, amphetamine, into n. accumbens (Hoebel, Hernandez, McLean, Stanley, Aulissi, Glimcher, & Margolin, 1981). It seems probable, therefore, that the powerful reinforcing effects of the common drugs of abuse stem, at least in part, from their capacity to release dopamine in n. accumbens and so to activate (in a manner whose details, however, are as yet obscure) the BAS.

Personality

These, then, are the three postulated fundamental emotion systems, each: (1) Defined in terms of a set of behavioral input-output relationships, in which the inputs consists of specific subsets of reinforcing events; and (2) attributed to the functioning of a particular subsystem in the brain. In the case of two of these systems (the BIS and BAS), the analysis (speculative as it is) has been extended also to the third, cognitive, level, at which specific information-processing functions are attributed to the neural system concerned. We next turn to the relation between these three systems and temperament (it should be noted that, in what follows, I use the terms "temperament" and "personality" interchangeably; I take them both to mean what remains of individual differences once general intelligence and such special cognitive characteristics as visuo-spatial or verbal ability have been removed).

As noted at the outset of the chapter, it is assumed that temperament reflects individual differences in predispositions towards particular kinds of emotion. We may now rephrase that assumption thus: temperament reflects parameter values (Gray, 1967) that determine, for a particular individual, the operating characteristics of our three emotion systems, alone and in interaction with one another. A further basic assumption is that the major dimensions of personality, as measured by such multivariate statistical techniques as factor analysis (e.g., Eysenck & Eysenck, 1985; Zuckerman *et al.*, 1988), are created by individual differences in such parameter values. However, while these techniques are able to determine the number of independent sources of variation in a given matrix of correlations (obtained, e.g., from a battery of questionnaires or other instruments for the measurement of personality), they cannot by themselves establish a nonarbitrary location of the factors used to describe these sources of variation. Thus it cannot be assumed that a particular dimensional description of personality—e.g., introversion-extraversion (E), neuroticism (N) and psychoticism (P) in the Eysenckian system—embodies a one-to-one correspondence between the dimensions employed and the fundamental emotion systems whose variation between individuals gives rise, *ex hypothesi*, to personality.

Analyses of personality such as those offered by Eysenck & Eysenck (1985) or Zuckerman *et al.* (1988) start from human individual differences measured directly, but in tests whose relation to the postulated underlying emotion systems is unknown. Suppose, instead, that we start the other way round and use our current understanding of these systems to predict the likely structure of human personality. We would then expect to observe dimensions of personality that correspond to individual differences in the functioning of each of our three emotion systems. In other words, we would expect to see (1) a dimension of personality corresponding to individual differences in the intensity of functioning of the BIS, of which the high pole would presumably correspond to high-trait anxiety (Gray, 1982a); (2) a dimension corresponding to individual differences in the functioning of the F/FLS, of which the high pole might correspond to a high propensity to aggressive-defensive behavior; and (3) a dimension corresponding to individual differences in the functioning of the BAS, of which the high pole might correspond to a high propensity to behavior motivated by positive reinforcement and to accompanying pleasurable emotions (hope, happiness, elation).

It is in connection with the first of these postulated dimensions (trait anxiety) that most progress has been made in bringing these general notions into the laboratory. This process has been aided by the existence of good instruments for measuring trait anxiety at the human level (e.g., Spence & Spence, 1966; Spielberger, 1976); and also by the fact that the location of this trait within an overall three-dimensional personality space is well established. Thus, in terms of the Eysenckian axes, high trait anxiety corresponds to high N, low E, and low P, the alignment with N being the closest. These known correspondences have permitted a series of laboratory tests designed to pit predictions from Eysenck's (e.g., 1981) theory against those derived from the BIS model. The key predictions concern learning and performance in tasks which use either positive or negative reinforcers. Presentation of these predictions will be aided by reference to Figure 7.11 (Gray, 1970).

Trait anxiety is depicted in this figure as a diagonal (from high N, low E, to low N, high E) running across the Eysenckian two-dimensional space defined by N and E. In addition, a second theoretical personality dimension derived from the emotion-system approach, impulsivity, orthogonal to trait anxiety, is postulated as reflecting individual

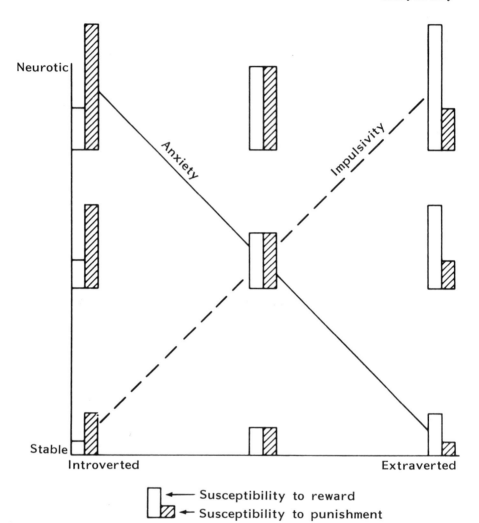

Figure 7.11. Relations between sensitivity to stimuli associated with reward (impulsivity) and with punishment (anxiety), neuroticism and introversion-extraversion.

differences in the functioning of the BAS. When this proposal was first made (Gray, 1970), it took no account of the third Eysenckian dimension, nor of individual differences in the F/FLS. Since there is still no clear indication as to how best to extend the model into this necessary third dimension (though see Gray, 1983, for one suggestion), I shall continue here to leave it out of account. The simplified two-dimensional model has the advantage that predictions from Eysenck's (1981) theory (far and away the best validated of those that have emerged from the direct study of human individual differences) are clearly different from those derived from the emotion-system approach.

According to Eysenck (1981; Eysenck & Eysenck, 1985), introverts should show superior conditioning and learning, relative to extraverts, unless level of arousal is high, in which case the relationship between E and conditioning is reversed. This hypothesis takes no account of the difference between conditioning and learning based on appetitive or aversive reinforcers respectively. Gray's (1970) hypothesis, in contrast, critically depends on the latter distinction: it predicts that, other things being equal, performance and learning will be facilitated for introverts if aversive rather than appetitive reinforcers are used; while for extraverts performance and learning will be facilitated if appetitive rather than aversive reinforcers are used (compare the heights of adjacent bars making up each pair in Figure 7.11). Note that Gray's hypothesis cannot be derived from Eysenck's by recourse to the differences in arousal level that might be associated with the polarity of reinforcement. It would normally be supposed that aversive reinforcement is more arousing than appetitive, which should therefore, on average (according to Eysenck's theory), work to the advantage of extraverts; yet Gray's hypothesis predicts that aversive reinforcement should favor introverts. The outcome of a large number of experiments, using a variety of methods, in which these predictions have been investigated, has uniformly been in agreement with Gray's model (see Gray 1981, for review; also Boddy *et al.*, 1986; Gupta, 1984; Gupta & Gupta, 1984; Gupta & Shukla, in press; Newman, 1987).

The results of this type of experiment, then, are very encouraging for the approach to the study of temperament advocated here. At the very least, they demonstrate the heuristic value of the approach. But it would be a mistake to overinterpret them. They certainly cannot be regarded as outweighing the considerable body of data which supports Eysenck's (1981) theory of introversion-extraversion and which cannot as yet be derived from the emotion-system approach. What is needed, rather, is a careful empirical study of behavior under conditions in which processes predictable from each theory can simultaneously be demonstrated. Experiments of this kind (e.g., Gupta, 1984; Gupta & Gupta, 1984) should allow one to determine whether either model can be reduced to the other; or whether each is correct, but with a different domain of applicability, perhaps because each reflects the operation of different brain mechanisms.

One possibility of the former kind is that level of arousal (the key concept in Eysenck's, 1981, theory) is determined by the relative balance between the BIS and BAS. The possibility follows naturally, in fact, from the assumption (see above) that, other things being equal, aversive reinforcers are more arousing than the appetitive variety. Suppose that for any given situation there exists a range of actual and potential reinforcing events; and that, on average across all situations, positive and negative reinforcers are roughly equal in frequency and potency. Then, on average, an individual who is relatively more sensitive to aversive reinforcers (i.e., an introvert) will be at a higher level of arousal than one (an extravert) who is relatively more sensitive to appetitive reinforcers. In this way, it might be possible to deduce the fundamental Eysenckian postulate (that introverts are normally at a higher level of arousal than extraverts) from the relationships between, on the one hand, E, and, on the other, the reactivities of the BIS and BAS, as depicted in Figure 7.11.

While perhaps plausible, this proposal is at present quite speculative; it lacks detailed theoretical analysis, let alone empirical support. But it is in this direction, I believe, that the most promising lines of investigation are to be found. The analysis of temperament would take a great stride forward if one could properly relate fundamental biological data, of the kind with which this chapter has mostly been concerned, to the great storehouse of information about human individual differences which, while they are well described by current dimensional models, are still difficult to link to the workings of the brain.

References

Adams, D. B. Brain mechanisms for offence, defense, and submission. *Behavioral and Brain Sciences*, 1979, *2*, 201–241.

Amsel, A. Frustrative nonreward in partial reinforcement and discrimination learning: Some recent history and a theoretical extention. *Psychological Review*, 1962, *69*, 306–328.

Berlyne, D. E. *Conflict, arousal and curiosity*. New York: McGraw-Hill, 1960.

Boddy, J., Carver, A., & Rowley, K. Effect of positive and negative verbal reinforcement on performance as a function of extraversion-introversion: Some tests of Gray's theory. *Personality and Individual Differences*, 1986, *7*, 81–88.

Deutch, J. A. *The structural basis of behaviour*. Cambridge: Cambridge University Press, 1964.

Di Chiara, G., & Imperato, A. Ethanol preferentially stimulates dopamine release in the nucleus accumbens of freely moving rats. *European Journal of Pharmacology*, 1985, *115*, 131–132.

Evenden, J. L., & Robbins, T. W. Increased response switching, perseveration and perseverative switching following d-amphetamine in the rat. *Psychopharmacology*, 1983, *80*, 67–73.

Eysenck, H. J. (Ed.), *A model for personality*. New York: Springer, 1981.

Eysenck, H. J., & Eysenck, M. W. *Personality and individual differences: A natural science approach*. New York: Plenum, 1985.

Fowles, D. The three arousal model: Implications of Gray's two-factor learning theory for heart rate, electrodermal activity and psychopathy. *Psychophysiology*, 1980, *17*, 87–104.

Graeff, F. G. The anti-aversive action of drugs. In T. Thompson, P. B. Dews, & J. Barrett (Eds.), *Advances in behavioural pharmacology*. Vol. 6. Hillsdale, NJ: Erlbaum, 1987.

Gray, J. A. Disappointment and drugs in the rat. *Advancement of Science*, 1967, *23*, 595–605.

Gray, J. A. The psychophysiological basis of introversion-extraversion. *Behaviour Research and Therapy*, 1970, *8*, 249–266.

Gray, J. A. Learning theory, the conceptual nervous system and personality. In V. D. Nebylitsyn & J. A. Gray (Eds.), *The biological bases of individual behaviour*. New York: Academic Press, 1972.

Gray, J. A. *Elements of a two-process theory of learning*. London: Academic Press, 1975.

Gray, J. A. Drug effects on fear and frustration: Possible limbic site of action of minor tranquillizers. In L. L. Iversen & S. D. Snyder (Eds.), *Handbook of psychopharmacology*. Vol. 8. New York: Plenum, 1977.

Gray, J. A. A critique of Eysenck's theory of personality. In H. J. Eysenck (Ed.), *A model for personality*. New York: Springer, 1981.

Gray, J. A. *The neuropsychology of anxiety: An enquiry into the functions of the septo-hippocampal system*. Oxford: Oxford University Press, 1982a.

Gray, J. A. Précis of 'The neuropsychology of anxiety: An enquiry into the functions of the septo-hippocampal system'. *Behavioral and Brain Sciences*, 1982b, *5*, 469–484.

Gray, J. A. On mapping anxiety. *Behavioral and Brain Sciences*, 1982c, *5*, 506–525.

Gray, J. A. Where should we search for biologically based dimensions of personality? *Zeitschrift für Differentielle und Diagnostische Psychologie*, 1983, *4*, 165–176.

Gray, J. A. The hippocampus as an interface between cognition and emotion. In H. L. Roitblat, T. G. Bever, & H. S. Terrace (Eds.), *Animal cognition*. Hillsdale, NJ: Erlbaum, 1984.

Gray, J. A. Anxiety and the brain: Pigments aren't colour names. *Bulletin of the British Psychological Society*, 1985, *38*, 299–300.

Gray, J. A. *The psychology of fear and stress* (2nd ed.). Cambridge: Cambridge University Press, 1987.

Gray, J. A., Feldon, J., Rawlins, J. N. P., Hemsley, D. R., & Smith, A. D. The neuropsychology of schizophrenia. *Behavioral and Brain Sciences*, 1991, *14*, in press.

Gray, J. A., & McNaughton, N. Comparison between the behavioural effects of septal and hippocampal lesions: A review. *Neuroscience and Biobehavioral Reviews*, 1983, *7*, 119–188.

Groves, P. M. A theory of the functional organization of the neostriatum and the neostriatal control of voluntary movement. *Brain Research Reviews*, 1983, *5*, 109–132.

Gupta, U. Phenobarbitone and the relationship between extraversion and reinforcement in verbal operant conditioning. *British Journal of Psychology*, 1984, *75*, 499–506.

Gupta, B. S., & Gupta, U. Dextroamphetamine and individual susceptibility to reinforcement in verbal operant conditioning. *British Journal of Psychology*, 1984, *75*, 201–206.

Gupta, S., & Shukla, A. P. Verbal operant conditioning as a function of extraversion and reinforcement. *British Journal of Psychology*, in press.

Hebb, D. O. Drives and the C.N.S. (conceptual nervous system). *Psychological Review*, 1955, *62*, 243–259.

Hoebel, B. G., Hernandez, L., McLean, S., Stanley, B. G., Aulissi, E. F., Glimcher, P., & Margolin, D. Catecholamines, enkephalin, and neurotensin in feeding and reward. In B. G. Hoebel & D. Novin (Eds.), *The neural basis of feeding and reward*. Brunswick, GE: Haer Institute, 1981.

Imperato, A., Mulas, A., & Di Chiara, G. Nicotine preferentially stimulates dopamine release in the limbic system of freely moving rats. *European Journal of Pharmacology*, 1986, *132*, 337–338.

Mathews, A. Anxiety and the processing of threatening information. In V. Hamilton, G. H. Bower, & N. Frijda (Eds.), *Cognitive perspectives on emotion and motivation*. Dordrecht: Kluwer Academic Publishers, 1988.

Millenson, J. R. *Principles of behavioral analysis*. New York: Macmillan, 1967.

Miller, N. E. Learnable drives and rewards. In S. S. Stevens (Ed.), *Handbook of experimental psychology*. New York: Wiley, 1951.

Mitchell, S. N., Brazell, M. P., Joseph, M. H., Alavijeh, M. S., & Gray, J. A. Regionally specific effects of acute and chronic nicotine on rates of catecholamine and indoleamine synthesis in rat brain. *European Journal of Pharmacology*, 1989, *167*, 311–322.

Mowrer, O. H. On the dual nature of learning: A re-interpretation of "conditioning" and "problem-solving." *Harvard Education Review*, 1947, *17*, 102–148.

Mowrer, O. H. *Learning theory and behavior*. New York: Wiley, 1960.

Newman, J. P. Reaction to punishment in extraverts and psychopaths: Implications for the impulsive behavior of disinhibited individuals. *Journal of Research in Personality*, 1987, *21*, 464–480.

Oades, R. D. The role of NA in tuning and DA in switching between signals in the CNS. *Neuroscience and Biobehavioral Reviews*, 1985, *9*, 261–282.

Olds, J., & Olds, M. Drives, rewards, and the brain. In F. Barron, W. C. Dement, W. Edwards, H. Lindmann, L. D. Phillips, J. Olds, & M. Olds (Eds.), *New directions in psychology*. Vol. 2. New York: Holt, Rinehart and Winston, 1965.

Penney, J. B., & Young, A. B. GABA as the pallidothalamic neuro-transmitter: Implications for basal ganglia function. *Brain Research*, 1981, *207*, 195–199.

Phillipson, O. T., & Griffiths, A. C. The topographical order of inputs to nucleus accumbens in the rat. *Neuroscience*, 1985, *16*, 275–296.

Reiman, E. M., Raichle, M. E., Butler, F. K. Hersovitch, P., & Robins, E. A focal brain abnormality in panic disorder, a severe form of anxiety. *Nature*, 1984, *310*, 683–685.

Rolls, E. T. Information representation, processing and storage in the brain: Analysis at the single neuron level. In R. Ritter & S. Ritter (Eds.), *Neural and molecular mechanisms of learning*. New York: Springer, 1986a.

Rolls, E. T. A theory of emotion, and its application to understanding the neural basis of emotion. In Y. Oomura (Ed.), *Emotions: Neural and chemical control*. Tokyo: Japan Scientific Societies Press, and Basel: Karger, 1986b.

Rolls, E. T., & Williams, G. V. Sensory and movement-related neuronal activity in different regions of the primatestriatum. In J. S. Schneider & T. I. Kidsky (Eds.), *Basal ganglia and behaviour: Sensory aspects and motor functioning*. Bern: Hans Huber, 1987.

Shapiro, S. K., Quay, H., Hogan, A., & Schwartz, K. Response perseveration and delayed responding in undersocialized aggressive conduct disorder. *Journal of Abnormal Psychology*, 1988, *97*, 251–264.

Spence, J. T., & Spence, K. W. The motivational components of manifest anxiety: Drive and drive stimuli. In C. D. Spielberger (Ed.), *Anxiety and behavior*. New York: Academic Press, 1966.

Spielberger, C. D. The nature and measurement of anxiety. In C. D. Spielberger & R. Diaz-Guerrero (Eds.), *Cross-cultural anxiety*. Washington: Hemisphere, 1976.

Stewart, J., de Wit, H., & Eikelboom, R. Role of unconditioned and conditioned drug effects in the self-administration of opiates and stimulants. *Psychological Review*, 1984, *91*, 251–268.

Swerdlow, N. R., & Koob, G. F. Dopamine, schizophrenia, mania and depression: Toward a unified hypothesis of cortico-striato-pallido-thalamic function. *Behavioral and Brain Sciences*, 1987, *10*, 215–217.

Zuckerman, M. Leaping up the phylogenetic scale in explaining anxiety: Perils and possibilities. *Behavioral and Brain Sciences*, 1982, *5*, 505–506.

Zuckerman, M., Kuhlman, D. M., & Camac, C. What lies beyond E and N? Factor analyses of scales believed to measure basic dimensions of personality. *Journal of Personality and Social Psychology*, 1988, *54*, 96–107.

8

Biotypes for Basic Personality Dimensions?

"The Twilight Zone" between Genotype and Social Phenotype

Marvin Zuckerman

The nineteenth-century "science" of phrenology proposed that each personality trait had a particular locus in the brain that shaped the skull above it. Today, we view this kind of brain localization as fallacious. But in the search for simplicity we may be creating a new kind of phrenology, one more in accord with real brain entities and modern neurophysiology, but still inaccurate. The new "phrenology" suggests that each personality trait is based on one particular brain structure or system or one biochemical.

Personality traits are elaborations of what once were relatively simple reflexive mechanisms. A simple organism like a paramecium has two basic "personality traits": approach and withdrawal. While these are largely a function of external stimuli they are conditionable, and one could conceive of individual differences in the traits based on variations in the stimulus-response mechanisms or "life experiences." Analogous tendencies like impulsivity and anxiety traits in higher organisms may have origins in early evolution, but the mechanisms mediating them have become quite complex. Anxiety, for instance, requires "anticipation," including abstraction from the common elements of past situations of danger, storage of them in memory, their control over behavior in the appropriate circumstances, and a rapid shift in the physiology of the body toward the demands of defense and survival. Any personality trait involves a variety of behavioral mechanisms and each behavioral mechanism is likely to be mediated by a number of biological mechanisms. It is these biological mechanisms that are most directly under the control of the genotype through its assembling of chemical components.

Given this kind of complexity in brain behavior relationships, a "top down" rather

Marvin Zuckerman • Department of Psychology, University of Delaware, Newark, Delaware 19716.

than a "bottom up" approach to defining basic personality traits may be best. A "top down" approach (e.g., Eysenck) is (1) definition of personality dimensions at the highest or broadest level; (2) delineation of narrower traits composing them; (3) identification of behavioral mechanisms involved in the personality traits; and (4) finding the biological mechanisms controlling the behavioral ones and thereby the personality traits. A "bottom up" approach (e.g., Gray) starts with the biological bases of behavioral mechanisms, as developed from comparative studies of other species, followed by extrapolation to the behavior and personality traits of humans. Theoretically, both approaches could yield the same isomorphic solution. Because of the problem of finding the appropriate animal models for human traits, it is more likely that different solutions will be reached by those starting from the top and those working up from the bottom. Gray (in press), for instance, has attempted to redefine the basic dimensions of personality within Eysenck's (Eysenck, 1967; Eysenck & Eysenck, 1985) model by drawing the axes at peculiar angles through the three-dimension space without regard for the empirically derived structure of personality traits as revealed in factor-analytic studies. While Gray has identified basic biobehavioral mechanisms in rats, their involvement in human personality traits is open to question. What will be described in this chapter is a more complex hypothetical relationship between basic personality traits and their biological substrates at several levels between the genotype and the social phenotype as shown in Figure 8.1.

Personality Traits

Personality trait dimensions, based on self-report questionnaires or ratings by others, represent the most abstract level of description. A recent factor analysis of questionnaire scales (Zuckerman, Kuhlman, & Camac, 1988) has shown that the three broad personality dimensions postulated by Eysenck (1967) can be identified in both men and women. Eysenck's scales, Extraversion (E), Neuroticism (N), and Psychoticism (P) are good markers for these dimensions. Data in this study and a more recent one suggest that Aggression (Agg) and Hostility may constitute an equally reliable fourth factor, located between the P and N dimensions, although somewhat closer to N than to P. Activity, suggested by Buss and Plomin (1984) as a primary dimension of temperament, particularly in children, can also be reliably identified in a five-factor analysis; but at higher levels it tends to divide up into the other factors. The major component of the E factor is consistently Sociability. The N factor at the broadest level consists of scales measuring negative affectivity: anxiety, hostility, and anger. Although markers for trait depression were not included they would probably fall into this factor. While the factor is labeled General Emotionality, it should be understood that this pertains primarily to dysphoric emotions, not to positive affect. The latter emotional trait is primarily related to the E dimension, and when it is related to the N dimension, the relationship is an inverse one. "Personality in the third dimension" (Zuckerman, 1989) or P is more complex in terms of its constituent personality traits.

I have argued that Eysenck's label "Psychoticism" is not an accurate description of the trait. If a clinical term must be used, "Psychopathy" or "Antisocial Personality" would be more appropriate, since this disorder incorporates the traits and many of the

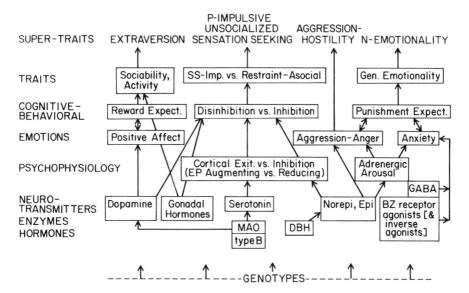

Figure 8.1. A psychobiological model for personality. Dopamine refers particularly to the A10 dopaminergic pathway from the ventral tegmental area to the nucleus accumbens via the medial forebrain bundle and the A9 pathway from the substantia nigra to the caudate putamen. Low levels of type B monoamine oxidase (MAO) may deregulate these systems. High levels of gonadal hormones, particularly testosterone, may furnish a basis for both sociability and disinhibition. High levels of serotonin in conjunction with high levels of both type A and B MAO may provide the basis for strong inhibition; low levels of serotonin together with high activity of dopaminergic systems bay be involved in disinhibition, impulsivity, and aggression or hostility. Regions of the septal area are particularly involved in inhibition-disinhibition of behavior. Norepinephrine (Norepi), particularly in the dorsal ascending noradrenergic pathways from the locus coeruleus, is also involved in the adrenergic arousal found in both anxiety and anger. Low levels of norepinephrine, perhaps related to low levels of the enzyme dopamine-beta-hydroxylase (DBH), may be involved in the traits of disinhibition and impulsivity. Stimulation from the central nucleus of the amygdala to the ventral tegmental areas and the locus coeruleus may increase activity in dopaminergic and noradrenergic systems. At low levels this catecholamine system activity may be rewarding and facilitating, but at high levels may be associated with anxiety, distractibility, inhibition, and adrenergic arousal. When adrenergic arousal is combined with high activity of benzodiazepine receptor inverse agonists and low levels of GABA inhibition, the result may be anxiety. Specific combinations of these biological traits may underlie the disposition of trait anxiety and emotionality in general.

biological constituents of the dimension better than psychotic disorders like schizophrenia. I have called the dimension "Impulsive, Unsocialized Sensation-Seeking" (ImpUSS) to summarize the narrower traits involved. Impulsivity can be distinguished from the other traits in the P-ImpUSS dimension in factor analyses rotating six or seven factors, but at these levels there is less reliability of the factors across gender or samples. The clustering of narrower factors within broader ones does not mean that there is no point in assessing narrow as well as broad ones because some of them seem to be more closely related to behavior mechanisms or biological factors, as will be shown.

Cognitive Affective and Behavioral Mechanisms

The model I am proposing would characterize the mechanisms underlying the E and N dimensions in cognitive terms rather than conditioning ones. Extraverts can be characterized in terms of a strong "Generalized Reward Expectancy" and introverts in terms of a weaker one. The normal (average N and P) extravert is generally an opitimist, with high self-esteem and self-efficacy beliefs, particularly in search of social reinforcements. Neurotics or high anxiety-trait persons can be characterized in terms of a strong "Generalized Punishment Expectancy." Generalized anxiety is associated with a cognitive component (worry) which involves excessive apprehension about possible negative outcomes and a feeling low efficacy (helplessness) in coping with stress. Recent data correlating scales of "Generalized Reward and Punishment Expectancies" (GRAPES) with the E and N scales from the Eysenck Personality Questionnaire (EPQ) tend to support these hypotheses (Ball & Zuckerman, 1990).

The basic mechanism underlying the P dimension is hypothesized to be one of Disinhibition vs. Inhibition. The combination of sensation-seeking (incautious risk-taking in pursuit of reward), impulsivity (inability to restrain behavior even where it might lead to punishment) and a lack of socialization (need or desire to follow the rules and abide by the values of society) all suggest a deficit in inhibition and a low threshold for disinhibition. The defect in behavioral restraint may operate at a brain level that short-circuits cognitive analyses. The impulsive and incautious person typically thinks after acting, rather than before. The characteristic learning problem in psychopaths is one of learning when not to act (passive avoidance), rather than learning when to act (Newman & Kosson, 1986). Their failure to learn from punishment experience may reflect a classical conditioning deficit when the unconditioned stimulus is aversive (Lykken, 1957; Hemming, 1981). Originally, Eysenck (1965) proposed a deficiency in general "conditionability" as the basis for extraversion. At that time extraversion was conceived of and assessed as a dual component trait including *sociability* and *impulsivity*. Eyelid-conditioning studies (Barratt, 1971; Eysenck & Levey, 1972) showed that conditioning was only related to the impulsivity component of E, particularly to a measure of narrow impulsivity (Frcka & Martin, 1987). However, the introduction of the P dimension into the personality instrument resulted in a dropping of impulsivity type items from the E scale and the closer alignment of impulsivity with P. The P scale itself predicted conditioning in a study where paraorbital shock was used instead of an air puff as the unconditioned stimulus (Bytes, Frcka, Martin, & Levey, 1983). Perhaps the more aversive nature of the UCS provided clearer evidence of the influence of P than an earlier study (Frcka, Beytes, Levey, & Martin, 1983). Impulsive and high P individuals seem to be poor conditioners in response to aversive UCSs. This would mean that they would have a difficult time in learning inhibition from physical punishment of the type that is often used in an attempt to discipline them.

Tellegen (1985) has suggested that basic dimensions of personality are strongly related to independent dimensions of positive and negative affect. Meyer and Shack (1989) have shown that both trait and state positive affect are aligned with extraversion, while negative affect items fall on a dimension defined by neuroticism. As shown in Figure 1, the present model accepts this idea that there is a tendency of sociable persons to experience frequent states of positive affect which may account for their high reward expectancy. Given the same positive reinforcement, reward effects (positive affect) would be stronger in the extravert than in the introvert. The punishment expectancy in neurotics would be based on their more frequent experience of states of negative affect. One could cogently argue that the generalized expectancies affect the occurrence of positive or negative affects more than the other way around. Affect and expectancy undoubtedly influence each other. However, emotions stem from more basic and earlier evolved parts of the nervous system than cognitions. Emotional discriminations may be made on the basis of partial, incomplete stimulus processing. While cognitions may modify and direct emotional responses, the initial emotional reactivity occurs at a lower level of the nervous system (Le Doux, 1987). As Zajonc (1980) says, "Preferences need no inferences." This question will be addressed again when I discuss a neuropsychological basis for the N dimension.

Psychophysiology

Most of the research with humans on the biological basis of personality has come from the field of psychophysiology, primarily because these non-invasive bioelectrical recording techniques are more accessible to psychologists than biochemical methods. Much of the research has been based on arousal theories of personality (Strelau & Eysenck, 1987) which have survived and even flourished despite criticisms. Eysenck's (1967) theory postulates that arousal and arousability of the reticulocortical activation system are the biological basis of extraversion and introversion.

The most relevant evidence for a cortical arousal theory of E-I comes from EEG studies since these provide the most direct psychophysiological measure of cortical arousal. The results from these studies have been equivocal (Gale & Edwards, 1986; O'Gorman, 1984). There are many methodological problems in this type of research, like defining the conditions in which to measure tonic arousal. But even when the analysis of the literature is limited to the most conceptually and methodologically sound studies, as agreed on by Gale and O'Gorman, the results are still inconclusive (Zuckerman, 1991).

Recent evidence suggests that the cortical arousal hypothesis may be relevant for some traits involved in the P dimension rather than the E dimension. O'Gorman and Lloyd (1987) used the EPQ-E scale, which unlike previous versions of E is largely devoid of impulsivity items, and the Eysenck and Eysenck's (1977) broad Impulsivity scale. They measured EEG in two conditions, one of which was suggested by Gale to be optimal for revealing differences between introverts and extraverts. While E and broad impulsivity measures were not related to EEG arousal, *narrow impulsivity* was related: impulsives were less aroused. Narrow impulsivity (responding quickly without restraint) was also the type related to eyelid conditioning, as discussed previously. Since arousal may be a primary basis for conditionability, the findings are consistent, but the emphasis must be shifted from E, as currently defined, to a specific component of the P dimension. Goldring and Richards (1985) also report that the P scale itself is related to low cortical arousal.

Eysenck's theory suggests an interaction between stimulus intensity and cortical arousability due to the sensitivity of introverts to stimulation in the lower range of intensity and their transmarginal (cortical) inhibition in response to high intensity stimuli. The cortical evoked potential (EP) *augmenting-reducing* paradigm developed by

Buchsbaum and Silverman (1968) provides an ideal way of testing this hypothesis, since it measures the cortical responsivity at each of several stimulus intensities covering a range of intensity. Augmenting describes the tendency for a linear increase in EP amplitude with increasing stimulus intensity, while reducing refers to either the lack of increase or a reduction of EP amplitude at the highest stimulus intensities.

No relationship has been found between extraversion and EP augmenting-reducing, but a very robust relationship has been found between the *Disinhibition* sensation-seeking scale and augmenting of visual and auditory EPs. This literature involving 15 studies has been recently summarized (Zuckerman, 1990). In 5 of 7 analyses of the visual EP and 7 of 9 analyses of the auditory EP there was a significant relationship between at least one of the sensation-seeking scales (usually Disinhibition) and augmenting: high disinhibitors tend to be augmenters, while low disinhibitors tend to be reducers. Barratt, Pritchard, Faulk, and Brandt (1987) found a similar relationship between impulsivity, particularly "cognitive impulsiveness," and augmenting.

The augmenting-reducing source of individual differences has also been demonstrated in cats (Hall, Rappaport, Hopkins, Griffin, & Silverman, 1970; Lukas & Siegel, 1977; Saxton, Siegel, & Lukas, 1987) where it has been related to natural behavior characteristics. Augmenter cats tend to be active and exploratory while reducers are inhibited and tend to withdraw from novel stimuli. The augmenter cats performed poorly on an experimental task requiring the animal to delay or inhibit response in order to get reward, despite the fact that they performed better than reducers on a simple fixed interval reward schedule. The pattern of performance seen in augmenter cats is also one seen in septal-lesioned rats and Gorenstein and Newman (1980) have suggested a parallel between the behavior of these rats and the "disinhibitory psychopathology" in humans, particularly in the antisocial personality. Another part of the pattern in septal-lesioned rats is enhanced "stimulus-seeking" behavior.

The evidence strongly suggests that the cortical augmenting-reducing paradigm is a marker for at least some of the traits in the P dimension, particularly disinhibition and impulsivity. Reducing represents the capacity for behavioral inhibition and augmenting is associated with a deficit in this capacity. This interpretation is consistent with the clinical correlates of EP augmenting including alcoholism, delinquency, drug use, and bipolar disorders (Zuckerman, Buchsbaum, & Murphy, 1980).

A particularly challenging line of research has been conducted by Pivik, Stelmack, and Bylsma (1988). They measured excitability of a spinal motoneuronal reflex with stimulation applied to the leg. High scorers on both E and Disinhibition scales showed reduced motoneuronal excitability as assessed by reflex recovery functions. The arousal hypothesis has been centered on the cortex, but there is a possibility that it might apply to neurons at subcortical levels as well. While the functional significance of reduced motoneuronal excitability is not clear, it has been associated with increased dopaminergic function, suggesting a possible link with the biochemical level.

Autonomic Arousal and Arousability

Eysenck (1967) hypothesized that the N dimension is biologically based on the limbic brain which regulates emotionality and the peripheral adjustments of the autonomic nervous system in reaction to stress. Adrenergic arousal is reflected in a variety of measurable psychophysiological changes such as heart rate, blood pressure, peripheral vasoconstriction, respiration rate, and skin conductance fluctuations and level. However, most studies have not shown a relationship between levels of adrenergic physiological activity and N in normal populations (e.g., Fahrenberg, 1987). Eysenck and Eysenck (1985) acknowledged the general failure of the hypothesis linking N with sympathetic-autonomic arousal, but said that this might be due to the fact that most studies did not expose subjects to stress or aversive stimuli. However, Fahrenberg (1987) describes large-scale studies where physiological measures were taken during resting, basal conditions, and during a variety of stressor situations, including physical stress (blood taking, cold-pressor tests) and social stress (interview, performance). While the stressors were effective in increasing physiological responsivity in all subjects, there was no evidence of a relationship with N.

However, a survey of studies (Zuckerman, 1991, chapter 8) comparing controls and patients shows that all groups of anxiety disorders, except those with simple phobias, have higher levels of *basal* heart rate and skin conductance fluctuations than normals. Physiological reactivity in response to general kinds of stress does not differentiate normals from anxiety patients; in fact, normals tend to show greater response to stress situations simply because they start at a lower level than patients. However, when phobic patients are exposed to objects or situations which normally elicit their fears, they do show heart rate reactions that are greater than those of normals exposed to the same stimuli. Unlike patients with anxiety disorders, high N subjects from the normal population cannot be characterized by a general dysregulation of the adrenergic arousal systems. Like the phobic patients among the anxiety disorders, their anxiety response may be only to specific kinds of stressors or persons, or the trait of neuroticism in normals may be more related to cognitive mechanisms than to arousal ones.

Biochemistry

Catecholamines (Dopamine, Norepinephrine, and Epinephrine)

Many theorists have suggested that the neurotransmitter dopamine is the basis of some kinds of general motivational trait involving exploration directed toward primary rewards in animals (Gray, in press; Stein, 1978) and novelty and sensation seeking in humans (Cloninger, 1987; Zuckerman, 1979). Moderate doses of dopamine agonists, like stimulant drugs, increase social behavior and activity; higher doses may reverse these effects (Zuckerman, 1984). Dopamine is vital to the intrinsic reward effects produced by self-stimulation or self-infusion of stimulant drugs (Bozarth, 1987). When dopamine is depleted, as in Parkinsonism, the result is an anhedonic, apathetic personality, not interested in the environment and lacking in positive emotionality or joy. All of the effects of dopamine depletion or release suggest that it must be involved in the positive affect, high activity, and sociability of extraversion.

However, there are also suggestions of a link to sensation-seeking and impulsivity found in the P dimension. Drug abusers tend to show high levels of sensation-seeking and antisocial tendencies (Zuckerman, 1987) and many of the drugs abused act through the dopaminergic systems, stimulants like cocaine and amphetamine having their primary effects on the nucleus accumbens, while opiate reward is mediated in the ventral tegmental area (Bozarth, 1987). Perhaps the non-drug using extravert has a high level of tonic activity in one or more of the dopamine systems, while the disinhibiting or boredom susceptible individual has a low level and therefore is particularly attracted to drugs or exciting activities that act on brain dopamine systems. But the only empirical correlations found thus far are between norepinephrine (in cerebrospinal fluid) and plasma dopamine-beta-hydroxylase (the enzyme which converts dopamine to epine-phrine in the neuron) and sensation-seeking. Both correlations are negative, suggesting that high sensation-seekers have low levels of both the neurotransmitter and the enzyme involved in its production.

While adrenergic arousal may be an essential component of clinical anxiety, it is not the entire story. Adrenergic arousal can be pleasurable when it occurs at an optimal level in sensation-seeking or sexual activities, neutral when it occurs in physical exercise, or displeasurable when it occurs during a panic attack. Drugs, like yohimbine, that stimu-late activity of the norepinephrine system in the brain, produce anxiety and panic attacks in persons who already have these disorders. But other drugs like lactate and caffeine, which do not stimulate catecholamine activity, also produce anxiety in these patients (Gorman, Fyer, Liebowitz, & Klein, 1987). All of these drugs do *not* produce panic and major anxiety in most normals, even though they do increase their physiological arousal.

The common denominator of all drugs which have an anxiogenic effect is that they produce peripheral sympathetic nervous system effects such as tachycardia. However, such arousal is not intrinsically associated with the subjective dysphoria characterizing anxiety. Perhaps recurrent arousal may result in the internal sensations of arousal becom-ing conditioned cues for the full panic or anxiety attacks. This would produce a positive feed-back in which apprehension of arousal would increase arousal.

Benzodiazepine-GABA System

Something else must dispose the person to perceive internal arousal as a sign of threat. Is there a particular mechanism for the emotion of fear or anxiety, as distin-guished from general emotionality? The benzodiazepines seem to reduce the subjective sense of anxiety without the generalized, intensive, sedative effects of barbiturates or alcohol. They act on recently discovered receptors in the brain called "benzodiazepine receptors." These receptors work by potentiating the effects of GABA, an inhibitory neurotransmitter widely distributed in the nervous system. However, the ben-zodiazepines (BZs) do not work by general sedation, so the GABA effects must be specific to certain pathways. These will be discussed in a subsequent section. The very existence of the BZ receptors suggests that there must be natural receptor agonists (which would dampen anxiety) or inverse agonists (which would be anxiogenic). A natural polypeptide produced from rat brain, called diazepam-binding inhibitor (DBI) has an affinity for the BZ receptor and also facilitates suppression of behavior in a conflict situation (Guidotti, Forchetti, Corda, Konkel, Bennett, & Costa, 1983). Beta-carbolines produced in the laboratory, but with a natural affinity for benzodiazepine receptors, have been shown to produce "apprehension" in normal subjects (Dorow, Duka, Holler, & Sauerbrey, 1987).

These early studies suggest that a balance between natural BZ receptor agonists and inverse agonists, when combined with catecholamine-mediated arousal, may produce the full-blown phenomenon of anxiety. An inverse agonist like DBI could be what "tags" arousal as "fear." Another possibility is that the number and distribution of BZ receptors may be what underlies the vulnerability to anxiety or N trait. Decreased concentrations of BZ receptors have been found in an anxious strain of mice and BZ-binding is higher in an emotionally nonreactive strain of rats than in one characterized by high emotionality (Robertson, Martin, & Candy, 1978). Whatever their precise role in emotionality in general or anxiety in particular, endogenous biochemicals acting on the BZ receptor sites are likely to play a crucial role in the generalized apprehensiveness characterizing the N dimension of personality.

Serotonin

The case for serotonin as a mediator of anxiety (Cloninger, 1987; Gray, 1982, in press) is largely based on its role in inhibition of approach behavior in conflict situations (Soubrie, 1986) or emotional systems in general (Panksepp, 1982). The case for anxiolytic effects of serotoninergic drugs is far less conclusive (File, 1988). As a matter of fact, the comparative and human clinical literature suggests that it is *low* levels of serotonin that are related to anxiety and more so to depression. But serotonin is primarily correlated with the P dimension, impulsivity and aggressiveness. Persons with low levels of the serotonin metabolite 5 hydroxyindoleacetic acid (5-HIAA) tend to score high on Eysenck's P scale (Schalling, Asberg, & Edman, 1984), and on hostility and psychopathy scales (Brown, Ebert, Goyer, Jimerson, Klein, Bunney, & Goodwin, 1982). Such persons also are found among those personality disorders who are behaviorally aggressive (Brown, Goodwin, Ballenger, Goyer, & Major, 1979) in contrast to more passive forms of disorders. Low levels of 5-HIAA are found in persons who have attempted or committed suicide in impulsive, violent ways, and in impulsive murderers (Van Praag, 1986). Van Praag, Kahn, Asnis, Wetzler, Brown, Bleich, and Korn (1987) have suggested that low 5-HIAA is more indicative of aggressive disregulation than depression. The human data suggest that low serotonin is related primarily to the disinhibition of behavioral impulse associated with the P dimension and only secondarily to anxiety and depression characteristic of the N dimension. These findings are consistent with the animal data suggesting that serotonin regulates impulsive behavior associated with the possibility of punishment.

Testosterone

Eysenck (1967) proposed that testosterone may be involved in the P dimension of personality, largely on the basis of the human sex difference in violent aggressiveness and the well-demonstrated association of aggressiveness with testosterone in other species. Studies have demonstrated a direct relationship between testosterone in males and the sensation-seeking trait of Disinhibition (Daitzman & Zuckerman, 1980; Daitzman,

Zuckerman, Sammelwitz, & Ganjam, 1978), and Monotony Avoidance (Schalling, 1987). Testosterone also correlates with social extraversion (Daitzman & Zuckerman, 1980; Schalling, 1987).

The evidence from both normals and prisoner samples suggest that testosterone in both sexes is related to dominant sociability and interest in sex as well as sexual experience. In the prisoner samples, testosterone also seems to be associated with a high degree of unprovoked violence (Dabbs, Ruback, Frady, Hopper, & Sgoutas, 1988; Ehrenkrantz, Bliss, & Sheard, 1974; Mattson, Schalling, Olweus, Low, & Svensson, 1980; Rada, Laws, & Kellner, 1876). But in the normal population the association with aggressiveness of this type is not found; instead testosterone is associated with both the E and P dimensions, the latter through sensation-seeking and the capability for normal aggressiveness as a defensive reaction in adolescent boys (Olweus, 1987).

Monoamine Oxidase (MAO)

While the implications of platelet measures MAO for activity in the three mono-amine systems are not certain, its relationships to at least two major dimensions of personality are clear from a wealth of correlational data. Low MAO levels have been related to high levels of general activity in neonates during the first three days of life (Sostek, Sostek, Murphy, Martin, & Born, 1981), and high levels of social activity in adult humans (Coursey, Buchsbaum, & Murphy, 1979), and general and social activity in colony-dwelling monkeys (Redmond, Murphy, & Baulu, 1979). MAO has been found to be negatively correlated with extraversion or positively correlated with introversion scales in several studies, but not in some others. If we weigh the behavioral data more highly than the questionnaire findings, there does seem to be a relationship between MAO and the E or sociability dimension.

There also appears to be a relationship between MAO and some traits within the P dimension. In the Coursey *et al.* (1979) study contrasting high and low MAO types in the normal population, the low MAO group reported more convictions for criminal offenses and more alcohol and drug use. The low-MAO male monkeys in the Redmond *et al.* (1979) study engaged in more aggressive and sexual activity than the high MAO ones. General sensation-seeking and Monotony Avoidance scales have been found to be negatively correlated with MAO in males in a number of studies (see Zuckerman, 1987, for review). While the results are not always significant, and the correlations tend to be low, the total pattern confirms an inverse relationship between MAO and sensation seeking. To these personality trait findings we may add the fact that low MAO levels are also found in alcoholics and chronic marijuana users.

While the relation of MAO to sensation-seeking in particular and the E and P dimensions in general is clear, the mechanism is not. MAO is not a direct behavioral inhibitor or activator but only affects behavior through its effects on the monoamine systems. All we can infer is that the monoamine systems are somehow involved in the biological substrates for personality. Perhaps the role of MAO is one of regulating or stabilizing these systems in response to environmental stimulation. Bipolars, who already have low levels of MAO even in the depressed state, tend to shift to the manic state when given monoamine oxidase inhibitors, perhaps due to a buildup of dopamine with insufficient MAO to metabolize the neurotransmitters accumulating in the neurons.

Dopamine-beta-hydroxlase (DBH) is an enzyme involved in the conversion of dopamine to norepinephrine in the neuron. Plasma DBH has been found to be negatively related to sensation-seeking in several studies. Low DBH has been associated with severe psychopathic disorder in alcoholics (Major, Lerner, Goodwin, Ballenger, Brown, & Lovenberg, 1980) and emotionally disturbed boys (Rogeness, 1984). The relationship of DBH to the P dimension must be mediated through its limiting effect on production of norepinephrine. Perhaps there is a link with the low adrenergic levels which are predictive of adult criminality and aggressiveness (Olweus, 1987).

Neuropsychology

The designation of particular brain structures as the locus of personality traits is a dangerous flirtation with the type of thinking that produced 19th century phrenology. A structure like the amygdala contains many types of neurotransmitters, and different nuclei within the discernible structure mediate different functions.

Reward and Activity

On the assumption that the trait of extraversion is specifically associated with reward sensitivity or expectancy and activity, three dopamine systems in the brain are likely candidates to be involved with this trait, as well as having some involvement in sensation-seeking (Zuckerman, 1979). The A10 system originates in the ventral tegmentum and projects to the nucleus accumbens via the medial forebrain bundle (MFB). About 85% of the projections from ventral tegmentum to accumbens are dopaminergic (Stellar & Stellar, 1985). The MFB is a highly active site of self-stimulation reward effect, and the nucleus accumbens is the primary site of action for reward by stimulant drugs (Bozarth, 1987). Another dopamine system originates in the subtantia nigra (A9) and projects to the neostriatum, caudate nucleus, and putamen. This system is necessary for regulation of activity and is the one severally damaged in Parkinson's disease. It is also largely dopaminergic. The subtantia nigra and caudate also support brain stimulation (Stellar & Stellar, 1985). Projections from both systems reach the lateral and medial prefrontal cortex as well as limbic areas such as the septum and amygdala. Since the A10 system is vital in reward and the A9 in motivated activity, individual differences in their physiology could very well be the source for the activity and search for reward typical of extraversion and sensation-seeking.

Behavioral Inhibition

Gray suggested that the core of anxiety is a "behavioral inhibition system" (BIS) in which the underlying neurological substrate is the septohippocampal system. The function of the BIS is to check incoming stimuli against the memory of the previous experience with those stimuli. If the stimuli are novel or associated with past punishment, the system is activated producing arousal, inhibition of ongoing behavior, and orienting (diversion of attention) to the stimulus.

While inhibition is an immediate reaction involved in anxiety, it is also involved in other kinds of activity including approach behavior. Orienting to novel stimuli is not necessarily associated with anxiety. Strong orienting responses (ORs) have been positively associated with sensation-seeking and state anxiety seems to dampen ORs to neutral but novel stimuli (Zuckerman, 1990). The inhibition of behavior in an approach-avoidance conflict situation may be a function of anxiety, but it is also a function of the disinhibition tendency postulated to be the core of the P dimension. This is why Gray (in press) regards anxiety and psychopathy traits as the two ends of a bipolar dimension of personality.

The septohippocampal system may be more relevant for the disinhibition vs inhibition mechanism than for an anxiety mechanism and therefore more related to the P dimension than to the N dimension of personality. The inhibition mechanism, triggered by signals of punishment, would be weakened in persons with high P traits like impulsivity and sensation-seeking. Serotonin pathways may be the main ones involved in inhibition of behavioral approach.

Emotionality

Where then should we look for a locus for the system underlying general emotionality or N? The amygdala seems to be at the center of such a system. The amygdala has been called the "sensory gateway to the emotions" by Aggleton and Mishkin (1986). This term is used because this structure serves as the central target for converging inputs from several cortical processing areas involving all of the sensory modalities. The olfactory input is even more direct, reflecting the early evolutionary control of emotional and behavioral response from this modality. LeDoux (1987) points out that there are direct pathways between the thalamus and amygdala which would allow emotional reactions to stimuli before they are fully processed by higher centers in the hippocampus and cortex. The amygdala seems to serve as a comparator, as does the hippocampus, but probably begins the process at an earlier stage than the hippocampus. Human anxiety of the panic and generalized type is often triggered by unknown stimuli. The amygdala may respond to partial cues that cannot be identified in consciousness, perhaps accounting for its important role in classical fear-conditioning.

The temporal lobe is a major source of input to the amygdala. Reiman, Raichie, Robins, Mintun, Fusselman, Fox, Price, and Heikman (1989) used positron emission tomography on patients with panic disorders before and after lactate infusion. Those who panicked showed significant increases in regional blood-flow in the bilateral temperopolar cortex as well as deeper limbic structures. The original Kluver-Bucy (1939) effect of removal of the temporal lobes was produced by damage to the amygdala lying within them. The syndrome was one of "psychic blindness"; animals could perceive stimuli but seemed ignorant of their emotional significance. The operated animals were also usually tame (no fear of handlers) and did not show fear of snakes. The amygdala receives such information from the inferotemporal cortex via the entorhinal cortex, a region of limbic cortex that is the major source of input into the hippocampus. Many of the input sources for the amygdala are also sources of input for the hippocampus. LeDoux's (1987) view is that the hippocampus mediates the more cognitive aspects of emotions transmitting thoughts or memories to the amygdala for reappraisal of emotional significance. But is this role of the hippocampus in emotions a primary one, or just one of its memory-related functions? The amygdala seems to be more central to an emotion-generating system, and therefore a likely basis for the dimension of personality based on emotionality.

Behavior Genetics

The direction of this chapter has been downward from the social trait through the different levels of the biotypes to the genotypes. The usual question asked by behavior geneticists is the extent to which a behavioral or biological phenomenon is determined by heredity and to what extent by environment. Questions asked by the more sophisticated analyses concern the kinds of genetic mechanisms and environmental factors involved. Given that we do not inherit personality traits as such, what is it (the biological characteristic) that we do inherit that influences them?

Personality Traits

Various large-scale studies of identical twins (ITs) and fraternal twins (FTs) reared together, some involving thousands of each type, have shown a fair uniformity of results. For most broad traits, such as E, N, and P, the estimates of heritability range from 40 to 60% with the typical figure around 50%. Usually the correlation for ITs is about .50, while that for FTs ranges from 0 to .3. For E there is some evidence of non-additive genetic factors, as indicated by very low FT correlations. The heritability is the same for the N and P dimension traits, but the genetic mechanism is purely additive. The results suggest little effect of shared environment; the main environmental effects seem to be specific.

While the comparisons of twins raised together is valuable as an estimate of broad heritability, the separated twin studies make no assumptions about the similarity of shared environments in ITs and FTs. Two such recent studies (Pederson, Plomin, Mc-Clearn, & Friberg, 1988; Tellegen, Lykken, Bouchard, Wilcox, Segal, & Rich, 1988) used samples of ITs and FTs raised in separate families and larger twin samples raised together. Both studies used a model that allowed a test for non-additivity in the genetic variance and separated the environmental variance into shared and non-shared sources. Heritabilities for the broad E, N, and P factors ranged from 31% (for N in the Pederson *et al.* study) to 58% for the Constraint (P) factor in the Tellegen *et al.* study. Heritability was about 40 % for E in both studies, with some evidence for an influence of shared environmental variance (7–22%) and non-shared environmental influence (38–52%). E also showed some evidence of non-additive types of genetic variance (dominance or epistasis). N and P showed little influence of non-shared environment or non-additive types of genetic influence.

Biological Traits

While the heritability of personality traits is much higher than most psychologists dreamed of 20 years ago, it must be emphasized that personality traits are not directly inherited, but are only a manifestation of particular combinations of inherited biological traits. Since the latter are closer to the genotype we would expect higher heritabilities for them than for the behavioral traits which result from the interactions of our neurophysiological makeup with the environment. But this is only true to the extent that the particular biological factors are stable rather than reactive over a wide range to the day-to-day environmental contingencies. The enzymes that govern the production and metabolism of the neurotransmitters seem to be more stable than levels of the neurotransmitters themselves at any given time (at least using the indirect methods currently available for human studies).

MAO, as measured in blood platelets, is a fairly stable biological trait. Twin studies (summarized in Zuckerman, 1989, 1991) suggest uncorrelated heritabilities of 76 and 86% respectively for the enzymes DBH and MAO, but somewhat lower heritabilities for metabolites of norepinephrine, dopamine, and serotonin. Heritabilities for the brain evoked potentials, augmenting-reducing of EPs, and EEG spectrum characteristics are quite high (80–89%); but heritabilities for peripheral autonomic responses like skin conductance levels and reactivity (54–60%) and heart rate levels and reactivity (40–60%) are more moderate. The higher heritability of measures of brain activity than peripheral autonomic measures may reflect the more complex influences affecting the latter including central nervous functions and specific kinds of environmental factors (there was no effect of shared environment on these variables).

The results suggest that the heritability of personality probably depends on individual differences in neurotransmitters, particularly in regulating enzymes and their effects on the psychophysiology of the central nervous system. New methodologies, like the PET scan applied to twins, may aid in the identification of more of these central biological traits which constitute the building blocks of the biological foundation of personality.

Conclusions

The descent from the neat and reasonably discrete factors of personality traits has become more tortuous at each level, finally ending in the intricate maze of brain circuitry. As Crick (1988) has pointed out, simplicity cannot be the goal of biological research and this must be even more true of psychobiological research. Attempting to link structure, physiology, and function of biological mechanisms in humans from experimental research largely conducted on other species seems hopeless from the start. What begins by seeming complex turns out on further inspection to be even more complex rather than simple. There is precious little light in this twilight zone between the genotype and biosocial phenotype.

I have proposed that E and N personality traits are based on generalized cognitive expectancies for reward and punishment, while the traits in the P dimension are based on the capacity to inhibit behavior in the service of social adaptation or, conversely, the tendency to become disinhibited and impulsive in the pursuit of novel and intense sensations, and a disregard for social conventions. Underlying outcome expectancies are affect mechanisms like anxiety and positive affect, which are closer to the biological mechanisms of the limbic brain than cognitions. Most of the biochemical mechanisms are associated with more than one dimension of personality. There are no plus or minus signs attached to the arrows in Figure 1. The direction of involvement of a particular system trait may not be easily predictable because some of the relationships are curvilinear and the direction of relationship depends on which leg of the curve you are dealing with.

The situation is further complicated by horizontal interactions between neurotransmitter systems, not even shown in the diagram. The most problematic level is that of brain neurology. The strong involvement of dopamine in activity and reward implicates the brain pathways mediated by this neurotransmitter in E and P dimensions, although correlational evidence for this hypothesis is still lacking. The septal-hippocampal system is involved in inhibition and arousal, some of it produced by anxiety, but a weak system may underlie disinhibition in the P dimension. Psychopathy has been conceptualized as a "septal disinhibition disorder" (Gorenstein & Newman, 1980) and augmenter cats behave much like septal lesioned rats (Saxton *et al.*, 1987). Recent evidence places the amygdala at the hub of a system identifiable as general emotionality. The temporal cortex and entorhinal cortex are major sources of input to the system. The orbitofrontal cortex has inputs into both inhibitory and emotionality systems.

Most theorists attempting to formulate grand psychobiological theories conclude with a modest statement that most of what they are saying is bound to be proven wrong. If we cannot predict the outcome of future research, at least we can predict the failure of our own theories with some reliability. But there is also a hubris that suggests that much of it may be right, even if imprecise in the details. With the current pace of research in the neurosciences we should not have to wait too long to find out.

References

Aggleton, J. P., & Mishkin, M. The amygdala: Sensory gateway to the emotions. In *Emotion: Theory, research and experience*. Vol. 3. New York: Academic Press, 1986.

Ball, S. A., & Zuckerman, M. Sensation seeking, Eysenck's personality dimensions and reinforcement sensitivity in concept formation. *Personality and Individual Differences*, 1990, *11*, 343–353.

Barratt, E. S. Psychophysiological correlates of classical differential eyelid conditioning among subjects selected on the basis of impulsivity and anxiety. *Biological Psychiatry*, 1971, *3*, 339–346.

Barratt, E. S., Pritchard, W. S., Faulk, D. M., & Brandt, M. E. The relationship between impulsiveness subtraits, trait anxiety, and visual N100 augmenting/reducing: A topographic analysis. *Personality and Individual Differences*, 1987, *8*, 43–51.

Beyts, J., Frcka, I. M., & Levey, A. B. The influence of psychoticism and extraversion on classical eyelid conditioning using a paraorbital shock UCS. *Personality and Individual Differences*, 1983, *4*, 275–283.

Bozarth, M. A. Ventral tegmental reward system. In J. Engel *et al.* (Eds.), *Brain reward systems and abuse*. New York: Raven Press, 1987.

Brown, G. L., Ebert, M. H., Goyer, P. F., Jimerson, D. C., Klein, W. J., Bunney, W. E., & Goodwin, F. K. Aggression, suicide, and serotonin: Relationships to CSF amine metabolites. *American Journal of Psychiatry*, 1982, *139*, 741–746.

Brown, G. L., Goodwin, F. K., Ballenger, J. C., Goyer, P. F., & Major, L. F. Aggression in humans correlates with cerebrospinal fluid amine metabolites. *Psychiatry Research*, 1979, *1*, 131–139.

Buchsbaum, M. S., & Silverman, J. Stimulus intensity control and cortical evoked response. *Psychosomatic Medicine*, 1968, *30*, 12–22.

Buss, A. H., & Plomin, R. *Temperament: Early developing personality traits*. Hillsdale, NJ: Erlbaum, 1984.

Calhoon, L. L. Exploration into the biochemistry of sensation-seeking. *Personality and Individual Differences*, 1988, *9*, 941–949.

Cloninger, C. R. A systematic method for clinical description and classification of personality. *Archives of General Psychiatry*, 1987, *44*, 573–588.

Coursey, R. D., Buchsbaum, M. S., & Murphy, D. C. Platelet MAO activity and evoked potentials in the identification of subjects biologically at risk for psychiatric disorders. *British Journal of Psychiatry*, 1979, *194*, 372–381.

Crick, F. D. *What mad pursuit: A personal view of scientific discovery*. New York: Basic Books, 1988.

Dabbs, J. M., Ruback, R. B., Frady, R. L., Hopper, C. H., & Sgoutas, D. S. Saliva testosterone and criminal violence among women. *Personality and Individual Differences*, 1988, *9*, 269–275.

Daitzman, R., & Zuckerman, M. Disinhibitory sensation-seeking personality and gonadal hormones. *Personality and Individual Differences*, 1980, *1*, 103–110.

Daitzman, R., Zuckerman, M., Sammelwitz, P., & Ganjam, V. Sensation-seeking and gonadal hormones. *Journal of Biosocial Science*, 1978, *10*, 401–408.

Dorow, R., Duka, T., Holler, L., & Sauerbrey, N. Clinical perspectives of carbolines from first studies in humans. *Brain Research Bulletin*, 1987, *19*, 319–326.

Ehrenkranz, J., Bliss, E. S., & Sheard, M. H. Plasma testosterone: Correlation with aggressive behavior and social dominance in man. *Psychosomatic Medicine*, 1974, *36*, 469–475.

Eysenck, H. J. Extraversion and the acquisition of eyeblink and GSR conditioned responses. *Psychological Bulletin*, 1965, *63*, 258–270.

Eysenck, H. J. *The biological basis of personality*. Springfield, IL: Thomas, 1967.

Eysenck, H. J., & Eysenck, M. W. *Personality and individual differences: A natural science approach*. New York: Plenum, 1985.

Eysenck, S. B. G., & Eysenck, H. J. The place of impulsiveness in a dimensional system of personality description. *British Journal of Social and Clinical Psychology*, 1977, *13*, 57–68.

Eysenck, H. J., & Levey, A. Conditioning introversion-extraversion and the strength of the nervous system. In V. D. Nebylitsyn & J. A. Gray (Eds.), *Biological bases of individual behavior*. New York: Academic Press, 1972.

Fahrenberg, J. Concepts of activation and arousal in the theory of emotionality (neuroticism): A multivariate conceptualization. In J. Strelau & H. J. Eysenck (Eds.), *Personality dimensions and arousal*. New York: Plenum, 1987.

File S. The psychopharmacology of anxiety. In B. Breckon (Ed.), *Emotion and emotional disorders*. Reports on first Maudsley conference on new developments in psychiatry. Basle: Roche, 1988.

Frcka, G., Beyts, J., Levey, A. B., & Martin, I. The influence of psychoticism on classical conditioning. *Personality and Individual Differences*, 1983, *4*, 189–197.

Frcka, G., & Martin, I. Is there— or is there not— an influence of impulsiveness on classical eyelid conditioning? *Personality and Individual Differences*, 1987, *8*, 241–252.

Fulker, D. W., Eysenck, S. B. G., & Zuckerman, M. The genetics of sensation seeking. *Journal of Personality Research*, 1980, *14*, 261–281.

Gale, A., & Edwards, J. A. Individual differences. In M. G. H. Coles, E. Donchin, & S. W. Porges (Eds.), *Psychophysiology: Systems, processes, and applications*. New York: Guilford, 1986.

Goldring, J. F., & Richards, M. EEG spectral analysis, visual evoked potentials and the photic-driving correlates of personality and memory. *Personality and Individual Differences*, 1985, *6*, 67–76.

Gorenstein, E. E., & Newman, J. P. Disinhibitory psychopathology: A new perspective and a model for research. *Psychological Review*, 1980, *87*, 301–315.

Gorman, J. M., Fyer, M. R., Liebowitz, M. R., & Klein, D. F. Pharmacologic provocation of panic attacks. In H. Y. Meltzer (Ed.), *Psychopharmacology: The third generation of progress*. New York: Raven Press, 1987.

Gray, J. A. *The neuropsychology of anxiety: An enquiry into the functions of the septo-hippocampal system*. Oxford: Oxford University Press, 1982.

Gray, J. A. Neural systems, emotion, and personality. In J. Madden, S. Matthysee, & J. Barchas (Eds.), *Adaptation, learning and affect*. New York: Raven Press, in press.

Guidotti, A., Forchetti, C. M., Corda, M. G., Konkel, D., Bennett, C. D., & Costa, E. Isolation, characterization, and purification to homogeneity of an endogenous polypeptide with agonistic action on benzodiazepine receptors. *Proceedings of the National Academy of Science USA*, 1983, *80*, 3531–3535.

Hall, R. A., Rappaport, M., Hopkins, H. K., Griffin, R. B., & Silverman, J. Evoked response and behavior in cats. *Science*, 1970, *170*, 998–1000.

Hemming, J. H. Electrodermal indices in a selected prison sample and students. *Personality and Individual Differences*, 1981, *2*, 37–46.

Kluver, H., & Bucy, P. C. Preliminary analysis of the temporal lobes in monkeys. *Archives of Neurology and Psychiatry*, 1939, *42*, 979–1000.

Le Doux, J. E. Emotion. In F. Plum (Ed.), *Handbook of physiology: The nervous system*. Vol. 5. Bethesda, MD: American Physiological Society, 1987.

Lukas, J. H., & Siegel, J. Cortical mechanisms that augmenting or reduce evoked potentials in cats. *Science*, 1977, *196*, 73–75.

Lykken, D. T. A study of anxiety in the sociopathic personality. *Journal of Abnormal Psychology*, 1957, *55*, 6–10.

Major, L. F., Lerner, P., Goodwin, F. K., Ballenger, J. C., Brown, G. L., & Lovenberg, W. Dopamine-beta-hydroxylase in CSF. *Archives of General Psychiatry*, 1980, *37*, 308–310.

Mattson, A., Schalling, D., Olweus, D., Low, H., & Svensson, J. Plasma testosterone, aggressive behavior, and personality dimensions in young male delinquents. *Journal of the American Academy of Child Psychiatry*, 1980, *19*, 476–490.

Meyer, G. J., & Shack, J. R. Structural convergence of mood and personality: Evidence for old and new directions. *Journal of Personality and Social Psychology*, 1989, *57*, 691–706.

Newman, J. P., & Kosson, D. S. Passive avoidance learning in psychopathic and nonpsychopathic offenders. *Journal of Abnormal Psychology*, 1986, *95*, 252–256.

O'Gorman, J. G. Extraversion and the EEG I: An evaluation of Gale's hypothesis. *Biological Psychology*, 1984, *19*, 95–112.

O'Gorman, J. G., & Lloyd, J. E. M. Extraversion, impulsiveness, and EEG alpha activity. *Personality and Individual Differences*, 1987, *8*, 169–174.

Olweus, D. Testosterone and adrenaline: Aggressive antisocial behavior in normal adolescent males. In S. A. Mednick, T. E. Moffitt, & S. A. Stack (Eds.), *The causes of crime: New biological approaches*.

Panksepp, J. Toward a general psychobiological theory of emotions. *The Behavioral and Brain Sciences*, 1982, *5*, 407–422.

Pederson, N. L., Plomin, R., McClearn, G. E., & Friberg, L. Neuroticism, extraversion, and related traits in adult twins reared apart and reared together. *Journal of Personality and Social Psychology*, 1988, *55*, 950–957.

Pivik, R. T., Stelmack, R. M., & Bylsma, F. W. Personality and individual differences in spinal motoneuronal excitability. *Psychophysiology*, 1988, *25*, 16–24.

Rada, R. T., Laws, D. R., & Kellner, R. Plasma testosterone levels in the rapist. *Psychosomatic Medicine*, 1976, *38*, 257–258.

Redmond, D. E., Jr., Murphy, D. L., & Baulu, J. Platelet monoamine oxidase activity correlates with social affiliative and agonistic behaviors in normal rhesus monkeys. *Psychosomatic Medicine*, 1979, *41*, 87–100.

Reiman, E. M., Raichie, M. E., Robins, E., Mintun, M. A., Fusselman, M. J., Fox, P. T., Price, J. L., & Haikman, K. A. Neuroanatomical correlates of a lactate-induced anxiety attack. *Archives of General Psychiatry*, 1989, *46*, 493–500.

Robertson, H. A., Martin, I. L., & Candy, J. M., Differences in benzodiazepine receptor binding in Maudsley reactive and Maudsley nonreactive rats. *European Journal of Pharmacology*, 1978, *50*, 455–457.

Rogeness, G. A. Clinical characteristics of emotionally disturbed boys with very low activities of dopamine-beta-hydroxylase. *Journal of the American Academy of Child Psychiatry*, 1984, *23*, 203–208.

Saxton, P. M., Siegel, J., & Lukas, J. H. Visual evoked potential augmenting/reducing slopes in cats. 2. Correlations with behavior. *Personality and Individual Differences*, 1987, *8*, 511–519.

Schalling, D. Personality correlates of plasma testosterone levels in young adolescents: An example of person situation interaction? In S. Mednick, E. Moffit & S. A. Stack (Eds.), *The causes of crime: New biological approaches.* Cambridge: Cambridge University Press, 1987.

Schalling, D., Asberg, M., & Edman, G. *Personality and CSF monoamine metabolites.* Unpublished manuscript. Department of Psychiatry and Psychology, Karolinska Hospital and the Department of Psychology, University of Stockholm, Sweden, 1984.

Sostek, A. J., Sostek, A. M., Murphy, D. L., Martin, E. B., & Born, W. S. Cord blood amine oxidase activities relate to arousal and motor functioning in human newborns. *Life Sciences*, 1981, *28*, 2561–2568.

Soubrie, P. Reconciling the role of central serotonin neurons in human and animal behavior. *Behavioral and Brain Science*, 1986, *9*, 319–364.

Stein, L. Reward transmitters: Catecholamines and opioid peptides. In M. A. Lipton, A. Di Mascio, & K. F. Killam (Eds.), *Psychopharmacology: A generation of progress.* New York: Raven Press, 1978.

Stellar, J. R., & Stellar, E. *The neurobiology of motivation and reward.* New York: Springer, 1985.

Strelau, J., & Eysenck, H. J. (Eds.). *Personality dimensions and arousal.* New York: Plenum, 1987.

Tellegen, A. Structures of mood and personality and their relevance to assessing anxiety, with an emphasis on self-report. In A. H. Tuma & J. D. Maser (Eds.), *Anxiety and the anxiety disorders.* Hillsdale, NJ: Erlbaum, 1985.

Tellegen, A., Lykken, D. T., Bouchard, T. J., Wilcox, K., Segal, N., & Rich, A. Personality similarity in twins reared together and apart. *Journal of Personality and Social Psychology*, 1988, *54*, 1031–1037.

Van Praag, H. M. Biological suicide research: Outcome and limitations. *Biological Psychiatry*, 1986, *21*, 1305–1323.

Van Praag, H. M., Kahn, R. S., Asnis, G. M., Wetzler, S., Brown, S. L., Bleich, A., & Korn, M. L. Denosologation of biological psychiatry on the specificity of 5-HT disturbances in psychiatric disorders. *Journal of Affective Disorders*, 1987, *13*, 1–8.

Zajonc, R. B. Feeling and thinking: Preferences need no inferences. *Americal Psychologist*, 1980, *35*, 151–175.

Zuckerman, M. *Sensation seeking: Beyond the optimal level of arousal.* Hillsdale, NJ: Erlbaum, 1979.

Zuckerman, M. Sensation seeking: A comparative approach to a human trait. *The Behavioral and Brain Sciences*, 1984, *7*, 413–471.

Zuckerman, M. Biological connection between sensation seeking and drug abuse. In J. Engel & L. Oreland (Eds.), *Brain reward systems and abuse.* New York: Raven Press, 1987.

Zuckerman, M. Personality in the third dimension: A psychobiological approach. *Personality and Individual Differences*, 1989, *10*, 391–418.

Zuckerman, M. The psychophysiology of sensation seeking. *Journal of Personality*, 1990, *58*, 313–345.

Zuckerman, M. *The psychobiology of personality.* New York: Cambridge University Press, 1991.

Zuckerman, M., Buchsbaum, M. S., & Murphy, D. L. Sensation seeking and its biological correlates. *Psychological Bulletin*, 1980, *88*, 187–214.

Zuckerman, M., Kuhlman, D. M., & Camac, C. What lies beyond E and N? Factor analyses of scales believed to measure basic dimensions of personality. *Journal of Personality and Social Psychology*, 1988, *54*, 96–107.

9

Biochemical Variables in the Study of Temperament
Purposes, Approaches, and Selected Findings

Petra Netter

Introduction

The present chapter will be concerned with the question why biochemical measures are employed in psychological investigations of temperament and what additional information they can provide for understanding basic mechanisms of temperament-related functions or theories. Within the limited space available, no complete review can be provided; rather, the presentation will be restricted to selected findings on peripheral catecholamines and cortisol and on central neurotransmitters which will serve as examples for elucidating salient ideas.

When analyzing the aims of researchers envisaged when including biochemical measures into their publications on psychological processes, one has to be aware that only very few are explicitly directed toward investigation of temperament. But, as many authors have pointed out (Prior, Crook, Stripp, Power, & Joseph, 1986; Strelau, 1983), the term *temperament* has considerable overlap with dimensions of personality and with emotional, cognitive, and behavioral functions. The relevance of these psychological fields for research in temperament is outlined in several chapters of this book, and it is understood that without further definitions the reader will conceive temperament as referring to dimensions such as activity, reactivity, adaptability, or stability as encountered in several temperament scales and inventories (Strelau, 1983; Buss & Plomin, 1975; Thomas & Chess, 1968).

Since dimensions of intensity and spontaneity of a reaction, its duration and flexibility, as well as its positive or negative affect, are reflected in many other personality-

Petra Netter • Department of Psychology, University of Giesen, D-6300 Giesen, Federal Republic of Germany.

related functions, the biochemical correlates of these will also be relevant to temperament.

The following sections will demonstrate approaches for the study of biochemical variables. They will be divided according to reasons for including them and will report some selected findings of causal or at least correlational relations between biochemical and psychological variables.

Approaches to the Study of Biochemical Variables

If we consider possible approaches to studying psychobiochemical relationships, we may be guided by the two axes of state (S) versus trait (T) and psychological (P) versus biochemical (B) variables as outlined in Figure 1.

The six lines drawn between the four angles of the figure reflect approaches starting with either the psychological (P) or the biochemical (B) variable as the independent one as indicated by index 1 or 2, respectively. Examples for each of the approaches will be mentioned in the respective sections. Since temperament is the major goal of interest, the state variables of either P or B origin may be represented in the experiments as indicators of temperament (for example, cognitive, emotional, motivational, or motor actions (= P) or hormones, neurotransmitters, measures of metabolism (= B).

Most approaches, however, using experimental procedures instead of correlational ones, imply the application of a treatment which again can be either of a psychological nature, like a mental or emotional stressor predominantly designed to elicit psychological reactions, or of a biochemical nature such as drugs, hormones, or nutrients with a primarily somatic site of action. The intervening variable investigated usually is the temperamental trait or state of interest. Several purposes for including biochemical variables may be distinguished.

Explanation of Theories on Temperament

Many theories or constructs relating behavior to biological processes rely on biochemical investigations as, for instance, Zuckerman's sensation seeking construct or Eysenck's extraversion/introversion theory, Strelau's dimensions of temperament based on the Pavlovian concept of strength of the nervous system, Henry and Stephen's theory of dominance and submission, or Seligman's learned helplessness theory of depression. These may be grouped according to the population on which they are developed.

Theories Based on Psychological Observations in Humans

If biochemical investigations are based on healthy human subjects they usually start with a trait like extraversion or emotionality and explore the set of biochemical variables most likely associated with this trait. The dependent measures may be those of levels, i.e., trait-like stable tonic measures as depicted by approach a_1 in Figure 9.1. An example

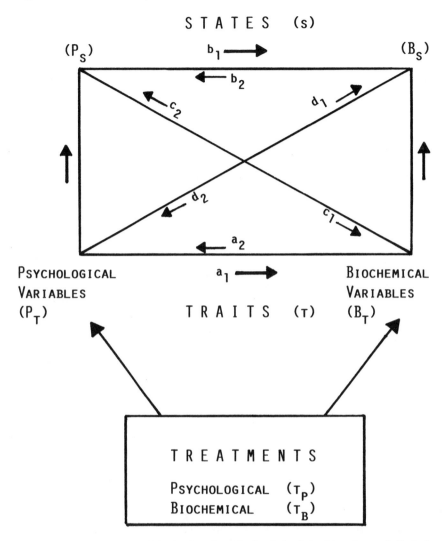

Figure 9.1. Approaches to the investigation of psychochemical relationships. Arrows indicate from which point researchers start when grouping their subjects: 1 = from psychological variables; 2 = from biochemical variables. B = biochemical, P = psychological variables or treatments. Index T or S = trait or state, respectively.

for this procedure would be the measurement of MAO B in blood platelets, which has been found to be lower in high sensation seekers than in lows (Zuckerman, 1983).

Another approach would be to apply treatments of psychological stressors or biochemical treatments like drugs eliciting states representative of traits (approach b_1 in Figure 9.1). This approach has been used by Eysenck applying sedative or stimulant drugs in order to make subjects more introvert or extravert in their cortical arousal system, although, in his work, measures of information processing and vigilance have been employed rather than biochemical measures as dependent variables. It is of course easier to change the quality of emotional states than actually to change the dimensions of temperament (speed, intensity, duration, and changeability of emotions).

Yet, the application of alcohol, tranquilizers, sedatives, and hypnotics may release neuronal inhibitory control and thus facilitate motor responses and slow down afferent arousal induced by sensory input, whereas caffeine, low doses of nicotine, and amphetamine-like substances would have opposite effects. These changes in input and output nervous reactivity may all be conceived as reflections of temperament.

In summary, in these theories based on healthy humans, biochemical measures are mainly used for *exploration* of the psychological construct under investigation with the purpose of elucidating its biological roots.

Theories Based on Biochemical Observations in Animal Models

A number of psychological theories have been developed on the basis of animal models in which by experimental manipulation of behavior or by chemical or mechanical lesions of the brain the concomitant biochemical or behavioral changes have been analyzed. An example is Henry and Stephens' (1977) theory of dominance and submission which claims that dominance is associated with the sympathetic-adrenomedullary system and submission with the hypothalamic-pituitary-adrenocortical function. When researchers try to look for a human behavior analogue of this model they may start by measuring cortisol and catecholamine levels and look for trait-like analogues of the social behavior observed in rats (approach a_2 in Figure 1). The more common approach, however, is to identify the psychological analogues of dominance and submission for instance by experimental induction of effort and distress. These showed the same biochemical correlates as the respective types of behavior in rats in an experiment conducted by Lundberg and Frankenhaeuser (1980): A factor analysis revealed that subjective distress was associated with high factor loadings on increase of cortisol, and that subjective feelings of effort rather loaded on a factor together with increase in adrenaline.

Seligman's theory of learned helplessness (Seligman, 1975) in which distress is defined as lack or loss of control was also investigated with respect to cortisol. Thus uncontrollable noise (Breier, Albus, Pichar, Zahn, Wolkowitz, & Paul, 1987) or experimentally induced failure (Netter, Croes, Merz, & Mueller, in press) could indeed be shown to raise cortisol levels in healthy subjects, demonstrating that animal models can be confirmed in experiments on humans.

A third theory less elaborate but also relating cortisol to aspects of temperament is the one put forward by Ursin (Ursin, Baade, & Levine, 1978) that the adrenocorticotropic hormone (ACTH) and consequently cortisol respond to change in expectancies derived from changes in environmental contingencies. This would mean that an increase in cortisol is rather an indicator of mismatch between external world and internal expectancies than a specific expression of distress. An experiment by Coover, Goldman, & Levine (1971) provided data on which this assumption was based: Animals trained to press a lever for food reward showed an increase in corticosterone when the reward was eliminated and a decrease when only the lever was eliminated but the food continued. Also other experiments performed by the same group (Levine & Coover, 1976) showed that a shift from predictable to unpredictable conditions was associated with increase in corticosterone and the reverse shift with no change in levels of the hormone.

The question whether controllability or predictability is the salient condition for increase in cortisol has also puzzled researchers coming from Seligman's (1975) theory of learned helplessness. Experiments performed by Overmier on dogs (Dess, Linwick, Patterson, Overmier, & Levine, 1983) suggested that controllability is the salient condition in the training phase for increase in cortisol and predictability in the test phase. Situational control as manipulated in these animal experiments has been related to personality theories such as the concept of type A or coronary-prone behavior (Friedman & Rosenman, 1975). Since control of environmental conditions and constant activity are the salient features of the type A personality, it was hypothesized that deprivation of control and action would mean a particular threat to these subjects, and it was indeed shown in an experiment by Frankenhaeuser, Lundberg, and Forsman (1980) that type A persons responded by higher cortisol increases when exposed to involuntary inactivity and type B persons when subjected to hard mental stress. These findings demonstrate that interactions between habitual aspects of temperament and situational ones have to be taken into account when aiming at *confirmation* of theories developed on animals in the human field.

Theories Based on Psychopathology

As in the old days of Kretschmer (1926) modern biological psychiatry also yields suitable models for extrapolating from psychopathology to normal variations in temperament. One example comes from research in depression where modern biochemical techniques revealed that "upregulation," i.e., increase in number and sensitivity of beta-receptors in the brain is a major biological change in depression (Sulser, 1979). Therefore, depletion of noradrenaline in the brain as a source of this process has been suspected to be responsible for or related to sadness in the normal range. Except for drug studies, it is, of course, hard to corroborate this hypothesis in healthy subjects, but peripheral noradrenaline or the noradrenaline metabolite MHPG in urine was taken as a substitute indicator of central nervous function and has been shown to be lower in level and less inducible by stress in neurotic depressed individuals than in well-adapted ones (Ballenger, Post, Jimerson, Lake, & Zuckerman, 1984; Frankenhaeuser, 1978).

A second parameter is cortisol, which has been observed to be elevated in some depressed patients (Depue, 1979). Therefore it was supposed that depressive states in healthy subjects would also be associated with high cortisol. This has been proven in field studies of subjects exposed to long-term uncontrollable life stress, such as a dying relative (Wolff, Friedman, Hofer, & Mason, 1964) or threatening uncontrollable disaster as experienced by the inhabitants of Three Mile Island (Schaeffer & Baum, 1984).

Similarly, the clinical observation of decreased levels of the serotonin metabolite 5-HIAA in cerebrospinal fluid of depressed patients having a history of particularly cruel attempts of suicide (Åsberg, Martensson, & Wägner, 1985) led to the theory of a genetically low synthesis or turnover of serotonin in brain cells in these patients and in psychopaths, alcoholics, and pathological aggressors (Coccaro, Siever, Klar, Maurer, Rubinstein, Cooper, Mohs, & Davis, 1989). Therefore, the hypothesis that lack of impulse control in nonpsychiatric subjects might be characterized by the same marker of low brain or blood platelet serotonin was tested and confirmed in several studies in which cerebrospinal fluid could be obtained from healthy subjects (Schalling, Åsberg, Edman, & Klinteberg, 1989; Schalling, Edman, & Åsberg, 1983) or in which responses to serotonergic drugs were used as tests for assessing sub- or supersensitivity of serotonin-receptors in the brain (Netter, Nowak, & Leithoff, 1988; Netter & Rammsayer, 1989; see next section).

The benefit of deriving one's hypotheses on biological correlates of temperament from psychopathology is twofold: gaining insight into biological markers and proving whether there is a linear continuum between psychopathology and normal behavior. Both these goals serve the purpose of *confirmation* of hypotheses derived from a different population.

Explanation of Underlying Biochemical Processes of Psychological Functions Indicative of Differences in Temperament

Growing interest in molecular processes of behavior has led researchers to explore the biochemical concomitants and mechanisms of psychomotor, cognitive, and emotional functions and of complex processes like coping behavior. Although the biochemical findings tend to elucidate these functions themselves rather than their temperamental aspects such as speed of onset, duration, flexibility, and intensity, a few examples may be mentioned where biochemical responses relate to these temperamental factors.[1]

It must be kept in mind, however, that one transmitter or hormone is involved in many functions and, conversely, one type of behavior is mediated by a variety of transmitters and peripheral biochemical variables.

Psychomotor Functions

Both alpha- and beta-adrenergic action of brain noradrenaline is known to induce motor behavior, i.e., to increase activity level in terms of temperament. Dopamine, however, besides inducing spontaneous activity, also affects flexibility or plasticity of behavior. In high concentrations it elicits stereotypies, and depletion of dopamine leads to tremor and rigor, as in Parkinson's disease (Mason, 1984). The type of behavior change is not only dose-dependent but also varies with localization of dopamine activity

---

[1]Motivational behavior, though thoroughly investigated in the fields of eating, sexual behavior, aggression, and harm avoidance, will not be treated separately, since it is partly represented in the theories presented in the first section, or is part of motor, emotional, or coping behavior.

in the brain: the cortex, the caudate nucleus, striatum, and deeper layers are organized in a hierarchical way contributing different steps in programming the order and sequence of behavior without or only with the help of external or proprioceptive cues (Cools, 1988). Thus, rigidity or spontaneity of motor behavior may also be guided by dopamine in the normal range.

The dopaminergic activity of the nucleus accumbens in the neostriatum is also responsible for converting emotional arousal into motor responses. This is mediated via concomitant activation of neostriatal GABAergic fibres and inhibition of those in lower layers of the brain providing a link between motor and emotional activity and plasticity.

Cognitive Functions

Cognitive styles such as the concept of impulsivity versus reflexivity, focused versus broad attention, or intentional versus incidental learning, have been conceived as reflections of temperament. An example demonstrating the aspect of cognitive flexibility may be given by experiments performed by Cools (1988). He could show that in case of reduced dopamine turnover or destruction of dopamine pathways in the striatum of the brain, animals lack the capacity to change their strategy in learning. The same has been observed in humans suffering from Parkinson's disease, which is associated with dopamine reduction in the basal ganglia. They lack the capacity of changing their strategy of thinking according to changing stimulus material. These "artificial" changes of temperament could indicate that, also in the normal range, the dimension of flexibility and adaptability may be related to the dopamine system.

Similarly, selectivity versus breadth of attention induced by nicotine versus scopolamine could be shown to be related to the acetylocholine system, which is possibly involved in habitual cognitive styles (Warburton & Wesnes, 1981).

Emotional Functions

Habitual differences in hedonic tone and intensity of emotional expression have always been linked to temperament and have been explored with respect to their biochemical correlates via experimental induction of emotions or via relating personality traits to biochemistry. Since positive emotions are related to the reward system in the brain, the role of opioids and dopamine has been investigated in relation to mood. Any kind of positive reinforcement seems to be associated with the release of beta-endorphin (Dum & Herz, 1987; Morley, 1983) and intracranial self-stimulation in rats, the classical animal model for investigating reward, has been shown to be associated with activation of dopaminergic fibers (Mason, 1984) and with activation of noradrenergic alpha-receptors (Stein, Wise, & Beluzzi, 1977).

In the periphery, examples for relationships to biochemistry may sometimes be found when constellations of catecholamines are inspected rather than absolute single values. Thus, in several evaluations subjects high in trait and state anxiety could be identified as exhibiting low noradrenaline and high adrenaline concentrations (Netter,

1983), whereas those who exhibited a high level of activity and self-confidence had the opposite constellation. These examples, of course, are far from advocating these measures as sensitive and reliable diagnostic instruments. Rather, they may serve to indicate the lines of research strategies and hypotheses for further experimentation.

Coping Processes

Coping strategies reflect types of emotional and behavioral control and therefore aspects of temperament. No matter whether the underlying processes are of a more conscious nature, like restraint, or unconscious mechanisms like denial. Wolff *et al.* (1964) have observed that in mothers of leukemic children destined to die within a limited period of time, the level of denial as rated by experienced interviewers was negatively correlated with the level of cortisol, and that shortly prior to death of the child when defense broke down, the cortisol level rose. Similarly, suppressed anger and overt aggression seem to differ with respect to their level of noradrenaline. Subjects scoring high on overt aggression tend to show lower levels of peripheral noradrenaline than those with low anger out scores (Mills, Schneider, & Dimsdale, 1989), a finding also observed in a large sample of hypertensives and healthy controls (Netter & Neuhaeuser-Metternich, 1988). One of the problems encountered in relating peripheral cortisol and catecholamines to these coping processes is that the relationship may sometimes only hold for a moderate level of defense, whereas after breakdown of the defense mechanism, resources of catecholamines and cortisol may be depleted, resulting in very low levels, as predicted by Selye's theory of the adaptation syndrome (Selye, 1950). Therefore, in some experiments, high cortisol as well as high catecholamine levels may be found in subjects who are in good control of a situation, whereas nonreactivity may be a sign of extreme exhaustion (Netter *et al.*, in press).

Explanation of Underlying Biochemical Processes of Somatic Response Differences Related to Temperament

Drug Responses

Numerous investigations report a great variability in drug response (for review, see Janke, 1983) the underlying basis of which is of interest to the investigator of temperament, since the detection of sub- or supersensitivity of brain or vascular receptors or of ion channel systems may explain velocity, intensity, and duration or flexibility of behavioral responses.

An example may be taken from our own experiments (Netter, 1989) where the biphasic action of nicotine was used to identify subjects who showed increases in vigilance at low doses and decreases at higher doses, whereas other subjects could not increase their cortical arousal by a low dose of nicotine, but only by a higher one. Inspection of personality characteristics of these subjects revealed that low nicotine sensitivity was associated with high sensory suggestibility as measured by a test battery developed by Gheorghiu (Gheorghiu, Hodapp, & Ludwig, 1975). The measure of sensory suggestibility seems to be related to broad as opposed to narrow attention (Warburton & Wesnes, 1981) and to the capacity of shifting from one state of mind to the other, as shown by EEG experiments in high and low hypnotizable subjects (Crawford, 1989) or by differences in perceptual shifts in high and low suggestible subjects (Kruse & Gheorghiu, unpublished data). This capacity of flexible shifting from one state of mind to the other can be viewed as an indicator of temperamental adaptability and flexibility on the cognitive level.

Psychophysiological Responses

Some psychophysiologists interested in the reactivity of the autonomic nervous system have investigated personality correlates of response differences which are also reflected in a variety of metabolic and endocrine parameters such as salivary response, changes of blood cell populations, blood glucose, triglycerides, and catecholamines (Fahrenberg, 1984).

Several papers have shown, however, that biochemical as well as physiological changes upon stress are sometimes lower in subjects characterized by high emotional reactivity as measured by questionnaires (Guski, 1976; Netter, 1987; Othmer, Netter, Golle, & Meyer, 1969), or they may be inadequate or delayed (Lienert & Netter, 1985). Again, the lack of adapting to the requests of a stressor may be indicative of the low flexibility of response systems in subjects reporting that they are easily emotionally aroused. The reason many researchers could not find associations between emotional responsivity and changes in single biochemical (and physiological) parameters (Fahrenberg, 1987) may be explained by the fact that systemic lack of the capacity to shift, and not intensity, speed, or duration of response, are associated with the temperament-related dimension of emotional reactivity.

Detection of Psychochemical Relationships in the Development of Psychosomatic Diseases Related to Temperament

Historical attempts to relate temperament to certain diseases like stroke or tuberculosis (*homo apoplecticus* and *homo phthisicus*) are revived by, for instance, the temperament-related concept of type-A personality (Friedman & Rosenman, 1975) and by the theory that unconscious conflicts may determine the development of predominantly parasympathetically or sympathetically induced diseases (Alexander, 1950). Modern biochemistry has tried to detect the underlying molecular pathways by which somatic stress or coping-induced processes may be mediated. For instance, the relation between type-A behavior and myocardial infarction may be explained by the vicious circle in which lack of oxygen supply due to sclerosis of coronary arteries in combination with type A-like search for control may lead to an increase in heart rate and to coronary pain and by this to an increase in anxiety which again, via output of adrenaline, will stimulate sympathetic activity of the organism and by increase of cortisol will facilitate thrombotic aggregation of platelets.

Also, associations between cancer and suppression of emotions, when exposed to unavoidable stressors of life (Eysenck, 1988), have been investigated biochemically by measuring immune responses after exposing animals to inescapable stress or humans to experimental conditions of uncontrollability (Lloyd, 1987). Suppression of lymphocyte proliferation in these situations may explain why growth of cancer is facilitated if subjects cannot cope adequately with a situation.

Heuristic Purposes

Most approaches of index 2 in Figure 9.1 do not easily provide hypotheses as to which psychological variables are expected to be associated with the biochemical measure. The reason is that biochemical responses have a much lower specificity for a certain stimulus than psychological ones. Therefore, studies starting from the biochemical response and looking for psychological correlates may sometimes have the nature of exploring the unknown. Good experimentalists in psychology usually detest this kind of approach which they call data-snooping or the "I-wonder-what-would-happen" approach; but it may provide valuable hypotheses for further research.

Since usually we do not deal with only a single parameter but with a bunch of biochemical responses, identification of patterns may provide the investigator with new sets of data for grouping subjects. By this approach, for instance, high adrenaline/high noradrenaline (A+/N+) responders and high adrenaline/low noradrenaline (A+/N−) responders were identified to reflect subjects with high activation and anxiety, respectively (Netter, 1983), and, in another study, constellations of A/N responses to pain of venipuncture were found to represent two different subtypes of the impulsivity personality pattern described by Eysenck's narrow impulsivity (A+/N+) and his risk-taking impulsivity (A+/N−) (Netter, 1988). These evaluations suggest that intraindividual relationships of monoamines can help to define temperamental groups of reactivity and that starting with the biochemical instead of with the psychological variable may help to establish new hypotheses.

Considerations of Validity

Validity of biochemical measures is threatened because of several reasons mentioned below.

1. Biochemical measures lack the specificity mentioned in the last section. Cortisol, for instance, is not only ambiguous with respect to whether its elevation reflects successful coping or inescapable stress, it is also influenced by nutritional, metabolic, immunological, hormonal, and circadian factors.
2. Sensitivity of the parameters depends on method of assessment: Lack of comparability between, for instance, fluorimetric, chemical detection, radioenzymatic, or mass spectrometry methods may all yield slightly different values of catecholamines.
3. For neurotransmitters there is no direct access to brain levels, and peripheral fluids like plasma or urine only reflect 5% of the brain turnover.

4. There is a rapid re-uptake into the nerve cell, and turnover, the salient parameter, may hardly be assessed.
5. There are many compensatory feedback loops between release of a transmitter and inhibition of its release by stimulation of autoreceptors. Therefore, levels of the metabolite in the cerebrospinal fluid may demonstrate high release in one instance or low re-uptake or high inhibition of a transforming enzyme in others.
6. There is no one-to-one relationship between a stimulus and a neurotransmitter and between a neurotransmitter and a behavioral response, so that the relationship established between transmitters and dimensions of temperament can only be described as the probability that, among other things, a certain transmitter is involved. The lack of stable relationships is further complicated by the fact that the same neurotransmitter may mediate different behaviors if released in different brain areas.

Furthermore, when considering the inclusion of biochemical variables into our analysis of temperament we have to be careful to separate: (1) Different parameters (latency, amplitude, duration, and gradient); (2) consistency across time, across situations, and across persons; and (3) measures indicating levels and those indicating responses.

Conclusions

Although it is very premature to provide any suggestions as to what biochemical measures and parameters might be suitable for assessing aspects of temperament described in other chapters of this book, a crude, tentative summary is given in Table 1.

Although authors of temperament scales and theories will disagree about setting equivalent certain terms and dimensions, the rough grouping tries to relate some subcategories of temperament to certain aspects of peripheral and central biochemical indicators of psychological processes. We are far from being able to describe any aspect of temperament by concomitant biochemical changes, but for some of them, such as impulsivity or plasticity of motor or cognitive control, more detailed information is available, while for others, such as persistence, almost nothing is known about biochemical indicators.

In summary, given the unreliability and unfavorable signal to noise ratio of biochemical variables encountered in temperament research, what recommendations may the researcher receive before starting his/her investigation? The tentative advices are:

1. To go back to a very molecular level.
2. To derive hypotheses from physiological knowledge, and, if it is not possible to test them in the human, an animal model should be used.
3. To apply pharmacological techniques of blockade and stimulation in humans which are used for animal or *in-vitro* experimentation.
4. To aggregate data from approaches based on trait versus trait investigations and create states that mimic traits by experimental treatments, and to modify traits by treatments.
5. To use cross validation by starting from groups defined according to psychologi-

Table 9.1. Possible Biochemical Indicators of Aspects of Temperament Described in Different Theories

Dimension of temperament	T & C	B & P	S	R	Biochemical variables	Parameters
Approach/withdrawal	+				catecholamines (plasma), ACTH, cortisol	level, response / relationship between / the two systems
Sociability		+				
Ergonicity, social				+		
Activity level		+		+	NA, A (plasma), any indicators of sympathetic arousal	ratio, level, amplitude, duration, number of variables
Ergonicity, object-related				+		
Intensity	+					
Strength of excitation			+		NA, DA (CNS)	level, turnover
Strength of inhibition			+			
Plasticity			+	+	DA (CNS)	level
Mobility	+				any (plasma)	return to baseline
Adaptation	+					no ISR, no SSR = bad adaptation / SSR-pattern = flexible, good adapt.; ISR = rigid
Flexibility/Rigidity	+					
Rhythmicity	+				cortisol, ACTH, 5-HT	regularity of chronobiological pattern
Impulsivity		+			5-HT	level, receptor sensitivity
Distractibility	+				NA, DA, ACh (CNS)	level? turnover?
Persistence	+				NA?	
Speed				+	any (plasma)	latency
Lability			+		NA, DA, 5-HT (CNS)	turnover
Emotionality	+				catecholamines (plasma, CNS)	threshold
Emotional reactivity			+	+	catecholamines, ACTH, cortisol (plasma)	levels, ratios or configurations of / NA & A level, turnover
Mood	+				NA, DA, opioids (CNS)	

NA = noradrenaline; A = adrenaline, 5-HT = serotonin, DA = dopamine; ACh = acetylcholine; ACTH = adrenocorticotropic hormone; CNS = central nervous system; ISR = individual specific response; SSR = stimulus-specific response.
T & C = Thomas & Chess; B & P = Buss & Plomin; S = Strelau; R = Rusalov.

cal traits (or traits plus treatment) and by starting from biochemical response groups and by checking if the same results can be found.

6. To use all combinations of parameters for predicting individual differences, i.e., single levels and responses, patterns of different cross-sectional responses, patterns of single responses across time and across situations, and, if possible, temporal patterns of patterns of parameters.

7. To group subjects according to intraindividual predictability, i.e., according to intraindividual covariation between biochemical and temperament data accumulated across time and to compare predictable individuals to nonpredictable ones.

Since temperament is that part of a person's psychological characteristics which is early detectable and genetically determined to a large extent, the search for physiological and biochemical correlates is certainly not altogether useless. Better biochemical methods of assessment and growing interest in interdisciplinary research in the field of personality research and individual differences will presumably yield more detailed knowledge about the biochemistry of temperament in the near future.

References

Alexander, F. *Psychosomatic medicine*. New York: Norton, 1950.

Åsberg, M., Martensson, B., & Wägner, A. Biochemische Indikatoren für die Funktion von Serotonin bei affektiven Erkrankungen. In H. Hippius & N. Matussek (Eds.), *Differentialtherapie der Depression: Möglichkeiten und Grenzen*. Basel: Karger, 1985.

Ballenger, J. C., Post, R. M., Jimerson, D. C., Lake, R., & Zuckerman, M. Neurobiological correlates of depression and anxiety in normal individuals. In R. M. Post & J. C. Ballenger (Eds.), *Neurobiology of mood disorders*. Baltimore: Williams & Wilkins, 1984.

Breier, A., Albus, M., Pichar, D., Zahn, T. P., Wolkowitz, O. M., & Paul, S. M. Controllable and uncontrollable stress in humans: Alterations in mood and neuroendocrine and psychophysiological function. *American Journal of Psychiatry*, 1987, *144*, 1419–1425.

Buss, A. H., & Plomin, R. *Temperament: Early developing personality traits*. Hillsdale, NJ: Erlbaum, 1984.

Coccaro, E. F., Siever, L. J., Klar, H., Maurer, G., Rubinstein, K., Cooper, T. B., Mohs, R. C., & Davis, K. L. Serotonergic studies in affective and personality disorder patients: Correlates with behavioral aggression and impulsivity. *Archives of General Psychiatry*, 46, 587–599.

Cools, A. R. Transformation of emotion into motion: Role of mesolimbic noradrenaline and neostriatal dopamine. In D. Hellhamner, I. Florin, & H. Weiner (Eds.), *Neurobiological approaches to human disease*. Stuttgart: Hans Huber, 1988.

Coover, G. D., Goldman, L., & Levine, S. Plasma corticosterone increases produced by extinction of operant behavior in rats. *Physiology and Behavior*, 1971, *6*, 261–263.

Crawford, H. J. Cognitive and physiological flexibility: Multiple pathways to hypnotic responsiveness. In V. A. Gheorghiu, P. Netter, H. J. Eysenck, & R. Rosenthal (Eds.), *Suggestion and suggestibility*. Heidelberg: Springer, 1989.

Depue, R. A. (Ed.), *The psychobiology of depressive disorders*. New York: Academic Press, 1979.

Dess, N. K., Linwick, D., Patterson, J., Overmier, J. B., & Levine, S. Immediate and proactive effects of controllability and predictability on plasma cortisol in dogs. *Behavioral Neuroscience*, 1983, *97*, 1005–1016.

Dum, J., & Herz, A. Opioids and motivation. *International Science Reviews*, 1987, *12*, 181–190.

Eysenck, H. J. The respective importance of personality, cigarette smoking, and interaction effects for the genesis of cancer and coronary disease. *Personality and Individual Differences*, 1988, *9*, 453–464.

Fahrenberg, J. Psychophysiological individuality: A pattern analytic approach to personality research and psychosomatic medicine. In S. Rachman & T. Wilson (Eds.), *Advances in behavior research and therapy*. Vol. 8. London: Pergamon, 1986.

Fahrenberg, J. Concepts of activation and arousal in the theory of emotionality (neuroticism): A multivariate conceptualization. In J. Strelau & H. J. Eysenck (Eds.), *Personality dimensions and arousal*. New York: Plenum, 1987.

Frankenhäuser, M. Psychoneuroendocrine approaches to the study of emotion as related to stress and coping. *Nebraska Symposium on Motivation*, 1978, *26*, 126–161.

Frankenhaeuser, M., Lundberg, U., & Forsman, L. Note on arousing type A persons by depriving them of work. *Journal of Psychosomatic Research*, 1980, *24*, 45–47.

Friedman, M., & Rosenman, R. H. *Der A Typ und der B Typ*. Hamburg: Rowohlt, 1975.

Gheorghiu, V. A., Hodapp, V., & Ludwig, C. M. Attempt to construct a scale for the measurement of the effect of suggestion on perception. *Educational Psychology Measurement*, 1975, *35*, 341–352.

Guski, R. Psychophysiologische Korrelate der emotionalen Labilität. *Zeitschrift für Experimentelle und Angewandte Psychologie*, 1976, *23*, 586–604.

Henry, J. P., & Stephens, P. M. *Stress, health, and the social environment*. New York: Springer, 1977.

Janke, W. (Ed.), *Response variability to psychotropic drugs*. Oxford: Pergamon, 1983.

Kretschmer, E. *Körperbau und Charakter* (5th ed.). Berlin: Springer, 1926.

Levine, S., & Coover, G. D. Environmental control of suppression of the pituitary-adrenal system. *Physiology and Behavior*, 1976, *17*, 35–37.

Lienert, G. A., & Netter, P. Die Konfigurationsfrequenzanalyse XXIb: Typenanalyse bivariater Verlaufskurven von Hyper- und Normotonikern. *Zeitschrift für Klinische Psychologie, Psychopathologie und Psychotherapie*, 1985, *33*, 77–88.

Lloyd, R. *Exploration in psychoneuroimmunology*. New York: Grune & Stratton, 1987.

Lundberg, U., & Frankenhäuser, M. Pituitary-adrenal and sympathetic adrenal correlates of distress and effort. *Journal of Psychosomatic Research*, 1980, *24*, 125–130.

Mason, S. T. *Catecholamines and behavior*. London: Cambridge University Press, 1984.

Mills, P. J., Schneider, R. H., & Dimsdale, J. E. Anger assessment and reactivity to stress. *Journal of Psychosomatic Research*, 1989, *33*, 379–382.

Morley, J. E. Neuroendorine effects of endogenous opioid peptides in human subjects: A review. *Psychoneuroendocrinology*, 1983, *8*, 361–379.

Netter, P. Activation and anxiety as represented by patterns of catecholamine levels in hyper- and normotensives. *Neuropsychobiology*, 1983, *10*, 148–155.

Netter, P. Psychological aspects of catecholamine response patterns to pain and mental stress in essential hypertensive patients and controls. *Journal of Clinical Hypertension*, 1987, *3*, 727–742.

Netter, P. Brain systems as mediators between behavior and bodily disease: Implications from a psychological viewpoint. In D. Hellhamner, J. Florin, & H. Weiner (Eds.), *Neurobiological approaches to human disease*. Stuttgart: Hans Huber, 1988.

Netter, P. Sensory suggestibility: Measurement, individual differences, and relation to placebo and drug effects. In V. A. Gheorghiu, P. Netter, H. J. Eysenck, & R. Rosenthal (Eds.), *Suggestion and suggestibility*. Heidelberg: Springer, 1989.

Netter, P. Aggression as a modulating factor in dopamine related drug effects on cortical and emotional arousal. *Personality and Individual Differences*, in press.

Netter, P., Croes, S., Merz, P., & Müller, M. Emotional and cortisol response to uncontrollable stress. In C. D. Spielberger, I. G. Sarason, J. Strelau, & J. Brebner, (Eds.), *Stress and anxiety*. Vol. 13. Washington: Hemisphere, in press.

Netter, P., & Neuhäuser-Metternich, S. *Aggression, hypertension, and catecholamine response*. Paper presented at the meeting of the 3rd European Conference on Personality, Stockholm, June, 1988.

Netter, P., Nowak, R., & Leithoff, G. Ritanserin, a 5-HT$_2$ blocker with personality dependent agonistic effects? *XVIth CINP Congress Abstracts*, 1988, 244.

Netter, P., & Rammsayer, T. Performance, motivation and personality dimensions as instruments for detecting mechanisms of action of a 5-HT$_2$ receptor antagonist. *Pharmacopsychiatry*, 1989, *22*, 210.

Othmer, E., Netter, P., Golle, R., & Meyer, A. E. Autonome Steuerung bei psychischen und vegetativen Extremlagen. *Zeitschrift für Experimentelle und Angewandte Psychologie*, 1969, *16*, 307–333.

Prior, M., Crook, G., Stripp, A., Power, M., & Joseph, M. The relationship between temperament and personality: An exploratory study. *Personality and Individual Diffrences*, 1986, *7*, 875–881.

Schaeffer, M. A., & Baum, A. Adrenal cortical response to stress in Three Mile Island. *Psychosomatic Medicine*, 1984, *46*, 227–238.

Schalling, D., Åsberg, M., Edman, G., & Klinteberg, B. Lack of behavioral constraint—The shared variance between impulsivity and aggressivity and its biochemical correlates. *Personality and Individual Differences*, 1989, *10*, VII (abstract).

Schalling, D., Edman, G., & Åsberg, M.Impulsive cognitive style and inability to tolerate boredom: Psychobiological studies of temperamental vulnerability. In M. Zuckerman (Ed.), *Biological bases of sensation seeking, impulsivity, and anxiety*. Hillsdale, NJ: Erlbaum, 1983.

Seligman, M. E. *Helplessness: On depression, development, and death*. San Francisco, CA: Freeman, 1975.

Selye, H. Stress and general adaptation syndrome. *British Medical Journal*, 1950, *1*, 1383–1392.

Stein, L., Wise, C. D., & Beluzzi, J. D. Neuropharmacology of reward and punishment. In L. L. Iversen, S. D. Iversen, & S. H. Snyder (Eds.), *Drugs, neurotransmitters, and behavior*. New York: Plenum, 1977.

Strelau, J. *Temperament—personality—activity*. London: Academic Press, 1983.

Sulser, F. New perspectives on the mode of action of antidepressant drugs. *Trends in Pharmacological Sciences*, 1979, *1*, 92–94.

Thomas, A., Chess, S., & Birch H. G. *Temperament and behavior disorders in children*. New York: New York University Press, 1968.

Ursin, H., Baade, E., Levine, S. (Eds.), *Psychobiology of stress*. New York: Academic Press, 1978.

Warburton, M., & Wesnes, K. Cholinergic mechanisms and attentional dysfunction. In C. Perris, G. Struwe, & B. Jansson (Eds.), *Biological psychiatry*. Amsterdam: Elsevier, 1981.

Wolff, C. T., Friedman, S. B., Hofer, M. A., & Mason, J. W. Relationship between psychological defenses and mean urinary 17-hydroxycorticosteroid excretion rates. *Psychosomatic Medicine*, 1964, *26*, 576–591.

Zuckerman, M. A biological theory of sensation-seeking. In M. Zuckerman (Ed.), *Biological bases of sensation seeking, impulsivity, and anxiety*. Hillsdale, NJ: Erlbaum, 1983.

10

Temperament and the Person-Situation Debate

Guus L. Van Heck

A Paradigm Crisis in Personality Psychology

The last two decades were a period of crisis and critical self-examination for Western personality psychology. Until the late 1960s, by far the most prominent model of personality was the dispositional model reflecting the conviction that a person's strivings, beliefs, feelings, typical ways of behaving, etc., could be condensed in a rather limited set of personality traits. In this model it was further assumed that these traits are stable and consistent enough to be powerful predictors, not only of general behavioral trends across time and across situational domains, but also of single reactions in specific situations (see, e.g., Ozer, 1986).

At the end of the 1960s, however, doubts increasingly arose concerning the usefulness of dispositions and traits. The continuous confrontation especially with limited success in predicting behavior in specific situations added fresh fuel to this critical attitude. Initially, the criticism was rather modest (Hunt, 1965; Peterson, 1968; Vernon, 1964); but the publication of Mischel's (1968) *Personality and Assessment* was a full-blown frontal attack.

Mischel's Attack on the Generality of Behavior

Mischel (1968, 1969) claimed that existing research showed impressive evidence that correlations between a particular behavior (indicator for trait A in a particular situation) and a second behavior (also an indicator of A) in another situation were usually less than .30. According to Mischel, on virtually all nonintelligence-related dispositional

---

Guus Van Heck • Department of Psychology, Tilburg University, 5000 LE Tilburg, The Netherlands.

measures, substantial changes occur in personal characteristics longitudinally over time and, especially, across seemingly similar settings cross-sectionally. For that reason, only modest links—ironically labeled "personality coefficients" by Mischel—should be expected; not only between two behaviors that according to theory reflect the same trait, but also between scores on an "omnibus" questionnaire for a particular trait and non-self-report measures of the same trait.

In his critical review Mischel (1968) pointed at the strong situational control of behavior. Therefore, he argued that in predicting behavior the emphasis should be on observable, specific stimulus conditions, rather than on broad intrapsychic dispositions.

Mischel's (1968) publication generated an upsurge of an old debate about the relative value of situationist and personological models in personality, which took place in the 1930s (e.g., Allport, 1937; Hartshorne & May, 1928; Newcomb, 1929). Again, at the center of the controversy was the question whether behavior that is described by a particular trait is relatively stable from situation to similar situation, and at the same time consistently manifested in different situations (e.g., Alker, 1972; Block, 1977; Endler & Magnusson, 1976; Epstein,1979, 1980; Hogan, DeSoto, & Solano, 1977; Mischel, 1968, 1969).

Outcomes of the Person-Situation Debate

The attack on the trait model elicited a plethora of reactions (see, e.g., Epstein & O'Brien, 1985; Hettema & Kenrick, 1989; Kenrick & Funder, 1988; West, 1983). Some defended the generality of trait-related behaviors across situations by accusing Mischel of intolerable selectivity in his review (Block, 1977; Craik, 1969). Others suggested various reconceptualizations of the original trait model, or propagated a paradigmatic shift by introducing alternative, non-dispositional models.

First, the revival of the person-situation controversy gave new impulses to the moderator variable approach. Self-reported consistency (Bem & Allen, 1974), observability (Kenrick & Stringfield, 1980), and trait relevance (Zuckerman, Koestner, DeBoy, Garcia, Maresca, & Sartoris, 1988) have been tested with varying success (see also Amelang & Borkenau, 1986; Chaplin & Goldberg, 1985; Cheek, 1982; Paunonen & Jackson, 1985; Van Heck, Janssen, & Lamberts, 1986). Second, Epstein (1979, 1980) suggested refraining from trying to predict single instances of behavior. This "solution" boils down to the use of aggregation procedures to predict behavior averaged over situations and occasions. Third, Buss and Craik (e.g., 1983, 1984) reconceptualized traits in terms of trends of overt behaviors, which trends can subsequently be used as predictors of future global act trends. Fourth, Wright and Mischel (1987, 1988) challenged the tendency to exclude contextual referents from dispositional constructs, and called attention to the view that traits summarize specific condition-behavior contingencies.

It is impossible to imagine personality psychology today without these moderator, aggregation, act frequency, and conditional, context-dependent approaches. Besides these "adjustments," however, other lessons have emerged from the controversy (cf. Kenrick & Funder, 1988), such as a growing awareness of systematic sources of judgmental bias, systematic effects of situations, and systematic interactions between persons and situations.

Several methodological frameworks have been suggested which permit the identification and examination of these systematic sources of lawful behavioral variability. First, taking factor-analytic experimental designs as his point of departure, Cattell (1979, 1982, 1988) has proposed a multidimensional data relations matrix aimed at finding quantitative laws predicting significant connections between the various vectors of the model, viz. traits, states, roles, environmental backgrounds, focal stimuli, response types, and observers. Ozer (1986) has specified a conceptual framework with five basic concepts: (1) persons, (2) situations, (3) time, (4) response classes, and (5) behavioral frequency, intensity, or saliency. He proposes the use of generalizability theory (Cronbach, Gleser, Nanda, & Rajaratnam, 1972) for studying the internal relations. Generalizability theory also takes a central place in Hettema's (1989b) conceptual framework for viewing various types of stability and consistency. Finally, within the context of research on temperament, Plomin and Daniels (1984) described a general approach for the analysis of person-environment interactions using hierarchical multiple regression, permitting analyses of continuous variation.

So, the last upturn of the person–situation debate has had important implications for the field of personality, which has, according to Kenrick and Dantchik (1983, p. 300), " . . . risen from its funeral pyre adorned with new and colorful plumage." One of the most salient implications is the *interactionist* invasion of personality.

According to Kenrick and Dantchik (1983), the dynamic interactionist position can be summarized as follows: First, the individual selects environments to play out personal characteristics. Second, the characteristics of the individual can reciprocally alter the environment. Third, neither personality factors alone, nor situational factors alone, are sufficient in predicting behavior; both must be considered jointly. Finally, the pattern of the individual's responses to situations in a particular domain is idiosyncratic. So, crucial in interactionism is the notion of *reciprocal, dynamic, transactional interactions* (Buss, Gomes, Higgins, & Lauterbach, 1987; Emmons, Diener, & Larsen, 1986; Endler, 1983; Hettema, 1979; Magnusson, 1980; Mischel, 1977; Secord, 1977).

In the next paragraph, I will discuss the role of *temperament* variables in the person–situation debate. In particular, I will examine to what extent temperament has attracted the attention of attackers and defenders of the dispositional model. The attention received is rather modest, due not least to the fact that the temperament approach never was within the mainstream of American psychology of personality (cf. Endler, 1989).

Mischel (1968), in questioning the generality and especially the transsituational consistency of traits, made an explicit exception for intelligence and intelligence-related concepts such as cognitive styles. No exceptional position, however, was claimed for temperament variables. As a matter of fact, "temperament" is not one of the entries in the subject index of Mischel's (1968) book. This is rather astonishing since it is not too far-fetched to expect relatively greater stability and consistency in the case of temperament variables as compared with nontemperamental personality traits. One has only to point to the major characteristics of temperament variables. Temperament refers to those traits or mechanisms which (1) form the biological basis of personality, (2) reflect style rather than content of behavior, and (3) have a high heritability (e.g., Buss & Plomin, 1984; Goldsmith, 1983; Goldsmith, Buss, Plomin, Rothbart, Thomas, Chess, Hinde, & McCall, 1987; Strelau, 1983, 1987). All three characteristics could lead to more generality of behavior than, by and large, will be found for personality variables with a lower heritability, which are not so clearly biologically based, and which are more content-oriented. Let us see what is known about the stability and consistency of temperament variables.

Stability of Temperament

With respect to stability, Buss and Plomin (1984) state that emotionality, activity, and sociability appear to be "among the most stable personality traits" (p. 146). They support this assertion by pointing to long-term longitudinal research (e.g., Buss & Plomin, 1975; Halverson & Waldrop, 1976; McDevitt & Carey, 1978; see also Beckwith, 1979, for a detailed review).

According to Buss and Plomin (1984), in the case of emotionality, moderate stability has been found for relatively short periods, viz. from 11 to 32 months/21 to 32 months, or 3-year periods from 6 to 9, 9 to 12, or 12 to 15 years. Then, all coefficients are in the .33–.66 range. However, for a longer 9-year period from 6 to 15 years, correlations are more modest, all in the .15–.44 range. Concerning activity level, stability coefficients are in excess of .45. Sociability—"the most stable of the temperaments" (Buss & Plomin, 1975, p. 118)—appears to stabilize increasingly during childhood. For 2-year periods early in life (e.g., from 2 to 4, or from 4 to 6 years) an appropriate summary statement is that stability varies from about .35 to about .50. For adolescence and adulthood the range is about .45 to about .65. Recently, Kagan (1989) compared shy and emotionally subdued children with consistently sociable and affectively spontaneous children. A moderate but significant preservation of these inhibited and uninhibited behavioral styles was found from the first assessments, at either 21 or 31 months, through 7½ years of age.

Besides emotionality, activity, sociability, and temperamental inhibition, the stability of other temperament variables has been studied. The following results give an idea of the extent of their stability.

Costa, McCrae, and Arenberg (1980) reported retest coefficients for temperamental traits measured by the Guilford-Zimmerman Temperament Survey at 6- and 12-year intervals. Results showed stability coefficients ranging from .59 to .87. Costa and McCrae (1977), using the 16PF, found that 10-year coefficients ranged from .70 to .84 for extraversion and from .58 to .69 for neuroticism. Using their own NEO Personality Inventory, comparable results were obtained (Costa & McCrae, 1988). Conley (1984) reported moderate longitudinal stability in the .40–.45 range for neuroticism and introversion-extraversion across several decades of adult life.

Summarizing, it can be said that temperament variables show moderate to high stability across time.

Transsituational Consistency of Temperament

A great deal of the evidence for transsituational specificity in personality psychology arose out of variance components studies in which the percentages of variance due to persons, situations, responses, and interaction effects were determined. A major role in this type of research was played by stimulus–response inventories (cf. Endler, Hunt, & Rosenstein, 1962). Some years ago, Furnham and Jaspars (1983) published a critical analysis and comparative review of nearly all studies (over 30) in which this type of instrument and this method of analysis were used. None of the reviewed studies, however, focused on a temperament variable. As far as I know, there is only one study, missed by Furnham and Jaspars, which features a temperament variable. In 1980, Lantermann reported a study featuring an S–R Questionnaire of Extraversion with situations and reactions based on Eysenck's (e.g., 1963) theoretical framework. For groups of self-reported consistent and variable subjects, Lantermann found that the magnitude of the triple Persons × Situations × Responses (PSR) interaction was 4.00 and 14.98%, respectively. The less complex interaction terms showed very modest P × S effects (2.23 and 4.17%, respectively, for consistent and variable subjects) and rather substantial P × R interactions (24.88 and 11.98, respectively). Compared with the main effect of Persons (13.82% for consistent subjects; 11.22% for variable subjects), these interactions are rather substantial.

Thus, the outcomes of the Lantermann (1980) study provide, at least for those persons who describe themselves as variable, evidence for the existence of a certain degree of situation specificity for extraversion. It is self-evident that the extreme scarcity of studies dealing explicitly with transsituational consistency does not permit to formulate far-reaching conclusions. It can be expected that in the near future the current growing interest for interactionist approaches within the study of temperament—an interest that is growing despite the absence of systematic interaction studies of the sort described above (see also Endler, 1989)—will stimulate (1) the construction of temperament scales that take account of the influence of situational factors, and (2) the use of experimental designs that make it possible to scrutinize the cross-situational consistency of temperamental variables.

Temperament and the Interactionist Approach to Personality

One of the questions in the roundtable "What Is Temperament?" (Goldsmith *et al.*, 1987) was "To what extent do you consider temperament to be a personological versus a relational or interactive construct?" The discussion reflects a growing tendency toward interactive conceptualizations. This takes two forms. First, there is the use of the "goodness-of-fit" concept, or concepts such as "match" and "mismatch." These concepts reflect consonances and dissonances between (1) environmental opportunities, expectations, and demands, and (2) the temperament characteristics of the person. Discrepancies between person and environment are seen as antecedents of distorted psychological development (e.g., Lerner, 1984; Thomas & Chess, 1977). Second, it is increasingly recognized that temperament variables play an important role in the elicitation of reactions from others in the social environment, but also in situation perception, situation selection, and the development of strategies that individuals use when trying to satisfy their needs (cf. Rothbart, in Goldsmith *et al.*, 1987; see also Buss, 1987). These latter aspects of a person–environment interactional analysis reflect the view of persons as intentional, active agents in the adaptation to the environment (see Endler, 1983; Endler & Magnusson, 1976; Hettema, 1979, 1989a; Magnusson, 1980; Plomin, De-

Fries, & Loehlin, 1977). In the roundtable discussion Buss and Plomin formulated this as follows:

> Individuals are often able to select environments, . . . Thus, an active person gravitates toward fast-paced or high-energy situations, a sociable person selects activities with people, and an emotional person tends to avoid situations involving stress. The extremes of temperament may be important in determining the nature of the social environment. Thus, an active person may quicken the tempo of a situation, a sociable one may make the context more interactive, and an emotional person may cause the situation to be laden with tension. Even when the environment is already in place, it can be altered by the actions of those extreme in temperament. (Goldsmith et al., 1987, p. 520)

In the following paragraphs I will review studies that lend support to this view of temperament as an active mechanism by which individuals adapt to their environment.

"Niche Picking": Temperament and Situation Selection

According to Mischel (1977, p. 248), "some of the most striking differences between persons may be found not by studying their responses to the same situation but by analyzing their selection and construction of stimulus conditions." As Diener, Larsen, and Emmons (1984) have noted, this type of interaction is quite compatible with more traditional trait theories. For instance, Snyder (1981, p. 310) has stated: "Quite possibly, one's choice of the settings in which to live one's life may reflect features of one's personality: An individual may choose to live his or her life in serious, reserved, and intellectual situations precisely because he or she is a serious, reserved, and thoughtful individual." Several studies have systematically investigated such links. Here, I will present the studies involving temperamental variables.

Strelau (1983) reported that high-reactive individuals tend to prefer situations (e.g., occupational situations, sport situations, etc.) of low stimulative value, whereas low-reactive persons showed the opposite tendency.

Snyder (1983) presented the empirical finding that extraverted, low self-monitoring individuals were particularly eager to enter sociable situations, while introverted, low self-monitoring persons were distinctly unwilling to enter situations that might foster behaviors incompatible with their introverted dispositions. Diener et al. (1984) found that extraversion correlated with time spent recreating socially. In a later study, Emmons et al. (1986) found that extraversion was positively correlated with the percentage of time spent in chosen social situations—a finding also reported by Furnham, 1981—and negatively correlated with the percentage of time spent in imposed social situations. The same correlational pattern holds for sociability. Furthermore, Zuckerman (1974) found that sensation-seekers actively seek sensation-providing leisure situations. In addition, evidence has been reported for substantial relations between preferences for different types of situations and temperament factors such as arousal-seeking (Mehrabian, 1978) and neuroticism (Furnham, 1981).

In a recent study of temperament (Van Heck, Hettema, & Leidelmeijer, 1990) it was found that male adolescents with high scores on sensation-seeking reported a preference for excesses. High scorers on Disinhibition and Experience Seeking scales had a high appreciation of interpersonal conflict situations and a markedly lower preference for relatively quiet situations that focus on joint working and sponsored teaching. High scorers on the Thrill and Adventure Seeking scale reported a more pronounced preference for interpersonal conflicts compared with low scorers. Impulsivity was connected to relaxation (negatively), sport (positively), and excesses (positively). Emotionality was linked to a preference for serving, and extraversion was correlated negatively with situations such as judgment, examination, lesson, etc. The latter study is a good illustration of active genotype–environment interactions (cf. Plomin, 1986), which occur when individuals seek environments to match their genotypes.

Temperament, Response Preferences, and Situation Transformation

In addition to situation selection, the modification of situations is another possibility to play out temperamental characteristics. To a certain extent, individuals create their own environment as a function of their personal characteristics. Buss (1985) uses the term *manipulation* to indicate the various ways in which people shape their environments. Hettema (1979, 1989c) uses the term *transformation* to specify this particular person–environment mechanism.

Empirical results concerning the relationship between temperament factors and transformational activities are scarce.

In a recent study, Buss *et al.* (1987) found clear links between extraversion and neuroticism and the use of specific sorts of manipulation tactics, these being means that people use to elicit and terminate the actions of others. For instance, positive correlations were found between extraversion and the employment of charm (e.g., making compliments) and reason (e.g., asking, explaining). Neurotics especially used silent treatment (e.g., ignoring, refusing to do something), regression (e.g., whining), and, to a lesser extent, debasement (e.g., acting humble) and coercion (e.g., demanding).

A striking aspect of the Buss *et al.* (1987) study is that alteration of the environment is studied in terms of actions deliberately directed at influencing the state of affairs. It is reasonable to assume that such means vary with the goals toward which they are directed. This very idea forms one of the cornerstones of Hettema's (1979, 1989a) open-system conception of psychological adaptation.

Using general systems theory as a comprehensive framework, Hettema (1979, 1989a) has conceived of personality as an open system encompassing the person as well as the immediately prevailing environment. According to this model, the internal as well as the external activities of the individual are governed by the leading principle of *psychological adaptation*, that is, the acquisition and maintenance of control over the environment. This requires a continuous process of transaction between the person and the environment. In this transactional process the person has to define the environment in order to behave adequately. In addition, from time to time the person has to *transform* the current situations in order to maintain or increase mastery. *Situation concepts* and *transformation rules* are the necessary tools persons have at their disposal for these tasks. Besides a means aspect, which will be left aside here due to space limitations, transformation rules—ways to change situations in a specified direction—also have a *goal* aspect.

This direction or goal aspect of behavior has been studied recently by Van Heck *et al.* (1990). Based on the work of Schank and Abelson (1977), the following goal categories were discerned: *Social Control* (the intention to gain power or authority), *Control* (the intention to gain control over physical objects), *Proximity* (the intention to move to a new location or to another person), *Knowledge* (the intention to increase knowledge), *Agency* (the intention to get someone else to pursue a goal on one's own behalf), and *Preparation* (the intention to make all sorts of preparations regarding specific goals). It was found that highly emotional persons, males as well as females, had a preference for Agency, Preparation, and Control. In addition, for males, but not for females, a significant positive correlation was obtained between emotionality and Proximity. Furthermore, male extraverts showed a tendency to refrain from preparatory activities and from calling others in to assist (Agency). Female extraverts, on the other hand, showed a clear preference for proximity-seeking and the amassing of knowledge. Moreover, impulsive males showed a reluctance to make thorough preparations. In the case of impulsive females a negative correlation was obtained with Agency. Finally, positive relationships were found between thrill and adventure-seeking and Proximity, Knowledge, Social Control, and Control. Another aspect of sensation-seeking, disinhibition and experience-seeking, appeared to be related to the intention to increase authority and social power. These significant correlations between sensation-seeking scales and general goal preferences were only found in male subjects.

Summarizing, it can be said that there is evidence for substantial links between temperament and goals. These relationships are examined in the study that is briefly described in the next paragraph.

An Illustrative Study

The primary purpose of this study was to explore how the temperamental variables "emotionality," "sociability," and "activity" were related to general goal preferences.

Two hundred eleven students (115 females and 96 males) of two high schools participated in the study. Their ages ranged from 15 to 19 years.

Temperament was assessed with a Dutch version of the EASI-III Temperament Survey (Buss & Plomin, 1975). The 30-item Dutch EAS employs a Yes—?—No response format. It was developed as part of the present research by Van Heck and Leidelmeijer. It comprises all the EASI-III items with the exception of the 20 Impulsivity items (cf. Buss & Plomin, 1984). Factor analysis of these items led to the identification of four factors: two Emotionality factors, namely Fear and Anger, and Sociability and Activity factors.

To define situations, we made use of a large-scale study by Van Heck (1984, 1989) aiming at the construction of a general taxonomy of situations. In this study situation concepts were defined and classified in terms of prototypical cues (e.g., locations, persons, acts, and objects).

Individual goals were measured, using a procedure developed by Hettema and Hol (1989). In a test booklet, subjects were presented with 30 descriptions of slightly problematic situations occurring regularly in everyday life. The descriptions of the situations were based on the prototypicality ratings obtained in the taxonomic study mentioned above. Each situation was followed by 21 response alternatives, equally representing the six goal categories (cf. Schank & Abelson, 1977) plus a general category. Subjects had to indicate the degree of preference for each of the particular responses on 5-point scales, ranging from "Applicable" to "Not applicable."

Table 10.1 shows, separately for females and males, the correlations between temperament variables and general goal preferences calculated across all 30 situations.

Fear was related to Agency in the case of males and females. In males, fear was also linked to Social Control and Preparation. Anger appeared to go together with the intention to increase authority/social power and mastery of physical elements of the environment. This effect was found in both sexes. Sociability and activity were related to goal preferences in only one of the sexes: Sociability was connected to proximity-seeking in women, while activity was related to Proximity, Knowledge, and Preparation in men.

Final Remarks

The scarcity of research studies prevents the formulation of more or less definite statements. It must be admitted that the study of interactions involving temperament is

Table 10.1. Correlations Between Temperament and General Preferences for Goals

| | EAS-scales | | | |
Goals	Fear	Anger	Sociability	Activity
Females (N = 115)				
SOCCONT	0.04	0.24**	0.11	0.03
CONTROL	0.08	0.26**	0.08	0.09
PROX	0.03	0.11	0.22*	0.14
KNOW	0.02	0.06	0.11	0.08
AGENCY	0.17*	0.12	0.06	0.13
PREP	0.10	0.15	0.10	0.08
Males (N = 96)				
SOCCONT	0.35**	0.31**	−0.03	−0.02
CONTROL	0.17	0.24*	0.04	0.19
PROX	0.12	−0.01	−0.03	0.31**
KNOW	0.02	0.03	0.10	0.38***
AGENCY	0.25*	0.11	−0.05	0.11
PREP	0.20*	0.16	−0.03	0.22*

SOCCONT = Social Control; CONTROL = Control; PROX = Proximity; KNOW = Knowledge; AGENCY = Agency; PREP = Preparation.
*$p < 0.05$ **$p < 0.01$ ***$p < 0.001$; one-tailed tested.

172   Guus L. Van Heck

still in an embryonic stage. Therefore, it can go in several unexplored directions (Plomin & Daniels, 1984). However, it becomes increasingly clear that the analysis of the goal and means aspect of actions forms a promising way to gain a clear insight into the ways individuals attempt—often with great success—to alter their environment to correspond more closely to their temperamental (and other personality) characteristics.

Using a prototype approach, situations can be defined equivocally in terms of acts (cf. Van Heck, 1989; see also Cantor, Mischel, & Schwartz, 1982, for empirical support). Assuming that all acts can be classified in terms of a limited set of goal categories, it follows that situations can be characterized in terms of prototypical goals (see Hettema, 1989c, for an extended treatment). How is this connected with the purposive, intentional, goal-directed ways in which individuals will bend situations to their will? Transformation of the situation is the alteration of the "character" of the situation. This can be accomplished by behaving in non-prototypical ways. Manifestation of acts that are highly prototypical for a given situation, like dancing, drinking, or chatting at a party, will not alter the situation considerably. The manifestation of acts that do not "belong" to the situation, on the other hand, will change the behavioral context considerably. For instance, a party can be transformed quite easily in a quarrel or a fight by "not behaving party," that is, by pursuing other goals than the typical party goals. Recently, Hettema (1989c) has developed a series of rules indicating when and in what direction situations are transformed as a function of behavior.

Thus, goals provide an integrative concept linking initial situations to end situations, that is, the outcomes of transactions with the environment. Knowledge of the goal structure of situations and the individuals' preferred goals will give insight in the conservation and transformation activities of persons when dealing with the continuous stream of events.

The preliminary data presented here show convincingly that temperament plays a substantial role in this dynamic interplay of persons and their environment. It remains an important task to conduct further studies of these interactions and the role of temperamental variables therein.

ACKNOWLEDGMENTS. I thank Kees C. M. Leidelmeijer and Frans Van Kasteren for their assistance in the data collection and the data analysis of the illustrative study.

References

Alker, H. A. Is personality situationally specific or intrapsychically consistent? *Journal of Personality*, 1972, *40*, 1–16.
Allport, G. W. *Personality: A psychological interpretation*. New York: Holt, 1937.
Amelang, M., & Borkenau, P. The trait concept: Current theoretical considerations, empirical facts, and implications for personality inventory construction. In A. Angleitner & J. S. Wiggins (Eds.), *Personality assessment via questionnaires: Current issues in theory and measurement*. Berlin: Springer, 1986.
Beckwith, I. Prediction of emotional and social behavior, In J. D. Osofsky (Ed.), *Handbook of infant development*. New York: Wiley-Interscience, 1979.
Bem, D. J., & Allen, A. On predicting some of the people some of the time: The search for cross-situational consistencies in behavior. *Psychological Review*, 1974, *81*, 506–520.

Block, J. Advancing the psychology of personality: Paradigmatic shift or improving the quality of research. In D. Magnusson & N.S. Endler (Eds.), *Personality at the crossroads: Current issues in interactional psychology*. Hillsdale, NJ: Erlbaum, 1977.

Buss, A. H., & Plomin, R. *A temperament theory of personality development*. New York: Wiley, 1975.

Buss, A. H., & Plomin, R. *Temperament: Early developing personality traits*. Hillsdale, NJ: Erlbaum, 1984.

Buss, D. M. Human mate selection. *American Scientist*, 1985, *73*, 47–51.

Buss, D. M. Selection, evocation, and manipulation. *Journal of Personality and Social Psychology*, 1987, *53*, 1214–1221.

Buss, D. M., & Craik, K. H. The act frequency approach to personality. *Psychological Review*, 1983, *90*, 105–126.

Buss, D. M., & Craik, K. H. Acts, dispositions, and personality. In B. A. Maher & W. B. Maher (Eds.), *Progress in experimental personality research*. Vol. 13. New York: Academic Press, 1984.

Buss, D. M., Gomes, M., Higgins, D. S., & Lauterbach, K. Tactics of manipulation. *Journal of Personality and Social Psychology*, 1987, *52*, 1219–1229.

Cantor, N., Mischel, W., & Schwartz, J.C. A prototype analysis of psychological situations. *Cognitive Psychology*, 1982, *14*, 45–77.

Cattell, R. B. *Personality and learning theory: The structure of personality and its environment*. Vol. 1. New York: Springer, 1979.

Cattell, R. B. The development of attribution theory into spectrad theory, using the general perceptual model. *Multivariate Behavioral Research*, 1982, *17*, 169–192.

Cattell, R. B. Handling prediction from psychological states and roles by modulation theory. In S. G. Cole, R. G. Demaree, & W. Curtis (Eds.), *Applications of interactionist psychology: Essays in honor of Saul B. Sells*. Hillsdale, NJ: Erlbaum, 1988.

Chaplin, W. F., & Goldberg, L. R. A failure to replicate the Bem and Allen study of individual differences in cross-situational consistency. *Journal of Personality and Social Psychology*, 1985, *47*, 1074–1090.

Cheek, J. Aggregation, moderator variables, and the validity of personality tests: A peer-rating study. *Journal of Personality and Social Psychology*, 1982, *43*, 1254–1269.

Conley, J. J. Longitudinal consistency of adult personality: Self- reported psychological characteristics across 45 years. *Journal of Personality and Social Psychology*, 1984, *47*, 1325–1333.

Costa, P. T., Jr., & McCrae, R. R. Age differences in personality structure revisited: Studies in validity, stability, and change. *Aging and Human Development*, 1977, *8*, 261–275.

Costa, P. T., Jr., & McCrae, R. R. Personality in adulthood: A six-year longitudinal study of self-reports and spouse ratings on the NEO Personality Inventory. *Journal of Personality and Social Psychology*, 1988, *54*, 853–863.

Costa, P. T., Jr., McCrae, R. R., & Arenberg, D. Enduring dispositions in adult males. *Journal of Personality and Social Psychology*, 1980, *38*, 793–800.

Craik, K. H. Personality unvanquished. *Contemporary Psychology*, 1969, *14*, 147–148.

Cronbach, L. J., Gleser, G. C., Nanda, H., & Rajaratnam, N. *The dependability of behavioral measurements: Theory of generalizability for scores and profiles*. New York: Wiley, 1972.

Diener, E., Larsen, R. J., & Emmons, R. A. Person × situation interactions: Choice of situations and congruence response models. *Journal of Personality and Social Psychology*, 1984, *47*, 580–592.

Emmons, R. A., Diener, E., & Larsen, R. J. Choice and avoidance of everyday situations and affect congruence: Two models of reciprocal interactionism. *Journal of Personality and Social Psychology*, 1986, *51*, 815–826.

Endler, N. S. Interactionism: A personality model, but not yet a theory. In M. M. Page (Ed.), *Nebraska Symposium on Motivation*. Lincoln, NE: University of Nebraska Press, 1983.

Endler, N. S. The temperamental nature of personality. *European Journal of Personality*, 1989, *3*, 151–165.

Endler, N. S., Hunt, J. McV., & Rosenstein, A. An S-R Inventory of Anxiousness. *Psychological Monographs*, 1962, *536*, 1–31.

Endler, N. S., & Magnusson, D. Toward an interactional psychology of personality. *Psychological Bulletin*, 1976, *83*, 956–974.

Epstein, S. The stability of behavior: I. On predicting most of the people much of the time. *Journal of Personality and Social Psychology*, 1979, *37*, 1079–1126.

Epstein, S. The stability of behavior: II. Implications for psychological research. *American Psychologist*, 1980, *35*, 790–806.

Epstein, S., & O'Brien, E. J. The person-situation debate in historical and current perspective. *Psychological Bulletin*, 1985, *98*, 513–537.

Eysenck, H. J. Biological basis of personality. *Nature*, 1963, *199*, 1031–1034.

Fiske, D. W. The limits for the conventional science of personality. *Journal of Personality*, 1974, *42*, 1–11.

Furnham, A. Personality and activity preference. *British Journal of Social and Clinical Psychology*, 1981, *20*, 57–68.

Furnham, A., & Jaspars, J. The evidence for interactionism in psychology. A critical analysis of the situation-response inventories. *Personality and Individual Differences*, 1983, *4*, 627–644.

Goldsmith, H. H. Genetic influences on personality from infancy. *Child Development*, 1983, *54*, 331–355.

Goldsmith, H. H., Buss, A. H., Plomin, R., Rothbart, M. K., Thomas, A., Chess, S., Hinde, R. A., & McCall, R. R. Roundtable: What is temperament? Four approaches. *Child Development*, 1987, *58*, 505–529.

Halverson, C. F., & Waldrop, M. F. Relations between preschool activity and aspects of intellectual and social behavior at age 7.5. *Journal of Developmental Psychology*, 1976, *12*, 107–112.

Hartshorne, H., & May, M. A. *Studies in the nature of character: Studies in deceit.* Vol. 1. New York: Macmillan, 1928.

Hettema, P. J. *Personality and adaptation.* Amsterdam: North-Holland, 1979.

Hettema, P. J. (Ed.). *Personality and environment: Assessment of human adaptation.* Chichester: Wiley, 1989a.

Hettema, P. J. Principles of personality assessment. In P. J. Hettema (Ed.), *Personality and environment. Assessment of human adaptation.* Chichester: Wiley, 1989b.

Hettema, P. J. Transformation rules: Towards a taxonomy of everyday behavior. In P. J. Hettema (Ed.), *Personality and environment. Assessment of human adaptation.* Chichester: Wiley, 1989c.

Hettema, P. J., & Hol, D. P. The assessment of behavioral strategies. In P. J. Hettema (Ed.), *Personality and environment. Assessment of human adaptation* Chichester: Wiley, 1989.

Hettema, P. J., & Kenrick, D. T. Biosocial interaction and individual adaptation. In P. J. Hettema (Ed.), *Personality and environment. Assessment of human adaptation.* Chichester: Wiley, 1989.

Hogan, R., DeSoto, C. B., & Solano, C. Traits, tests, and personality research. *American Psychologist*, 1977, *32*, 255–264.

Hunt, J. McV. Traditional personality theory in the light of recent evidence. *American Scientist*, 1965, *53*, 80–96.

Kagan, J. Temperamental contributions to social behavior. *American Psychologist*, 1989, *44*, 668–674.

Kenrick, D. T., & Dantchik, A. Interactionism, idiographics, and the social-psychological invasion of personality. *Journal of Personality*, 1983, *51*, 286–307.

Kenrick, D. T., & Funder, D. C. Profiting from controversy: Lessons from the person-situation debate. *American Psychologist*, 1988, *43*, 23–34.

Kenrick, D. T., & Stringfield, D. O. Personality traits and the eye of the beholder: Crossing some traditional philosophical boundaries in the search for consistency in all of the people. *Psychological Review*, 1980, *87*, 88–104.

Lantermann, E. D. *Interaktionen. Person, Situation und Handlung.* München: Urban & Schwarzenberg, 1980.

Lerner, J. V. The import of temperament for psychosocial functioning: Tests of a "goodness of fit" model. *Merrill-Palmer Quarterly*, 1984, *30*, 177–188.

Magnusson, D. Personality in an interactional paradigm of research. *Zeitschrift für Differentielle und Diagnostische Psychologie*, 1980, *1*, 17–34.

McDevitt, S. C., & Carey, W. B. The measurement of temperament in 3- to 7-year-old children. *Journal of Child Psychology and Psychiatry*, 1978, *19*, 245–253.

Mehrabian, A. Characteristic individual reactions to preferred and unpreferred environments. *Journal of Personality*, 1978, *46*, 717–731.

Mischel, W. *Personality and assessment*. New York: Wiley, 1968.

Mischel, W. Continuity and change in personality. *American Psychologist*, 1969, *24*, 1012–1018.

Mischel, W. On the future of personality measurement. *American Psychologist*, 1977, *32*, 246–254.

Newcomb, T. M. *Consistency of certain extrovert-introvert behavior patterns in 51 problem boys*. New York: Columbia University, Teachers College, Bureau of Publications, 1929.

Ozer, D. J. *Consistency in personality: A methodological framework*. New York: Springer, 1986.

Paunonen, S. V., & Jackson, D. N. Idiographic measurement strategies for personality and prediction: Some unredeemed promissory notes. *Psychological Review*, 1985, *92*, 486–511.

Peterson, D. R. *The clinical study of social behavior*. New York: Appleton-Century-Crofts, 1968.

Plomin, R. Behavior genetic methods. *Journal of Personality*, 1986, *54*, 226–261.

Plomin, R., & Daniels, D. The interaction between temperament and environment: Methodological considerations. *Merrill-Palmer Quarterly*, 1984, *30*, 149–162.

Plomin, R., DeFries, J. C., & Loehlin, J. C. Genotype-environment interaction and correlation in the analysis of human behavior. *Psychological Bulletin*, 1977, *84*, 309–322.

Schank, R. C., & Abelson, R. *Scripts, plans, goals, and understanding: An inquiry into human knowledge structures*. Hillsdale, NJ: Erlbaum, 1977.

Secord, P. F. Social psychology in search for a paradigm. *Personality and Social Psychology Bulletin*, 1977, *3*, 41–50.

Snyder, M. On the influence of individuals on situations. In N. Cantor & J. Kihlstrom (Eds.), *Personality, cognition, and social interaction*. Hillsdale, NJ: Erlbaum, 1981.

Snyder, M. The influence of individuals on situations: Implications for understanding the links between personality and social behavior. *Journal of Personality*, 1983, *51*, 497–516.

Strelau, J. *Temperament—personality—activity*. London: Academic Press, 1983.

Strelau, J. The concept of temperament in personality research. *European Journal of Personality*, 1987, *1*, 107–117.

Thomas, A., & Chess, S. *Temperament and development*. New York: Brunner/Mazel, 1977.

Van Heck, G. L. The construction of a general taxonomy of situations. In H. Bonarius, G. L. Van Heck, & N. Smid (Eds.), *Personality psychology in Europe: Theoretical and empirical developments*. Vol. 1. Lisse: Swets and Zeitlinger, 1984.

Van Heck, G. L. Situation concepts: Definitions and classification. In P. J. Hettema (Ed.), *Personality and environment. Assessment of human adaptation*. Chichester: Wiley, 1989.

Van Heck, G. L., Hettema, P. J., & Leidelmeijer, K. C. M. Temperament, situatie-voorkeuren en situatie-transformaties. *Nederlands Tijdschrift voor de Psychologie*, 1990, *45*, 1–16.

Van Heck, G. L., Jansen, J. H., & Lamberts, C. L. H. Cross-situationele variabiliteit en de voorspelbaarheid van personen. *Nederlands Tijdschrift voor de Psychologie*, 1986, *41*, 346–357.

Vernon, P. E. *Personality assessment: A critical survey*. New York: Wiley, 1964.

West, S. G. Personality and prediction: An introduction. *Journal of Personality*, 1983, *51*, 275–285.

Wright, J. C., & Mischel, W. A conditional approach to dispositional constructs: The local predictability of social behavior. *Journal of Personality and Social Psychology*, 1987, *53*, 1159–1177.

Wright, J. C., & Mischel, W. Conditional hedges and the intuitive psychology of traits. *Journal of Personality and Social Psychology*, 1988, *55*, 454–469.

Zuckerman, M. The sensation seeking motive. In B. Maher (Ed.), *Progress in experimental personality research*. Vol. 7. New York: Academic Press, 1974.

Zuckerman, M., Koestner, R., DeBoy, T., Garcia, T., Maresca, T. B. C., & Sartoris, J. M. To predict some of the people some of the time: A reexamination of the moderator variable approach in personality theory. *Journal of Personality and Social Psychology*, 1988, *54*, 1006–1019.

11

The Concepts of Personality and Temperament

Willem K. B. Hofstee

This chapter is about the conceptual relation between personality and temperament. I propose to define the psychology of personality as the study of traits. I argue against both social and biological conceptions of personality in the context of the psychological subdiscipline of personality. In attempting a restoration of the orthodox personological approach, I enlist the aid of temperamentalists on the one hand, but go against tendencies to explain temperament in biological terms on the other.

The structure of the chapter is as follows: I start out by discussing at some length the personological approach, which has all but passed into oblivion during the past decades. After thus having set the stage for my argument, I turn to the concept of temperament, in particular, to the problematic relation between it and biological explanation.

The Personological Twist

The specific assignment of personality psychology is to explain behavior in terms of individual differences: No other branch of psychology does that. Loftier conceptions of personality psychology are possible, and do indeed prevail in texts on theories of personality: Freud, Jung, Rogers, Kelly, Maslow, and other giants have left us their exegesis of the drama of human existence. Their emphasis, however, was not on individual differences but, quite to the contrary, on universal dynamics of the human predicament. Also, their mission has not been specific: novelists, playwrights, ministers, and philosophers have shared their endeavor. For the specific task of personality psychology, our more

Willem K. B. Hofstee • Department of Psychology, University of Groningen, 9712 HV Groningen, The Netherlands.

pedestrian giants, from Heymans to Eysenck, from Binet to Guilford, will appear to be of greater significance in the long run.

Doubts have been raised about the legitimacy of attempting the scientific study of individual differences. The societal and political acceptance of the mere existence of such differences was at an all-time low during the 1960s and 1970s; and, also, person-ologists have found themselves intellectually in a defensive position. Explanations of behavior in terms of individual differences have been judged to be circular, invalid, and grossly atheoretical. These reproofs need to be refuted for the present argument.

The Alleged Circularity of Personological Explanation

The structure of a personological explanation is: [actor] [behaved in a certain way] because he or she is [trait], for example: The reason Mary hit John is that she is aggressive. In this explanation the trait is itself a summary label compiling relevant behaviors; for example, aggressive acts. It follows that the structure of these explana-tions is: [actor] [behaved in a certain way] because he or she is [someone who generally shows that behavior]. Superficially, such propositions may impress one as being taut-ological or circular. That impression, however, is deceptive.

Upon closer inspection, personological explanations cannot be tautological, be-cause they are falsifiable. They deny other explanations, most notably, situational expla-nations: The statement about Mary may be wrong, for example, because it appears that Mary and John were performing an act whose script dictated the hitting, or because John behaved in such a way that there was hardly an alternative for Mary but to hit him, or because John is a masochist (which does not necessarily make Mary a sadist), and so on. In systematic research, the way to pit the personological and the situational—and the third, interactional—explanations against each other is the two-way ANOVA design. In daily life, we perform informal or thought-experiment versions of it, by observing or imagining the same person in other situations, or by observing or imagining other persons in the same situation.

The allegation of circularity may be caused by the somewhat peculiar character of personological explanations. "Why does he do that?" "Well, because he tends to." Compare: "Daddy, why is our grass green?" "Well, 'cause grass tends to be." I discuss the seeming superficiality of such explanations below. Another reason for suspicion is the undeniable tendency of the human inference-maker to jump to conclusions. If this jump is made with a single observation as the take-off point, the conclusion is indeed circular: Mary hit John because she is aggressive, and Mary is judged aggressive because she hit John. In the first place, however, people jump to all sorts of conclusions: personal, situational, and other, so there is no specific reason for suspicion. In the second place, personologists are trained not to. In the third place, overreactions may be adaptive in the broader context of a subjective cost-benefit analysis that extends different weights to false negatives and false positives: If obnoxious behavior is displayed by a relative stranger whom we can easily avoid in the future, little cost is attached to blaming the person; if it is displayed by our own children, we had better find a way to blame the situation.

The Alleged Invalidity of Personological Explanation

Over the past decades, the more or less collective impression has arisen that personological explanations are wrong all or most of the time, and that situational and/or interactional explanations are right. Note that this impression presupposes that personology is at least falsifiable and thus not tautological. Let us consider the logical and empirical status of the two main competitors of personological explanation, situationism and interactionism.

Situationism is either a position that denies individual differences altogether and therefore cannot be taken seriously; or it hypothesises differential perceptions of the same situation, which amounts to abandoning situational explanation: If, at a party, John talks his head off, dances, and flirts, whereas Mary sits in a corner all by herself, we may indeed entertain the scientific hypothesis that John and Mary have different perceptions of the situation. But the difference is either located in the persons or in the interaction between them and the situation; logically, there can only be personological or interactional, not situational, interpretations for individual differences in reaction to a situation.

Attached to situationism is the phantom called "fundamental attribution error" (Jones, Kanouse, Kelley, Nisbett, Valins, & Weiner, 1971), which has haunted personology for quite some time. The pertinent reasoning was as follows: Actors attribute their own behavior to the situation, whereas they attribute others' behavior to traits. These attributions are logically incompatible. Therefore, personologists are victims to the "fundamental attribution error" that ascribes behavior to traits. In perspective, just about everything is wrong with this thesis. Firstly, the differential attribution effect is in the order of magnitude of a (significant but) small effect. Secondly, it is moderated by content; for example, it makes a difference whether causes for success or failure are attributed. Thirdly, and mainly, it is based on a *non sequitur*: In each specific case, either the personal or the situational attribution, or both, may be wrong (Funder, 1987; Quattrone, 1982); in fact, both these errors are familiar in everyday life. We may fail to excuse behaviors that later appeared to be dictated by the situation, and we may wrongly excuse other behaviors.

The most prominent source of the idea that personological explanations are wrong has been interactionism rather than situationism. Interactionism has at least two meanings. Static interactionism is the position that person main effects are trivial in comparison to person × situation interaction effects. Dynamic interactionism, or transactionalism, holds the view that persons act upon the situation, which in turn acts upon them, and so on, so that stable traits cannot exist.

The position that over-all individual differences do not exist is not tenable (see, e.g., Epstein, 1979). The idea that the (static) interaction effect between persons and situations is far more important than the person main effect, stems mainly from research on state anxiety (see Van Heck, 1981, for an overview), which is at best a peripheral concept in personology. The proper way to conceive of the claim of static interactionism is a cost-benefit analysis: How much more variance is explained by taking situations into account, and does the gain outweigh the extra effort? With respect to central variables in the personality domain, such as extraversion, agreeableness, conscientiousness, emotional stability, and intellect (e.g., Angleitner & Ostendorf, in press; Goldberg, 1980), the answer may well be negative in most cases.

Dynamic interactionism is even more vulnerable to cost-benefit analysis. The dynamic interplay between the person and the situation is difficult to study, and would result in short-term predictions at best. The continuous monitoring of the subject that this paradigm requires would itself influence behavior, and therefore become an obstacle against external generalizability.

Philosophically, interactionism seems to be based upon a striving towards full understanding with supreme disregard of parsimony considerations. Once this attitude is adopted, it is easy to pinpoint the shallowness of the personological paradigm: Improvement of understanding, marginal though it may be, is always possible at the cost of introducing situational and/or temporal variables. Full explanation without a restriction upon the number of explanatory factors, however, cannot be a scientific ideal.

The Alleged Atheoretical Nature of Personological Explanations

As I noted above in passing, one of the possible reasons for the allegation of circularity of personological explanations is their seeming superficiality or atheoretical nature. This issue deserves a more thorough treatment, especially in the present context: For, the underlying question is whether temperamental accounts of behavior should refer to biological factors (Strelau, 1987) in order to be theoretically acceptable.

What precisely goes on when, in answer to the question, "Why is our grass green?" Daddy says, "well, because it tends to be"? Technically there is nothing wrong with an explanation that consists of subsumption of a singular proposition (Mary hit John) under a rule (Mary tends to do things like that); particularly for predictive purposes, subsumption is a powerful tool: Uncle Bill's grass may also be expected to be green. Nonetheless, our youngster may well feel cheated out of a satisfactory answer, that is, a true explanation. Daddy's answer seems to imply that there is no problem, and may be taken as an exercise in promoting superficiality in his youngster.

The reason for this delicate misunderstanding is not hard to find: If our youngster feels practiced upon, it is because the emphasis in the question was not upon *our* grass, but upon grass in general. Why is grass green? Why does Mary terrorize other people? Those are the deeper questions, which are brushed off by the subsumptive, personological, or botanical, explanation.

For the psychology of personality, the dilemma is whether personality should be conceived as the *explanans*, that which explains, or as the *explanandum*, that which is to be explained. In the former case, representing the personological position, individual differences constitute one of the explanations of human behavior, in competition with other accounts. In the latter case, individual differences constitute the dependent variable, to be explained by social, developmental, and other factors.

The answer to the dilemma depends on the aims we want to reach: prediction or control. As I noted, the subsumptive personological approach is eminently suitable for predictive purposes. The fundamental approach, which would explain individual differences, is at best indirectly relevant in this respect; at worst, it distracts the predictivist's attention by producing accounts in general terms (oedipal conflict, archetypes, self-actualization) that may—or may not—contribute to the understanding of behavior but were never geared to the prediction of individual differences. On the other hand, the predictive personological approach has little or nothing to contribute to the manipulation, change, or control of personality, while the fundamental approach tries to do just that.

The methodological paradigm for the predictive approach is the correlational design, for the fundamental approach, the experimental design; the application perspective for the predictivist is diagnosis and selection, in particular, personnel selection; for the fundamentalist, the application perspective is treatment, in particular, psychotherapy. These amplifications may serve to explain the low status of personology in the Western world over the past decades, in which treatment gained popularity at the cost of diagnosis and selection; the traditionally perceived superiority of experimentation over correlation may have boosted that shift. This must have been what Sechrest (1976) meant when he referred to the clinical "spelling" of personality. Funder (1987) notes that during this latency period of personology, industrial psychologists were among the few who carried on with the business of prediction.

Because of its correlational nature, personology does not provide causal conclusions and is therefore not in that sense explanatory. It shares this feature with other branches of science such as zoology and botany. Nonetheless it impresses some as incomplete for lack of a causal layer. This uneasiness rests upon a reductionist argument. Scientific reduction has two sides. The valid one is that in all scientific explanation, something is written in function of something else, and in that sense reduced: Full veridical description is not an aim of science. The other, however, which is in order here, is the explanation of phenomena at one level in terms of another, supposedly more fundamental level: biology in terms of chemistry, chemistry in terms of physics. The idea is that explanation is between levels, not within. That idea is impractical, if only because it leads to a regress that is usually denoted as physicalism. It is anything but widely accepted, and cannot serve as an argument against the shallow program of personology.

Temperament and Personology

In this section, I argue in favor of a personological conception of temperament, and against a biological reduction of it. Whereas the contribution of temperamentalists in liberating personology from an era of social-psychological and clinical imperialism can only be gratefully acknowledged, personality should not therefore solicit a new, biological occupation; on the other hand, temperamentalists may also be better off in joining the personological ranks. Naturally, the argument has to be more qualified than that. But to the temperamentalist, it should read like an invitation to personology.

By its nature, this section is partly a comment on Strelau's (1987) articulate statement on the relation between the concepts of personality and temperament, in which the two are drawn apart rather than fused. Strelau's point of departure with respect to the concept of personality, however, is radically different from mine. After discussing his proposals, I turn to the role of biological explanation in the study of temperament, and finally, to methodological issues.

Strelau on Temperament and Personality

Strelau (1987) all but concedes the territory of personality to nontemperamentalists. He rightly notes that most personality theories—psychoanalytic, social learning, phenomenological, cognitive—have no use for temperament at all, with the notable exception of trait theories, which he explicitly excludes from his conceptual analysis. Noting that temperament has been regarded as one of the elements of personality, as a synonym of personality, and as a phenomenon not belonging to the structure of personality, he opts for the latter view. He discusses five respects in which there is at least a polar difference between temperament and personality:

1. Temperament is biologically determined, whereas personality is a product of the social environment (cf. Leontev, 1978).
2. Temperamental features may be identified from early childhood, whereas personality is shaped in later periods of development.
3. Individual differences in temperamental traits like anxiety, extraversion–introversion, and stimulation-seeking are also observed in animals, whereas personality is the prerogative of humans.
4. Temperament stands for stylistic aspects, personality for content aspect of behavior.
5. Unlike temperament, personality refers to the integrative function of human behavior. (What Strelau seems to say at this point is that personality is a teleological, temperament a causal concept).

The opposition between Strelau's view and the personological stance set out above is a great deal resolved by considering it as a semantic difference: Strelau himself acknowledges the close correspondence between the temperament and the personological, or trait-theoretical, or individual differences approach of personality for which I have argued in conformity with, most notably, Eysenck (Eysenck & Eysenck, 1985). There is a difference in strategy, however. To put it dramatically, personologists are busy trying to liberate what they consider to be their territory from alien invaders, whereas the temperamentalist, for fear of being himself overrun by the forces of the grand personality theories, has resigned himself to abandoning the territory of personality and retreating to his own stronghold, awaiting better times. My argument, in this admittedly dubious metaphor, is that the time has come to join forces with the resistance in the land of personality.

Let us examine Strelau's arguments against identifying personality with temperament. The first is that many personality psychologists would disagree with statements like Eysenck's (1986) that genetic factors are the main determinants of personality. There are two sides to this issue. One is the debate on heritability coefficients—their database, and their susceptibility to restriction of range: for example, the more the general level of measured intelligence goes up, reflecting the influence of environmental optimalization, the higher the heritability coefficient, because the contribution of environmental factors to individual differences has decreased correspondingly. Thus there may be substantive disagreement without rejecting the viewpoint as such. The other side is that reduction to biological factors ought not play a central role either in personology or in the study of temperament, as I shall argue more extensively below; consequently, that the objection is also peripheral. Strelau's second argument is that personality is at least in part socially determined. I have spent the major part of this chapter arguing against that view. His third point is that a temperamental conception of personality can lead to socially harmful consequences such as racism. This is a tenuous argument, for two reasons: neglecting or denying temperamental differences can also be socially harmful; and, generally speaking, the misuse of scientific points of view is not prevented by abandoning them, since they will be revived by others if the need arises.

A secondary question, if the personological viewpoint is accepted, is whether all traits outside the intelligence domain are temperamental (as Buss & Plomin, 1984; Eysenck & Eysenck, 1985, state or imply) or whether temperament is a proper subset of personality. There are several ways to approach this issue. I shall use lexical analysis, which thus far has not been applied to this issue.

To select personality-descriptive terms from the lexicon (for a historical review of this research paradigm, see John, Angleitner, & Ostendorf, 1988) is to construct an implicit or extensional definition of personality. Such listings of trait terms are far more concrete than abstract, intensional definitions of personality. Ideally, we should have a listing of temperamental traits at our disposal, in addition to the lists of personality traits that have been made available (Angleitner, Ostendorf & John, 1989; Brokken, 1979; Goldberg, 1980). As no such list of temperament traits has yet been produced, only tentative and indirect comparisons can be made. I shall argue that temperament is the core of personality, that is: On the one hand, temperament does not coincide with personality, but is a proper subset of it; on the other hand, temperamental traits are a central subset rather than a peripheral one.

Five personality factors have emerged from the lexical research tradition: Extraversion, Agreeableness, Conscientiousness, Emotional Stability, and Intellect or Openness (Angleitner & Ostendorf, in press; Goldberg, 1980; McCrae & Costa, 1985). Temperamentalists (e.g., Buss & Plomin, 1984; Eysenck & Eysenck, 1985; Fey, 1978; Strelau, 1983; Zuckerman, 1979) have usually distinguished fewer dimensions, which can be conceived as rotations of two or more of these factors, or have made finer distinctions within dimensions. Especially the dimension of Intellect or Openness does not seem to belong to the temperament domain as defined thus far, even though there is some overlap between the temperamental variable of Sensation-Seeking and certain facets of Openness.

Interestingly, some temperamental variables emphasize the opposite pole of personality factors. Conscientiousness, for example, does not sound very temperamental, whereas its approximate polar opposite, Impulsivity, does; the same relation holds for Agreeableness and Aggressiveness. Such differences of emphasis do not impress one as very deep, but this conceptual issue may deserve further study.

With regard to the central position of temperamental traits, a finding by Brokken (1979) in his study of trait-descriptive adjectives is relevant. Brokken had subjects rate the 1203 Dutch adjectives on fundamentality, that is, the extent to which these terms were judged fundamental versus superficial in describing people's personalities. Over adjectives, he correlated this rating with the terms' scores on the two criteria on which they were selected. These criteria consisted of whether a term could be substituted in the following two framing sentences: (1) "He or she is a [adjective] person" (Person criterion), and (2) "He or she is [adjective] by nature" (Nature criterion). The fundamentality rating correlated .52 with the Nature criterion, and .26 with the Person criterion; the correlation between the criteria was .41. Thus the answer to the question whether an adjective stands for a trait in a superficial or a more fundamental manner is more closely associated with the Nature criterion than with the Person criterion, the former having a more temperamental connotation. The impression that arises is that trait adjectives are a fuzzy set, at the core of which are temperamental traits.

In this lexical framework, the most convincing argument in favor of a central position of temperamental traits is found in comparing the fundamentality ratings of the five personality factors. Hofstee, Brokken, & Land (1981) constructed marker scales for the Dutch language, without any regard for the fundamentality ratings of the items. *Post hoc* calculation of the average fundamentality per factor gives the following results: Introversion and Emotional Stability have the highest ratings on fundamentality (1.9 and 1.7, respectively, on a scale ranging from 0–3); Conscientiousness and Agreeableness follow next with 1.5 and 1.4, respectively; the lowest ratings are for factor V (1.1), which is best interpreted as Lack of Civilizedness. This order of fundamentality corresponds perfectly to what one would expect in answer to the question of whether these factors have a temperamental connotation. Therefore, the more temperamental a trait is, the more fundamental it is judged to be with respect to the concept of personality.

The above analysis may be found peculiar in that "temperamental connotation" is treated as a relative and continuous concept; many theorists may feel more at ease with a dichotomous approach in which a trait is either temperamental or not. In the abstract, one may be able to make such neat distinctions. At the more specific and operational level, however, fuzziness is inevitable. Consider a thought experiment in which a number of terms, or other items, are presented to a number of independent judges with the question whether these items indicate temperament. Three predictions can be made with near certainty about the outcome: (1) Agreement between judges will not be perfect; (2) the judgments will be positively correlated over items; and (3) it will not make a great deal of difference whether the judges are experts or laypeople. Within limits, this prediction also holds for many other tasks like clinical diagnosis, personnel selection, peer review of grant requests and journal articles, and so forth. One may arbitrarily take a particular expert's opinion (preferably one's own) and declare it to be the standard. It may be more profitable in the long run, however, to search for the core of consensus, and to accept a certain degree of fuzziness in the social language game of science.

The Role of Biological Explanations

Personality and temperament are defined by their relative permanence; attitudes, likings, and interests that are easy to reprogram do not come under that heading. An obvious consequence of this definition is to try to inspect the person's hardware, that is, the biological makeup of the individual. The grapevine of biology comprises the person's genes, glands, and nerves. I distinguish three ways to connect biology and temperament, and recommend against two of these.

The prime distinction concerns direction: Do biological variables function in the framework of a biological reduction of temperament, or do they serve to construct-validate temperamental concepts? In the former case, personology is a subdiscipline of biology; in the latter, biology is used as an auxiliary science.

In the first section of this chapter, I have argued that there is no need to explain something in terms of something else if one wishes to be scientific. In addition, the familiar argument against reduction of phenomena at a higher level of aggregation to variables at a lower level is inefficiency. The point is illustrated by Kohn's (this volume) review of the relation between psychometrically measured reactivity and classical laboratory indices. Kohn concludes that the results of the pertinent studies are discouraging. More promising appears to be his work relating psychometrically measured reactivity to subjective intensity and tolerance of pain. Quite evidently, tolerance of pain is a psychological, not a biological variable. More generally, anyone's educated guess should be that the search for direct mappings of psychological onto biological variables is going to be less than completely successful.

My recommendation against biologistic reductionism is not to be construed as a depreciation of research on biological correlates of personality in the process of construct validation. Finding such correlates strengthens the interpretation of the pertinent psychological variable as a relatively permanent disposition, that is, a temperamental trait. With respect to the five factors of personality, for example, there is a running debate on whether Agreeableness, Conscientiousness, and Culture are equally central and important to personality as are Extraversion-Introversion and Mental Stability. Knowing more about the heritability coefficients and the neurophysiological correlates of the former factors would help resolve the issue.

There exists a third, albeit apocryphal, strategy of connecting psychological and biological (or other natural-scientific) concepts, best named the metaphorical strategy, which cannot be rejected strongly enough. It consists of a conceptual flirtation with concepts and models from a more established discipline, at the level of mere analogy. Such concepts and models function as expletives lending supposed impressiveness, authority, and eloquence to one's enterprise. Diagnostic of this strategy is the selective mention of positive results—if mention of data is made at all. Surely, analogies and metaphors have their place as heuristic devices in hypothesis formation. They can also be profitably applied for quite a different purpose, that is, uncovering the latent rhetoric that underlies a grand theory. In no case, however, is hermeneutics to be substituted for empirical research and logical deduction.

A Judgmental Conception of Temperament

How should one assess temperamental traits? After having argued against a reductionist conception that would explain (or measure) temperament through biological variables, I shall propose to conceive of temperament—and personality in general—in intersubjective terms. Like justice and like artistic or scientific quality, personality and temperament are best viewed as judgmental variables. Objective elements enter into, but do not exhaust, these assessments. We may be able to automatically record or reliably observe a person's elementary behaviors that are relevant to a particular trait—although this is often easier said than done and may well amount to conducting science in a clumsy way if at all successful—but if a discrepancy would arise between the observational compound and our judgment of the person's standing on that trait, we would at the very least search for additional indicators. Therefore, instead of trying to escape from our predicament, we had better capitalize on the vast array of methodological erudition that psychology has accumulated to deal with the frailties of human judgment.

The preeminent liability of human judgment is idiosyncrasy. Idiosyncrasies come in two sorts: unpredictable, which we treat like random error, lowering reliability, and predictable, which we call bias, lowering validity. The distinction between the two is relative, reflecting the manner in which we treat idiosyncrasies rather than any intrinsic property.

Two strategies present themselves to overcome unreliability: objective measurement, and panel formation. Objective measurement solves the problem by definition, but in most cases provides a pseudosolution: In exchange for an unreliable assessment of the target concept, we obtain a reliable measure of something else. In the representative case, the correlation (or association in general) between the measure and the judgment, corrected for unreliability of the latter variable, will not be perfect. In other words, by avoiding the Scylla of unreliability we come down to the Charybdis of invalidity. No such risk is involved in using the other strategy, which consists of increasing the number of judges, thus Spearman–Browning the reliability *and* validity of the averaged judgments. Consensual assessment is traditionally the approved manner of evaluating scientific plans, programs, and products; what is good enough for that purpose should be good enough for us. It should be noted that actual face-to-face discussion between judges is not necessary and may even detract from the Spearman–Brown effect. Another note is that objective scores may be used as booster variables (Hofstee, 1988) if a sufficient number of judges is hard to reach: In the boostered multiple regression equation, the true score component of the judgments serves as the criterion, and the observed judgments and the scores as the predictors; the composite amounts to a more reliable version of the judgment variable.

The issue of bias is not as easily solved. In the area of personality measurement, it manifests itself in systematic discrepancies between self and peer ratings, but also in different perspectives attached to social roles: Mothers and fathers, for example, may have systematically different views of their children's temperamental traits (Martin, this volume). Interesting though these discrepancies may be from a social-psychological point of view, they are a nuisance from a personological perspective: To entertain the idea of multiple personalities on the part of our subjects would amount to sacrificing the king in the chess game of personology. A preferable solution is to adopt one of these perspectives as the most veridical approximation to the target. In contrast to current practice, which capitalizes heavily on self-judgments through personality inventories, the outside observer's point of view is a more likely candidate for this adoption. A forceful methodological reason is that, in many cases, several more or less exchangeable raters can be found, whereas the individual's own point of view is not replicable. On the substantive side, even though one may argue *ad infinitum* on the metaphysical question of who is a person's best judge or friend, it may be possible to reach agreement on which point of view is more consequential: Here again, the person is heavily outnumbered by the set of relevant others.

The argument in favor of the observer's rather than the actor's point of view implies no objection against the content of temperament questionnaires; translating these instruments into the third person singular may be a better approach than asking an observer to rate persons directly on traits. I also do not argue for abolishing self-ratings: The actor perspective can profitably be used as an auxiliary variable, boosting the reliability and validity of the prime measure (Hofstee, 1988), and it may serve as a surrogate when observers' ratings are not available.

Conclusion

In an attempt to draw together the concepts of personality and temperament, I have started out by highlighting a personological, individual differences conception of personality at the cost of grand-theoretical and interactionist conceptions. Subsequently, I have tried to temper the biological aspirations of the temperamentalist tradition by arguing against reductionism and by accentuating the judgmental nature of personality measurement including the assessment of temperamental dispositions.

In many respects, this chapter is in the spirit of a refractory comment on some of the developments that can be discerned in this area, in particular, tendencies toward comprehensiveness with respect to biological and/or social determinants of personality. I am convinced that such programs are far too ambitious at best, leading to loose theorizing, underdetermined and equivocal results, and abandonment of any practical application perspective; at worst, they reflect a misconception of what science is about: parsimony rather than completeness, elegance rather than laboriousness, modesty instead of pretense. I wish the study of temperament a most pedestrian future.

References

Angleitner, A. & Ostendorf, F. Personality factors via self- and peer-ratings based on a representative sample of German trait-descriptive terms, in press.

Angleitner, A., Ostendorf, F., & John, O. P. *Towards a taxonomy of German personality-descriptors.* 1989. Submitted for publication.

Brokken, F. B. *The language of personality.* Unpublished doctoral dissertation, University of Groningen, 1979.

Buss, A. H., & Plomin, R. *Temperament: Early developing personality traits.* Hillsdale, NJ: Erlbaum, 1984.

Epstein, S. The stability of behavior: I. On predicting most of the people much of the time. *Journal of Personality and Social Psychology,* 1979, *37,* 1079–1126.

Eysenck, H. J. Models and paradigms in personality research. In: Angleitner, A., Furnham, A. & Van Heck, G. (Eds.) *Personality Psychology in Europe: Current trends and controversies.* Vol. 2. Lisse: Swets & Zeitlinger, 1986.

Eysenck, H. J., & Eysenck, M. W. *Personality and individual differences: A natural science approach.* New York: Plenum, 1985.

Fey, J.A. *Temperament.* Amsterdam: Academische Pers, 1978.

Funder, D. C. Errors and mistakes: Evaluating the accuracy of social judgment. *Psychological Bulletin,* 1987, *101,* 75–90.

Goldberg, L. R. Some ruminations about the structure of individual differences: Developing a common lexicon for the major characteristics of human personality. Invited paper, Convention of the Western Psychological Association, Honolulu, Hawaii, 1980.

Hofstee, W. K. B. *Booster variables in expert judgment*. Unpublished manuscript, 1988.

Hofstee, W. K. B., Brokken, F. B., & Land, H. Constructie van een standaard-persoonlijkheids-eigenschappen-Lijst (SPEL). *Nederlands Tijdschrift voor de Psychologie*, 1981, *36*, 443–452.

John, O. P., Angleitner, A., & Ostendorf, F. The lexical approach to personality: A historical review of trait taxonomic research. *European Journal of Personality*, 1988, *2*, 171–203.

Jones, E. E., Kanouse, D. E., Kelley, H. H., Nisbett, R. E., Valins, S., & Weiner, B. *Attribution: Perceiving the causes of behavior*. Morristown, NJ: General Learning Press, 1971.

Leontev, A. N. *Activity, consciousness, and personality*. Englewood Cliffs, NJ: Prentice-Hall, 1978.

McCrae, R. R., & Costa, P. T., Jr. Updating Norman's "Adequate Taxonomy": Intelligence and personality dimensions in natural language and in questionnaires. *Journal of Personality and Social Psychology*, 1985, *49*, 710–721.

Quattrone, G. A. Overattribution and unit formation: When behavior engulfs the person. *Journal of Personality and Social Psychology*, 1982, *43*, 593–607.

Sechrest, L. R. Personality. *Annual Review of Psychology*, 1976, *27*, 1–27.

Strelau, J. *Temperament—personality—activity*. London: Academic Press, 1983.

Strelau, J. The concept of temperament in personality research. *European Journal of Personality*, 1987, *1*, 107–117.

Van Heck, G. L. M. *Anxiety: The profile of a trait*. Unpublished doctoral dissertation, University of Tilburg, 1981.

Zuckerman, M. *Sensation seeking: Beyond the optimal level of arousal*. Hillsdale, NJ: Erlbaum, 1979.

II

Diagnostic and Methodological Issues

Part II, which discusses diagnostic and methodological problems, contains seven chapters. The first three (Chapters 12–14) deal with psychometric issues. Angleitner and Riemann (Chapter 12) present important methodological issues in the construction of temperament inventories, arguing that the conceptual differences between temperament and personality should find their expression in the item content and the strategies used in constructing temperament scales. In Chapter 13, Slabach, Morrow, and Wachs delineate the current state of affairs in the psychometric measurement of temperament in infants and children while, in Chapter 14, Martin and Halverson provide evidence for the existence of low interrater agreement between parents in the diagnosis of children's temperament.

Goldsmith and Rothbart (Chapter 15) give very useful information on a series of questionnaire- and laboratory-based instruments the authors have developed for diagnosing temperament in early childhood.

Chapters 16–18 center on the dilemma concerning psychometric versus laboratory measures of temperament traits. This issue is discussed by Kohn (Chapter 16) with reference to studies on reactivity and anxiety, and by Amelang and Ullwer (Chapter 17), who present a variety of data illustrating the laboratory-psychometric dissonance in diagnosing extraversion and neuroticism. Fahrenberg (Chapter 18), referring to neuroticism and anxiety, argues that multimodel (multimethod and multisituation) assessments are needed in laboratory and field studies on temperament in order to raise the generalizability of psychophysiological diagnosis of temperament.

12

What Can We Learn from the Discussion of Personality Questionnaires for the Construction of Temperament Inventories?

Alois Angleitner and Rainer Riemann

The intention of this chapter is to analyze common and distinct procedures and problems that are prevalent in the construction and use of temperament and personality questionnaires. We start from the assumption that meaningful differences exist between the concepts of personality and temperament, and outline some consequences of these differences for the generation of questionnaire items and the subsequent item-selection process. The main focus of this chapter is the assessment of temperament in adults.

Personality and Temperament: Where Are the Differences?

The terms personality and temperament are both used to refer to temporarily relatively stable individual differences in behavior. Researchers in both fields make use of the trait concept for a convenient description of individual differences. Despite this obvious communality, and notwithstanding the fact that the border between both concepts is fuzzy, "personality" and "temperament" can be meaningfully differentiated.

A brief look at a few prominent definitions reveals both substantial agreement in the conceptualization of temperament, as well as some distinct features of the two concepts. Wundt (1903) defines temperament as the habitual emotional reactivity of an individual. In addition, physiological and biochemical factors are accentuated by McDougall (1923). Typical motor reactions of an individual as belonging to the realm of tempera-

---

Alois Angleitner and **Rainer Riemann** • Department of Psychology, University of Bielefeld, D-4800 Bielefeld, Federal Republic of Germany.

ment have been emphasized in early textbooks (Bloor, 1928; Downey, 1923). In the view of Allport (1937), personality is defined as a psychophysical system. The raw materials of personality are physique, intelligence, and temperament. These raw materials are seen as dependent on the genetic inheritance. Temperament is defined by Allport as follows:

> The characteristic phenomena of an individual's emotional nature, including his suscep-
> tibility to emotional stimulation, his customary strength and speed of response, the quality
> of his prevailing mood, and all pecularities of fluctuation and intensity in mood, these
> phenomena being regarded as dependent upon constitutional make-up, and therefore
> largely hereditary in origin. (Allport, 1961, p. 34)

Cattell (1946, p. 14) views temperament as a part of personality referring to temper, emotionality, and constitutional reactivity. Later he refines his view:

> Temperamental traits are definable by exclusion as those traits which are unaffected by
> incentive or complexity. These are traits like highstrungness, speed, energy, and emotion-
> al reactivity, which common observation suggests are largely constitutional. (Cattell,
> 1950, p. 35)

In a more recent publication by Buss and Poley (1976, p. 76) we read:

> The concept of temperament is rather straightforward and presents little difficulty—
> referring as it does to individual differences in "temper," that is, characteristics which are
> largely stylistic ways of behaving in social situations.

Summarizing the numerous approaches to the study of temperament and the rela-
tion of temperament to personality, Strelau (1987) stresses five discriminatory features in which temperament and personality are different:

1. Determinants of development (temperament: biological, personality: social).
2. Developmental stages of shaping (temperament: childhood, personality: adulthood).
3. Referring populations (temperament: animals and man, personality: man).
4. Content-saturated behavior (temperament: absent, personality: present).
5. Central regulating function (temperament: insignificant, personality: significant).

In agreement with these classifications is also the definition of temperament given by Plomin (1981). He states that temperament involves those dimensions of personality that are largely genetic or constitutional in origin, exist in most ages and most societies, show some consistency across situations, and are relatively stable. We would conclude from this statement that temperament is most clearly detectable in formal behavioral characteristics.

How to Find the Real Temperament Traits

The fundamental question for both personality and temperament research concerns the universe of traits that are considered for study. We may find stable individual differences to a large degree. Not all differences are relevant for temperament even if they meet the above-mentioned criteria. We may think of an example given by Goldberg: Some people are able to wiggle their ears, some are not. Two basic approaches for the selection of relevant traits can be distinguished: the inductive lexicographic strategy and the hypothetico-deductive.

The lexicographic approach is based on the "sedimentation hypothesis" formulated by Cattell in the 1940s. This hypothesis states that those individual differences are encoded in our language that are necessary and important for human conduct. Thus, the personality/temperament vocabulary represented in natural languages (personality-descriptive adjectives, nouns, and verbs) is analyzed to yield a finite set of attributes that denote socially relevant individual differences (see John, Angleitner, & Ostendorf, 1988). The lexicographic approaches by Allport and Odbert (1936), Norman (1963), Goldberg (1981, 1982) in the USA, Hofstee (1976, 1977) and Brokken (1978) in the Netherlands, and by Angleitner, Ostendorf, and John (1990) in Germany include a broad category labeled "stable temperament and character traits." The sets of adjectives and nouns assigned to this category should be checked for the selection of temperament traits using the following criteria:

1. *Nature criterion.* In the Dutch trait taxonomy studies Hofstee and his coworkers developed the person and the nature criterion for the selection of trait terms. For the nature criterion, judges were given the following instruction: "Call an adjective a personality descriptive adjective if it may replace the dots in the following sentence: He (She) is . . . . by nature" (Brokken, 1978). Rusalov (personal communication) used this criterion independently formulated in the opposite direction. He asked his subjects to indicate to what degree a trait (e.g., aggression) can be changed by social influences (e.g., education, training). Trait terms judged with good agreement as high on the nature criterion and little changeable could be considered as temperament traits.

2. *Independence of Culture.* A trait term that is found in more than one language should be regarded with more confidence as a temperament trait, compared to one found in only one language. If we compare the trait terms listed in the English, German, and Dutch lists, we have an empirical base for the selection of temperament traits.

3. *Applicability to children.* Experienced judges could be used to find out whether a trait term can literally be used to denote individual differences among young children and adults. However, ratings of the applicability to animals seem less practicable.

4. *Content saturation.* In the same way, judges could be asked whether a trait term refers more to *what* a person does or to *how* the person performs certain behaviors.

We expect that these criteria are not independent of each other. Trait terms that can be applied to children and adults should be rated as little content-saturated and high on the nature criterion. In addition, these traits should be found in other languages too.

However, we are convinced that the number of temperament traits may still be large. Thus, robust higher order factors should be established in cross-cultural self- and peer-rating studies. These factors could be considered as temperament factors insofar as there is independent evidence that they meet the criteria proposed by Strelau (1987).

The taxonomy of personality-descriptive verbs, begun by Goldberg (1982) and De Raad, Mulder, Klosterman, and Hofstee (1988), seems promising for the temperament domain. For the selection of personality-descriptive verbs, De Raad *et al.* used the instructions: "If, under the circumstances, one person (verb)s more than others, does that

tell something about his/her personality?" This frame sentence could also be adapted for
the temperament domain. This procedure allows one to establish a behavioral terminology that avoids situational and context specifity—a problem in act and item
formulations—as well as broad generalizations—a problem in using trait adjectives or
nouns.

No doubt the lexicographic approach, which starts from an exhaustive sampling of
terms and requires a cumbersome reduction, is not very economical. However, if we are
interested in the comprehensive study of temperament expressed in behavior, there is no
alternative way.

The hypothetico-deductive approach takes its starting point from more or less
elaborated temperament theories. The basic constructs of these theories may be derived
from physiological research (e.g., the numerous theories based on the Pavlovian properties of the nervous system), clinical observation (e.g., Carey, 1970; Thomas & Chess,
1977), factorial studies of selected variables (e.g., Eysenck, 1944) or other sources.
Take as an example Pavlov's theorizing about the concepts "strength of exitation,"
"strength of inhibition," "balance," and "mobility." Strelau (1983) reformulated these
conceptualizations and operationalized them in behavioral terms. For the construction of
the STI-R (Strelau, Angleitner, Bantelmann, & Ruch, 1990) each scale definition was
partitioned in several units referring to smaller behavioral domains. For example, the
mobility component includes the following five behavioral domains:

1. Reacts adequately to unexpected changes in the environment.
2. Adapts quickly to new surroundings.
3. Passes easily from one activity to another.
4. Changes mood lightly from positive to negative and the reverse, according to
   the meaning of the situation.
5. Prefers situations which require to perform different activities simultaneously.

These behavioral units constituted the basis for the generation of items which were
nominated by experts familiar with the theory.

At the first glance the hypothetico-deductive approach seems much more efficient
than the lexicographic approach for finding relevant temperament traits. However, as
there are numerous theories of temperament, which are at least partially supported by
empirical results, the question of the structure of temperament traits and the relative
importance of postulated constructs arises again. To find universal dimensions of temperament large-scale construct validation studies are needed.

Temperament and the Item Content of Temperament Scales

Given the clarifications referring to the differences between the concepts of temperament and personality it may be argued that the items of temperament scales should
differ from personality scale items in several respects. We refer here again to the features
of temperament traits given by Strelau (1987) and examine their implications for the
construction of questionnaire items.

1. *Biological factors play a crucial role in determining temperament.* This criterion requires focus on behaviors or characteristics of persons that are probably determined

by their biological makeup, instead of formulating items that refer to learned reactions. Typical items capture psychophysiological reactions and symptoms that are not under voluntary control, including motor reactions and their inhibition (e.g., "I move a lot in bed," DOTS-R, Windle & Lerner, 1985, 1986). The assumption that individual differences in temperament are inherited may be given more weight in using appropriate designs, for example, the comparison between monozygotic and dizygotic twins for the item selection, as was done by Buss and Plomin (1975) in their construction of the EASI. The use of heritability coefficients as a criterion for the construction of tests was already suggested by Jones (1971).

2. *Temperament traits focus on formal, stylistic characteristics of behavior.* This feature of temperament traits has obvious consequences for the construction of questionnaire items. The items should refer to how people perform behaviors rather than what behaviors are performed. Descriptions of specific contexts and social situations should be absent in temperament items. For covering the stylistic characteristics adverbs can be used, because adverbs express these characteristics most clearly (e.g., "Do you speak rapidly?" STI, Strelau, 1983).

3. *Temperament is shaped in childhood.* Behavioral characteristics that show stability over a person's life span meet this criterion best. Thus, the item stability over reasonably long time periods might be regarded as a criterion in the item-selection process. In addition, items should refer to behavior reactions that are observable in children and adults.

4. *Temperament refers to phenomena that can be observed in man and animal.* Obviously this postulate cannot be utilized directly for the construction of temperament items. However, it can be deduced that temperament questionnaires should consist of items that can be judged reliably by observers. Those items should be dismissed that refer exclusively to nonobservable internal reactions (e.g., "Can you suppress momentary moods of dejection?" STI).

5. *Central regulating functions are insignificant for temperament traits.* This criterion excludes cognitive aspects of behavior and items that refer to attitudes, values, and goals. Instead, the individuals' regulation of the stimulative value of activities and surroundings should be studied by focusing on preferences for certain types of activities and environmental conditions.

To explore the differences between temperament and personality questionnaires currently in use, the items of the following temperament questionnaires were classified according to a taxonomy proposed by Angleitner, John, and Loehr (1986): (1) the Strelau Temperament Inventory (STI, Strelau, 1983), (2) the short version of the revised STI (STI-RS, Strelau, Angleitner, Bantelmann, & Ruch, 1990), (3) the Questionnaire for the Measurement of the Structure of Temperament (QST, Rusalov, 1989), (4) the adult version of the Revised Dimensions of Temperament Survey (DOTS-R, Windle & Lerner, 1985, 1986), and (5) the Emotionality Activity Sociability Impulsivity Temperament Survey (EASI-III, Buss & Plomin, 1975).

The taxonomy consists of seven central categories: (1) descriptions of reactions, which are subdivided into overt, covert, and bodily reactions (symptoms); (2) trait attributions, subdivided into unmodified or modified by, for example, situational context specifications or frequency qualifiers; (3) wishes and interests; (4) biographical facts; (5) attitude and belief statements; (6) reactions of other persons to the subject; and (7) bizarre item content. Three raters independently provided these classifications. The average percentage agreement between the raters was 60%. For further analysis, each item was assigned to the category that had been selected by the majority of judges. The results of this categorization are reported in Table 1, together with the classifications presented by Angleitner et al. (1986) for the MPI and MMQ (Eysenck, 1962, 1943), the EPI (Eysenck & Eysenck, 1964), the 16PF (Cattell & Eber, 1964), and the MMPI (Hathaway & McKinley, 1964). In the study of Angleitner et al. the judges were given the additional option not to subclassify an item.

In Table 1 the percentage of items assigned by the majority of the raters to each category is presented separately for each questionnaire. In the column headed "left unclassified," the percentage of those items is given that were not assigned to the same category by more than 50% of the judges. This percentage is particularily high for the EASI III. An example may illustrate the reading of Table 1: 58% of the STI items (N = 134) were assigned to the category descriptions of overt reactions, 27% were regarded as "covert reactions," 4% and 1% asked for unmodified and modified trait attributions, and 2% for the subjects' wishes and interests. No item was assigned to the remaining categories. Eight percent of the items were left unclassified.

A look at the temperament scales reveals that they are made up mostly by items asking for:

1. Overt reactions of the testperson that are in principle observable by the public (see Column 1a in Table 1).
2. Covert reactions or internal reactions that are private and generally not observable by others (internal sensations, feelings, cognitions; see Column 1b in Table 1). Some examples may illustrate this:

"I smile often." (DOTS-R)
"I move a lot in bed." (DOTS-R)
"Do you wake quickly and without difficulty?" (STI)
"I often feel like crying." (EASI-III)
"Do you feel bored or sleepy when performing monotonous work?" (STI)

The percentages of items assigned to these categories are much higher for the temperament inventories (including Eysenck's questionnaires) than for the 16PF and MMPI. However, substantial differences can be observed between the different temperament scales within the same questionnaire (see Angleitner et al., 1986, for details). For measuring emotionality (neuroticism) the test constructors concentrate on covert reactions regarding item content (partly also on symptoms), whereas for the scales measuring activity, rhythmicity, sociability, or impulsivity, they generate items with mostly overt behavioral item content. For example, the EPI (forms A and B) extraversion scales are build by 51% of items asking for overt reactions, the neuroticism scales are made up largely of items referring to covert reactions (53%) and physical symptoms (25%).

Items asking for trait attributions (Colums 2a and 2b in Table 1) were not found in the STI-RS and were rare in the STI, the QST, and the DOTS-R. However, a substantial portion of the items of the EASI-III and Eysenck's questionnaires was assigned to this category. The percentage of "trait attributions" found in these questionnaires is comparable to that of personality inventories. Examples for this category are:

"Are you hot-tempered?" (STI)

Table 12.1. Relative Frequencies of Items in Each Category from Temperament and Personality Questionnaires

Questionnaire	Number of items	Description of reactions[1]				Trait attributions			Indirect references					Left unclassified
		1a overt	1b covert	1c symptoms	Not subclassified	2a unmodified	2b modified	Not subclassified	3 Wishes	4 Biography	5 Attributions	6 Others	7 Bizarre	
STI	134	58.21	26.87	0.0	0.0	3.73	0.75	0.0	2.24	0.0	0.0	0.0	0.0	8.21
STI-RS	84	67.86	27.38	0.0	0.0	0.0	0.0	0.0	0.0	0.0	0.0	0.0	0.0	4.76
QST	105	54.29	34.29	0.0	0.0	3.81	0.0	0.0	0.0	0.0	0.95	0.0	0.0	6.67
DOTS-R	54	70.37	24.07	0.0	0.0	3.70	0.0	0.0	0.0	0.0	0.0	0.0	0.0	1.85
EASI III	50	30.00	30.00	0.0	0.0	14.00	2.00	0.0	0.0	0.0	0.0	0.0	0.0	24.00
MPI[2]	48	18.80	41.70	2.1	8.2	18.80	4.20	2.0	0.0	0.0	0.0	0.0	0.0	4.20
MMQ[2]	56	19.60	23.20	17.9	8.9	10.70	7.10	7.2	0.0	1.8	0.0	0.0	0.0	3.60
EPI-A/B[2]	57/57	33.35	29.80	10.5	7.95	7.00	4.40	0.85	0.0	0.9	0.0	0.0	0.0	5.25
16PF-A/B[2]	171/171	17.80	22.55	2.65	12.60	2.95	0.30	2.60	12.55	3.2	12.3	1.5	0.0	9.05
MMPI[2]	404	10.40	27.00	13.10	11.10	3.20	1.00	2.00	4.70	5.7	5.9	2.2	3.0	10.60

[1] See text for description of the categories.
[2] Data taken from Angleitner et al., 1986.

"I am very sociable." (EASI-III)

The "trait attributions" do not meet the above-mentioned criterion of public observability.

Items referring to wishes and interests (Column 3 in Table 1), to biographical facts (Column 4), attitudes and beliefs (Column 5) and other persons' reactions (Column 6) as well as bizarre items (Column 7) are nearly absent from temperament scales. Items assigned to these categories make up a substantial part of the 16PF and the MMPI.

Although not all temperament and personality questionnaires were compared, the results point at meaningful differences between the questionnaires in both domains. The high percentage of items referring to overt reactions is especially in line with the criteria derived for temperament items. The fact that authors of personality questionnaires include items in their original item pools which do not refer to specific reactions and that these items "survive" the empirical item-selection process may reflect the higher weight given to integrative functions of behavior. Systems of values and motivational constructs can be operationalized in questions that refer to a person's "wishes and interests" and "attitudes and beliefs." The social nature of personality constructs may find its expression in items referring to a person's biography and other persons' reactions.

In our reflection on the item contents of temperament scales we will now concentrate on three unsolved problems:

1. A glance at different temperament scales documents that the test constructors are probably not aware of their mixing together frequency and intensity aspects in their item formulations, for example, "I frequently get upset," "I am somewhat emotional" (EASI-III), and "I often stay still for long periods of time," "Even when I am supposed to be still, I get very fidgety after a few minutes" (DOTS-R).

It may be the case that some temperament traits, for such as the various constructs referring to a person's activity, are more connected with frequency assumptions, others more with intensity assumptions, such as emotionality, impulsivity, or arousability. Following the arguments by Strelau (1987) in defining temperament, it seems reasonable that an intensity conception is theoretically more adequate than a frequency conception. People may differ in their actions dependent on their different living circumstances, but still they may be similar in the intensity by which they perform their actions: They are called phlegmatic or choleric.

In the future it may be worthwhile to compare items based on frequency assumptions with items measuring the intensity of reactions. The missing correspondence between the postulated physiological mechanism and the proposed psychometric scales (Strelau, 1990) may find a partial explanation in the fact that most psychophysiological measures capture the intensity of reactions, whereas frequency conceptualizations are preferred in the psychometric tradition. No one would *a priori* expect much convergence between these different conceptualizations.

A look at the descriptions and items of temperament scales reveals that the authors are somewhat inclined to use an abilities conception. Examples of such items are: "Do you have difficulties in adapting to a new daily schedule?" (STI); "Are you able to work while waiting for guests?" (STI); and "I get bored easily" (EASI-III). The abilities conception of personality was proposed from independent perspectives by Fiske and Butler (1963) and Wallace (1966). The main focus of the abilities conception are individual differences in persons' capabilities to perform behaviors required by the situation rather than in their typical or average behaviors. It may be worthwhile to consider the abilities conception in temperament research more explicitly, not only for the generation of questionnaire items, but also for the construction of laboratory tests of behavioral performance.

2. The vast majority of authors claim in their writings that stylistic components of behavior are central for temperament constructs. How should these stylistic components of behavior be incorporated into the item formulations? In general, we see two solutions:

1. The items for temperament should be formulated in a broader way, covering different content domains. However, this may lead to very abstract formulations involving much interpretation on behalf of the answering subject. Examples are:

"Are you capable of adapting your conduct to the behavior of others in a group when necessary?" (STI)

"My life is fast-paced." (EASI-III)

"I move towards new situations." (DOTS-R)

2. A second possibility would be to start from the opposite direction: Items should be generated that refer to specific actions in a variety of different contexts, using verbs instead of "I like," "I tend," "Do you easily," "Are you able," "Can you," etc. This means that one concentrates on the actions that a hot-tempered person is likely to show (e.g., "I raise my voice in a debate," instead of "I have trouble controlling my impulses") and gathers these reactions across many different situations. The strategy developed by Buss and Craik (1980) in their act-frequency approach may be used for eliciting relevant actions for different temperament traits.

3. A serious problem arises if "parallel" versions of a questionnaire are constructed, with the intention to measure the same temperament dimensions in young children and adults. No generally accepted procedure exists that ensures the equivalence of items across age groups. What are the behavioral expressions for impulsivity that are equivalent in meaning for different age periods, especially in children? In general, authors of temperament questionnaires have developed two strategies for solving this issue: (1) For each age group different items are formulated, which ask for appropriate behavioral reactions. The equivalence of these items across age groups is accepted by face validity. For example, the item "My child splashes hard in the bath and plays actively," is seen to be equivalent to the item "Child seems to have difficulty in sitting still, may wriggle a lot or get out of seat" (NYLS-scales, Thomas & Chess, 1977); and (2) either the scales or the items are constructed in such a way that they can be used in a broad range of age groups with minor modifications (EASI-III; DOTS-R).

Steps in the Construction of a Temperament Scale

Suppose we know the relevant temperament traits for which we would like to develop an inventory. The question arises, what should a test constructor consider in developing a successful instrument? Several issues should be considered:

1. *Use of a rational scale construction strategy.* A strategy similar to the procedure of eliciting behavioral acts used by Buss and Craik (1980, 1983) may be adopted. We

may ask subjects (parents, teachers, etc.) if they know somebody whom they will call, for instance, "active," and then ask how this person typically behaves to elicit this impression. However, to avoid the problem of specifity of context, these items would most likely have to be reformulated.

Another strategy is to bring together experts of these temperament concepts for which scales should be developed (preferably from different nations) and to ask them to generate items. It is important to define the behavioral domains very precisely beforehand and to find agreement concerning some basic rules about what constitutes a good item. The suggestions given by Jackson (1970) are recommended.

The items should be (1) short and clearly understandable, (2) free from extreme levels of social desirability, (3) diverse in content as to cover the universe of human conduct, (4) applicable to adults in different cultures and not biased toward particular populations, as for example, college students or males, (5) logically related to the construct under consideration and at the same time not overlapping with similar but irrelevant constructs, and (6) balanced in their keying.

To reduce the item pool to a manageable size, the items may be judged for prototypicality following Rosch and Mervis's (1975) procedures. Only items that are regarded as good examples for the behavioral domain in question should be considered for the empirical scale construction. The application of such strategies limits the personal idiosyncrasies which may enter if one researcher alone generates the whole item pool. It allows a more representative sampling of the items.

2. *Checking the syntactic characteristics of the items.* The empirical fact that, for example, about 30–40% of the items of Eysenck's inventories are judged as not immediately understandable (Angleitner et al., 1986) should alert us to the linguistic characteristics of items. It has been documented that syntactic properties are related to the psychometric item and scale characteristics (see Angleitner et al., 1986).

3. *Consider the item stability and the homogeneity issue.* It has been argued above that item stability should be given an important rank for the selection of items. The homogeneity/heterogeneity of items for a proposed scale has to be considered in advance. Theoretical arguments have to be considered to decide whether the trait under study covers a narrow domain of behaviors or is conceptualized more broadly and includes a variety of facets. Keeping the number of items constant, the internal consistency of a broader scale should be lower compared to a narrow scale. Therefore, lower internal consistencies of a scale may be acceptable. However, the values should not fall short of a critical border of about .70. In line with Loevinger's (1957) emphasis on the substantial validity issue, we do not recommend the *blind* application of item-analytical strategies for finding homogeneous scales. Really homogeneous scales are yielded if items are repeated or phrased tautologically.

In case the temperament traits are postulated to be orthogonal, the use of factor-analytic strategies to warrant unidimensionality is preferable (Windle, 1988). However, if the concepts are theoretically correlated, the application of factor analysis is not justified. Take the example of the correlated Pavlovian concepts "strength of exitation" and "mobility." In constructing scales for these concepts, the authors of the STI-R relied on the multitrait-multimethod approach formulated by Campbell and Fiske (1959). In the STI-R, only items that correlated higher with their own scale compared with the related or unrelated scales in question have been accepted (Strelau et al., 1990). The procedure is similar to the differential reliability index as proposed and used by Jackson (1967) for developing the Personality Research Form (PRF).

4. *Consider response distortions in the item generation and in the construction process.* In hundreds of studies it has been shown that personality scale values may be distorted by several factors. These factors have been called tendencies to say yes or no, faking good or bad, social desirability, etc. In principle, response distortions cannot be avoided, but it seems possible to reduce them. For instance, the yes-saying tendency may be reduced by balancing the item-keying. Furthermore, if the subjects are informed about such distortions in the instructions, the chance to avoid response distortions may be enhanced.

Numerous strategies to control social desirability have been proposed. However, until now no procedure could be established that clearly helps to increase the validity of a scale. In the construction of the STI-R this problem was treated in the following way: All the items were rated by 20 judges concerning their social desirability value. The items with the most extreme mean ratings were selected for a social desirability scale. However, although the items selected for the content scales correlated higher with their own scales than with the social desirability scale, it turned out that the content scales showed high correlations with this new social desirability scale (SD). Furthermore, this SD scale did not correlate substantially with other social desirability or control scales (EPQ-Lie scale, PRF-Infrequency scale). This result shows that the initial item pool for the STI-R was already very high in content saturation. Nevertheless, rating the items' social desirability values is recommended for reformulating or eliminating items with extreme values. This brings more balance and neutralization in social desirability.

In his reexamination of response tendencies Paulhus (1986) made a distinction between self-deception and impression-management. He underlines that "items asking about overt behavior were minimally subject to self-deception" (p. 153). He also concludes that "impression management may also be usefully controlled by asking about behaviors with neutral desirability value" (p. 153). It follows that the application of these procedures helps to reduce the possible influence of response distortions.

5. *Consider convergent and discriminant validity in construction.* Temperament scales contain mainly items that express overt behaviors. This implies that they are good candidates for using samples of observers (peers, spouses, friends, colleagues, parents, relatives, etc.). Self- and observer ratings on the item as well as on the scale or facet levels can easily be carried out, resulting in a multitrait-multimethod design (Campbell & Fiske, 1959). In general, researchers continue to document the validity of their scales in pointing to the convergent validities by correlating scales with conceptually similar scales. But very seldom do authors consider some possible item-overlap. Likewise, a clear theoretical deduction regarding for which concepts zero or moderate correlations are expected is missing in almost all studies. This seems to be true for personality as well as temperament inventories.

The application of these guidelines, which are the result of our experience with personality scales, will, it is hoped, improve the construction of temperament scales. In asking for specific reactions, temperament inventories are relying more on direct modes of self-description. Such direct modes have already been shown to possess more satisfactory item-response statistics (Angleitner *et al.*, 1986). It follows that temperament traits should be good candidates for self-report measures.

The Cross-Cultural Adaptation of Temperament Scales

Temperament traits should be measurable in different cultures. The applicability of items in diverse cultures and nations should be considered in the initial item-generation process. By using experts, a fairly representative sample of items for a temperament trait in question can be developed. This initial item pool may then be considered as the item universe, and translated by several independent translators. The translators should be instructed about the concepts, which should be measured by this item set. Bilingual samples of subjects may be used for checking the equivalence of item meanings. Furthermore, it seems important to us that, for the empirical construction process, the procedures are comparable and standardized. The aim of such a cross-cultural research cooperation would be the development of comparable, multi-language temperament scales that are relatively culture-free.

Conclusions

In this chapter we have argued that the conceptual differences between "temperament" and "personality" should find their expression in the item content and construction strategies of temperament scales. Despite the fact that individual differences in temperament are regarded as biologically determined—and, therefore, that psychophysiological assessment may seem to be more appropriate—sufficient variation in behavior is observable to warrant the measurement of temperament via self-reports. We see five major and largely unresolved issues that require further theoretical and empirical efforts:

1. The scope and structure of the universe of temperament traits measured via self-reports is as yet not studied systematically.
2. Robust correlations of self-report data and psychophysiological measures have to be established.
3. Cross-cultural research programs are rare and scattered.
4. The equivalence of temperament scales across age groups needs further clarification.
5. Item formulations that refer to the frequency of performing certain behaviors, the intensity of behavioral expressions, and the capability of showing a behavior, when it is required by the situation, should be disentangled.

References

Allport, G. W. *Personality: A psychological interpretation*. New York: Holt, 1937.
Allport, G. W. *Pattern and growth in personality*. London: Holt, Rinehart & Winston, 1961.
Allport, G. W., & Odbert, H. S. Trait-names: A psycho-lexical study. *Psychological Monographs*, 1936, *47*, No. 211.
Angleitner, A., John, O. P., & Loehr, F. J. It's what you ask and how you ask it: An itemmetric analysis of personality questionnaires. In A. Angleitner & J. S. Wiggins (Eds.), *Personality assessment via questionnaires: Current issues in theory and measurement*. Berlin: Springer, 1986.

Angleitner, A., Ostendorf, F., & John, O. P. Towards a taxonomy of personality-descriptors in German: A psycho-lexical study. *European Journal of Personality*, 1990, *4*, 89–118.

Bloor, C. *Temperament*. London: Methuen, 1928.

Brokken, F. B. *The language of personality*. Unpublished doctoral dissertation, University of Groningen, 1979.

Buss, A. H., & Plomin, R. *A temperament theory of personality development*. New York: Wiley, 1975.

Buss, A. H., & Poley, W. *Individual differences: Traits and factors*. New York: Gardner, 1976.

Buss, D. M., & Craik, K. H. The frequency concept of disposition: Dominance and prototypically dominant acts. *Journal of Personality*, 1980, *48*, 379–392.

Buss, D. M., & Craik, K. H. The act frequency approach to personality. *Psychological Review*, 1983, *90*, 105–126.

Campbell, D. T., & Fiske, D. W. Convergent and discriminant validation by the multitrait-multimethod matrix. *Psychological Bulletin*, 1959, *56*, 81–105.

Carey, W. B. A simplified method for measuring infant temperament. *Journal of Pediatrics*, 1970, *77*, 188–194.

Cattell, R. B. *Description and measurement of personality*. New York: World Book, 1946.

Cattell, R. B. *Personality: A systematic theoretical and factual study*. New York: McGraw-Hill, 1950.

Cattell, R. B., Eber, H. W. *The Sixteen Personality Factor Questionnaire*. Champaign, IL: Institute for Personality and Ability Testing, 1964.

De Raad, B., Mulder, E., Kloosterman, K., & Hofstee, W. K. B. Personality-descriptive verbs. *European Journal of Personality*, 1988, *2*, 81–96.

Downey, J. E. *The will temperament and its testing*. Yonkers, NY: World Book, 1923.

Eysenck, H. J. Types of personality: A factorial study of seven hundred neurotics. *Journal of Mental Science*, 1944, *90*, 851–861.

Eysenck, H. J. *The Maudsley Personality Inventory*. (Manual prepared by R.R. Knapp). San Diego: Educational and Industrial Testing Service, 1962.

Eysenck, H. J. *MMQ*. Göttingen: Hogrefe, 1964.

Eysenck, H. J., & Eysenck, S. B. G. *Manual of the Eysenck Personality Inventory*. London: University of London Press, 1964.

Fiske, D. W., & Butler, J. M. The experimental conditions for measuring individual differences. *Educational and Psychological Measurement*, 1963, *23*, 249–266.

Goldberg, L. R. Language and individual differences: The search for universals in personality lexicons. In L. Wheeler (Ed.), *Review of Personality and Social Psychology*. Vol. 2. Beverly Hills: Sage, 1981.

Goldberg, L. R. From Ace to Zombie: Some explorations in the language of personality. In C. D. Spielberger, & J. N. Butcher (Eds.), *Advances in Personality Assessment*. Vol. 1. Hillsdale, NJ: Erlbaum, 1982.

Hathaway, S. R., & McKinley, J. C. *Manual for the Minnesota Multiphasic Personality Inventory*. New York: Psychological Corporation, 1943.

Hofstee, W. K. B. *Dutch traits: The first stages of the Groningen taxonomy study of personality descriptive adjectives*, University of Groningen, The Netherlands, 1976.

Hofstee, W. K. B. *Preliminary steps in structuring the set of 1.204 Dutch personality-descriptive adjectives*. Heymanns Bulletins, HB-77–302 IN, University of Groningen, The Netherlands, 1977.

Jackson, D. N. *Personality Research Form. Manual*. Goshen, NY: Research Psychologists Press, 1967.

Jackson, D. N. A sequential system for personality scale development. In C. D. Spielberger (Ed.), *Current topics in clinical community psychology*. Vol. 2. New York: Academic Press, 1970.

John, O. P., Angleitner, A., & Ostendorf, F. The lexical approach to personality: A historical review of trait taxonomic research. *European Journal of Personality*, 1988, *2*, 171–203.

Jones, M. B. Heritability as a criterion in the construction of psychological tests. *Psychological Bulletin*, 1971, *75*, 92–96.

Loevinger, J. Objective tests as instruments of psychological theory. *Psychological Reports*, 1957, *3*, 635–694.

McDougall, W. *An outline of psychology*. New York: Scribners, 1923.

Norman, W. T. Toward an adequate taxonomy of personality attributes: Replicated factor structure in peer nomination personality ratings. *Journal of Abnormal and Social Psychology*, 1963, *66*, 574–583.

Paulhus, D. L. Self-deception and impression management in test responses. In A. Angleitner & J. S. Wiggins (Eds.), *Personality assessment via questionnaires. Current issues in theory and measurement*. Berlin: Springer, 1986.

Plomin, R. Heredity and temperament: A comparison of twin data for self-report questionnaires, parental ratings, and objectively assessed behavior. In L. Gedda, P. Parisi, & W. E. Nance (Eds.), *Progress in clinical and biological research: Twin research III, Part B. Intelligence, personality, and development* Vol. 69B. New York: Alan R. Liss, 1981.

Rosch, E., & Mervis, C. B. Family resemblances: Studies in the internal structure of categories, *Cognitive Psychology*, 1975, *7*, 563–605.

Rusalov, V. M. Object-related and communicative aspects of human temperament: A new questionnaire of the structure of temperament. *Personality and Individual Differences*, 1989, *10*, 817–827.

Strelau, J. *Temperament—personality—activity.* London: Academic Press, 1983.

Strelau, J. The concept of temperament in personality research. *European Journal of Personality*, 1987, *1*, 107–117.

Strelau, J. *Are psychophysiological scores good candidates for diagnosing temperament/personality traits and for a demonstration of the construct validity of psychometrically measured traits?* Paper submitted for publication, 1990.

Strelau, J., Angleitner, A., Bantelmann, J., & Ruch, W. The Strelau temperament inventory revised (STI-R): Theoretical considerations and scale development. *European Journal of Personality*, 1990, *4*, 209–235.

Thomas, A., & Chess, S. *Temperament and development.* New York: Brunner/Mazel, 1977.

Wallace, J. An abilities conception of personality: Some implications for personality measurement. *American Psychologist*, 1966, *21*, 132–138.

Windle, M., & Lerner, R. M. *Revised Dimensions of Temperament Survey-Adult.* Unpublished manuscript, 1985.

Windle, M., & Lerner, R. M. Reassessing the dimensions of temperamental individuality across the life span: The Revised Dimensions of Temperament Survey (DOTS-R). *Journal of Adolescent Research*, 1986, *1*, 213–230.

Windle, M. Psychometric strategies of measures of temperament: A methodological critique. *International Journal of Behavioral Development*, 1988, *11*, 171–201.

Wundt, W. *Grundzüge der physiologischen Psychologie* (5th ed.). Vol. 3. Leipzig: W. Engelmann, 1903.

13

Questionnaire Measurement of Infant and Child Temperament
Current Status and Future Directions

Elizabeth H. Slabach, Judy Morrow, and
Theodore D. Wachs

Introduction

In 1982 Hubert, Wachs, Peters-Martin, and Gandour published a review on the psycho-metric adequacy of various paper-and-pencil measures used to assess temperament. This review documented a number of problems with available instruments, including incon-sistent stability, low interparent agreement and questionable construct, and concurrent and predictive validity. In spite of the pessimistic conclusions of this review, plus the equally pessimistic conclusions of more recent reviews involving such issues as the definition of temperament (Crockenberg, 1986; Bornstein, Gaughran, & Homel, 1986), research on temperament continues at an "exponential" pace (Bates, 1986). Given that this continued interest involves efforts to generate new measures of temperament, as well as to revise old measures, an updated review of the psychometric adequacy of tempera-ment questionnaires seems in order. Specifically, our concern was whether the psycho-metric problems documented by Hubert *et al.* in 1982 have continued to exist.

The present review will be based on research appearing *since* the Hubert *et al.* (1982) review. As in the 1982 review, the present paper will be restricted to studies involving children (birth–18 years) and will be limited to questionnaire measures of temperament. Readers wishing more detail on the use of laboratory or observational

Elizabeth H. Slabach, Judy Morrow and Theodore D. Wachs • Department of Psychological Sci-ences, Purdue University, West Lafayette, Indiana 47907.

approaches to the assessment of temperament can find this information in a number of available reviews (Goldsmith & Rieser-Danner, in press; Rothbart & Goldsmith, 1985).

As in the 1982 review, our prime concern is with the psychometric adequacy of questionnaire measures of temperament, regardless of how temperament is defined. While there seems to be increasing agreement that temperament is biologically based, appears early in life, and is relatively stable across situations and over time, it is also clear that there are still a number of major unresolved issues in the definition of temperament (Bates, 1987, 1989; Goldsmith, Buss, Plomin, Rothbart, Thomas, Chess, Hinde, & McCall, 1987; Strelau, 1987). While there continues to be controversy about the precise definition of temperament, McCall (Goldsmith *et al.*, 1987) has proposed that we accept a working definition of temperament and get on with assessing the utility of the construct. Ultimately we will need to develop a more precise definition of temperament, but for now the authors of this chapter endorse the approach of using a working definition.

The fact that we are adopting a working definition clearly puts more emphasis on the need to have psychometrically adequate measures of temperament. When a working definition is utilized, in practice the working definition often reduces to an *operational definition*; that is, temperament is defined on the basis of instruments used. An example of this is seen in the comment by Rothbart (Goldsmith *et al.*, 1987), that certain concepts were discarded from their list of temperamental dimensions because of an inability to develop appropriate psychometric measures for these variables.

Comparison of instruments cited in the original Hubert *et al.* (1982) review with those found in the current data search indicated that there were a number of measures for which no more than two published research references had been discovered since 1982. This group of instruments may be considered as inactive, and will not be covered in the current review. A listing of these instruments is shown in Table 13.1.

In addition, since 1982, a number of instruments were revised or shortened. These revisions are also listed in Table 13.1. A description of the revisions for specific instruments are to be found in Table 13.2. Finally, since 1982, a number of new temperament questionnaires have emerged. These are listed in Table 13.1 and described in Table 13.2 [viable instruments which have not been revised since 1982, and are described in the Hubert *et al.* (1982) review will not be redescribed here, but are also listed in Table 13.1]. A notable omission from Table 13.1 involves both the Brazelton Neonatal Assessment Scale (BNAS) and the Bayley Infant Behavior Record (IBR), both of which received considerable usage between 1982 and the present.

While some BNAS items may measure aspects of temperament (i.e., rapidity of buildup, irritability, activity), other items have little or no theoretical or intuitive link with the temperament construct (i.e., habituation, pull-to-sit, and lability of skin color). Most temperament researchers using this measure do not identify, *a priori*, which items are relevant for their particular purposes.[1] For a recent review on the psychometric properties of the BNAS, see Brazelton, Nugent, and Lester (1987).

---

[1] Similar concerns also exist for the possible future use of the newly developed "neurobehavioral maturity assessment" for preterms—Korner, Kraemer, Reade, Forrest, Dimiceli, & Thom, 1987—as a measure of temperament.

Table 13.1. The Status of Temperament Instruments: 1982–1988

Instruments minimally investigated since 1982

Temperament Characteristics Inventory
Clinical Behavior Observation Instrument
Nurses Scale for Rating Neonates
Child Stimulus Screening Scale
Parent Temperament Scale Revised
EASI—III
Abbreviated Temperament Questionnaire
Swedish 6, 12 and 24 Month Temperament Questionnaires
Child's Characteristics Questionnaire
EASI—I
Baby Behavior Questionnaire
Toddler Behavior Questionnaire
Neonatal Perception Inventory

Instruments revised since 1982*

Dimensions of Temperament Scale (Revised—DOTS-R)
Teacher Temperament Questionnaire (Short form—STTQ)
Revised Infant Temperament Questionnaire (Short form—SITQ)

Instruments in active use since 1982

Parent Temperament Questionnaire (PTQ—72 items; age range: 3–7 years)
Revised Infant Temperament Questionnaire (RITQ—95 items; age range: 4–12 months)
Toddler Temperament Scale (TTS—97 items; age range: 1–3 years)
Behavioral Styles Questionnaire (BSQ—100 items; age range: 3–7 years)
Middle Childhood Temperament Questionnaire (MCTQ—99 items; age range: 8–11 years)
Perception of Baby Temperament (PBT—56 item Q sort; age range: first year)
Infant Behavior Questionnaire (IBQ—87 items; age range: 3–18 months)
Infant Characteristics Questionnaire (ICQ—24 items; age range: 4–24 months)
Colorado Childhood Temperament Inventory (CCTI—30 items; age range: 5 months–9 years)

Instruments developed since 1982*

Maternal Perception Questionnaire (MPQ)
Temperament Assessment Battery (TAB)
Toddler Behavior Assessment Questionnaire (TBAQ)
Temperament Q Sort (Q Sort)

*Details on instrument format and standardization are shown in Table 13.2.

Table 13.2. New and Revised Temperament Instruments

New Instruments

Instrument	Content	Format/Response mode	Standardization sample
Maternal Perceptions Questionnaire *(MPQ)* (Olson *et al.*, 1982)	At 13 months, 4 factors: language competence; unresponsive to mother; psychomotor incompetence, unsociable. At 24 months, 5 factors: language competence, unresponsive to mother, unsociable, compliant, mature	26-item questionnaire 2 Forms, 13 and 24 month versions	N = 375 13 months N = 120 24 months SES na
Temperament Assessment Battery *(TAB)* (Martin, 1984)	Parent and teacher forms assess 6 characteristics: activity, adaptability, approach, emotional intensity, distractibility, & persistence. Clinician form assesses 5 characteristics: Activity, adaptability, approach, distractibility, & persistence.	7-point ratings based on frequency of behavior. 48 items on parent and teacher forms. 24 items on clinician form used for children 3–7 years	3–7 years parent form; N = 603, 8 different samples from preschool to 2nd grade. Teacher form: N = 605, preschool to 2nd grade. Most from southern or Rocky Mountain regions. Clinician Form: na
Toddler Behavior Questionnaire *(TABQ)* (Goldsmith *et al.*, 1986)	Five affect-based scales: Joy, duration of interest, fear, anger, activity. Also 2 validity scales which assess careless responding and social desirability.	107 items. 7 point ratings, plus "does not apply" option. For use from 18–36 months	165 mothers of twins filled out scale for each twin. Age of twins na,* but other psychometric data collected with 18–24-month-olds.
Temperament Q-Sort *(Q Sort)* (Goldsmith & Alansky, 1987)	4 hypothetical dimensions; (positive emotionality; negative emotionality; interest-persistence; activity level)	Q-sort based on Water's 100 item attachment Q-sort	8–9 trained judges performed Q-sort for hypothetical child who was supposed to be high in a particular construct
Dimensions of Temperament Survey Revised *(DOTS-R)* (Windle & Lerner, 1986)	9 factors: activity-general, activity-sleep; approach, flexibility; mood; rhythmicity-sleep; rhythmicity-eating; rhythmicity-daily habits; Task orientation.	4-point ratings depending on age, either rated by parent or child. 54 items. For use from 4 years–adolescence	N = 114 preschoolers (4 years old) mother rated scale: Child rated scale: 6th graders (12 years old)

Table 13.2. (continued)

New Instruments

Instrument	Content	Format/Response mode	Standardization sample
Shortened Teacher Temperament Questionnaire (STTQ) (Cadwell & Pullis, 1983)	3 factors: task orientation; adaptability; reactivity	23-item questionnaire selected from original TTQ for use from K thru grade school	
Short Infant Temperament Questionnaire (SITQ) (Sanson, Prior, Garino, Oberklaid, & Sewell, 1985)	9 NYLS categories	30-item questionnaire; items selected from RITQ	4–8 months; Australian infants, n = 46, representative of population of State of Victoria

*na = information not available.

In contrast, the majority of the items on the IBR *can* be construed as temperament-related (i.e., social orientation, cooperativeness, fearfulness, reactivity). However, the IBR is primarily an observational tool (based on the examiner's impressions of the infant after a developmental assessment), and thus is beyond the scope of this article (see Bradshaw, Goldsmith, & Campos, 1987 for recent relevant psychometric data on the IBR).

Reliability[2]

Internal Consistency

In their 1982 review, Hubert *et al.* concluded that moderate internal constency appeared to be the norm for most measures. To some extent the same pattern of results is shown in the present survey. Once again, the Colorado Childhood Temperament Inventory (CCTI—Buss & Plomin, 1984; Palisin, 1986), Middle Childhood Temperament Questionnaire (MCTQ—Hegvik, McDevitt, & Carey, 1982), and the Infant Behavior Questionnaire (IBQ—Bradshaw, Goldsmith, & Campos, 1987; Goldsmith & Campos, 1986; Rieser-Danner, 1986; Worobey & Blajda, 1989) continue to demonstrate the highest levels of internal consistency (mean or median $r > .80$). The toddler version of the Infant Behavior Questionnaire (Temperament Behavior Assessment Questionnaire— TBAQ—Goldsmith, 1987; Goldsmith, Elliott, & Jaco, 1986), revised Dimensions of Temperament Scale (DOTS-R—Windle & Lerner, 1986) the teacher form of the Tem-

[2]Originally, all data on reliability were placed in tables detailing information available from each study. Because of page limitations these tables had to be dropped. Readers wishing a copy of the reliability tables can obtain this information by writing to T. D. Wachs, Department of Psychological Sciences, Purdue University, West Lafayette, Indiana 47907.

perament Assessment Battery (TAB—Martin, 1984), short form of the Teacher Temperament Questionnaire (STTQ—Bender, 1985a) and the recently developed Goldsmith Q Sort procedure (Q Sort—Goldsmith & Alansky, 1987) also show highly satisfactory internal consistency ($r > .75$). Lower but acceptable levels of internal consistency ($r > .60$) continue to be shown for the Infant Characteristics Questionnaire (ICQ—Mebert, 1989), as well as for the parent and clinical forms of the Temperament Assessment Battery (Martin, 1984) and the Perception of Baby Temperament Scale (PBT—Sirignano & Lachman, 1985).

The most puzzling results in terms of internal consistency continue to be seen with the set of scales developed by Carey and his associates. The 1982 review indicated that, for the Revised Infant Temperament Questionnaire (RITQ), internal consistency was highly variable. The same degree of variability (across the 9 subscales) is seen in the present survey, not only in terms of the RITQ (Sanson, Prior, Garino, Oberklaid, & Sewell, 1987), but also in terms of the Toddler Temperament Scale (TTS) designed for use with toddlers (Fullard, McDevitt, & Carey, 1984; Gibbs, Reeves, & Cunningham, 1987; Prior, Kyrios, & Oberklaid, 1986) and the Behavioral Styles Questionnaire (BSQ), designed for use with preschoolers (Gibbs *et al.*, 1987; Goldstein, Rollins, Jay, & Miller, 1986; Palisin, 1986). Across all of these scales, the lowest level of internal consistency are most often found for sensory threshold, adaptability, and intensity. As in the 1982 review, the highest internal consistency is most often reported for approach.

While the reasons are not yet clear, the overall pattern of results with the RITQ, as well as with the TTS and BSQ, indicates that caution must be exercised in assuming internal consistency for these scales, if not for the whole instrument, then at least for certain selected subscales such as *sensory threshold, adaptability and intensity.*

Test-Retest Reliability

In their 1982 review Hubert *et al.* concluded that the majority of temperament instruments showed only moderate levels of test-retest reliability. However, in the 1982 review, test-retest reliability was evaluated when the same instrument was given at two different time periods. Thus, retest intervals of anywhere from one week to one year were accepted. Given this liberal definition it could be argued that Hubert *et al.* were confounding test-retest reliability and stability. In the present review, a more *stringent* age relevant criteria for test-retest reliability was utilized. Specifically, for infants in the first year of life a maximum *1-month* test-retest interval was allowed. For toddlers between 12 and 24 months a *2-month* gap was the maximum interval utilized; for children between two years and school age a 3-month interval was utilized, and for school age children a 6-month gap was the maximum interval allowed for test-retest reliability. Test-retest intervals longer than these were considered to be indices of *stability*, regardless of whether the same instrument was used at both occasions. The intervals used, while arbitrary, in our judgment reflect a satisfactory integration of the stability of children's development at different time periods, psychometric criteria, and the theoretical construct of temperament.

Using this more stringent criteria, the available results indicate a higher and much less variable range of test-retest correlations than was previously described. Satisfactory test-retest reliability (mean or median $r > .70$) is found for the Toddler Temperament Scale (with the exception of rhythmicity—Fullard *et al.*, 1984; Gibbs *et al.*, 1987), the Middle Childhood Temperament Questionnaire (Hegvik *et al.*, 1982; Maziade, Cote, Boudreault, Thivierge, & Boutin, 1986) the Colorado Childhood Temperament Inventory (with the exception of sociability—Buss & Plomin, 1984) and the recently developed Maternal Perception Questionnaire (MPQ—Bornstein *et al.*, 1986; Olson, Bates, & Bayles, 1982) and Temperament Assessment Battery (with the exception of adaptability—Martin, 1984). For the Revised Infant Temperament Questionnaire, satisfactory test-retest reliability is shown both for the short form (SITQ) (Sanson *et al.*, 1987) and for the full RITQ, even when used in different cultural settings (Hsu, Soong, Stigler, Hong, & Liang, 1981). Given the wide range of reported correlations (Gibbs *et al.*, 1987; Simonds & Simonds, 1982), the test-retest reliability of the Behavioral Styles Questionnaire must be considered questionnable. Unfortunately there are no new data available on the Infant Characteristics Questionnaire, which, in the 1982 review, showed satisfactory reliability on the fussy-difficult factor, but less satisfactory 1-month test-retest reliability on the remaining three factors.

Stability of Temperament

In their 1982 review Hubert *et al.* concluded that the highest stability appeared to occur for subscales tapping *affective dimensions and activity*. The present review encompassing the *RITQ* (Peters-Martin & Wachs, 1984; Sanson *et al.*, 1987; Washington, Minde, & Goldberg, 1986), *TTS* (Earls & Jung, 1987), *IBQ* (Goldsmith, *et al*, 1986; Rothbart, 1986a; Thompson & Lamb, 1982) and the *CCTI* (Field, Vega-Lahr, Scafidi, & Goldstein, 1987) tends to confirm this earlier conclusion.

In terms of *individual scales*, moderate stability (median or mean $r \pm .30$) is seen for the *PTQ* (Maziade *et al.*, 1986), *RITQ* (Peters-Martin & Wachs, 1984, Sanson *et al.*, 1987), *TTS* (Earls & Jung, 1987; Guerin & Gottfried, 1988), *BSQ* (Guerin & Gottfried, 1988), *IBQ* (Rothbart, 1986a; Sutton, Bell, Luebering, & Aaron, 1988; Thompson & Lamb, 1982) *ICQ* (Lee & Bates, 1985), *MPQ* (Olson *et al*, 1982) and the *TAB* (Martin, Wisenbaker, Mathews-Morgan, Holbrook, Hooper, & Spalding, 1986). Highly variable stability is reported for the CCTI (Field *et al*, 1987). However, these conclusions must be qualified in several ways. *First*, the highest levels of stability appear primarily when stability intervals are no greater than six months. With some exceptions, (eg., Lee & Bates, 1985; Field *et al.*, 1987), particularly for infants and toddlers, stability begins to decline as test-retest intervals increase. *Secondly*, if different raters are used at different ages (Martin *et al*, 1986), or if different instruments are used at different ages (Guerin & Gottfried, 1988), stability also is lower than if the same raters or the same instruments are used at different ages. Finally, there may be differential stability on different dimensions for males and females (Earls & Jung, 1987) or for mothers and fathers (Zenah, Keener, & Anders, 1986).

What are the implications of the above results? The overall results for psychometric stability are consistent with those models of temperament that allow for change in the *behavioral expression of temperament* across time. What is unclear at present is how much of this change is due to genuine variability in temperament across time, as opposed to instrument problems. One approach to distinguishing between these two sources may come from advances in assessing the underlying physiological basis of temperament. Parallel physiological and behavioral changes would suggest that changes in temperament reflect more than just measurement error. Alternatively, research indicating reliable relations between environment and temperament over time would also aid in distinguishing actual changes in temperament from measurement artifact. Until these types of studies are done, the exact meaning of changes in the behavioral expression of temperament over time will continue to remain unclear.

Interrater and Interparent Agreement

In their 1982 review, Hubert *et al.* indicated that interrater or parent-observer reliability estimates were "generally high." However, this was based upon a limited number of instruments for which data were available, including instruments such as the Brazelton or Bayley IBR which assess the child's ongoing behavior during test situations. More recent data indicate that a much more pessimistic conclusion is in order. Specifically, where actual figures are given, parent-observer agreement is generally low ($r < .30$—ICQ Bates & Bayles, 1984; TAB, Martin, 1984) to moderate ($r < .40$—CCTI, Field *et al.*, 1987). While higher interrater agreement is shown for the Q-Sort (Goldsmith & Alansky, 1987) the figures reported refer to interjudge agreement on sorting for one hypothetical child. As will be discussed below, this degree of variability in interrater agreement offers a major problem for temperament researchers.

One of the more serious concerns expressed in the 1982 review involved the tremendous variability and moderate levels of interparent agreement shown. However, this conclusion was based only on results for eight instruments for which data were available. Only two of these instruments, the ICQ and the Parent Temperament Questionnaire (PTQ), have had further study since that time. One study (Black, Gasparrini, & Nelson, 1981) using developmentally disabled children, indicates that interparent agreement (median $r = .66$) for the PTQ is higher than previously reported. At least for the ICQ Fussy-Difficult factor, good interparent agreement ($r = .61$) is again shown (Bates & Bayles, 1984). However, new evidence on four instruments (CCTI, PBT, TAB, TTS) again indicates moderate interparent agreement and high variability in interparent agreement, not only *across* instruments and studies (median interparent agreement across 5 instruments = .43, range .35–.70; Field *et al.*, 1987; Hefferman, Black, & Poche, 1982; Huitt & Ashton, 1982; Martin, 1984; Simons, McCluskey, & Mullett, 1985; Sirignano & Lachman, 1985; Washington *et al.*, 1986; Zenah *et al.*, 1986), but also *within* instruments across temperament dimensions. Thus, both for interparent agreement and interobserver agreement, moderate and highly variable relations appear to be the norm.

As noted earlier, one of the major assumptions underlying the construct of temperament is that temperament is a stable characteristic of the child. As such, the ratings of different observers should reflect this assumed stability. Potential reasons why such cross-rater stability is lacking include problems in adequacy of wording of scale items or instructions, rater response sets, differential weighting of rarely occurring child behaviors, differential amounts of contact leading to different ratings, *or* the possibility that the child is displaying different temperaments for different individuals (Bates, 1989; Hubert *et al.*, 1982; Rothbart & Goldsmith, 1985). However, only a few of the available possibilities have been systematically investigated.

If children were varying their temperamental pattern for each parent, we would expect either to find stable relations between variations in parent interaction patterns and variations in child temperament, or parent-observer coefficients which were higher than mother-father coefficients, (assuming that the contexts in which mothers and fathers see their infants are not substantially different from the contexts in which parents and outside observers see the infant). Both the 1982 review and more recent studies again offer little support for the first (Crockenberg, 1986) or second (Field *et al.* 1987) prediction. In terms of the hypothesis that degree of agreement would be a function of the amount of time spent by the rater with the child, both previous research (Hubert *et al.*, 1982) and more recent research (Martin, 1984) indicate that agreement between mothers and pre-school teachers (both of whom presumably had a good deal of contact with the child) was not significantly higher than agreement between outside observers. Based on what little evidence is available, degree of contact also does not appear to be a viable explanation. A third hypothesis which has been investigated involves the possibility that mothers, fathers, and observers may be either using different behaviors when rating temperament dimensions, or using different criteria for rating child behaviors. Available evidence indicates that while parents may perceive specific infant behaviors differentially in terms of contributing to easiness/difficulty (Hubert & Wachs, 1985), reliable differential perceptions by mothers and fathers on behaviors underlying specific temperamental dimensions have not been demonstrated (Hubert, 1989a, 1989b; Hubert & Wachs, 1985).

The only remaining hypothesis which has been systematically investigated involves the impact of nontemperamental dimensions upon parent or observer ratings. Hubert (1989b) has reported that child characteristics (age and gender) generally did not moderate differences in parents' *pleasure* with their child's temperament. One exception was approach. Pleasure with approach was more salient for mothers of six-months-olds, as compared with mothers of 24-month-olds. For fathers, gender rather than age seemed more salient, with fathers expressing more pleasure at approach by sons than daughters. Child age and parity may also differentially influence parents' assessments, with mothers' ratings being more influenced by child age (Hubert, 1989a; 1989b; Hubert & Wachs, 1985), while fathers reactions are more related to child parity (Hubert, 1989a). These findings suggest that it may be important to assess whether part of the variability in interparent agreement may be due to differential perceptions of behaviors by parents of younger vs older, male and female, or first- versus later-born children.

Validity Issues

In the present review we have divided studies into two validity categories.[3] The first class, *Weak Validity* studies, refers to research based on predictions derived from specific

---

[3]A third validity category, quasi-validity studies, will not be covered here due to space limitations. This category involves research where there is no theoretical or empirical reason to expect predictive relations

models of temperament. In this case, significant findings not only support the theory but also, by implication, lend support to the validity of the instrument used in the study. However, for this class of studies, when there are nonsignificant results, it is difficult to determine if nonsignificance represents a flaw in the temperament instrument or an invalid or oversimplified theory. As a result, studies in this class have only limited utility for establishing the validity of specific temperament instruments. The final class of studies, *Strong Validity* studies, represents research derived either from fundamental postulates about the nature of temperament, or research predicting relations which have already been well documented in other domains. In this case, nonsignificant results are most likely due to instrument failure.

Weak Validity Studies

Temperament and Behavior Problems

Within the framework of the New York Longitudinal Study (NYLS) approach (Thomas, Chess, & Birch, 1986), a major emphasis has been on the relation of temperament to children's behavior problems. While logical, such a proposed relation is not a fundamental test of the temperament construct. In terms of finding predicted relations between *difficult temperament* and behavior problems, significant results are found for the *PTQ* (Maziade, Caperaa, Laplante, Boudreault, Thivierge, Cote, & Boutin, 1985), *RITQ* (DiBlasio, Bond, Wasserman, & Creasey, 1988; Sanson *et al.*, 1985), *BSQ* (Wolfson, Fields, & Rose, 1987), *MCTQ* (Wertlieb, Weigel, Springer, & Feldstein, 1987), *ICQ* (Bates, Olson, Pettit, & Bayles, 1982); Bates, 1987), *MPQ* (Bates, Maslin, & Frankel, 1985), *DOTS* fit score (Lerner, 1984) and the *TAB* (Martin, 1984).

While these significant results support the validity of the instruments used, inconsistent results must also be noted. Differential patterns of relations have been reported for girls and boys (DiBlasio *et al.*, 1988), and for pre- versus postpubescent girls (Lerner, 1984). Evidence is also inconsistent in regard to whether difficulty *equally* predicts both internalizing and externalizing problems (Bates, 1987) or is differentially related (Wertlieb *et al.*, 1987). Whether these inconsistent results reflect instrument or model failure is unclear. Judgment about utility of these studies may also be tempered by the possibility of *item overlap* between temperament and behavior problem scales (Wertlieb *et al.*, 1987). While systematic studies of content overlap do not appear to be available, a brief inspection of the content of temperament scales and behavior problem checklists suggests item overlap between temperament items involving activity and problem checklist items assessing hyperactivity, and between temperament items assessing intensity and problem checklist items assessing noncompliance. When early temperament is

for temperament. For this class of studies, significant findings tell us little about the validity of either the instrument or the theory, especially when there is variability of results across studies. Examples in this category include studies comparing temperament patterns of developmentally disabled and non-disabled children, studies of cross-cultural patterns of temperament, or studies relating temperament to IQ. A listing of relevant studies in this category can be obtained by writing to T. D. Wachs at the address given in Note 2.

used to predict later behavior problems, content overlap may not be so critical, in that temperament-related behaviors may develop into what are later called behavior problems. However, for concurrent prediction, content overlap seems a much more critical problem.

A second set of results involves the validity of specific temperament *dimensions* as predictors of behavior problems. Across studies covering an age range from 2–12 years, the most consistent predictors of behavior problems appear to be the dimensions of *intensity* and *mood* as assessed on the TTS (Earls & Jung, 1987), BSQ (Earls & Jung, 1987; Wolfson *et al.*, (1987), MCTQ, (Hegvik *et al.*, 1982) and unrevised DOTS, (Skarpness & Carson, 1986). It could be argued that the observed consistency is due to common rater variance since, in most cases, the child's caregiver filled out both the temperament questionnaire and the behavior problem measure. However, observed relations for these dimensions also occur when mothers fill out the DOTS and teachers fill out the Child and Adolescent Adjustment Profile (Skarpness & Carson, 1986), making it difficult to attribute results solely to artifact. More serious is the fact that neither adaptability, intensity, nor mood were found to predict when the TAB (Martin, 1984) or STTQ (Bender, 1985a) were correlated with behavior problems in a school setting. It could be argued that different dimensions of temperament are salient for behavior problems in different settings. For example, Klein (1982) has reported that threshold was found to be the best predictor of behavior problems in kindergarten, whereas persistence was found to be the best predictor of behavior problems in a head start classroom.

While different dimensions of temperament may be salient for behavior problems in different settings, until specific theoretically based *predictions* are made about which dimensions of temperament are salient in different settings, it is difficult to separate out actual relations from random correlations. The consistency of evidence, however, does support the validity of the difficult cluster score, as well as the mood and intensity categories of the instruments cited above, as predictors of behavior problems, at least within the home setting.

Temperament and Attachment

It has been argued (Kagan, 1982) that the infant's fear of new people and situations is an early-appearing stable temperamental trait which should influence the child's level of distress, and thus the child's attachment pattern in a strange situation. Available evidence on this question appears to be inconsistent (Bates & Bayles, 1988), with relations between temperament and attachment varying as a function of attachment classification (Belsky & Rovine, 1987), type of behavior assessed in the strange situation (Bates *et al.*, 1985; Bradshaw *et al.*, 1987; Thompson, Connell, & Bridges, 1988), specific temperament dimension and age of infant (Bates *et al.*, 1985). Whether these inconsistent results are due to instrument or theory failure is a subject for future research.

Factor Structure

Most studies in this area have attempted to validate the nine dimension system proposed by the NYLS. Obviously, failure to validate can reflect either instrument failure or a weakness in the NYLS model. Available evidence using a variety of scales such as the *RITQ* (Sanson *et al.*, 1987), *TTS* (Gibbs *et al.*, 1987), *BSQ* (Gibbs *et al.*, 1987), *PBT* (Huitt & Ashton, 1982), and *DOTS-R* (Windle & Lerner, 1986) yields a variety of factor solutions, *none* of which appear to fit the hypothesized nine-dimension solution postulated by Thomas & Chess (1977). Along the same lines, individual scale items which correlate with their hypothesized dimensions are the exception rather than the rule for the *TTS* and *BSQ* (Gibbs *et al.*, 1987), though significant item factor correlations have been reported for the PTQ (Black *et al.*, 1981).

Differences in factor structure across studies may be due to a variety of reasons, including the use of sample sizes that are clearly inadequate for obtaining stable factor structures, use of subjects at different ages, and use of different factor solutions or rotations (Windle, 1988). However, the consistent failure to duplicate the nine-dimensional NYLS model suggests that it may be the theory rather than the instrument that is at fault in this regard.

The above conclusion, implicating theory rather than instrument failure, is strengthened by the fact that, in some cases, stable factor structures have been reported in the literature. For the STTQ, four studies have reported the identification of a *task orientation* and a *reactivity* factor (Cadwell & Pullis, 1983; Mevarech, 1985; Paget, Nagle, & Martin, 1984; Pullis, 1985), while three of the studies have also identified a third factor—*adaptability* (Cadwell & Pullis, 1983; Paget *et al.*, 1984; Pullis, 1985). Similarly, for the PTQ, the first factor described by Maziade, Cote, Boudreault, Thivierge, and Caperaa (1984) appears to be equivalent to that found with this instrument by Thomas *et al.* (1968) in the United States and Persson-Blennow & McNeil (1982) in Sweden. Other studies with the TAB (Martin *et al.*, 1986), STTQ (Cadwell & Pullis, 1983) and the DOTS-R (Windle & Lerner, 1986) indicate stability of factor structure across ages. However, in the case of the DOTS-R (Windle & Lerner, 1986) this is in part a function of the methodology, in that repeated factor analyses were done and items were dropped until there was factor congruence across ages.

Temperament and Parent Characteristics

A number of reports have appeared indicating that temperament questionnaire variability may be influenced by a variety of parent characteristics, including parent anxiety (Affleck, Allen, McGrade, & McQueeney, 1983; Bates & Bayles, 1984; Sameroff, Seifer, & Elias, 1982; Vaughn, 1983), and indices of parental mental illness (Affleck *et al.*, 1983; Sameroff *et al.*, 1982). While it seems clear that parental characteristics may act as a potential confounding factor for questionnaire measures of temperament, this confounding is not considered a strong validity problem, for several reasons. First, as noted in a number of studies (Bates & Bayles, 1984; St. James-Roberts & Wolke, 1984), while most temperament instruments contain both objective and subjective factors, there is no evidence that the influence of subjective factors (parent characteristics) outweigh those of objective factors (child temperament).

A second reason is based on the fact that many of the available studies assume that parents' characteristics influence their report of their child's temperament. An alternative hypothesis is that the child's temperament may influence the parents' characteristics. Evidence for this hypothesis is reported by Cutrona & Troutman (1986). Using path analyses, these authors report that infant difficult temperament both directly and indirectly influences the mother's level of postpartum depression.

The evidence cited above suggests that we cannot automatically assume that relations between parents' characteristics and their reports on temperament questionnaires are evidence against the validity of the temperament questionnaires. This is not to say that we should necessarily ignore subjective factors. To the extent that we can specify which dimensions of temperament are most likely to be influenced by parent characteristics, it may be possible to adopt a strategy proposed by Bates (1987), and use appropriate correction procedures to minimize the confounding influence of parent characteristics.[4]

Temperament as a Mediator

The concept of temperament as a mediator is derived from theoretical statements, which suggests that temperament could influence the individual's reaction to the environment (Thomas & Chess, 1977). While evidence in this area is scarce, Wachs & Gandour (1983) have reported that infants assessed as difficult on the *RITQ* were more influenced by noise and crowding stress in the home than were temperamentally easy infants. Using the *TTS*, this result was replicated by Wachs (1987); Wachs also reported evidence indicating that more active infants had less need of adult mediation of the environment than did less active infants. Using a different outcome measure, this latter result has also been replicated by Gandour (1989), also using the TTS. Evidence congruent with this set of results is also seen in a study by Affleck *et al.* (1983), using the *PBT*, which indicated that high-risk infants rated as more active show greater developmental progress relative to corrected age than do less active infants.

In contrast, Plomin and Daniels (1984) report few interactions between temperament scores on the *CCTI* and measures of the child's home environment, as these influence adjustment at four years. Inconsistent evidence is seen in regard to the *DOTS* or the *DOTS-R*. These instruments are based on the "goodness-of-fit model," which predicts that behavioral outcomes are a function of the degree to which temperamental attributes are congruent or incongruent with environmental demands (Windle, 1988). While some evidence has supported the goodness-of-fit model (i.e., Lerner, 1983, 1984; Lerner & Galambos, 1985; Lerner *et al.*, 1985), other studies report nonsignificant interactions between environmental context and scores on either the DOTS (Lerner, 1984) or the DOTS-R (Windle, Hooker, Lernez, East, Lerner, & Lerner, 1986). Whether these inconsistencies are a function of the weakness of the Thomas-Chess goodness-of-fit theory, weakness of the CCTI, DOTS, and DOTS-R, or the inappropriateness of hierarchical multiple regression for assessing interaction (Windle *et al.*, 1986) remains unclear.

Overall, available evidence supports the sensitivity of the RITQ and TTS when

[4]While measurement issues such as social desirability or response bias are consistently raised in the personality assessment literature (e.g., Paulhus, 1986), there appears to be surprisingly little concern in the temperament literature about potential problems in this area. Given available evidence on the potential influence of parent characteristics upon their temperament ratings of their child, more emphasis on these basic measurement issues also would seem an obvious direction for future psychometric research on temperament scales.

investigating the role of temperament as a mediator. The validity status of the CCTI and the DOTS/DOTS-R remains ambiguous for this line of investigation.

Strong Validity Studies

Temperament and Child Behavior

As noted by Bates (1989), at this level of definition, "temperament" refers to stable cross-situational patterns in observed behavior. While the construct of temperament, defined on this level, represents more than a given specific behavior, it must be assumed that valid measures of temperament will, *at least to some degree*, reflect the observed behavior of the child; i.e., there should be at least a moderate degree of correlation between temperament scores and corresponding behaviors. For this class of studies, validity can be approached both through *convergent validity* (predicting which relations should occur) and *divergent validity* (predicting which relations should not occur). While a variety of convergent relations are reported in the literature, evidence for divergent validity is sorely lacking.

Temperament and Child Behavior in the Classroom

The majority of studies in this area have used the *STTQ* as their measure of temperament. A number of findings support the convergent validity of the STTQ. For example, lower STTQ task orientation has been found to be related to higher distractibility in the classroom (Bender, 1985a) and to the child's need for monitoring by the teacher (Pullis, 1985). Higher STTQ reactivity has also been found for children who need more classroom monitoring (Pullis, 1985). However, there are also an equal number of nonsignificant results. Bender (1985a) has reported nonsignificant relations between STTQ task orientation and the child's task-related behavior in the classroom; Bender also reports that STTQ reactivity and classroom distractibility are related only for learning-disabled children. Paget *et al.* (1984) have reported that STTQ sociability is unrelated to the number of contacts between child and teacher or the number of child-initiated contacts.

One reason for the discrepancies may be methodological. In those studies reporting significant relations, teachers fill out *both* the STTQ and the ratings of the child. When nonsignificant relations are reported, the child's behaviors are typically rated by independent observers. Given the possibility of halo effects when the same rater fills out both instruments, the above pattern does not offer a high level of support for the convergent validity of the STTQ.

Research using the *BSQ* in classroom settings has generally reported nonsignificant results (Carson, Skarpness, Schultz, & McGhee, 1986). For the unrevised *DOTS*, while there is some evidence for convergent validity, results for divergent validity are poor. For example, Skarpness and Carson (1986) report that DOTS attention span bears a low but significant positive relation to the child's rate of productivity in the classroom; however, a similar relation is also shown between mood and productivity. Similarly, Lerner, Lerner, & Zabski, (1985) have reported that fourth-graders who rate themselves as adaptable are also rated as more able by their teacher. However, a similar relation is also shown for activity and teacher ability ratings. Similar inconsistencies, indicating problems with divergent validity, are found for the *TAB*. Martin (1984) reports that TAB activity is positively related to observer ratings of classroom distractibility and gross motor behavior, while children who are disliked by the teacher are rated as more active and more distractible. However, TAB approach negatively relates to peer interaction, while TAB approach and persistence also predict motor activity.

Temperament and Behavior in the Home

In this domain, the strongest validity evidence is shown for the RITQ and the IBQ. For the *RITQ*, studies have reported that temperamentally difficult and moody infants sleep less during the night (Weissbluth, 1981), have difficulty going to sleep or staying asleep (Sanson, Prior, & Oberklaid, 1985) and are more likely to have colic (Sanson *et al.*, 1985). Using a sample of Kenyan infants, DeVries (1984) has reported that infants scored as difficult on the RITQ were more likely to survive famine conditions then temperamentally easy infants. DeVries attributes these differences to difficult infants being more likely than easy infants to elicit caregiving patterns such as feeding. Supporting this interpretation, Carey (1985) has reported that infants who gained 30% or more of weight for length between 6 and 12 months were overrepresented on the RITQ difficult cluster. The relation between temperament and weight gain has also been documented for the *BSQ* and *MCTQ* (Carey, Hegvik, & McDevitt, 1988).

For the *IBQ*, Worobey and Blajda (1989) report that, in the first two months of life, while infant activity and responsivity clusters on the IBQ are unrelated to infant behavior, irritability was positively related to crying and negatively related to alertness. Rothbart and Goldsmith (1985) report that all 5 IBQ scores converge with corresponding observationally based behavioral categories at 3 months (average $r = .47$), and that 4 out of the 5 scales converged at 6 months (average $r = .40$) and at 9 months (average $r = .67$). At the same ages, Rothbart (1986a) reports significant converging relations between observer ratings and IBQ scores for activity, smiling, distress at limits, fearfulness, and positive and negative reactivity. The results, while moderate in magnitude, are consistent. The pattern of results of these two latter studies also suggests that, as children get older, there is a greater degree of convergence between parent reports of temperament and observed child behavior.

For the *ICQ*, evidence is inconsistent across studies. Bates *et al.* (1982), using 6-month-old infants, report that ICQ difficulty scores are significantly and positively correlated with observed fussiness, demandingness, and the degree to which the child is unable to entertain itself. In contrast, both Isabella, Ward, and Belsky (1985) and Fish and Belsky (1988), using infants observed from 3 to 9 months, report that none of the ICQ scales related to observed measures of fussiness or crying. One possible reason for the discrepancy may be methodological. Specifically, the observational data of Bates *et al.* were aggregated across three home visits, whereas those by Fish and Belsky were based on only a single visit, while Isabella *et al.* used two visits. It may well be that multiple observations are necessary before stable relations can be found between child behavior and ICQ scores.

In terms of other research in this area, for the *PTQ*, Gordon (1983) reports that

220   Elizabeth H. Slabach *et al.*

there are no differences between difficult and easy children on a variety of behavioral patterns. For the *PBT*, Affleck *et al.* (1983) report that babies rated as more positive in mood on the PBT were also rated by observers as showing less distress. However, evidence for divergent validity is inconsistent, in that Affleck *et al.* also report that babies showing more optimal interaction patterns with their mothers are rated as more active on the PBT. For the *MPQ*, Olson *et al.* (1982) report that, at 24 months, babies scored as more troublesome are reported as having more conflict interactions with their mothers, whereas babies scored as more compliant are scored as having positive interactions. At 13 months babies who are rated as showing sociability toward strangers (i.e., less shyness) on the MPQ are also rated as showing lower levels of dependency behavior toward their mothers.

Overall, the above results suggest that if one wishes to study relations between temperament and ongoing child behavior patterns, the strongest instruments appear to be the RITQ and the BQ. Both the ICQ and the MPQ, also appear to be potentially useful.

Temperament and Child Behavior in a Laboratory Situation

For the RITQ, the few available studies are too inconsistent to yield a clear pattern of results. Feinman and Lewis (1983) report that, at 10 months, easy infants display more interest and approach toward strangers after positive interaction with their mothers than difficult infants. Berberian and Snyder (1982) report difficult infants show more stranger acceptance at 5–7 months but the reverse at 8–9 months. Wenckstern, Weizman, and Leenars (1984) report that children who are slow responders in laboratory play situations show lower intensity and threshold on the RITQ.

For the TTS, Matheny, Wilson, and Thoben (1987) factor-analyzed the 9 dimensions and reported evidence for a tractability factor. Significant positive correlations between the TTS tractability factor and an objective laboratory measure of tractability were found at 12, 18, and 24 months.

For the IBQ the pattern of evidence is also mixed. Convergent validity between corresponding child behaviors and temperament scores are reported for IBQ *positive emotionality* (Goldsmith & Campos, 1986; Rothbart, 1988; Rothbart & Goldsmith, 1985; Thompson & Lamb, 1982), IBQ *fear* (Goldsmith & Campos, 1986; Rieser-Danner, 1986; Rothbart, 1988; Rothbart & Goldsmith, 1985; Thompson *et al.*, 1988; Thompson & Lamb, 1982), IBQ *activity* (Rieser-Danner, 1986) and IBQ *duration of orientation* (Rothbart & Goldsmith, 1985). Divergent validity is shown by the lack of relation between non-corresponding child behaviors and IBQ *positive emotionality* (Goldsmith & Campos, 1986) and IBQ *fear* scores (Goldsmith & Campos, 1986; Thompson *et al.*, 1988).

While the above offers evidence supporting both the convergent and divergent validity of the IBQ, non-consistent evidence also exists. Some studies report a lack of relation between IBQ and laboratory measures of *activity* (Goldsmith & Campos, 1986; Rieser-Danner, 1986) *fear* (Goldsmith & Campos, 1986) and *orientation* (Rieser-Danner, 1986). Other studies report different patterns of results as a function of age of the child (Rothbart, 1988) or type of laboratory task used (Bradshaw *et al.*, 1987). Questionable divergent validity for the IBQ is also seen in the results of Goldsmith and Campos (1986), who report that IBQ activity is negatively related to distress both during stranger approach and on the visual cliff. Similarly, Thompson and Lamb (1982) report that 19$^1/_2$-month social behavior in the laboratory is negatively related both to IBQ activity and distress at limits. In the one study using the TBAQ (Sutton *et al.*, 1988) a similar inconsistent pattern of results is shown.

In analyzing the above evidence, the most inconsistent findings, either directly or in terms of divergent validity, are found for the IBQ activity and orientation dimensions. While available evidence supports the utility of the TTS tractability and IBQ affect scores as predictors of child behavior in laboratory situations, it also seems important to establish whether these scores are equally useful across all laboratory situations or across all ages. It will also be important to establish whether more consistent relations can be obtained with longer and/or repeated laboratory observations of children's behavior, given that reliability of behaviors seen in single, short-term laboratory observations may be suspect (Rothbart & Goldsmith, 1985).

Temperament and the Child's Behavior During Test Situations

While most studies attempting to relate temperament to global measures of cognitive functioning have not been particularly useful, there are some situations where one can make specific predictions about temperament-performance relations, such that failure of prediction suggests problems with the dimension of temperament under study.

For example, one would expect, based on the hypothesized characteristics of specific dimensions, that children with more negative moods, less adaptability, more withdrawal, or more difficultness might be more resistant in testing situations. Evidence supporting this viewpoint is seen in a recent paper by Wachs, Morrow, and Slabach (1990), indicating that greater intra-infant variability during visual recognition memory testing was related to less adaptability, higher difficultness, greater negative mood, and higher persistence on the *RITQ*. Similarly, Olson *et al.* (1982) report that children scored as more sociable on the MPQ at 13 months were found to be more responsive and less fearful during testing at 13 and 24 months. A similar pattern was seen between unsociability and test responsiveness and fear during testing at 24 months.

Other studies in this area, unfortunately, are less consistent. Some studies report the occurrence of unpredicted relations (problems with divergent validity). Using the *RITQ*, Dunst and Lingerfelt (1985) report that persistence and distractibility predict 2- to 3-month-old infants performance in a conjugate reinforcement task; unfortunately, rhythmicity is a stronger predictor than persistence or distractibility. Unless one assumes that more rhythmic infants are better able to detect regularities in conjugate reinforcement tasks, there appears to be no logical reason for this particular relation.[5] Similarly, preterms who scored high on activity and low in persistence on the TTS were also rated as more sociable during testing, a relation which would not necessarily be predicted (Roth *et al.*, 1984). Using both the *TTS* and the *BSQ* Bathurst & Gottfried (1987) reported that children who were categorized as "untestable" on cognitive measures given

---

[5]Though Bates (personal communication) has argued that rhythmic infants may be more predictable, so that mothers' estimates of when their child will be at its optimal state for a lab visit (not tired, not hungry) are more likely to be correct. Obviously, infants in an optimal state will pay more attention to task variables during testing.

between 24 and 60 months scored lower on approach, as might be expected. However, other possible temperamental mediators such as adaptability, which should also relate to untestability, were not found to be predictive. Fagen and Ohr (1985) report that infants who cried when expectancies were violated during cognitive testing scored higher on IBQ activity than infants who did not cry; though significant, this latter relation would not be expected. Utilizing a conjugate reinforcement task, Worobey and Butler (1988) report a relation between *IBQ* duration of orienting and measures of retention/encoding; however, fear and smiling/laughter also predict performance in the conjugate reinforcement task. Fagen, Singer, Ohr, and Fleckenstein (1987a) also report that expected differences between criers or non-criers on mood did not occur. Other studies report predicted relations for the *RITQ* (Roth, Eisenberg, & Seu, 1984) *IBQ* (Fagen, Ohr, Singer, & Fleckenstein, 1987b), *ICQ* (Bates & Bayles, 1984; Wachs & Smitherman, 1985), and *STTQ* (Mevarech, 1985), but also report that these relations unexpectedly vary by the age, sex or risk status of the child.

For preschool-age children, Goldstein *et al.* (1986) reported that the BSQ persistence score related to errors and the BSQ distractibility score related to initial response latency in the Matching Familiar Figures (MFF) test. These positive findings must be tempered by the fact that while all nine BSQ scales were related to overall MFF impulsivity, only distractibility was found to be in the predicted direction.

Overall, results relating temperament to performance or behavior during testing are inconsistent. Individual differences as a function of group or age make it difficult to interpret the positive findings found with the RITQ and ICQ. Inconsistent findings or problems with divergent validity call into question the utility of the STTQ, TTS, BSQ, and IBQ.

Temperament and Parent Child Interaction

One of the major assumptions from the New York Longitudinal Study is that the path from difficult temperament to behavior problems is mediated via the effect of the child upon the parent (Thomas *et al.*, 1968). While this assumption is not central to the construct of temperament, available evidence from other domains (i.e., Bell & Harper, 1988; Sameroff & Chandler, 1975) would suggest that child characteristics should influence caregiver behavior. Hence we regard this domain as a strong test of instrument validity.[6]

While, on both theoretical and empirical grounds, there should be a relation between the child's temperament and caregiver behaviors, earlier reviews (e.g., Crockenberg, 1986) do not find a consistent set of findings supporting this hypothesis. The present review, incorporating some of the studies described by Crockenberg, as well as others not considered, also indicates an inconsistent pattern of findings.

For the RITQ, while Klein (1984) reports significant temperament-parent behavior relations at 6 and 12 months, data from two other studies report little or no relation between RITQ scores and caregiving pattern at 12 months (Peters-Martin & Wachs,

[6]Studies in which child behavior scores are derived from parent report will not be considered, due to the obvious confounding of parent report measures for both temperament and child behavior (Gunn & Berry, 1985; Simonds & Simonds, 1981). Only studies using independent observations of child behavior will be considered.

1984; Wachs, 1988). Using the IBQ in the first month of life, Worobey and Blajda (1988) also report no relation between observed maternal behaviors and infant irritability, activity, or responsivity. Using the *ICQ*, Lounsbury and Bates (1982) report that, in a laboratory test situation, adults expressed more irritation and anger at the cries of difficult and average infants, as opposed to the cries of easy infants. However, difficult temperament on the ICQ was unrelated to specific patterns of mother infant interaction at either 6 (Bates *et al.*, 1982; Pettit & Bates, 1984) or 13 months (Pettit & Bates, 1984). For the *PTQ*, while significant relations are reported between PTQ easy-difficult scores and maternal interactions with their 3–7-year-old children, the types of caregiver behaviors associated with PTQ scores are not necessarily what would be predicted for parents of children with difficult temperament (Gordon, 1983). Finally, Olson *et al.* (1982) report that 13-month-old infants categorized as unresponsive on the *MPQ* had mothers who made greater use of control interaction techniques at 13 months and lower use of nonpunitive techniques at 24 months. However, in both cases the correlations were quite modest ($r = .18$ at 13 months and $-.20$ at 24 months), and there was no relation between troublesomeness, unresponsiveness, or sociability on the MPQ at 24 months and any measure of parent-child interaction.

Obviously, the possibility that the above pattern of inconsistent results are due to instrument failure cannot be dismissed. However, before dismissing existing instruments as insensitive, other methodological and contextual factors need to be considered. Crockenberg (1986) has emphasized the need to have samples of sufficient size to produce enough statistical power to detect existing relations. Other studies suggest that sex differences may mediate the relation between temperament and interaction (Gordon, 1983; Klein, 1984). A third factor that needs to be considered is whether caregiver characteristics moderate relations between temperament and parent behavior. Lounsbury and Bates (1982) have reported that experienced mothers are less upset by the cries of average and difficult infants than less experienced mothers. Hubert and Wachs (1985) report that the temperament characteristics that cause parents to label their infant as difficult may vary from parent to parent. Finally, while it is important to have adequate measures of temperament, it is also important to have adequate measures of caregiving patterns. As noted by Wachs (1987), short-term, single observations of caregiver behavior may not produce measures with sufficient stability to allow detection of existing relations. Until these problems are dealt with, the failure to find consistent patterns cannot be attributed solely to instrument failure. Obviously, however, the difficulty in finding consistent relations between temperament and caregiver behavior does not, at present, offer support for the validity of existing instruments either.

Expected Group Differences

Most studies on group differences in temperament contribute little to assessing instrument validity, given that there are few theoretically derived or empirically based predictions that can be made about group differences in temperament. One exception is where previous research indicates that group differences do exist. In this situation existing group differences should be reflected in available measurement of temperament. Two examples are noted below.

Based on previous research on the nature of learning disabilities (Bender, 1985b), one would expect differences between normal and learning-disabled children on dimensions such as task orientation in school situations. Evidence available from two studies using the STTQ (Bender, 1985a, 1987) indicates that, in fact, learning-disabled school-age children are rated lower by teachers on task orientation than non-learning-disabled children. Since the teachers knew which children were learning-disabled, these differences are not based on blind ratings. Ideally, a more stringent validity test would utilize blind ratings.

A second expected group difference comes in the area of activity. In a major review, Eaton and Enns (1986) reported evidence from a variety of sources indicating that males are higher in activity level than females. For those temperament studies that have looked at sex differences in activity level, available evidence indicates that expected differences in activity ratings are reflected on a variety of instruments including the *BSQ* (Hegvik *et al.*, 1982; Simonds & Simonds, 1982), *TTS* and *MCTQ* (Hegvik *et al.*, 1982), and the *CCTI* (Buss & Plomin, 1984). The one exception is a study using the *TTS* (Matheny, Wilson, & Nuss, 1984), which indicates no significant sex differences in rated activity level (although these differences did occur in laboratory assessments). Thus, with the exception of the TTS, where the evidence is inconsistent, available evidence indicates the construct validity of each of the above instruments in terms of reflecting expected group differences.

Biological Aspects of Temperament

As noted earlier, one of the major assumptions underlying the construct of temperament is that it is constitutional-biologically based. Variability in temperament scores on specific instruments which are related to variability in biological/constitutional factors would clearly support the construct validity of the particular temperament instrument under study. Unfortunately, at present there is little if any evidence on this particular question. Of the available studies some are inappropriate, either because of the relatively crude nature of biological parameters measured (i.e., pregnancy complications—DeVries & Sameroff, 1984), or because the studies appear to reflect stability in temperamental characteristics rather than biological influences (i.e., relations between neonatal activity and later approach and activity—Korner, Zeanah, Linden, Berkowitz, Kraemer, & Agras, 1985).

Of the few studies available, Ross (1987) has indicated that neonatal acidosis (which is frequently related to respiratory problems) predicts lower activity, rhythmicity, approach, and adaptability on the *TTS* at 12 months of age; higher levels of neonatal supplemental oxygen needed also relates to less approach and slow adaptability on the TTS at 12 months, whereas initial blood oxygen level relates to lower activity. The suggestion of a relation between early respiratory status and later temperament is also seen in the work of Weissbluth, Hunt, Brouillette, Hanson, David, and Stein (1985). Specifically, these authors report that more sleep apnea and periodic (irregular) breathing, between 3–5 weeks, predicted lower RITQ ratings of infant intensity and threshold at four months.

Curiously, for the *IBQ*, which is derived from one of the most constitutionally based theories of temperament (Rothbart, 1986b), there is little evidence for physiological correlates, though there is some evidence for the physiological basis of temperament-related behaviors such as intensity of smiling (Rothbart, 1986b). For the TBAQ, which is the upward extension of the IBQ, Sutton *et al.* (1988) report that lower heart-rate variability was related to higher TBAQ interest, while higher EKG variability, (which relates to uninhibited expressive behavior) was associated with higher pleasure and anger scores on the TBAQ. While research on biological aspects of temperament is sparse, that which is available suggests that further exploration of respiratory and cardiac correlates of temperament may prove fruitful.

Summary and Conclusions

The Psychometric Adequacy of Temperament Questionnaires

In their 1982 review, Hubert *et al.* identified five major problems that limit the psychometric adequacy of existing temperament questionnaires. The present review indicates a resolution of problems in three of these areas. In terms of the problem of *unsatisfactory test/retest reliability*, we have suggested that the criterion for differentiating test/retest reliability from stability utilized in the earlier review was unsatisfactory. When a shorter interval for defining test/retest reliability is utilized, available evidence suggests that most existing temperament questionnaires show a pattern of *significant* short-term test/retest reliability as well as a moderate level of cross-time stability. This pattern is congruent with those theories of temperament which allow for a gradual shift in the behavioral expression of temperament.

In terms of the second problem area, namely a *lack of convergent validity*, studies appearing over the past seven years clearly support the convergent validity of at least five available measures of temperament. In terms of the third problem, *factorial divergence*, while the hypothesized nine dimension NYLS structure is rarely seen, stable factor structures have been demonstrated for several temperament instruments.

While available evidence indicates improvement in the psychometric adequacy of temperament questionnaires for three previously identified problem areas, difficulties continue to exist in the remaining two areas. Specifically, both the Hubert *et al.* review and the present review continue to report *low and variable interparent or interrater agreement figures*. As noted in the present review, available evidence does not support the hypotheses that children are displaying different temperament patterns for different raters, or that agreement is a function of the amount of time spent with the child, or that different raters are using different conceptual schemes when evaluating specific child behaviors. Further, the fact that satisfactory *intraparent* agreement exists for most measures (i.e., there is congruence between a parent's rating of their child on a temperament questionnaire and on their global rating of specific temperament dimensions—Fullard, McDevitt, & Carey, 1984; Gibbs *at al.*, 1987; Hegvik *et al.*, 1982; Ross, 1987), suggests that the source of the problem is not the inability of individual raters to score a child's behavior reliably. At present, the most promising explanation seems to involve the possibility that individual nontemperamental child characteristics, such as age, birth order, or sex, may differentially influence the temperament ratings of different observers or mothers versus fathers. Continuing research defining what aspects of parent perceptions are influenced by nontemperamental child characteristics, along the lines established by Hubert (1989a, 1989b), would seem to be an essential step if progress is to be made in this area.

A second continuing area of concern involves the inconsistent findings relating child temperament to patterns of *parent-child interaction*. Many of the reasons for these inconsistencies have been documented by Crockenberg (1986). What has been highlighted by the present review is the potential relevance of *nontemperamental mediating variables* for this question. Child characteristics such as age, sex, and risk status have all been shown to mediate relations between child temperament and parent caregiving patterns. Similarly, parent characteristics such as anxiety, previous experience with children, and individual preferences for different child behaviors have also been implicated as mediators. The above pattern suggests that the fault may not be so much in the instruments used to assess temperament, but rather in the usage of an oversimplified model of how child temperament influences caregiver behaviors. Specifically, the available evidence suggests that temperament may be a *necessary*, but not a *sufficient* influence upon variability in caregiver behavioral patterns. Rather than continuing to assume a direct correspondence between temperament and caregiver behavior patterns, what seems necessary is the development of models integrating *both* temperamental and nontemperamental individual characteristics, as these relate to subsequent caregiver behaviors (Cutrona & Troutman, 1986). Obviously such a research strategy assumes an adequate measure of child temperament, but this assumption may be necessary for the present. If more complex models are generated and temperamental influences still are not found, then this would be at least indirect evidence against the validity of the temperament instruments used.

In addition to the above problems, the present review also defined a problem area which was not noted in the earlier review, namely the question of *divergent validity*. As noted earlier, the present review documents good convergent validity for a number of existing temperament instruments. However, the importance of finding predicted relations between temperament and specific criterion variables is diminished when unexpected or counterintuitive relations occur with *equal or greater frequency*. This occurrence of unexpected or counterintuitive relations basically defines the divergent validity problem noted in the present review.

In highlighting the divergent validity problem we fully recognize that, while the construct of temperament has had a long history, detailed research and systematic theorizing on temperament are relatively recent. Under these conditions it would be asking too much to initially expect a high degree of accuracy in terms of predicting which relations should not be occurring. Rather, our concern is the lack of emphasis on divergent validity that we see in the literature. While convergent predictions are common, divergent predictions are rare. Significant non-predicted results, while reported, are rarely discussed in terms of whether these results make any sense within the framework of the temperament model or instrument being utilized. While *precise* divergent predictions may not now be possible, it should be possible to begin to specify, *a priori*, which patterns of results are *basically unacceptable* for a specific instrument or model. One conclusion of this review is that temperament researchers must begin to approach the divergent validity problem, at least at this level of prediction, if further progress is to be made in both measurement and theory.

If future results do not yield evidence supporting divergent validity, two possible alternatives should be considered. First there is the possibility that the problem is *conceptual*. Buss and Plomin (1984) have made a distinction between broad and narrow temperament traits, and have suggested that a variety of individual narrow traits can be subsumed under a single broad trait (i.e., fearfulness, shyness, and difficultness may all be examples of a general emotionality trait). Following the Buss and Plomin (1984) hypothesis, one approach would be to use oblique rotations, to determine if supposedly distinct temperament dimensions are, in fact, intercorrelated (Windle, 1988). If Buss and Plomin are correct, the divergent validity problem should disappear if narrow traits are reconceptualized and reclustered into more appropriate broad traits.

The other alternative is *instrument failure*. It may well be that supposedly homogeneous temperamental dimensions are, in fact, heterogeneous in structure. While a unidimensional trait, if adequately measured, should produce evidence indicating both convergent and divergent validity, a heterogeneous multidimensional trait could simultaneously yield evidence supporting convergent validity while rejecting divergent validity. This hypothesis may seem surprising, given the evidence for good internal consistency of most temperament instruments, as noted earlier in this review. However, as noted by Windle (1988), internal consistency is not the same thing as homogeneity. Internal consistency refers to the degree of covariation among items measuring an attribute, whereas homogeneity refers to a set of items measuring the same dimension (Windle, 1988). Thus, there may be high internal consistency in a situation where multiple factors contribute to common score variance. While a dimension which has factorial homogeneity will also have relatively high internal consistency, a dimension which is internally consistent need not necessarily be homogeneous. To assess instrument failure, one approach could involve investigating the actual factor structure of the instrument used. For example, a factor structure where individual items loaded on multiple factors could suggest the existence of heterogeneous temperamental dimensions.

The Utilization of Questionnaires

In their review Hubert *et al.* (1982, p.578) concluded that "no single psychometrically sound and adequately validated measure of early temperament is currently available." These authors suggested that it may be necessary to select specific temperament instruments for specific purposes, rather than assuming that a single instrument will be useful across all situations. While improvements have been made in a number of the available temperament instruments, we are still a long way from having a "benchmark" temperament questionnaire, against which other procedures can be validated, or which is valid for all domains of investigations. Clearly, some instruments appear to be better suited for certain questions than others. For example, the authors of this review would feel comfortable recommending the IBQ for studies involving temperamental contributions to children's normal behavior patterns, the ICQ for studies relating temperament to subsequent behavior problems and the TTS when the question involves the role of temperament as a mediator of environmental influences. However, the lack of research on certain instruments, plus the methodological flaws in some of the available research, indicates that it would be premature at present to classify instruments as valid or invalid. Ultimately, there will be a process of natural selection, resulting in a limited number of psychometrically sound instruments. Indeed, this process may be already occurring. As noted in Table 1, more instruments have become moribund over the past seven years than have been newly developed or revised. For the present, it is hoped that researchers will consider closely the psychometric characteristics of instruments when choosing a temperament questionnaire to use in a study. For example, if the demands of a study call for an instrument with good internal consistency, or adequate stability, or a replicable factor structure, certain instruments may be more appropriate than others.

It could be argued that efforts should more properly be directed at defining the biological underpinnings of temperament, rather than upon improving questionnaire measures. However, to the extent that temperament is a multilevel construct, encompassing both biological and behavioral levels (Bates, 1989), adequate instruments must be available at all levels. It could also be argued that, at a behavioral level, laboratory or observational measures of temperament may be a more appropriate direction than further refinement of questionnaires. However, both laboratory or observation measures of temperament have to deal with the same psychometric problems as questionnaires (Rothbart & Goldsmith, 1985). More importantly the latter argument assumes that utilization of a *single* behavioral measurement approach is the most optimal strategy. However, available evidence on the advantage of using multimethod assessment procedures (i.e., Rushton, Brainerd, & Pressley, 1983) does not support the viability of this assumption. Ideally, we should be able to integrate questionnaires, lab assessments, and direct observations to maximize sensitivity of measurement of temperament. Having psychometrically sound questionnaire measures represents a definite step in this direction.

ACKNOWLEDGMENTS. The authors gratefully acknowledge the detailed and incisive comments of Jack Bates and Nancy Hubert during the writing of this chapter. Special thanks are also owed to Cris Pecknold for her patience in retyping multiple ongoing drafts of the chapter. Requests for reprints or disagreements about conclusions should be addressed to Theodore D. Wachs, at the address given.

References

Affleck, G., Allen, D., McGrade, J., & McQueeney, M. Maternal and child characteristics associated with mothers' perceptions of their high risk/developmentally delayed infants. *The Journal of Genetic Psychology*, 1983, *142*, 171–180.
Bates, J. E. The measurement of temperament. In R. Plomin & J. Dunn (Eds.), *The study of temperament: Changes, continuities and challenges*. Hillsdale, NJ: Erlbaum, 1986.
Bates, J. E. Temperament in infancy. In J. D. Osofsky (Ed.), *Handbook in infant development* (2nd ed.). New York: Wiley, 1987.
Bates, J. E. Concepts and measures of temperament. In G. A. Kohnstamm, J. E. Bates, & M. K. Rothbart (Eds.), *Temperament in childhood*. Chichester: Wiley, 1989.
Bates, J. E., & Bayles, K. Objective and subjective components in mothers' perceptions of their children from age 6 months to 3 years. *Merrill-Palmer Quarterly*, 1984, *30*, 111–130.
Bates, J. E., & Bayles, K. The role of attachment in the development of behavior problems. In J. Belsky & J. Nezworski (Eds.). *Clinical implications of attachment*. Hillsdale, NJ: Erlbaum, 1988.

Bates, J. E., Maslin, C. A., & Frankel, K. A. Attachment security, mother-child interactions and temperament as predictors of behavior-problem ratings at age 3 years. In I. Bretherton & E. Waters (Eds.), Growing points of attachment theory and research. *Monographs of the Society for Research in Child Development*, 1985, *50* (1–2, Ser. No. 209).

Bates, J., Olson, S. L., Pettit, G. S., & Bayles, K. Dimensions of individuality in the mother-infant relationship at 6 months of age. *Child Development*,1982, *53*, 446–461.

Bathhurt, K., & Gottfried, A. Untestable subjects in child development research: Developmental implications. *Child Development*, 1987, *58*, 1135–1144.

Bell, R., & Harper, L. *Child effects on adults*. Hillsdale, NJ: Erlbaum, 1977.

Belsky, J., & Rovine, M. Temperament and attachment security in the strange situation: An empirical rapprochement. *Child Development*, 1987, *58*, 787–795.

Bender, W. N. Differences between learning disabled and non-learning disabled children in temperament and behavior. *Learning Disability Quarterly*, 1985a, *8*, 11–18.

Bender, W. N. Differential diagnosis based on task-related behavior of learning disabled and low-achieving adolescents. *Learning Disability Quarterly*, 1985b, *8*, 261–266.

Bender, W. N. Behavioral indicators of temperament and personality in the inactive learner. *Journal of Learning Disabilities*, 1987, *20*, 301–305.

Berberian, K., & Snyder, S. S. The relationship of temperament and stranger reaction for younger and older infants. *Merrill-Palmer Quarterly*, 1982, *28*, 79–94.

Black, W., Gasparrini, B., & Nelson, R. Parental assessment of temperament in handicapped children. *Journal of Personality Assessment*, 1981, *45*, 155–158.

Bornstein, M. H., Gaughran, J. M., & Homel, P. Infant temperament: Theory, tradition, critique, and new assessments. In C. E. Izard & P. B. Read (Eds.), *Measuring emotions in infants and children*. Vol. 2. Cambridge: Cambridge University Press, 1986.

Bradshaw, D., Goldsmith, H., & Campos, J. Attachment, temperament, and social referencing: Inter-relationships among three domains of infant affective behavior. *Infant Behavior and Development*, 1987, *10*, 223–231.

Brazelton, T., Nugent, J., & Lester B. Neonatal behavioral assessment scale. In J. Osofsky (Ed.), *Handbook of infant development* (2nd ed.). New York: Wiley, 1987.

Buss, A. H., & Plomin, R. *Temperament: Early developing personality traits*. Hillsdale, NJ: Erlbaum, 1984.

Cadwell, J., & Pullis, M. Assessing changes in the meaning of children's behavior: Factorial invariance of teachers' temperament ratings. *Journal of Educational Psychology*, 1983, *75*, 553–560.

Carey, W. B. Temperament and increased weight gain in infants. *Developmental and Behavioral Pediatrics*, 1985, *6*, 128–131.

Carey, W., Hegvik, R., & McDevitt, S. C. Temperamental factors associated with rapid weight gain and obesity in middle childhood. *Developmental and Behavioral Pediatrics*, 1988, *9*, 194–198.

Carson, D., Sharpness, L., Schultz, N., & McGhee, P. Temperament and communicative competence as predictors of young children's humor. *Merrill-Palmer Quarterly*, 1986, *32*, 415–426.

Crockenberg, S. B. Are temperamental differences in babies associated with predictable differences in caregiving. In J. Lerner, & R. Lerner (Eds.), *Temperament and psychosocial interaction in children*. San Francisco: Jossey-Bass, 1986.

Cutrona, B., & Troutman, B. Social support, infant temperament and parenting self-efficacy. *Child Development*, 1986, *57*, 1507–1518.

DeVries, M. Temperament and infant mortality among the Masai of East Africa. *American Journal of Psychiatry*, 1984, *141*, 1189–1194.

DeVries, M., & Sameroff, A. Culture and temperament: Influences on infant temperament in three East African societies. *American Journal of Orthopsychiatry*, 1984, *54*, 83–96.

DiBlasio, C., Bond, L., Wasserman, R., Creasey, G. *Infant temperament and behavior problems at 6 to 7 years*. Paper presented at the International Conference of Infant Studies. Washington, DC, April, 1988.

Dunst, C., & Lingerfelt, B. Maternal ratings of temperament and operant learning in two- to three-month old infants. *Child Development*, 1985, *56*, 555–563.

Earls, F., & Jung, K. Temperament and home environment characteristics as causal factors in the early development of childhood psychopathology. *Journal of the American Academy of Child and Adolescent Psychiatry,* 1987, *26,* 491–498.

Eaton, W. O., & Enns, L. Sex differences in human motor activity level. *Psychological Bulletin,* 1986, *100,* 19–28.

Fagen, J., & Ohr, P. Temperament and crying in response to the violation of a learned expectancy in early infancy. *Infant Behavior and Development,* 1985, *8,* 157–166.

Fagen, J., Ohr, P., Singer, J., & Fleckenstein, L. Infant temperament and subjects loss due to crying during parent conditioning. *Child Development,* 1987a, *58,* 497–504.

Fagen, J., Singer, J., Ohr, P., & Fleckenstein, L. Infant temperament and performance on the Bayley Scales of Infant Development at 4, 8, & 12 months of age. *Infant Behavior and Development,* 1987b, *10,* 505–512.

Feinman, S., & Lewis, M. Social referencing at ten months: A second order effect on infant' response to strangers. *Child Development,* 1983, *54,* 878–887.

Field, T., Vega-Lahr, N., Scafidi, F., & Goldstein, S. Reliability, stability and relationships between infant and parent temperament. *Infant Behavior and Development,* 1987, *10,* 117–122.

Fish, M., & Belsky, J. *Continuity and discontinuity in infant temperament.* Paper presented at the International Conference of Infant Studies. Washington, DC, April, 1988.

Fullard, W., McDevitt, S. C., & Carey, W. B. Assessing temperament in one-to-three-year-old children. *Journal of Pediatric Psychology,* 1984, *9,* 205–216.

Gandour, M. Activity level as a dimension of temperament in toddlers: Its relevance for the organismic specificity hypothesis. *Child Development,* 1989, *60,* 1092–1098.

Gibbs, M., Reeves, D., & Cunningham, C. The application of temperament questionnaires to a British sample: Issues of reliability and validity. *Journal of Child Psychology and Psychiatry,* 1987, *28,* 61–77.

Goldsmith, H. *The Toddler Behavior Assessment-Questionnaire Manual.* Department of Psychology, University of Oregon, 1987.

Goldsmith, H., & Alansky, J. *Construction of Q sort measures of temperament and their relation to security of attachment.* Paper presented at the Society for Research in Child Development. Baltimore, April, 1987.

Goldsmith, H. H., Buss, A. H., Plomin, R., Rothbart, M. K., Thomas, A., Chess, S., Hinde, R. A., & McCall, R. R. Roundtable: What is temperament? Four approaches. *Child Development,* 1987, *58,* 505–529.

Goldsmith, H. H., & Campos, J. J. Fundamental issues in the study of early temperament: The Denver Twin Temperament Study. In M. E. Lamb, A. L. Brown, & B. Rogoff (Eds.), *Advances in developmental psychology.* Vol. 4. Hillsdale, NJ: Erlbaum, 1986.

Goldsmith, H. H., Elliot, T. K., & Jaco, K. L. Construction and initial validation of a new temperament questionnaire. *Infant Behavior and Development,* 1986, *9,* 144.

Goldsmith, H. H., & Rieser-Danner, L. Assessing early temperament. In C. R. Reynolds, & R. Kamphaus (Eds.), *Handbook of psychological and educational assessment of children.* Vol. 2. *Personality, behavior and context.* New York: Guilford, 1989.

Goldstein, F., Rollins, H., Jay, R., & Miller, S. Temperament and cognitive style in school age children. *Merrill-Palmer Quarterly,* 1986, *32,* 263–273.

Gordon, B. Maternal perception of child temperament and observed mother-child interaction. *Child Psychiatry and Human Development,* 1983, *13,* 153–167.

Guerin, D., & Gottfried, A. Correlations of temperament from infancy through eight years. Paper presented at the International Conference on Infant Studies. Washington, DC, April, 1988.

Gunn, P., & Berry, P. Down syndrome temperament and maternal response to description of child behavior. *Developmental Psychology,* 1985, *21,* 842–847.

Heffernan, L., Black, W., & Poche, P. Temperament patterns in young neurologically impaired children. *Journal of Pediatric Psychology,* 1982, *7,* 415–423.

Hegvik, R., McDevitt, S., & Carey, W. The Middle Childhood Temperament Questionnaire. *Developmental and Behavioral Pediatrics,* 1982, *3,* 197–200.

Hsu, C., Soong, W., Stigler, J., Hong, C., & Liang, C. The temperamental characteristics of Chinese babies. *Child Development*, 1981, *52*, 1337–1340.

Hubert, N. C. *Parental attributions regarding their young children's temperamental easiness/ difficultness.* Paper presented at the meeting of the Society for Research in Child Development. Kansas City, April, 1989a.

Hubert, N. C. Parental reactions to perceived temperament behaviors in their 6 and 24 month old children. *Infant Behavior and Development*, 1989b, *12*, 185–198.

Hubert, N. C., & Wachs, T. D. Parental perceptions of the behavioral components of infant easiness/difficultness. *Child Development*, 1985, *56*, 1525–1537.

Hubert, N. C., Wachs, T. D., Peters-Martin, P., & Gandour, M. J. The study of early temperament: Measurement and conceptual issues. *Child Development*, 1982, *53*, 571–600.

Huitt, W., Ashton, P. Parent's perception of infant temperament: A psychometric study. *Merrill-Palmer Quarterly*, 1982, *28*, 95–109.

Isabella, R., Ward, M., & Belsky, J. Convergence of multiple sources of information on infant individuality: Neonatal behavior, infant behavior, and temperament reports. *Infant Behavior and Development*, 1985, *8*, 283–291.

Kagan, J. *Psychological research on the human infant*. New York: Grant Foundation, 1982.

Klein, H. The relationship between children's temperament and adjustment to kindergarten and Head Start settings. *Journal of Psychology*, 1982, *112*, 259–268.

Klein, P. Behavior of Israeli mothers toward infants in relation to infants' perceived temperament. *Child Development*, 1984, *55*, 1212–1218.

Korner, A., Kraemer, H., Reade, E., Forrest, T., Dimiceli, S., & Thom, V. A methodological approach to developing an assessment procedure for testing the neurobehavioral maturity of pre term infants. *Child Development*, 1987, *68*, 1478–1487.

Korner, A., Zeanah, C., Linden, J., Berkowitz, R., Kraemer, H., & Agras, W. The relation between neonatal and later activity and temperament. *Child Development*, 1985, *56*, 38–42.

Lee, C., & Bates, J. Mother-child interaction of age two years and perceived difficult temperament. *Child Development*, 1985, *56*, 1314–1325.

Lerner, J. V. The role of temperament in psychological adaptation in early adolescents: A test of a "goodness of fit" model. *Journal of Genetic Psychology*, 1983, *143*, 149–157.

Lerner, J. V. The impact of temperament for psychosocial functioning: Tests of a "goodness of fit" model. *Merrill-Palmer Quarterly*, 1984, *30*, 177–188.

Lerner, J. V., & Galambos, N. Maternal role satisfaction, mother-child interaction, and child temperament: A process model. *Developmental Psychology*, 1985, *21*, 1157–1164.

Lerner, J. V., Lerner, R. M., & Zabski, S. Temperament and elementary school children's actual and rated academic performance: A test of a "goodness-of-fit" model. *Journal of Child Psychology and Psychiatry*, 1985, *26*, 125–136.

Lounsbury, M., & Bates, J. The cries of infants of differing levels of perceived temperamental difficultness: Acoustic properties and effects on listeners. *Child Development*, 1982, *53*, 677–686.

Martin, R. P. *The Temperament Assessment Battery manual*. University of Georgia. Athens, GA, 1984.

Martin, R. P., Wisenbaker, J., Mathews-Morgan, J., Holbrook, J., Hooper, S., & Spalding, F. Stability of teacher temperament ratings over 6 and 12 months. *Journal of Abnormal Child Psychology*, 1986, *14*, 167–179.

Matheny, A. P., Jr., Wilson, R., & Nuss, S. Toddler temperament: Stability across settings and over ages. *Child Development*, 1984, *55*, 1200–1211.

Matheny, A. P., Jr., Wilson, R., Thoben, A. Home and mother: Relation with infant temperament. *Developmental Psychology*, 1987, *21*, 486–494.

Maziade, M., Cote, R., Boudreault, M., Thivierge, J., & Boutin, P. Family correlates of temperament continuity and change across middle childhood. *American Journal of Orthopsychiatry*, 1986, *56*, 195–203.

Maziade, M., Cote, R., Boudreault, M., Thivierge, J., & Caperaa, P. The New York Longitudinal Study's Model of Temperament: Gender differences in demographic correlates in a French-speaking population. *Journal of American Academy of Child Psychiatry*, 1984, *233*, 582–587.

Maziade, M., Caperaa, P., Laplante, B., Boudreault, H., Thivierge, J., Cote, R., & Boutin, P. Value of difficult temperament among 7 year-olds in the general population for predicting psychiatric diagnosis at age 12. *American Journal of Psychiatry*, 1985, *142*, 943–946.

Mebert, C. Stability and change in parent perception of infant temperament: Early pregnancy to 13.5 months postpartum. *Infant Behavior and Development*, 1989, *12*, 237–244. Paper presented at the International Conference on Infant Studies. Washington, DC, April, 1988.

Mevarech, Z. The relationships between temperament characteristics, intelligence, task-engagement, and mathematics achievement. *British Journal of Educational Psychology*, 1985, *55*, 156–163.

Olson, S., Bates, J., & Bayles, K. Maternal perceptions of infant toddler behavior: A longitudinal, construct validation study. *Infant Behavior and Development*, 1982, *5*, 397–410.

Paget, K., Nagle, R., & Martin, R. Interrelationships between temperament characteristics and first-grade teacher-student interactions. *Journal of Abnormal Child Psychology*, 1984, *12*, 547–560.

Palisin, H. Preschool temperament and performance on achievement tests. *Developmental Psychology*, 1986, *12*, 766–770.

Paulhus, D. L. Self-deception and impression management in test responses. In A. Angleitner & J. S. Wiggins (Eds.), *Personality assessment via questionnaires. Current issues in theory and measurement*. Berlin: Springer, 1986.

Persson-Blennow, I., & McNeil, T. Factor analysis of temperament characteristics in children at 6 months, 1 year, and 2 years of age. *British Journal of Educational Psychology*, 1982, *52*, 51–57.

Peters-Martin, P., & Wachs, T. D. A longitudinal study of temperament with its correlates in the first 12 months. *Infant Behavior and Development*, 1984, *7*, 285–298.

Pettit, G., & Bates, J. Continuity of individual differences in the mother-infant relationship from six to thirteen months. *Child Development*, 1984, *55*, 729–739.

Plomin, R., & Daniels, D. The interaction between temperament and environment: Methodological considerations. *Merrill-Palmer Quarterly*, 1984, *30*, 1449–162.

Prior, M., Kyrios, M., & Oberklaid, F. Temperament in Australia, American, Chinese, and Greek infants. *Journal of Cross-Cultural Psychology*, 1986, *17*, 455–474.

Pullis, M. LD students' temperament characteristics and their impact on decisions by resource and mainstream teachers. *Learning Disability Quarterly*, 1985, *8*, 109–121.

Rieser-Danner, L. *Measures of infant temperament: A convergent validity study*. Paper presented at the International Conference on Infant Studies. Los Angeles, April, 1986.

Ross, G. Temperament of preterm infants: Its relationship to perinatal factors and one-year outcome. *Journal of Developmental and Behavioral Pediatrics*, 1987, *8*, 106–110.

Roth, K., Einsenberg, N., & Seu, E. The relation of preterms and full term infants' temperament to test-taking behaviors and developmental status. *Infant Behavior and Development*, 1984, *7*, 495–505.

Rothbart, M. K. Longitudinal observation of infant temperament. *Developmental Psychology*, 1986a, *22*, 356–365.

Rothbart, M. K. A psychobiological approach to the study of temperament. In G. A. Kohnstamm (Ed.), *Temperament discussed*. Lisse: Swets & Zeitlinger, 1986b.

Rothbart, M. K. Temperament and the development of inhibited approach. *Child Development*, 1988, *59*, 1241–1250.

Rothbart, M. K., & Goldsmith, H. H. Three approaches to the study of infant temperament. *Developmental Review*, 1985, *5*, 237–250.

Rushton, P., Brainerd, C., Pressley, M. Behavioral development and construct validity: The principle of aggregation. *Psychological Bulletin*, 1983, *94*, 18–38.

Sameroff, A., & Chandler, M. Reproductive risk and the continuum of caretaking casuality. In F. Horowitz (Ed.), *Review of child development research IV*. Chicago: University of Chicago Press, 1975.

Sameroff, A. J., Seifer, R., & Elias, P. K. Sociocultural variability in infant temperament ratings. *Child Development*, 1982, *53*, 564–578.

Sanson, A., Prior, M., Garino, E., Oberklaid, F., & Sewell, J. The structure of infant temperament: Factor analysis of the Revised Infant Temperament Questionnaire. *Infant Behavior and Development*, 1987, *10*, 97–104.

Sanson, A., Prior, M., & Oberklaid, F. Normative data on temperament in Australian infants. *Australian Journal of Psychology*, 1985, *37*, 185–195.

Simonds, J., & Simonds, M. Nursery school children's temperament related to sex birth position and socioeconomic status. *Journal of Pediatric Psychology*, 1982, *7*, 49–59.

Simonds, M., & Simonds, J. Relationship of maternal parenting behaviors to preschool children's temperament. *Child Psychiatry and Human Development*, 1981, *12*, 19–31.

Simons, C., McCluskey, K., & Mullett, M. Interpersonal ratings of temperament for high and low risk infants. *Child Psychiatry and Human Development*, 1985, *15*, 167–179.

Sirignano, S., & Lachman, M. Personality change during the transition to parenthood: The role of perceived infant temperament. *Developmental Psychology*, 1985, *21*, 558–567.

Skarpness, C., & Carson, D. Temperament, communicative competence. The psychological adjustment of kindergarten children. *Psychology Reports*, 1986, *59*, 1299–1308.

St. James-Roberts, I., & Wolke, D. Comparison of mothers' with trained observers' reports of neonatal behavior style. *Infant Behavior and Development*, 1984, *7*, 299–310.

Strelau, J. The concept of temperament in personality research. *European Journal of Personality*, 1987, *1*, 107–117.

Sutton, D., Bell, M., Luebering, A., & Aaron, N. *Laboratory and maternal report measures of temperament and their relationship to heart rate variability.* Paper presented at the International Conference on Infant Studies. Washington, DC, April, 1988.

Thomas, A., & Chess, S. *Temperament and development.* New York: Brunner/Mazel, 1977.

Thomas, A., Chess, S., & Birch, H. *Temperament and behavior disorders in children.* New York: New York University Press, 1968.

Thompson, R. A., Connell, J. & Bridges, L. Temperament, emotion and social interactive behavior in the strange situation: A component process analysis of attachment system function. *Child Development*, 1988, *59*, 1102–1110.

Thompson, R., & Lamb, M. Stranger sociability and its relationship to temperament and social experience during the second year. *Infant Behavior and Development*, 1982, *5*, 277–287.

Vaughn, B. *Maternal personality variables measured prenatally predict perception of infant temperament.* Paper presented at the biannual meeting of the Society for Research in Child Development. Detroit, April, 1983.

Wachs, T. D. Short-term stability of aggregated and nonaggregated measures of parental behavior. *Child Development*, 1987, *58*, 796–797.

Wachs, T. D. Relevance of physical environment influences for toddler temperament. *Infant Behavior and Development*, 1988, *11*, 431–446.

Wachs, T. D., & Gandour, M. J. Temperament, environment, and six-month cognitive-intellectual development: A test of the organismic specificity hypothesis. *International Journal of Behavioral Development*, 1983, *6*, 135–152.

Wachs, T. D., Morrow, J., & Slabach, E. Intra-individual variability in infant visual recognition performance: Temperamental and environmental correlates. *Infant Behavior and Development*, 1990, *13*, 401–407.

Wachs, T. D., & Smitherman, C. H. Infant temperament and subject loss in an habituation procedure. *Child Development*, 1985, *56*, 861–867.

Washington, J., Minde, K., & Goldberg, S. Temperament in pre-term infants. *Journal of American Academy of Child Psychiatry*, 1986, *25*, 493–502.

Weissbluth, M. Sleep duration and infant temperament. *Journal of Pediatrics*, 1981, *99*, 817–819.

Weissbluth, M., Hunt, C., Brouillette, R., Hanson, D., David, R., & Stein, I. Respiratory patterns during sleep and temperament ratings in normal infants. *Journal of Pediatrics*, 1985, *106*, 688–690.

Wenckstern, S., Weizman, F., & Leenars, A. Temperament and tempo of play in eight month old infants. *Child Development*, 1984, *55*, 1195–1199.

Wertlieb, D., Weigel, C., Springer, T., & Feldstein, M. Temperament as a moderator of children's stressful experiences. *American Journal of Orthopsychiatry*, 1987, *57*, 234–245.

Windle, M. Psychometric strategies of measures of temperament: A methodological critique. *International Journal of Behavioral Development*, 1988, *11*, 171–201.

Windle, M., Hooker, K., Lenerz, K., East, P. L., Lerner, J. V., & Lerner, R. M. Temperament, perceived competence, and depression in early- and late-adolescents. *Developmental Psychology*, 1986, *22*, 384–392.

Windle, M., & Lerner, R. M. Reassessing the dimensions of temperamental individuality across the life-span: The Revised Dimensions of Temperament Survey (DOTS-R). *Journal of Adolescent Research*, 1986, *1*, 213–230.

Wolfson, J., Fields, J., & Rose, S. Symptoms, temperament, resiliency, and control in anxiety-disordered preschool children. *Journal of the American Academy of Child and Adolescent Psychiatry*, 1987, *26*, 16–22.

Worobey, J., & Blajda, V. M. Temperamental ratings at 2 weeks, 2 months, and 1 year: Differential stability of activity and emotionality. *Developmental Psychology*, 1989, *25*, 257–263.

Worobey, J., & Butler, J. Memory learning and temperament in early infancy. Paper preseted at the International Conference on Infant Studies. Washington, DC, April, 1988.

Zenah, C., Keener, M., & Anders, T. Developing perceptions of temperament and their relation to mother and infant behavior. *Journal of Child Psychology and Psychiatry*, 1986, *27*, 499–512.

14

Mother-Father Agreement in Temperament Ratings
A Preliminary Investigation

Roy P. Martin and Charles F. Halverson, Jr.

There is a sizeable literature which demonstrates that temperament ratings by parents predict meaningful psychological outcomes. In the seminal New York Longitudinal Study, for example, (Thomas, Chess, Birch, Hertzig, & Korn, 1963; Thomas, Chess, & Birch, 1968; Thomas & Chess, 1977) parent reports in the form of interviews were used and were found to be reliable, and to relate in meaningful ways to a variety of outcomes. Building on this work and research from other traditions (e.g., behavior genetics), many parent-rating scales have been developed and several have been widely used. These include the Infant Temperament Questionnaire (Carey & McDevitt, 1978), the Toddler Temperament Questionnaire (Fullard, McDevitt, & Carey, 1978), The Middle Childhood Questionnaire (Hegvik, McDevitt, & Carey, 1982), the Behavior Style Questionnaire (McDevitt & Carey, 1978), the Dimensions of Temperament Survey (Lerner, Palermo, Spiro, & Nesselroade, 1982), and Infant Behavior Questionnaire (Rothbart, 1981). Each of the more widely used measures demonstrated acceptable though varying levels of temporal stability and internal consistency, and substantial concurrent and predictive validity.

Despite such successes, those of us who use questionnaires to measure temperament are humbled by the fact that the rater and the instrument are really inseparable parts of the measurement process, and raters are known to be subject to a variety of influences affecting the ratings provided. Maternal depression and anxiety, for example, have been found to affect mothers' descriptions of their children on behavior problem checklists (Brody & Forehand, 1986; Forehand, Wells, McMahon, Griest, & Rogers, 1982; Sears,

Roy P. Martin • Department of Educational Psychology, University of Georgia, Athens, Georgia 30602.   **Charles F. Halverson, Jr.** • Department of Child and Family Development, University of Georgia, Athens, Georgia 30602.

Maccoby, & Levin, 1957) as well as on temperament measures (Sameroff, Seifer, & Elias, 1982; Vaughn, Bradley, Joffe, Seifer, & Barglow, 1987).

A survey of characteristics of instruments designed to measure temperament indicates that one of the weakest aspects of parental ratings is indexed by estimates of interrater agreement. For example, for the Temperament Assessment Battery for Children (TABC, Martin, 1988), a measure designed for children 3 through 7 years of age, internal consistencies for mothers and fathers typically range from .60 to .90 across the six scales of the instrument, and stabilities over a one-year period from .40 to .70. Interrater agreement indexed by the correlation between mothers' and fathers' ratings show more variability and a lower mean level than other reliability indices. For example, the interrater correlations for mothers and fathers reported in the TABC manual (Martin, 1988) generally ranged from .00 to .70, with a mean around .40. Persons using other scales have obtained somewhat similar results. Jacob, Grounds, and Haley (1982) reported correlations ranging from .18 to .73 across three scores on the Behavior Problem Checklist (Quay, 1977), and Lyon and Plomin (1981) found correlations between mothers and fathers on the EASI (Emotionality, Activity, Sociability & Impulsivity Scale; a temperament measure) rating from .27 to .57. Goldsmith (1981) found parental correlations for the Infant Behavior Questionnaire were all below .60, and Bates (1980) reports, in a brief review of parental agreement studies, correlations between .06 and .69.

One of the interesting aspects of reliability on the TABC is that agreement seems to be related to identifiable characteristics of the sample; that is, samples composed of "normal" preschool and early elementary school children seem to have higher levels of parental agreement, while samples referred for psychological evaluation due to parental concern seem to have lower levels of parent agreement (Pfeffer & Martin, 1983).

With these differences in mind, the authors have begun a series of investigations into factors that may be related to variation in parental agreement in temperament ratings. It is the purpose of this chapter to report on some of this research. More specifically, the chapter reviews four indices of agreement, and presents some of the initial results of research designed to isolate correlates of variation in parental agreement.

It should be noted that the approach taken in this research differs from most attempts to isolate factors that affect parent ratings of children. The most typical approach to this problem is to obtain measures of characteristics of the rater, the child rated, or the situation in which ratings are obtained, and to correlate these with parental ratings. Examples of research of this type which focus on temperament ratings include Bates and Bayles (1984); Sameroff et al., (1982); and Vaughn et al., (1987). The approach taken here is to compute indices of parental agreement (usually across several samples) and then determine if variation in the agreement index is systematically related to characteristics of the parents, the child, or the situation.

Method

Participants

Research on four samples is reported. The first sample, referred to here as the *Georgia Longitudinal Study Sample*, consists of children from 154 intact families who are participating in a short-term longitudinal study still in progress on the effect of family factors on child behavior. Each family had both parents in the home and at least one child between three and six years of age (referred to as the target child) with no child over ten years of age. Families were recruited from preschools, day-care centers, and radio and newspaper announcements. Families and teachers were paid for their participation. The sample was predominantly white and middle-class with mean education level of mothers being a college degree and for fathers some graduate training. The data reported here are for target child temperament ratings by mothers and fathers in the third year of the study (mean age of sample was approximately 6.9 years, range 5 to 9 years).

The second sample, referred to as the *Georgia Preschool Clinic Sample*, consisted of 170 children between the ages of 3 and 7 years of age who had been referred to the University of Georgia Preschool Clinic. Most of the children were white, and from middle-class homes, with an overrepresentation of university faculty families. The clinic served any parent who wanted information about their preschool child for whatever reason. Some had concerns about the poor developmental level of their child, but the majority wanted documentation of their own perception that their child was developing well and had above-average ability. In fact, many of the children were in the gifted range of cognitive ability: the mean IQ of the sample was 116. This clinic serves as a training clinic for psychologists, so each child was administered a large battery of tests, and parents and teachers completed several questionnaires describing the child, including ratings of temperament.

Sample 3, referred to here as the *Preschool Sample (PS)*, consisted of 48 children (27 males, 21 female) with a mean age of 49.9 months, selected from three private preschools in the greater Philadelphia, Pa. area. These children were selected as a "normal" control group for a sample of similar-age children who had been referred for psychological evaluations in a study of temperament differences between referred and nonreferred children (Pfeffer & Martin, 1983). Children were systematically drawn from each socioeconomic strata of the community, ranging from Warner's (1960) category "1" through "7."

The "referred" sample of 48 children from the Pfeffer and Martin (1983) study constituted the fourth sample for which data are reported here, and this sample is known as the *Pennsylvania Child Find Sample*. It was so named because these children had been referred by their parents to a team of evaluators (medical, psychological, speech, and language specialists) in response to radio and other mass-media announcements designed to notify parents of the importance of identifying preschool children who might have developmental delays or emotional problems. The sample studied in this research consisted of those children who had been referred because of behavior problems, particularly those who exhibited noncompliant or conduct problems. Children exhibiting anxiety, withdrawn behavior, or shyness were excluded. The sample consisted of 33 males and 15 females, with a mean age of 49.4 months. Children were drawn from all socioeconomic levels, as was documented by Warner (1960) categorizations of families fairly evenly divided from category "1" through category "7" (see Pfeffer & Martin, 1983).

Instrument

For all four samples, temperament was assessed using the Temperament Assessment Battery for Children—Parent Form (Martin, 1988). This is a revision of the

Thomas, Chess, and Korn Parent Temperament Questionnaire (Thomas & Chess, 1977), designed to improve the psychometric characteristics of the original instrument. For theoretical as well as psychometric considerations, three of the original scales (Mood, Threshold, and Rhythmicity) were eliminated, leaving six scales: Activity Level (motoric vigor), Adaptability (ease and speed of adjustment of new social situations), Approach/Withdrawal (initial tendency to approach or withdraw from new situations), Emotional Intensity (particularly intensity of negative emotions), Ease-of-Management-Through-Distraction (extent to which the parent can manage inappropriate behavior through use of distraction), and Persistence (attention span, and tendency to continue a learning task despite obstacles).

Extensive reliability and validity data are reported in the manual (Martin, 1988). Internal consistency as indexed by coefficient alpha ranges from .60 to .87 for the six scales of the Parent Form. The Activity Level, Ease-of-Management-Through-Distraction and Approach/Withdrawal Scales tend to have higher internal consistencies than the remaining scales. Stability of mother ratings over one year range from .43 for Ease-of-Management-Through-Distraction to .70 for Persistence. For fathers, one year stabilities range from .37 for Ease-of-Management-Through-Distraction to .62 for Persistence and Approach/Withdrawal.

Data Analysis Procedures

As one begins to examine the issue of agreement between raters, it becomes clear that there is not one index of agreement but a family of such indices. Four indices of agreement were investigated in this research: (1) comparisons of differences in means and standard deviations of ratings provided by mothers and fathers for each sample; (2) correlations between ratings of mothers' and fathers' of the same characteristic (e.g., activity level) for each sample; (3) calculation of absolute differences between mothers' and fathers' ratings across all temperamental characteristics rated for each child; and (4) intraclass correlations for mothers' and fathers' ratings for each child. For the latter two indices, correlations were calculated between the index and selected characteristics of the situation, the child, and the raters.

Results

Mean Differences in Ratings of Mothers and Fathers

One of the most straightforward methods of determining degree of agreement between raters is to compare mean differences in ratings for one or more samples. Such data for four samples are presented in Table 14.1. Differences were calculated by substracting the mean rating of fathers from the mean rating of mothers for each scale; thus a positive mean difference indicates that mothers' ratings were higher than fathers' ratings. Mean differences were tested for statistical significance by t-tests for correlated samples. (The correlated-samples t-test was used because mothers' and fathers' ratings correlate modestly).

Inspection of the means in Table 14.1 indicates that for some temperament characteris-

**Table 14.1. Mean Differences Between Ratings of Mothers
and Fathers: Four Samples**

Temperament scale and sample	N	Mean Diff.*	t-test** p
Activity			
Georgia Longitudinal Study	154	-1.20	<.01
Georgia Preschool Clinic	170	.69	ns
Kindergarten Sample	48	-1.92	ns
Pennsylvania Child Find Sample	48	1.44	ns
Adaptability			
Georgia Longitudinal Study		1.20	<.001
Georgia Preschool Clinic		.77	ns
Kindergarten Sample		.72	ns
Pennsylvania Child Find Sample		-1.44	ns
Approach/Withdrawal			
Georgia Longitudinal Study		1.15	<.01
Georgia Preschool Clinic		.04	ns
Kindergarten Sample		1.52	ns
Pennsylvania Child Find Sample		1.12	ns
Emotional Intensity			
Georgia Longitudinal Study		-.34	ns
Georgia Preschool Clinic		.70	ns
Kindergarten Sample		-.05	ns
Pennsylvania Child Find Sample		-.80	ns
Ease of Management Through Distraction			
Georgia Longitudinal Study		1.91	<.001
Georgia Preschool Clinic		2.34	<.001
Kindergarten Sample		11.28	<.001
Pennsylvania Child Find Sample		-8.72	<.001
Persistence			
Georgia Longitudinal Study		1.10	<.01
Georgia Preschool Clinic		.32	ns
Kindergarten Sample		1.28	ns
Pennsylvania Child Find Sample		1.92	ns

*Mean difference was calculated by subtracting father's scores from mother's score.
**t-test for correlated samples, mothers' and fathers' ratings.

tics, there is a tendency for mothers' ratings to be higher than fathers' (e.g., Approach/Withdrawal), and for others (e.g., Emotional Intensity), fathers' rating are higher than mothers'. However, only in the case of the Ease-of-Management-Through-Distraction are the differences consistently significant.

These results at first appear confusing. They are more comprehensible, however, when the ease of management of each temperament characteristic and the composition of each sample is taken into account. With regard to ease of management, Activity Level and Emotional Intensity are scored in a direction such that a high score is less desirable from a management point of view (higher activity, more emotional intensity). For these characteristics there is no clear tendency for mothers or fathers to provide higher ratings. For characteristics that are scored in a more desirable direction from the point of view of parental management, (Adaptability, Approach/Withdrawal, Ease-of-Management-Through-Distraction, Persistence), there is a tendency for mothers to have higher means than fathers (14 of 16 means are in this direction) although only six of 16 differences are statistically significant, and two of these differences are in the contrary direction.

The contrary direction for the Pennsylvania Child Find Sample may be attributable to the characteristics of the sample. Unlike the other samples studied, this sample is made up of children who were referred by at least one parent for an evaluation because the parents felt there were significant behavioral problems. Thus, in the only sample studied for which there were high levels of perceived child behavior problem, the mothers rated these children in a less positive direction (i.e., as being less adaptable, and less easy to manage through distraction).

These results lead us to the following tentative hypothesis: In normal samples, mothers tend to rate positive temperamental characteristics more positively than fathers, and in samples of more "troubled" children, mothers tend to rate negative temperamental characteristics more negatively. This fosters the interpretation that mothers are more discriminating raters than fathers perhaps because mothers have more experience with children. This difference in rating pattern is most clearly observed for the characteristic labeled, Ease-of-Management-Through-Distraction. This variable is related to "distractibility" as measured in some other temperament questionnaires such as Behavior Style Questionnaire (McDevitt & Carey, 1978), but is limited to ease of distracting the child away from inappropriate behaviors. This scale of the TABC may be related to measures of tractability or behavioral flexibility, and is probably related to parental perceptions of general ease of management.

Differences in Variation of Mothers' and Fathers' Ratings

The variance of the ratings of mothers and fathers for each sample were calculated and differences were tested through the t-test for variance differences for correlated samples. In 19 of 24 comparisons (comparisons for four samples across six temperament scales) the direction of the difference was that mothers' responses were more variable than fathers'. This result might be seen as consistent with the hypothesis that mothers are more discriminating than fathers in temperament ratings. However, this conclusion is limited by the fact that only three of the differences were significant. This indicates that the variance differences observed were too small to be reliable, given the moderate-to-small sizes of the samples studied.

Correlations between Ratings of Mothers and Fathers

Table 14.2 presents data for four samples in which the correlation between mothers and fathers was calculated for each scale of the TABC. If the results for the Pennsylvania

Table 14.2. Interrater Correlations Between Mothers and Fathers

Temperament scale	Sample	N	r
Activity	Georgia Longitudinal Study	154	.42
	Georgia Preschool Clinic	170	.58
	Kindergarten Sample	48	.30
	Pennsylvania Child Find Sample	48	−.21
Adaptability	Georgia Longitudinal Study		.38
	Georgia Preschool Clinic		.34
	Kindergarten Sample		.58
	Pennsylvania Child Find Sample		.08
Approach/Withdrawal	Georgia Longitudinal Study		.66
	Georgia Preschool Clinic		.64
	Kindergarten Sample		.42
	Pennsylvania Child Find Sample		.04
Emotional Intensity	Georgia Longitudinal Study		.42
	Georgia Preschool Clinic		.57
	Kindergarten Sample		.51
	Pennsylvania Child Find Sample		.12
Distractibility	Georgia Longitudinal Study		.30
	Georgia Preschool Clinic		.43
	Kindergarten Sample		.49
	Pennsylvania Child Find Sample		.09
Persistence	Georgia Longitudinal Study		.31
	Georgia Preschool Clinic		.50
	Kindergarten Sample		.42
	Pennsylvania Child Find Sample		.35

Child Find Study are not considered, the results are quite similar across samples. In general, correlations range from .30 to .66 across all scales with little difference in the interrater correlations for the separate scales. The only exception is that there is a tendency for the ratings on the Approach/Withdrawal scale to be higher than the other scales. This tendency is strengthened by the fact that the two highest correlations were for the larger samples.

The findings for the Pennsylvania Child Find Sample are clearly different from the other three. They range from −.21 to .35, with only one being significantly different from zero. Children in this sample were distinct from those in the other three samples in that they had been referred by their parents for an evaluation by a child study team to determine if some type of developmental delay were present (speech and language delays were most common, but some general intellectual slowness was found), and all of the children were reported to have externalizing behavior problems to some degree. Lower correlations between mothers' and fathers' ratings have also been obtained for "disturbed child families" than for families with "normal" children by other researchers (e.g., Jacob *et al.*, 1982) using different instruments.

The reason for the lower correlation in the Child Find Sample studied here is unclear, but the clinic staff had the impression that the mother had been the member of the family who had been most concerned about the developmental delays and behavior problems, and had been the member of the family in most instances who had initiated the referral. Thus, the mother may have sensed a problem in situations where the father did not. The fathers may have been resistant to the referral because they were denying the problem, or were simply unaware of the behaviors that were indicative of the problem.

For the Georgia Preschool Clinic Sample, an effort was made to determine if the interrater correlations between mother and father were affected by gender of the child, IQ of the child, mother and father education, and the extent to which the child was a behavior problem. In all cases, two subsamples were formed by splitting the sample at the mean on the continuous variable (e.g., IQ, father's education), then comparing the interrater correlations for each of the subsamples. No significant effects were found for age, gender, IQ, or parental education. Some provocative results were obtained for the extent to which the child was a behavior problem. When correlations for children with more than three conduct problems (as indicated by their mother on a modified form of the Quay-Peterson Behavior Problem Checklist) were compared to those for children with less than three conduct problems, there were differences between interrater correlations for activity level and emotional intensity that approached significant levels, and a significant difference for a persistence factor made up of a linear combination of the activity and persistence scales ($p < .05$). In these cases, the interrater correlations were higher when the child exhibited *more* conduct problems (in the .70 range) than when there were *few* conduct problems reported by the mother (.40 to .50 range).

To check on the replicability of these findings, similar analyses were carried out on the Georgia Longitudinal Study Sample. Again, age and gender of child did not have any significant effect. When an extreme-groups analysis was carried out on mother-rated behavior problems [the 26 highest behavior problem (HBP) children and the 14 children with no behavior problems (LBP) indicated], there was tendency for the LBP group to have a higher interrater correlation than the HBP group on Adaptability (.28 HBP, .69 LBP), but for Distractibility (.33 HBP, −.10 LBP), and Activity level (.33 HBP, −.10 LBP) this pattern was reversed. Taken at face value, these results lend some support to the notion that interrater correlations are higher for children with more behavior problems, at least for temperament characteristics that are related to behavior problems (e.g., Activity level, Distractibility, Emotional Intensity).

These two sets of results from "normal" samples are at odds with the results from the "referred" sample (Pennsylvania Child Find Study). In the first instance, higher agreement was found for children with more behavior problems, whereas the correlations for the "referred" sample were much lower than for the normal sample. One interpretation of inconsistency is that the results are due to sampling error, and are not reliable. However, the differences in outcome may result from the behaviors of the child and perceptions of the parent that lead to a referral for psychological assessment and intervention. For example, the most problematic children in the "normal" samples were probably not considered as serious by their parents as the least problematic child in the "referred" sample, at least based on the idea that parents of children in the normal samples had not sought professional help for their children. Thus, there had been no breakdown in family coping mechanisms for the normal samples. It is possible, when problems become overwhelming, that there is a breakdown in perceptions and in communication between husband and wife, or that differences in perceptions predate such breakdowns. In the normal samples, this breakdown threshold has not been reached, so there is more parental communication about child-rearing problems, and thus more rater agreement on the more problematic children.

Based on these results, the following tentative hypotheses are offered: Interrater correlations between mothers and fathers are mediated by the extent to which the parents view the child as a behavior problem. The relationship is hypothesized to be curvilinear; that is, for clinically difficult children (defined as children from families in which behavior problems or the perception of them by the parent is severe enough to cause the parent to seek professional help) agreement is expected to be poor. However, for difficult children in the normal range, agreement is higher than for clinically difficult children, and higher than for children who are rated as having few behavior problems by their parents.

Absolute Differences between Ratings of Mother and Father

Another index of agreement was calculated by determining the sum of the differences across the six measures of the TABC for each pair of raters (the mother and father of each subject in the sample). Then the relationship of this index to parent characteristics (mother's education, father's education, maternal adjustment, satisfaction with parenting, dyadic adjustment, a measure of marital communication), and child characteristics (gender, temperament, IQ, conduct problem status) was calculated for the Georgia Preschool Clinic Sample, and the Georgia Longitudinal Study Sample (all variables were not available in both samples, but a subset of these variables was available for each sample with some overlap in variables studied).

Parental characteristics were generally unrelated to this index of agreement. The only exception to this rule was that mother-father agreement for girls was significantly positively related to parental education, particularly to mother's education for the Georgia Preschool Clinic sample. However, this relationship was not obtained for the Georgia Longitudinal Study Sample. In a similar study using absolute value differences on the Behavior Problem Checklist (Quay, 1977), Jacobs et al. (1982) found father's education and years married to be significantly positively related to agreements for male children, but not for females.

The absolute difference index was also correlated with the teacher ratings of temperament for the Preschool Clinic Sample. When correlations for the entire sample were calculated, few significant correlations were obtained for either sample. However, when the sample was divided by sex a clear picture emerged. As can be seen by inspection of Table 14.3, substantial correlations were obtained between parental agreement and teacher temperament ratings for boys, but not for girls. Another interesting finding revealed in Table 14.3 is that the greater the degree of parental agreement, the more socially desirable was the temperament rating. Thus, there appears to be a tendency for parents to agree more on boys with positive characteristics as viewed by the teacher when agreement is assessed using the absolute difference index. This finding was not replicated in the Georgia Longitudinal Study Sample. However, using the Behavior Problem Checklist, Jacob et al. (1982) found that there was significantly more agreement between parents of "normal" boys, using an absolute difference index, than between parents of disturbed boys. Also,

**Table 14.3. Correlations of Absolute Value
Index with Teacher-Rated Temperament**

	Correlations	
	Male	Female
Temperament Scale		
Activity	ns	ns
Adaptability	ns	ns
Approach/Withdrawal	.29*	ns
Emotional Intensity	ns	ns
Distractibility	−.43***	ns
Persistence	.34**	ns
Factor Scale		
Emotionality Factor	ns	ns
Sociability	.41**	ns
Persistence	ns	ns

*p < .05   **p < .01   ***p < .001

Ferguson, Partyka, and Lester (1974), using the Children's Behavior Checklist, found that parents agreed more on the behavior of younger (5 to 7 years) males in a "non-clinic group" than on younger males in a "clinic" group.

While the results are far from unequivocal, the following tentative hypothesis is offered: Using an absolute difference index in ratings calculated across scales of a temperament measure, mothers and fathers will have higher agreement for boys who have fever behavior problems than for boys who have more behavior problems, where the extent of behavior problems is determined by teacher rating or professional diagnosis.

Intraclass Correlations between Ratings of Mother and Father

The absolute difference index is in some ways analogous to the mean difference index reported on above; the former deals with differences in absolute rating level within pairs, while the latter deals with differences in level of ratings across pairs. It is also possible to develop a *within-pair* index that is analogous to the across-pair correlation coefficient, an index that is sensitive to the pattern of rating levels across the different scales of a measure (in this case, the six scales of the TABC). Simple correlations can be calculated for each rating pair. However, the intraclass correlation was utilized because it represents agreement in term of elevation, scatter, and profile (Robinson, 1957), as opposed to simply being sensitive to profile, as is the case for the traditional correlation coefficient. The index was calculated by entering into the correlation the standardized data for each pair twice; data are entered in such a manner that the data from the mother in each mother-father pair were entered first, then with fathers first.

There was no indication that this index was related to the age or gender of the rated child, or the education level of the parents. However, for boys (N = 81), there was a pattern of significant relationships with the teachers ratings of temperament for the preschool clinic sample. That is, this index correlated .26 with Distractibility ($p < .05$), and $-.32$ with Persistence ($p < .01$). Thus, as the child's temperamental characteristics became more positive (easier to manage), as viewed by the teacher, there was less agreement in temperament ratings by the parents.

These results suggest the following tentative hypothesis: When agreement between mothers and fathers is indexed through the intraclass correlation, there is a relationship with teacher-rated temperament such that as characteristics that are more easily managed by the teacher are rated higher, parental agreement decreases.

Discussion

The purpose of this chapter is to review several methods for studying agreement in temperament ratings between mothers and fathers, and to develop a set of hypotheses about factors that affect rater agreement using these methods.

The results reported here can legitimately be interpreted in two ways. The most conservative interpretation is that while there clearly is variation across studies and across rating pairs in level of agreement (no matter what index is used), this variation is determined by idiosyncratic aspects of the rating situation to such an extent that it is not worthwhile to search for factors that consistently relate to these indices across samples and rating circumstances. This interpretation is supported by the lack of strong and consistent findings for any index across samples.

An alternative interpretation is that there were enough significant findings to support further efforts to track down meaningful relationships between parent, child, and situation characteristics, and mother-father agreement in temperament ratings. This is the interpretation favored by the authors of this chapter. This interpretation is in part based on the importance of the phenomena under study, and the strong face validity of the proposition that perceptions of parents affect their children. Logically, it seems unlikely that the degree to which mothers and fathers share a common perception of their child does not have an effect on their behavior toward the child in the home, how they go about seeking professional help with problem behaviors, and how they interact with school personnel.

With regard to a general finding across all indices, it can be said that parental characteristics were not generally significantly related to parental agreement on temperament. Variables studied included parental education, years married, socioeconomic status, and attitudes about the marriage. Characteristics of the child, however, were related to rater agreement, particularly the extent to which the child was viewed as a behavior problem, or as possessing temperamental characteristics that are more difficult to manage.

Several aspects of these results have led us to believe that mothers are more discriminating raters of temperament than fathers. That is, for "normal" healthy children, mothers tend to rate their children more positively or as more easily managed than do fathers. For children experiencing behavior problems, mothers tend to rate them as less positive on temperamental characteristics relating to child management. The most likely explanation for this tentatively held hypothesis is that mothers are more sensitive to the behavior of their children, at least in the early years (infancy through grade school), and have a better knowledge of the typical behavior of other children, so that comparative judgments are made more accurately. This heightened sensitivity may be the result of better training in child behavior for mothers than for fathers, or it may simply be the result of more time spent in child care by mothers.

The most common index of agreement between rating pairs is the correlation coefficient calculated for rating pairs across all the subjects in the sample. It is often referred to as an interrater reliability coefficient. The results from this study were somewhat difficult to interpret regarding correlates of this index. Results seem to indicate that for normal samples, as the child becomes more difficult, parental agreement increases; however, in clinical samples, as the child becomes seen as very problematic, parental agreement declines. These different findings are not easily integrated, and further attempts at replication seem to be the only meaningful way to clarify the issue.

One of the interesting findings is that parents tend to have more agreement on some scales than others. Interrater correlations were stronger, for example, on the Approach/Withdrawal scale than on the others. Three related sets of explanations for this phenomenon are possible. First, it may be that both mothers and fathers are more aware of variation in initial tendencies to withdraw or approach novel situations because they are more stable than other behaviors. Martin (1988) has shown that both parents and teachers ratings of the approach/withdrawal tendency are among the most temporally stable over periods of one year. Second, this scale has the strongest internal consistency characteristics on the parent form of the TABC. Perhaps item selection produced a more coherent set of items that are more meaningful to parental raters. Finally, there may be something about the behavior being measured that make it more easily observed than other behaviors tapped by the TABC. For example, parents may find it noteworthy that their normally outgoing child withdraws in novel social situations.

This paper presents data on two of a set of agreement indices that are seldom utilized in this kind of research. These include the absolute difference index and the intraclass correlation which are examples of a class of agreement indices that focus on comparisons between two individuals, rather than across all individuals in the sample, as is the case for the interrater coefficient. Care must be exercised in interpreting these indices since they have characteristics that are not generally understood. For example, the apparently contrary findings for the absolute difference index and the intraclass correlation with regard to effects on parental agreement of teacher-rated child behavior were very difficult to interpret until we determined that the two indices were correlated $-.51$. Given this finding, it became clear that these indices would be expected to be related in opposite directions to similar criterion variables.

Research such as that reported here has led to speculation about usefulness of parental-rating agreement indices of children as indicators of the integrity of the marital unit. Halverson (unpublished data) has found significant relationships between parental agreement on child temperament and parental agreement on child rearing, as well as observer ratings of parental competence. Another important line of research would be to study agreement between parents and teacher to determine the relationships of such agreement to child behavior (see Victor, Halverson, & Wampler, 1988, for data on this point). As these types of research proceed, we may find that our concept of interrater reliability changes from a problematic source of error variance to a sensitive indicator of stress in caretaker systems.

In conclusion, it seems clear that persons interested in determining the temperament of children must be sensitive to the often demonstrated problem of low rater agreement on temperament ratings between parents. Further, the findings of this research indicate that variation in agreement between parents on temperament ratings may be systematically related to identifiable characteristics of the temperament characteristics being measured, characteristics of the child, and perhaps to characteristics of the family. Such findings should foster more research into such phenomena, and more qualified statements with regard to the outcomes of temperamental research.

ACKNOWLEDGMENT. Portions of this chapter were supported by Grant MH39899.

References

Bates, J. E. The concept of difficult temperament. *Merrill-Palmer Quarterly*, 1980, *26*, 299–319.

Bates, J. E., & Bayles, K. Objective and subjective components in mothers' perceptions of their children from age 6 months to 3 years. *Merrill-Palmer Quarterly*, 1984, *30*, 111–130.

Brody, G. H., & Forehand, R. Maternal perceptions of child maladjustment as a fuction of the combined influence of child behavior and maternal depression. *Journal of Consulting and Clinical Psychology*, 1986, *54*, 237–240.

Carey, W. B., & McDevitt, S. Revision of the Infant Temperament Questionnaire. *Pediatrics*, 1978, *61*, 735–739.

Ferguson, L. R., Partyka, L. B., & Lester, B. M. Patterns of parent perception differentiating clinic from nonclinic children. *Journal of Abnormal Child Psychology*, 1974, *2*, 169–181.

Forehand, R., Wells, K. C., McMahon, R. J., Griest, D., & Rogers, T. Maternal perception of maladjustment to clinic-referred children: An extension of earlier research. *Journal of Behavioral Assessment*, 1982, *4*, 145–151.

Fullard, W., McDevitt, S. C., & Carey, W. B. *Toddler Temperament Scale*. Temple University. Unpublished test form, 1978.

Goldsmith, H. H. *Multi-method, theory-based assessment of infant temperament: A twin study.* Paper presented at the annual meeting of the Society for Research in Child Development, 1981.

Hegvik, R., McDevitt, S., & Carey, W. The Middle Childhood Temperament Questionnaire. *Developmental and Behavioral Pediatrics*, 1982, *3*, 197–200.

Jacobs, T., Grounds, L., & Haley, R. Correspondence between parents' reports on the Behavior Problem Checklist. *Journal of Abnormal Child Psychology*, 1982, *10*, 593–608.

Lerner, R. M., Palermo, M., Spiro, A., & Nesselroade, J. Assessing the dimensions of temperamental individuality across the life-span: The Dimensions of Temperament Survey (DOTS). *Child Development*, 1982, *53*, 149–160.

Lyon, M. E., & Plomin, R. The measurement of temperament using parental ratings. *Journal of Child Psychology and Psychiatry*, 1981, *22*, 47–53.

Martin, R. P. *The Temperament Assessment Battery for Children: Manual*. Brandon, VT: Clinical Psychology Press, 1988.

McDevitt, S. C., & Carey, W. B. The measurement of temperament in 3- to 7-year old children. *Journal of Child Psychology and Psychiatry*, 1978, *19*, 245–253.

Pfeffer, J., & Martin, R. P. Comparison of mothers' and fathers' temperament ratings of referred and nonreferred preschool children. *Journal of Clinical Psychology*, 1983, *39*, 1013–1020.

Quay, H. Measuring dimensions of deviant behavior: The Behavior Problem Checklist. *Journal of Abnormal Child Psychology*, 1977, *5*, 277–287.

Robinson, W. S. The statistical measurement of agreement. *American Sociological Review*, 1957, *22*, 17–25.

Rothbart, M. K. Measurement of temperament in infancy. *Child Development*, 1981, *52*, 569–578.

Sameroff, A. J., Seifer, R., & Elias, P. K. Sociocultural variability in infant temperament ratings. *Child Development*, 1982, *53*, 564–578.

Sears, R., Maccoby, E., & Levin, H. *Patterns of Child Rearing*. New York: Harper & Row, 1957.

Thomas, A., & Chess, S. *Temperament and development*. New York: Brunner/Mazel, 1977.

Thomas, A., Chess, S., & Birch, H. *Temperament and behavior disorders in children*. New York: New York University Press, 1968.

Thomas, A., Chess, S., Birch, H. G., Hertzig, M., & Korn, S. *Behavioral individuality in early childhood*. New York: New York University Press, 1963.

Vaughn, B. E., Bradley, C. F., Joffe, L. S., Seifer, R., & Barglow, P. Maternal characteristics measured prenatally are predictive of ratings of temperament 'difficulty' on the Carey Infant Temperament Questionnaire. *Developmental Psychology*, 1987, *23*, 152–161.

Victor, J. B., Halverson, C. F., Jr., & Wampler, K. S. Family-school context: Parent and teacher agreement on child temperament. *Journal of Consulting and Clinical Psychology*, 1988, *56*, 573–577.

Warner, W. L. *Social class in America*. New York: Harper & Row, 1960.

15

Contemporary Instruments for Assessing Early Temperament by Questionnaire and in the Laboratory

H. H. Goldsmith and Mary Klevjord Rothbart

Research in behavioral science often succeeds or fails depending on the quality of its assessment instruments. Recognizing this, many temperament researchers have proposed questionnaires, interview schedules, home observation coding systems, and laboratory methods for assessing early temperament. These assessment instruments have been reviewed and evaluated from several perspectives (e.g., Bornstein, Gaughran, & Homel, 1986; Crockenberg & Acredolo, 1983; Goldsmith & Rieser-Danner, 1990; Hubert, Wachs, Peters-Martin, & Gandour, 1982; Neale & Stevenson, 1989; Rothbart & Goldsmith, 1985; Seifer & Sameroff, 1986; Slabach, Morrow, & Wachs, this volume). In this chapter, we preview some new instruments and review recent data on an established questionnaire, all developed in our laboratories. These instruments include the Infant Behavior Questionnaire, the Toddler Behavior Assessment Questionnaire, and the Children's Behavior Questionnaire, as well as a battery of laboratory temperament assessment techniques.

Any broad assessment effort requires the investigator to set certain priorities. We were guided by the standard psychometric priorities of constructing scales that were theoretically grounded, conceptually independent, inclusive of varied facets of each temperament construct, internally consistent, and empirically distinctive. We also set high research priority on establishing convergence with other methods of assessing the same constructs. Other assessment efforts have subscribed to similar priorities. In fact, these psychometric considerations apply broadly to personality assessment at any age.

H. H. Goldsmith and **Mary K. Rothbart** • Department of Psychology, University of Oregon, Eugene, Oregon 97403-1227.

However, we also attempted to be sensitive to developmental considerations, and this priority sets our research apart from the broader field of personality assessment.

Assuming one accepts the basic premise that "temperament" refers to a set of phenomena with important developmental histories (Rothbart, 1989b) rather than pre-formed or hard-wired characteristics, we can derive at least three assessment principles.

The first principle is that *behavioral manifestations of temperamental dispositions change during development.* The overt form of temperament-related behavior changes as the child matures. Activity level is an obvious case in which activity is first indexed mainly without locomotion, which gives way to crawling, which in turn subsides as walking begins. Less obvious are emotional indicators of temperament. For example, in the positive affective domain, the social smile is evident from about 6 weeks of age, but laughing often does not appear in the laboratory until 3–4 months and then is infrequent until later (Rothbart, 1973; Sroufe & Wunsch, 1972). Also, although fearful facial expressions appear in early infancy, behaviorally inhibited signs of fear to novel and intense stimuli are not observed until 8 months or later (Rothbart, 1988, 1989a; Schaffer, 1974). Similarly, angry facial expressions have been reported during the first weeks of life, but a clear-cut angry cry tends not to occur until later. Angry facial, vocal, and mo-toric components apparently become organized into coherent responses that can be re-liably elicited in the laboratory at about age 5 months (Stenberg & Campos, in press). As methods for eliciting temperament-related behaviors become more sensitive, the ages when components are thought to come "on line" are revised, but the essential point is that change in overt manifestation of temperament is the rule rather than the exception during early development.

After infancy, the primary behavioral indicators of temperamental dispositions can be modified by a wide array of processes subsumed by the rubric "socialization of emotions" (Gordon, 1989) as well as by other emerging skills. Thus, valid assessment of temperamental reactivity after infancy may require observation in special circumstances where socialization and advanced cognitive skills are less likely to operate.

By suggesting that behavioral manifestations of temperament change with develop-ment, we do not mean to imply that the neurophysiological underpinnings of tempera-ment are immutable. Indeed, the evidence is strong that these underpinnings also follow an extended postnatal developmental course (Gunnar, 1986; Rothbart, 1989c). The assessment instruments presented in this chapter are all confined to the behavioral level of analysis, so these neurophysiological considerations are, for present purposes, a background consideration.

A second principle of developmentally sensitive assessment of temperament is that *the elicitors of temperament-related behaviors change during development.* Not only temperament-related responses but also temperament-related eliciting stimuli change with development. For example, it is widely acknowledged that novel stimuli that threaten the individual are prototypical elicitors of fearfulness. Just what constitutes novelty changes with development. In general, stimuli that highlight individual differ-ences in emotionality become more symbolic and probably more individualized.

A third developmental assessment principle is that *observed individual differences in temperament can be due to either rate of development of temperament-related be-havior or characteristic level (or strength) of disposition, or to a combination of the two factors.* We customarily ascribe the same meaning to identical personality questionnaire scores of a 20-year-old college sophomore and a 21-year-old college junior. However, it is an entirely different matter to ascribe the same meaning to identical scores of a 1-year-old and a 2-year-old, even if exactly the same questions are asked about each child. Although this may seem an obvious point, there is usually a conflict in temperament research between needing to change the surface form of assessment to accommodate the child's changing behavioral repertoire and needing to retain the same assessment procedures to be confident that the underlying temperamental trait is the same. Psychometricians will recognize parallels to the "factor invariance problem" that haunts many aspects of assessment research (Nesselroade, 1977).

Given these developmental assessment principles, one approach would be simply to ask the caregivers of children of all ages questions such as, "How fearful is your child?" and assume that the caregiver will take the appropriate developmental principles into account when answering the questions. However, this approach assumes substantial developmental knowledge on the part of caregivers and fails to consider caregivers' differences in such knowledge. A more analytic approach that we favor requires specifying situation and response for every query about temperament and producing instruments tailored for different age groups. We have attempted to produce such instruments in both laboratory and questionnaire formats. Combined with appropriate research designs, these instruments are sensitive to the three principles we have elaborated.

The Infant Behavior Questionnaire

The Infant Behavior Questionnaire (IBQ) (Rothbart, 1981) assesses temperamental dimensions of Activity Level, Smiling and Laughter, Fear, Distress to Limitations (Frustration), Duration of Orienting and Soothability through caregiver report. It was designed for 3–12-month-old children, and item analyses were performed separately for samples of infants 3-, 6-, 9- and 12-months of age. The IBQ has been employed in research with infants aged 2 weeks to 19½ months (Thompson & Lamb, 1984; Worobey & Blajda, 1989), and this broad range may prove to define the outer limits of the IBQ's applicability.

Development of the IBQ

A major aim of the initial work on the IBQ was to develop, refine, and validate a caregiver report assessment for infant temperament that would not necessarily be tied to the nine temperament dimensions developed by Thomas and Chess (1977) and their colleagues in the New York Longitudinal Study (Thomas, Chess, Birch, Herzig, & Korn, 1963; Thomas, Chess, & Birch, 1968). We further wished to assess dimensions of temperament that would be conceptually independent, that is, designed with no conceptual overlap among operational definitions of the measures. By following this strategy, we hoped to observe intercorrelations among measures that would not be an artifact of overlapping item content across scales. Both the Thomas *et al.* work cited above and Carey's questionnaires (Carey, 1970; Carey & McDevitt, 1978) include such overlap. Choice of initial dimensions was based upon the New York Longitudinal Study

Table 15.1. Internal Consistency Estimates for IBQ Scales

Scale	Number of items	3	6	9	12
		Alpha estimates (in months)			
AL—Activity level	17	.73	.77	.81	.84
SL—Smiling and laughter	15	.85	.77	.73	.80
FR—Fear	16	.80	.81	.84	.81
DL—Distress to limitations	20	.84	.80	.75	.78
SO—Soothability	11	.84	.75	.73	.82
DO—Duration of orienting	8	.72	.67	.75	.72

research but was also influenced by the work of Shirley (1933) and Escalona (1968), the studies of temperament and behavioral genetics reviewed by Diamond (1957), and reviews of more recent studies of behavioral genetics and longitudinal studies of personality in human subjects. Eleven dimensions were selected for investigation. Four tapped general characteristics of response as assessed across differing sensory receptors and response channels: threshold, intensity, and adaptability (including soothability) of response, and rhythmicity. Seven involved activation of more specific motor and emotional responses: activity level, fear, distress to limitations (frustration), overall negative emotionality, smiling and laughter, duration of orienting, and distractibility.

We reasoned that parent reports are subject to rater biases, but that these biases might be expected to operate most strongly when judgments are retrospective, global, or involve comparing one's own child with others. Thus instead of asking parents to make global judgments about their children as do, for example, Buss and Plomin (1975, 1984), we asked them instead about the relative frequency of occurrence of concrete behaviors in carefully defined situations. To minimize memory-related distortions, parents were asked to report the relative frequency of their child's behaviors within the past week or, for some items, within the past two weeks. Data reviewed by Hasher and Zacks (1979) suggest that frequency judgments of even nonattended items are remembered with some accuracy. We also avoided comparative judgments, such as "my child is very active," by aggregating information about children's specific responses to concrete situations. Information about other infants is unavailable to many parents, especially to new parents. Interviews with 26 parents aided in writing IBQ items.

An illustrative item is the following: "During the past week, when being undressed, how often did your baby: wave his/her arms and kick?" Responses ranged from 1 = never, through 4 = about half the time, to 7 = always, with X = does not apply (meaning, "I did not see my baby in this situation.") A number of items were worded in a reverse direction to counteract acquiescence response sets. The preliminary version of the IBQ included 244 items.

Four hundred sixty-three Infant Behavior Questionnaires were filled out by parents of 3-, 6-, 9-, and 12-month-old infants. Item analyses were performed for all scales separately at each age, retaining only those items correlating .20 or better with scales scores for a given age.

Two kinds of analyses were performed on the initial scales: conceptual and item analyses. In the conceptual analysis, we eliminated all scales whose operational definitions overlapped with those of other scales. Those discarded included negative emotionality (overlap with fear and distress to limitations scales), and distractibility (overlap with duration of orienting). Three scales were eliminated due to unsatisfactory item characteristics and internal reliability: threshold, rhythmicity, and intensity. In addition, only the soothability items of the original adaptability scale had satisfactory inter-item correlations, and they were extracted to form a soothability scale. Internal reliabilities of the scales based on coefficient alpha are given in Table 15.1.

Household Reliability

A subsample of 22 mothers filled out the questionnaire along with a second adult in the household (father or baby-sitter) who spent time caring for the infant. Although mothers were asked not to discuss the items with the other individual filling out the questionnaire, we did not have direct control over such discussion; questionnaires were all mailed to the parents' homes. Product-moment correlations for agreement of the 22 matched pairs of questionnaires were: Smiling and Laughter, $r = .45$, Duration of Orienting, $r = .46$, Soothability, $r = .54$, Fear, $r = .66$, Distress to Limitations, $r = .60$, Activity Level, $r = .69$. All correlations were significant at $p < .05$.

Content of the IBQ

Current operational definitions and sample items for IBQ scales are given below:

Activity Level: The child's gross motor activity, including movement of arms and legs, squirming and locomotor activity. Sample item: ". . . During feeding, how often did the baby: lie or sit quietly?" (coded as a reverse item).
Smiling and Laughter: Smiling and laughter from the child across a range of situations. Sample item: "When being dressed or undressed, how often did the baby: smile or laugh?"
Fear: The child's distress and/or extended latency to approach an intense or novel stimulus. Sample item: "When introduced to a strange person, how often did the baby: hang back from the stranger?"
Distress to Limitations: The child's distress while waiting for or refusing food, being confined, dressed or undressed, or being prevented access to a desired object or activity. Sample item: "During feeding, how often did the baby: fuss or cry when given a disliked food?"
Soothability: The child's reduction of distress when soothing techniques are applied. Sample item: "In the last week, how often did the method soothe the baby: rocking?"
Duration of Orienting: The child's extended visual, vocal, or physical interaction with objects when there has been no sudden change in stimulation. Sample item: "After

sleeping, how often did the baby: coo and vocalize for a period of five minutes or longer?"

Intercorrelations Among Scale Scores

Temperament scales were designed to avoid conceptual overlap, allowing us to examine empirical intercorrelations among temperament scale scores. Intercorrelations among scale values for 6- and 12-month-infants from the item-refinement sample are reported in Table 15.2. Positive correlations are found at both ages between Activity Level and Distress to Limitations, and between Distress to Limitations and Fear. Negative correlations are found between Smiling and Laughter and Fear.

Theoretical Approach to Temperament

Our theoretical approach to temperament has developed in parallel with the development of the IBQ scales (see Rothbart, 1986; Rothbart in Goldsmith, Buss, Plomin, Rothbart, Thomas, Chess, Hinde, & McCall, 1987; Rothbart, 1989d; Rothbart, this volume), and it describes a much broader domain for temperament than is covered by the IBQ measure. We have proposed that temperament includes constitutionally based individual differences in reactivity and self-regulation, with reactivity referring to the arousability of emotional and motor processes as reflected in response parameters of threshold, latency, intensity, rise time, and recovery time (Rothbart & Derryberry, 1981). Self-regulation refers to processes that modulate (facilitate or inhibit) reactivity, including attention, responsiveness to cues signaling reward and punishment, behavioral inhibition to novel or intense stimuli, and effortful inhibitory control (Rothbart & Posner, 1985).

In this view, temperament is expressed behaviorally in emotional expression, motor activity, including approach versus behavioral inhibition, and shifting and focusing of attention. The IBQ assesses emotionality through three negative affect scales: Fear, Distress to Limitations (frustration), and Soothability (the duration parameter of negative affect); one positive affect scale: Smiling and Laughter; one motor activity scale: Activity Level; and one attentional scale: Duration of Orienting. Behavioral inhibition is

Table 15.2. Intercorrelations of IBQ Scales

Scale	AL	FR	DL	SL	SO	DO
AL—Activity level		.07	.28	.11	.03	−.01
FR—Fear	.02		.36	−.22	−.01	.05
DL—Distress to limitations	.33	.29		−.19	−.12	−.14
SL—Smiling and laughter	.00	−.34	−.30		.29	.19
SO—Soothability	−.02	.00	−.13	.17		.05
DO—Duration of orienting	.05	.04	−.16	.19	.19	

Note: Six-month correlations above diagonal ($N = 93$); 12-month correlations below diagonal ($N = 106$).

captured through the items in the Fear scale assessing latency to approach novel and intense stimuli.

Stability

Table 15.3 combines data from 3 initial longitudinal cohorts described in Rothbart (1981) with data from a fourth longitudinal cohort reported in Rothbart (1986). The latter included data only for activity level, smiling and laughter, fear, and distress to limitations. Correlations reported are averages across at least two cohorts, except for those with superscript (b), which were based on only one cohort. The data show general tendencies for stability to be higher over shorter intervals and to increase as the infant matures. However, the patterns of changing stability vary across the temperamental dimensions, and the basis for these different patterns requires investigation.

Validation of the IBQ

Although this section does not represent a complete review of research investigating the validity of the IBQ, we can identify some of the approaches to validating the instrument, as well as results on validity studies done with children of different ages.

Convergence with other Questionnaires

We first consider the convergence of IBQ scale scores with scale scores from other temperament questionnaire scales. Goldsmith and Rieser-Danner (1987) reported convergence among the IBQ, Carey and McDevitt's (1978) Revised Infant Temperament Questionnaire (the RITQ), and Bates' Infant Characteristics Questionnaire (the ICQ; Bates, Freeland, & Lounsbury, 1979). Mothers ($n = 32–33$) and day-care teachers ($n = 51–63$) completed these three instruments for infants aged 2.5–8.2 months. Predicted correlations with magnitudes ranging from .51–.73 were found between the IBQ Fear

Table 15.3. Stability Correlations for IBQ Scales[a]

Scale	Months					
	3–6	3–9	3–12	6–9	6–12	9–12
AL—Activity level	.58	.48	.48[b]	.56	.60	.68
SL—Smiling and laughter	.55	.55	.57[b]	.67	.72	.72
FR—Fear	.27	.15	.06[b]	.43	.37	.61
DL—Distress to limitations	.23	.18	.25[b]	.57	.61	.65
SO—Soothability	.30[b]	.37[b]	.41[b]	.50	.39	.29
DO—Duration of orienting	.36[b]	.35[b]	.11[b]	.62	.34	.64

[a]See text for explanations.
[b]Correlations based on only one cohort.

and RITQ Approach/Withdrawal scales, the IBQ Fear and ICQ Unadaptable scales, the IBQ Distress to Limitations and the RITQ Negative Mood scales, the IBQ Distress to Limitations and the ICQ Fussy/Difficult scales, and the IBQ Activity Level and RITQ Activity scales (the ICQ does not have an activity scale).

In addition, Rothbart and Mauro (1990) have reviewed item-level factor analyses of questionnaires based on Thomas and Chess's (1977) nine temperament dimensions. In these studies, support is found for two distress-related factors, one in response to novelty (similar to our Fear scale) and one more general irritability or distress-proneness (similar to our Distress to Limitations scale), as well as a positive emotionality factor (similar to our Smiling and Laughter scale), an activity-reactivity factor (similar to our Activity Level scale), an attention span factor (similar to our Duration of Orienting Scale), and a rhythmicity factor (which is not reflected in the IBQ). Thus, with the exception of Rhythmicity, the nine dimensions of temperament originally identified by Thomas and Chess may be combined into a smaller number of factors assessing individual differences in emotionality, activity, and attention.

Convergence with Home Observations

In home observation, (Rothbart, 1986) we investigated the relation between IBQ scores and measures derived from observational codes of Activity Level, Smiling and Laughter, Distress to Limitations, Fear and Vocal Activity in a longitudinal sample of 46 infants seen at 3, 6, and 9 months of age. We were not able to code Duration of Orienting, and our home observations of Soothability were too unreliable to include in our analysis. In spite of some reliability problems with the home observations and the fact that the content of the IBQ items and our home observation measures were not highly overlapping, we found extensive convergence between the two sets of measures. This was especially clear for 9 months, where we found that, uncorrected for attenuation, four of our five individual scales, as well as aggregated positive and negative reactivity and overall reactivity measures showed significant positive relations between IBQ and home observation. At 3 and 6 months, fewer of the uncorrected scale scores showed significant convergence, but with correction for attenuation, moderate-to-high convergence was found for all measures at 3 months and 4 of the 5 measures at 6 months. Uncorrected IBQ aggregated positive and negative and overall reactivity measures showed convergence at both of these ages, with the exception of positive reactivity at 3 months.

In research involving home observation (Worobey & Blajda, 1989) and the use of actometers at 3 months (Eaton & Dureski, 1986), convergence between IBQ Activity Level and the other measures of activity has not been found. When this is considered in conjunction with our .15 uncorrected correlation at 3 months for IBQ and home observation (Rothbart, 1986), it suggests that Activity Level is not appropriately measured by the IBQ at 3 months. McKeen and Eaton (1989) used the IBQ Activity Level scale at 6 months and found convergence between it and actometer measures. When this is considered in conjunction with our findings of convergence with home observation at 6 months (discussed above), there is good support for using the IBQ scales with older infants. Worobey and Blajda (1989) also found positive relations between the IBQ measures and negative reactivity as measured in the home for very young infants (under 3 months), as did Crockenberg and Acredolo (1983) for 3-month-old infants.

Convergence with Laboratory Measures

In laboratory work, convergence between the Fear measure and infant reaction during a stranger approach has been found in the Denver Twin Temperament Study for 9-month-olds and a study by Rieser-Danner on 12-month-olds (these results are reported by Goldsmith & Rieser-Danner, 1987). Thompson and Lamb (1982) reported significant convergence between IBQ Fear and stranger sociability at ages $12^1/_2$ and $19^1/_2$ months in a longitudinal sample. In the Denver Twin Temperament Study, Goldsmith and Campos (1986) reported some positive correlations with 9-month-olds between IBQ Smiling and Laughter and positive reactions to laboratory games with the mother and an experimenter.

In a laboratory study performed on a longitudinal sample of over 60 infants at Oregon (Rothbart, 1989), we found further evidence for convergence. Infants were seen at 3, 6.5, 10, and 13.5 months. Stimuli were presented to evoke emotional reactions: stimuli assessing smiling and laughter included small attractive squeeze toys, a sound-light display, a rapidly opening parasol, a bell, mechanical and musical toys. Stimuli assessing fear included mechanical moving and sound-producing toys, and a social episode with a stranger. Stimuli assessing frustration or distress to limitations included toys out of reach and toys placed behind a plexiglass barrier. For these episodes, the parameters of latency to an emotional reaction, peak intensity and duration of the emotional expression were coded and combined with unit weighting. At 13.5 months only, we coded the amount of time before the child lost interest in toys to assess duration of orienting. Significant low-to-moderate levels of convergence between lab and IBQ measures were found for Smiling and Laughter at 6.5, 10, and 13.5 months, and for Fear at 6.5 and 10 months, with the 13.5 measure related to peak fearful distress. Low but significant convergence was found between duration of distress and Soothability at 6.5, 10, and 13.5 months, with a trend for 3 months. Our laboratory measure of sustained interest was positively correlated with Duration of Orienting. For Distress to Limitations, however, we did not find convergence between laboratory and parent report.

Summary of Validity Evidence

To date, the IBQ has fared least well for assessment of infant temperament at 3 months, although home observations suggest that it can be used to assess negative reactivity. More research will be needed on the frustration measure, but we may note that none of the laboratory measures involved the mother, and the frustration reaction may prove to be highly susceptible to social context effects. If so, we may wish to reconceptualize the distress-to-limitations dimension as more general distress-proneness or irritability. If this were done, revisions in the scale would be needed.

Evidence reviewed for infants older than 3 months, as well as other studies not cited, lend substantial support for the validity of the IBQ as a temperamental measure.

Advice to Potential Users

The Infant Behavior Questionnaire has been developed for research purposes only. It does not include a measure of infant "difficulty" and there is no evidence for its appropriateness in clinical settings.

The Toddler Behavior Assessment Questionnaire

Rationale

The motivation for constructing the initial version of the Toddler Behavior Assessment Questionnaire (TBAQ) was partially practical and partially theoretical. The practical side was that Goldsmith and Campos began, in 1980, a longitudinal follow-up of an infant sample that had been tested with the IBQ, and no comparable temperament questionnaire for toddlers existed. Also in that year, Goldsmith and Campos (1980) presented the first version of their theoretical approach that defined infant temperament as differences in the characteristic expression of emotions. Thus, the original version of the TBAQ tapped aspects of emotionality and followed the general scheme of the IBQ in construction technique and item type.

Construction

We constructed the TBAQ in a three-part, iterated process (Goldsmith, 1988; Goldsmith, Elliott, & Jaco, 1986). First, six individuals, working as teams, wrote items that systematically combined situations and responses postulated as relevant to one of the targeted dimensions. We solicited input from mothers and other researchers during this period of item writing and revision. Second, we administered the candidate items to samples of mothers—and sometimes fathers—with children in the appropriate age range. We computed item statistics and discarded items that correlated lower than .25 (in most cases) with their intended scale. To heighten discriminant properties, we also eliminated items that correlated highly with other scales. Examining the content of items that we discarded led to slight revisions in how the underlying dimensions were conceptualized in some cases. For instance, what initially was to be a "fearfulness" scale, became a more narrowly conceptualized Social Fearfulness scale because items concerning fearful reactions to animals, loud sounds, the dark, and so forth, failed to correlate with other, more social, fear items. Also, the final Interest/Persistence scale primarily measures sustained attention, rather than responses to distractions or being stubborn.

After the first round of revision, we wrote new items and administered the revised scale to a new sample. This process continued for four waves of data collection, with more than one sample assessed in some waves. However, the Interest/Persistence and Anger Proneness scales were used in only the last two waves, which comprised a total of five samples. In all, some 500 TBAQ records were used in the scale derivation process. The percentage of items on the current version that were also included in essentially the same form on the initial 1980 version are as follows: Social Fearfulness (100%), Pleasure (47%), and Activity Level (75%).

Our goal was to achieve final versions of the scales with about 20 items each and to avoid undue narrowing of content while retaining high internal consistency.

Validity Scales

The basic approach to avoiding response sets in the TBAQ was the same that Rothbart had adopted in constructing the IBQ: asking parents to report frequencies of clearly described behaviors in specific contexts during a recent time interval. We also sought to avoid language that would elicit a social desirability response set. Neverthe-less, we judged that a direct measure of social desirability would be a useful addition to the TBAQ.

A well-known dilemma in measuring social desirability is that some traits, such as Pleasure, are more valued by society and by caregivers than others, such as Anger Proneness. To help unconfound biased responding on different scales from real de-sirability differences between the scales, we constructed a content-balanced Social De-sirability scale. We borrowed the basic notion from Tellegen (1982), but implemented it somewhat differently than he did in the Multidimensional Personality Questionnaire. We chose two pairs of items from each of the five TBAQ content scales, all of which were keyed in the socially desirable direction for the Social Desirability scale.

The scale is content-balanced because one item in each pair is keyed in the high direction for its content scale and the other member of the pair is keyed in the low direction. Furthermore, we attempted to match, as nearly as possible, the situation and response described in members of a pair. If this strategy was successful, a high score on Social Desirability could be obtained only by contradicting oneself regarding the content of the child's behavior. A complication arose because a few of the 20 Social Desirability items had to be rephrased to increase or decrease their desirability. This sometimes resulted in lower correlations with the content scales, and the items in question were thus removed from their content scale, leaving them only on the Social Desirability scale. At present, we do not know whether the Social Desirability scale is valid; however, we present its correlations with each of the content scales in Table 4 below. The results imply that responses to the Pleasure scale may be affected by social desirability con-siderations.

We also gathered data to create a Low Frequency validity scale for the TBAQ. This scale could be useful for identifying invalid records due to carelessness. No data to validate this scale have been collected, and the scale is not discussed further in this report. Additional research will clarify whether inclusion of validity scales significantly improves temperament questionnaires.

Scale Definitions and Sample Items

Below, we describe the content and provide a sample item for each TBAQ scale:

Activity Level: Limb, trunk, or locomotor movement during a variety of daily situations, including free play, confinement, or quiet activities. Sample item: "When playing on a movable toy, how often did your child attempt to go as fast as s/he could?"

Anger Proneness: Crying, protesting, hitting, pouting, or other signs of anger in situations involving conflict with the respondent or another child. Sample item: "When you removed something your child should not have been playing with, how often did s/he try to grab the object back?"

Social Fear: Inhibition, distress, withdrawal (versus approach), or signs of shyness in novel or uncertainty-provoking situations. Sample item: "When your child was being approached by an unfamiliar adult while shopping or out walking, how often did your child show distress or cry?"

Table 15.4. Some Psychometric Properties of TBAQ Scales[a]

Scale	Number of items	Alpha	Average item-total r	r with social desirability
AL—Activity level	20	.78	.44	−.22
PL—Pleasure	19	.80	.47	.45
SF—Social fearfulness	19	.83	.49	−.21
AP—Anger proneness	28	.82	.41	−.07
IP—Interest/persistence	22	.79	.45	.32

[a]See text for explanations.

Pleasure: Smiling, laughter, and other hedonically positive vocalizations or playful activity in a variety of nonthreatening or mildly novel situations. Sample item: "When in the bathtub, how often did your child babble or talk happily?"

Interest/Persistence: Duration of task engagement in ongoing solitary play. Sample item: "How often did your child play alone with her/his favorite toy for 30 minutes or longer?"

Reliability and Validity

Internal Consistency

Given the scale construction procedures and the iterated process, it is unsurprising that the internal consistency of each scale is high. Table 4 presents reliability estimates as well as other psychometric data. The data are all averages from two samples gathered in Eugene, Oregon; the total number of subjects was 102.

As Table 15. 4 shows, the TBAQ scales are approximately equal in length, internal consistency (alpha), and level of item-scale intercorrelation. This property is desirable because differential correlations with other measures are unlikely to be due to differential reliability of the TBAQ scales, a problem with some other temperament questionnaires. The scales are relatively long compared to some temperament questionnaires. This is because we chose to sample each content domain fairly broadly, resulting in lower item-total correlations than we could have obtained with more similar content. The item-total correlations given in Table 4 were computed with all items included in the scale score so that they are somewhat inflated by part-whole correlations. The social desirability correlations were explained above.

Currently, we do not have sufficient data on parental agreement. Our only information is from an earlier version of the TBAQ that included only the Fearfulness, Pleasure, and Activity Level scales in their initial form. Correlations for parental agreement ranged from .20 to .41. These values should be understood in terms of the item overlap between the initial and current versions, as reported above.

Discriminant Properties

We take the view that interscale correlations should be low but not necessarily near zero. For example, we expect some inverse relation between the positive and negative affect scales. Also, Activity Level and Anger Proneness should be positively related simply because expression of anger often involves high energy levels. Table 5 shows average interscale correlations from the two most recent samples tested.

As Table 15. 5 shows, the TBAQ scales are largely independent. The modest intercorrelations mostly involve the Pleasure scale, and they imply that broad hedonic tone and arousal dimensions may affect the responses. That is, Pleasure correlates positively with the other, milder hedonically positive scale, Interest/Persistence, and negatively with the hedonically negative Social Fearfulness scale. Pleasure also correlates positively with the Anger Proneness and Activity Level scales, for which high scores imply substantial behavioral activation.

Correlation with other Temperament Questionnaires

The early three-scale version of the TBAQ was administered to mothers and teachers of a sample of toddlers in day-care settings along with the Toddler Temperament Scale (TTS) (Fullard, McDevitt, & Carey, 1984) and the EASI (Buss & Plomin, 1975). The results indicate substantial convergence for conceptually related scales in maternal report data. The TBAQ Social Fear scale correlated strongly with TTS Approach/Withdrawal ($r = .79$) and moderately with EASI Sociability ($r = -.49$) and TTS Mood ($r = .36$). The TBAQ Activity Level scale correlated strongly with activity scales on the TTS ($r = .73$) and EASI ($r = .54$). Convergence for activity (but not fear) scales was also apparent in day-care teachers' data. See Goldsmith & Rieser-Danner (1986) and Goldsmith, Rieser-Danner, and Briggs (in press) for details.

More recently, Goldsmith (unpublished) administered the five-scale version of the TBAQ along with Bates's Infant Characteristics Questionnaire (ICQ) (Bates & Bayles, 1984; Bates *et al.*, 1979). With our sample of 54 mothers, three scales showed significant ($p = .05$, 1-tailed) correlations with the ICQ overall difficulty index: Activity Level (.57); Anger Proneness (.54); and Pleasure ($-.22$). These same three scales were similarly correlated with the largest factor of the ICQ, Fussy/Difficult. Other notable correlations between the TBAQ and ICQ subscales were between TBAQ Activity Level and ICQ Persistence ($r = .64$), TBAQ Fear and ICQ Unadaptability ($r = .20$), and TBAQ Pleasure and ICQ Unsociability ($r = -.41$).

Thus, data from two studies suggest moderate to strong correlations between TBAQ scales and conceptually similar scales from other questionnaires. However, few of these correlations are so high that the scales involved could be considered interchangeable.

Table 15.5. Intercorrelations of TBAQ Scales[a]

Scale	AL	PL	SF	AP
AL—Activity level				
PL—Pleasure	.19			
SF—Social fearfulness	−.01	−.21		
AP—Anger proneness	.22	.19	−.03	
IP—Interest/persistence	−.01	.32	−.03	.07

[a] See text for explanations.

Initial Analyses Relating the TBAQ to Laboratory Measures

In ongoing research, we have begun to correlate the TBAQ with composites of objective behavioral measures from the Laboratory Temperament Assessment Battery (LAB-TAB). The initial results relating the TBAQ and LAB-TAB promise convergent validation at a reasonable level for both instruments (see a later section of this chapter that describes LAB-TAB).

Relation between IBQ and TBAQ

The TBAQ derives from Rothbart's (1981) Infant Behavior Questionnaire and would, of course, be the appropriate instrument to use when following a sample previously tested with the IBQ. The corresponding scales are as follows (IBQ scale/TBAQ scale): Distress to Limitation/Anger Proneness; Smiling & Laughter/Pleasure; Fear/Social Fear; Duration of Orienting/Interest/Persistence; Activity Level/Activity Level. There is no TBAQ counterpart to the IBQ Soothability scale. Despite the corresponding scales, the TBAQ items were not derived from the IBQ items, with a few exceptions. The scale content varies in an age-appropriate fashion, and the underlying nature of the constructs is probably not identical. In general, the TBAQ contains a greater variety of item content, which reflects toddlers' more extensive behavioral repertoire. In particular, TBAQ Social Fear has substantially more shyness-related content than IBQ Fear.

Preliminary correlational analyses from a longitudinal twin study that employed the IBQ and the early 3-scale version of the TBAQ showed modest, but highly significant, stability of mothers' reports from 9 to 22 months of age for the Fear and Joy/Pleasure scales, but not the Activity scale. More detailed analyses that will document the relations between IBQ and TBAQ scales are in progress. Ultimately, understanding the stability of questionnaire-based assessment of early temperament will require large-sample longitudinal studies that span the infant, toddler, and preschooler periods.

Applicability

The TBAQ should be employed for research purposes only. There is no evidence for its clinical utility; its content is oriented toward normal range behavior; and there is no evidence that its scales are predictive of childhood behavioral problems.

Two other cautions about use of the TBAQ are in order. It is a common practice to shorten scales before inclusion in some studies. We strongly advise against this practice for the TBAQ. One reason is that the current item content is carefully balanced in several ways. For instance, we know that eliminating certain items can change the interscale correlations substantially, as well as reduce internal consistency, a point which is also relevant to the second caution. We advise against omitting items on the basis of low item-total correlations in a new sample unless the sample is quite different from those used in constructing the TBAQ. Because the current items "survived" screening in from five to eight samples (with the exception of a few items which have been screened in

only two samples), it is likely that any low item-total correlation in a new sample—
unless it is very large—is due to random sampling fluctuation.

Companion Instruments Developed by Rothbart

Questionnaire for Preschoolers and Early School-Age Children

The Children's Behavior Questionnaire (CBQ) is currently being developed for use
between 3–7 years of age. The outside age boundaries for its use have not yet been
determined. The CBQ is a caregiver-report measure that assesses the following dimensions (scales with counterparts in the IBQ are italicized): *Activity Level, Anger*, Ap-
proach/Anticipation, Attentional Shifting and Focusing, Discomfort, *Fear*, Pleasure to
High and Low Stimulus Intensities, Impulsivity, Inhibitory Control, *Falling Reac-
tivity/Soothability*, Sadness, Shyness, and *Smiling and Laughter*. Internal-consistency
estimates of the CBQ for a sample of 262 children range from .67 to .94, and continuing
analyses are in progress. Our work predicting seven-year temperament on the CBQ from
infant laboratory assessments (Rothbart, Derryberry, & Hershey, 1990) suggests that the
measure will be very useful for longitudinal work.

Questionnaire for Adolescents

A self-report questionnaire for early adolescents, the Early Adolescent Temperament Questionnaire (EATQ) has also been developed by Deborah Capaldi and Mary
Rothbart for use with boys and girls in early and mid-adolescence, approximately ages
11–14 (Capaldi & Rothbart, 1990). The scales developed for this measure include
Activity Level, Autonomic Reactivity, Attention, Fear, Irritability, Low-Intensity Pleasure, High Intensity Pleasure/Risk Seeking, Motor Activation, Inhibitory Control, Sensitivity, Shyness, and Sadness. For an item analysis sample of 97 children, coefficient
alphas ranged from .65 to .79; average convergence between adolescent self-report and
parent report was .30. The scale contains 99 items.

Questionnaire for Adults

Derryberry and Rothbart (1988) have constructed a self-report questionnaire for use
with adult subjects, the Physiological Reactions Questionnaire (PRQ). Several of the
dimensions assessed in the caregiver-report scales for children and adolescents were
derived from this work with adults. In this research, the general constructs of emotionality, reactivity, and self-regulation were decomposed into subconstructs, and homogeneous scales developed through item analysis for assessing each subconstruct. Scales
include External and Internal Sensitivity, Cognitive and Autonomic Reactivity, Rising
and Falling Reactivity, Motor Activation and Tension (all reactivity dimensions), Discomfort, Fear, Frustration, and Sadness (negative emotionality), Pleasure to Low or

High Intensity Stimulation and Relief (positive emotionality) and Attentional Focusing and Shifting and Inhibitory Control (self-regulation). More recently, scales have also been developed to assess Approach/Anticipation and Shyness.

In all, the questionnaires available nearly allow a life-span approach to the measurement of temperament. In particular, the questionnaires for the three oldest ages (the CBQ and beyond) provide a highly detailed assessment of dimensions of temperamental reactivity and self-regulation.

Need for Non-Questionnaire Measures

No construct should be equated with only one method of assessment, however refined that method might become. Although the bulk of available evidence suggests that our questionnaires are not substantially biased by parental characteristics or response sets, respondent characteristics must flavor any questionnaire approach. For some purposes, access to the more extensive observational base of the parent must be sacrificed for more rigorously objective assessment techniques.

Behavioral Assessment of Early Temperament in the Laboratory: The Laboratory Temperament Assessment Battery

This section describes procedures we have developed to measure behavioral aspects of temperament during infancy (Goldsmith & Rothbart, 1988). The Laboratory Temperament Assessment Battery (LAB-TAB) is available in a locomotor version that is being standardized for 12- and 18-month-olds and a prelocomotor version that is initially being standardized with 6-month-olds.

Our goal in developing LAB-TAB is to make available a standardized instrument for laboratory assessment of early temperament. We expect that LAB-TAB will prove useful in laboratories besides our own. With the availability of LAB-TAB, it no longer will be necessary to develop laboratory measures of temperament anew for every study. Appropriate standardization data on large samples will allow assignment of more accurate scores, rather than relying on standardization in individual samples. LAB-TAB will also facilitate comparison of results across studies from different laboratories.

The full standardization data are not yet available and validation studies are still under way. Nevertheless, the LAB-TAB procedures described in this chapter represent some 7 years of research, and other investigators may be able to take advantage of that effort.

Terminology

In describing LAB-TAB, we strive to use certain terminology consistently. The content areas of temperament covered by LAB-TAB are called *dimensions*. These dimensions include activity level, fearfulness, anger proneness, interest/persistence, and joy/pleasure. The 20 settings, four per dimension, that we use to assess temperament are called *episodes*. Sometimes the stimulus is presented on multiple *trials*. To facilitate scoring, the longer episodes are typically divided in shorter intervals called *epochs*. Within each epoch or trial, a number of infant *responses*, such as smiling, reaching, or crying, are scored. Sometimes the presence or absence of a response is simply noted; however, more often *parameters* of the response, such as latency, duration, and intensity, are scored.

Physical Setting, Equipment, and Laboratory Routine

LAB-TAB is designed to be used in a developmental research laboratory without unusual or expensive equipment. The standard setting consists of two experimental rooms and one control room with windows suitable for videotaping activity in the experimental rooms. One of the rooms should be similar to a living room, whereas the other can be much smaller, perhaps like an interviewing room. To minimize distractions, some episodes are best carried out in a small, partially enclosed booth that has an opening for presenting stimuli.

At least one videorecording system is necessary; two systems facilitate rapid transition from one episode to another. In our laboratory, a programmable timing light cues participants to change activities and aids scoring. For cuing the mother as to her role and instructing her about how to react to unexpected behavior from her child, we use a small FM transceiver for some episodes. However, the transceiver is unnecessary for successful use of LAB-TAB. We have rejected numerous ideas for "high-tech" enhancement of stimulus presentation and scoring in order that the episodes can be easily adopted elsewhere.

Two experimenters can carry out the LAB-TAB episodes. One female experimenter interacts with the mother and child during a warm-up period that typically lasts about 10 minutes. The warm-up continues until the child appears at ease in the laboratory setting. The experimenter who has interacted with the child during the warm-up period serves as the "familiar experimenter" throughout the visit. The LAB-TAB procedures assume that the primary caregiver accompanies the child to the laboratory.

For 18-month-olds, it is usually possible to conduct about seven episodes in one visit. However, this varies with the actual episodes being run, as well as with the particular child's characteristics. Testing should cease if the child becomes fatigued or drowsy.

Carryover Effects and Sequencing of Episodes

Any time multiple assessments are carried out during a single laboratory visit, carryover effects from one episode to another are a potential danger. We employ several practices to minimize carryover effects. First, we provide brief rests between episodes. Second, we avoid consecutive, potentially stressful episodes in the same room. The change of rooms reduces situational carryover. Third, the familiar experimenter is responsible for ensuring that the child is in a quiet, alert state before a new episode begins.

Finally, the sequencing of the episodes is designed to minimize carryover effects. We generally begin with a nonstressful episode drawn from the Pleasure or Interest domains. Fear and Anger episodes are interspersed, and we position the Free Play episode of Activity Level midway through the laboratory visit to provide a longer period of play.

The episodes in the locomotor version of LAB-TAB are listed below. After the brief descriptive title of each episode, a designation of LR (living room), TT (testing at table), or EC (enclosed chamber) indicates the setting.

Fearfulness Episodes

- Large, novel, remotely controlled toy enters room (LR).
- Mechanical toy dog races across table toward child (TT).
- Male stranger approaches and picks up child (LR).
- Plastic masks of human-like faces are displayed (EC).

Anger Proneness Episodes

- Gentle arm restraint by parent while playing with toy (TT).
- Attractive toy placed behind Plexiglas barrier (TT).
- Brief separation from mother (LR).
- Restraint in car seat (LR).

Pleasure Episodes

- Reaction to sound and light display in nonsocial setting (EC).
- Puppet game (TT).
- Reaction to perceiving contingent control of toy's movement (TT).
- Modified peek-a-boo game with mother's face appearing behind various doors (TT).

Interest/Persistence Episodes

- Task orientation while playing with blocks (TT).
- Interest and engagement in toy that displays lights and sounds (TT).
- Interest in person not engaged in interaction with child (LR).
- Attention to repeated presentation of photographic slides (EC).

Activity Episodes

- Activity while in corral filled with large rubber balls (LR).
- Fine motor manipulation of simple pegboard and shapeboard (TT).
- Fidgeting while watching video clips (LR).
- Locomotor activity during free play (LR).

Maternal Interview

Prior to the LAB-TAB episodes, we administer a brief structured interview to the mother. The interview obtains the mother's predictions about how her child would typically respond to the impending laboratory episodes. We hope it will help establish the ecological validity of LAB-TAB. The interview begins with a description of the episodes; then the mother looks at the stimuli, and we ask her a series of questions. For example, for the Anger Proneness: Arm Restraint episode, we first ask how the child is expected to react in a multiple choice format, i.e., "How do you think (your child) will react?"

- Will take it in stride—will not be bothered at all.
- Will protest only mildly.
- Will protest mildly at first then get quite upset.
- Will get quite upset rapidly.
- Don't know.
- Other

Then, the mother is asked to rate, on a 4-point scale (Definitely Yes, Probably Yes, Probably No, Definitely No) whether she thinks her child will (1) look angry; (2) fuss or whine; and (3) squirm and try to pull arms away. If these questions are answered in the affirmative, we ask about more intense reactions. Finally, we ask the mother to rate how confident she feels about her predictions. The questions are, of course, modified according to the likely responses for each of the 20 episodes.

The interview format is flexible, and researchers could add questions about the importance of each behavior to the mother, about how much pleasure or concern each response might evoke in the mother, or about other topics that might be relevant to the temperament-related hypotheses under investigation.

Summary of Research

Most of the episodes yield from 5 to 10 composite measures, each based on several behavioral events. Interrater agreement for most of these composite measures ranges from 87% to 100%, according to initial analyses. The scoring is straightforward and calls for few subjective judgments.

There are many reliability and validity issues that we shall examine as our database grows. However, analyses of the existing data show promising results. An example comes from the first episode that was ready for analysis: Pleasure: Reaction to Sound and Light Display for 18-month-olds. This rather simple episode was scored with high agreement. The discrete measures scored in this episode were latency to the first smile, duration of smiling, laughter, positive vocalizations, hedonically positive motoric acts, and intensity ratings of smiling. A square root transformation proved useful for expressing the latency variable. These six measures were scored on four trials. Intercorrelations across trials averaged .66, which encouraged us to form within-response, cross-trial composites. In this episode, the only possible examination of convergence across parameters was for latency, duration, and intensity of smiling composites; the average intercorrelation was .68, supporting a temperamental interpretation, according to the theoretical approaches of Goldsmith and Campos (1986) and Rothbart and Derryberry (1981). Next, we examined cross-modal correlations within the episode (e.g., laughter with motoric acts, motoric acts with smiling intensity, etc.). A positive manifold in the correlation matrix was confirmed by a first principal component that loaded all variables. We formed a simple unit-weighted composite of the six measures. Its internal consistency (alpha) was estimated as .67, an encouraging value considering that only six items entered into the composite and the broader measure of temperamental pleasure from LAB-TAB would incorporate data from the other three Pleasure episodes.

As a methodological check, we examined the composite's correlation with sex of infant and order of the Sound and Light Display episode within the visit; as expected, these correlations were near-zero. We then correlated the overall Sound and Light Display Pleasure composite with the new TBAQ scales. Both convergent and discriminant validity were supported as only the TBAQ Pleasure scale significantly predicted our lab measure ($r = .47$). Pleasure expressed during the episode was unrelated to TBAQ Social Fear, Activity, Persistence, or Anger Proneness. Another Pleasure episode, the Cognitive Assimilation task at age 18 months correlated .37 with TBAQ Pleasure scale reported by the mothers. Correlations of the Pleasure: Cognitive Assimilation task with the other TBAQ scales averaged .01.

The maternal interview contained seven items concerning the mother's predictions about the infant's likely behavior in the Sound and Light Display episode. We formed a composite from these seven interview items that predicted the infant's actual behavior in LAB-TAB ($r = .61$), supporting convergent validity. Not surprisingly, the TBAQ Pleasure scale and the interview composite were correlated .52.

The first Fear episode we analyzed was Display of Masks. Again, latency, duration, and intensity parameters of the same response were highly intercorrelated (mean $r = .77$). Cross-response convergence was even stronger than in the analogous pleasure measures; for instance, average latencies to show fear in the facial, vocalic, and bodily avoidance domains averaged .79. Alpha for a preliminary 10-item Fear: Masks composite was .70, which would, of course, increase as other fear measures are added.

The first Activity episode analyzed was Free Play. The pattern of results was similar to those described above. Interestingly, alpha for a 4-item composite comprising only the "change in locomotor activity" measures was .85, higher than for an overall Free Play composite. As in other analyses, sex of infant and order of the Free Play episode were uncorrelated with behavior. In these preliminary analyses, we did *not* observe good convergence with the TBAQ Activity scale. The apparent explanation is that pleasure-related content in the "toy play measures" from the Free Play episode led to contamination with the Pleasure questionnaire scale. This is the sort of problem that will require additional attention—not in revision of laboratory procedure but in fine-tuning scores and selecting the best component measures for temperament summary scores. On the other hand, the summary LAB-TAB free-play variable did correlate .59 with mothers' interview-based predictions that the child would avoid examining just one toy closely, and convergence with other interview measures was also apparent.

We also examined some of the initial 18-month data from the anger proneness episodes. We estimated alpha at .89, .91, and .92 for three of the 18-month Anger episodes. Reasonable levels of lab by questionnaire convergence and specificity was found for the Anger episodes (e.g., Anger: Maternal Separation by TBAQ Anger Proneness scale, $r = .52$). Cross-episode consistency for the LAB-TAB anger proneness episodes are promising thus far. For instance, Anger: Barrier Task × Anger: Placement in Car Seat summary scores correlated .42. We noted an interesting exception to the general pattern of convergence in that anger in the context of maternal interaction was relatively independent of anger expressed during frustrating tasks. This finding highlights the importance of LAB-TAB's systematic variation of social context of assessment across the various episodes.

In summary, results from the 18 month episodes presented above, which are simply the first that we have analyzed, suggest promising psychometric properties for the locomotor version of LAB-TAB. Thus far, we have only undertaken a few analyses of the prelocomotor data; however, the initial results are quite similar to those reported above for the 18-month locomotor battery.

Earlier research in our respective laboratories sets the expectation that the validity of the LAB-TAB measures will eventually be supported. For instance, Rothbart (1988, 1989) demonstrated significant convergence for laboratory measures of fear, pleasure, and sustained play with, respectively, questionnaire scales tapping fearfulness, smiling and laughter, and duration of orienting. Her laboratory measures were precursors of some of the episodes that we have refined for LAB-TAB. Similarly, Goldsmith and Campos (1986) demonstrated lab-questionnaire convergence for stranger distress and fearfulness assessed via questionnaire. In previous work, we also found indications that test-retest reliability should eventually prove satisfactory: Goldsmith and Campos (1989) found 2-week retest correlations of about .50 for Fear and Pleasure composites; this degree of stability was noteworthy because the composites showed only modest internal consistency. Rothbart showed that laboratory measures of distress, fear, frustration, and pleasure showed stability coefficients of about .30 over the period from 10 to 13.5 months, a period of tremendous behavioral reorganization. It should be clear that the data mentioned in this paragraph do not refer to the current LAB-TAB; they are encouraging because we believe that the LAB-TAB measures are clear improvements over the ones we used previously.

The preliminary nature of these analyses should be emphasized. We are currently beginning new standardization, reliability, and validity studies for LAB-TAB.

Anticipated Use

We expect that most investigators will use only a subset of the episodes in any particular study. We hope users will arrange for repeated testing to reduce temporal variation. We also expect that LAB-TAB will typically be used in conjunction with caregiver report via the Infant Behavior Questionnaire or the Toddler Behavior Assessment Questionnaire.

Investigators who wish to use LAB-TAB should contact the authors for more complete information, including specific information about stimuli, scoresheets for each episode, and current standardization and validity data.

Conclusion

Research on temperament is in a phase of proliferation of theories and assessment instruments. In this chapter, we have reported on the development of a series of questionnaire and laboratory-based instruments to assess temperament. Although some of these instruments require further development and validation, they show sufficient evidence of reliability, convergent validity, and discriminant validity to justify their expanded use. As they and other theory-based instruments are employed in a variety of research designs, we should begin to appreciate the intricacies of their construct validity. Undoubtedly, the resulting theoretical tension will eventually lead to increased understanding of the role of temperament in social, cognitive, and personality development.

ACKNOWLEDGMENTS. This work was supported by NSF grant BNS-8508927 and NIMH grant MH-41200 to Goldsmith and Rothbart, by NIMH grants MH21674 and MH43361 to Rothbart, and by grants from the University of Texas Research Institute, the Spencer Foundation, and the Foundation for Child Development to Goldsmith. Goldsmith was supported by Research Career Development Award HD00694. Jennifer Alansky, Lori Bowden, Karen Hershey, Karen Jaco, and Loretta Rieser-Danner contributed to the construction of LAB-TAB. Kate Duncan, Patricia East, Teri Elliott, and Karen Jaco contributed to the construction of the TBAQ. Suzanne Kelly, Lita Furby, and Mark Layman contributed to the construction of the IBQ.

References

Bates, J. E., & Bayles, K. Objective and subjective components in mothers' perceptions of their children from age 6 months to 3 years. *Merrill-Palmer Quarterly*, 1984, *30*, 111–130.

Bates, J. E., Freeland, C. A. B., & Lounsbury, M. L. Measurement of infant difficultness. *Child Development*, 1979, *50*, 794–803.

Bornstein, M. H., Gaughran, J. M., & Homel, P. Infant temperament: Theory, tradition, critique, and new assessments. In C. E. Izard & P. B. Read (Eds.), *Measuring emotions in infants and children*. Vol. 2. Cambridge: Cambridge University Press, 1986.

Buss, A. H., & Plomin, R. *A temperament theory of personality development*. New York: Wiley, 1975.

Buss, A. H., & Plomin, R. *Temperament: Early developing personality traits*. Hillsdale, NJ: Erlbaum, 1984.

Capaldi, D. M., & Rothbart, M. K. (March, 1990). Development of an adolescent temperament measure. Paper presented at the meetings of the Society for Research on Adolescence, Atlanta, Georgia.

Carey, W. B. A simplified method for measuring infant temperament. *Journal of Pediatrics*, 1970, *77*, 188–194.

Carey, W. B., & McDevitt, S. Revision of the Infant Temperament Questionnaire. *Pediatrics*, 1978, *61*, 735–739.

Crockenberg, S. B., & Acredolo, C. Infant temperament ratings: A function of infants, mothers, or both? *Infant Behavior and Development*, 1983, *6*, 61–72.

Derryberry, D., & Rothbart, M. K. Arousal, affect and attention as components of temperament. *Journal of Personality and Social Psychology*, 1988, *55*, 953–966.

Diamond, S. *Personality and temperament*. New York: Harper & Row, 1957.

Eaton, W. O., & Dureski, C. M. Parent and actometer measures of motor activity level in the young infant. *Infant Behavior and Development*, 1986, *9*, 383–393.

Escalona, S. K. *The roots of individuality: Normal patterns of development in infancy*. Chicago: Aldine, 1968.

Fullard, W., McDevitt, S. C., & Carey, W. B. Assessing temperament in one-to-three-year-old children. *Journal of Pediatric Psychology*, 1984, *9*, 205–216.

Goldsmith, H. H. *Preliminary manual for the Toddler Behavior Assessment Questionnaire*. Oregon Center for the Study of Emotion technical report No 88-04, University of Oregon, Eugene, OR, 1988.

Goldsmith, H. H., Buss, A. H., Plomin, R., Rothbart, M. K., Thomas, A., Chess, S., Hinde, R. A., & McCall, R. R. Roundtable: What is temperament? Four approaches. *Child Development*, 1987, *58*, 505–529.

Goldsmith, H. H., & Campos, J. J. *The nature of determinants of infant temperament and its implications for attachement formation: A reconceptualization.* Developmental Psychobiology Research Group Conference. Estes Park, CO, May 1980.

Goldsmith, H. H., & Campos, J. J. Fundamental issues in the study of early temperament: The Denver Twin Temperament Study. In M. E. Lamb, A. L. Brown, & B. Rogoff (Eds.), *Advances in developmental psychology.* Vol. 4. Hillsdale, NJ: Erlbaum, 1986.

Goldsmith, H. H., & Campos, J. J. The structure of temperamental fear and pleasure in infants: A psychometric perspective. *Child Development,* 1990, *61,* 1944–1964.

Goldsmith, H. H., Elliot, T. K., & Jaco, K. L. Construction and initial validation of a new temperament questionnaire. *Infant Behavior and Development,* 1986, *9,* 144.

Goldsmith, H. H., & Rieser-Danner, L. Variation among temperament theories and validational studies of temperament assessment. In G. A. Kohnstamm (Ed.), *Temperament discussed: Temperament and development in infancy and childhood.* Lisse: Swets & Zeitlinger, 1986.

Goldsmith, H. H., & Rieser-Danner, L. Assessing early temperament. In C. R. Reynolds, & R. Kamphaus (Eds.), *Handbook of psychological and educational assessment of children: Personality, behavior, and context.* Vol. 2. New York: Guilford, 1990.

Goldsmith, H. H., Rieser-Danner, L., & Briggs, S. Convergent and discriminant validity for infant, toddler, and preschooler temperament questionnaires. *Developmental Psychology,* in press.

Goldsmith, H. H., Rothbart, M. K. *The Laboratory Temperament Assessment Battery (LAB-TAB): Locomotor Version.* Oregon Center for the Study of Emotion, technical report No 88-01, 1988.

Gordon, S. The socialization of children's emotions: Toward a unified constructionist theory. In C. Saarni, & P. L. Harris (Eds.), *Children's understanding of emotion.* New York: Cambridge University Press, 1989.

Gunnar, M. R. Human developmental psychoneuroendocrinology: A review of research on neuroendocrine responses to challenge and threat in infancy and childhood. In M. E. Lamb, A. L. Brown, & B. Rogoff (Eds.), *Advances in developmental psychology.* Vol. 4. Hillsdale, NJ: Erlbaum, 1986.

Hasher, L., & Zacks, R. T. Automatic and effortful processes in memory. *Journal of Experimental Psychology. General,* 1979, *108,* 356–388.

Hubert, N. C., & Wachs, T. D. Peters-Martin, P., & Gandour, M. J. The study of early temperament: Measurement and conceptual issues. *Child Development,* 1982, *53,* 571–600.

McKeen, N., & Eaton, W. O. *Infant motor activity: Temperament, behavior and sex differences.* Paper presented at the meeting of the Society for Research in Child Development. Kansas City, MO, April 1989.

Neale, M. C., & Stevenson, J. Rater bias in the EASI temperament scales: A twin study. *Journal of Personality and Social Psychology,* 1989, *56,* 446–455.

Nesselroade, J. R. Isssues in studying developmental change in adults from a multivariate perspective. In J. E. Birren & K. W. Schaie (Eds.), *Handbook of the psychology of aging.* New York: Van Nostrand Reinhold, 1977.

Rothbart, M. K. Laughter in young children. *Psychological Bulletin,* 1973, *80,* 247–256.

Rothbart, M. K. Measurement of temperament in infancy. *Child Development,* 1981, *52,* 569–578.

Rothbart, M. K. Longitudinal observation of infant temperament. *Developmental Psychology,* 1986, *22,* 356–365.

Rothbart, M. K. Temperament and the development of inhibited approach. *Child Development,* 1988, *59,* 1241–1250.

Rothbart, M. K. Behavioral approach and inhibition. In S. Reznick (Ed.), *Perspectives on behavioral inhibition* (pp. 139–157). Chicago: University of Chicago Press, 1989a.

Rothbart, M. K. Temperament and development. In G. A. Kohnstamm, J. A. Bates, & M. K. Rothbart (Eds.), *Temperament in childhood* (pp. 187–248). Chichester: Wiley, 1989b.

Rothbart, M. K. The biological processes of temperament. In G. A. Kohnstamm, J. A. Bates, & M. K. Rothbart (Eds.), *Temperament in childhood* (pp. 77–110). Chichester: Wiley, 1989c.

Rothbart, M. K. Temperament in childhood: A framework. In G. A. Kohnstamm, J. A. Bates, & M. K. Rothbart (Eds.), *Temperament in childhood* (pp. 59–75). Chichester: Wiley, 1989d.

Rothbart, M. K. Convergences between laboratory and parent report measures of temperament. In C.

Garcia Coll, Chair, "Behavioral assessments of infant temperament: Issues in validity and continuity." Meetings of the Society for Research in Child Development, Kansas City, Missouri (1989e, April).

Rothbart, M. K., & Derryberry, D. Development of individual differences in temperament. In M. E. Lamb & A. L. Brown (Eds.), *Advances in developmental psychology*. Vol. 1. Hillsdale, NJ: Erlbaum, 1981.

Rothbart, M. K., Derryberry, D., and Hershey, K. Stability of early temperament: Laboratory infant assessment to parent report at seven years. Manuscript in preparation, 1990.

Rothbart, M. K., & Goldsmith, H. H. Three approaches to the study of infant temperament. *Developmental Review*, 1985, *5*, 237–250.

Rothbart, M. K., & Mauro, J. A. Questionnaire measures of infant temperament. In J. W. Fagen & J. Colombo (Eds.), *Individual differences in infancy: Reliability, stability and prediction* (pp. 411–430). Hillsdale, NJ: Erlbaum, 1990.

Rothbart, M. K., & Posner, M. I. Temperament and the development of self-regulation. In L. C. Hartlage & C. F. Telzrow (Eds.), *The neuropsychology of individual differences: A developmental perspective*. New York: Plenum Press, 1985.

Schaffer, H. Cognitive components of the infant's response to strangeness. In M. Lewis & L. Rosenblum (Eds.), *The origins of fear*. New York: Wiley, 1974.

Seifer, R., & Sameroff, A. J. The concept, measurement, and interpretation of temperament in young children: A survey of research issues. In M. L. Wolraich, & D. Routh (Eds.), *Advances in developmental and behavioral pediatrics*. Vol. 7. Greenwich, CN: JAI Press, 1986.

Shirley, M. *The first two years: Personality manifestations*. Vol. 3. Minneapolis: University of Minnesota Press, 1933.

Sroufe, L. A., & Wunsch, J. The development of laughter in the first year of life. *Child Development*, 1972, *43*, 1326–1344.

Stenberg, C., & Campos, J. J. The development of anger expressions in infancy. In N. L. Stein, T. Trabasso, & B. Leventhal (Eds.), *Psychological and biological approaches to emotion* (pp. 247–282). Hillsdale, NJ: Erlbaum, 1990.

Tellegen, A. *Brief manual for the Differential Personality Questionnaire*. Department of Psychology, University of Minnesota, 1982.

Thomas, A., & Chess, S. *Temperament and development*. New York: Brunner/Mazel, 1977.

Thomas, A., Chess, S., & Birch, H. *Temperament and behavior disorders in children*. New York: New York University Press, 1968.

Thomas, A., Chess, S., Birch, H. G., Hertzig, M., & Korn, S. *Behavioral individuality in early childhood*. New York: New York University Press, 1963.

Thompson, R. A., & Lamb, M. E. Stranger sociability and its relationships to temperament and social experience during the second year. *Infant Behavior and Development*, 1982, *5*, 277–287.

Thompson, R. A., & Lamb, M. E. Continuity and change in socioemotional development during the second year. In R. N. Emde & R. J. Harmon (Eds.), *Continuities and discontinuities in development*. New York: Plenum, 1984.

Worobey, J., & Blajda, V. M. Temperamental ratings at 2 weeks, 2 months, and 1 year: Differential stability of activity and emotionality. *Developmental Psychology*, 1989, *25*, 257–263.

16

Reactivity and Anxiety in the Laboratory and Beyond

Paul M. Kohn

Psychometric versus Experimental Measures of Reactivity

Reactivity as a concept (Strelau, 1983) is the psychological obverse of strength of the nervous system (Nebylitsyn, 1972a). Thus, highly reactive people, ones with a weak nervous system, are sensitive to weak stimulation, have a low optimum level of stimulation and arousal, are distractible and lack "functional endurance." The last term means that they are less able than others to respond adaptively to increasingly intense, prolonged, or repetitive stimulation. Their reaction time, for example, should stop quickening and, in fact, slow down in response to increasingly loud auditory stimuli at a lower volume than is characteristic of low reactives. In technical language, high reactives have a lower "threshold of transmarginal inhibition" than other people (Keuss & Orlebeke, 1977; Nebylitsyn, 1972a). Low reactives, persons with strong nervous systems, of course, show the opposite characteristics.

Because the concepts of reactivity and strength of the nervous system are neo-Pavlovian in origin, it is understandable that the original techniques of measuring them were experimental rather than psychometric: e.g., slopes and mean judgments for brightness and loudness magnitude estimation (Reason, 1968; Sales & Throop, 1972), and slopes and mean reaction times to lights and tones of varying intensities (Keuss & Orlebeke, 1977; Strelau, 1983). More recently, however, psychometric tests of reactivity have been developed such as the Reactivity Scale (RS; Kohn, 1985) and the Strength of Excitation subscale of the Strelau (1972a) Temperament Inventory (STI-SE). There are also measures of such related constructs as extraversion (Eysenck & Eysenck, 1968) and augmenting-reducing (Vando, 1974) which are so conceptually similar and empirically

Paul M. Kohn • Department of Psychology, York University, North York, Ontario M3J 1P3, Canada.

correlated with reactivity measures that I elsewhere suggested referring to them all as indexes of "arousability" (Kohn, 1987), an important aspect of temperament.

Recently my associates and I (Kohn, Cowles, & Lafreniere 1987) reported a study in which the RS, the STI-SE, the Extraversion subscale of the Eysenck Personality Inventory (EPI-E; Eysenck & Eysenck, 1968) and the Reducer-Augmenter Scale (RAS; Vando, 1970, 1974) were intercorrelated with the above-cited experimental measures plus personally set volume for listening to popular music (Davis, Cowles, & Kohn, 1984; Kohn, Hunt, Cowles, & Davis, 1986). We found that, although the psychometric tests intercorrelated highly (from .45 to .66 in absolute magnitude) and there were a few high intercorrelations among the experimental indexes, the cross-correlations between experimental and psychometric measures were generally low and nonsignificant.

We (Kohn, 1987; Kohn et al., 1987) attributed the lack of correspondence between the two kinds of indexes to the distinction between general and partial properties of the nervous system (Nebylitsyn, 1972b; Strelau, 1983). Although such properties as reactivity or strength of the nervous system were originally conceived as general across sensory modalities, evidence suggests that they are also somewhat partial in terms of differing individually within modalities as well as across them (Ippolitov, 1972; Strelau, 1972b, 1983). It is argued that test scores in this domain are largely general across modalities in their significance, whereas experimental measures are *necessarily* modality-specific, mostly either visual or auditory. The prospect of great success in relating measures of corresponding general and partial properties, as we did, thus seems remote.

This raises the question with which I ended a previous presentation (Kohn, 1987): Namely, if relating reactivity (or, more generally, arousability) to laboratory measures of the usual kind is unlikely to prove fruitful, what could one usefully relate it to (Kohn, 1987, p. 247)? Because the definition of reactivity is clearly relevant to the experience and tolerance of distress, and because this is an interesting and humanly important area, I chose initially to examine that relationship, notably as it pertains to pain tolerance and adverse reactions to everyday stresses.

Reactivity and Response to Pain

Dubreuil and Kohn (1986) had already demonstrated a modest relationship between reactivity on one hand and perceived severity and tolerance for pain on the other. The fact that high reactives found painful stimulation more severe and tolerated it less well than did low reactives reinforced previous findings with the related constructs of extraversion (Barnes, 1975; Eysenck & Eysenck, 1985) and augmenting-reducing (Barnes, 1985; Petrie, 1967, Vando, 1974).

One point, however, was puzzling: The reported relationships between arousability measures and pain tolerance were generally modest, with the notable exception of Vando (1974), who reported an astonishing correlation of .84 between pain tolerance and his Reducer-Augmenter Scale. A logically possible reason for this is simply that the RAS is more valid than other measures of arousability. However, the fact that others have obtained weaker correlations between the RAS itself on one hand and pain tolerance and rated severity of pain on the other somewhat undercuts this interpretation (Barnes, 1985; Mahoney, Shumate, & Worthington, 1980).

An alternative interpretation reflects the fact that Vando's (1970, 1974) instructions differed importantly from ones commonly used in pain experiments. Notably, whereas the latter typically ask subjects to endure as much pain as possible, Vando (1970, p. 32) used the analogy of a minor surgical procedure:

> In some surgical procedures pain is an important signal for the doctor. He wants to know when you first feel pain, and your reports of pain guide him in his work. Of course, he has no desire to hurt you and has an anaesthetic spray ready to deaden the area any time you wish. . . . You are asked to say "now" when you first experience pain and you are asked to say "stop" at that point when you might flinch and hinder the procedure.

(The above comes from Vando's instructions for the first of two trials. Instructions for the second trial differ in that subjects were told not to say "stop" until they were sure they could not help flinching.)

Pain-tolerance measures apparently reflect a combination of true pain tolerance, i.e., the *real* maximum pain that a person can endure voluntarily, and immediate inclination to undergo pain voluntarily which varies with personal state and circumstance. Demonstrations that variables like competition and the presence of others (Murphy & Murphy, 1931) and apparent competition between a salient membership group and some other group (Lambert, Libman & Poser, 1960) increase pain tolerance support this conception of pain-tolerance measurement.

Our interpretation of Vando's (1970, 1974) results was that his "surgical-analogy" instructions reduced the social-desirability demand implicit in more standard instructions to endure as much pain as possible. In fact, he himself abandoned such instructions because, in response to them, subjects endured pain levels so high as to risk self-injury under his procedure (Vando, 1970, p. 32). Thus, in our terms, Vando's surgical-analogy instructions evoke social-desirability demands less and hence true pain tolerance proportionally more than do standard instructions. Accordingly, measures of arousability such as the RAS or the RS should relate more strongly to pain tolerance under surgical-analogy instructions than under standard instructions; however, the opposite should be true of a measure of need for social approval, such as Marlowe and Crowne's (1961) Social Desirability Scale (SDS).

My colleagues and I did two experiments to test the above reasoning (Kohn, Cowles, & Dzinas, 1989). The first was designed simply to determine whether standard instructions are more fraught with social-desirability demands than are surgical-analogy instructions. Students in an introductory-psychology class rated either a printed set of surgical-analogy instructions ($n = 27$) or a printed set of standard instructions ($n = 28$) on a series of five-point scales for social-evaluation threat, physical threat, mundane threat, unfamiliar threat, and overall threat.

The standard instructions asked subjects to endure finger-pressure stimulation (Forgione & Barber, 1971) "for at least one minute, and for as long after that as you can take." In contrast, the surgical-analogy instructions, modeled on Vando's (1970), requested subjects to undergo stimulation for at least one minute and after that "only until you think you are at real risk of flinching or moving unexpectedly, and, thus, hypothetically risking surgical accident." Receipt of either set of instructions by a subject was randomly predetermined.

Two-way multivariate analysis of variance (MANOVA) for Gender x Instructions yielded only a significant main effect for instructions, $F(5,47) = 3.02, p < .02$. Univariate analyses (ANOVAs) within this overall effect implicated only the dependent variable of social-evaluation threat, $F(1,51) = 4.95, p < .05$. As expected, the standard instructions ($M = 3.29$) were more socially threatening than the surgical-analogy instructions ($M = 2.48$). Thus, subjects seem to find the thought of showing low pain tolerance more socially threatening after standard than after surgical-analogy instructions.

Accordingly, we conducted a second experiment wherein undergraduate volunteer subjects underwent pain-tolerance testing under either standard ($n = 45$) or surgical-analogy ($n = 45$) instructions after having responded to measures of arousability and need for social approval. Vando's (1970, 1974) Reducer-Augmenter Scale and Kohn's (1985) Reactivity Scale were used to assess arousability, and Marlowe and Crowne's (1961) Social Desirability Scale to test need for social approval. Pain-tolerance testing involved applying 2300 g of pressure to the dorsal surface of the medial phalanx of the dominant hand's index finger (Forgione & Barber, 1971), and assignment to instructional conditions was, of course, randomly predetermined. Judgments of pain intensity on an 11-point scale were solicited at 30s and 60s, and pain tolerance was defined by how many seconds up to a predetermined limit of 5 min a subject voluntarily endured stimulation.

We hypothesized that the arousability measures, the RS and the RAS, would correlate more highly with rated severity and pain tolerance after surgical-analogy instructions than after standard instructions. In contrast, we expected the SDS to relate more strongly to the pain measures after standard instruction than after surgical-analogy instructions.

Cronbach's alpha reliabilities for the psychometric tests were adequate here as in previous work: .70 for the SDS, .82 for the RAS, and .81 for the RS. The correlation between the RS and the RAS was negative, r (88) $= -.42, p < .001$, as befits oppositely keyed indexes of arousability. Neither arousability measure correlated reliably with the SDS, $r = -.08$ for RS and .04 for RAS. The 30s and 60s pain ratings correlated highly with one another, $r = .82. p < .001$, and with pain tolerance, $r = -.55$ and $-.63$ respectively, $p < .001$ in both cases.

Two-way MANOVA on the pain measures for Gender × Instructions yielded only a significant main effect for gender F (3,78) $= 12.05, p < .001$. Univariate ANOVAs within this overall effect revealed that men rated the pain as less severe at 30s and 60s and endured it longer than did women, $F(1,78) = 8.99, 21.61$ and 31.80 respectively, $p < .005$ in all three cases. Men were also more likely to score high, i.e., as reducers, on the RAS, t (88) $= 2.44, p < .02$, and low on the RS, t (88) $= 3.80, p < .001$. There was no significant sex difference on the SDS.

Of greatest interest were the cross correlations between the pain indexes on the one hand and gender and the personality tests on the other. These appear in Table 16.1. The following findings are notable: (1) Gender correlates appreciably with the pain measures across instructional conditions, except for its failure to correlate significantly with the 30s rating in the surgical-analogy condition—again, males are less sensitive to pain and more tolerant of it than are females; (2) RS correlates significantly and substantially with all three pain measures across instructional conditions—that is, high reactives describe their pain as more severe and endure it less protractedly than do low reactives; (3) SDS does not relate significantly to any pain index under either condition; and (4) Although the RAS correlates significantly with the 30s rating (negatively) and pain tolerance

Table 16.1. Cross-Correlations Between Personality and Pain Measures under Standard and Surgical-Analogy Instructions

	Standard instructions (n = 45)			Surgical-analogy instructions (n = 45)		
	30-second rating	60-second rating	Tolerance	30-second rating	60-second rating	Tolerance
Gender	−.40**	−.46**	.60**	−.19	−.47**	.42**
Social Desirability Scale	−.03	.01	−.05	−.18	−.25	.10
Reducer-Augmenter Scale	−.09	−.11	−.02	−.32*	−.21	.45**
Reactivity Scale	.37**	.43**	−.50**	.35*	.45**	−.42**

Note: Actual *n*'s vary slightly because one subject couldn't tolerate the pain long enough to reach the 30 sec rating point, and four others failed to reach the 60 sec rating point.
*p < .05, two-tailed.
**p < .01, two-tailed.

(positively) after surgical-analogy instructions, it does not relate significantly to any pain measure after standard instructions. The difference between correlations for RAS and pain tolerance across instructional conditions is significant, $z = 2.23, p < .05$. Figure 16.1 illustrates the relationship between reactivity and pain tolerance under standard and surgical-analogy instructions. It shows that reducers or high RAS-scorers are more pain-tolerant than augmenters or low RAS-scorers after surgical-analogy instructions, but not after standard instructions.

Elsewhere (Kohn *et al.*, 1989), we have reported regression analyses which support the conclusions based on the correlations in Table 16.1, i.e., that gender and reactivity predict response to pain quite well, that the social-approval measure does not do so at all, and that the Reducer-Augmenter Scale does so under surgical-analogy instructions only. These findings support our initial reasoning practically but not conceptually. That is, our surmise that "surgical-analogy instructions" contributed to Vando's obtaining an outlandishly high correlation, .84, between his arousability measure, the RAS, and pain tolerance appears to be correct. The fact remains, however, that the corresponding correlation in our own surgical-analogy condition, .45, is *still* significantly lower than his, $z = 3.84, p = < .01$. On the other hand, our theorizing about the role of social-approval motivation remains unsubstantiated. The SDS did not relate to pain tolerance in our study, nor in other recent work (Otto & Dougher, 1985).

Figure 16.1 suggests that the major impact of the surgical-analogy instructions was to diminish the pain tolerance of the augmenters, i.e., low RAS-scorers. This might suggest relaxation of a *social norm* to be pain tolerant which, after standard instructions, affects mainly those who are predisposed to be most intolerant of pain, i.e., highly arousable subjects. The obvious flaw in this interpretation is that it only works when the RAS is used as the index of arousability, not when the RS is so used. Indeed, the fact that

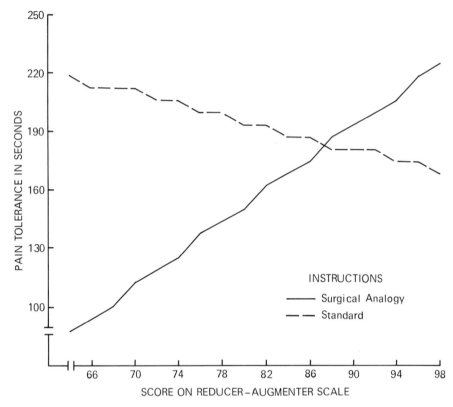

Figure 16.1. Pain tolerance as a function of instructions and score on the Reducer-Augmenter Scale.

the RS predicted pain response effectively across conditions whereas the RAS only did so after surgical-analogy instructions is difficult to interpret at all.

On the positive side, the effectiveness of the RS as a predictor of pain tolerance across conditions supports its validity as a measure of predisposition for distressed responding to high levels of stimulation. This encouraged me to examine its possible role as a predisposing factor in adverse reactions to stress.

Reactivity, Anxiety, and Adverse Reactions to Stress

Research relating cumulative stressful experiences to adverse health consequences began with Holmes and Rahe's (1967) classic work on major life events. Several changes in our understanding of this relationship have since occurred. First, contrary to Holmes and Rahe, positive events requiring adjustments, e.g., job promotions or financial windfalls, appear not to predict adverse health consequences (Antoni, 1985; McGrath & Burkhart, 1983; Taylor, 1986). Second, everyday stressors or "hassles" relate more strongly to adverse consequences than do major life events (Burks & Martin,

1983; De Longis, Coyne, Dakof, Folkman, & Lazarus, 1982; Eckenrode, 1984; Kanner, Coyne, Schaefer, & Lazarus, 1981; Monroe, 1983; Weinberger, Hiner, & Tierney, 1987).

Accordingly, a simple design occurred to us (Kathryn Lafreniere, Maria Gurevich and me): We would have subjects respond to a measure of daily hassles, the Reactivity Scale, a trait-anxiety measure (as an additional probably relevant personality variable, hitherto overlooked in the hassles literature), and measures of physical and mental health. Unfortunately, our literature review revealed that there were serious criticisms that the most commonly used Hassles Scale (Kanner *et al.*, 1981) was contaminated by items and a format which implied distressed physical and mental responses to stress rather than mere exposure to daily hassles (e.g., Burks & Martin, 1983; Dohrenwend, Dohrenwend, Dodson, & Shrout, 1984; Dohrenwend & Shrout, 1985; Green, 1986; Marziali & Pilkonis, 1986). Thus, such contamination could inflate observed relationships between the Hassles Scale and adverse health consequences to an unknown degree. We therefore decided that our simple design required a *decontaminated* hassles measure, and set out to develop one.

A Psychometric Detour

Since we planned to do our initial work with college students, we devised items suitable for that population. We attempted also to avoid items which, in our view, could likely reflect physical or mental health symptoms or distressed functioning. Finally, instead of calling our measure a "hassles scale" and having subjects indicate how severe particular hassles were which they had recently encountered, we named it the "Inventory of College Students' Recent Life Experiences" (ICSRLE) and simply asked them to rate the intensity of each listed experience over the past month on the following four-point scale: 1 = *not all* part of my life; 2 = *only slightly* part of my life; 3 = *distinctly* part of my life; and 4 = *very much* part of my life. The initial item pool consisted of 85 items. These were generally brief, e.g., "not enough leisure time," "financial burdens," and "separation from people you care about."

The ICSRLE, along with Cohen, Kamarack, and Mermelstein's (1983) Perceived Stress Scale (PSS) was administered to 208 undergraduate subjects. An item analysis was run on the first 100 subjects' data to select items which correlated positively and significantly with the PSS at a one-tailed alpha of .05. (We didn't necessarily expect *single* hassles items to correlate extremely highly with perceived stress.) We selected 49 items for the final scale which appears elsewhere (Kohn, Lafreniere, & Gurevich, 1990). Their individual correlations with the PSS ranged from .17, $p < .05$, to .48, $p < .0005$. The alpha reliability of the final scale on the item-selection subsample was .89, and its correlation against the PSS was .67, $p < .0005$.

Because capitalization on chance could have inflated the above estimates, we cross-replicated them on the remaining 108 subjects. The alpha reliability of the ICSRLE for the latter subsample was .88, and its correlation against the PSS was .59, $p < .0005$. If one accepts perceived stress as an appropriate validity criterion for a decontaminated hassles scale, ours appears reliable and valid.

Predicting Adverse Reactions to Stress

Everyday observation suggests that day-to-day stresses do affect people's physical and mental well-being. Thus, our new decontaminated hassles scale, the ICSRLE, should predict to measures of well-being. Observation also suggests that some of us are more vulnerable than others to such stressors, i.e., that temperamental and personality factors affect vulnerability to the adverse effects of daily hassles.

We were interested in the possible role of reactivity as a moderator of the impact stress has on physical and mental health. We reasoned that highly reactive persons would tend to overreact to stress. This is partly because much stress involves overstimulation, stemming from time pressure, excessive and conflicting demands, and information overload. Also, insofar as the ability to solve problems under pressure is important, the distractibility of high reactives and their low functional endurance or capacity to keep functioning under high levels of stimulation should put them at a cognitive disadvantage.

We also decided to examine the possible role of anxiety in mediating adverse reactions to everyday hassles. This is because of numerous demonstrations that specific stressors, e.g., impending surgery (Auerbach, 1973; Auerbach, Kendall, Cutter, & Levitt, 1976; Auerbach, Martelli, & Mercuri, 1983) or a stressful interview (Johnson, 1968), evoke more state anxiety in high than low trait-anxious persons. Assuming that state anxiety, notably if prolonged, intense, or frequent, contributes to the adverse consequences of stress, highly trait-anxious people should be especially vulnerable to such consequences.

These theoretical considerations led us to administer the following measures to 211 college students: the Inventory of College Students' Recent Life Experiences, described above; Kohn's (1985) Reactivity Scale; the Trait subscale of the State-Trait Anxiety Inventory (STAI-T; Spielberger, Gorsuch, & Lushene, 1970); the Perceived Stress Scale (Cohen *et al.*, 1983); the Hopkins Symptom Checklist (HSCL; Derogatis, Lipman, Rickels, Uhlenhuth, & Covi, 1974), an index of psychiatric symptomatology; and the Health Problem Inventory (HPI), a specially constructed ten-item measure of frequency of common minor ailments, e.g., colds, headaches, and digestive upsets. Except for the RS and the STAI-T, all measures were time-referenced to the preceding month.

Alpha reliabilities and intercorrelations were computed for all the measures. These appear in Table 16.2 along with the corresponding means and standard deviations. Hierarchical-entry stepwise multiple regressions were run on perceived stress (the PSS), psychiatric symptomatology (the HSCL), and common health problems (the HPI). Trait-anxiety, reactivity, hassles, and gender (as a dummy variable) were the main-effect predictors. In addition, the following interaction terms entered the initial model: Gender × Hassles, Gender × Anxiety, Gender × Reactivity, Hassles × Anxiety, Hassles × Reactivity, Gender × Hassles × Anxiety, and Gender × Hassles × Reactivity. Nonsignificant terms at each level of analysis were dropped unless they were marginal to a significant interaction. Thus, the final models, which appear in Table 3, include only effects which are either significant or implicated in a significant interaction.

As Table 16.2 shows, all measures were adequately reliable with Cronbach's alphas ranging from .74 to .95. The major findings from the regression analyses summarized in Table 3 were as follows: (1) Anxiety, beta = .52, $p < .001$, and hassles, beta = .33, $p < .001$, both contributed positively to perceived stress with a substantial combined effect,

**Table 16.2. Means, Standard Deviations, Reliabilities and Intercorrelations
of the ICSRLE, RS, STAI-T, PSS, HSCL and HPI**

Variable	1	2	3	4	5	6
1. ICSRLE	—	—	—	—	—	—
2. RS	.20	—	—	—	—	—
3. STAI-T	.58	.34	—	—	—	—
4. PSS	.63	.28	.71	—	—	—
5. HSCL	.68	.25	.75	.69	—	—
6. HPI	.45	.26	.40	.36	.58	—
M	95.63	77.05	42.55	26.16	100.21	17.43
SD	16.73	10.92	9.77	7.56	21.95	4.62
α	.89	.75	.91	.84	.95	.74

ICSRLE = Inventory of College Students' Recent Life Experiences; RS = Reactivity Scale; STAI-T = Trait Subscale of State-Trait Anxiety Inventory; PSS = Perceived Stress Scale; HSCL = Hopkins Symptom Checklist; HPI = Health Problems Inventory. All correlations are significant at the .005 level, two-tailed.

$R^2 = .58$, $p < .001$. Surprisingly, trait anxiety affected perceived stress even more strongly than hassles did. (2) Hassles and trait anxiety had a significant interactive effect on psychiatric symptomatology, beta $= 1.02$, $p < .005$, which along with the marginal main effects accounted for 67% of the variance, $p < .001$. This interaction is illustrated in Figure 16.2 which shows the lines of best fit for persons scoring at the 25th, 50th, and 75th percentiles on trait anxiety for the relationship between hassles and psychiatric symptomatology. The positive impact of hassles on symptomatology increases as trait anxiety grows; likewise, the pathogenic effect of trait anxiety increases as exposure to hassles rises. (3) Both hassles, beta $= 41$, $p < .001$, and reactivity, beta $= .17$, $p < .01$, had significant positive impact on minor ailments, together accounting for 23% of the variance, $p < .001$.

**Table 16.3. Final Regression Models for Perceived Stress Scale,
Hopkins Symptom Checklist, and Health Problem Inventory**

Criterion	Predictor	β	t	p	R^2	F	df	p
PSS	ICSRLE	.33	5.92	<.001				
	STAI-T	.52	9.36	<.001	.58	141.32	2,204	<.001
HSCL	ICSRLE (A)	−.12	0.73	NS				
	STAI-T (B)	−.11	0.49	NS				
	A × B	1.02	3.00	<.005	.67	137.62	3,206	<.001
HPI	ICSRLE	.41	6.52	<.001				
	RS	.17	2.77	<.01	.23	30.49	2,202	<.001

PSS = Perceived Stress Scale; HSCL = Hopkins Symptom Checklist; HPI = Health Problems Inventory; ICSRLE = Inventory of College Students' Recent Life Experiences; STAI-T = Trait Subscale of State-Trait Anxiety Inventory; RS = Reactivity Scale.

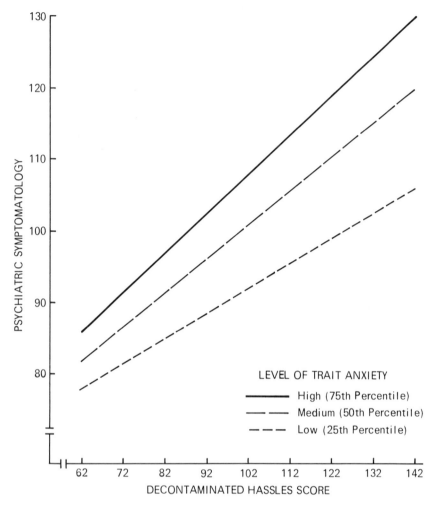

Figure 16.2. Psychiatric symptomatology as a function of trait-anxiety level and decontaminated hassles score.

Thus, trait anxiety seems to affect mainly the perception of stress and adverse mental health reactions to it. Two curious facts about the effect of trait anxiety on perceived stress are notable: (1) That it is additive to rather than interactive with the effect of hassles; and (2) that it exceeds the latter effect in magnitude. Perhaps, the relationship between the PSS and measures of *state* anxiety deserves investigation because it may be greater than one would expect, possibly approaching identity.

Reactivity, unlike trait anxiety, apparently affects people's vulnerability to physical illness, but not their subjective perception of being stressed, nor their psychiatric well-being. High reactivity thus seems to operate covertly and insidiously. Furthermore, reactivity's contributions to minor physical complaints are additive to rather than interactive with those of hassles, at least within the range of variation of daily stressors which our subjects reported experiencing over the previous month. Conceivably, reactivity might interact with stress, given a wider range of variation in the latter.

Also noteworthy are the positive correlations of hassles with reactivity, $r = .20$, $p < .005$, and trait anxiety, $r = .58$, $p < .001$. These findings suggest that cumulative stress over intervals as short as a month may increase trait anxiety and, to a lesser degree, reactivity. On the other hand, if level of exposure to hassles is quite stable on average, the impact of hassles may reflect a longer cumulation than superficially appears. The obvious alternative interpretation that highly anxious and reactive people seek out hassled life-styles seems theoretically unlikely in both cases and empirically so with respect to reactivity (Kohn, 1987; Strelau, 1983).

Overview

In earlier work, my associates and I found that psychometric measures of arousability generally and reactivity specifically did not relate consistently to theoretically relevant experimental indexes of strength of the nervous system (Kohn et al., 1987). Our explanation was that the psychometric tests measure arousability as a *general* property of the nervous system, whereas the experimental indexes, being modality-specific, necessarily tap *partial* properties of the nervous system (Nebylitsyn, 1972b; Strelau, 1983).

This raised the question of what can one usefully relate arousability in general and reactivity specifically to (Kohn, 1987, p. 247). In this chapter, we have accordingly discussed the relationships, theoretical and empirical, between reactivity on one hand and responses to pain and to stress on the other. We also related response to stress to another temperamental variable, namely trait anxiety. Briefly, the empirical work reported herein supports the following conclusions:

1. Reactivity is associated with high sensitivity and low tolerance for pain.
2. Hassles do affect perceived stress, psychiatric symptomatology, and minor physical illness independently of measurement contamination by these factors.
3. Reactivity apparently contributes to minor physical illness independently of hassles-based stress. It apparently does not, however, affect either psychiatric symptomatology or the subjective perception of being stressed.
4. Trait anxiety contributes to perceived stress independently and more strongly than does hassles-based stress.
5. Trait anxiety and hassles affect psychiatric symptomatology interactively such that the adverse impact of hassles increases with trait anxiety, and the pathogenic effect of trait anxiety increases with hassles. However, trait anxiety appears not to affect minor physical ailments, either alone or interactively.

ACKNOWLEDGEMENT. The author gratefully acknowledges the facilitation of his work by grants from the Social Sciences and Humanities Research Council of Canada's Small Grant Program, administered by the Office of Research Administration, York University.

References

Antoni, M. H. Temporal relationship between life events and two illness measures: A cross-lag panel analysis. *Journal of Human Stress*, 1985, *11*, 21–26.

Auerbach, A. Trait-state anxiety and adjustment to surgery. *Journal of Consulting and Clinical Psychology*, 1973, *40*, 264–271.

Auerbach, S .M., Kendall, P. C., Cutter, H. F., & Levitt, N. R. Anxiety, locus of control, type of preparatory information and adjustment to dental surgery. *Journal of Consulting and Clinical Psychology*, 1976, *44*, 809–818.

Auerbach, S. M., Martelli, M. F., & Mercuri, L. G. Anxiety, information,interpersonal impact and adjustment to a stressful health-care situation. *Journal of Personality and Social Psychology*, 1983, *44*, 1284–1296.

Barnes, G. E. Extraversion and pain. *British Journal of Social and Clinical Psychology*, 1975, *14*, 303–308.

Barnes, G. E. The Vando R-A Scale as a measure of stimulus reducing-augmenting. In J. Strelau, F. H. Farley, & A. Gale (Eds.), *The biological bases of personality and behaviour: Theories, measurement techniques, and development*. Vol. 1. Washington, DC.: Hemisphere, 1985.

Burks, N., & Martin, B. Everyday problems and life-change events: Ongoing versus acute sources of stress. *Journal of Human Stress*, 1983, *11*, 27–35.

Cohen, S., Kamarack, T., & Mermelstein, R. A global measure of perceived stress. *Journal of Health and Social Behavior*, 1983, *24*, 385–396.

Davis, C. A., Cowles, M. P., & Kohn, P. M. Behavioural and physiological aspects of the augmenting-reducing dimension. *Personality and Individual Differences*, 1984, *5*, 683–691.

DeLongis, A., Coyne, J. C., Dakof, G., Folkman, S., & Lazarus, R. S. Relationship of daily hassles, uplifts and major life events to health status. *Health Psychology*, 1982, *1*, 119–136.

Derogatis, L. R., Lipman, R. S., Rickels, K., Uhlenhuth, E. H., & Covi, L. The Hopkins Symptom Checklist (HSCL): A self-report symptom inventory. *Behavioral Science*, 1974, *19*, 1–15.

Dohrenwend, B. P., & Shrout, P. E. "Hassles" in the conceptualization and measurement of life-stress variables. *American Psychologist*, 1985, *40*, 780–785.

Dohrenwend, B. S., Dohrenwend, B. P., Dodson, M., & Shrout, P. E. Symptoms, hassles, social supports and life events: Problem of confounded measures. *Journal of Abnormal Psychology*, 1984, *93*, 222–230.

Dubreuil, D. L., & Kohn, P. M. Reactivity and response to pain. *Personality and Individual Differences*, 1986, *6*, 907–909.

Eckenrode, J. Impact of chronic and acute stressors on daily reports of mood. *Journal of Personality and Social Psychology*, 1984, *46*, 907–918.

Eysenck, H. J., & Eysenck, M. W. *Personality and individual differences: A natural science approach*. New York: Plenum, 1985.

Eysenck, H. J., & Eysenck, S. B. G. *Manual of the Eysenck Personality Inventory*. San Diego CA: Educational and Industrial Testing Service, 1968.

Forgione, A., & Barber, T. X. A strain gauge pain stimulator. *Psychophysiology*, 1971, *8*, 102–106.

Green, B. L. On the confounding of "hassles" stress and outcome. *American Psychologist*, 1986, *41*, 714–715.

Holmes, T., & Rahe, R. The Social Readjustment Rating Scale. *Journal of Psychosomatic Research 11*, 213–218.

Ippolitov, F. V. Interanalyzer differences in the sensitivity-strength parameter for vision, hearing and cutaneous modalities. In V. D. Nebylitsyn & J. A. Gray (Eds.), *Biological bases of individual behavior*. New York: Academic Press, 1972.

Johnson, D. T. Effects of interview stress on measures of state and trait anxiety. *Journal of Abnormal Psychology*, 1968, *73*, 245–251.

Kanner, A. D., Coyne, J. C., Schaefer, C., & Lazarus, R. S. Comparison of two modes of stress measurement: Daily hassles and uplifts versus major life events. *Journal of Behavioral Medicine*, 1981, *4*, 1–39.

Keuss, P. J. G., & Orlebeke, J. F. Transmarginal inhibition in a reaction time task as a function of extraversion and neuroticism. *Acta Psychologica*, 1977, *41*, 139–150.

Kohn, P. M. Sensation seeking, augmenting-reducing, and strength of the nervous system. In J. T. Spence & C. Izard (Eds.), *Motivation, emotion, and personality: Proceedings of the XXIII International Congress of Psychology*. Amsterdam: North Holland-Elsevier, 1985.

Kohn, P. M. Issues in the measurement of arousability. In J. Strelau & H. J. Eysenck (Eds.), *Personality dimensions and arousal*. New York: Plenum, 1987.

Kohn, P. M., Cowles, M. P., & Dzinas, K. Arousability, need for approval, and situational context as factors in pain tolerance. *Journal of Research in Personality*, 1989, *23*, 214–224.

Kohn, P. M., Cowles, M. P., & Lafreniere, K. Relationships between psychometric and experimental measures of arousability. *Personality and Individual Differences*, 1987, *8*, 225–231.

Kohn, P. M., Hunt, R. W., Cowles, M. P., & Davis, C. A. Factor structure and content validity of the Vando Reducer-Augmenter Scale. *Personality and Individual Differences*, 1986, *7*, 57–64.

Kohn, P. M., Lafreniere, K., & Gurevich, M. The Inventory of College Students' Recent Life Experiences: A decontaminated hassles scale for a special population. *Journal of Behavioral Medicine*, 1990, *13*, 619–630.

Lambert, W. E., Libman, E., & Poser, E. G. The effect of increased salience of a membership group on pain tolerance. *Journal of Personality*, 1960, *28*, 350–357.

Mahoney, J., Shumate, M., & Worthington, E. L., Jr. Is the Vando Scale a valid measure of perceptual reactance? *Perceptual and Motor Skills*, 1980, *51*, 1035–1038.

Marlowe, D., & Crowne, D. P. Social desirability and response to perceived situational demands. *Journal of Consulting Psychology*, 1961, *25*, 109–115.

Marziali, E. A., & Pilkonis, P. A. The measurement of subjective response to stressful life events. *Journal of Human Stress*, 1986, *12*, 5–12.

McGrath, R. E., & Burkhart, B. R. Measuring life stress: A comparison of the predictive validity of different scoring systems for the Social Readjustment Rating Scale. *Journal of Clinical Psychology*, 1983, *39*, 573–581.

Monroe, S. M. Major and minor life events as predictors of psychological distress: Further issues and findings. *Journal of Behavioral Medicine*, 1983, *6*, 189–205.

Murphy, G., & Murphy, L. B. *Experimental social psychology*. New York: Harper & Row, 1931.

Nebylitsyn, V. D. *Fundamental properties of the human nervous system*. New York: Plenum, 1972a.

Nebylitsyn, V. D. The problem of general and partial properties of the nervous system. In V. D. Nebylitsyn & J. A. Gray (Eds.), *Biological bases of individual behavior*. New York: Academic Press, 1972b.

Otto, M. W., & Dougher, M. J. Sex differences and personality factors in responsivity to pain. *Perceptual and Motor Skills*, 1985, *61*, 383–390.

Petrie, A. *Individuality in pain and suffering*. Chicago: University of Chicago Press, 1967.

Reason, J. T. Individual differences in auditory reaction time and loudness estimation. *Perceptual and Motor Skills*, 1968, *236*, 1089–1090.

Sales, S. M., & Throop, W. F. Relationship between kinesthetic aftereffect and "strength of the nervous system." *Psychophysiology*, 1972, *9*, 492–497.

Spielberger, C. D., Gorsuch, R. L., & Lushene, R. E. *STAI Manual for the State-Trait Anxiety Inventory*. Palo Alto CA: Consulting Psychologists' Press, 1970.

Strelau, J. A diagnosis of temperament by nonexperimental techniques. *Polish Psychological Bulletin*, 1972a, *3*, 97–105.

Strelau, J. The general and partial nervous-system types—data and theory. In V. D. Nebylitsyn & J. A. Gray (Eds.), *Biological bases of individual behavior*. New York: Academic Press, 1972b.

Strelau, J. *Temperament—personality—activity*. London: Academic Press, 1983.

Taylor, S. *Health psychology*. New York: Random House, 1986.

Vando, A. *A personality dimension related to pain tolerance*. Dissertation Abstracts International, 1970, 31, 2292B-2293B. (University Microfilms No. 70–18,865)

Vando, A. The development of the R-A Scale: A paper-and-pencil measure of pain tolerance. *Personality and Social Psychology Bulletin*, 1974, *1*, 28–29.

Weinberger, M., Hiner, S. L., & Tierney, W. M. In support of hassles as a measure of stress in predicting health outcomes. *Journal of Behavioral Medicine*, 1987, *10*, 19–31.

17

Correlations between Psychometric Measures and Psychophysiological as Well as Experimental Variables in Studies on Extraversion and Neuroticism

Manfred Amelang and Ulrike Ullwer

Theoretical Outline, Methodological Criticisms, and Some Unresolved Questions

Extraversion/Introversion (E/I) and Neuroticism (N) are the two "great" dimensions for the description of individual differences in temperament. Corresponding factors can be found—with varying emphases—in the theoretical systems by Guilford, Cattell, and Eysenck. They also hold a central position in the discussion on the Norman (1963) five-factor-model (Costa & McCrae, 1988; McCrae & Costa, 1987). Several monographs dealing with Extraversion/Introversion and Neuroticism have been published (e.g., Eysenck, 1971, a,b; 1973; Eysenck & Eysenck, 1985; Morris, 1979) and scarcely a textbook fails to devote special sections to it. The reasons for this are the relative invariance in the extraction of these dimensions in factor analyses on the one hand and the fairly high validity of E/I and N test scores in predicting peer ratings for both dimensions on the other hand (e.g., Amelang & Borkenau, 1982; Costa & McCrae, 1988).

Compared to most other proposed dimensions, there are specific theories available for E/I and N. These are mainly connected to the name of H.J. Eysenck (1967) who, unlike most workers in the field of personality and individual differences, rises above the

---

Manfred Amelang and **Ulrike Ullwer** • Department of Psychology, University of Heidelberg, D-6900 Heidelberg, Federal Republic of Germany.

level of the purely descriptive and traces the E/I as well as the N differences back to anatomic structures and psychophysiological processes. Statements concerning the E/I dimensions have become more differentiated and far-reaching than those on N (cf. Brocke & Battmann, 1985). The common elements in the approaches to explain both dimensions are activation processes which, according to their respective intensity, are regarded as the cause for interindividual variance in E/I and N scores.

In particular, Eysenck (1967) relates interindividual differences on the neuroticism continuum to the activity of the limbic system, assuming a lower excitation threshold for neurotic persons and a higher excitation threshold for emotionally stable persons. Under conditions otherwise identical, the limbic system, according to the theory, is already activated in emotionally unstable persons at a lower intensity of external stimuli. Correspondingly, it leads to "autonomous limbic activation" with all the resultant reactions, such as taking a considerably longer time to return to a normal state after stressful experiences, whereas higher degrees of stimulation are necessary to bring this about among the emotionally more stable.

As regards to the extraversion/introversion dimension, Eysenck bases his assumptions on a genetically determined relationship between nervous excitatory and inhibitory processes. According to the theory, extraverts lie near the inhibition pole on the excitation-inhibition continuum, whereas introverts are found nearer the excitation pole. The excitation threshold of the ascending reticular activating system (ARAS) is seen as the neurophysiological correlate of the "excitation-inhibition balance," that is, with quicker responsiveness in the case of introverted persons and a slower response rate in the case of extraverted persons. Thus, under conditions which are otherwise identical, more intensive cortical arousal reactions take place for the introverted than the extraverted.

The relationship between reticular activation and cortical arousal is only monotonic and positive up to the point where "transmarginal inhibition" in the sense of a protective mechanism starts, thus counteracting further activation. Beyond this point, paradoxically, the level of arousal is higher for persons who are habitually less excitable, or have "stronger nerves": the extraverted.

Thus the Yerkes-Dodson Law, which specifies an inverse U-function between level of activation and performance holds differentially for the extreme groups of introverts and extraverts; the points of optimal arousal are different: extraverts should reach their level of optimal arousal—and at the same time their optimal hedonic tone—under stronger stimulation than introverts (cf. Eysenck, 1967, p. 109).

Apart from these stable typological differences in arousal between extraverted and introverted persons, Eysenck (1981) also assumes activating situational factors which are related to the tasks performed. In their systematic discussion and partial reconstruction of Eysenck's notion, Brocke and Battmann (1985) call this part "theory of situational excitation." Performance and behavior therefore result from the interaction between the personality-specific amount of arousal, the situational arousal, and the optimal hedonic tone. By this, a few findings incompatible with the theory can be "explained" *post hoc*, but predictions become much more difficult (Brocke & Liepmann, 1985, report an experiment relevant to this point, but the results were only partly as expected).

The theory described, especially the one on E/I, led to the deduction of many hypotheses which were tested in a large number of empirical and experimental studies.

The domain of investigated phenomena covered by the theory ranges from physiological processes, perception, and verbal and motor learning to social and political attitudes, humor, sexual behavior, and health/illness as well as crime. Additionally, psychiatric symptoms and the effects of psychopharmacological substances have been dealt with. The numerous publications by Eysenck, especially the books of 1971a, 1971b, 1973, and 1976, as well as the ones by Eysenck & Eysenck (1985), Brody (1972, 1988), Morris (1979) and Amelang & Bartussek (1989) inform in detail about theories and hypotheses, investigative procedures, and results.

The methodological approach in all the studies reported there and elsewhere is almost always the same (and here our *criticism* starts). From the theory, an empirically/experimentally testable statement for a certain variable is deduced (for instance, higher pain tolerance should be observable in extraverts due to their low arousal-inhibition quotient). A sample of subjects is then obtained, out of which extreme groups of extraverts and introverts are drawn, according to their scores in the MPI-E scale. Finally, the subjects are compared with regard to their scores in the dependent variable (e.g., tolerance to pain).

Particularly noticeable is the fact that, with the exception of very few studies (see below literature overview), it was only rarely attempted to simultaneously incorporate *several* dependent variables within a single study using one and the same sample of subjects.

Correlations between the dependent variables themselves could, however, only be computed in this way. If, as the numerous individual studies indicate, correlations can be found between Extraversion and Neuroticism on the one hand and the experimental variables on the other, the dependent variables themselves could also be intercorrelated (see Figure 17.1, model A)—unless the variance components explained by the questionnaires are nonoverlapping (as illustrated in Figure 17.1, model B).

The findings reported in the literature frequently show significant but numerically low correlations between questionnaire and experimental variables. Although this does not exclude conditions as schematically illustrated in Figure 17.1(B), a situation following principle Figure 17.1(A) would have to be expected on the basis of the theory.

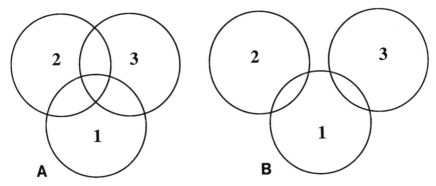

Figure 17.1. Two models of the intercorrelations and mutual overlap between three groups of variables. 1 = questionnaire; 2 = experimental/psychophysiological variable (e.g., pain tolerance); 3 = experimental/psychophysiological variable (e.g., flicker fusion).

Furthermore, only a simultaneous inclusion of several experimental variables allows us to check the question which of the measured components are especially "close" to the postulated arousal-inhibition balance and which are related to (questionnaire) extraversion only in a more indirect way. This question cannot be answered conclusively by comparing results across different studies, considering the differences in samples, their relative extremity, the experimental procedures, and so on.

Finally, although Eysenck and Eysenck (1969, 141–149) themselves speak of the "dual nature" of the (questionnaire) E/I dimension and distinguish the two primary factors "Impulsiveness" and "Sociability," all further analyses are concerned almost exclusively with E/I considered as a singular dimension. With regard to this, it should be investigated in detail to what extent the primary factors of extraversion differ from each other in their explanatory value. It seems an obvious assumption that "Impulsiveness" is more closely related to the excitation-inhibition balance than "Sociability," inasmuch as "Impulsiveness" refers to the aspects of drive and intensity of behavior (Levy & Lang, 1966), whereas "Sociability" refers only to the content of behavior. Evidence for this statement in the sense of construct validity can, for instance, be found in the observation by Giambra, Quilter, and Phillips (1988), that "Impulsiveness" correlates (negatively) with age but "Sociability" does not.

Therefore, our *hypothesis* for the experimental and psycho-physiological variables was that their correlation with extraversion is dependent upon the correlation with the Impulsiveness rather than the Sociability subfactor of extraversion.

These, then, are the problems, open questions, and hypotheses which occasioned the various experiments at the Heidelberg Institute. First of all, the work done was partly concerned with the factor structure of the E/I and N dimensions, and partly with the external validity of various instruments for measuring both dimensions, among them being the methods developed by Eysenck himself. Further large-scale studies dealt with the postulated excitation-inhibition balance, i.e., psychophysiological and experimental variables. In the following, we will report our findings in both of these areas.

Psychometric Studies: Pro-Eysenck Findings

The "great" factor-analytic personality systems in the literature refer, at least at a secondary or a tertiary level, to the temperamental dimensions of Extraversion/ Introversion and Neuroticism. Despite this agreement in the use of linguistic labels, marked discrepancies exist with regard to the content of the factors. This divergence is partially due to the diversity of the research approaches, partly to the relative flexibility of the theoretical framework, or to the particular technique of factorization and rotation. All of these aspects have contributed to these differences in interpretation of the "true" structure of the extraversion factor, in particular those between Guilford (1975) and Eysenck (1977). A comparative study on the empirical clarification of this unresolved controversy was first carried out in the German language area (see Amelang & Borkenau, 1982). Here, a random sample of persons (N = 424) of both sexes aged between 18 and 30 completed a battery of personality questionnaires, which included, among other things, scales of the 16 Cattell Personality Factors, scales from the Guilford-Factors, and the

Extraversion and Neuroticism scales of the Eysenck Personality Inventory, each of which was comprised of 24 questions.

For 346 subjects within this sample, it was possible to collect ratings from three peers, relatives and/or acquaintances on 23 trait polarities. Two examples for the format are given below:

Sociability

sociable, lively	7	6	5	4	3	2	1	unsociable
casual, informal								restrained
outgoing								still

Anxiety

| anxious, insecure | 7 | 6 | 5 | 4 | 3 | 2 | 1 | self-confident |
| worried | | | | | | | | unconcerned |

These ratings were used as criteria for the questionnaire-scores. The results are presented in Figure 17.2.

Guilford (1975) suggested the structure in the upper half of Figure 17.2 as a hierarchical model of the scales he had developed earlier. In particular, he repeatedly emphasized the affinity of the primary factors "Restraint" and "Thoughtfulness," which, according to him, together constitute the factor "Introversion/Extraversion." In opposition to this, Eysenck (1977) expects "Restraint" to coincide with "Sociability," which is the reason, in the development of the Extraversion scale of EPI, he based his scale construction on a common sample of "Restraint" *and* "Sociability" items.

As it is to be seen, our results support Eysenck's approach quite decisively and suggest that the Guilford model has to be reformulated in the manner illustrated. At the same time, the results show that the E- and N scales of the EPI, which Eysenck assigns to a secondary level, measure to a large extent the same dimensions as the factors of a higher order as defined in the Guilford model. The correlations of the EPI scales with the Guilford factors lie in the range of the EPI reliabilities, thus being even higher than in the study by Campbell and Reynolds (1984) where EPI-E correlated .52 with Guilford's GZTS-Introversion-Extraversion, and EPI-N correlated .72 with Emotional Health.

The same can be said of the correlations between the EPI scales and the 16 Cattell Personality Factors. A secondary analysis of the scales in the item-assignment by Schneewind (1977) led to the extraction of four factors; the two containing most of the variance by far can be seen in Figure 17.3

With the two dimensions, which can be interpreted as extraversion/introversion and anxiety or neuroticism, the similarly named EPI scales again correlate at the level of their reliability. In other words, the information which can be aggregated across the primary factors of the 16 PF can also be gathered in a similar way using the Extraversion and Neuroticism scales of the EPI, but with far fewer items.

Such results confirm Eysenck's general conception and argue in favor of the quality of the instruments developed by him. This applies to the external validity as well. The individual scores on the EPI-E scale (Form A) correlated with the peer ratings in the assigned scales for "Sociability" $r_{tc} = .50$, "Desire for Contact" $r_{tc} = .44$ and "Friendliness" $r_{tc} = .42$, EPI-N with "Depressiveness" $r_{tc} = .48$, "Emotional Instability" $r_{tc} =$

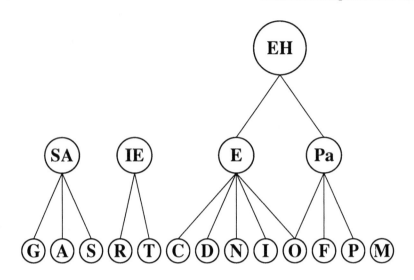

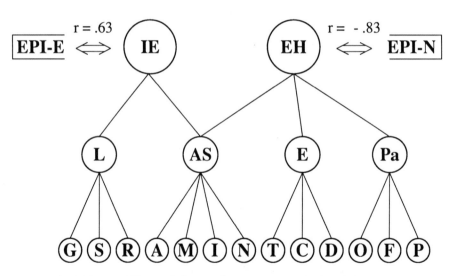

Figure 17.2. Guilford's (1975) model of personality (upper part) and reformulation of model, as suggested by our results (Amelang & Borkenau, 1982). EH = Emotional Health; SA = Social Activity; IE = Introversion-Extraversion; E = Emotional Stability; Pa = Paranoid Disposition; G = General Activity; A = Ascendance; S = Sociability; R = Restraint; T = Thoughtfulness; C = Cycloid Disposition; D = Depression; N = Lack of Nervous Tenseness; I = Inferiority Feelings; O = Objectivity; F = Friendliness; P = Personal Relations; M = Masculinity.

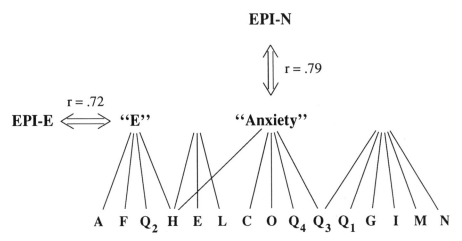

Figure 17.3. Results of 16 PF-Cattell secondary factorization (N = 344; from Amelang, 1987). E = Dominance; A = Affectothymia; F = Surgency; Q2 = Self-Sufficiency; H = Parmia; L = Protension; C = Ego Strength; O = Guilt Proneness; Q4 = Ergic Tension; Q3 = Self-Sentiment; Q1 = Radicalism; G = Superego Strength; I = Premsia; M = Autia; N = Shrewdness.

.45 and "Anxiety" r_{tc} = .44, i.e., an average of about r_{tc} = .45. The coefficients rise to r_{tc} = .54 if the trait polarities are grouped together through factorial analysis into more complex dimensions for "Extraversion" and "Neuroticism."

No other personality test was more successful in the explanation of variance of these two criterion dimensions than the EPI scales E and N. Moreover, it rarely occurred that a specific subscale from one of the test batteries correlated *to a higher extent* with a specific peer rating score than one of the scales of the EPI. This is additional evidence for the value of higher-level information. It shows the possibility of successfully forecasting consistent temperamental differences in several areas at one and the same time with a few, broadly generalized dimensions.

However, the internal structure of the EPI scales does not seem to correspond with the tables in which Eysenck & Eysenck (1985, 14–15) list various primary factors of E and N. More specifically, the factorization of the E/I and N items on our data set, using very difficult techniques, constantly led to only *one* global neuroticism factor and two moderately intercorrelated extraversion factors, which could be labeled "Impulsiveness" and "Sociability." We will return to this point later.

Psychophysiological and Experimental Variables: A Selective Literature Overview

Multivariate Studies

Considering the fact that Stelmack (1981) gives an excellent overview on the psychophysiology of Extraversion and Neuroticism, it does not seem necessary to go into that in detail once again. Rather, the following remarks may be sufficient:

1. Due to the close interconnection between limbic system and reticular formation, an absolute independence of limbic activation and reticular arousal cannot be expected. In this regard, Eysenck makes the assumption that reticular arousal does not necessarily influence limbic activation but that, conversely, limbic activation inevitably causes an increase in reticular as well as in cortical arousal. This supposed mechanism would explain the negative correlation between E and N in subjects with higher N scores (e.g., Eysenck, 1959a). Especially for this reason, it is virtually incomprehensible that Eysenck and Eysenck (1969), in their construction of the EPI, tried to establish the orthogonality of the E/I and N dimensions. Assuming the correctness of the theory, this inevitably leads to a distortion of the "actually true" conditions in the individual measurement of E and N.

2. Studies at the Freiburg Institute, which are unprecedented with regard to the sample of persons, parameters, and situations, showed, moreover, that the even more basic assumption of relatively consistent dimension or a coherent pattern of autonomous instability is untenable. Therefore, Fahrenberg (1987) suggests the development of multicomponent models of activation and an appropriate strategy for measuring reaction patterns and their possible hierarchical organization.

An extensive discussion of the multitude and variety of the experimental and psychophysiological variables would not lead to any definite conclusions, as the general experimental approach already outlined (i.e., usually having only one dependent variable) is obviously insufficient for answering the questions which are of importance here, viz., the problems of:

- The intercorrelations between the different psychophysiological/experimental variables.
- The relative magnitudes of the correlations between (questionnaire) measures for Extraversion and Neuroticism on the one hand and psychophysiological and experimental variables on the other.
- The presumably different influence of the primary factors "Sociability" and "Impulsiveness."

What can sensibly be done here is to give a description of those studies in which more than only one dependent or experimental variable was included in one and the same group of subjects. Among the 64 studies assembled by Eysenck (1971b), only two meet this requirement, those by Holmes (1967) and by Lynn (1960).

Holmes (1967) measured in 49 female students (1) the speed of pupillary reaction to different levels of illumination as a criterion for concentration of acetylcholine in the cholinergic synapses; and (2) the learning rate in a verbal conditioning task, giving special attention to the perception of reinforcement contingencies ("awareness") by the subjects.

Only the pupillary constriction, and not the pupillary dilation, showed significant correlations ($r = .33, .44,$ and $.52$ for the intervals 1, 2, and 3 seconds after presentation of the light stimuli) with the result of the learning task; above that, it is reported that the extreme group of "fast constrictors" was more introverted (MPI) than the "slow constrictors." Thus, the conclusion seems to indicate that learning rate in conditioning, too, is related to Extraversion, although further details are not given. For pupillary dilation, there was also a correlation in that the "fast dilators" were more extraverted than the "slow dilators," but the author does not comment on this apparent anomaly vis-à-vis the results for pupillary constriction.

Lynn (1960) investigated the amount of reminiscence writing down the alphabet backwards and the length of the figural aftereffect in 40 male students. Correlations with extraversion were $r = .42$ for the former and $r = .43$ for the latter variable. The correlation between reminiscence effect and aftereffect was $r = .34$.

A third experiment was done by Eysenck (1960), but he himself, members of his team, or other authors quote it only rarely and superficially if at all. Sometimes the quotations are even incorrect. It is notable that in three experiments related to one another, three different authors realized the following program for one and the same sample of 100 students:

1. Willet (1960) conducted conditioning experiments in four different paradigms (eyelid, salivary, spatial, verbal). The correlations of each of these experiments with Extraversion scales were, on the whole, insignificant.

2. Holland (1960) administered six perception tests which were all supposed to measure reactive inhibition. There were no significant correlations of the measures either with one another or with the questionnaires.

3. Eysenck (1960) used the most valid and algebraically independent variables from the Willett and Holland results, combining them in a factor analysis, and obtained, apart from an "artifact" dimension and one that was "not interpretable," the two factors Extraversion and Neuroticism on which the respective questionnaire measures had the highest loadings by far. On the E dimension, the spiral "distance" score and the spiral "slope" score had loadings only a little over .20, the figural aftereffect with two measures only around .10, but—contrary to expectations!—on the introversion pole these two measures had loadings about .50, as well as spatial conditioning and the spiral "aftereffect." Eyelid and verbal conditioning showed only very low loadings which, in addition, were partly higher in numbers on the N factor.

Altogether, these results were disappointing. To our knowledge, such complex designs were not implemented anymore. When in the recent past multivariate approaches have been implemented, this has simply amounted to using different questionnaire (i.e., "predictor") measures (e.g., Furnham, 1984). Other authors have based their studies on more than one experimental variable, but those were partly taken from one and the same task (e.g., Giambra et al., 1988).

In an experiment by O'Gorman and Lloyd (1987), the correlation between narrow impulsiveness and alpha activity turned out according to the hypotheses, but none of the other personality variables correlated with this psychophysiological variable. Here, two dependent variables and conditions were available, but the intercorrelations between them were not computed, or at least not reported.

Something similar applies to the 30 variables for pulse rate and galvanic skin response during different stages of sleep in the experiment by Thompson and Mueller (1984). These authors found only weak indications for a higher level of arousal in extraverts as compared to introverts. However, such a result can be taken as an objection against the theory only insofar as the reliability of the scores and their intercorrelations has been established. Both aspects could have been investigated even with the fairly small sample of 18 Ss, but this was not done.

The study by Matthews (1987) is part of the growing number of studies aimed at measuring arousal by using, among other things, self-reports. Matthews (1987) had 40 male college students work through the 16 PF. The scores for the scale "Exvia" stood for Extraversion and those in the scales 16 PF-F and H for primary factors of Extraversion. Two self-report measures for arousal (among them the Thayer, 1978, Dimension B) as well as 16 PF-Exvia and F correlated in the direction expected (arousal variables positive, personality scales negative) with a score for "physiological arousal." This variable had been formed by combining a heart rate and skin conductance level measure. Heart rate and skin conductance did, however, not correlate significantly either with each other or with a third physiological arousal score, namely oral temperature. By and large, the results confirm the expectations but, in addition, the correlations of the 16 PF factor Anxiety with the physiological variables would be of interest. Details regarding this are missing.

De Pascalis and Montirosso (1988) did find a significant correlation of $r = .45$ between Neuroticism and the N2 peak latency in event-related potentials, but this was only the case for one of two experimentally realized conditions. Again, details concerning the consistency of N2 peak latency, as well as the intercorrelations between those variables are missing. All these correlations could have been computed (on the problems of any EEG research on E/I, cf. Bartussek, 1984).

Finally, there are studies using more than one experimental variable in which results that confirm the hypotheses have been obtained, such as that by Geen (1984), who was able to show that extraverts preferred a higher noise level when reading pair associates than did introverts: the two variables were, however, taken from different experiments.

This short overview justifies the following statements: Those studies including more than one psychophysiological or experimental variable (1) usually do not report intercorrelations between these variables, or (2) in cases where these data are reported, intercorrelations are numerically low and statistically insignificant. In cases where expected correlations with questionnaire data did not turn out (e.g., Roger & Jamieson, 1988), it cannot be determined whether insufficient reliability is responsible for this. When correlations of questionnaire data were scarce in some psychophysiological variables and altogether lacking in other variables that were supposedly similar or equally representative, this may be due to the relative orthogonality between the dependent variables and/or the inflation of random significances.

The "Dual Nature of Extraversion": Rediscovered

Since the 1960s Eysenck and Eysenck (1969, pp. 141–149) themselves have spoken of the "dual nature" of the (questionnaire) E/I-dimension in the sense of an internal differentiation according to "Impulsiveness" and "Sociability." Nevertheless, all analyses refer almost exclusively to the global dimension, even though it is to be expected that the excitation-inhibition balance, or even the cortical arousal, would have been found to be related more closely to Impulsiveness (as the energetic component of Extraversion) than to Sociability.

Indeed, in various studies the E-scale discriminated between groups of "normal" and delinquent persons, and this effect was based only on those items which had high loadings on the "Impulsiveness" component (e.g., Eysenck & Eysenck, 1971), whereas the Sociability items discriminated in a direction contrary to expectations, or not at all. It is remarkable that for a long time such analyses were missing for variables like pain tolerance, reactive salivation, and reminiscence effect, which are much more direct indicators for the excitation-inhibition balance, and for which the findings reported in the literature are less contradictory than for those concerning the relationship between Extraversion and deviant behavior (e.g., Barnes, 1975; Deary, Ramsay, Wilson, & Riad, 1988).

It is only more recently that the differentiation between Impulsiveness and Sociability has been dealt with in several experimental studies. Revelle, Humphreys, Simon, and Gilliland (1980) administered morning and evening doses of caffeine and found consistent results for Impulsiveness but not for Sociability (day 1). From this, they concluded "that impulsivity and not sociability is related to the diurnal rhythm of arousal" (p. 22).

Also, in a psychopharmacological experiment, Smith, Rypma and Wilson (1981) observed, from the electrodermal orienting response, a higher tonic level and stronger phasic responses in introverts under placebo, whereas extraverts showed stronger phasic reactions and a higher tonic level under the influence of caffeine. The findings of extraversion were by and large in agreement with the hypotheses and a confirmation of Eysenck's theory. Those results concerning the differentiation along the impulsiveness dimension, were very similar to those of the global extraversion dimension, whereas the sociability effects were insignificant.

Rocklin and Revelle (1981) not only stressed the importance of a differentiation between Impulsiveness and Sociability but also stated: "While impulsivity has been shown to have relationships relevant to the arousal theory of extraversion, sociability has not" (p. 282).

The results of experiments carried out at the Heidelberg Institute are in agreement with this conclusion (Amelang & Breit, 1983). In a tapping task, in which a Morse button had to be pressed as fast as possible for two minutes, only those extreme groups which were formed on the basis of an (EPI-E) Impulsiveness scale differed from each other in the sense of the hypothesis. Those which were assembled according to the Sociability scale did not so differ.

In an investigation by Campbell (1983), individuals studying in locations that provided greater external stimulation had significantly higher extraversion and impulsivity, but not sociability scores, than individuals studying elsewhere in the library. Impulsivity was more strongly associated than sociability with preferred noise levels, frequency of study breaks, and importance and preferred levels of socializing opportunities.

Other studies have dealt with the influence of complexity, color and novelty in visual stimuli on the arousal level, thus establishing a connection between personality and the experience of art. According to early observations by Eysenck, Granger, and Brengelmann (1957), extraverts seem to prefer more complex visual patterns than introverts and colorful modern paintings to less colorful classical paintings. In the study by Zuber & Ekehammar (1988) there were only correlations on the part of Impulsivity but not Sociability for the preference of color and selective attention to the salient feature (form complexity) of present stimuli. Neuroticism showed no relationship to perception.

In the already-mentioned study by Matthews (1987), only 16 PF-F, as a factor related to Impulsivity, but not 16 PF-H as an equivalent to Sociability, interacted with the time of day. The author, however, concedes that there is no obvious way in which to account for this result.

As Eysenck and Eysenck (1974), while constructing the EPQ, had largely replaced the impulsiveness items within the E dimension by those for sociability (Rocklin & Revelle, 1981), therefore EPI-Sociability has a higher correlation with EPQ-E than EPI-Impulsivity (Campbell & Heller, 1987), the hypothesis that impulsivity is of primary importance for the arousal theory of extraversion should also have implications for those studies in which EPI- and EPQ-Extraversion were simultaneously used for the selection of extreme groups. In fact, in the experiments by Gilliland (1977) it was found that EPI-E but not EPQ-E related to verbal ability under stress induced by caffeine.

Similar to this, O'Gorman and Lloyd (1987) report that subjects with high scores on narrow impulsiveness were found to show less alpha activity than subjects with low scores, whereas no significant relationships with alpha activity emerged for the other personality scales. They concluded "that impulsiveness rather than EPQ-E is the major correlate of differences in EEG-defined arousal" (p. 169).

With respect to this, the results of some studies indicate that the arousal theory of extraversion has mainly to do with impulsivity as one primary factor of Extraversion. In other words, the differences between extraverts and introverts observed in various experimental and psychophysiological tasks seem to find their main explanation in the Impulsivity dimension.

Neuroticism

Gray (1973) came to the conclusion that extraverts do not show, as Eysenck assumes, a generally lower rate of conditioning than introverts. Instead, they appear to be insensitive to punishment or its threat (which is normally used as UCS in the form of the unpleasant air puff or electrical shock in classical eyelid or PGR conditioning) and oriented to reward or any kind of positive reinforcement, whereas an increase in neuroticism goes along with a rise in susceptibility to punishment. According to Gray, this relationship is moderated by the score on the respective other scale in that the highest increase in susceptibility to punishment is to be expected from the combination extravert/stable to introvert/neurotic, and the highest increase in susceptibility to reward from the combination introvert/stable to extravert/neurotic. Gray (1973) interprets the dimension between the poles introvert/stable and extravert/neurotic, which he obtains by a 45° rotation of the E/I and N factors, as "Impulsivity." Therefore, special Impulsiveness scales in appropriately designed studies would have to have a higher explanatory value than E/I and N alone.

The Gray theory (see also Gray, 1981, 1987) has been repeatedly investigated. Early studies with mostly positive results were, among other things, carried out by Gray and Nicholson (1974), Seunath (1975), Nagpal and Gupta (1979), McCord and Wakefield (1981) as well as Bartussek, Collett, and Naumann (1984). In these studies, primary focus was on the dimension of E/I. In Gray's theory, extraversion-introversion is determined by the *relative* sensitivities of the behavioral inhibition system and the behavioral activation system whilst N is determined by the *absolute* sensitivities of these systems. The scope of the studies reported above did not allow us adequately to evaluate the relationship of N to the effects of different types of reinforcement. Such work is still required and the prediction is, as Boddy, Carver, and Rowley (1986, p. 88) state, "that subjects high on neuroticism should display greater sensitivity to both positive and negative reinforcement, the relative sensitivities being determined by the degree of extraversion/introversion."

Additionally, the aforementioned authors, in whose experiments with two tasks extraverts performed better under positive than negative reinforcement, while introverts performed better under negative than positive reinforcement, point out that even those results which seem to be in accordance with Gray's theory cannot be concisely interpreted:

> The covert nature of cognitive operations carried out in the experimental tasks precludes unequivocal attribution of superior task performance in negatively reinforced introverts to the accentuated excitation of the Behavioral Inhibition System. (Boddy *et al.*, 1986, p. 81)

Implications for the subjective internal processes can also be found in the studies by Patterson, Kosson, and Newman (1987; cf. also Pearce-McCall & Newman, 1986, Nichols & Newman, 1986). In two experiments, longer pausing following punishment predicted better learning from punishment for both introverts and extraverts.

> These results suggested that in the presence of *silent cues for rewards* (emphasized by the authors) extraverts' characteristic reaction to punishment interferes with processing punished errors and may contribute to their most general propensity for impulsive, nonreflective action. (Patterson *et. al.*, 1987, p. 365)

As could be shown hereby, a clear explanation in the sense of Gray's theory is dependent on several additional conditions. Eysenck (1987), however, questions the appropriateness of the theory itself. His view is that "practically all the large-scale factor analytic studies in the literature have found factors corresponding to E and N (. . .) but none have found two major factors corresponding to anxiety and impulsivity, when large enough samples of trait and items were used" (p. 491). The second criticism is that measures of anxiety regularly fail to locate at an angle of 45° from E to N.

These objections are weighty, although they do not reduce the heuristic value of Gray's ideas, without which numerous original designs would not have been realized. Over and above that, by embedding his system in the coordinates of N and E, Gray (1987) once again stressed the necessity of a *simultaneous* examination of the two dimensions.

Even though the structural orthogonality of E and N is central in Eysenck's analyses, some networks have to be taken into consideration under a functional aspect. According to his conception, reticular arousal does not necessarily influence limbic activation but limbic activation necessarily causes an increase in reticular as well as cortical arousal. As already mentioned under (1), Eysenck connects E/I with the arousal threshold of the reticular system and N with the one of the limbic system. Interindividual differences in psychophysiological or behavioral criteria can, according to these assumptions, only then be reduced to the arousal level of the reticular formation, when the limbic system fires at a low rate only, in the ideal case: when it is not aroused at all. This is more likely the fewer the emotionally affecting stimuli that are present.

In all other cases, an observed cortical arousal has to be explained by the overlapping and presumably interacting effects of reticular and limbic system. If we assume, for the sake of simplicity, an additive model for a given stimulus functioning as "stressor," states of cortical arousal would have to be expected for the combination low E/high N, and states of low arousal for high E/low N (poles of highest and lowest anxiety, in the sense of Gray).

As the definition and empirical assessment of "stress" is extremely difficult, there are two options for the precise tests of both extraversion theories: one would be to implement situations that are definitely emotionally "neutral," and the other, which is also proposed by Gale (1973, 1980), would be to exclusively select subjects with low Neuroticism scores.

None of these two possible designs was taken into account throughout in the previous work reported above—a possible reason for the fact that in many cases correlations between E/I and physiological or experimental variables were only low or even insignificant.

For future work this mandates an investigation of the influence of E/I on psychophysiological and experimental variables under simultaneous control of N, that is, a test of the hypothesis that N functions to moderate the correlation between E/I on the one hand and experimental variable on the other, for these correlations would have to be higher for subjects scoring low on N than for those scoring high on N. Testing this moderator hypothesis was one of the central objectives of the experiments to be discussed below.

Report of a (Nearly) Comprehensive Study

The review of the literature shows that studies in which the following aspects are being considered *simultaneously* are entirely missing: (1) use of more than one psychophysiological and/or experimental variable in one and the same sample of subjects; (2) reliability checks for these variables (e.g., by repeated measurements under identical or systematically varied conditions); (3) consideration of various aspects of E/I, especially the primary factors Impulsivity and Sociability; and (4) testing the hypothesis of a moderator function of N on the relationship between (questionnaire) extraversion and the psychophysiological/experimental variables.

At the Heidelberg Institute a series of experiments meeting these requirements was carried out: Data analysis continues, but for some variables the results have already been computed in detail. Even these findings can, due to the limited space, be presented only partially. (Additional results are reported in Amelang and Ullwer, 1990, 1991a, 1991b.)

Method

Sample of Subjects

The sample of subjects consisted of 181 persons (102 females) with a mean of age of 23.7 years (range 19 to 35). Due to the recruitment strategy (advertising for participation in a local paper and by notices in University Departments), the socioeconomic structure of the sample was quite heterogeneous. The main categories were "students" (about 50%), "working persons," "housewives," and "unemployed." The subject received a payment of DM 130 for their participation. This amount could be increased by performing extraordinarily well in some learning experiments and in a motor task.

Sample of Variables

The subjects provided individual scores in a total of n = 950 items from personality tests and self-assessment scales assembled *ad hoc*. Moreover, they worked through the scales "1 + 2 Verbal Comprehension" and "3 Inductive Reasoning" from the "Test System for School and Educational Counseling" (PSB) by Horn (1969), which is a widely used intelligence test in Germany.

Among others, the items belonged to the following tests:EPI (form A & B; Eysenck & Eysenck, 1968)—Extraversion, Neuroticism; EPQ (Eysenck & Eysenck, 1974)—Extraversion, Neuroticism, Psychoticism (each of them omitting the items already included in the EPI); Experimental Versions for Impulsiveness by Eysenck and Eysenck (1977)—Impulsiveness, Risk-Taking, Non-Planning, and Liveliness. The variables were developed by Eysenck's research group and were subsequently applied by that group. For this reason they are crucial to our argument.

Along with these, further questionnaires with similar claims to validity were applied, in order to cover the extraversion and neuroticism sector comprehensively, among them the Mainz Impulsiveness Scales by Vossel and Safian (1985), scales from Guilford's STDCR, Cattell's 16 PF, and the Freiburg Personality Inventory by Fahrenberg, Hampel, and Selg (1984).

Moreover, some scales dealing with the wider context of extraversion (Motivation for Variation: Fischer & Wiedl, 1973) were also included, as well as scales for the assessment of Actual States (Adjective Check List, EWL—Janke & Debus, 1978) and for controlling response sets (e.g., Lie scales from EPI and EPQ; Acquiescence: Buse, 1970).

This program was completed by a total of 73 self-ratings on 7-point two-pole trait dimensions, of which two examples are given in the following:

aggressive	7	6	5	4	3	2	1	nonaggressive
extraverted	7	6	5	4	3	2	1	introverted

For 26 of these trait polarities and about half of the subject sample (N = 80), their relatives, acquaintances or friends provided peer ratings as external criteria. With the exception of only a few scales, the interrater reliability was satisfactory so that, for the vast majority of the rating dimensions, a mean score could be computed for the ratings by the three peers per subject.

The experimental program included the variables and tasks listed in Table 17.1.

All of these variables had been selected in such a way that Eysenck's extraversion theory allowed the deduction of directional hypotheses about behavior or the performance of the extraverted and introverted subjects, respectively; reference studies were available from the literature on most experimental tasks.

The experiments for each subject took a total of 8 hours, divided into two sessions. Due to the scope and density of the experimental program, it was not possible to conduct

**Table 17.1. Psychophysiological
and Experimental Variables as
Operationalizations of the
Excitation-Inhibition Theory**

Psychophysicological variables

Evoked potentials
Spontaneous EEG
Salivation test
Sleep duration

Variables of perception

Pain threshold and pain tolerance
Critical flicker fusion
Rate of fluctuation of "leaping pictures"
Estimating weights
Estimation time intervals

Learning

Pursuit rotor tracking
Writing down the alphabet backwards
Eyelid conditioning
Operant conditioning
Verbal conditioning
Verbal learning

Motor performance

Rapid tapping
Appropriate speed of simple movements
Endurance of maximal power

all experimental sessions at constant times of day. Seven experimenters administered the
tests and experiments. The experimental conditions were systematically varied and
reliability checks were carried out whenever possible.

To illustrate, the secretion of saliva after stimulation of the tongue was tested using
distilled water, artificial lemon acid, and freshly pressed lemon juice, both with the same
pH-value. As another example, a spontaneous electroencephalogram was recorded twice
each time under the following conditions: "rest with eyes closed," "eyes fixed on a
point," and "mental arithmetic." As a third example, pain threshold was measured at the
right and the left hand, etc.

Due to the abundance of data gathered, only a portion of our findings can be
presented here. We have chosen to focus on a few variables, and to describe relatively
simple experimental tasks the explanation of which do not require lengthy description of
detail. Furthermore, we were guided by the proviso that each of the afore-mentioned
blocks (Psychophysiological Variables, Variables of Perception, Learning, and Motor
Performance) should be represented by at least one variable. Thus constrained, we will
deal here only with the following five variables:

1. *Salivation Test.* Each subject received 4 drops of (a) distilled water, (b) artificial lemon acid (pH = 2.6), and (c) freshly pressed lemon juice (pH = 2.6). These drops were dribbled on the subject's tongue. The amount of salivation secreted within 20 seconds after fluid application was soaked up with a cotton-wool ball whose weight difference (in $^1/_{100}$g) before/after made up the score. Each of the conditions was repeated after about 10 minutes.

2. *Pain Threshold and Pain Tolerance.* Each subject dipped his or her hand up to the wrist into icewater. The time measured until the sensation of pain was reported was used to define "pain threshold": the time between the occurrence of the sensation of pain and the removal of the hand from the water defined "pain tolerance." The instructions were purposely given so as *not* to induce achievement-motivation. The comparison between the right and the left hand provided an indication of reliability.

3. *Flicker Fusion.* A generator provided rectangular impulses for a bulb. The frequency of the impulses could be continuously varied between 19 and 80 Hz. The point of subjective fusion was measured twice for both ascending and descending direction. The mean score in the four trials defined the individual score. This score was obtained under normal background noise (quiet room, low noise level) as well as under 60 and 75 dB white noise (medium and high level). The order of low-medium-high level was invariant.

4. *Eyelid Conditioning.* Using an apparatus with a fixed program available on the market, the number of conditioned reactions (eyeblinks) to an air puff of 3 pound-inch^2 was registered in eight blocks of five trials each. A sound of 1000 Hz and 75 dB exposed 500 msec before the UCS and ending with the UCS served as the Conditioned Stimulus. In this phase, the trials had 100% contingency. In the extinction phase, the UCS was missing in three blocks of five trials each.

5. *Rapid Tapping.* For two minutes, the subjects pressed a Morse button with the index finger of their dominant hand as rapidly as possible, putting their wrist on the table. Any on-and-off contact was measured (in milliseconds) separately for twelve sections lasting 10 seconds each.

There were four conditions: (1) Slow tapping (instruction: "Choose the speed which is most pleasant for you;" (2) Rapid tapping I ("As fast as possible"); (3) Rapid tapping II [Repetition of (2)]; and (4) Rapid tapping III [like (2) but with increased motivation by offering a financial reward for especially high performance]. The order of conditions was the same for all subjects, with an interval of at least 30 minutes. We will report only about condition (2) and about reliability over conditions (2) and (3).

Results

There were significant sex differences for EPI-N and EPQ-N, for several Impulsiveness scales, and for the scales of the FPI (belonging to the Anxiety factor), 16 PF, and a few self-rating polarities (higher scores in the female sex). For this reason, all analyses were carried out separately for male and female subjects.

For both self and peer ratings on each of the test scales, separate factor analyses were carried out. In all sets of data, clear factors of Extraversion, Neuroticism, and Impulsiveness (among others) could be identified. These factors were subsequently included as additional variables in the group of predictors, i.e., the questionnaire variables. The correlations between peer ratings and the factor scores for these variables are shown in Table 17.2.

As can be seen from the table, the coefficients are of satisfactory magnitude throughout, especially the ones for E and N. Only the predictability of the peer rating factor "Impulsiveness" is relatively low. On the whole, these results—and many others which are not documented here—show that the questionnaire data are very reliable and valid.

Looking at Tables 17.3–17.7, it becomes obvious that the same is true for the psychophysiological/experimental variables: depending upon the options available for computing adequate coefficients, the reliability and/or consistency across experimental conditions was not only significant throughout but also of considerable magnitude— elementary requirements for possible correlations between all these variables and the questionnaire scores.

Most of the variables show clear effects of sex. This is obviously not only the case for measures more strongly influenced by motivational factors (like, e.g., pain threshold and tolerance, rapid tapping) but also for variables in which the motivational component is less important (e.g., flicker fusion, salivation test). With regard to sex, however, Eysenck's extraversion theory is indifferent; as far as the psychophysiological variables are concerned, sexually determined differences were *not* to be expected. On the other hand, they certainly cannot be taken as a reason for rejecting the theory as untenable.

The results listed in Table 17.8 are, however, more crucial. As can be seen, only very few out of a total of 200 coefficients computed for each of the sexes separately are significant (12 coefficients for the male and 7 for the female). All coefficients computed

Table 17.2. Correlations between the Individual Scores in the Questionnaire Scales ("Predictors") and the Peer-Rating Factors*

	Peer-rating-factor scores		
	Extraversion	Neuroticism	Impulsivity
EPI { E	.59		
EPI { N		.50	
EPQ { E	.57		
EPQ { N		.51	
I (from EPI-E)	.39		
Sociability (from EPI-E)	.57		
I (Exp.-versions)	.35		.39
MIS (Mainz-I-Scales)	.32		.43
E (Factorized tests)	.53		
N (Factorized tests)		.53	
I (Factorized tests)		.41	
E (Factorized self-ratings)	.66		

*The coefficients were separately computed for both sexes. For reasons of space only the arithmetic mean from both sexes is listed. Only coefficients > .31 are included (which equals to 1% with N = 70).

Table 17.3. Mean Volume of Salivation in 1/100 g after Stimulation of the Tongue with Four Drops of Water (W), Artificial Lemon Acid (ALA), or Freshly Pressed Lemon Juice (FPLJ), Separate for Male (m) and Female (f) Ss. Reliability- and Cross-Conditions Coefficients Listed in Lower Part of Table.

		W	ALA	FPLJ
$\bar{x}$ (s)	m	21.8 (16.8)	44.6 (38.1)	55.3 (42.0)
	f	17.9 (14.4)	44.5 (39.6)	64.7 (60.2)
Difference m/f		ns	ns	ns
r_{tt}	m	.79**	.61**	.80**
	f	.55**	.66**	.81**
r_{cond}		.41** (W/ALA)	.54** (ALA/FPLJ) .34** (W/FPLJ)	

Note. $\bar{x}$ = mean. s = standard deviation. r_{tt} = reliability. r_{cond} = correlations between conditions.

Table 17.4. Mean Times (in Seconds) until Occurrence of Pain ("Threshold") and Time between Occurrence of Pain and Drawing Back the Hand from the Water ("Tolerance"), Separate for Left and Right Hand, Male (m) and Female (f) Ss. Correlations between Hands (as an Equivalent to Reliability) and Variables Are Listed in Lower Part of Table.

		Threshold			Tolerance		
		Left (1)	Right (r)	1 + r	Left (1)	Right (r)	1 + r
$\bar{x}$ (s)	m	19.7 (13.3)	24.1 (14.5)	43.6 (26.4)	65.8 (44.3)	68.1 (48.0)	132.6 (87.6)
	f	15.9 (9.9)	18.7 (11.2)	34.3 (20.0)	49.1 (40.4)	49.9 (38.5)	99.0 (76.8)
d	m/f	*	*	*	*	*	*
$r_{r/l}$	m	.78**			.78**		
	f	.79**			.89**		
r_{cond}	m	.41**					
	f	.42**					

Note. $\bar{x}$ = mean. s = standard deviation. d = difference. $r_{r/l}$ = correlation right/left hand. $r_{cond.}$ r = correlation between conditions.

**Table 17.5. Mean Frequency (and Standard Deviation)
for Flicker Fusion under Low, Medium, and High
White Noise, Separate for Male (m) and Female (f) Ss.
Correlations between Experimental Treatments
Are Listed (as Equivalents for Cross-Conditions
Consistency) in Lower Part of Table.**

		Low (L)	Medium (M)	High (H)
$\bar{x}$ (s)	m	67.1 (4.7)	66.9 (4.5)	66.2 (4.3)
	f	66.0 (3.8)	64.8 (3.6)	64.1 (4.1)
Difference m/f		ns	**	**
r_{cond}	m	.90** (L/M)	.94** (M/H)	
	f	.80**	.84**	
	m	.86** (L/H)		
	f	.71**		

Note. $\bar{x}$ = mean. s = standard deviation. $r_{cond.}$ = correlations between conditions.

for the sample of females show a sign contrary to the predictions. Looking at the significant coefficients, 10 of these are from the two variables of the tapping test (9 of them for the male sample; all in accordance with hypotheses). Correlations of Extraversion, Impulsiveness, and Sociability scores with tapping performance appear to be fairly similar, both in terms of percentage of significances and in terms of magnitude. Only in

**Table 17.6. Mean Number of Conditioned
Responses during Last Three Trials
of Learning Phase and First Three Trials
of the Extinction Phase, Separate for Male
(m) and Female (f) Ss.**

		Learning phase	Extinction phase
$\bar{x}$ (s)	m	5.69 (5.4)	3.81 (4.6)
	f	8.31 (5.7)	4.91 (4.7)
Difference m/f		*	ns
r_{cond}	m	.57**	
	f	.60**	

Note. $\bar{x}$ = mean. s = standard deviation. $r_{cond.}$ = correlations between conditions.

Table 17.7. Mean OFF-Times during the Twelve 10-Second Intervals of Rapid Tapping and Retest-Reliability for Each Interval. Correlations between OFF-Times of Successive Intervals Are Listed in Lower Part of Table.

		1	2	3	4	5	6	7	8	9	10	11	12
							Intervals or sections						
$\bar{x}$ (s)	m	112.2	119.7	121.6	124.6	124.0	127.1	124.8	121.3	122.6	119.8	121.0	124.2
	f	137.5	132.6	136.6	139.3	140.6	140.7	142.2	143.2	141.9	142.1	141.0	147.8
d	m/f	*	*	**	*	**	*	*	**	**	**	**	**
r_{tt}	m	.40	.35	.55	.56	.68	.63	.71	.70	.69	.66	.70	.55
	f	.22	.49	.40	.52	.45	.50	.55	.53	.55	.53	.50	.40

		1/2	2/3	3/4	4/5	5/6	6/7	7/8	8/9	9/10	10/11	11/12
						Correlations between intervals or sections						
r_{tc}	m	.88	.76	.81	.82	.93	.86	.85	.86	.87	.93	.84
	f	.35	.88	.91	.85	.90	.91	.91	.92	.92	.90	.50

Note. Each coefficient is significant at least with p = 0.05. $\bar{x}$ = mean. d = difference. r_{tt} = retest-reliability. r_{tc} = correlation between intervals.

Table 17.8. Correlations between Selected Questionnaire Scales and Psychophysiological/Experimental Variables, Separate for Male (m) and Female (f) Ss

	Salivation				Pain				Rapid Tapping			
	Ala		FPLJ		Threshold		Tolerance		Sections 1–6		Sections 7–12	
	m	f	m	f	m	f	m	f	m	f	m	f
EPI-E		.24*			−.29 / .08 / .31				.33**		.31*	
EPQ-E					−.41* / −.03 / .29				.28*		.29*	
E (Test-factor)					−.41* / −.07 / .20							
E (Self-rating-factor)		.22*			−.30 / .11 / .39*				.28*			

	1	2	3	4	5	6	7	8
Sociability (from EPI-E)	.21*			−.26 .04 .33		.28*		.33**
I (from EPI-E)		−.26*		−.16 .07 .20				
I (Exp.-versions)	.20*		.06 −.07 −.16	−.10 .21 .33				.29*
MIS (Mainz-I-Scales)		−.27*	.08 −.04 −.13		−.27*			
I (Self-rating factor)					.17 −.19 −.36*			
I (Test-factor)			.11 −.05 −.16			.53** .26* .10	−.23*	

Notes. E = Extraversion. N = Neuroticism. I = Impulsivity. ALA = Artificial Lemon Acid. FPLJ = Freshly Pressed Lemon Juice. The upper coefficient stands for the group of emotionally unstable, the lower for the group of emotionally stable subjects in terms of EPI-Neuroticism. Only coefficients which were significant for the subgroups of male or female persons or which were significantly moderated by N are listed.

one case does the EPI-N scale significantly moderate a predictor-"criterion" correlation (test factor Impulsivity and sum score of the first six tapping trials) but here the results are contrary to the hypothesis.

As far as the salivation variables are concerned, the two significant coefficients in the male subsample (from two Impulsiveness scales) are in accordance with the hypothesis. The five significant correlations for the female sex are, without exception, contrary to hypotheses (not in Table 17.8: self-rating factor Extraversion and salivation variable water in the female sample $r_{tc} = .22$; $p < .05$). For the sum total of the three steps of flicker fusion, the only significant coefficient is the one for the male subjects with the self-rating factor Impulsiveness ($r_{tc} = -.24$; $p < .05$).

With regard to moderation, a systematic tendency can be observed only for the correlations related to pain threshold. Moderator effects were found only for the male sex, all such effects being in accordance with hypotheses in that for subjects with low N scores, the predictor-criterion correlations were higher than for persons scoring high on N. These moderator effects existed for only two of the five Impulsiveness scales but for all Extraversion and Sociability scales.

The results for the conditioning paradigm are not listed in the table since correlations were, with one exception, insignificant. This exception, which can be regarded as a "random significance," concerns the correlation between E and percentage of learned conditioned responses within the reinforcement trials: here coefficients in the male sample were .15 for the emotionally unstable, and −.25 for the emotionally stable subjects (total male $r = -.03$).

Similar results were obtained when the correlations between questionnaire scales and experimental variables were computed via analyses of variance. These were carried out in several designs, but even the selection of extreme groups on the E and N dimensions did not produce clear effects. The moderator effects were even rarer when, instead of EPI-N, the factor score for the test factor "Neuroticism" was used. In no case did correlations turn up between scores from *different* experimental variables (e.g., conditioning/rapid tapping; pain variables/salivation, etc.).

Discussion and Concluding Remarks

Overall, the results do not provide any confirmation of the Eysenck Activation theory of E/I. None of the hypotheses concerning the excitation-inhibition-balance could be confirmed with sufficient consistency. Further analyses not discussed here show, moreover, that N does not substantially explain the individual differences in the experimental variables, either.

A possible criticism of the findings could be formulated around the objection that the subjects were considerably strained by the multitude of experimental tasks and the duration of the experiments, thus changing the variables' meaning. Especially, time of day should have been controlled, since, e.g., Knorring, Mernstad, Forsgren, and Holmgren (1986) and Deary et al. (1988) found a higher correlation between Saliva Secretion and Extraversion in the morning than in the afternoon. In addition, some of the studies mentioned under (2) revealed influences attributable to diurnal rhythm. In response to such criticism, however, one could argue that the scores obtained in our study are demonstrably reliable and cross-situationally consistent. Nevertheless, a *post hoc* analysis of effects attributable to time of day is possible, and it is our intention to carry out such an analysis.

Pending the results of those analyses, the following statements seem justified on the basis of the findings observed so far:

1. Despite the proven reliability and consistency across the varied conditions, the psychophysiological and the experimental variables do not correlate in any significant degree with the various questionnaire-based indices of extraversion. The same applies to the factor of "Emotional Lability."

2. In view of the positive results reported from England, it is either the case that interculturally significant influences (the specific nature of which remains to be explicated) underlie the discrepancies, or it is instead the case that the published results reflect atypical effects of an idiosyncratic combination of authors, subjects, and experimental tasks, as well as evaluation and publication strategies. Even the Freiburg research group was able to establish only zero-correlations between the questionnaire scales and psychophysiological variables in spite of extremely careful work, which is why Fahrenberg (1987) calls this a "frustrating state of affairs."

The following implications can be drawn for further research:

1. Further aggregation of questionnaire data as well as of the physiological experimental variables has been called for by many. The implementation of this strategy, however, has had no clear effect on the results we have been obtaining.

2. Precise specification of suitable intensities of total stimulation through stress, as defined by the theory, on a dimension which reflects the experimental situation, the demands of the setting as a whole, and the individual coping styles.

The burden of this work, which is essential for an empirical differentiation between activation and arousal, falls primarily upon the originator of the theory or its proponents. The subsequent inclusion of situational activating concepts in the theory by Eysenck (1981) has further aggravated this problem. The mesh of interacting factors must not be allowed to become too complex, however, to the point that an empirical test of the theory is rendered impossible (see Eysenck, this book). It is not acceptable, however, that a theory be made invulnerable by the claim that operationalization, based on a critical study, is inadequate.

ACKNOWLEDGMENTS. This work was supported by the German Research Association (DFG) Am 37/5, 37/7-1, 37/8-1 and 37/8-2. We thank the DFG as well as research assistants Christiane Breit, Thomas Schneyer, Peter Borkenau, and Joachim Schahn for their energetic and inventive help. Thanks are also due to the total of about 2600 participants who were subjects in various stages of the sometimes tedious experiments. We thank Silke Kroening and Jim Lamiell for the help they gave to the English language expression of our thoughts.

References

Amelang, M. Fragebogen-Tests und experimentell-psychologische Variablen als Korrelate der Persön-lichkeitsdimensionen Extraversion/Introversion (E/I) und Neurotizismus (N). In M. Amelang (Ed.), *Bericht über den 35. Kongress der Deutschen Gesellschaft für Psychologie in Heidelberg 1986*. Vol. 2. Gottingen: Hogrefe, 1987.

Amelang, M., & Bartussek, D. *Differentielle Psychologie und Persönlichkeitsforschung* (3rd ed.). Kohlhammer: Stuttgart, 1989.

Amelang, M., & Borkenau, P. Über die faktorielle Struktur und externe Validität einiger Fragebogen-Skalen zur Erfassung von Dimensionen der Extraversion und emotionalen Labilität. *Zeitschrift für Differentielle und Diagnostische Psychologie*, 1982, *3*, 119–146.

Amelang, M., & Breit, C. Extraversion and rapid tapping: Reactive inhibition or general cortical activation as determinants of performance differences. *Personality and Individual Differences*, 1983, *4*, 103–105.

Amelang, M. & Ullwer, U. Untersuchungen zur experimentellen Bewährung von Eysencks Extraver-sions-theorie. [Experimental tests of Eysenck's Extraversion theory], *Zeitschrift für Differentielle und Diagnostische Psychologie*, 1990 *11*, 121–148.

Amelang, M. & Ullwer, U. Ansatz und Ergebnisse einer (fast) umfassenden Überprüfung von Eysencks Extraversionstheorie. [Method and results of a (nearly) comprehensive study on Eysenck's Extraver-sion theory], *Psychologische Beiträge*, 1991a *33* (in press).

Amelang, M. & Ullwer, U. Some results of a large scale test of Eysenck's Extraversion theory. 1991b Manuscript submitted for publication.

Barnes, G. E. Extraversion and pain. *British Journal of Social and Clinical Psychology*, 1975, *14*, 303–308.

Bartussek, D. Extraversion und EEG: Ein Forschungsparadigma in der Sackgasse? In M. Amelang & H. J. Ahrens (Eds.), *Brennpunkte der Persönlichkeitsforschung*. Göttingen: Hogrefe, 1984.

Bartussek, D., Collet, W., & Naumann, E. *Der Einfluss von Gewinn und Verlust auf das evozierte EEG-Potential in Abhängigkeit von Extraversion und Neurotizismus*. Paper presented at the 25th Con-ference of Experimental Psychologists, Hamburg, 1983 (summarized in Bartussek, 1984).

Boddy, J., Carver, A., & Rowley, K. Effect of positive and negative verbal reinforcement on perfor-mance as a function of extraversion-introversion: Some tests of Gray's theory. *Personality and Individual Differences*, 1986, *7*, 81–88.

Brocke, B., & Battmann, W.. Die Aktivierungstheorie der Personlichkeit. Eine systematische Darstellung und partielle Rekonstruktion. *Zeitschrift fur Differentielle Psychologie*, 1985, *6*, 189–213.

Brocke, D., & Liepmann, D. Eysenck's Theorie der situativen Erregung: Einige Befunde zu einer interaktionistischen Erganzung der Aktivierungstheorie der Persönlichkeit. *Zeitschrift für Differ-entielle und Diagnostische Psychologie*, 1985, *6*, 19–31.

Brody, N. *Personality research and theory*. New York: Academic Press, 1972.

Brody, N. *Personality: In search of individuality*. San Diego: Academic Press, 1988.

Buse, L. *Untersuchung zur Akquieszenz an einem Extraversions-Fragebogen*. Unpublished manuscript, Hamburg, 1970.

Campbell, J. B. Differential relationships of extraversion, impulsivity, and sociability to study habits. *Journal of Research in Personality*, 1983, *17*, 308–314.

Campbell, J. B., & Heller F. Correlations of extraversion, impulsivity, and sociability with sensation seeking and MBTI-introversion. *Personality and Individual Differences*, 1987, *8*, 133–136.

Campbell, J. B., & Reynolds, J. H. A comparison of the Guilford and Eysenck factors of personality. *Journal of Research in Personality*, 1984, *18*, 305–320.

Costa, P. T., Jr., & McCrae, R. R. Personality in adulthood: A six-year longitudinal study of self-reports and spouse ratings on the NEO Personality Inventory. *Journal of Personality and Social Psychology*, 1988, *54*, 853–863.

Deary, I. J., Ramsay, H., Wilson, J. A., & Riad, M. Stimulated salivation: Correlations with personality and time of day effects. *Personality and Individual Differences*, 1988, *9*, 903–909.

De Pascalis, V., & Montirosso, R. Extraversion. neuroticism and individual differences in event-related potentials. *Personality and Individual Differences*, 1988, *9*, 353–360.

Eysenck, H. J. *A manual for the Maudsley Personality Inventory.* London: University of London Press, 1959.

Eysenck, H. J. A factor analysis of selected tests. In H. J. Eysenck (Ed.), *Experiments in personality: Psychodiagnosis and psychodynamics.* Vol.2. London: Routledge & Kegan Paul, 1960.

Eysenck, H. J. *The biological basis of personality.* Springfield, IL: Thomas, 1967.

Eysenck, H. J. *Readings of extraversion. Bearings on basic psychological processes.* London: Staples Press, 1971a.

Eysenck, H. J. *Readings on extraversion. Fields of application.* London: Staples Press, 1971b.

Eysenck, H. J. *Eysenck on extraversion.* London: Crosby Lockwood Staples, 1973.

Eysenck, H. J. *The measurement of personality.* Lancaster: Medical and Technical Publishers, 1976.

Eysenck, H. J. Personality and factor analysis: A reply to Guilford. *Psychological Bulletin*, 1977, *84*, 405–411.

Eysenck, H. J. General features of the model. In H. J. Eysenck (Ed.), *A model for personality.* New York: Springer, 1981.

Eysenck, H. J. The place of anxiety and impulsivity in a dimensional framework. *Journal of Research in Personality*, 1987, *21*, 489–492.

Eysenck, H. J., & Eysenck, M. W. *Personality and individual differences: A natural science approach.* New York: Plenum, 1985.

Eysenck, H. J., & Eysenck, S. B. G. *Manual of the Eysenck Personality Inventory.* San Diego CA: Educational and Industrial Testing Service, 1968.

Eysenck, H. J., & Eysenck, S. B. G. Crime and personality: Item-analysis of questionnaire responses. *British Journal of Criminology*, 1971, *11*, 49–62.

Eysenck, S. B. G., & Eysenck, H. J. *The dual nature of extraversion.* Paper presented at the XXII International Congress of Psychology, 311. Leipzig: Abstract Guide, 1969.

Eysenck, S. B. G., & Eysenck, H. J. *Manual of Personality Questionnaire.* London: University London Press, 1974.

Eysenck, H. J., Granger, G. W., & Brengelmann, J. C. *Perceptual processes and mental illness.* London: Chapman & Hall, 1957.

Fahrenberg, J. Concepts of activation and arousal in the theory of emotionality (neuroticism): A multivariate conceptualization. In J. Strelau, & H. J. Eysenck (Eds.), *Personality dimensions and arousal.* New York: Plenum, 1987.

Fahrenberg, J., Hampel, R., & Selg, H. *Das Freiburger Persönlichkeitsinventar FPI.* Göttingen: Hogrefe, 1984.

Fischer, M., & Wiedl, K. H. Variationsmotivation. *Psychologische Beiträge*, 1973, *65*, 478–521.

Furnham, A. Extraversion, sensation seeking, stimulus screening and Type A behaviour pattern: The relationship between various measures of arousal. *Personality and Individual Differences*, 1984, *2*, 133–140.

Gale, A. The psychophysiology of individual differences: Studies of extraversion and the EEG. In P. Kline (Ed.), *New approaches in psychological measurement.* London: Wiley, 1973.

Gale, A. *Electroencephalografic correlates of extraversion- introversion.* XXII International Congress of Psychology, 311. Leipzig: Abstract Guide, 1980.

Geen, R. G. Preferred stimulation levels in introverts and extraverts: Effect of arousal and performance. *Journal of Personality and Social Psychology*, 1984, *46*, 1303–1312.

Giambra, L. M., Quilter, R. E., & Phillips, P. B. The relationship of age and extraversion to arousal and performance on a sustained attention task: A cross-sectional investigation using the Mackworth Clock-Test. *Personality and Individual Differences*, 1988, *9*, 225–230.

Gilliland, K. The interactive effect of introversion/extraversion with caffein-induced arousal on verbal performance. *Dissertation Abstracts International*, 1977, *37*, 58, 55B.

Gray, J. A. Causal theories of personality and how to test them. In J. R. Royce (Ed.), *Multivariate analysis and psychological theory.* New York: Academic Press, 1973.

Gray, J. A. A critique of Eysenck's theory of personality. In H. J. Eysenck (Ed.), *A model for personality*. New York: Springer, 1981.

Gray, J. A. Perspectives on anxiety and impulsivity: A commentary. *Journal of Research in Personality*, 1987, *21*, 493–509.

Gray, J. A., & Nicholson, J. N. Behavior measures of susceptibility to frustration in children: Relation to neuroticism and introversion. *Studia Psychologica*, 1974, *16*, 21–39.

Guilford, J. P. Factors and factors of personality. *Psychological Bulletin*, 1975, *82*, 802–814.

Holland, H. C. Measures or perceptual functions. In H. J. Eysenck (Ed.), *Experiments in personality: Psychodiagnostics and psychodynamics*. Vol. 2. London: Routlege & Kegan Paul, 1960.

Holmes, D. S. Pupillary response, conditioning and personality. Journal of Personality and Social Psychology, 1967, 5, 98–103.

Horn, W. *Prüfsystem fur Schul- und Bildungsberatung PSB*. Göttingen: Hogrefe, 1969.

Janke, W., & Debus, G. *Die Eigenschaftswörterliste EWL*. Göttingen: Hogrefe, 1978.

Knorring, L. von, Mernstad, H., Forsgren, L., & Holmgren, S. Saliva secretion rate and saliva composition in relation to extraversion. *Personality and Individual Differences*, 1986, *7*, 33–38.

Levy, P, & Lang, P. J. Activation, control and the spiral aftermovement. *Journal of Personality and Social Psychology*, 1966, *3*, 105–112.

Lynn, R. Extraversion, reminiscence and satiation effects. *British Journal of Psychology*, 1960, *51*, 319–324.

Matthews, G. Personality and multidimensional arousal: A study of two dimensions of extraversion. *Personality and Individual Differences*, 1987, *8*, 9–16.

McCord, R. R., & Wakefield, J. A. Arithmetic achievement as a function of introversion-extraversion and teacher presented reward and punishment. *Personality and Individual Differences*, 1981, *2*, 145–152.

McCrae, R. R., & Costa, P. T., Jr. Validation of the five-factor model of personality across instruments and observers. *Journal of Personality and Social Psychology*, 1987, *52*, 81–90.

Morris, L. W. *Extraversion and introversion*. Washington: Hemisphere, 1979.

Nagpal, M., & Gupta, B. S. Personality, reinforcement and verbal conditioning. *British Journal of Psychology*, 1979, *70*, 471–476.

Nichols, S. L., & Newman, J. P. Effects of punishment on response latency in extraverts. *Journal of Personality and Social Psychology*, 1986, *50*, 624–630.

Norman, W. T. Toward an adequate taxonomy of personality attributes: Replicated factor structure in peer nomination personality ratings. *Journal of Abnormal and Social Psychology*, 1963, *66*, 574–583.

O'Gorman, J. G., & Lloyd, J. E. M. Extraversion, impulsiveness, and EEG alpha activity. *Personality and Individual Differences*, 1987, *8*, 169–174.

Patterson, C. M., Kosson, D. S., & Newman, J. P. Reaction to punishment, reflectivity, and passive avoidance learning in extraverts. *Journal of Personality and Social Psychology*, 1987, *52*, 565–575.

Pearce-McCall, D., & Newman, J. P. Expectation of success following noncontingent punishment in introverts and extraverts. *Journal of Personality and Social Psychology*, 1986, *50*, 439–446.

Revelle, W., Humphreys, M. S., Simon, L., & Gilliland K. The interactive effect of personality, time of day and caffeine: A test of the arousal model. *Journal of Experimental Psychology. General*, 1980, *109*, 1–31.

Rocklin, C., & Revelle, W. The measurement of extraversion: A comparison of the Eysenck Personality Inventory and the Eysenck Personality Questionnaire. *British Journal of Social Psychology*, 1981, *20*, 279–284.

Roger, D., & Jamieson, J. Individual differences in delayed heart-rate recovery following stress: The role of extraversion, neuroticism and emotional control. *Personality and Individual Differences*, 1988, *9*, 721–726.

Schneewind, K. Entwicklung einer deutschsprachigen Version des 16 PF-Tests von Cattell. *Diagnostica*, 1977, *23*, 188–191.

Seunath, O. M. Personality, reinforcement and learning. *Perceptual and Motor Skills*, 1975, *41*, 459–463.

Smith, B. D., Rypma, C. B., & Wilson, R. J. Dishabituation and spontaneous recovery of the electrodermal orienting response: Effects of extraversion, impulsivity, sociability and caffeine. *Journal of Research in Personality*, 1981, *15*, 233–240.

Stelmack, R. M. The psychophysiology of extraversion and neuroticism. In H. J. Eysenck (Ed.), *A model for personality*. New York: Springer, 1981.

Thayer, R. E. Towards a theory of multidimensional activation (arousal). *Motivation and Emotion*, 1978, *2*, 1–33.

Thompson, W. B., & Mueller, J. H. Extraversion and sleep: A psychophysiological study of the arousal hypothesis. *Personality and Individual Differences*, 1984, *5*, 345–353.

Vossel, G., & Safian, P. Dimensionen der Impulsivität. In D. Albert (Ed.), *Bericht über den 34. Kongress der Deutschen Gesellschaft für Psychologie in Wien 1984*. Vol. 1. Göttingen: Hogrefe, 1985.

Willett, R. A. Measures of learning and conditioning. In H. J. Eysenck (Ed.), *Experiments in personality: Psychodiagnostics and psychodynamics*. Vol. 2. London: Routledge & Kegan Paul, 1960.

Zuber, I., & Ekehammar, B. Personality, time of day and visual perception: Preferences and selective attention. *Personality and Individual Differences*, 1988, *9*, 345–352.

18

Differential Psychophysiology and the Diagnosis of Temperament

Jochen Fahrenberg

Introduction

Constitutional research that relates temperament, physiological-biochemical features, and physique has a long but disappointing history. Empirically, the assumed psycho-morphological as well as psychophysiological and psychochemical correlations proved to be generally low, and inconsistent at best. The majority of initially suggestive findings have suffered an identical fate: the optimistic publication attracts other researchers' interest, although rarely do they attempt identical replication, and a series of more or less similar studies is undertaken that usually results in a contradictory pattern of partial agreement and obvious refutation. Such inconsistencies eventually lead to a decline in research motivation and the originally claimed relationship seems to fade out—sometimes to be revived with fresh hope. This state of affairs is not restricted to constitutional research and psychophysiological personality research but is paralleled by frustrating research experience in related fields, e.g., research on specificity issues in psychosomatic medicine and the search for biological markers of psychotic and neurotic disorders.

The constitutional basis of personality development and psychophysiological disorders has recently attracted renewed interest. Behavioral assessment of the neonate has shown that basic differences in temperament and somatic functions appear at this initial stage of life (see the relevant contributions to this volume). The search for the genetic and early-learning basis of normal infant behavior and for risk dispositions in developmental psychobiology thus reinitiates basic concepts of constitutional theory and of constitutional pathology outlined at the beginning of this century in Germany, France, and other European countries. Research on individual-specific response patterns that is

Jochen Fahrenberg • Institute of Psychology, Albert-Ludwigs-University, D-7800 Freiburg i. Br., Federal Republic of Germany.

conducted in the psychophysiological laboratory and the concept of vulnerability to disease also resume the traditional constitutional theory (for a summary, see Fahrenberg, 1986; Iacono & Ficken, 1989).

A recent review on the psychophysiology of neuroticism and anxiety (Fahrenberg, 1989) concludes that decades of research in this field have failed to substantiate consistent psychophysiological personality traits. Nevertheless, biologically oriented psychologists will insist that individual differences in emotionality as assessed psychologically in subjective and behavioral terms must have either a specific or a nonspecific neurophysiological and biochemical basis. The persistent discrepancy between theoretical view and empirical evidence suggests a thorough evaluation of theoretical approach and research methodology. Some of these issues will be addressed in the following sections.

The research outcome with respect to extraversion-introversion (Eysenck & Eysenck, 1985; Stelmack, 1981) or the more recently introduced sensation-seeking and impulsivity concepts (Zuckerman, 1983; 1989) may be more encouraging. However, many inconsistencies are evident and a thorough meta-analysis that applies advanced techniques from evaluation methodology, e.g., quantification of effect strength and ratings of precisely defined design features of internal and external validity, are entirely lacking in this field.

Recent advances in analytic techniques have facilitated research into neuroendocrine, neuroimmunological, and biochemical functions. Many investigators seem to be convinced that significant relationships between such data and personality variables already have been identified (see Hellhammer, Florin, & Weiner, 1989). But again, inconsistencies between findings from various laboratories emerge. The Dexamethasone Suppression Test in the psychobiological research on depressives may serve to illustrate this point, and previous reviews (e.g., Cattell & Scheier, 1961) refer to a number of such failures. Much of the recent research on transmitter substances, hormones, and immunological parameters seems to replicate the same methodological deficiencies. Small sample univariate designs with low level data handling and a general disregard of the principle that identical replications must be achieved through cross-laboratory cooperation will restrict adequate development in this research domain.

Biologically oriented personality researchers, by recognizing the doubtful evidence for psychophysiological traits, would profit from critical reevaluation of traditional research questions and research methodology. An essential step in this direction would be to acknowledge advances in differential psychophysiology concerning, for example, the multivariate approach, differentiation of response patterns, and multimodal assessment strategies. An outline of such developments (reviewed in more detail elsewhere; Fahrenberg, 1983, 1988; Stemmler & Fahrenberg, 1989) will provide a frame of reference for the subsequent discussion of two especially relevant issues: (1) psychophysiological laboratory data versus questionnaire (psychometric) data in the diagnosis of temperament, and (2) the generalizability of psychophysiological assessments extending from the laboratory to the field.

Multivariate Activation Theory

Activation processes are higher nervous system functions of varying intensity and synergistic patterning; their study requires a complementary and multivariate psychological-physiological approach. Autonomic and cortical activation (arousal) are essential concepts in theories of temperament because individual differences in these functions are related to the well-known dimensions of emotionality (neuroticism), extraversion-introversion, sensation-seeking, etc. Psychophysiological personality research has been strongly influenced by these postulates, although autonomic and cortical arousal are theoretical constructs that still lack consistent operationalizations. Research has not yet produced standard patterns or dimensions of physiological processes specifying the CNS, ANS, and behavioral parameters that define the concepts and those that do not. No standardized assessment has been put forth to measure individual differences reliably and to allow for cross-laboratory comparison and thus for possible integration of experimental results.

The generally small amount of common variance in psychophysiological measures and its consequences for methodology and application constitute one of the most important issues for differential psychophysiology. For decades the phenomenon of response fractionation has troubled investigators interested in individual differences and prediction. In fact, a considerable proportion of the methodological discussion in psychophysiology is a consequence of this covariation problem and the motive to eventually find a sufficient explanation in the particular and perhaps inadequate research methodology. Many sources of error have been revealed that could threaten the internal validity of psychophysiological experiments (for overviews, see Fahrenberg, 1983, 1988; Gale & Edwards, 1983; Myrtek, 1984; Rösler, 1984; Stemmler & Fahrenberg, 1989).

However, it is highly improbable that the frustrating state of affairs concerning physiological correlates of personality traits could be explained merely by errors of measurement. Such an interpretation ignores recent investigations that have carefully analyzed methodological issues by conducting parameter studies, employing many experimental and statistical controls, and developing more precise assessment strategies.

Multivariate methodology has served to substantiate the position traditionally held in constitutional research and in systemic physiology that physiological responses are patterned depending on the individual's dispositions, situational demands, and subject-task interactions. It is a major challenge to present-day psychophysiology to advance more precise definition of such patterns and corresponding standard assessment procedures eventually validated against pharmacologically induced reference patterns. It is a notable trend further to differentiate global concepts by employing multiple recordings of autonomic and somatic functions, more specific parametrization, and increased sampling rates to aid functional analysis of system dynamics.

In some laboratories, considerable progress has been made in assessing individual differences in activation (arousal) processes. The basic facts of response fractionation and response patterning in physiological data demand methodological consequences. The scope of this multimodal approach (Cattell, 1966; critical multiplism, see Cook, 1985; principles of symmetry and representative designs, see Wittmann, 1988) will provoke criticism concerning its feasibility and practical application. The search for more valid assessments may strain many laboratories and thus hinder practical applications of psychophysiological concepts and methods. However, conventional single-channel physiological measurement approaches are obsolete in most psychophysiological research orientations.

The Search for Psychophysiological Traits

Basic Assumptions

Personality traits and abilities, like any psychological phenomena, must have a physiological basis in brain function. This statement may seem trivial; however, there is obvious disagreement about the nature and specificity of their representation in the central nervous system. Individual differences in temperament could be represented in rather diffuse, essentially semantic activity in the associative neocortex and all areas where symbolic-semantic analyses, for example, problem solving, moral and aesthetic evaluations, and the like, take place. Biologically oriented personality researchers seem to share the assumption that relatively consistent and stable traits (in particular, features of temperament) are based on the activity of anatomically distinct neuronal subsystems, particular receptor-transmitter systems, and/or on distinct properties of certain functional subsystems, e.g., differential thresholds and patterns of regulation.

There is much evidence from other fields like developmental neurobiology, behavioral assessments in the neonate, genetic, and twin research; behavioral neuropharmacology; or brain surgery, that such assumptions in principle are sound. But it remains an unsettled task for psychophysiological research to substantiate hypothetical personality dimensions as distinct psychobiological traits.

Concepts of arousal/activation in this context traditionally play an important role and still exert considerable influence in current theory, although an integration of the various, often vague theoretical and heterogeneous empirical strategies still proves to be extremely difficult (see Strelau & Eysenck, 1987). Activation and arousal define an area of research rather than a set of coherent theoretical constructs at present.

The search for the biological basis of personality as advocated, for example, by Eysenck (1967), can be understood as a general research program that is split up into many rather specialized research questions. The majority of investigations focus on a particular trait, but some research has a broader scope by evaluating the basic covariation problem within and between various modes of assessment. Psychophysiological assessment theory, including attempts at explaining obvious discrepancies between different levels of observation has in itself become an important area of research.

Correlational research that conforms to the Multitrait-Multimethod rationale would be the adequate approach to testing the convergent and discriminant validity of psychological and physiological variables relating to a particular trait and thus to provide evidence for the psychophysiological construct itself. Unfortunately, such MTMM-analyses have not been undertaken. Instead, there have been many attempts to correlate various physiological measures with questionnaire scores and other personality data; but this approach in many instances has proved frustrating because simple covariation between most parameters of psychological and physiological-biochemical subsystems and even among various physiological subsystems were inconsistent, low, or even negligible.

Emotionality as a trait concept, together with anxiety and nervousness/neuroticism, probably is the oldest and most prominent psychophysiological trait concept in modern psychology, and has given rise to a large number of empirical investigations. The gradual progress in this line of research toward falsifying and clarifying essential issues should be of some interest to temperament researchers, since many of the issues refer to methodological advances and thus are applicable to research on more recent psychophysiological trait theories.

Overgeneralization, of course, should be avoided, because the outcome for other traits may be more positive and rewarding. Fresh attempts should not be discouraged, provided the methodological advances are acknowledged and more sophisticated research designs are attained.

The Psychophysiology of Neuroticism and Anxiety

The personality dimension emotionality (neuroticism) derived from questionnaire data is related to individual differences in emotional and autonomic responsiveness. The limbic system of the brain is thought to be the neuroanatomical basis for this trait because it appears to be largely involved in the regulation of emotions. Eysenck's (1967) notion of this traditional concept of nervousness was very influential in psychophysiological personality research, an empirically valid trait concept bridging from self-ratings and behavior ratings to autonomic and endocrine data that would be extremely important to many research questions and practical applications.

As the psychophysiology of neuroticism and anxiety is discussed in two recent articles (Fahrenberg, 1987, 1989), it may suffice here to refer to the major issues and conclusions. This evaluation is essentially based on a series of psychophysiological studies conducted in our laboratory at the University of Freiburg. These investigations were large-scale, multiparameter, and multisituation studies that included systematic replications (Fahrenberg, Walschburger, Foerster, Müller, & Myrtek, 1979; Fahrenberg, Foerster, Schneider, Müller, & Myrtek, 1984; Myrtek, 1984). Compared to earlier research the more recent multivariate investigations controlled for many sources of variance as well as experimental and statistical artifacts.

As long as the correlation analysis is restricted to the questionnaire level, there can be no serious doubt that the empirical data strongly suggest the notion of a second-order trait dimension of emotionality (neuroticism). Many investigators have observed substantial positive correlation coefficients between an individual's N-score and the reported frequencies, as well as subjectively rated intensity of complaints on various autonomic, sensory, and somatic functions, fatigue, and so on.

There is, however, strong empirical evidence against Eysenck's theoretical postulate that emotionality scores from questionnaires are substantially correlated with physiological responsiveness. This conclusion, in principle, does not exclude the vague possibility that even more refined methodology eventually could shift the evidence. But at present there is virtually no distinct psychophysiological correlation related to emotionality that has been reliably replicated across studies and across laboratories. Strong evidence for retaining the null hypothesis has brought psychophysiological research on emotionality to a near standstill.

This state of affairs could lead one either to resign or to argue for advancing conceptual clarification and revising research programs. Some of these issues will be pointed out in the following.

Relevant Issues in Testing Psychophysiological Trait Postulates

Several authors have discussed the negative results found in the psychophysiology of emotionality (Fahrenberg, 1987, 1989; Gale & Edwards, 1984; Myrtek, 1984; Stelmack, 1981). Gale and Edwards (1983) specified several principles of error in this field that mostly pertain to internal validity of experimentation. Still other conceptual and methodological issues exist that also deserve consideration.

Conceptual Issues

1. Investigations that attempt to relate questionnaire scores to single psychophysiological-biochemical measures in an isolated fashion appear to be obsolete and should be replaced by a systemic approach to physiological regulation. Activation, arousal, thresholds of the limbic system, and the like, in contrast are global, psychophysiologically vague concepts. They lack standardized assessment procedures and indicators of established empirical discriminant-convergent validity and thus must lead to confusion.

2. A semantic analysis and structuring of arousal-activation theories as proposed by Brocke and Battmann (1985) could lead to more precise operationalization of essential terms and eventually allow for adequate discrimination of theoretically related and interacting traits, for example, extraversion and emotionality.

3. Certain parameters of testing, i.e., types of stressors, stimulus parameters, appropriate experimental setting, and types of physiological measures, are crucial according to Eysenck (1981), for testing his trait theory. Since he does not provide operational definitions, a fundamental methodological issue ensues as to precisely under what conditions an adequate test of Eysenck's hypothesis must be conducted.

4. In psychophysiological research little concern appears regarding commensurable concept levels of physiological measures and psychological scores. Top-down and bottom-up strategies, i.e., decomposition of second-order trait dimensions and aggregation of single physiological measures, should complement each other in a systematic fashion. More specific physiological-neuroendocrine assessments, further differentiation of regulatory pattern, and development of multicomponent models of activation processes raise the essential issue how psychological concepts could be specified to meet adequately this differentiation concerning systemic level and type of aggregation, i.e., averaging across time intervals, classes of situation, or areas of content.

5. Attempts at decomposing global trait concepts have been made in order to attain more precise and empirically consistent findings. A similar tendency is apparent, for example, in research on impulsivity and sensation-seeking subscales (Zuckerman, 1989) or the hostility component in coronary-prone behavior pattern (Dembroski & Williams, 1989). However, with emotionality, the task of identifying primaries, probably due to the traditional, highly consistent item pool, is still unsolved.

6. With respect to the emotionality dimension, revisions have been proposed. Noteworthy are Gray's (1981) reformulation of Eysenck's theory by suggesting a different rotational solution to be theoretically superior and Andresen's (1987) bipolar concept of emotionality that separates a positively toned and a negatively toned dimension of activation.

7. The theoretical discussion on the validity of psychophysiological trait theories should extend to the more recent information processing approach which challenges the

basic assumption that a distinct biological correlate of temperament traits exists. The notion of emotionality as a multireferential cognitive scheme would assist understanding basic inconsistencies and discrepancies in emotionality research. Illustrative examples of the information-processing approach are provided by Hallam (1985), who regards anxiety as a multireferential, often metaphorical lay construct, and by Buse and Pawlik (1984), who have applied the analysis of social stereotypes and self-attribution processes to explain the association of temperament and somatotype.

Issues in Assessment.

1. Assessments of individual differences in activation processes have to acknowledge response fractionation and patterning of physiological-biochemical measures. As compared to speculations on unitary arousal dimension, a multicomponent approach is much more demanding; but gradually psychophysiologists are more readily following the lead of physiologists in applying more refined methods for differentiating functional systems, for example, alpha- and beta-adrenergic as well as cholinergic systems, or for recognizing the many feedback loops in neuroendocrine subsystems.

2. Internal validity and reliability of assessments have improved considerably over the years by refining measurement and sampling rates, e.g., multiparameter beat-to-beat analysis in cardiovascular recordings, radio-immune-assays in the biochemical laboratory; by improving experimental tasks and controls; and by applying multivariate procedures for partitioning of covariance, response pattern analysis, etc. Research on the external validity, however, could become more interesting in the future.

3. External validity may be discussed concerning three aspects:

• Generalizability of assessed individual differences across various laboratory conditions and conditions outside the laboratory.
• Validity of laboratory measures to predict real-life criterion situations for healthy subjects and patients.
• Practical utility of psychophysiological assessments in decision making based on cost-benefit analyses.

Psychophysiological research has not yet provided such standardized assessments to predict relevant criteria so that the practical utility can be evaluated. But in the future more effort will likely be devoted to defining new paradigms and applications that may then be explored in complementary strategies of laboratory-field research and especially by ambulant monitoring of psychophysiological events.

Generalizability of Psychophysiological Assessments

An Extension from the Laboratory to the Field

The issue of external validity and the demand for more ecological validity in psychological work are both well known (e.g., Patry, 1982; Pawlik, 1988). Data acquisition in naturalistic settings is increasingly aided by the development of microprocessor-based systems for multichannel monitoring of physiological, behavioral, and self-report data outside the laboratory. There can be little doubt that psychologists should follow these new research options.

Only recently in differential psychology have more advanced designs and computer-based methods been introduced to assess simultaneously the individual's subjective state as well as behavioral and environmental data in field settings. Instead of employing diaries (Chesney & Ironson, 1989) or a beeper-and-diary combination (Hormuth, 1986), these data are recorded by the subject on a preprogrammed pocket computer in response to a sequence of items and categories presented on an LED-display. Research by Pawlik and Buse (1982) and Perrez (1988) indicates the feasibility and reliability of such methods in investigating trait consistency, subject-situation interaction, coping-characteristics, etc.

Field studies (ambulatory monitoring) in psychophysiology are designed to search for naturally occurring behavior episodes that may qualitatively (type of behavior, spontaneity) and quantitatively (range of obtained measures) differ from the laboratory settings (Fahrenberg et al., 1984; Turpin, 1985). Noteworthy is the investigation on gradients of psychophysiological activation in parachutists as a function of an approaching jump (Fenz, 1973), and also the analysis of mood states during 24-hour cardiac monitoring (Roth, Tinklenberg, Doyle, Horvath, & Kopell, 1976). Concerning psychophysiological personality traits, little research has been conducted based on ambulatory monitoring, although the many restrictions of laboratory settings are evident (see, for example, Gale & Baker, 1981). With respect to data acquisition in naturalistic settings, medical research appears to be much more advanced. Ambulatory monitoring of ECG or blood pressure in risk patients is common practice today.

The strategic combination of laboratory and field assessments can be seen as an extension of the multimodal approach. Several authors have, for example, pointed out the importance of combined laboratory-field studies in stress research (e.g., Fenz, 1973; Laux & Vossel, 1982); but only recently have psychophysiologists begun to actually test the predictability and generalizability of individual differences in activation processes (Dimsdale, 1984; Fahrenberg et al., 1984, 1986; Turner & Carroll, 1985).

The issue of laboratory-field generalizability arises particularly in blood pressure recordings. Does a casual blood pressure reading taken in the office reliably predict the individual's habitual blood pressure level during the course of daily activities (Harshfield, Hwang, Blank, & Pickering, 1989)? The external validity of psychophysiological measures, too, is an important issue in practical application of psychophysiological methods and no less so in research on trait theories which postulate psychophysiological temperament features that are relatively consistent across various situations and relatively stable across replications.

Therefore, we have conducted laboratory-field studies to test whether or not individual differences in intensity and pattern of activation exhibited in certain naturalistic field situations outside the laboratory can be reliably predicted from standardized assessment procedures in the laboratory.

The First Study

Male students of physical education (N = 58) were examined under various emotionally activating and physically demanding conditions (mental arithmetic, reaction time, free speech, cold pressor test, bicycle ergometer). The assessment included multi-channel recordings of prestart phases in an athletic stadium and performance on a 1000 m run. This multisituational assessment was repeated after three weeks, three months, and, for most (N = 42) subjects, after one year. These data together with two ECG-sleep recordings at the subject's home, which provided baseline estimates, were used to investigate predictability and generalizability of physiological and self-report measures based on a broad variety of conditions.

Maximum exercise on a bicycle ergometer in the laboratory and during a 1000 m run in the stadium is employed as a physical challenge and as a reference of the upper limit of normal physiological functioning. Would we expect a correlation coefficient between both heart rate measures of—let us say—.60 or .70 to provide for substantial prediction? Likewise, pairs of laboratory and field situations are designed for quiet conditions of psychological significance: conditions of active relaxation and conditions of anticipation of exercise.

The correlation coefficients shown in Table 18.1 indicate that significant relationships are present between individual differences found in activation in particular field situations and in corresponding conditions in the laboratory. The correlation coefficients are highest for heart rate and respiration rate between conditions of rest and relaxation in the laboratory and in the stadium, and between anticipation of ergometer exercise and relaxation prestart. Heart rate at maximal physical exertion in the laboratory and field correlate $r = .35$ (in the first examination). A prediction based on 13% of common

Table 18.1. Prediction of Individual Differences in Three Field Conditions Based on Corresponding Laboratory Assessments (see Fahrenberg et al., 1984, 1986)

Laboratory conditions	Examination	Heart rate	Respiration rate	Systolic blood pressure	Diastolic blood pressure	Tenseness
Stadium: Relaxation In-Door						
Relaxation	1	.58**	.70**	.23	.36**	.10
	2	.67**	.54**	.34**	.45**	−.07
	3	.66**	.68**	.17	.27*	.07
Stadium: Relaxation Pre-start						
Anticipation	1	.53**	.39**	.22	.42**	.01
exercise	2	.48**	.43**	.26	.17	.15
	3	.51**	.44**	.48**	.25	.01
Stadium: 1000 m Run						
Exercise	1	.35**	.39**	.32*	.33*	.11
max-	2	.38**	.39**	.33*	.25	.38**
imum	3	.56**	.48**	.56**	.37*	.42**

Correlation coefficients are based on n = 46 to n = 58 due to missing data. The examination was repeated after three weeks and three months.
*p < .05 **p < .01.

variance seems to be of little practical relevance. The coefficients for blood pressure and for self-reported tenseness are still lower and in several instances too small to reach significance. Large effects, according to Cohn's rule of thumb ($r \pm .50$ and $p < .01$), thus exist (1) for heart rate in conditions of relaxation and anticipation (but not for conditions of physical exercise); and (2) for respiration rate in relaxation conditions only.

The generalizability of measures according to Cronbach *et al.* (1972) can be investigated to provide a comprehensive statistical description of the observed variability (Jones, 1977). Generalizability coefficients depend on the relationship between variance components and allow the comparison of psychophysiological measures differentiating such essential aspects as relatively stable individual differences and the effects due to conditions and replications. In this way, too, the suitability of certain parameters for trait studies may be tested.

The generalizability study was performed for psychological and physiological data using four laboratory conditions (mental arithmetic, reaction time test, anticipation of free speech, and cold pressor test) in the first place. Noteworthy are pulse wave velocity, heart rate, respiration rate, and ventricular ejection time. These four parameters will more likely represent habitual characteristics of physiological responding than other measures in this study (Fahrenberg, Foerster, Schneider, Mueller, & Myrtek, 1986). After including four conditions from the field setting, generalizability coefficients are reduced roughly in proportion. But if both conditions of intense strain are added to the analysis, the generalizability coefficients for physiological parameters, especially for heart rate and respiration rate, sharply decrease, while the coefficients for psychological variables remain fairly consistent.

In the present context it will be interesting to examine the predictive validity of psychometric measures, especially emotionality (N-score derived from the Freiburger Persoenlichkeitsinventar, FPI) and total score of somatic complaints. Table 18.2 depicts a selection of criterion variables from the laboratory and from the field conditions. Very few significant correlations exist and generally the retention of the null hypothesis is appropriate. This conclusion likewise holds for single physiological variables and for various composite measures obtained by different modes of aggregation employing a four-component model of activation and a total score within and across the conditions of measurement.

According to these results, the psychometric assessment of emotionality would not allow any prediction of individual differences in physiological responsiveness to a variety of arousal conditions (for a more detailed research report, see Fahrenberg *et al.*, 1984, 1986).

These results have to be considered within the restrictions imposed by imperfect stability. Substantial differences in relative stability are evident between variables obtained during rest conditions. Heart rate and respiration rate appear to be the most stable physiological parameters when assessed at intervals of about three weeks, three months, and one year. Blood pressure measures seem to be less stable and individual differences in self-reported state are even less reproducible. The same pattern prevails when coefficients of stability are computed for other conditions of this experiment (Fahrenberg *et al.*, 1987).

It appears unlikely that these findings can be attributed predominantly to error of measurement, because instrumental reliability in most of the physiological methods is

**Table 18.2. Predictive Validity of Questionnaire Scores
of Emotionality (FPI-N) and Frequency
of Somatic Complaints (FBL-11) in a Multiparameter
Multisituation Study (see Fahrenberg et al., 1984, 1986)**

	Predictor	
	FPI-N	FBL-11
Laboratory: Rest		
Tenseness	.01	−.29*
Heart rate	−.10	−.03
Respiration rate	.04	.03
Systolic blood pressure	−.09	−.12
Diastolic blood pressure	.17	.15
Laboratory: Change scores rest to mental arithmetic		
Tenseness	−.09	.08
Heart rate	.21	.00
Cardiovascular component	.11	.05
Respiratory component	−.15	−.22
Eye motility component	−.13	−.12
Electrodermal component	−.17	.20
Composite score	−.19	−.06
Field: Relaxation stadium anticipating 1000 m run		
Tenseness	.20	.10
Heart rate	.03	.14
Pulse wave velocity	−.06	−.02
Respiration rate	−.08	−.08
Systolic blood pressure	.20	.23
Diastolic blood pressure	.15	.14
Field: 1000 m run		
Tenseness	.01	.04
Heart rate	.12	.04
Respiration rate	−.29*	−.24
Field: Recovery after 1000 m run		
Systolic blood pressure	−.05	.05
Diastolic blood pressure	−.01	−.15
Performance data		
Performance time 1000 m	.26*	.28*
Ergometer maximum watt	.20	−.08

Correlation coefficients based on n = 46 to n = 58 due to missing data.
*$p < .05$.   **$p < .01$.

remarkably high. These coefficients—46 variables were examined in this study—indicate that only a few assessments from a typical psychophysiological study truly depict relatively stable individual differences. Measures of individual differences that are hardly reproducible under equivalent retest conditions obviously are not suited for reliable estimation of an individual's habitual reactivity. We believe stability coefficients of at least $r = .70$ (based on an interval of three weeks) to be mandatory.

Results from our first laboratory-field comparison contradict conventional beliefs and simple diagnostic strategies which implicitly consider laboratory assessments to substantially predict an individual's physiological responsiveness in conditions of daily life that are roughly equivalent to laboratory settings. Although significant correlations may exist, the effect size generally is only low-to-medium, and thus insufficient to allow for practically relevant predictions. However, the stabilities of many physiological measures appear to be insufficient for substantial prediction of habitual characteristics, although the instrumental reliability is satisfactory in most instances. Lengthening recording intervals and aggregating systematically across intervals and conditions could further increase stabilities.

Laboratory-field comparison inevitably will evoke the basic criticism whether corresponding conditions can be considered functionally equivalent regarding their demand characteristics and specific synergisms of the activation process. Even in the present investigation that employed pairs of conditions, for example, standardized performance of physical exercise in the laboratory and field, it remains questionable to what extent an equivalent type of event ("*gleicher Geschehenstyp*," Lewin, 1927, p. 419) is present. The methodology of the laboratory-field issue and aspects of external validity have been reviewed (e.g., Patry, 1982; Stokols, 1987; Winkel, 1987); however, operational definitions concerning the equivalence of events and actual investigations concerning this issue are rare. We have studied situation aspects based on similarity ratings obtained from subjects and experts and have examined stimulus-specific response patterns in additional multivariate statistical analyses (see Fahrenberg *et al.*, 1984). The discussion of a possible alternative led to a second investigation that provides a different database, now extending to the individual's usual course of daily activities.

The Second Study

In our second laboratory-field investigation we conducted a 24-hour monitoring of largely unrestricted daily activities and sleep instead of the highly standardized conditions of pre-start and athletic performance in the stadium. The ambulatory monitoring has obvious advantages, since naturally occurring episodes of emotions, social interactions, and other behaviors may be observed. We are thus following the usual practice in ECG and blood pressure monitoring in which for medical purposes the patient's cardiovascular condition is assessed on an arbitrary day.

The multimodal assessment approach to ambulatory monitoring as recently developed in our laboratory (Heger, 1990) is a new methodology. The device consists of three recorders cased in a leather shoulder bag: the microprocessor-based 4-channel Physio-Port recorder (PAR NATIC) for noninvasive measurement of blood pressure, heart rate, respiration rate, and activity, the Walkman recorder for the subject's free commentaries on particular events, and the pocket computer CASIO PB1000. This computer is programmed to obtain self-report data from the subject at a fixed interval of one hour or even more frequently if the subject believes this to be appropriate. In this study 19 items were employed to assess environmental aspects, behavior, and momentary as well as retrospective self-ratings of mood, social interaction, and activity. Subjects receive these systems after the conventional psychophysiological assessment in the laboratory, which employs a variety of standardized physical and psychological tasks; and when returning the next day the subjects are thoroughly interviewed to obtain an additional, retrospective account of their daily course of activities.

With this equipment we have advanced to a multimodal assessment of 110 male students selected for normotensive and borderline blood pressure. The quality of these 24-hour ambulatory monitoring records were evaluated concerning several aspects like technical failures, input errors, recording artifacts, and record length, and subsequently about 80% were considered to be of sufficient overall quality for further analysis. The statistical analyses revealed substantial interindividual and intraindividual variability in psychophysiological activation process (Heger, 1990).

The primary research interest is to investigate group differences between normotensives and borderline hypertensives with respect to cardiovascular reactivity and hemodynamic pattern. These extensive recordings, however, provide a large set of data to examine further hypotheses that relate to personality reserach, especially state-trait aspects of psychophysiological activation processes and the issue of laboratory-field generalizability.

Based on these multimodal assessments, a series of hypotheses can be tested concerning whether (1) self-ratings of tenseness, positive mood, and other dimensions of well-being; and (2) physiological measures obtained by ambulatory monitoring can be predicted reliably from (1) corresponding self-ratings and (2) physiological measures recorded during various mental and physical tasks in the laboratory sessions. Generally speaking, what is the portion of ambulatory reactivity accounted for by laboratory reactivity (Fahrenberg, Heger, Foerster, & Müller, 1991)?

Predictability and generalizability will be examined for single measures and for composite scores that are aggregated across conditions and variables in terms of both state levels and change scores. It should be especially interesting to examine whether individual scores from standardized personality inventories (e.g., scores for emotionality, anxiety, anger, impulsiveness, strain, and somatic complaints) have their own predictive validity with regard to self-ratings or physiological measures obtained by ambulatory monitoring. Therefore, a set of correlation coefficients will be obtained that depict relationships between questionnaire and self-report data (psychometric data) and physiological measures of activation within the laboratory and under approximately naturalistic conditions.

The disadvantages of this design are also obvious. There is little chance of knowing whether the particular day is representative for the subject's usual life. The population of events from which the 24-hour sample comes remains unknown, although about 70% of the subjects rated this particular day as fairly or highly representative. The physiological recording represent a mixture of effects due to physical activities, movement artifacts, accidental events, and psychologically relevant episodes. In medical examinations this overall variability on an arbitrary day would be of diagnostic relevance. In psychophysiology, however, a differentiation of principal sources of variance would be more important, demanding segmentation of records and categorizing situations with respect to psychological content and amount of physical activity. The recording equipment will impose some restrictions upon the subject and may induce changes in the usual daily behavior or even phenomena of reactance in the volunteer subject. Such side effects in ambulatory monitoring will depend on the equipment and the perceived inconveniences. The general experience is that such monitoring is not too inconvenient under conditions of daily activities.

Findings from our study indicate that the blood pressure measurement and the hourly beeping of the pocket computer on the average cause significant but small heart rate changes of about 1 to 2 beats per minute; however, not an accelerating response (alarm reaction) but—probably due to interrupting ongoing physical activity— deceleration (Heger, 1990). Evaluating psychological effects of self-monitoring, of having blood pressure measurements taken automatically, and of possible reactance phenomena, of course, appears to be more difficult (for overviews, see Haynes & Horn, 1983; Chesney & Ironson, 1989; Harshfield *et al.*, 1989). It should be noted that nearly any psychological or physiological assessment will introduce additional variance due to method effects and interactions. Method variance is not specific to multimodal assessments, but of course there are characteristic sources with such procedures.

This second study should also be regarded as an exploration into the methodology of field recordings. The basic difficulties and demands for methodological refinement are quite obvious: improving recorder reliability and strategies in outlier detection, improving the measurement of physical activity to eventually adjust cardiovascular data accordingly, adapting the subjects to reduce first-day reactance effects, developing conceptually adequate sampling schedules, and theoretical structuring to advance from impressionistic data acquisition to precise hypothesis testing. Practical on-line methods to assess situational demand characteristics are not available at present and there are no elaborated contextual theories to provide a frame of reference. However, we expect to improve upon a minitypology of psychophysiological response patterns under field conditions by examining laboratory-field predictability and generalizability of individual differences. And again, we are especially interested in correlating personality traits that are defined by questionnaires, e.g., emotionality, extraversion, and impulsivity, with means and variances of self-report data and physiological measures obtained by ambulatory monitoring of these 110 subjects. These statistical analyses are not yet completed.

Conclusions

Psychophysiological personality research is in need of a critical reevaluation of traditional research questions and research methodology. Attempts to advance operationalizations of emotionality/neuroticism and anxiety as psychophysiological trait concepts have not achieved convergent validity. Recognizing this state of affairs, biologically oriented personality researchers could profit from recent advances in differential psychophysiology. Essential contributions have been made in terms of documenting response specificities, developing multicomponent models of activation processes, and refining assessment strategies to account for patterning and hierarchical organization.

Additionally, more adequate parameters of physiological systemic functioning have acquired accessibility for measurement.

Empirical evidence indicates that we need multimodal assessments, i.e., multimethod and multisituation data to depict validly an individual's patterned behavior in the relevant context of the laboratory, clinic, or field. Multimodal assessment strategies are available to personality researchers, but the general lack of interest in application and development of such methodology is noteworthy. With respect to data acquisition in naturalistic settings, medical research, on the other hand, appears to be much more advanced. Ambulatory monitoring of ECG or blood pressure are common practice today.

It is advocated that an extension of multimodal assessments from the laboratory to the field would be a rewarding approach in differential psychophysiology. Complementary research strategies that take into account aspects of external validity provide a new research option for testing psychophysiological trait theories in temperament research.

References

Andresen, B. *Differentielle Psychophysiologie valenzkonträrer Aktivierungsdimensionen.* Frankfurt/M: Peter Lang, 1987.

Brocke, B., & Battmann, W.. Die Aktivierungstheorie der Persönlichkeit. Eine systematische Darstellung und partielle Rekonstruktion. *Zeitschrift für Differentielle und Diagnostische Psychologie*, 1985, *6*, 189–213.

Buse, L., & Pawlik, K. Kretschmers Konstitutionstypologie als implizite Persönlichkeitstheorie: Selbst-Attribuierungs-Effekte in Abhängigkeit vom Körperbau-Persönlichkeits-Stereotyp. *Zeitschrift für Differentielle und Diagnostische Psychologie*, 1984, *5*, 111–129.

Cattell, R. B. The data box: Its ordering of total resources in terms of possible relational systems. In R. B. Cattell (Ed.), *Handbook of multivariate experimental psychology*. Chicago: Rand-McNally, 1966.

Cattell, R. B., & Scheier, I. H. *The meaning and measurement of neuroticism and anxiety.* New York: Ronald Press, 1961.

Chesney, M. A., & Ironson, G. H. Diaries in ambulatory monitoring. In N. Schneiderman, S. M. Weiss, & P. G. Kaufmann (Eds.), *Handbook of research methods in cardiovascular behavioral medicine.* New York: Plenum, 1989.

Cook, T. D. Postpositivist critical multiplism. In R. L. Shotland & M. M. Mark (Eds.), *Social science and social policy*. Beverly Hills, CA: Sage, 1985.

Cronbach, L. J., Gleser, G. C., Nanda, H., & Rajaratnam, N. *The dependability of behavioral measurements: Theory of generalizability for scores and profiles.* New York: Wiley, 1972.

Dembroski, T. M., & Williams, R. B. Definition and assessment of coronary-prone behavior. In N. Schneiderman, S. M. Weiss, & P. G. Kaufmann (Eds.), *Handbook of research methods in cardiovascular behavioral medicine.* New York: Plenum, 1989.

Dimsdale, J. E. Generalizing from laboratory studies to field studies of human stress physiology. *Psychosomatic Medicine*, 1984, *46*, 463–469.

Egeren, van, L. F., & Sparrow, A. W. Laboratory stress testing to assess real-life cardiovascular reactivity. *Psychosomatic Medicine*, 1989, *51*, 1–9.

Eysenck, H. J. *The biological basis of personality.* Springfield, IL: Thomas, 1967.

Eysenck, H. J. Book Review. *Personality and Individual Differences*, 1981, *2*, 173–174.

Eysenck, H. J., & Eysenck, M. W. *Personality and individual differences: A natural science approach.* New York: Plenum, 1985.

Fahrenberg, J. Psychophysiologische Methodik. In K. J. Groffmann & L. Michel (Eds.), *Enzyklopädie der Psychologie. Psychologische Diagnostik.* Vol. 4. *Verhaltensdiagnostik.* Göttingen: Hogrefe, 1983.

Fahrenberg, J. Psychophysiological individuality: A pattern analytic approach to personality research and psychosomatic medicine. In S. Rachman & T. Wilson (Eds.), *Advances in behaviour research and therapy.* Vol. 8. London: Pergamon Press, 1986.

Fahrenberg, J. Concepts of activation and arousal in the theory of emotionality (neuroticism): A multivariate conceptualization. In J. Strelau & H. J. Eysenck (Eds.), *Personality dimensions and arousal.* New York: Plenum, 1987.

Fahrenberg, J. Psychophysiological processes. In T. R. Nesselroade & R. B. Cattell (Eds.), *Handbook of multivariate experimental psychology* (2nd ed). New York: Plenum, 1988.

Fahrenberg, J. Psychophysiology of neuroticism and anxiety. In A. Gale & M. W. Eysenck (Eds.), *Handbook of individual differences: Biological perspectives.* Chichester: Wiley, in press.

Fahrenberg, J., Foerster, F., Schneider, H. J., Müller, W., & Myrtek, M. *Aktivierungsforschung im Labor-Feld-Vergleich.* München: Minerva, 1984.

Fahrenberg, J., Foerster, F., Schneider, H.J., Müller, W., & Myrtek, M. Predictability of individual differences in activation processes in a field setting based on laboratory measures. *Psychophysiology,* 1986, *23,* 323–333.

Fahrenberg, J., Heger, R., Foerster, F., & Müller, W. (1991) Differentielle Psychophysiologie von Befinden, Blutdruck und Herzfrequenz im Labor-Feld-Vergleich. *Zeitschrift für Differentielle und Diagnostische Psychologie, 12* (in press).

Fahrenberg, J., Schneider, H. J., & Safian, P. Psychophysiological assessments in a repeated-measurement design extending over a one-year interval: Trends and stability. *Biological Psychology,* 1987, *24,* 49–66.

Fahrenberg, J., Walschburger, P., Foerster, F., Myrtek, M., & Müller, W. *Psychophysiologische Aktivierungsforschung. Ein Beitrag zu den Grundlagen der multivariaten Emotions- und Stress-Theorie.* München: Minerva, 1979.

Fenz, W. D. Stress and its mastery: Predicting from laboratory to real life. *Canadian Journal of Behavioral Science,* 1973, *5,* 332–346.

Gale, A., & Baker, S. In vivo or in vitro? Some effects of laboratory environments, with particular reference to the psychophysiology experiment. In M. J. Christie & P. G. Mellet (Eds.), *Foundations of psychosomatics.* New York: Wiley, 1981.

Gale, A., & Edwards, J. A. A short critique of the psychophysiology of individual differences. *Personality and Individual Differences,* 1983, *4,* 429–435.

Gray, J. A. A critique of Eysenck's theory of personality. In H. J. Eysenck (Ed.), *A model for personality.* New York: Springer, 1981.

Hallam, R. S. *Anxiety: Psychological perspectives on panic and agoraphobia.* London: Academic Press, 1985.

Harshfield, G. A., Hwang, C., Blank, S. G., & Pickering, T. Research techniques for ambulatory blood pressure monitoring. In N. Schneiderman, S. M. Weiss, & P. G. Kaufmann (Eds.), *Handbook of research methods in cardiovascular behavioral medicine.* New York: Plenum, 1989.

Haynes, S. N., & Horn, W. F. Reactivity in behavioral observation: A review. *Behavioral Assessment,* 1983, *4,* 369–385.

Haynes, S. N., & Wilson, C. C. *Behavioral assessment. Recent advances in methods, concepts, and applications.* San Francisco, CA: Jossey Bass, 1979.

Heger, R. *Psychophysiologisches 24-Stunden-Monitoring.* Doctoral dissertation, Universität Freiburg i.Br., Frankfurt: Peter Lang, 1990.

Hellhammer, D., Florin, I., & Weiner, H. *Neurobiological approaches to human disease.* Toronto: Hans Huber, 1989.

Hormuth, S. E. The sampling of experience in situ. *Journal of Personality,* 1986, *54,* 262–293.

Iacono, W. G., & Ficken, J. W. Research strategies employing psychophysiological measures: Identifying and using psychophysiological markers. In G. Turpin (Ed.), *Handbook of clinical psychophysiology.* Chichester: Wiley, 1989.

Jones, R. R. Conceptual versus analytic uses of generalizability theory in behavioral assessment. In J. D. Cone & R. P. Hawkins (Eds.), *Behavioral assessment: New directions in clinical psychology.* New York: Brunner/Mazel, 1977.

Laux, L., & Vossel, G. Paradigms in stress research: Laboratory versus field and traits versus processes. In L. Goldberger & S. Breznitz (Eds.), *Handbook of stress. Theoretical and clinical aspects.* New York: Free Press, 1982.

Lewin, K. Gesetz und Experiment in der Psychologie. *Symposium*, 1927, *1*, 375–421.

Myrtek, M. *Constitutional psychophysiology.* New York: Academic Press, 1984.

Patry, J. L. (Ed.). *Feldforschung.* Bern: Hans Huber, 1982.

Pawlik, K. "Naturalistische" Daten für Psychodiagnostik: Zur Methodik psychodiagnostischer Felderhebungen. *Zeitschrift für Differentielle und Diagnostische Psychologie*, 1988, *9*, 169–181.

Pawlik, K., & Buse, L. Rechnergestützte Verhaltensregistrierung im Feld: Beschreibung und erste psychometrische Überprüfung einer neuen Erhebungsmethode. *Zeitschrift für Differentielle und Diagnostische Psychologie*, 1982, *3*, 101–118.

Perrez, M. Bewältigung von Alltagsbelastungen und seelische Gesundheit. Zusammenhänge auf der Grundlage computer-unterstützter Selbstbeobachtungs- und Fragebogendaten. *Zeitschrift für Klinische Psychologie*, 1988, *17*, 292–306.

Rösler, F. Physiologisch orientierte Forschungsstrategien in der differentiellen und diagnostischen Psychologie. II. Zur Systematisierung psychophysiologischer Untersuchungen. *Zeitschrift für Differentielle und Diagnostische Psychologie*, 1984, *5*, 7–36.

Roth, W. T., Tinklenberg, J. R., Doyle, C. M., Horvath, T. B., & Kopell, B. S. Mood states and 24-hour cardiac monitoring. *Journal of Psychosomatic Research*, 1976, *20*, 179–186.

Stelmack, R. M. The psychophysiology of extraversion and neuroticism. In H. J. Eysenck (Ed.), *A model for personality.* New York: Springer, 1981.

Stemmler, G., & Fahrenberg, J. Psychophysiological assessment: Conceptual, psychometric, and statistical issues. In G. Turpin (Ed.), *Handbook of clinical psychology.* Chichester: Wiley, 1989.

Stemmler, G., & Meinhardt, E. Personality, situation and physiological arousability. *Personality and Individual Differences*, 1990, *11*, 293–308.

Stokols, D. Conceptual strategies of environmental psychology. In D. Stokols & I. Altman (Eds.), *Handbook of environmental psychology.* New York: Wiley, 1987.

Strelau, J., & Eysenck, H. J. (Eds.). *Personality dimensions and arousal.* New York: Plenum, 1987.

Turner, J. R., & Carroll, D. The relationship between laboratory and 'real world' heart-rate reactivity: An exploratory study. In J. F. Orlebeke, G. Mulder, & L. J. P. van Doornen (Eds.), *Psychophysiology of cardiovascular control: Models, methods, and data.* New York: Plenum, 1985.

Turpin, G. Ambulatory psychophysiological monitoring: Techniques and applications. In D. Papakostopoulos, S. Butler, & I. Martin (Eds.), *Clinical and experimental neuropsychophysiology.* London: Croom Helm, 1985.

Winkel, G. H. Implications of environmental context for validity assessments. In D. Stokols & I. Altman (Eds.), *Handbook of environmental psychology.* New York: Wiley, 1987.

Wittmann, W. W. Multivariate reliability theory: Principles of symmetry and successful validation strategies. In J. R. Nesselroade & R. B. Cattell (Eds.), *Handbook of multivariate experimental psychology* (2nd ed.). New York: Plenum, 1988.

Zuckerman, M. (Ed.). *Biological bases of sensation seeking, impulsivity and anxiety.* Hillsdale, NJ: Erlbaum, 1983b.

Zuckerman, M. Brain monoamine systems and personality. In D. Hellhammer, I. Florin, & H. Weiner (Eds.), *Neurobiological approaches to human disease.* Toronto: Hans Huber, 1989.

III

Addendum

In the Addendum, Strelau outlines the most typical features of contemporary temperament research. The main reference for his discussion is a list of temperament traits and the psychometric methods aimed at measuring temperament in adults.

19

Renaissance in Research on Temperament
Where To?

Jan Strelau

Introduction

"The modern history of temperament research began in the late 1950s with the New York Longitudinal Study conducted by Alexander Thomas, Stella Chess, and their colleagues" (Plomin, 1986, p. ix). This statement holds true for the United States only.

Exactly the same can be said in referring to the research on temperament conducted since the mid-1950s by Boris M. Teplov (Moscow) and Vulf S. Merlin (Perm, Ural) and their students in Russia.

Credit should be given to the New York researchers first of all for their interactional approach to temperament and for their unique longitudinal study in children temperament.

The Russian psychologists and psychophysiologists adapted the Pavlovian typology of the nervous system (NS) properties to man. They developed Pavlov's idea of the significance of temperamental traits in human adjustment and behavior and concentrated on studying the physiological backgrounds of the separate NS traits considered as the basis for temperament.

The question arises whether there is something in common in the schools mentioned above (Thomas and Chess, Teplov and Merlin), considered the initiators of the contemporary approach in temperament research.

First of all, it has to be stated that both groups rejected the constitutional approach to temperament, represented in Europe by E. Kretschmer (1944) and in the United States by W. H. Sheldon (Sheldon & Stevens, 1942). For constitutional psychologists, tempera-

Jan Strelau • Department of Individual Differences, Faculty of Psychology, University of Warsaw, 00-183 Warsaw, Poland.

ment, strongly connected with the content of behavior, has been regarded almost as a synonym for personality. The title of Kretschmer's classic monograph *Koerperbau und Charakter* (with more than 20 editions to date), in which he describes his typology of temperament, may serve as a synthetic argument for the statement given above. Thomas and Chess, as well as Teplov and Merlin, have limited the phenomenon of temperament to rather formal aspects of behavior. For the New Yorkers it is the stylistic side (the "how") of behavior. In the case of the Russians it is the energetic and temporal characteristic of human activity.

Also, the argument that there exist links between the constitutional makeup, understood as the shape of the physique, and the temperamental (personality) traits has been rejected by both groups as scientifically groundless. For the same reason, the notion of links between temperament and proneness to psychiatric illnesses has declined.

Finally, both groups—the Russians and the New Yorkers—did not limit their research to the description of temperamental traits, mostly combined into types, as was typical of the constitutional approach. The new tendency, present in both schools, was to bind the individual's temperament with real-life situations and with behavior in these situations.

One more feature shared by both schools, and negative in essence, has to be mentioned. This is a complete or almost complete isolation from each other, as well as from temperamental studies conducted by individuals representing other lines of thinking in this area. This isolation, which cannot be explained by political and language reasons only, bore consequences for the next decades of research in temperament.

As mentioned earlier, credit has to be given to the initiators of modern research in temperament—Thomas and Chess and Teplov and Merlin—for different reasons. This also means that in the 1950s there existed essential differences[1] in the theoretical backgrounds and in the ways of studying temperament between the two groups living in separate hemispheres. The following three seem to be the most important:

1. Teplov and Merlin developed their theory of temperament referring to nervous system properties understood as explanatory concepts. In Thomas and Chess's theory no use was made of any physiological interpretation in order to explain the status of temperamental traits.
2. Experimental and laboratory studies, including psychophysiological and electrophysiological methods, were typical for the Russian experts in temperament, whereas Thomas and Chess mainly used clinical and "paper-and-pencil" techniques (interviews and inventories) as means for studying temperament.
3. Adults were the main population to which research on temperament conducted in Teplov's and Merlin's laboratories refers. The American scholars studied temperament only or preponderantly in children.

The Last Three Decades in Studies on Temperament

The three decades which have passed since the beginning of the modern approach to studies on temperament may be characterized as a period of essential development of

---

[1]There also exist remarkable differences between Teplov's and Merlin's approach to temperament described in detail elsewhere (Strelau, 1983a, 1985a).

temperament research which grew both in the number of studies and the range of problems being attacked. Bates (1986), who computed the abstracts dealing with temperament in children being published between 1967 and mid-1983, stated that 62% of the publications (comprising 162 articles) have been published since 1980. Plomin, analyzing *Psychological Abstracts*, concluded that "since 1970 the number of articles on temperament has increased by 50% each 5 years" (Plomin, 1986, p. ix). The growing interest in studies on temperament has been also cited by Strelau and Angleitner (see Introduction, this volume).

In spite of this development, there still do not exist lines of communication between researchers centered around Thomas and Chess[2] and the followers of Teplov and Merlin. In Thomas and Chess's 1977 monograph *Temperament and Development*, Pavlov's name was mentioned only once. No study or name from Eastern Europe is included. Only one temperament researcher representing other lines of thought is mentioned—W. H. Sheldon. Almost the same may be said of other publications stemming from the Thomas and Chess group, as, for example, *The Study of Temperament: Changes, Continuities and Challenges* edited by Plomin[3] and Dunn (1986). Among the chapters included in this volume, written by 24 American experts in temperament, in only one (Buss & Plomin, 1986) has an East European temperament researcher been cited. The same holds true if we consider the books and papers on temperament published by Soviet psychologists, where the achievements of the American temperament researchers are not taken into account. Only recently may growing interest in studies on temperament conducted in the United States be observed (see, e.g., Ravich-Shcherbo, 1988).

The Warsaw temperament group seems to be one of the rare exceptions as regards international communication in this field of study. The regulative theory of temperament developed by Strelau and his students (see Eliasz, 1985; Klonowicz, 1987; Strelau, 1983a, 1983b, 1985a, 1985b) takes into account the theories and facts stemming from the Soviet Union as well as from the West, including the Thomas-Chess group (see, e.g., Strelau, 1983a, 1984, 1987a, 1987b).

The statement that cooperation does not exist between the East European researchers in temperament and representatives in this field of research in the West should be limited, however, to the Thomas-Chess group.

Since the 1960s, efforts have been undertaken to build bridges between the Pavlovian and neo-Pavlovian concepts of temperament and biologically based personality dimensions, also labeled temperamental traits (see Eysenck & Eysenck, 1985; Gray, 1973; Mangan, 1982; Strelau, 1983a; Zuckerman, 1985), introduced by psychologists from the West. Gray (1964), who rendered part of the contribution of the Teplov-Nebylitsyn school for the English-speaking reader, has shown that there exist similarities between the strength of the NS and the arousability concept, to which most of the biologically based personality (temperament) dimensions refer (see Strelau & Eysenck,

[2]When the Thomas-Chess followers or group is mentioned, this has to be understood very broadly. Many of the researchers covered by this label do not identify themselves with the Thomas and Chess theory of temperament (e.g., Goldsmith, Rothbart, Plomin, etc.). All or most of them participate, however, in the so-called "Occasional Temperament Conferences" initiated by Thomas and Chess and taking place in the United States only.
[3]Plomin belongs to the small group of American researchers who pay attention to temperamental studies based on other than their own theoretical backgrounds.

1987). In a paper presented in 1966 at the XXI International Congress of Psychology in Moscow, Eysenck has shown the links between the strength of the NS and extraversion-introversion (Eysenck, 1966, 1972; see also Gray, 1967). From the beginning of 1972, several initiatives have been undertaken to search for similarities and differences between the Pavlovian and neo-Pavlovian properties and such temperament dimensions as extraversion, neuroticism, psychoticism, anxiety, sensation-seeking, and augmenting/reducing (see, e.g., Claridge, 1985; Corulla, 1989; Kohn, Cowles, & Lafrenier, 1987; Mangan, 1982; Nebylitsyn & Gray, 1972; Strelau, 1983a; Strelau, Angleitner, & Ruch, 1989; Strelau & Eysenck, 1987; Strelau, Farley, & Gale, 1985, 1986).

It is worth stating that researchers studying the temperament (personality) dimensions listed above in fact do not refer at all to the contribution of Thomas and Chess and their followers, and the opposite is true, though with some exceptions (e.g., Buss & Plomin, 1984; Plomin & Dunn, 1986; Windle, 1989).

This state of affairs in research on temperament, of which isolation between groups and schools is typical, challenges us to raise the question whether the notion "temperament" has, in all the theories and conceptualizations mentioned until now, the same meaning. The answer to this question is no, and pages of definitions of the concept "temperament" might be given in support of this statement. Recently a roundtable discussion on *What Is Temperament?* was published (Goldsmith, Buss, Plomin, Rothbart, Thomas, Chess, Hinde, & McCall, 1987). Seven discussants, mostly bound with the Thomas-Chess group in studying temperament, have given seven different definitions of temperament.

In spite of differences in the understanding of temperament, it seems that all researchers in this field, independent of their specific subject of study and approach to solving problems, refer to the same category of phenomena having in common several features which give reason to consider them under the label "temperament."

Recently I have described these features in order to show how the notions "temperament" and "personality" can be differentiated (Strelau, 1987a; see also Hofstee, this volume). Taking this comparison into account, it can be stated that temperament reveals itself in relatively stable individual differences in behavior. These differences are present since early childhood (see Bates, 1987; Buss & Plomin, 1984; Thomas & Chess, 1977) and they may be seen not only in man but also in animals (see Broadhurst, 1975; Eysenck & Eysenck, 1985; Matysiak, 1980; Simonov, 1987; Zuckerman, 1979). They refer mainly to the formal characteristics of behavior (see Strelau, 1983a; Teplov, 1985; Thomas & Chess, 1977), and the variance of this behavior is determined to a high degree by biological factors (Buss & Plomin, 1984; Eysenck, 1967; Eysenck & Eysenck, 1985; Nebylitsyn, 1972; Rothbart & Posner, 1985; Strelau, 1983a; Zuckerman, 1985).

Taking these characteristics of the concept "temperament" as a point of departure, it might be concluded that the variety of studies represented by different schools, groups, and individuals, like the research conducted by Thomas, Chess, and their followers, the Pavlovian and neo-Pavlovian approach to NS properties, the majority of studies concerned with such dimensions as, for example, extraversion-introversion, sensation-seeking or augmenting/reducing and the investigations conducted by Strelau and his students, refer to temperament.

Taking into account the variety of approaches and studies to be met in the field of temperament, the question may be put forward, what are the most typical features of contemporary temperament research? A list of them, far from being complete, comprises the following characterisitics:

1. An enormous number of traits (dimensions) is covered by the label "temperament" and concomitant with this is an unbelievable growth of diagnostic methods (see, e.g., Hubert, Wachs, Peters-Martin, & Gandour, 1982; see also Slabach, Morrow, & Wachs, this volume).

2. Psychometric methods dominate experimental studies in diagnosing temperament, this being especially typical in studies on children (see Bates, 1986; Buss & Plomin, 1984; Plomin & Dunn, 1986; Thomas & Chess, 1977; see also Goldsmith & Rothbart, this volume).

3. The quest for determinants of individual differences in temperament shows an increasing number of studies in behavior genetics (e.g., Goldsmith, in press; Matheny & Dolan, 1980; Plomin, 1982; Ravich-Shcherbo, 1988; Torgersen, 1985).

4. Inquiries after physiological mechanisms underlying temperament—psychophysiological, electrophysiological, neuropsychological, and biochemical studies on man and animals—are conducted on selected temperament dimensions with special attention to mechanisms regulating the level of arousal (see Gray, 1982; Schalling, Edman, & Asberg, 1983; Simonov, 1987; Zuckerman, 1979, 1985, 1988; see also Eysenck, Gray, Netter, and Zuckerman, this volume).

5. Studies on temperament comprise the whole range of ages—from infancy to old age—with a new tendency to develop a life-span approach (e.g., Lerner & Lerner, 1983; Plomin, Pedersen, McClearn, Nesselroade, & Bergeman, 1988; Thomas & Chess, 1977).

6. Search for consistency of temperamental characteristics with a special interest in early childhood development (see, e.g., Giuganino & Hindley, 1982; Hagekuell, 1989; Matheny, 1983; Plomin & Dunn, 1986; see also Rothbart, this volume).

7. Exposure is given the regulatory functions of temperament and studies based on contextual and interactional approaches to temperament (e.g., Carey, 1985; Eliasz, 1981, 1985; Klonowicz, 1987; Rothbart & Posner, 1985; Strelau, 1983a, 1983b; Thomas & Chess, 1977; see also Rothbart and Van Heck, this volume).

8. Concentration on the role of temperament in human adaptation and real life situations with special attention to behavior in family, school, and occupational environments and to developmental and behavioral disorders (e.g., Burks & Rubenstein, 1979; Carey & McDevitt, 1989; Chess & Thomas, 1986; Eliasz & Wrzesniewski, 1986; Klonowicz, 1985, 1987; Strelau, 1983a, 1988; see also Chess & Thomas, and Talwar, Nitz, Lerner, & Lerner, this volume).

9. Expansion of the interdisciplinary approach to research on temperament: studies on temperament are conducted, among others, by psychologists, psychophysiologists, neuropsychologists, behavior geneticists, psychiatrists, pediatricians, and pedagogists, thus ensuring a variety of perspectives on temperament investigations (e.g., Carey & McDevitt, 1989; Kohnstamm, Bates, & Rothbart, 1989; Plomin & Dunn, 1986; Strelau, Farley, & Gale, 1985, 1986).

It must be noted that no one of the temperament theories, research groups, or schools comprises all of the characteristics typical for contemporary research on temperament. This is, among other factors, due to limited possibilities individuals and groups have in searching for regularities and laws of human behavior. It is also not possible to present here in detail the whole state of affairs in modern temperament psychology. For this very reason I have decided to concentrate on the first itemized characteristic only. Where possible, however, I shall refer to other features of modern temperament studies.

Invation of Traits (Dimensions) and Diagnostic Tools in Temperament Research

The statement that research on temperament concentrates on an enormous number of traits, accompanied by a variety of methods for measuring them, should be first considered in categories of positive evaluations. It reflects the concern to comprise the whole riches of human behavior, the aspiration to study temperament from many different perspectives, as well as the high level of research activity in this field. In the context of efforts to reduce the whole personality, including temperament, to three dimensions, as proposed by Eysenck (1970), to the "big five" factors, as suggested by Norman (1963), or even to sixteen, as proposed by Cattell (1965), it has to be asked whether proliferation of temperamental traits is the course to take.

On the basis of accessible psychometric tools used for diagnosing temperament in adults, a list of over 80 traits (dimensions, factors) is presented in Appendix 1. Since the number of "paper-and-pencil" temperament measures seems far from exhausted, it might be expected that the quantity of temperamental traits under study goes far beyond a hundred. The variety of traits can be subjected to analysis from many points of view, some of which are presented below.

One versus Many Temperament Dimensions

Temperament theories differ, among other elements, in the number of dimensions to be comprised by the label "temperament." This depends to a high degree on whether temperament refers to some aspect of all kinds of behavior (see, e.g., Rothbart & Posner, 1985; Strelau, 1983a; Thomas & Chess, 1977), or whether it is limited to selected behaviors. A good example of the latter is Goldsmith and Campos's (1982) concept of temperament, where temperament comprises emotionality only. Taking our list of temperament variables as the point of departure, it can be easily stated that in several temperament theories the structure of adult temperament comprises a large number of traits (factors). For example, according to Windle and Lerner (1986), adult temperament comprises 10 traits. The same number, however, different in quality, has been offered by Guilford, Zimmerman, and Guilford (1976). The question arises, how do these traits relate to the temperament characteristics present in other theories?

In temperament research, examples may be found where, in spite of the consciousness that temperament comprises more then one trait, only one dimension is the subject of investigation, as is the case in studies on reducing-augmenting, or sensation-seeking. Their main disadvantage consists in very fragmentary characteristics of temperament, generally isolated from other traits. At the same time, some of these studies have virtues not to be met in other temperament approaches. For example, research on sensation-seeking, as conducted by Zuckerman (1979, 1984), gives detailed information about: the structure of this trait, the physiological mechanism underlying it, the determinants of individual differences in sensation-seeking, its relation to certain other temperamental traits, its importance in human behavior, and the ways to study it.

The Many Traits and Cumulative Value of Temperament Research

It seems reasonable that studies on temperament are conducted within a given theoretical framework. This means, among other principles, that they are limited to traits hypothesized by the given theory. The more than 80 temperamental traits listed stem from many theories and concepts, which means that, in fact, only a few of the traits are taken into account in a real study.

Research can be characterized as progressive if facts to be discovered can be cumulated and related to each other. This requires that at least two steps be taken in temperament studies. First, data obtained within a given theoretical framework have to be compared with data to be found in other temperament approaches. This obvious principle is not realized in practice, since most temperament researchers are secluded in their own worlds without taking notice of other facts and theories in temperament research. Only recently, some studies have been undertaken in order to show how the different temperament concepts and traits relate to each other (see, e.g., Strelau *et al.*, 1989; Windle, 1989).

Second, the large number of traits has to be reduced to a reasonable quantity, taking into account the specific developmental stages in which differences in the behavioral expression of temperament occur. This task waits to be undertaken. There are different ways of reducing or of clustering traits (dimensions) to a reasonable number and to the proper level of generality. Probably the most common approach is factor analysis based on traits (scales) taken from different diagnostic tools (see, e.g., Corulla, 1989; Mangan, 1982; Zuckerman, Kuhlman, & Camac, 1988). However, this way has not yet led, at least in the psychology of temperament, to satisfactory solutions. Another method, which gains more and more popularity in personality research, is the lexical approach. As is known, it led, among other things, to the solution of the so-called "big five" factors to which the variety of personality traits, including some temperament characteristics (as e.g., extraversion, neuroticism) tend to be reduced (see Costa & McCrae, 1988; John, Angleitner, & Ostendorf, 1988; Norman, 1963).

The Structure of Temperament Needs to Be Described by Traits Representing the Same Level of Behavior Organization

The traits presented in Appendix 1 represent different levels of generality. For example, activity and extraversion seem to be traits which refer to a broad range of behavioral characteristics, whereas attention span and affect intensity are very narrow concepts.

Some traits from the list should be regarded as subcomponents of more general factors (traits). This is, for example, the case with rhythmicity, which assumes a more specific shape, like rhythmicity-daily habits, rhythmicity-eating, or rhythmicity-sleep

(Windle & Lerner, 1986). The question arises, however, whether such specific traits, rather considered as habits (see Eysenck, 1970), should be on the temperament list at all.[4] More important, it should be clear which of the traits have to be regarded as first-order (e.g., rhythmicity-eating), second-order (e.g., rhythmicity) and third-order factors (e.g., extraversion). The most reasonable comparison of traits takes place if it is carried out on the same level of the structure of temperament.

The Temperamental Traits Less Diverse Than Names Suggest

Many of the traits having different labels indeed refer to very similar aspects of behavior, thus suggesting that factor-analytic studies in which these traits are included should essentially reduce their number. To give one example, the following dimensions may be mentioned: activity, approach, arousability, ergonicity, extraversion, sensation-seeking, impulsivity, intensity, reactivity, reducing-augmenting, sociability, and strength of the nervous system. Evidence for links between some of the traits listed above already exists. For example, we know today pretty much about the relationships among extraversion, sensation-seeking, reducing-augmenting, strength of the NS and impulsivity (see Kohn et al., 1987; Strelau & Eysenck, 1987; Zuckerman, 1983; Zuckerman et al., 1988; see also Windle 1989 for studying relationships between scales taken from EPI, EASI, and DOTS-R).

In one of our studies (Ruch, Angleitner, & Strelau, 1990) conducted on 102 adult subjects, eight different temperament and personality diagnostic tools were used with the purpose of examining the relationships among the traits being measured. The application of the Personality Research Form (PRF), Eysenck Personality Questionnaire-Revised (EPQ-R), I_7 Impulsiveness Questionnaire (I_7), Claridge and Broks's STQ, Affect Intensity Measure (AIM), Telic Dominance Scale (TDS), and the German Adjective List (GAL)[5] aimed at diagnosing the 5 Norman factors, allowed to measure 34 temperament/personality traits (dimensions). A factor analysis with Varimax rotation and Scree test resulted in separating 5 factors which illustrate the interdependencies among the traits under discussion. The factors, with loadings only $> .30$ are presented in Table 19.1.

Not to go into details elsewhere described (Ruch et al., in press), the factor analysis shows that the traits being measured are in many cases not orthogonal to each other. The many relationships being found stimulate thinking about links between the different temperament/personality dimensions, or even concepts.

Not All So-Called Temperament Traits Pertain to Temperament

Among the many traits listed in Appendix 1 are those which, according to our understanding of temperament, should not appear on the temperament list. Taking the characteristics of temperament given on page 341 as the basis for our judgment, for

---

[4]This does not contradict the fact that information about these habits concerning rhythmicity may be important for clinical purposes or in early education.
[5]For a detailed description of these inventories see Ruch et al. (in press).

Table 19.1. Factor Analysis (with Varimax Rotation) of 34 Temperament/Personality Traits—with Loadings > .30 (adapted from Ruch et al., in press)

Scales		I	II	III	IV	V
EPQ	P	.69				
	E	.33			.72	
	N		−.76			
I₇	Imp	.60	−.34			
	Ven	.70			.32	
	Emp			.80		
TDS	SM					
	PO	−.65				
	AA	−.77				
AIM	AI		−.34	.62		
STQ	STA		−.65			
	STB		−.70			
GAL	Sur		.35		.60	
	Agr		.56			
	Con	−.62	.34		.41	
	EmS		.79			
	Cul		.37		.39	
PRF	Ac					.71
	Af			.71	.33	
	Ag		−.64			
	Do				.70	
	En					.64
	Ex				.73	
	Ha	−.59				
	Im	.70				
	Nu			.71		
	Or	−.74				
	Pl	.52				−.55
	Sr			.57		
	Su			.68		
	Un	.39				
STI	SE	.39		−.33	.41	.37
	SI		.69			
	MO	.37	.59			

example, some of the factors to be measured by the Guilford-Zimmerman Temperament Survey should be excluded. One can hardly accept the view that individual differences in such traits as, for example, ascendance or objectivity are mainly determined by biological factors or that they are present in early stages of human development. These strongly content-saturated traits, the variance of which is essentially the result of the social environment, are good examples of personality characteristics. Taking as a criterion the features of items from which inventories are composed, Angleitner and Riemann (this volume) have shown that whereas items taken from personality inventories are mostly content-saturated, the temperament items refer mainly to the formal, stylistic aspects of behavior.

Temperamental Traits Differ in Evidence for Heritability

Most of the temperament theories or concepts dealing with single temperament dimensions are based on the assumption that individual differences in temperament have an evident biological background (see Eysenck, 1967, 1970; Goldsmith, 1983; Rothbart & Derryberry, 1981; Strelau, 1983a; Teplov, 1985; Zuckerman 1985), genetically determined, or as a result of the genotype-environment interaction. The most extreme position regarding the determination of individual differences in temperament is represented by Buss and Plomin, who regard as temperamental dimensions only ". . . inherited personality traits present in early childhood" (Buss & Plomin 1984, p. 84; see also Buss, this volume).

The idea that individual differences in temperament have strong biological determination has engendered increasing interest in temperament studies based on behavior genetics. Eysenck, on the basis of many studies comprising extraversion, neuroticism, and psychoticism, concludes that ". . . twin studies suggest a narrow heritability for temperamental traits of around 50%, which, when corrected for attenuation, suggests heritabilities between 60 and 70%" (Eysenck & Eysenck, 1985, p. 96). Also, the genetic determination of individual differences in sensation-seeking has broad evidence (see Eysenck, 1983; Zuckerman, 1979). The same may be said about such temperamental traits as activity, emotionality, and sociability (see Buss & Plomin, 1984), as well as about some other traits referring to the Thomas-Chess theory of temperament (see Goldsmith, 1983; Torgersen, 1985). Since the end of the 1960s, Soviet psychophysiologists of the Teplov-Nebylitsyn school have conducted a series of studies to examine the genetic backgrounds of individual differences in such traits as strength of excitation (e.g., Shlakhta & Panteleyeva, 1978), mobility and lability of nervous processes (e.g., Ravich-Shcherbo, 1976), and activatability (arousability) of the nervous system (e.g., Ravich-Shcherbo, Shlakhta, & Shibarovskaya, 1969). As summarized by Strelau (1983a), the results of these studies are far from being unequivocal regarding the influence of the genotype in determining individual differences in these traits.

In the case of many traits mentioned in the list, no studies concerning the determinants of their variance have been conducted. This refers to such traits as affect intensity, reactivity, or reducing-augmenting. It has to be stressed, however, that biological determination, essential for a temperamental trait, does not prejudge whether a trait has high or low heritability (see Goldsmith *et al.*, 1987; Strelau, 1983a).

Different Temperamental Traits under the Same Label and Differences in their Popularity

Some of the traits listed in Appendix 1 are specific for given schools or research groups, as, for example, adaptability, rhythmicity, and distractability, which originate, among other traits, from the Thomas-Chess theory, or strength of the nervous system and mobility of nervous processes, to be studied by neo-Pavlovian researchers. In the case of these traits we know approximately what they mean and how they can be measured. There are also, however, traits which, in spite of having the same label, stem from different theoretical approaches. Activity, approach, reducing-augmenting, or impulsivity seem to be good examples here. Referring to these traits without the specific theoretical context in which they occur leads to many misunderstandings. For example, according to Wilson, Barrett, and Gray (1989) approach is considered as a temperament trait which refers to the responsiveness to stimuli in the environment that are associated with primary rewards, whereas Windle and Lerner (1986) characterize approach by typical response patterns to new persons, situations, or events.

As can be seen from the list, some of the traits can be measured by several diagnostic tools (e.g., activity, impulsivity, sociability). In this case the comment in the last paragraph holds true. Other traits are rather unique, i.e., they occur isolated in specific diagnostic methods, mostly based on theories not having links to other temperament approaches (e.g., solidity or validity taken from the MNT questionnaire, ergonicity and plasticity as measured by the STQ, or active avoidance and fight from the GWPQ). There is no reason to ignore them, but the responsibility to show how they relate to other temperamental traits or theories belongs to the authors of those concepts.

Neutral Traits versus Traits with Evaluative Loading

Teplov and Nebylitsyn (1963) formulated in the beginning of the 1960s several methodological principles to be obeyed in studies on NS properties, understood as explanatory concepts in temperament research. One of the principles states:

> The student of TNS must renounce any evaluative attitude and take the view that NS properties are neither good nor bad, each being simply associated with the specific form of the organism's adjustment to the environment. (Strelau, 1983a, p. 28)

On the basis of our own studies we were able to show that temperamental traits play different regulatory functions, thus changing their value depending on the context in which they occur. For example, high reactivity which decreases performance under high stimulation increases work efficiency under low stimulation (see Strelau, 1983a, 1988). Temperamental traits, being bipolar, cannot as such be estimated in positive or negative categories. For this very reason evaluative labels in identifying temperamental traits should be avoided. This evaluative tendency is strongly expressed in temperament research on children. For example, Bates's Infant Children Questionnaire sets up to measure a trait called "difficult." The concept "difficult child," understood as a result of a specific configuration of temperamental traits and introduced by Thomas & Chess (1977), is well known among temperament researchers in children.

The interactional approach makes us treat temperamental traits as having different meanings and values, depending on with which external (environmental) and internal components they are in interaction. As Rothbart states: "What is seen as difficult in one situation may not be difficult in another" (Goldsmith et al., 1987, p. 521).

We should learn from the experience accumulated in intelligence studies that evaluative labels concerning traits remove from parents and educators the responsibility for inefficient teaching and upbringing. This is true too when a child is described as being difficult.

Uncontrolled Growth of Psychometric Methods in Temperament Research

The enormous number of temperamental traits (dimensions) goes together with an unusual increase in diagnostic techniques to be used in this field of study. Hubert *et al.* (1982), reviewing the instruments used in diagnosing early temperament and based mainly on the Thomas-Chess theory, describe 26 diagnostic tools. A few years later the number has grown to 30 psychometric measures of child temperament (see Slabach, Morrow, & Wachs, this volume). Taking into account only these psychometric tools which are aimed at diagnosing temperament in adults, I was able to identify 25 "paper-and-pencil" techniques (see Appendix 2). The list of psychometric tools for diagnosing temperament traits in adults comprises:[6]

1. Inventories which are labeled as temperament diagnostic tools (e.g., EASTS, STI-R) even if some of the traits, as in the case of GZTS, hardly can be considered as belonging to the domain of temperament.
2. Inventories which are aimed at measuring a single trait/dimension (e.g., RAS, RS, or AIM) believed to belong to the structure of temperament or to so-called primary (biologically determined) personality characteristics considered synonyms for temperament.
3. Personality inventories based on the assumption that temperament and personality are interchangeable concepts. This position is typical for biologically oriented researchers, as, e.g., Eysenck (Eysenck & Eysenck, 1985) or Gray (1983); and such inventories as EPI, EPQ, and GWPQ are good examples here.

For an expert in constructing questionnaires, it is not difficult to find among the many temperament methods those which are far from fulfilling the basic psychometric criteria for an acceptable instrument (see Angleitner & Riemann, this volume). In the field of psychometric methods aimed at diagnosing temperament in children, this state of affair has been shown by Hubert *et al.* (1982; see also Slabach *et al.*, this volume).

The number of psychometric methods does not go together with experimental studies on temperament, the latter being especially developed among East European researchers (see Mangan, 1982; Nebylitsyn, 1972; Strelau, 1983a; Teplov, 1985). Experimental manipulations in which temperamental traits are involved go beyond the descriptive level which dominates in temperament research. Experimental data should be used, among other evidences, as measures of validation of the psychometric tools. There exist, however, difficulties concerning the level of generality to which a given temperamental trait is expressed in behavior under experimental control (see Andresen, 1987; Fahrenberg, 1987; Nebylitsyn, 1972, Strelau, 1972, 1983a; see also Amelang & Ullwer, Fahrenberg & Kohn, this volume).

---

[6]Personality inventories which comprise the whole or a broad domain of personality traits (factors), such as values, interests, attitudes, etc., including temperament traits, are not listed here, as, e.g., Cattell's 16PF or Jackson's PRF.

Final Remarks

There is no ready recipe for what should be done to advance our knowledge of temperament. Indeed, many different recipes should be proposed, taking into account the specific approach in studying temperament. One conclusion, however, can be drawn from this chapter without any doubt. To summarize, more international, interdisciplinary, and intergroup cooperation is needed in order to raise the level of communication among temperament researchers and to increase the integration and cummulative value of data in this field of study.

ACKNOWLEDGMENT. Preparation of this chapter was supported by the Minister of National Education (Grant RPBP III.25).

Appendix 1. Temperamental Traits to Be Measured in Adults by Psychometric Tools

Active Avoidance
Wilson, Barrett, & Gray (GWPQ)

Activity (Active)
Buss & Plomin (EASTS)
Thomas & Chess (NYLSQ)
Thurstone (TTS)

Activity Level—Sleep
Windle & Lerner (DOTS-R Adult)

Adaptability
Thomas & Chess (NYLSQ)

Affect Intensity
Larsen & Diener (AIM)

Anger
Buss & Plomin (EASTS)

Approach (Withdrawal)
Windle & Lerner (DOTS-R Adult)
Wilson, Barrett, & Gray (GWPQ)

Arousability (Trait-Arousal)
Mehrabian (SSQ), (MTS)

Ascendance
Guilford & Zimmerman (GZTS)

Attention Span
Thomas & Chess (NYLSQ)

Balance of Nervous Processes
Strelau (STI)
Strelau, Angleitner, Bantelmann, & Ruch (STI-R)

Boredom Susceptibility
Zuckerman (SSS IV & V)

Choleric
Cruise, Blitchington, & Futcher (TI)

Cognitive Impulsiveness
Barratt (BIS-10)

Disinhibition
Zuckerman (SSS IV & V)

Distractability
Thomas & Chess (NYLSQ)
Windle & Lerner (DOTS-R Adult)

Distress
Buss & Plomin (EASTS)

Dominant (Trait-Dominance)
Mehrabian (MTS)
Thurstone (TTS)

Emotional Stability (Emotionally Stable)
Guilford & Zimmerman (GZTS)
Thurstone (TTS)

Emotional Susceptibility
Caprara, Cinanni, D'Imperio, Passerini, Renzi, & Travaglia (IESS)

Emotionality
Feij (ATL)
Rusalov (STQ)

Empathy
Eysenck, Pearson, Easting, & Allsopp (I_7 Questionnaire)

Ergonicity
Rusalov (STQ)

Experience Seeking
Zuckerman (SSS IV & V)

Extinction
Wilson, Barrett, & Gray (GWPQ)

Extraversion
Eysenck & Eysenck (EPI), (EPQ)
Feij (ATL)

Fearfulness
Buss & Plomin (EASTS)

Fight
Wilson, Barrett, & Gray (GWPQ)

Flexibility (Rigidity)
Windle & Lerner (DOTS-R Adult)

Flight
Wilson, Barrett, & Gray (GWPQ)

Friendliness
Guilford & Zimmerman (GZTS)

General Activity
Guilford & Zimmerman (GZTS)
Windle & Lerner (DOTS-R Adult)

Impulsiveness (Impulsivity, Impulsive)
Barratt (BIS-10)
Eysenck, Pearson, Easting, & Allsopp (I_7 Questionnaire)
Feij (ATL)
Thurstone (TTS)

Intensity
Thomas & Chess (NYLSQ)

Irritability
Caprara, Cinanni, D'Imperio, Passerini, Renzi, & Travaglia (IESS)

Masculinity
Guilford & Zimmerman (GZTS)

Melancholic
Cruise, Blitchington, & Futcher (TI)

Mobility
Gorynska & Strelau (TTI)

Mobility of Nervous Processes
Strelau (STI)
Strelau, Angleitner, Bantelmann, & Ruch (STI-R)

Mood
Thomas & Chess (NYLSQ)
Windle & Lerner (DOTS-R Adult)

Motor Impulsiveness
Barratt (BIS-10)

Neuroticism
Eysenck & Eysenck (EPI), (EPQ)

Nonplanning Impulsiveness
Barratt (BIS-10)

Objectivity
Guilford & Zimmerman (GZTS)

Passive Avoidance
Wilson, Barrett, & Gray (GWPQ)

Persistence
Gorynska & Strelau (TTI)
Windle & Lerner (DOTS-R Adult)

Personal Relations
Guilford & Zimmerman (GZTS)

Phlegmatic
Cruise, Blitchington, & Futcher (TI)

Plasticity
Rusalov (QST)

Psychoticism
Eysenck & Eysenck (EPQ)

Reactivity
  Kohn (RS)

Recurrence
  Gorynska & Strelau (TTI)

Reducing—Augmenting
  Vando (RAS)

Reflective
  Thurstone (TTS)

Regularity
  Gorynska & Strelau (TTI)

Restraint
  Guilford & Zimmerman (GZTS)

Rhythmicity
  Thomas & Chess (NYLSQ)

Rhythmicity—Daily Habits
  Windle & Lerner (DOTS-R Adult)

Rhythmicity—Eating
  Windle & Lerner (DOTS-R Adult)

Rhythmicity—Sleep
  Windle & Lerner (DOTS-R Adult)

Sanguine
  Cruise, Blitchington, & Futcher (TI)

Sensation-Seeking
  Zuckerman (SSS IV & V)
  Feij & Kuiper (ALT)

Sociability (Sociable)
  Buss & Plomin (EASTS)
  Guilford & Zimmerman (GZTS)
  Thurstone (TTS)

Social Emotionality
  Rusalov (STQ)

Social Ergonicity
  Rusalov (STQ)

Social Plasticity
  Rusalov (STQ)

Social Tempo
  Rusalov (STQ)

Solidity
  Marke & Nyman (MNT)

Speed
  Gorynska & Strelau (TTI)

Stability
  Marke & Nyman (MNT)

Stimulus Screening
  Mehrabian (SSQ)

Strength of Excitation
  Strelau (STI)
  Strelau, Angleitner, Bantelmann, & Ruch (STI-R)

Strength of Inhibition
  Strelau (STI)
  Strelau, Angleitner, Bantelmann, & Ruch (STI-R)

Tempo
  Gorynska & Strelau (TTI)
  Rusalov (STQ)

Thoughtfulness
  Guilford & Zimmerman (GZTS)

Threshold (Sensory)
  Thomas & Chess (NYLSQ)

Thrill- and Adventure-Seeking
  Zuckerman (SSS IV & V)

Trait-Pleasure
  Mehrabian (MTS)

Validity
  Marke & Nyman (MNT)

Venturesomeness
  Eysenck, Pearson, Easting, & Allsopp (I_7 Questionnaire)

Vigorous
  Thurstone (TTS)

Appendix 2. Psychometric Tools Used for Diagnosing Temperament Traits in Adults

1. Adolescenten Temperament Lijst (ATL)
   Feij, J. A., & Kuiper, C. D. (1984). *ATL Handleiding: Adolescenten Temperament Lijst.* Lisse: Swets & Zeitlinger.
   Traits to be measured: extraversion, emotionality, impulsivity, sensation-seeking.

2. Affect Intensity Measure (AIM)
   Larsen, R. J., & Diener, E. (1987). Affect intensity as an individual difference characteristic: A review. *Journal of Research in Personality, 21,* 1–39.
   Trait to be measured: affect intensity.

3. Barratt Impulsiveness Scale (BIS-10)
   Barratt, E. S. (1985). Impulsiveness subtraits: Arousal and information processing. In J. T. Spence & C. E. Izard (Eds.), *Motivation, emotion, and personality* (pp. 137–146). Amsterdam: North-Holland.
   Traits to be measured: motor impulsiveness, cognitive impulsiveness, non-planning impulsiveness.

4. EAS Temperament Survey (EASTS)
   Buss, A. H., & Plomin, R. (1984). *Temperament: Early developing personality traits.* Hillsdale, NJ: Erlbaum.
   Traits to be measured: distress, fearfulness, anger, activity, sociability.

5. Eysenck Personality Inventory (EPI)
   Eysenck, H. J., & Eysenck, S. B. G. (1968). *Manual of the Eysenck Personality Inventory.* San Diego, CA: Educational and Industrial Testing Service.
   Traits to be measured: extraversion, neuroticism.

6. Eysenck Personality Questionnaire (EPQ)
   Eysenck, H. J., & Eysenck, S. B. G. (1975). *Manual of the Eysenck Personality Questionnaire* (Junior & Adult). London: Hodder & Stoughton.
   Traits to be measured: extraversion, neuroticism, psychoticism.

7. Gray-Wilson Personality Questionnaire (GWPQ)
   Wilson, G. D., Barrett, P. T., & Gray, G. A. (1989). Human reactions to reward and punishment: A questionnaire examination of Gray's personality theory. *British Journal of Psychology, 80,* 509–515.
   Traits to be measured: approach, active avoidance, passive avoidance, extinction, fight, flight.

8. Guilford-Zimmerman Temperament Survey (GZTS)
   Guilford, J. S., Zimmermann, W. S., & Guilford, J. P. (1976). *The Guilford-Zimmerman Temperament Survey handbook: Twenty-five years of research and application.* San Diego CA: Edits Publishers.
   Traits to be measured: general activity, restraint, ascendance, sociability, emotional stability, objectivity, friendliness, thoughtfulness, personal relations, masculinity.

9. I$_7$ Impulsiveness Questionnaire (I$_7$ Questionnaire)
Eysenck, S. B. G., Pearson, P. R., Easting, G., & Allsopp, J. F. (1985). Age norms for impulsiveness, venturesomeness and empathy in adults. *Personality and Individual Differences*, 6, 613–619.
Traits to be measured: impulsiveness, venturesomeness, empathy.

10. Irritability and Emotional Susceptibility Scales (IESS)
Caprara, G. V., Cinanni, V., D'Imperio, G., Passerini, S., Renzi, P., & Travaglia, G. (1985). Indicators of impulsive aggression: Present status of research on irritability and emotional susceptibility scales. *Personality and Individual Differences*, 6, 665–674.
Traits to be measured: irritability, emotional susceptibility.

11. Marke-Nyman-Temperamentskala (MNT)
Baumann, U., & Angst, J. (1972). Die Marke-Nyman-Temperamentskala (MNT). *Zeitschrift fuer klinische Psychologie*, 1, 189–212.
Traits to be measured: validity, stability, solidity.

12. Mehrabian Temperament Scale (MTS)*
Mehrabian, A. (1978). Measures of individual differences in temperament. *Educational and Psychological Measurement*, 38, 1105–1117.
Traits to be measured: trait-pleasure, trait-arousal, trait-dominance.

13. New York Longitudinal Study Questionnaire for Early Adult Life (NYLSQ)
Thomas, A., Mittleman, M., Chess, S., Korn, S. Y., and Cohen, Y. (1982). A temperament questionnaire for early adult life. *Educational and Psychological Measurement*, 42, 593–600.
Traits to be measured: activity, adaptability, attention span, distractibility, mood, rhythmicity, threshold (sensory).

14. Structure of Temperament Questionnaire (STQ)
Rusalov, V. M. (1989). Object-related and communicative aspects of human temperament: A new Questionnaire of the structure of temperament. *Personality and Individual Differences*, 10, 817–827.
Traits to be measured: ergonicity, social ergonicity, plasticity, social plasticity, tempo, social tempo, emotionality, social emotionality.

15. The Reactivity Scale (RS)
Kohn, P. M. (1985). Sensation seeking, augmenting-reducing, and strength of the nervous system. In J. T. Spence & C. E. Izard (Eds.), *Motivation, emotion, and personality* (pp. 167–173). Amsterdam: North-Holland.
Trait to be measured: reactivity.

16. Revised Dimensions of Temperament Survey—Adult (DOTS-R Adult)
Windle, M., & Lerner, R. M. (1986). Reassessing the dimensions of temperament individuality across life span: The Revised Dimensions of Temperament Survey (DOTS-R). *Journal of Adolescent Research*, 1, 213–230.

---

*Since Mehrabian does not label his temperament inventory, for convenience the name Mehrabian Temperament Scale has been proposed by the author.

Traits to be measured: activity level-general, activity level-sleep, approach-withdrawal, flexibility-rigidity, mood quality, rhythmicity-sleep, rhythmicity-eating, rhythmicity-daily habits, low distractibility, persistence.

17. Sensation-Seeking Scale Form IV (SSS IV)
Zuckerman, M. (1979). Sensation seeking: Beyond the optimal level of arousal. Hillsdale, NJ: Erlbaum.
Traits to be measured: sensation-seeking, boredom susceptibility, disinhibition, experience seeking, thrill- and adventure-seeking.

18. Sensation Seeking Scale Form V (SSS V)
Zuckerman, M. (1979). Sensation seeking: Beyond the optimal level of arousal. Hillsdale, NJ: Erlbaum.
Traits to be measured: sensation-seeking, boredom susceptibility, disinhibition, experience-seeking, thrill- and adventure-seeking.

19. Stimulus Screening Questionnaire (SSQ)
Mehrabian, A. (1977). A questionnaire measure of individual differences in stimulus screening and associated differences in arousability. *Environmental Psychology and Nonverbal Behavior, 1,* 89–103.
Trait to be measured: stimulus screening-arousability.

20. Strelau Temperament Inventory (STI)
Strelau, J. (1983). Temperament—personality—activity. London: Academic Press.
Traits to be measured: strength of excitation, strength of inhibition, mobility of nervous processes, balance of nervous processes.

21. Strelau Temperament Inventory—Revised (STI-R)
Strelau, J., Angleitner, A., Bantelmann, J., & Ruch, W. (1990). The Strelau Temperament Inventory-Revised (STI-R): Theoretical considerations and scale development. *European Journal of Personality, 4,* 209–235.
Traits to be measured: strength of excitation, strength of inhibition, mobility of nervous processes, balance of nervous processes.

22. Temperament Inventory (TI)
Cruise, R. J., Blitchington, W. P., & Futcher, W. G. A. (1980). Temperament Inventory: An instrument to empirically verify the four-factor hypothesis. *Educational and Psychological Measurement, 40,* 943–954.
Traits to be measured: phlegmatic, sanguine, choleric, melancholic.

23. Temporal Traits Inventory (TTI)
Gorynska, E., & Strelau, J. (1979). Basic traits of the temporal characteristics of behavior and their measurement by an inventory technique. *Polish Psychological Bulletin, 10,* 199–207.
Strelau, J. (1983). Temperament—personality—activity. London: Academic Press.
Traits to be measured: persistence, recurrence, mobility, regularity, speed, tempo.

24. Thurstone Temperament Schedule (TTS)
   Thurstone, L. L. (1953). *Examiner manual for the Thurstone Temperament Schedule* (2nd ed.). Chicago IL: Science Research Associates.
   Traits to be measured: active, vigorous, impulsive, dominant, emotionally stable, sociable, reflective.

25. Vando Reducing-Augmenting Scale (RAS)
   Barnes, G. E. (1985). The Vando R-A Scale as a measure of stimulus reducing-augmenting. In J. Strelau, F. H. Farley, & A. Gale (Eds.), *The biological bases of personality and behavior: Theories, measurement techniques, and development* (Vol. 1, pp. 171–180). Washington, D.C.: Hemisphere.
   Trait to be measured: reducing-augmenting.

References

Andresen, B. *Differentielle Psychophysiologie valenzkonträrer Aktivierungsdimensionen.* Frankfurt/M: Peter Lang, 1987.

Bates, J. E. The measurement of temperament. In R. Plomin & J. Dunn (Eds.), *The study of temperament: Changes, continuities and challenges.* Hillsdale, NJ: Erlbaum, 1986.

Bates, J. E. Temperament in infancy. In J. D. Osofsky (Ed.), *Handbook in infant development* (2nd ed.). New York: Wiley, 1987.

Broadhurst, P. L. The Maudsley reactive and non-reactive strains of rats: A survey. *Behavior Genetics,* 1975, *5,* 299–319.

Burks, J., & Rubenstein, M. *Temperament style in adult interaction: Applications in psychotherapy.* New York: Brunner/Mazel, 1979.

Buss, A. H., & Plomin, R. *Temperament: Early developing personality traits.* Hillsdale, NJ: Erlbaum, 1984.

Buss, A. H., & Plomin, R. The EAS approach to temperament. In R. Plomin & J. Dunn (Eds.), *The study of temperament: Changes, continuities and challenges.* Hillsdale, NJ: Erlbaum, 1986.

Carey, W. B. Interactions of temperament and clinical conditions. *Advances in Developmental and Behavioral Pediatrics,* 1985, *6,* 83–115.

Carey, W. B., & McDevitt, S. C. (Eds.), *Clinical and educational applications of temperament research.* Amsterdam/Lisse: Swets & Zeitlinger, 1989.

Cattell, R. B. *The scientific analysis of personality.* Harmondsworth: Penguin Books, 1965.

Chess, S., & Thomas, A. *Temperament in clinical practice.* New York: Guilford Press, 1986.

Claridge, G. *Origins of mental illness: Temperament, deviance and disorder.* Oxford: Basil Blackwell, 1985.

Corulla, W. J. The relationship between the Strelau Temperament Inventory, sensation seeking and Eysenck's dimensional system of personality. *Personality and Individual Differences,* 1989, *10,* 161–173.

Costa, P. T., Jr., & McCrae, R. R. From catalog to classification: Murray's needs and the five-factor model. *Journal of Personality and Social Psychology,* 1988, *55,* 258–265.

Eliasz, A. *Temperament a system regulacji stymulacji.* Warszawa: Panstwowe Wydawnictwo Naukowe, 1981.

Eliasz, A. Transactional model of temperament. In J. Strelau (Ed.), *Temperamental bases of behavior: Warsaw studies on individual differences.* Lisse: Swets & Zeitlinger, 1985.

Eliasz, A., & Wrzesniewski, K. Type A behavior resulting from internal or external reinforcements. *Polish Psychological Bulletin,* 1986, *17,* 39–53.

Eysenck, H. J. *Conditioning, introversion-extraversion and the strength of the nervous system.* Paper presented at the XXI International Congress of Psychology, Moscow, SU, 1966.

Eysenck, H. J. *The biological basis of personality.* Springfield, IL: Thomas, 1967.

Eysenck, H. J. *The structure of human personality* (3rd ed). London: Methuen, 1970.

Eysenck, H. J. Human typology, higher nervous activity, and factor analysis. In V. D. Nebylitsyn, & J. A. Gray (Eds.), *Biological bases of individual behavior.* New York: Academic Press, 1972.

Eysenck, H. J. A biometrical-genetical analysis of impulsive and sensation seeking behavior. In M. Zuckerman (Ed.), *Biological bases of sensation seeking, impulsivity, and anxiety.* Hillsdale, NJ: Erlbaum, 1983.

Eysenck, H. J., & Eysenck, M. W. *Personality and individual differences: A natural science approach.* New York: Plenum, 1985.

Fahrenberg, J. Concepts of activation and arousal in the theory of emotionality (neuroticism): A multivariate conceptualization. In J. Strelau, & H. J. Eysenck (Eds.), *Personality dimensions and arousal.* New York: Plenum, 1987.

Giuganino, B. M., & Hindley, C. B. Stability of individual differences in personality characteristics from 3 to 15 years. *Personality and Individual Differences,* 1982, *3,* 287–301.

Goldsmith, H. H. Genetic influences on personality from infancy. *Child Development,* 1983, *54,* 331–355.

Goldsmith, H. H. Behavior-genetic approaches to temperament. In G. S. Kohnstamm, J. A. E. Bates, & M. K. Rothbart (Eds.), *Temperament in childhood.* Chichester: Wiley, 1989.

Goldsmith, H. H., Buss, A. H., Plomin, R., Rothbart, M. K., Thomas, A., Chess, S., Hinde, R. A., & McCall, R. R. Roundtable: What is temperament? Four approaches. *Child Development,* 1987, *58,* 505–529.

Goldsmith, H. H., & Campos, J. J. Toward a theory of infant temperament. In R. N. Emde & R. J. Harmon (Eds.), *The development of attachment and affiliative systems.* New York: Plenum, 1982.

Gray, J. A. (Ed.), *Pavlov's typology.* Oxford: Pergamon, 1964.

Gray, J. A. Strength of the nervous system, introversion-extraversion, conditionability and arousal. *Behavior Research and Therapy,* 1967, *5,* 151–169.

Gray, J. A. Causal theories of personality and how to test them. In J. R. Royce (Ed.), *Multivariate analysis and psychological theory.* New York: Academic Press, 1973.

Gray, J. A. Precis of "The neuropsychology of anxiety: An inquiry into the functions of the septo-hippocampal system." *Behavioral and Brain Sciences,* 1982, *5,* 469–484.

Gray, J. A. Where should we search for biologically based dimensions of personality? *Zeitschrift für Differentielle und Diagnostische Psychologie,* 1983, *4,* 165–176.

Guilford, J. S., Zimmerman, W. S., & Guilford, J. P. *The Guilford-Zimmerman Temperament Survey handbook: Twenty-five years of research and application.* San Diego, CA: Edits Publishers, 1976.

Hagekuell, B. Longitudinal stability of temperament within a behavioral style framework. In G. S. Kohnstamm, J. A. E. Bates, & M. K. Rothbart (Eds.), *Temperament in childhood.* Chichester: Wiley, 1989.

Hubert, N. C., Wachs, T. D., Peters-Martin, P., & Gandour, M. J. The study of early temperament: Measurement and conceptual issues. *Child Development,* 1982, *53,* 571–600.

John, O. P., Angleitner, A., & Ostendorf, F. The lexical approach to personality: A historical review of trait taxonomic research. *European Journal of Personality,* 1988, *2,* 171–203.

Klonowicz, T. Temperament and performance. In J. Strelau (Ed.), *Temperamental bases of behavior: Warsaw studies on individual differences.* Lisse: Swets & Zeitlinger, 1985.

Klonowicz, T. Reactivity and the control of arousal. In J. Strelau & H. J. Eysenck (Eds.), *Personality dimensions and arousal.* New York: Plenum, 1987.

Kohn, P. M., Cowles, M. P., & Lafreniere, K. Relationships between psychometric and experimental measures of arousability. *Personality and Individual Differences,* 1987, *8,* 225–231.

Kohnstamm, G. A., Bates, J. E., & Rothbart, M. K. (Eds.), *Temperament in childhood.* Chichester: Wiley, 1989.

Kretschmer, E. *Körperbau und Charakter* (5th & 17/18th ed.). Berlin: Springer, 1926 & 1944.

Lerner, J. V., & Lerner, R. M. Temperament and adaptation across life: Theoretical and empirical issues. In P. B. Baltes, & O. G. Brim, Jr. (Eds.), *Life-span development and behavior.* Vol. 5. New York: Academic Press, 1983.

Mangan, G. L. *The biology of human conduct: East-West models of temperament and personality*. Oxford: Pergamon, 1982.

Matheny, A. P., Jr. A longitudinal twin study of stability of components from Bayley's Infant Behavior Record. *Child Development*, 1983, *54*, 356–360.

Matheny, A. P., Jr., & Dolan, A. B. A twin study of personality and temperament during middle childhood. *Journal of Research in Personality*, 1980, *14*, 224–234.

Matysiak, J. *Roznice indywidualne w zachowaniu zwierzat w swietle koncepcji zapotrzebowania na stymulacje*. Wroclaw: Ossolineum, 1980.

Nebylitsyn, V. D. *Fundamental properties of the human nervous system*. New York: Plenum, 1972.

Nebylitsyn, V. D., & Gray, J. A. (Eds.). *Biological bases of individual behavior*. New York: Academic Press, 1972.

Norman, W. T. Toward an adequate taxonomy of personality attributes: Replicated factor structure in peer nomination personality ratings. *Journal of Abnormal and Social Psychology*, 1963, *66*, 574–583.

Plomin, R. Behavioural genetics and temperament. In R. Porter & G. Lawrenson (Eds.), *Temperament differences in infants and young children*. London: Pitman Books, 1982.

Plomin, R. Introduction. In R. Plomin & J. Dunn (Eds.), *The study of temperament: Changes, continuities and challenges*. Hillsdale, NJ: Erlbaum, 1986.

Plomin, R. & Dunn, J. (Eds.). *The study of temperament: Changes, continuities and challenges*. Hillsdale, NJ: Erlbaum, 1986.

Plomin, R., Pedersen, N. L., McClearn, G. E., Nesselroade, J. R., & Bergeman, C. S. EAS temperaments during the last half of the life span: Twins reared apart and twins reared together. *Psychology and Aging*, 1988, *3*, 43–50.

Ravich-Shcherbo, I. V. On the problem of the essence of psychophysiological bases of individuality. In V. S. Merlin & B. A. Nikityuk (Eds.), *Problems of differential psychophysiology related to genetics*. Moscow: SSSR Academy of Pedagogical Sciences, 1976 (in Russian).

Ravich-Shcherbo. I. V. (Ed.). *The role of environment and heredity in moulding human individuality*. Moscow: Pedagogika, 1988 (in Russian).

Ravich-Shcherbo, I. V., Shlakhta, N. F., & Shibarovskaya, G. A. A study of some typological indices in twins. In V. D. Nebylitsyn (Ed.), *Problems of differential psychophysiology*. Vol. 6. Moscow: Prosveshcheniye, 1969 (in Russian).

Rothbart, M. K., & Derryberry, D. Development of individual differences in temperament. In M. E. Lamb & A. L. Brown (Eds.), *Advances in developmental psychology*. Vol. 1. Hillsdale, NJ: Erlbaum, 1981.

Rothbart, M. K., & Posner, M. I. Temperament and the development of self-regulation. In L. C. Hartlage & C. F. Telzrow (Eds.), *The neuropsychology of individual differences: A developmental perspective*. New York: Plenum, 1985.

Ruch, W., Angleitner, A., & Strelau, J. (in press). The Strelau Temperament Inventory-Revised (STI-R): Validity studies. *European Journal of Personality, 5.*

Schalling, D., Edman, G., & Asberg, M.Impulsive cognitive style and inability to tolerate boredom: Psychobiological studies of temperamental vulnerability. In M. Zuckerman (Ed.), *Biological bases of sensation seeking, impulsivity, and anxiety*. Hillsdale, NJ: Erlbaum, 1983.

Sheldon, W. H., & Stevens, S. S. *The varieties of temperament*. New York: Harper & Row, 1942.

Shlakhta, N. F., & Panteleyeva, T. A. The investigation of genotypically determined strength of nervous system syndrome. In B. F. Lomov & I. V. Ravich-Shcherbo (Eds.), *The problems of genetic psychophysiology in man*. Moscow: Nauka, 1978 (in Russian).

Simonov, P. V. Individual characteristics of brain limbic structures interactions as the basis of Pavlovian/Eysenckian typology. In J. Strelau, & H. J. Eysenck (Eds.), *Personality dimensions and arousal*. New York: Plenum, 1987.

Strelau, J. The general and partial nervous-system types—Data and theory. In V. D. Nebylitsyn & J. A. Gray (Eds.), *Biological bases of individual behavior* . New York: Academic Press, 1972.

Strelau, J. *Temperament—personality—activity*. London: Academic Press, 1983a.

Strelau, J. A regulative theory of temperament. *Australian Journal of Psychology*, 1983b, *35*, 305–317.

Strelau, J. *Das Temperament in der psychischen Entwicklung.* Berlin: Volk und Wissen Volkseigener Verlag, 1984.

Strelau, J. Pavlov's typology and the regulative theory of temperament. In J. Strelau (Ed.), *Temperamental bases of behavior: Warsaw studies on individual differences.* Lisse: Swets and Zeitlinger, 1985a.

Strelau, J. (Ed.). *Temperamental bases of behavior: Warsaw studies on individual differences.* Lisse: Swets & Zeitlinger, 1985b.

Strelau, J. The concept of temperament in personality research. *European Journal of Personality,* 1987a, *1,* 107–117.

Strelau, J. Emotion as a key concept in temperament research. *Journal of Research in Personality,* 1987b, *21,* 510–528.

Strelau, J. Temperament dimensions as co-determinants of resistance to stress In M. P. Janisse (Ed.), *Individual differences, stress, and health psychology.* New York: Springer, 1988.

Strelau, J., Angleitner, A., & Ruch, W. Strelau Temperament Inventory (STI): General review and studies based on German samples. In J. N. Butcher & C. D. Spielberger (Eds.), *Advances in personality assessment.* Vol. 8. Hillsdale, NJ: Erlbaum, 1990.

Strelau, J., & Eysenck, H. J. (Eds.), *Personality dimensions and arousal.* New York: Plenum, 1987.

Strelau, J., Farley, F. H., & Gale, A. (Eds.), *The biological bases of personality and behavior: Theories, measurement techniques, and development.* Vol. 1. Washington: Hemisphere, 1985.

Strelau, J., Farley, F. H., & Gale, A. (Eds.), *The biological bases of personality and behavior: Psychophysiology, performance, and application.* Vol. 2. Washington: Hemisphere, 1986.

Teplov, B. M. *Complete works.* Vol. 2. Moscow: Pedagogika, 1985 (in Russian).

Teplov, B. M., & Nebylitsyn, V. D. The study of the basic properties of the nervous system and their significance in psychology of individual differences. *Voprosy Psikhologii,* 1963, *9,* 38–47 (in Russian).

Thomas, A., & Chess, S. *Temperament and development.* New York: Brunner/Mazel, 1977.

Torgersen, A. M. Temperamental differences in infants and 6-year-old children: A follow-up study of twins. In J. Strelau, F. H. Farley, and A. Gale (Eds.), *The biological bases of behavior: Theories, measurement techniques, and development.* Vol. 1. Washington: Hemisphere, 1985.

Wilson, G. D., Barrett, P. T., Gray, J. A. Human reactions to reward and punishment: A questionnaire examination of Gray's personality theory. *British Journal of Psychology,* 1989, *80,* 509–515.

Windle, M. Temperament and personality: An exploratory interinventory study of DOTS-R, EASI-II, and EPI. *Journal of Personality Assessment,* 1989, *53,* 487–501.

Windle, M., & Lerner, R. M. Reassessing the dimensions of temperamental individuality across the life-span: The Revised Dimensions of Temperament Survey (DOTS-R). *Journal of Adolescent Research,* 1986, *1,* 213–230.

Zuckerman, M. *Sensation seeking: Beyond the optimal level of arousal.* Hillsdale, NJ: Erlbaum, 1979.

Zuckerman, M. (Ed.), *Biological bases of sensation seeking, impulsivity and anxiety.* Hillsdale, NJ: Erlbaum, 1983.

Zuckerman, M. Sensation seeking: A comparative approach to a human trait. *The Behavioral and Brain Sciences,* 1984, *7,* 413–471.

Zuckerman, M. Biological foundations of the sensation-seeking temperament. In J. Strelau, F. H. Farley, & A. Gale (Eds.), *The biological bases of personality and behavior: Theories, measurement techniques, and development.* Vol. 1. Washington: Hemisphere, 1985.

Zuckerman, M. Brain monoamine systems and personality. In D. Hellhammer, I. Florin, & H. Weiner (Eds.), *Neurobiological approaches to human disease.* Toronto: Hans Huber, 1989.

Zuckerman, M., Kuhlman, D. M., & Camac, C. What lies beyond E and N? Factor analyses of scales believed to measure basic dimensions of personality. *Journal of Personality and Social Psychology,* 1988, *54,* 96–107.

Index

Goodness of fit concept (*Cont.*)
  theoretical approaches to, 24–25
  variability in, 21–23
Group differences, child temperament measure-
    ment, validity issues, 223–224
Heuristics, biochemistry and, 156
Hormones. *See* Endocrine system
Hyperactivity, EAS theory and, 58

Impulsivity, EAS theory and, 59
Individual differences
  biology and, 29–42
  child temperament measurement (early), 250–
    251
  developmental issues and, 62
  extraversion and neuroticism, 287
  personological approach and, 177–178
Infancy, developmental issues, 63–67
Infant Behavior Questionnaire (IBQ), 251–257
  content of, 253–254
  development of, 251–253
  household reliability of, 253
  intercorrelations among scorers, 254
  stability of, 255
  theory and, 254–255
  Toddler Behavior Assessment Questionnaire
    (TBAQ) compared, 262
  use of, 257
  validation of, 255–257
Interactionist approach
  personological approach and, 179–180
  person-situation debate and, 167–168
Internal consistency, child temperament measure-
    ment, 209–210
Interparent agreement, child temperament mea-
    surement, 212–213
Interrater agreement, child temperament mea-
    surement, 212–213

Laboratory Temperament Assessment Battery
    (LAB-TAB), described, 264–269
Language, trait identification and, 193
Learning
  activity and (EAS theory), 46
  emotionality and (EAS theory), 51–52
  extraversion and neuroticism, 294
  sociability and (EAS theory), 56–57
Learning disability, child temperament measure-
    ment, validity issues, 224
Life cycle perspective, developmental issues
    and, 69
Low sensory threshold, goodness of fit concept
    and, 23

MAO. *See* Monoamine oxidase (MAO)
Match and mismatch, goodness of fit and, 24–
    25
Metabolism, biochemistry and, 155
Monoamine oxidase (MAO)
  biochemistry and, 149
  biosocial approach and, 98–99
  biotypes and, 138–139
Mother-father agreement, 235–248
  analysis of, 245–247
  Infant Behavior Questionnaire (IBQ), 253
  methods, 236–238
    data analysis procedures, 238
    instrument, 237–238
    participants, 236–237
  overview of, 235–236
  results, 238–245
    absolute differences, 243–244
    correlations, 240–243
    differences in variation, 240
    intraclass correlations, 244–245
    mean differences, 238–240
Multitrait-multimethod analysis, differential psy-
    chophysiology and, 320
Multivariate activation theory, differential psy-
    chophysiology and, 318–319

Negative emotionality, EAS theory and, 53
Neuropsychology, 105–128
  behavioral approach system, 114–122
  behavioral inhibition system, 109–113
  biotypes and, 139–141
  defined, 105–106
  emotion analysis and, 106–109
  fight/flight system, 114
  personality and, 122–126
Neuroticism, 318, 321. *See also* Extraversion
    and neuroticism testing
Newborn period, developmental issues, 62–63
Niche
  biology and, 33–36
  person-situation debate and, 168–169
Norepinephrine, biotypes and, 135–136

Objectivity, personological approach and, 186
Ophthalmology
  biosocial approach and, 97
  extraversion and neuroticism, 294–295

Pain response, reactivity testing and, 274–278
Parent characteristics, child temperament mea-
    surement, 216–217